THE COLLABORATIVE CONSTITUTION

Constitutional scholars have long debated whether courts or legislatures should have the last word on rights. In this book, Aileen Kavanagh offers a new collaborative vision of how to protect rights in a democracy. Rejecting the false dichotomy between courts and legislatures, Kavanagh argues that protecting rights is a collaborative enterprise where all three branches of government play distinct but complementary roles, whilst working together in a spirit of comity, civility, and mutual respect. Connecting constitutional theory to the practice of protecting rights in a working democracy, this book offers an innovative understanding of the separation of powers, grounded in the values and virtues of collaborative constitutionalism.

AILEEN KAVANAGH is Professor of Constitutional Governance, Trinity College Dublin and Director of TriCON – the Trinity Centre for Constitutional Governance. Formerly Professor of Constitutional Law at the University of Oxford, Kavanagh has written widely on comparative constitutional law, human rights, and constitutional theory.

CAMBRIDGE STUDIES IN CONSTITUTIONAL LAW

The aim of this series is to produce leading monographs in constitutional law. All areas of constitutional law and public law fall within the ambit of the series, including human rights and civil liberties law, administrative law, as well as constitutional theory and the history of constitutional law. A wide variety of scholarly approaches is encouraged, with the governing criterion being simply that the work is of interest to an international audience. Thus, works concerned with only one jurisdiction will be included in the series as appropriate, while, at the same time, the series will include works which are explicitly comparative or theoretical – or both. The series editors likewise welcome proposals that work at the intersection of constitutional and international law, or that seek to bridge the gaps between civil law systems, the US, and the common law jurisdictions of the Commonwealth.

Series Editors
David Dyzenhaus
Professor of Law and Philosophy, University of Toronto, Canada
Thomas Poole
Professor of Law, London School of Economics and Political Science

THE COLLABORATIVE CONSTITUTION

AILEEN KAVANAGH

Trinity College Dublin

Shaftesbury Road, Cambridge CB2 8EA, United Kingdom

One Liberty Plaza, 20th Floor, New York, NY 10006, USA

477 Williamstown Road, Port Melbourne, VIC 3207, Australia

314–321, 3rd Floor, Plot 3, Splendor Forum, Jasola District Centre, New Delhi – 110025, India

103 Penang Road, #05-06/07, Visioncrest Commercial, Singapore 238467

Cambridge University Press is part of Cambridge University Press & Assessment, a department of the University of Cambridge.

We share the University's mission to contribute to society through the pursuit of education, learning and research at the highest international levels of excellence.

www.cambridge.org
Information on this title: www.cambridge.org/9781108493260

DOI: 10.1017/9781108680929

First published 2024

A catalogue record for this publication is available from the British Library.

A Cataloging-in-Publication data record for this book is available from the Library of Congress

ISBN 978-1-108-49326-0 Hardback

BRIEF CONTENTS

Introduction: The Call for Collaboration *page* 1

PART I INSTITUTIONS AND INTERACTIONS

1 Constitutionalism beyond Manicheanism 31

2 The Promise and Perils of Dialogue 58

3 The Case for Collaboration 86

PART II RIGHTS IN POLITICS

4 Governing with Rights 121

5 Legislating for Rights 150

6 Legislated Rights: From Domination to Collaboration 170

PART III JUDGE AS PARTNER

7 Judge as Partner 205

8 The HRA as Partnership in Progress 230

9 Calibrated Constitutional Review 266

10 Courting Collaborative Constitutionalism 297

PART IV RESPONSIVE LEGISLATURES

11 Underuse of the Override 333

12 Declarations, Obligations, Collaborations 363

Conclusion: The Currency of Collaboration 403

CONTENTS

Acknowledgements   *page* xi
List of Abbreviations   xvi

Introduction: The Call for Collaboration   1
1 Collaboration Calling   1
2 The Collaborative Constitution as Practice and Principle   13
3 Constitutions, Comparison, Context   18
4 Outline and Overview   23

PART I   INSTITUTIONS AND INTERACTIONS

1   Constitutionalism beyond Manicheanism   31
1 Introduction   31
2 Clash of the Titans   32
3 The Terror of the Twin Tyrannies   42
4 Political versus Legal Constitutionalism   50
5 Conclusion: A Farewell to Arms   55

2   The Promise and Perils of Dialogue   58
1 Introduction   58
2 Divining Dialogue   60
3 The Canadian Conversation: From Metaphor to Model   64
4 The UK Debate about Dialogue   70
5 Promises   73
6 Perils   76
7 Dialogue, Disagreement, Distortion   80
8 Conclusion   85

3   The Case for Collaboration   86
1 Introduction   86
2 Dividing Constitutional Labour   87
3 Curbing and Counteracting   94

4   Comity and Collaboration   97
5   Conflict within Constraints: From Showdown to Slowdown   106
6   Conclusion   116

PART II   RIGHTS IN POLITICS

4   Governing with Rights   121
    1   Introduction: A Shared Responsibility   121
    2   The Executive and the Constitution   123
    3   Executive Engagement with Rights   128
        a   Cabinet, Civil Servants, and Bill Teams   130
        b   The Office of Parliamentary Counsel   132
        c   The Attorney General and the Law Officers   134
        d   The Minister: Claiming Compatibility between Law
            and Politics   137
        e   The Joint Committee on Human Rights   138
    4   Raising Rights-Consciousness   139
    5   Envisioning Executive Constitutionalism   142
    6   Conclusion   147

5   Legislating for Rights   150
    1   Introduction   150
    2   Unpacking Parliament   151
    3   The JCHR as a Hybrid Constitutional Watchdog   156
    4   Raising Rights-Consciousness in Parliament   163
    5   Conclusion   168

6   Legislated Rights: From Domination to Collaboration   170
    1   Introduction   170
    2   Deconstructing Executive Dominance   172
    3   Legislating for Terror   179
    4   Legislative Decision, Judicial Distortion, Democratic Debilitation   184
    5   Detecting Debilitation?   186
    6   Discerning Distortion?   189
    7   Claiming Compatibility: A Case Study of Money in Politics   195
    8   Conclusion   201

PART III   JUDGE AS PARTNER

7   Judge as Partner   205
    1   Introduction: Between Supremacy and Subordination   205
    2   The Contribution Courts Make   206
    3   Janus-Faced Judging in a Joint Enterprise   208
    4   From Faithful Agent to Constitutional Partner   212

5 Of Common Law Rights and Clear Statements 215
6 The Principle of Legality as a Presumption of Partnership 220
7 Conclusion 227

8 The HRA as Partnership in Progress 230
1 Introduction 230
2 The Art of the Possible 233
3 Taking Interpretation to the Limit 238
4 Interpreting Rights, Declaring Wrongs 243
5 Declarations as Decision not Dialogue 250
6 The Hidden Strengths of Weak-Form Review 258
7 Conclusion 264

9 Calibrated Constitutional Review 266
1 Introduction: Between Abdication and Usurpation 266
2 Courts as Quality-Control 267
3 Mapping the Contours of Comity 272
4 Calibrated Constitutional Review 277
5 Courting Counter-Terrorism 281
6 Proportionality in Partnership 287
7 Conclusion 294

10 Courting Collaborative Constitutionalism 297
1 Introduction 297
2 Legislative Leeway at the End of Life 298
3 Proportionality and Political Process Review 302
4 Avoiding Pre-emption 308
5 Court as Catalyst, Judge as Nudge 311
   a Alerts, Prods, and Pleas 312
   b Judicial Advice and Soft Suggestions 314
   c Judicial Warnings 319
6 Stepping in Where Parliament Fears to Tread 322
7 From Passive Virtues to Collaborative Devices 327
8 Conclusion 329

PART IV   RESPONSIVE LEGISLATURES

11 Underuse of the Override 333
1 Great Expectations 333
2 Canada in Context 337
3 Reconciling Rights and Democracy UK-Style 344
4 Underuse by Design not Demonisation 346

5 From Dialogue and Disagreement to Comity and Collaboration   353
6 The Upshot of Understanding the Override   357
7 Conclusion   360

12 Declarations, Obligations, Collaborations   363
1 Introduction   363
2 Uncovering Conventions   364
   a What Are Conventions?   364
   b Regular Practice   365
   c Normative Obligation   367
3 Patterns of Political Response   368
4 Institutionalising a Compliance-Oriented Approach   370
5 Willing Compliance, Workaday Acceptance   372
6 An Open and Welcoming Response   376
7 Courting Controversy   379
   a When Life Means Life   380
   b Courting Counter-Terrorism   383
   c Rhetoric, Resistance, and Registering Sex Offenders   386
   d Political Wrangling about Prisoner Voting   391
8 A Convention to Comply with Declarations of Incompatibility?   397
9 Conclusion   400

Conclusion: The Currency of Collaboration   403
1 Collaborative Leitmotivs   403
2 Broadening the Collaborative Horizon   408
3 Collaboration as Currency   411

Bibliography   417
Index   486

ACKNOWLEDGEMENTS

This book is the culmination of many years of reflection and writing about constitutional government. Though much of the hard labour was done in solitary confinement, the process as a whole was deeply collaborative, and I am grateful to all those who helped along the way. When I started thinking about the idea of the collaborative constitution, I was working at the University of Oxford, where I benefited enormously from numerous discussions, seminars, and lectures which helped to sharpen and deepen my ideas. Many of the key principles underpinning this book were discussed as part of the postgraduate BCL Seminars in Constitutional Theory, which I co-taught over a number of years with Nick Barber, Les Green, and Richard Ekins. I am very grateful for their insight and engagement, as well as those from the excellent students who took the course. Whilst at Oxford, I was also involved in running the Graduate Course in Legal Research Method, which brought together a number of colleagues from diverse subject-areas to think through the challenges of legal research and writing. As part of this course, I benefited from excellent discussions on how to write about law with Alan Bogg, Hugh Collins, Anne Davies, Simon Douglas, Timothy Endicott, Liz Fisher, John Gardner, James Goudkamp, Tarunabh Khaitan, Jeremy Waldron, Alison Young, Lucia Zedner, and many more. I am hugely grateful for those discussions, which informed my approach to legal scholarship in lasting ways.

Beyond these seminars, I owe a debt of gratitude to a number of colleagues at Oxford who either read early versions of the material included in the book or generously discussed some inchoate ideas at crucial junctures. Paul Craig was especially helpful at the early stages. In numerous, insightful discussions over coffee at St John's, Paul helped me to formulate the pivotal questions as part of a structured inquiry. His support, encouragement, and critical engagement were enormously helpful in getting this book on the road. My colleague at St Edmund Hall, Adrian Briggs, applied his razor-sharp wit and acute legal mind to the preposterous proposals of a public lawyer. Timothy Endicott, Les Green, and John Gardner all read some parts of this book and I am hugely grateful for their generosity, support, and critical feedback. Les Green always put something original and insightful on the table. Timothy engaged with the material closely, critically, and collegially. We will all miss John Gardner's unique combination of sharp insight, good humour, and generous spirit.

As my ideas developed, I ran a seminar series on comparative constitutionalism at Oxford, which engaged with collaborative constitutional themes with a number of friends and colleagues who were working on related issues. That seminar series was both immensely enjoyable and enormously enriching. I am grateful to all the contributors and commentators, including Jesse Blackbourn, Chintan Chandrachud, Hasan Dindjer, Timothy Endicott, Graham Gee, Tamas Gyorfi, Max Harris, Tom Hickey, Jeff King, Helle Krunke, Murray Hunt, Mariano Melero de la Torre, Conrado Hübner Mendes, Robert Sharpe, Björg Thorarensen and Kate O'Regan. I am particularly grateful to Kate O'Regan for numerous, insightful discussions about judging in a democracy, and for her thoughtful and supportive engagement with all the ideas advanced in this book. Her feedback on early drafts of chapters was invaluable, and all of her comments bore fruit in the final text. When talking with Kate, the collaborative constitution became doubly collaborative.

In 2016, I hosted a symposium on *Protecting Rights, Engaging Parliament* at St John's College, Oxford, generously funded by the British Academy. By combining academics, judges, civil servants, parliamentary counsel, parliamentary officials, a Law Commissioner, a former Attorney General, a former Director of Public Prosecutions, the Legal Advisor to the Joint Committee on Human Rights, as well as members of the House of Lords Constitution Committee, this one-day symposium was a microcosm of the collaborative constitution in action. My gratitude goes to all the speakers for contributing to this event, including Graham Gee, Daniel Greenberg, Dominic Grieve, Janet Hiebert, Murray Hunt, Helena Kennedy, Jeff King, Liam Laurence-Smith, Robert Leckey, Ken MacDonald, Rick Rawlings, Stephen Sedley, Philip Sales, Stephen Tierney, and George Williams.

In 2019, I moved to Trinity College Dublin and I am immensely grateful for the supportive and stimulating academic environment provided by the Trinity Law School, especially insightful discussions with Oran Doyle, David Kenny, Andrea Mulligan, David Prendergast, Surya Roy, Des Ryan, and Rachael Walsh. As Head of School, Mark Bell steered the Law School through the choppy waters of the Covid pandemic, providing a steady, secure, and supportive environment which enabled us all to work as best we could under trying circumstances. I want to register my personal gratitude and professional admiration for that quiet and collaborative form of leadership. Whilst at Trinity, I co-taught a course in advanced constitutional law with Rachael Walsh, and many of her perceptive comments and probing questions have worked their way into the book. I am also grateful for lively and insightful discussions within the wider constitutional community in Ireland, including Justice Gerard Hogan, Chief Justice Donal O'Donnell, Maria Cahill, Laura Cahillane, Eoin Carolan, Conor Casey, Tom Hickey, Hilary Hogan, Davy Lalor, Conor O'Mahony, Ioanna Tourkochoriti, Eoin Daly, and many more.

The Annual Conference of the International Society of Constitutional Law (ICON-S) provided an enriching scholarly environment where I could test out the key ideas contained in this book. At the 2019 ICON-S Conference in Santiago de Chile, there was a panel on my book with Rosalind Dixon, Stephen Gardbaum, and Mark Tushnet, all of whose work is a deep inspiration for my own. At another ICON-S, I received insightful feedback on the book manuscript from Eoin Carolan, Michaela Hailbronner, James Fowkes and David Kosař. Both of these panels were a model of academic comity and collaboration where robust disagreement was combined with robust civility. When thinking about the arguments advanced in this book, I can rest assured that they have been tried and tested by the best in the business.

Whether in spoken or in written form, I have received invaluable feedback on aspects of this book from a number of colleagues and friends over the years, including Farah Ahmed, Richard Albert, Trevor Allan, Ittai Bar-Siman-Tov, David Bilchitz, Conor Casey, Cora Chan, Sam Bookman, Dan Coenen, Cathryn Costello, Erin Delaney, Rosalind Dixon, Oran Doyle, David Dyzenhaus, James Fowkes, Stephen Gardbaum, Graham Gee, Claudia Geiringer, Janneke Gerards, Tamas Gyorfi, Michaela Hailbronner, Carol Harlow, Tom Hickey, Janet Hiebert, Murray Hunt, Vicki Jackson, Jeff King, Dimitrios Kyritsis, Robert Leckey, Mary Liston, Janet McLean, Colm O'Cinnéide, Adam Perry, Gavin Phillipson, Jeff Pojanowski, Rick Rawlings, Denise Reaume, Kent Roach, Philip Sales, Fred Schauer, Stephen Sedley, Larry Solum, Scott Stephenson, Adrienne Stone, Maurice Sunkin, Yvonne Tew, Adam Tucker, Mark Tushnet, Adrian Vermeule, Rachael Walsh, Lulu Weis, Po-Jen Yap, and Jan Van Zyl Smit. I am grateful to them all. Robert

Leckey, Vanessa MacDonnell, and Kent Roach helped me to stake out the parameters of the collaborative constitution, whilst testing it against Canadian and comparative experience. Their combination of theoretical insight and practical application inspired my own approach. I am grateful to Dan Meagher and Matthew Groves for helping me to find a way into the impressive antipodean scholarship on the principle of legality. Murray Hunt shed light on the parliamentary protection of rights, particularly the role of the Joint Committee on Human Rights (JCHR), and made me think hard about the idea of the collaborative constitution and the role of justification within it. I am particularly grateful to David Dyzenhaus for nudging me over the finish line, and for insightful conversations on collaborative themes. Some of the central ideas for the book – including its title – were forged in lively discussion over dinner with David Dyzenhaus, Cheryl Misak, Murray Hunt, and Lois McNay.

Jeff King kindly and generously gave me his data-set on political responses to declarations of incompatibility in the first decade of the Human Rights Act (HRA). Together with Jeff's own insightful work on this issue, that data-set provided the initial grounding for Chapter 12 and I am extremely grateful to Jeff for sharing his data, and for the spirit of scholarly collaboration and collegiality which accompanied it. Throughout the book, I have drawn great inspiration from the work of Jeff King, Dimitrios Kyritsis, and Eoin Carolan, who were all working on collaborative themes from different angles. The intellectual debt I owe Jeff, Dimitrios, and Eoin is legible in every chapter of this book, but I also want to register my personal thanks for the numerous collaborative discussions over the years. At times, it was reassuring to have such insightful corroboration on collaboration.

I have been very fortunate to have had superb research assistance whilst writing this book, including from Eimear Dooley, Louis O'Carroll, Karl Laird, Lewis Graham, Daniel Gilligan, Samuel Lemire, and Adam Elebert. In particular, Louis O'Carroll did an enormous amount of excellent work on Chapter 12. Louis' transition from the undergraduate degree at Trinity College Dublin to the BCL at Oxford suited my geographically non-binary life perfectly. I am grateful to the British Academy and the University of Oxford for providing generous financial support for this research assistance, and to the Law School at Trinity College Dublin in the later stages. The book was also supported by Erasmus+ and the Jean Monnet Centre of Excellence in Law and Politics at Trinity College Dublin.

Huge thanks go to Finola O'Sullivan, Marianne Nield, and Rachel Imrie at Cambridge University Press, who shepherded this book through its long gestation with professionalism and patience. I am particularly indebted to Finola O'Sullivan for providing that vital support at the outset. I am honoured to be part of the great Cambridge Studies in Constitutional Law series, which Finola created in collaboration with David Dyzenhaus and other editors.

A few months before I completed the book, my doctoral supervisor, Joseph Raz, died. I was due to meet him after I had finished the book, but that was not to be. I want to register my deep admiration and heartfelt thanks to Joseph Raz as the most inspiring and exacting teacher any doctoral student could hope to have. It was an honour to have been supervised by him, and a pleasure to have known him.

The greatest debt I owe is to my husband, Matthew Robinson, whose deep reserves of loving support, patient forbearance and unstinting good humour made this book possible. I treasure our life-long partnership, in which I have learnt so much about the values and virtues of collaboration as part of a long-term relationship. I also want to thank our children, Seán and Una, for enriching our lives and reminding us of what matters most. I dedicate this book to my father, Patrick Kavanagh, in admiration, love and gratitude for all the support he has given me over the years and still to this day.

ABBREVIATIONS

AG	Attorney General
CA	Court of Appeal
CLR	Commonwealth Law Reports
CO	Cabinet Office
DoI	Declaration of Incompatibility
DPP	Director of Public Prosecutions
ECHR	European Convention on Human Rights
ECtHR	European Court of Human Rights
HC	House of Commons
HCA	High Court of Australia
HL	House of Lords
HRA	Human Rights Act
JCHR	Joint Committee on Human Rights
MoJ	Ministry of Justice
NIHRC	Northern Ireland Human Rights Commission
SSHD	Secretary of State for the Home Department
UKSC	United Kingdom Supreme Court

~

Introduction

The Call for Collaboration

1   Collaboration Calling

Which branch of government should we trust to protect rights in a democracy? Some take a court-centric approach to this question, arguing that the courts provide a 'forum of principle'[1] which makes judges uniquely situated to protect rights against the feared and fabled 'tyranny of the majority'. Others urge us to put our faith in the democratic legislature as a supremely dignified, diverse, and deliberative forum which can protect our rights against the oligarchic offensive of an ermined elite.[2] Rejecting the binary options of either the courts or the legislature, this book argues that protecting rights is a collaborative enterprise between all three branches of government, where each branch has a distinct but complementary role to play whilst working together with the other branches in constitutional partnership. Instead of advocating the hegemony and supremacy of one branch over another, this book articulates a collaborative vision of constitutionalism where the protection of rights is a shared responsibility between all three branches. On this vision, protecting rights is neither the solitary domain of a Herculean super-judge nor the dignified pronouncements of an enlightened legislature. Instead, it is a complex, dynamic, and collaborative enterprise, where each branch of government plays a valuable role whilst treating the other branches with comity and respect.

In making the case for the collaborative constitution, this book inscribes itself into a longer trajectory of scholarly attempts to work out which branch should protect rights in a democracy. In Chapter 1, I begin by exploring the Manichean narrative of 'courts versus legislature' and

---

[1] Dworkin (1985).
[2] Waldron (1993b); Webber et al. (2018).

1

'political versus legal constitutionalism'[3] which dominated the scholarly discourse on protecting rights in the late twentieth century. Rejecting these alternatives as false dichotomies between polarised extremes, I argue that we need to move 'beyond Manicheanism'.[4] Beyond the binaries of 'heroes versus villains' and 'good versus evil', this book offers a less dramatic but more realistic account of institutional roles, where all three branches of government are presented as 'imperfect alternatives',[5] each with its fair share of pros and cons. Whatever virtues the branches of government possess, I argue that they are necessarily 'partial virtues which must be integrated into an institutionally diverse constitutional order'.[6]

Instead of embracing 'nirvana solutions'[7] where paragons of principle are pitted against oligarchic ogres, what is urgently needed to advance this debate is a more grounded and granular institutional account which acknowledges the valuable, but necessarily imperfect, contributions of all three branches of government in a differentiated division of labour. The aim of this book is to provide that account. Once we accept that the protection of rights needs both legislation and adjudication – both elected politicians and independent judges – the key task, then, is to work out how these institutions act, interact and counteract in a complex, collaborative scheme. Abandoning the Manichean battlefield where democracy is presented as 'constitutionalism's nemesis'[8] and constitutionalism is portrayed as 'the constant object of a democrat's fear and suspicion',[9] this book recasts the debate in collaborative rather than purely conflictual terms. Between the dramatic forces of light and darkness, this book explores the many shades of grey.

In the twenty-first century, scholars began to explore ways of transcending the binary framing of this debate and the antagonistic picture on which it rests. Inspired by innovations in constitutional design in the UK and Commonwealth countries, scholars argued that we should view the relationship between the branches of government as a dialogue.[10] Instead of positing the hegemony of one branch over the other, the courts

---

[3] Kavanagh (2019).
[4] Hilbink (2006).
[5] Komesar (1994).
[6] Whittington (2000) 693.
[7] Komesar (1994) ix.
[8] Waldron (2016) 38.
[9] Ibid 38.
[10] Hogg & Bushell (1997); Sigalet, Webber & Dixon (2019a).

and the legislature could each have a say, albeit with the fall-back of legislative finality in circumstances of disagreement. Yet, whilst the metaphor of dialogue usefully highlighted the interaction between the branches, Chapter 2 argues that it lacked the analytical resources to capture the complexity of the constitutional relationships between the branches of government.[11] The malleability of the metaphor meant that it could be applied to any form of inter-institutional interaction, ranging from polite conversations between friends to no-holds-barred shouting matches between enemies locked in combat. For that reason, the idea of dialogue failed to take us beyond the Manichean narrative of 'courts versus legislature' and 'rights versus democracy'. In fact, it resurrected the antagonistic narrative, shifting the debate to which branch should get 'the last word'[12] in the dialogue: the legislature, as 'political constitutionalists' preferred, or the courts, as 'legal constitutionalists' claimed.[13] With its fixation on legislative finality and override of courts, the Manichean narrative reappeared in dialogic clothing.

In order to make sense of the subtleties of the relationships between the branches, this book argues that we need to dig deeper into the foundations of constitutional democracy, anchoring our analysis in a plausible and attractive account of the roles and relationships between the branches of government. In short, we need to ground our analysis in a conception of the constitutional separation of powers. This book makes the case for collaboration as the guiding value of such an account. Instead of squaring off against each other to get the last word on rights in fierce constitutional combat, or having a cosy constitutional conversation on the meaning of rights, the central chapter of this book – Chapter 3 – argues that they must work together in constitutional partnership marked by the values of comity, collaboration, and conflict management. On this vision of constitutionalism, the branches of government are not enemies at war. But they are not friends either. Instead, they are partners in a collaborative enterprise, where they are required to treat each other with constitutional comity and respect.

At the heart of this book lies a relational and collaborative conception of the separation of powers, where distinct branches of government perform different institutional roles whilst working together in a collaborative

---

[11] Kavanagh (2016a).
[12] For 'a hard look at the last word' in constitutional discourse, see Kavanagh (2015a).
[13] Bellamy (2011) 91–2; Kavanagh (2019) 56.

constitutional scheme.[14] When we look at how the branches of government carry out their distinctive roles, it is clear that they are not 'satellites in independent orbit'.[15] Instead, they are interdependent and interrelated actors who must work together in a system of 'separateness but interdependence, autonomy but reciprocity'.[16] Rather than viewing the separation of powers as a prescription for solitary confinement with 'high walls'[17] between the branches, this book explores the constitutional norms of respect and restraint, fortitude and forbearance, which frame and shape the interactive engagement between them. Beyond 'high walls', this book builds bridges. Delving deep into the interactive dynamics between the branches, it explores the myriad modes of constructive engagement which form 'the connective tissue'[18] between the different arms of government in a healthy body politic.

The collaborative constitution does not overlook the critical role of robust checks and balances between the branches. On the contrary, such checks and balances are partly constitutive of the collaborative enterprise. Comity and contestation are not mutually exclusive activities. However, alongside contestation, critique and mutual oversight, this book also discerns the inter-institutional dynamics of mutual respect and mutual support as the branches carry out their distinct but interconnected tasks. Situating checks and balances within a broader collaborative endeavour, my account emphasises that the branches of government 'do not merely counteract protectively; they also interact productively'.[19] In place of a static vision of separated functions and isolated authorities, the separation of powers is thus recast in relational terms as a dynamic process of interaction and engagement, framed and shaped by the norms of mutual respect, restraint and 'role recognition'[20] in a collaborative constitutional scheme.

So what is collaboration? Collaboration is the act of working together with others. As its etymology reveals, the ideas of combined labour and joint effort lie at its core.[21] In the constitutional context, collaboration

---

[14] Kavanagh (2022); Kyritsis (2017); Cartabia (2020).

[15] Bingham (2000) 230.

[16] *Youngstown Sheet and Tube Co v Sawyer* 1953 343 US 579, 635 (Jackson J); Kavanagh (2016b) 235ff.

[17] *Plaut v Spendthrift Farms Inc* 514 US 211 (1995) (Scalia J).

[18] Greene (2018) 94, 103; MacDonnell (2019) 204; McLean (2018) 412–13.

[19] Hickman (2005a) 335.

[20] Hodge (2015) 474; Kavanagh (2022) 539–41.

[21] 'Collaboration' comes from the Latin *collaboratus* meaning 'to labour together' – *com* (with) and *laborare* (to labour or work).

refers to a shared commitment by diverse actors to carry out their responsibilities in mutually responsive and respectful ways as part of a joint endeavour oriented towards a common goal.[22] Collaboration is a complex kind of 'acting together'[23] marked by three features: (1) mutual responsiveness; (2) mutual respect and support; and (3) a commitment to the joint enterprise as a 'shared cooperative activity'.[24] To be clear, collaboration does not require consensus or conformity. Nor does it require identity or even equality between the parties in the collaborative effort. On the contrary, collaboration 'signposts the coming together of distinct elements, espousing complementary goals but responding to a different set of incentives'.[25] Indeed, the value and point of many collaborative endeavours is precisely the desire to reap the collaborative advantage of combining a diverse range of abilities, aptitudes, skills, and perspectives in the joint resolution of a complex problem. Therefore, the collaborative constitution has institutional heterogeneity at its core. Embracing a 'principled plurality of governing institutions',[26] the collaborative constitution envisages a joint enterprise where each branch makes a distinct but complementary contribution to the joint constitutional effort. Achieving just government under the constitution is a 'common goal, differently realised'.[27]

Throughout this book, I use the term 'constitutional constitutional*ism*' in order to capture the dynamic and diachronic dimension of constitutional government as a 'going concern'[28] and a 'work in progress'.[29] Recalling the metaphor of constitutionalism as 'rebuilding the ship at sea',[30] I emphasise that this constitutional 'building' and 'rebuilding' is an ongoing, collaborative effort which requires all hands on deck in order to keep the ship afloat and maintain it on an even keel.[31] Instead of framing the separation of powers solely as a set of sanctions for constitutional malfeasance, or as a negative admonition to 'mind the

---

[22] Bratman (2014); Dyzenhaus (2006) 4–5.

[23] Gardner (2002) 495; Kutz (2000).

[24] Bratman (1992); Bratman (2014) (providing a philosophical analysis of the nature of 'shared cooperative activity').

[25] Joseph (2004) 334; Carolan (2016a) 221–5.

[26] Sabl (2002) 15.

[27] Levi (1976) 391; Jackson (2016) 1718; Bateup (2006) 1169

[28] Balkin (2016) 242–3; Vermeule (2007) 245ff.

[29] Paris (2016) 26; Bell (2016) 421ff; Balkin (2016) 241; Leckey (2015) 19; Dyzenhaus (2012) 257.

[30] Elster, Offer & Preuss (1998); Vermeule (2007) 245.

[31] Craiutu (2017) 20, 159; Daly (2017) 280ff.

institutional gaps', the collaborative constitution also embraces a form of positive constitutionalism which calls on the branches to care for the connections between them.[32]

Once we adopt a 'wide-scope vision of the constitutional order'[33] which encompasses multiple institutions, this raises the question of how we can bring diverse institutional perspectives together, combining them in a workable *system* of constitutional government or a 'constitutional *order*' as it is sometimes called.[34] After all, if there is a 'polyphony'[35] of constitutional voices, each singing to a different tune, this runs the risk of having either a variety of competing virtuoso performances or a constitutional cacophony with no coordination between them. The answer offered in this book is that constitutional government is an ensemble piece not a virtuoso performance, where each branch plays a different role as part of a broader collaborative enterprise whilst remaining responsive to – and respectful of – the distinct contributions made by their fellow participants in the constitutional scheme. This does not require each contributor to the collaborative process to play the same tune on the same instrument at exactly the same tempo. Nor does it require them to achieve perfect constitutional harmony. On the contrary, the aim of the collaborative constitution is to combine the different tones, timbre and tempo of many voices, where each participant acknowledges their distinctive role *as part* of a broader collaborative effort whilst respecting and supporting the valuable contribution of their fellow participants. Sometimes in harmony, sometimes in counterpoint – and sometimes with syncopated rhythms, discordant contributions, and a few wrong notes along the way – the constitutional actors must recognise their own voice – and those of their fellow contributors – as one amongst many.[36] What combines them together in a shared collaborative activity is their mutual responsiveness, recognition and commitment to each other, and to the larger ensemble piece.

Working together with others in a constructive, long-term partnership over time is hard work. Not only does it require each of the partners to

---

[32] Kavanagh (2019); Appleby, MacDonnell & Synot (2020) 447; Dyzenhaus (2006) 5.

[33] Kyritsis (2017) 6; also see Kavanagh (2019) 63.

[34] Möllers (2013) 44.

[35] Kyritsis (2017) chapter 2 (providing 'a moral map of constitutional polyphony'); Craiutu (2017) 23–4, 49 (describing constitutional governance as a 'complex polyphony'); Waldron (1999a) chapter 3 (applying the metaphor of 'many voices' to the legislature); Schapiro (2009) (on 'polyphonic federalism'); Bratman (1992) 327ff.

[36] Rosenblum (2008) 7, 12.

carry out their respective roles with integrity, commitment, and professionalism, it also requires them to exercise some *self-discipline*, which manifests in norms of mutual respect, self-restraint, and self-control. This self-control is necessary in order to keep the partnership going over the long haul. Accepting the complexity of comity and counterbalancing, contestation and collaboration, tension and tolerance in the collaborative constitutional order, I characterise the relationship between the branches of government as a difficult but dynamic *constitutional partnership in progress*.

Three leitmotivs are woven into the tapestry of the book, and bear emphasis at the outset. These are: *constitutional relationships, unwritten constitutional norms*, and *constitutional restraint*. Let us start with the idea of *constitutional relationships*. In many ways, this is a book about relationships. Resting on the insight that 'constitutions are shaped by the working relationships between their principal institutions',[37] this book presents constitutional government as a relational phenomenon, forged in a complex web of ongoing relationships between a multiplicity of constitutional actors.[38] Once we appreciate constitutional government *as relational*, new and exciting lines of constitutional inquiry come into view. Instead of asking 'who is the ultimate arbiter of rights: the courts or the legislature?', we can reject the false dichotomy presupposed by the question and acknowledge that all three branches of government have a shared responsibility for upholding rights. Shifting our focus 'from rivals to relationships',[39] we can begin to examine the health of those relationships, uncovering the norms of respect, restraint, and reciprocity which frame and shape the relational dynamics in a healthy body politic.[40]

The focus on relationships has other analytical payoffs. For one thing, it 'renders visible a number of constitutional actors and dynamics that are often invisible on traditional accounts'.[41] Widening the cast of key constitutional actors 'beyond the usual constitutional coterie',[42] this book appreciates civil servants, legal advisers, parliamentary drafters, the Loyal Opposition, the Upper Chamber of a bicameral legislature, the Attorney General and many more as key constitutional actors, each embedded in a

---

[37] Griffith (2001) 49; Kavanagh (2019) 50.
[38] On the relational nature of constitutionalism, see Cartabia (2020); Kavanagh (2019); Kavanagh (2022); Appleby, MacDonnell & Synot (2020); Weis (2020b) 625.
[39] Kavanagh (2019).
[40] Appleby, MacDonnell & Synot (2020) 448; Cartabia (2020) 3ff.
[41] Appleby, MacDonnell & Synot (2020) 439.
[42] Ibid 449.

'dense collaborative network'[43] within, between and beyond the branches of government. Recasting the separation of powers in relational terms, we can shift the focus away from the febrile adversarialism of the Manichean narrative towards a more productive inquiry into the interactive dynamics and collaborative interplay between the key constitutional actors. Putting constitutional relationships at the heart of our constitutional understanding, this book takes up the challenge of analysing the relational interplay between a multiplicity of actors, whilst articulating the normative values, constitutional virtues, and practical institutional skills required to make constitutional relationships work.

The second, and related, theme concerns the fundamental role of *unwritten constitutional norms* which lie at the foundation of the collaborative constitution. By 'unwritten constitutional norms',[44] I mean the rules, norms, and practices of constitutional government 'accepted as obligatory by those concerned in the working of the constitution'.[45] Though neither required nor enforced by law, these non-legal rules nonetheless provide the 'basic ground rules of constitutional practice'[46] – the constitutional rules of the game which are binding as a matter of 'constitutional morality'.[47] Whilst the written constitutional rules may specify the *powers* of the branches of government, it is the unwritten constitutional norms which articulate the constitutional *responsibilities* which attach to those powers.[48] These norms regulate the roles and relationships between the branches of government.[49] They put flesh on the bones of the body politic.

In the UK and Commonwealth constitutional orders, these unwritten constitutional norms have a particular salience. Known as 'constitutional conventions',[50] they distribute responsibilities and facilitate collaboration between 'the major organs and officers of government'.[51] They are 'the hidden wiring'[52] on which the constitutional system depends. Yet, whilst these norms are often associated with the Anglo-Commonwealth

---

[43] Krisch (2010) 228; Cohn (2013) (on 'network governance').
[44] Elster (2010).
[45] Marshall (1984) 7.
[46] Wilson (2004) 420
[47] Dicey (1964) 24.
[48] Jennings (1959) 81–2; Halberstam (2004) 734.
[49] Elster (2010) 21; Pozen (2014) 30.
[50] Marshall (1984).
[51] Ibid 1; Pozen (2014) 30.
[52] Hennessy (1995).

constitutional tradition, they are no mere peculiarity of the uncodified constitution. In fact, *all* constitutions rely to a significant extent on unwritten norms of constitutional behaviour, which frame and shape the roles and relationships between the branches of government.[53] Indeed, all constitutions ultimately rest on the most fundamental norm of all, namely, that the key branches of government must recognise and accept the constitution as an authoritative framework for their behaviour and for the polity as a whole.[54] Thus, even the most comprehensively crafted 'written constitution' ultimately rests on political will and constitutional commitment by the key political actors to abide by the constitutional rules of the game.[55] Absent that fundamental commitment, the constitution becomes a hollow hope, a parchment barrier devoid of authority because the key constitutional actors do not recognise it as binding on their behaviour.

The salience and significance of these norms for any well-functioning constitutional system is put into stark relief in contemporary times. In the vast literature on constitutional corrosion and democracy decay across the world, the deepest lament amongst constitutional lawyers is that powerful political figures are violating the 'unwritten democratic norms'[56] of mutual toleration, respect, and forbearance on which a well-functioning constitutional democracy depends. Leading American scholars observe that much of Donald Trump's 'most vexing political behaviour challenge[d] not the interpreted Constitution, but the unwritten norms that facilitate comity and cooperation in governance'.[57] In an insightful analysis, political scientists Steven Levitsky and Daniel Ziblatt emphasise the pivotal importance of norms of respect for the constitutional rules of the game and the 'shared codes of conduct'[58] about how political actors are expected to behave. Without such foundational rules, constitutional practice descends into chaos and corrosive conflict.[59]

---

[53] Griffith (2001) 43; Gardner (2012) 89; Fallon (2001) 8; Levinson (2011) 697ff; N Siegel (2017); Pozen (2014) 30ff (on the role of 'unwritten constitutional norms' in the US system); Dixon & Stone (2018) (on 'the invisible constitution in comparative perspective'); MacDonnell (2019); Endicott (2021) 14–15; Taylor (2014) (on conventions in German constitutionalism).

[54] Hart (2012) chapters 5 & 6 (famously describing this as the 'rule of recognition').

[55] Levinson (2011); Chafetz (2011).

[56] Levitsky & Ziblatt (2019) 8, 100ff.

[57] Pozen (2014) 9; Greene (2018); Balkin (2018) 24–8.

[58] Levitsky & Ziblatt (2019) 101.

[59] Pozen (2014) 9.

Indeed, if the key political actors stop observing those norms, then the constitutional checks and balances we rely on for security against constitutional abuse 'cannot serve as the bulwarks of democracy we imagine them to be'.[60]

This underscores the foundational Hartian point that all legal systems ultimately rely on a commitment of the key constitutional actors to abide by the rules of the constitutional game and treat them 'as normative'.[61] Beneath the constitutional architecture of legal rules lies constitutional attitudes as political norms. As Mattias Kumm observed, 'at the heart of constitutionalism is not a constitutional text but a constitutional cognitive frame'.[62] Instead of embracing the idea of 'constitution as architecture',[63] therefore, this book foregrounds the idea of 'constitutionalism as mindset',[64] grounded in the norms and beliefs, the attitudes and actions, the dispositions and commitments of the constitutional actors to make the system work. When Donald Trump became President of the United States, his 'norm-breaking' behaviour highlighted the fundamentality and fragility of these 'unwritten rules'[65] to a well-functioning constitutional order – norms which had been largely invisible to American constitutional scholars in previous generations because they had been taken for granted in a relatively well-functioning system. One of the aims of *The Collaborative Constitution* is to bring to these 'unwritten' norms to the surface of constitutional analysis, rendering them visible for all to see.

The third leitmotiv which echoes across this book is the theme of *constitutional restraint*. In all long-term working relationships, discord and disagreement, arguments and acrimony will inevitably arise at times. A healthy long-term relationship built on the firm foundations of mutual commitment, respect, and restraint can weather these storms, enabling the partners – and the partnership as a whole – to move forward in a constructive and collaborative fashion. However, if these flashpoints of friction become the pervasive, persistent and endemic mode of inter-institutional interaction, then this will undermine the fundamental norms of respect, trust and mutual recognition on which the working constitution depends.

---

[60] Levitsky & Ziblatt (2019) 7.
[61] Green (2012) xxi.
[62] Kumm (2009) 321.
[63] Bator (1990).
[64] Koskenniemi (2006).
[65] Levitsky & Ziblatt (2019) chapter 6 (on 'The Unwritten Rules of American Politics').

In order to avoid a downward spiral of escalating animosity and entrenched antagonism, the key constitutional actors need to carry out their constitutional roles with a modicum of constitutional restraint. Therefore, mutual respect begets mutual restraint, which bespeaks a concern to channel, constrain and manage interbranch conflict and rivalry in constitutionally constructive ways. Collaboration does not naively suggest an absence of tension or conflict between the branches. Instead, it discerns a duty of mutual respect and restraint between interdependent actors who have a responsibility to make the constitutional partnership work. If constitutions are shaped by the working relationships between the key constitutional actors, then there is a duty on all branches of government to work on their relationships and to treat each other with constitutional civility and mutual respect. On the collaborative vision, contestation and conflict must be mediated by the norms of comity, civility and collaboration. Fierce disagreement must be moderated by forbearance and a commitment to constitutional fair play.[66] Instead of celebrating interbranch conflict in the form of dramatic *constitutional showdowns*,[67] the collaborative constitution emphasises the quotidian demands of *constitutional slowdown* as a preferable *modus vivendi* for a successful long-term partnership over time.

In mapping the contours of the collaborative constitution, this book seeks to provide a new linguistic register in which to analyse constitutional dynamics, one that 'sounds more in responsibility and restraint'[68] than in conflict and confrontation. The collaborative constitution emphasises an 'ethics of responsibility'[69] and a collaborative mindset which frames and shapes inter-institutional engagement over time. Whilst leading theoretical accounts of constitutional government emphasise the inevitability of disagreement, foregrounding a conflictual narrative of 'constitutional hardball',[70] this book seeks to reorient the inquiry towards more constructive questions about how to manage, channel and frame those disagreements in order to make them politically productive in a constitutional democracy. Of course, we are naturally fascinated by the agonistic drama of high-stakes conflict and constitutional showdowns. Conflict sells copy, whilst quiet collaboration, compromise and civility behind the

---

[66] Levitsky & Ziblatt (2019) 107, 213; Heclo (2008) 3.
[67] Posner & Vermeule (2008).
[68] Pozen (2014) 63.
[69] Weber (1919) 32; Sabl (2002) 168; Chafetz (2011).
[70] Tushnet (2004); Balkin (2008).

scenes is hardly newsworthy. We are transfixed by narratives of 'competing supremacies'[71] locked in a 'contest for constitutional authority'.[72]

Yet, by focusing on the blockbuster cases and fiery flashpoints of political friction, we 'guarantee drama at the expense of perspective'.[73] We also risk mistaking the exception for the norm, thereby distorting our overall vision of the constitutional dynamics at stake. In calling for collaboration, this book aims to seed a more productive conversation about the laborious requirements of constitutional process, where constitutional actors agree to play by the rules of the game, acting in accordance with the demanding constitutional role-imperatives of a collaborative constitutional scheme. Though admittedly less glamorous and less dramatic than 'constitutional showdowns', these are the requirements that make constitutional democracy work. We may spend our evenings transfixed by cinematic narratives about relationships breaking down, but this book explores the quotidian practices of making long-term constitutional relationships work. Turning our backs on the high-octane drama of friction and rupture – where the key constitutional actors face off against each other in a heightened state of conflict and crisis – this book documents the slow, painstaking, and often invisible labour of developing constitutional meaning collaboratively over time.

Whilst leading theoretical accounts champion the idea of full-blooded disagreements on questions of justice, this book focuses on how such disagreements are negotiated, constrained and ultimately resolved in a constitutional democracy. One of the most basic rationales of constitutional government is to 'prevent the day-to-day political competition from devolving into no-holds-barred conflict'[74] and to manage disagreements about how to proceed as a political community.[75] The norms of

---

[71] Hunt (2003) 337; Dyzenhaus (2006) 7.

[72] Burgess (1992). Other book titles reveal our fascination with conflict: see e.g. Geyh (2006) (*When Courts and Congress Collide*); Burt (1992) (*The Constitution in Conflict*); Hampshire (2000) (*Justice Is Conflict*). For the related focus on constitutional crisis, see Graber, Levinson & Tushnet (2018a) (*Constitutional Democracy in Crisis?*) (though note the question mark); Runciman (2019) (*How Democracy Ends*); Levitsky & Ziblatt (2019) (*How Democracies Die*).

[73] Sabl (2002) 3.

[74] Issacharoff (2018) 449; Ginsburg & Huq (2016) 19; Ginsburg & Huq (2018); Balkin (2018) 15–16.

[75] Loughlin (2003) 39; Carolan (2009) 4; Levinson & Balkin (2009) 714 ('Disagreement and conflict are natural features of politics. The goal of constitutions is to manage them within acceptable boundaries').

collaborative constitutionalism are the keystone of that effort. In order to make the constitutional partnership work, this book draws on a cluster of undramatic though deeply demanding constitutional virtues, including comity,[76] forbearance,[77] civility,[78] moderation,[79] trust,[80] compromise,[81] democratic discipline, and constitutional self-restraint.[82] These are the virtues, traditions, and practices which are central to 'making democracy work'.[83] They lie at the heart of the collaborative constitution.

2 The Collaborative Constitution as Practice and Principle

In developing and defending the idea of the collaborative constitution, the argument of this book is forged through an iterative engagement between abstract theory and constitutional practice, perennially testing theoretical claims against common features of that practice. Proceeding in the mode of a 'reflective equilibrium',[84] I investigate how abstract propositions square with familiar features of constitutional practice, and then return to the theoretical inquiry with a series of insights, puzzles and problems which any credible constitutional theory must explain, or explain away. In striving to make sense of the roles and relationships between the branches of government in a constitutional democracy, I draw on the deep well of analytical legal philosophy, political theory, and constitutional theory. But I also take constitutional practice seriously as generative of its own insights and inspiration for the theoretical and comparative scholar.[85] Connecting theory and practice in a dialectical process of mutual correction, creative insight and critical import, I adopt

---

[76] On comity, see Endicott (2015a); Katzmann (1988).
[77] On forbearance, see Levitsky & Ziblatt (2019) 102, 106–7, 127–8, 212; Holland (2016).
[78] On civility and civic culture, see Bejan (2017); Calhoun (2000); Carter (1998); Shils (1997); Almond & Verba (1989); Bellah et al. (2008); Craiutu (2017) 23–5, 155–9.
[79] On moderation, see Craiutu (2012), (2007); Rosenblum (2008) 121
[80] On trust, see O'Neill (2002); Putnam (1994) 15, 89–90, 171–80. On the role of trust in 'making and breaking cooperative relations', see Gambetta (1988); Kramer (2000); Axelrod (1990).
[81] On compromise, see Gutmann & Thompson (2014); Fumurescu (2013); Margalit (2010); Sabl (2002) chapters 1 & 2; Craiutu (2017) 27–32, 119–20, 212–16, 222–3; Weinstock (2013).
[82] On the value and virtue of 'democratic restraint', see Wall (2007); Sabl (2002) 48.
[83] Putnam (1994); Stoker (2006).
[84] Rawls (1971) 18–22, 46–53; Pettit (2012) 20; Rosenblum (1998) 19.
[85] Kyritsis (2012) 299; Fallon (2001) chapter 1.

a theoretically informed but empirically grounded perspective which is internal to constitutional practice.[86]

One question which arises is whether the collaborative constitution *describes* a particular constitutional system or, alternatively, whether it *prescribes* a normative ideal to which constitutional democracy should aspire. The answer is that it does both. In defending the collaborative constitution, I argue that it rests on a phenomenologically plausible account of key features of constitutional practice, whilst simultaneously embodying a normatively attractive constitutional ideal. In short, *The Collaborative Constitution* combines descriptive and normative dimensions as part of an analytical account of constitutional government which is both grounded in practice and geared towards principle.[87] Taking constitutional law as it is currently practised, I try to 'reconstruct aspects of its immanent normative structure'[88] in a way which illuminates the practice and uncovers the ideals to which that practice aspires. Given the centrality of this methodological approach to the book as a whole, it is worth clarifying its contours at the outset.

Let us start with the idea that the collaborative account is *grounded in practice*. In this book, I adopt a phenomenological approach, which takes the institutions, practices, structures, norms and modes of decision making in a constitutional democracy as the primary object of analysis, whilst seeking to understand, explain and illuminate – in short, to make sense of – that practice in all its complexity.[89] In order to grasp the phenomenology of inter-institutional interaction, this book proceeds from the premise that normative theorising about what institutions *should* do must rest on an accurate picture of what those institutions *can* and *cannot* do.[90] Thus, if the central question animating this book is 'who should protect rights in a democracy, and how?', then philosophical analysis must be complemented by *institutional analysis* of *what* the key institutions do, *how* they do it, and *how they interact* with other actors in a differentiated institutional landscape.[91] On this approach, 'taking rights seriously' entails 'taking institutions seriously'[92] – not just as abstract instantiations of the

[86] Leckey (2015) chapters 1 & 2.
[87] Fowkes (2016a) 4; Fombad (2016a).
[88] Pozen (2014) 9, 74.
[89] Raz (1994) 44.
[90] Fallon (2001) 37; Friedman (2005) 270; Graber (2002) 332; King (2012) 2, 127; Young (2012) 3.
[91] Young (2012) 3; Komesar (1994).
[92] Whittington (2000) 697; Komesar (1984).

values we prize, but as concrete practices, structures and norms which frame and shape institutional behaviour in a plurality of institutional settings.

In striving to illuminate the roles and relationships between the branches of government, this book adopts an 'internal point of view',[93] appreciating the rules, practices, and norms of institutional behaviour from the perspective of those who are charged with making the constitution work.[94] Beginning with 'an inquiry into the mundane practices of actually existing constitutions',[95] I give credence to the 'observable self-understandings'[96] of judges, legislators and government Ministers about how they perceive their roles and relationships in the constitutional scheme. In doing so, I grapple with the tools of their trade, situating their decisions within the relevant institutional context. Thus, when examining the judicial role, I combine an appreciation of the insightful theoretical literature on the subject with a descent into the doctrinal detail and procedural rules of the adjudicative process, viewing judicial decision-making in the crucible of constitutional practice. Drawing on a close reading of cases in context – supplemented by practitioner manuals and academic textbooks – I listen to what judges have to say about the challenges of judging in a democracy.[97] Likewise, when striving to understand the role of the Executive and legislature in the constitutional scheme, I engage with the political science scholarship on what these institutions do. In short, I put the politics in 'political political theory'.[98] The resulting account may fall short of eulogies extolling the dignity of the legislature as the apotheosis of our most noble democratic ideals. But it has the countervailing value of being truer to the practice of Executive and legislative constitutionalism on the ground.[99]

The upshot of this approach is a book which ranges widely and deeply across disciplinary divides – from legal doctrinal analysis to normative argument, political science to political theory, and comparative

---

[93] Hart (2012) 89–90, 115–16, 242–3, 254; Harel (2014) 230.

[94] Heclo (2006) 733; Raz (1979) 181.

[95] Loughlin (2006) 436 (describing this as 'the immanent method' of constitutional theorising).

[96] Leckey (2015) 155. On the role of self-understandings in legal theory, see Smith (2000) 249; Dickson (2015a) 221, 225–8; Dickson (2015b) 578–85; Kyritsis & Lakin (2022) 5–6.

[97] In the UK, there has been a recent proliferation of judicial speeches, which are available at https://www.supremecourt.uk/news/speeches.html.

[98] Waldron (2016).

[99] Komesar (1994).

constitutional law to constitutional theory. This interdisciplinary approach is not borne out of a hubristic ambition for methodological multiplicity. On the contrary, it is rooted in a humble appreciation for the complexity of the institutional questions posed in this book. If constitutionalism is a collaborative enterprise between distinct and diverse institutional actors, then we need to attend to the diverse institutional contexts in which collaborative constitutionalism is forged.

So much for the collaborative constitution being *grounded in practice*. What about the other dimension of being *geared towards principle*? Beyond its use as an explanatory account, the collaborative constitution also articulates a normative constitutional ideal, i.e. a set of norms which govern – and *should* govern – the roles and relationships between the branches of government in a constitutional democracy. When the branches of government carry out their respective roles in the constitutional division of labour in a spirit of comity, civility and collaboration, this helps to make the constitution work. As American constitutional scholar Philip Bobbit observed, 'the most successful constitutional order is one that encourages collaboration . . . among the various constitutional institutions and actors, and thereby enhances its own stability'.[100] On my account, therefore, collaborative constitutionalism is what happens when constitutional government goes well.[101]

Of course, as with any ideal, reality has a way of falling short. The constitutional actors in any system may fail to live up to the norms and requirements of the collaborative constitution, either by overreaching the limits of their own institutional role, or by failing to treat their constitutional partners with comity and constitutional respect. Indeed, in contemporary times, the collaborative constitution is increasingly under threat. With the rise of populist authoritarianism across the world, we see the alarming spread of constitutional corrosion and democracy decay, where powerful political actors use strong-arm tactics to undermine the constitution from within.[102] Whilst maintaining the formal façade of constitutional democracy, they strip out the 'hidden wiring'[103] – the norms of comity, collaboration and constitutional commitment – required to make constitutional democracy work.[104] The result is 'a

---

[100] Bobbitt (1982) 182.
[101] Ibid 182.
[102] Sadurski (2019) 8, 253, 259.
[103] Hennessy (1995).
[104] Sadurski (2019) 8, 19, 179, 186, 253–61.

constitution without constitutionalism'[105] – a written document which endorses laudable constitutional ideals, without the hard work and constitutional commitment on which a well-functioning constitutional democracy depends. Less drastically, but no less insidiously, established democracies such as the UK and the US are experiencing a deterioration in respect for the inherited norms of constitutional fair play, and contempt for the accountability actors designed to keep the Executive in check.[106] These days, it feels as if we are all living in 'fragile democracies'.[107]

But this evolving picture of constitutional corrosion does not undercut the force of the collaborative conception of constitutionalism. It fact, it raises the stakes and heightens the imperative to take collaborative constitutionalism seriously as a way of sustaining the working constitution over time. The current decline in respect for constitutional norms highlights the critical importance of preserving the precious resources of the collaborative constitution, lending new urgency to claims that they should not be squandered through careless practice and raw political ambition devoid of an ethics of constitutional responsibility.[108] The creeping authoritarianism of contemporary regimes underscores the point that a working constitutional democracy is not guaranteed by parchment barriers, nor by an intricate matrix of checks and balances designed to run like constitutional clockwork. At the deepest level, all constitutions ultimately rest on a commitment by the key constitutional actors to abide by the norms of constitutional democracy under the rule of law.[109] In short, they depend on a fundamental commitment to the principles and practices of collaborative constitutionalism.

In a context where that commitment is fragile even in the most established constitutional democracies, we need to attend to the deep foundations of constitutional democracy, ensuring that we recognise the importance of unwritten norms of constitutionalism to making any written constitution work. Even when key political figures fall short of the ideal of collaborative constitutionalism – as they inevitably will from time to time – this is the ideal against which they should be understood and assessed, and towards which they should strive.[110] Given the practice-oriented, internal

---

[105] Fowkes (2016b) 205.
[106] Pozen (2014) 9.
[107] Issacharoff (2015).
[108] Weber (1919).
[109] Levinson (2011); Sadurski (2020a) 330.
[110] Raz (1979) 47; Dickson (2001) 138.

approach adopted in this book, which seeks to understand constitutional government from within, it should not be surprising that many constitutional democracies already conform – imperfectly but substantially – to the norms of collaborative constitutionalism.[111] This is because the norms of collaborative constitutionalism are already inherent in constitutional practice to some meaningful degree. Even if the key constitutional actors fall short, we can still articulate the ideal they have betrayed. Understanding institutions involves understanding the ideal to which they aspire – 'for that is how they are supposed to function, and that is how they publicly claim that they attempt to function'.[112] The argument of this book is that constitutionalism is, and should be, oriented towards the collaborative ideal.

In articulating and defending that ideal, this book does not pretend to provide a programmatic blueprint for detailed institutional behaviour in an ideal constitutional universe. There is no such place, and there is no such blueprint. Institutional behaviour and interaction is inevitably contingent and context-specific to a large degree, dependent on a myriad of historical, social, political, legal and cultural factors which no constitutional theory can hope to encompass. Moreover, the collaborative conception of the separation of powers accepts the inevitable and valuable variation in how that ideal is instantiated across diverse systems with discrete constitutional histories. Nonetheless, *The Collaborative Constitution* articulates a constitutional ideal with a 'prescriptive core',[113] thereby providing some theoretical, analytical, and institutional resources we can use to evaluate, appraise, and critique constitutional performance. In this spirit, I offer the idea of the collaborative constitution both as an explication of constitutionalism in practice and as an articulation of a constitutional ideal which informs – and should inform – institutional behaviour in a constitutional democracy.

3   Constitutions, Comparison, Context

In defending the collaborative constitution, I base my analysis on democratic constitutional orders, whose salient features include a general adherence to the principles of democracy, the separation of powers, the protection of rights, and the rule of law. Particularly in the first part of the book where I lay the theoretical foundations, I draw freely on

---

[111] Pozen (2014) 89.
[112] Raz (2009) 103–4; Raz (1979) 47, 181; Rawls (2005) 85ff.
[113] Kyritsis (2017) 211.

examples from a number of different jurisdictions which broadly share a commitment to these principles, even if that commitment appears shaky at times.[114] However, in order to illustrate the idea of the collaborative constitution in context, I provide a fine-grained analysis of rights protection in the UK constitutional order, alongside insightful comparators from the Commonwealth constitutional tradition.

On one level, choosing the UK as an illustrative case-study may seem strange. After all, given its famously 'unwritten constitution', the UK system is often presented as exceptional and aberrational in comparative terms.[115] However, there are two features of the UK constitution which make it an insightful theoretical and comparative case study in this context. First, all constitutions ultimately rest on unwritten norms of constitutional behaviour, including a commitment by the constitutional actors to treat the written text as authoritative, and norms of inter-institutional behaviour requiring the branches of government to treat each other with comity and respect.[116] At this fundamental level, the UK constitutional order is the same as all other constitutional systems.[117] Indeed, the very fact that the UK lacks a 'canonical constitutional master-text'[118] points up the particular importance of these norms in grounding a constitutional democracy. Therefore, rather than being an aberration, the UK constitutional order makes explicit the common constitutional foundations which all constitutional systems share.[119]

Second, the UK's exceptionalism was significantly reduced in the context of rights following the enactment of the Human Rights Act 1998 (HRA), where courts were empowered to evaluate legislation against a canonical set of rights and, if found wanting, to declare that the law is incompatible with rights. True, the HRA deliberately departed from some features of American-style judicial review, particularly in its determination to prevent courts having the power to strike down or invalidate legislation.[120] Nonetheless, the very act of enumerating rights in a canonical document which courts are then empowered to use as standards against which legislation is judged, brings the UK courts into

---

[114] For a similar approach, see King (2012) 10–13.
[115] See e.g. Graber, Levinson & Tushnet (2018b) 8 (who question whether the UK even counts as a constitutional democracy).
[116] Walters (2008) 260, 265; MacDonnell (2019) 191; McLean (2018) 395; Foley (1989).
[117] Gardner (2012).
[118] Ibid 90.
[119] Walters (2016); MacDonnell (2019).
[120] Human Rights Act 1998, section 4.

the common constitutional realm of reviewing legislation for compliance with rights. The recurrent political proposals to amend and repeal the HRA do not change this, since the Government has always proposed to put an alternative statutory or parliamentary Bill of Rights in its place.[121] In an era of statutory Bills of Rights, the gap between the 'written' and 'unwritten' – or, more accurately, between the codified and uncodified constitutions – begins to close.

But there are other reasons why the UK provides an insightful case-study of collaborative constitutionalism in action. For one thing, the HRA embodies an innovation in constitutional design which explicitly engages all three branches of government in a joint enterprise of protecting rights. Instead of positing the courts as the solitary and supreme guardian of rights, the HRA specifically enlisted the Executive and legislature to play a central and constructive rights-protecting role in a multi-institutional constitutional scheme.[122] The HRA was intended to 'weave acceptance and understanding of [rights] into the democratic process' so that 'positive rights and liberties would become the focus and concern of legislators, administrators and judges alike'.[123] By explicitly drawing the Executive and legislature into the joint enterprise of protecting rights, the HRA therefore provides both an illustrative case-study and instructive testing ground for collaborative constitutionalism in action.

There is another reason why the UK experience sheds light on broader comparative and theoretical themes. When the Human Rights Act was enacted, it was hailed by comparative constitutional lawyers as instantiating a 'new model of constitutionalism'[124] which – together with Canada, New Zealand, and some Australian states – carved out a constitutionally desirable middle path between the 'bipolar extremes'[125] of parliamentary supremacy on the one hand and US-style judicial supremacy on the other. Variously described as 'the new Commonwealth model',[126] the 'hybrid

---

[121] See e.g. the proposed Bill of Rights Bill 2022, which was eventually withdrawn, at www .gov.uk/government/publications/bill-of-rights-bill-documents. For claims that the HRA enacted a 'parliamentary Bill of Rights', see Kavanagh (2009a) 2; Ewing (2004); Hiebert & Kelly (2015) 1; Klug (2001) 370; Elliott (2011) 13 (describing the HRA and the New Zealand Bill of Rights Act as 'interpretative bills of rights').

[122] Section 19 HRA; White Paper *Rights Brought Home: Human Rights Bill*, Cm 1997 Cm 3782 [3.1].

[123] Irvine (2003a) 36; Straw (1999); Hiebert & Kelly (2015) 9, 251 ff; Hunt (2010) 601–2.

[124] Gardbaum (2013b).

[125] Gardbaum (2013b) 1, 51

[126] Gardbaum (2013b).

approach',[127] the 'dialogue model',[128] or 'weak-form review',[129] the distinctive feature of the new model was that it left the last word with the democratically elected legislature.[130] Thus, whilst the Canadian Charter of Rights and Freedoms empowered the courts to strike down rights-infringing legislative provisions, it nonetheless allowed the legislature to override some of those rights.[131] In the UK, the courts were empowered to make a declaration of incompatibility, but that declaration had no impact on the validity of the impugned legislation; nor did it place a legal obligation on Parliament to change the law to comply with the declaratory ruling.[132] As Stephen Gardbaum put it, the new model of constitutionalism 'decoupled' constitutional rights-based review 'from judicial supremacy by empowering the legislature to have the final word'.[133] The recurring leitmotiv of the new model was one of judicial decision and legislative dissent, judicial oversight and legislative override. The New Commonwealth Model was said to rest on a combination of weak – or at least 'weakened'[134] – courts, and strong, if not emboldened, legislatures.[135]

As an innovation in constitutional design which self-consciously departed from the American model, the New Commonwealth Model elicited great excitement amongst constitutional theorists and comparative lawyers. Not only did it provide a real-world instantiation of a new constitutional design, it also seemed to provide a seductively simple solution to the notorious 'counter-majoritarian difficulty'[136] which had vexed American scholars for decades. By shifting the last word from unelected courts to the democratic legislature, the New Commonwealth Model seemed to have found the Holy Grail of reconciling constitutionalism and democracy. Instead of allowing courts to displace the legislature, now the democratic legislature could displace the courts.[137] All at once,

---

[127] Goldsworthy (2003a) 483; Weill (2012) 349.
[128] Hogg & Bushell (1997); Roach (2016b); Young (2017); Hickman (2005a).
[129] Tushnet (2008b); Dixon (2012); Dixon (2019b); Bateup (2009).
[130] Kavanagh (2015c) 1009; Tushnet (2008b) 21; Yap (2015) 1–2.
[131] *Canadian Charter of Rights and Freedoms 1982*, section 33.
[132] Section 4 HRA.
[133] Gardbaum (2001) 709.
[134] Dixon (2019b).
[135] Tushnet (2008b); Kavanagh (2015c).
[136] Bickel (1986) 16.
[137] On the idea of institutional 'displacement' as pivotal to the distinction between 'strong-form' and 'weak-form' review, see Tushnet (2004) 1897; Tushnet (2003a) 2786; cf. Kavanagh (2015c) 1010–13.

the UK's position in comparative discourse shifted from constitutional pariah to constitutional paradigm, providing a 'better, more democratically defensible balance of power between courts and legislatures'[138] than traditional constitutional models.

As a leading exemplar of the New Commonwealth Model, the UK therefore provides a fertile testing ground for these ambitious theoretical and taxonomic claims. Not only has the distinction between 'strong-form' and 'weak-form review' become an enormously influential way of categorising constitutional systems,[139] the idea of 'weak-form review' has also garnered support amongst constitutional theorists who had long resisted rights-based review on grounds of democratic illegitimacy.[140] Therefore, alongside Canada, New Zealand, and some Australian states, the UK system provides a living laboratory to test some of the key theoretical and comparative claims which dominate contemporary constitutional scholarship. By offering a textured and nuanced narrative of how the UK system works – one which speaks back to the global, comparative, and theoretical field – this book makes a targeted intervention in the broader comparative and theoretical literature on how to uphold rights in a democracy. It speaks in the vernacular, whilst translating the Commonwealth experience into the *lingua franca* of global constitutional theory. Viewing comparative constitutional law as an 'expanded form of contextualisation'[141] where understanding is deepened by differentiation, I argue that some of that experience got lost in translation. Part of the aim of this book, therefore, is to make a key contribution to comparative constitutional law scholarship, in the form of a complement, corrective and challenge to leading comparative taxonomies.[142]

---

[138] Gardbaum (2013b) 75–6; Tushnet & Dixon (2014) 102; Gardbaum (2001) 744; Kavanagh (2015c) 1010–13

[139] Lavapuro, Ojanen & Scheinin (2011) (Finland); Hirschl (2011) (the Nordic countries); Khosla (2010) 759ff (India); Weill (2012) & Weill (2014) (Israel); Stone (2008) 30–2 (Australia); Kelly & Hennigar (2012) (Canada); Dixon (2012) (America, UK, Canada, New Zealand); Colón-Ríos (2012) & Colón-Ríos (2014) (Latin America); Kavanagh (2015c) 1009 (UK).

[140] Waldron (2016) 199–200; Dixon (2017).

[141] Dann (2005) 1465; see also Watt (2012) (on 'comparison as deep appreciation'); Lemmens (2012) (on comparison as an 'act of modesty'); Zweigert & Kötz (1998) 21, 40–41; Geiringer (2018) 323.

[142] For discussion of the complementarity between fine-grained contextual comparativism and broader taxonomies, see the *ICON-Debate* with Kavanagh (2015c) 1031; Gardbaum (2015) 1048; Kavanagh (2015d) 1052; see also Geiringer (2019).

The deeper point here is that collaborative constitutionalism is not inexorably tied to any particular constitutional design. It lives primarily in the unwritten norms of comity, collaboration, and constrained conflict which lie at the foundation of a constitutional order. Of course, some designs and decisional structures may bolster and enhance collaborative constitutionalism more than others. The HRA is one such option, especially given its explicit invitation to all three branches of government to contribute to the joint enterprise of protecting rights. The HRA wears its collaborative colours on its sleeve. Nonetheless, whilst this book uses the UK as an illustrative case–study and instantiation of the collaborative ideal, this has less to do with the precise institutional configurations of the HRA, and more to do with how the branches of government understand their constitutional roles, and how they engage with each other when implementing the constitutional framework in practice.

4   Outline and Overview

This book is divided into four parts. Part I lays the theoretical foundations of the collaborative constitution, examining 'Institutions and Interactions' through the lens of leading theoretical accounts. Proceeding dialectically, and to some extent chronologically, Chapter 1 addresses the 'Manichean narrative' which pits courts against legislatures. In order to make headway in the debate about who should protect rights in a democracy, this chapter argues that we need to move 'beyond Manicheanism'. Chapter 2 considers the influential theory of 'dialogue' which dominated the discourse on protecting rights in the early part of the twenty-first century. Acknowledging the insights that dialogue brought to the constitutional table – particularly its emphasis on the iterative and interactive nature of constitutionalism in context – I argue that 'dialogue' overpromised and underdelivered. By resting on an over-simplified picture of interbranch interaction, and succumbing to the polarities of the traditional Manichean narrative, it ultimately led to a distorted understanding of the key interactional dynamics at work in a well-functioning constitutional democracy.[143]

The pivotal chapter of this book is Chapter 3, which makes 'the case for collaboration' as a descriptively defensible and normatively attractive way of understanding and illuminating the relationship between the

---

[143] Geiringer (2019) 573.

branches of government in a constitutional democracy. Together with this Introduction and the Conclusion, Chapter 3 contains the main arc of the argument in favour of the collaborative constitution. Moving 'from rivals to relationships'[144] – and from conversation to collaboration – Chapter 3 sets out the key claims of collaborative constitutionalism, laying down the theoretical foundations on which the subsequent analysis rests. Instead of viewing the branches of government *in isolation, in opposition* or *in conversation,* Chapter 3 argues that they should be viewed instead *in collaboration* – as partners in a collaborative enterprise, based on a division of labour where each branch has a distinct but complementary role to play in upholding rights.[145]

The rest of the book puts collaborative constitutionalism in motion, examining in detail and in depth how a plurality of constitutional actors work together to make rights real. Part II presents the Executive and legislature as 'pro-constitutional actors',[146] exploring the iterative, interactive and collaborative dynamic between them in the Westminster system. The decision to begin the institutional analysis with the political actors and not the courts was deliberate. It bespeaks a constitutional perspective which views the Government and legislature as leading protagonists and full partners in the collaborative enterprise of protecting rights.[147] Starting with the Executive and legislature also has the advantage of following the constitutional chronology on the ground. After all, when courts adjudicate whether a legislative provision violates rights, they typically enter the picture *after* the legislation has been crafted, proposed, scrutinised and debated by the Executive and legislature acting in concert.[148] Therefore, in terms of defining, defending and specifying rights, the Executive and legislature *get there first.* My analysis follows this constitutional chronology, exploring the primacy of the political actors in making rights real in a constitutional democracy.

Part III turns to the role of judging in a democracy. Eschewing the image of the hero-judge, I defend a more modest but, I suggest, more accurate idea of 'judge as partner'. On the collaborative vision, judges are neither solitary crusaders for moral enlightenment nor our saviours from democratic depravity. Instead, they are independent decision-

---

[144] Kavanagh (2019).
[145] Coenen (2001) 1590.
[146] Jackson (2016).
[147] Kumm (2009) 305; King (2012) 57–8.
[148] Gardbaum (2013b) 80; Kyritsis (2012) 319.

makers in an interdependent constitutional scheme, whose role is to adjudicate legal disputes, whilst paying respect to the democratically elected legislature. Chapter 7 examines the anatomy of adjudication, revealing a significant but subsidiary role for the courts in the collaborative law-making enterprise. Building on this collaborative account, Chapter 8 analyses adjudication under the HRA, presenting it as a 'constitutional partnership in progress'. Chapter 9 defends the idea of 'calibrated constitutional review' as a way of operationalising the judicial duty of respect for the democratic legislature in the constitutional scheme. Charting a middle course between supremacy and subordination, I argue that judges must *calibrate* the mode, means and intensity of review out of respect for the relative institutional competence, expertise and legitimacy of the branches of government.[149] Chapter 10 rounds out the analysis by exploring the tools and techniques of collaborative constitutionalism in court, documenting the myriad doctrines and devices which courts use to give shape to the shared responsibility for protecting rights. Whilst the underlying theme of 'judge as partner' portrays judges as largely responsive actors in the constitutional scheme, this chapter highlights the catalytic function of courts in prompting and prodding the Executive and legislature to rise to their own responsibilities to promote rights. Framed under the rubric of 'court as catalyst'[150] and 'judge as nudge', the courts are portrayed as suitably responsive but subtly catalytic actors in the collaborative constitutional scheme.

The fourth and final part of this book turns to the idea of 'Responsive Legislatures', exploring the ways in which the Executive and legislature respond to judicial decisions that legislation violates rights. Given the pivotal importance of the legislature's 'right to disagree'[151] with courts in so-called weak-form systems or dialogic review, Chapter 11 undertakes a close, contextual and comparative assessment of the legislative powers to ignore, override or displace judicial decisions about rights in the UK and Canada. Exploring the conspicuous 'underuse of the override' in both jurisdictions, this chapter argues that the rare use of the legislative override was a feature, not a bug, in the constitutional design of both

---

[149] Komesar (1994) 23; Kavanagh (2015c) 1038 (arguing that the courts should 'calibrate their respect for the institutional competence and legitimacy of the elected branches of government, thus facilitating a division of labour between them').

[150] Scott & Sturm (2007).

[151] Yap (2012) 532–3.

of these systems from the outset. Though the legislature was *empowered* to override or reject judicial decisions, it was *expected* to exercise this power with caution and circumspection. Departing from the dominant scholarly narrative which treats the underuse of the override as a failure of democratic dialogue, I defend it as a potential success story in the collaborative constitution. Chapter 11 is an example of 'fine-grained, contextual comparativism'[152] in action, attuned to the way in which constitutional texts can only be properly understood when viewed in the context of constitutional culture.

Chapter 12 turns to the question of whether there is an emerging constitutional convention in favour of complying with declarations of incompatibility under the HRA. Following a comprehensive empirical analysis of all political responses to declarations of incompatibility since the HRA was enacted, I argue that there is a strong political presumption in favour of complying with declarations of incompatibility rather than defying them outright. Building on previous empirical accounts,[153] I discern the emergence of a constitutional convention in *statu nascendi* where the political actors believe themselves to be under a general constitutional obligation to comply with declarations of incompatibility, unless exceptional circumstances arise.

The book concludes with some broader reflections on 'the currency of collaboration' in contemporary times. In the fractured political landscape of the post-Brexit era, political actors in the UK are increasingly hostile to rights, manifesting a worrying impatience with constitutional constraints and the inherited norms of the collaborative constitution. Given this context, it is tempting to end the book with a 'eulogy for the constitution that was'[154] and a constitutional *cri de coeur* for the demise of the political constitution. I resist that temptation for two reasons. First, even acknowledging the current strains and pains in the collaborative constitutional order, I believe that the UK constitution is still a relatively well-functioning example of collaborative constitutionalism in action. The traditions of mutual respect between the organs of government and the discipline of responsible government in a parliamentary system, not to mention the abiding constitutional commitment to liberty and the rule of law, run so deep and wide in the British constitutional culture that I hesitate to conclude that they have been completely swept aside.

---

[152] Kavanagh (2015c) 1037; Geiringer (2019) 577; Gardbaum (2015) 1048.
[153] King (2015a); Crawford (2013); Sathanapally (2012); Young (2011).
[154] Webber (2014a).

Though it is tempting to pronounce a constitutional crisis, I reserve that diagnosis for circumstances more dire.[155]

My second reason is the flipside of the first. When we look around the world today, it is striking how gradual, incipient and insidious the shift from constitutional democracy to popular authoritarianism has been. Instead of wearing their authoritarian colours on their sleeve, these regimes have hidden the deep democratic decay and constitutional corrosion under a false façade of 'political constitutionalism'[156] and democratic government. Evoking a lost Eden of pure democracy, populist authoritarian leaders claim that they, and only they, can speak on behalf of the people. This toxic combination of populist rhetoric, potent nostalgia and the alluring ideal of giving 'power to the people,'[157] stands to threaten us all. In light of this challenge, the call for collaboration should be heard loud and strong. There is no room for constitutional complacency or a sanguine assumption that 'it can't happen here'.[158] It can. Instead of ending on a note of loss and lament, therefore, I conclude this book on a note of vigilance and vindication. Highlighting the fundamentality and fragility of collaborative constitutional norms, I argue that these norms are a precious resource of *constitutional capital* we squander at our peril. The book concludes, therefore, with a renewed call for commitment to the hard work and combined effort of the collaborative constitution. We must all do what we can to nourish the norms of comity, collaboration and constitutional partnership on which a healthy body politic depends.

---

[155] Balkin (2018) 14–15; Balkin (2008) 590; Levinson & Balkin (2009) 714.
[156] Sadurski (2018) 251–3.
[157] Tushnet & Bugaric (2021).
[158] Sunstein (2018a).

PART I

INSTITUTIONS AND INTERACTIONS

1

Constitutionalism beyond Manicheanism

1 Introduction

In twentieth-century constitutional theory, scholars divided deeply about who should protect rights in a democracy. In one corner, the *champions of courts* portrayed judges as Herculean heroes in a 'forum of principle',[1] valiantly defending our most basic liberties against the inevitable encroachments of a rights-infringing legislature. In the opposite corner, *defenders of democracy* lionised the legislature as the supremely dignified, diverse and deliberative forum in which everyone's rights would get their due.[2] Far from being the heroes in law's empire, the courts were now cast as 'the enemies of the people',[3] storming the citadel of our most precious democratic ideals, riding roughshod over the principle of political equality, and foisting their elite views on the unwilling masses in a deeply disrespectful and disempowering manner. In a battle between saints and sinners, heroes and villains, the debate was framed in starkly Manichean terms.

The argument of this chapter is that in order to establish who should protect rights in a democracy, we need to move 'beyond Manicheanism'.[4] Whilst the Manichean narrative dramatises the tension between constitutionalism and democracy, I argue that it has engendered an unduly polarised, dichotomised and distorted picture of the key institutional questions at stake.[5] In place of a Manichean narrative of 'courts versus legislature' and 'constitutionalism versus democracy', this chapter points towards a *shared responsibility* between all three branches of government, where each branch has a valuable, though limited, role to play. Instead of pitting Herculean heroes against power-hungry politicians - or enlightened legislators against 'the enemies of the people' - we should accept

---

[1] Dworkin (1985).
[2] Waldron (1999b); Webber et al. (2018).
[3] Slack (2016); Rozenberg (2020).
[4] Hilbink (2006).
[5] Kavanagh (2019).

that all institutions are 'imperfect alternatives'.[6] Whatever virtues courts and legislatures possess, they are necessarily 'partial virtues which must be integrated into an institutionally diverse constitutional order'.[7] Once we leave the Manichean battlefield behind us – and abandon the siege mentality which takes hold there – we can better appreciate the complexity of litigation and legislation under Bills of Rights. In order to do so, we need to move beyond the binaries of good versus evil and heroes versus villains.

This chapter begins with an analysis of the iconic debate between Ronald Dworkin and Jeremy Waldron, who, together, have staked out the most influential, insightful and, at times, ingenuous positions in the Manichean narrative.[8] Since Dworkin and Waldron have emerged as the theoretical Titans in the field, I open the chapter with a 'clash of the Titans'. Part 3 broadens out the analysis to consider 'the terror of the twin tyrannies' which lie at the heart of the Manichean narrative: the *tyranny of the majority* on the one hand, and the *tyranny of juristocracy* on the other. I argue that these twin tyrannies give expression to overstated and partly distorted concerns. Indeed, I argue further that we *need* counter-majoritarianism in democratic constitutional government, not only in the name of rights but in the name of democracy as well. Finally, I turn to the long-running schism in British public law theory between political and legal constitutionalism.[9] Whilst this oppositional dialectic has numerous affinities with the broader Manichean narrative, it possesses some distinctive and illuminating features which shed light on the broader debate about how constitutionalism and democracy combine and interact. I conclude with a plea to move beyond Manicheanism, thus paving the way for more measured and realistic accounts of the institutional division of labour in a constitutional democracy.

2   Clash of the Titans

In Ronald Dworkin's canonical constitutional analysis, the courts are revered as the 'forum of principle'[10] and the supreme custodians of

---

[6] Komesar (1994).

[7] Whittington (2000) 698.

[8] Sadurski (2002) 277 (describing Dworkin and Waldron as 'canonical points of reference against which most of the participants in this debate define their own views').

[9] For a detailed analysis of this debate, see Kavanagh (2019).

[10] Dworkin (1985), chapter 3.

rights in a democracy. In order to divide the labour between the courts and the legislature, Dworkin posited a distinction between principle and policy, where principle was defined as a 'requirement of justice or fairness or some other dimension of morality',[11] and policy was characterised as 'a kind of standard that sets out a goal to be reached, generally an improvement in some economic, political or social feature of the community'.[12] Whilst legislatures were confined to the grubby machinations of majoritarian politics, Dworkin argued that judges were uniquely positioned to deal with questions of justice and rights. Not only were judges peculiarly adept in dealing with 'matters of principle',[13] their insulation from 'the demands of the political majority'[14] allowed them to stand firm against the incoming tide of majoritarian prejudice and political self-dealing, thus rescuing rights 'from the battleground of politics'.[15]

If judges are the heroes in Dworkin's drama, the legislature is the unequivocal villain of the piece. By defining constitutionalism as 'the theory that the majority must be restrained to protect individual rights',[16] the clear implication is that we need the courts to issue the restraining orders to keep the democratic delinquents in check.[17] Throughout his writings, Dworkin revealed a deep distrust of democratically elected institutions, at times assuming political hostility to rights on grounds of majoritarian bias.[18] Dworkin also argued that allowing politicians to check legislation for compliance with rights was procedurally unfair, because it would make the legislature a 'judge in its own cause'.[19] As he observed, 'decisions about rights against the majority are not issues that in fairness ought to be left with the majority'.[20] Enter Hercules the hero

---

[11] Dworkin (1977) 22.

[12] Dworkin (1977) 22, 85; Dworkin (1985) chapters 1–3.

[13] Dworkin (1985).

[14] Dworkin (1977) 85.

[15] Dworkin (1985) 71.

[16] Dworkin (1977) 142–3, 147.

[17] Political scientist Keith Whittington pulls no punches when he describes Dworkin's account of democratic politics as 'empirically overstated, analytically confused, and normatively ungrounded', see Whittington (2002) 818; see also Komesar (1994) 256–70.

[18] Dworkin (1977) 143 (describing the US government's attitude towards rights throughout the twentieth century as 'homogenous and hostile'); Dworkin (1985) 70.

[19] On *nemo iudex in causa sua*, see Dworkin (1985) 24–5; Dworkin (1986) 375–7; Ely (1980) 103; cf. Waldron (1999a) 297.

[20] Dworkin (1977) 142.

to save us from the democratic depravities of a majoritarian legislature.[21] When rights are adjudicated in court, 'the deepest, most fundamental conflicts between individual and society will once, someplace, finally, become questions of justice'.[22]

In contrast to Dworkin's hagiography of Hercules as the bulwark of principle, Waldron puts the legislature in the limelight, issuing a passionate paean to the legislature as the unsung hero of constitutional theory.[23] Nobody puts the legislature in a corner. Instead of casting Parliament as a pantomime villain or as a 'monolithic entity in the grip of a desire to do down our rights',[24] Waldron made the legislature the star of the show, imbuing it with the dignity, discernment, and moral superiority which Dworkin had reserved for the Herculean judge.[25] For Waldron, the key problem with giving judges the power to make final decisions on rights was that we disagree about what rights require.[26] The only way of respecting those disagreements was to allocate decisions about rights to a majoritarian method of decision-making where 'we, in our millions'[27] can 'participate on equal terms in social decisions on issues of high principle and not just interstitial matters of social and economic policy'.[28]

By taking decisions about rights away from elected institutions and placing them in the hands of an unelected and unaccountable legal elite, Waldron argued that rights-based review constituted an unjustifiable 'disempowerment of ordinary citizens on matters of the highest moral and political importance'.[29] To add insult to injury, it evinced a profound distrust of our fellow citizens,[30] dubious disregard for their political equality,[31] and disdain for the dignity of legislation.[32] Since legislatures are clearly superior to courts in terms of democratic legitimacy and, *pace* Waldron, are fully capable of protecting rights in practice, there is no

---

[21] For an account of 'Hercules on Olympus', see Dworkin (1986) chapter 10; Sunstein (2015) 5–10 (on the constitutional persona of 'the hero-judge').
[22] Dworkin (1985) 71.
[23] For similar laments that the legislature is overlooked in constitutional scholarship, see Bauman & Kahana (2006); Webber et al. (2018); Weis (2020b) 622.
[24] Waldron (2004) 27.
[25] Waldron (1999b) 2.
[26] Waldron (1999a).
[27] Waldron (2016) 5 (parenthesis omitted); Waldron (2006) 1349.
[28] Waldron (1999b) 213.
[29] Waldron (1993b) 45.
[30] Ibid 27–8; Waldron (2016) 141; Kyritsis (2006) 740.
[31] Waldron (1999a); cf. King (2012) 154–6.
[32] Waldron (2003b) 374; cf. Kyritsis (2006) 740.

justification for letting unelected judges second-guess or overrule legislative decisions about rights. The upshot is clear: democratic decisions about what rights require should be treated as 'dispositive'[33] and rendered immune from judicial override.

If the debate about the legitimacy of rights-based review is a clash of the Titans, then Dworkin has surely met his match. The prophet of the American 'civic religion'[34] meets the high priest of participation. But regardless of whether judges are 'princes in law's empire'[35] delivering us from all evil, or 'robed roulette wheels'[36] wreaking havoc with the dignity of legislation, these radically opposed narratives nonetheless have a number of features in common. First, both Dworkin and Waldron pose the question about who should protect rights in stark, dichotomous terms, presenting us with a *binary choice* between either the courts or the legislature as our chosen champion of rights.[37] Second, they both present the institutions *in isolation*. When Hercules decides questions of rights, he does so in splendid isolation, oblivious to the goings-on elsewhere in the constitutional system.[38] When the Waldronian legislature deliberates about rights, it does so in the manner of a moral philosophy seminar, untroubled by what the courts or the Executive might have to say.[39] Third, Dworkin and Waldron present the courts and legislatures *in opposition*. They presuppose an adversarial paradigm where each branch of government is 'locked in an embrace of eternal and inevitable opposition',[40] each vying for supremacy to get the last word on what rights require.

Finally, Dworkin and Waldron succumb to what Adrian Vermeule described as 'the nirvana fallacy'[41] – that is, a tendency to compare an idealistic view of one institution with a dystopian picture of its perceived rival. Idealisation begets polarisation, and polarisation begets exaggeration.

---

[33] Waldron (2006) 1371.

[34] Mashaw (1997) 51 (noting that the American constitutionalism is often described as a 'civic religion').

[35] Dworkin (1986).

[36] Mashaw (1997) 181.

[37] Dyzenhaus (2009) 48; Stephenson (2016) 57; McLachlin (2019) 2.

[38] Mendes (2013) 91–2; Fallon (2001) 28; Michelman (1986) 76 (describing Hercules as a 'loner', an insular character whose narrative constructions are monologues).

[39] Waldron (1993b) 31; Waldron (1999a) 224–30.

[40] McLachlin (1999) 35 (though former Chief Justice McLachlin observed, but did not endorse, this conflictual narrative); McLachlin (2019) 2.

[41] Vermeule (2006) 10; see also Dyzenhaus (2009) 50; Gyorfi (2016) 141; Whittington (2002) 847.

The result is an imbalanced and distorted discourse where both sides are pressed into the trenchant defence of idealised positions, problematically detached from the complex institutional realities on the ground. Though Dworkin and Waldron each champion a different branch of government as the sole and supreme guardian of rights, they nonetheless share an institutionally insular, oppositional, and antagonistic narrative about how rights should be realised in a constitutional democracy.

Let us consider each of these issues in turn, starting with the binary framing of the question as an institutional either/or. When we look at how rights are protected in constitutional democracies, it is clear that the idea of a binary choice between the courts and the legislature as the sole and supreme guardian of our rights, radically oversimplifies the constitutional options we face. In order to make rights real in a constitutional democracy, we need both courts and legislatures to play different roles in upholding rights, whilst working alongside each other in multiple ways.[42] For example, we need the legislature to enact detailed regulatory frameworks to specify particular entitlements and impose duties on public authorities and administrative agencies.[43] Once legislated, we then need independent courts to interpret the legislation and resolve disputes about its meaning. Rights need legislatures as much as – if not more than – they need courts. Indeed, they also need a committed Executive to initiate rights-respecting legislation, to implement legislative frameworks, and specify the requirements of rights in multiple ways.[44] By presenting us with a binary choice between either the courts or the legislature, Dworkin and Waldron overlook the possibility that protecting rights is a joint institutional enterprise, where the branches of government play distinct but complementary roles. They fail to appreciate the protection of rights as a 'multi-institutional'[45] rather than single-institutional endeavour.

Second, Dworkin and Waldron view the courts and legislature *in opposition*, presenting the relationship between them in fundamentally antagonistic terms. Whilst Dworkin perceives legislatures as the aggressors of rights, Waldron views the courts as the destroyers of democracy. Either way, the binary alternatives become emboldened antagonists.

---

[42] McLachlin (2019) 2.

[43] King (2012) 41–4; Webber et al. (2018) 17–19.

[44] King (2012) 44–8; Endicott (2020b) 597ff.

[45] Komesar (1994); Schacter (2011) 1411; King (2012) 41; Roach (2015) 405; McMorrow (2018) 103.

The branches of government are locked in combat, hardwired to attack each other and undermine the values they each hold dear. But this relentlessly oppositional narrative ignores the fact that courts and legislatures in well-functioning democracies often engage with each other in mutually respectful and even mutually supportive ways.[46] Rather than vying with the legislature to seize the last word, the courts often leave space for democratic deliberation and defer to legislative decisions out of respect for the competence, expertise and legitimacy of the democratically elected legislature.[47] By the same token, the political actors often comply with court rulings rather than defy them.[48] As I show in Chapter 12, democratically elected politicians sometimes welcome 'adverse' court rulings on rights, supporting judicial decisions on their merits.[49] Moreover, there is a documented phenomenon across multiple jurisdictions where key political actors invite and actively encourage the courts to resolve controversial issues concerning rights in order to obviate further legislative intervention.[50]

This is not to deny that there can be friction and competition between the branches at times. As I argue in Chapter 3, a degree of interbranch contestation is an inevitable and constitutive feature of the relationship between the branches of government. My point here is simply that the observable dynamic of mutual respect and restraint complicates the assumption underpinning the Manichean narrative that the relationship between the branches of government is one of unbridled antagonism or conflict all the way down. In place of a uniformly confrontational struggle for supremacy, constitutional practice across multiple jurisdictions reveals a more complex and composite institutional environment, where comity and conflict, contestation and collaboration each have a role to play.[51]

---

[46] Levinson (2005) 957 (challenging the 'government-as-empire-building-Leviathan' image with widespread empirical counter-examples in the US context, where the picture of 'stubbornly passive Congresses bears only a very partial resemblance to the mutually rivalrous, self-aggrandising branches imagined by separations of powers law and theory').

[47] Kavanagh (2015a) 844; Kavanagh (2009a) chapter 7 (documenting the dynamics of judicial deference under the HRA); Hunt (2015) 17–19; Levinson (2011) 734 (arguing that in the American context, 'open defiance of the [Supreme] Court has been the exception rather than the rule', with the court normally remaining 'safely within the bounds of political tolerance'); Schauer (2006a).

[48] Levinson (2011) 724 ('In the real world, we often observe government units choosing to surrender power to, or cooperate with, their supposed competitors').

[49] Chapter 12 in this vol.; O'Regan (2019); Leckey (2015) 195.

[50] Graber (1993); Whittington (2005a); Katzmann (1988) 4; Leckey (2015) 88.

[51] Leckey (2015) 195.

If we want to make sense of the subtleties of the relationships between the branches of government, therefore, we must encompass the complexity of inter-institutional engagement, not just focus on the confrontational dimension alone.

Third, by pitting the legislature against the courts in a battle of 'competing supremacies',[52] there is a tendency to treat courts and legislatures not only as rivals, but also – ironically – as equivalents.[53] By focusing on which institution is 'superior' or 'better' than the other, Dworkin and Waldron use uniform criteria of assessment across the different branches of government. But this elides the institutional differences between these institutions, occluding the different roles they play in the constitutional scheme.[54] As Christoph Möllers observed, 'every critique of constitutional review that treats constitutional courts as somewhat illegitimate substitutes for parliaments misses the procedural differences between the two'.[55] We can agree with Waldron that courts lack 'the democratic representative credentials required for [enacting] legislation'.[56] But this is only a problem if the courts are expected to enact legislation as part of their institutional role – which they are not. Instead, they are tasked with a different role in the constitutional scheme, namely that of applying, interpreting, and reviewing legislation in the context of a bivalent legal dispute. By the same token, legislatures typically lack the institutional independence and legal expertise possessed by the courts. That is only a problem if legislatures are asked to adjudicate individual cases – which they are not. Just as it is futile to assess the courts against the standards we would expect of legislatures, it is equally misguided to assess the legislature against the standards we would expect of courts. What we need are differentiated, role-specific standards which are sensitive to the nature, limits and functions of particular institutions, not a monolithic demand for democratic or electoral legitimacy across the board.[57]

The most significant problem with this oppositional dialectic is that both Dworkin and Waldron succumb to 'the nirvana fallacy',[58] namely, the tendency to compare an idealistic picture of one institution with a dystopian picture of its perceived rival. The fact that Dworkin models his

---

[52] Dyzenhaus (2006) 10.
[53] Whittington (2000) 698; Mendes (2013) 77.
[54] Landau (2014) 1536.
[55] Möllers (2019) 250.
[56] Waldron (2016) 135.
[57] Kavanagh (2009b) 303; Kavanagh (2019) 58; Elliott (2013) 234, 258; Gyorfi (2016) 37.
[58] Vermeule (2006) 10; Kavanagh (2017) 70–1; Komesar (1988) 717; Lovell (2003) 22–3.

judge on a mythical demi-god of unrivalled moral and intellectual prowess alerts us to the fact that some idealisation is afoot. Even granting that Hercules is a heuristic, the invocation of a superhero sets the tone for how we should understand the division of labour between courts and legislatures in a constitutional democracy. Once Herculean judges are pitted against morally depraved political schemers, we know who to choose as the guardians of our rights. Mesmerised by the Dworkinian drama, we are primed to believe that Hercules should never defer to the decisions of the democratically elected legislature. After all, why would a mythical demi-god with a pipeline to truth ever defer to a bunch of moral degenerates hell-bent on violating rights?

Waldron rightly takes Dworkin to task for naively glorifying judges as platonic guardians whilst denigrating legislators as horse-trading egotists and self-serving schemers.[59] Now, you might think that the best way of countering Dworkin's Manichean narrative would be to provide a more accurate and realistic comparative account of both institutions, eschewing either starry-eyed glorification or cynical condemnation of either branch.[60] But Waldron decided to 'apply the canon of symmetry in the other direction'[61] presenting

> a rosy picture of legislatures and their structures and processes that matched, in its normativity, perhaps in its naivety, certainly in its aspirational quality, the picture of courts – "forum of principle" etc. – that we present in the more elevated moments of our constitutional jurisprudence.[62]

Hammering home the vices of courts and the virtues of legislatures, Waldron proposed a 'normative or aspirational model of legislation',[63] bestowing upon the legislature the aura of 'dignity and standing in the political community that we associate with ... the judicial process'.[64]

Now, it may be that Waldron perceived himself to be ambushed on all sides by an army of judge-worshippers. Therefore, he believed that he had no other option but to come out all guns blazing, armed with a litany of legislative virtues and a 'parade of [judicial] horribles'.[65] But it is not

---

[59] Waldron (1999b) 2.
[60] Whittington (2000) 692–3.
[61] Waldron (1999a) 32; Waldron (2016) 220.
[62] Waldron (1999b) 2; Waldron (1999a) 32, 90; cf. King (2012) 156–8; Posner (2000) 590–1.
[63] Waldron (1999b) 1.
[64] Ibid 31.
[65] Komesar (1994) 6, 140; Jackson (2016) 1734; Waldron (2016) 248, 220, 43–4, 269; Waldron (1999a) 31; Waldron (1999b) 1; Waldron (2014) 164.

clear that trading 'one optimistic picture for another'[66] is the best approach to tackling the court-centrism and far-fetched idealisation of judges which Dworkin advances and Waldron abhors. Sanguine judge-worship should certainly be avoided. But legislative romanticism is likewise unhelpful.[67] By giving legislatures the rose-tinted treatment and lambasting the courts at every turn, Waldron does not counteract the 'nirvana fallacy'.[68] He merely replicates it in the opposite direction.[69] This drives the debate into a 'dead end of polarised positions'[70] where opposing camps engage in mutual accusations of false idealisation and 'inappropriate demonisation'[71] of rival institutions. Either way, the 'nirvana fallacy' embraces a dystopian delusion which bears only a tentative relationship with institutional reality on the ground.[72]

What is needed to advance this debate is not more rosy pictures paired with excoriatingly caustic critiques but a more realistic portrait of both courts and legislatures, appreciating their relative strengths and weaknesses as part of a more holistic constitutional analysis. In short, we need clear-eyed 'comparative institutional analysis' not wide-eyed 'nirvana solutions'.[73] Most likely, elected legislatures in established democracies are not as uniformly hostile to rights as Dworkin dreads. But nor are courts as democratically deviant and institutionally aggressive as Waldron fears. In order to capture the truth about what these institutions do – and, crucially, what they *ought* to do as part of their constitutional role – we need to move 'beyond Manicheanism'.[74] Removing the rose-tinted spectacles, we need to look reality in the eye. Viewed in the cold light of day, we can see that all institutions are 'imperfect alternatives',[75] each with their fair share of pros and cons. Whatever virtues courts or legislatures possess, they are necessarily 'partial virtues that should be integrated into an institutionally diverse constitutional order'.[76]

---

[66] Waldron (2016) 220, 248.
[67] Green (1986) 1041; Kavanagh (2019) 71.
[68] Vermeule (2006) 3.
[69] Dyzenhaus (2009) 50; O'Donnell (2017) 205.
[70] Hunt (2015) 9; Kinley (2015) 29; Roach (2015) 405.
[71] Jackson (2020) 93.
[72] Webber et al. (2018); cf. Trueblood (2019) 577.
[73] Komesar (1994) ix; Young (2012) 3.
[74] Hilbink (2006).
[75] Komesar (1994).
[76] Whittington (2000) 693.

Whilst Dworkin waxes lyrical about the unsurpassed intellectual and moral prowess of the Herculean judge, he is stunningly silent about the epistemic and institutional limitations of judges in grappling with polycentric policy issues which come before the courts in disputes about rights. Similarly, whilst Waldron eulogises the legislature as a supremely dignified, deliberative forum with unsurpassed moral reasoning, he is remarkably reticent about the influence of electoral politics and representative responsibilities on legislative reasoning about rights.[77] In fact, it is striking that the greatest defenders of 'the dignity of legislation'[78] in contemporary legal theory studiously ignore the central role of representation and electoral accountability in the 'central case'[79] of what legislatures are expected to do in a representative democracy.[80] In these theoretical renderings, legislative reasoning is modelled on how we 'do philosophy'[81] in our philosophy colloquia, rather than how elected politicians do politics in a legislative assembly, in full view of the voting public to whom they are accountable.

In order to develop a credible role-conception for legislatures and courts, we need to 'take institutions seriously',[82] not just as expressions of abstract principles we cherish but as concrete practices, purposes, norms, and institutional constraints, situated within an interactive institutional setting. For legislatures, that means grappling with the role of electoral accountability in the working life of elected representatives. For courts, it means grappling with the doctrinal details, the institutional and epistemic limitations of adjudicative institutions, and the scope and limits of the judicial role in a collaborative constitutional scheme. Putting institutional flesh on the bare bones of Dworkin's and Waldron's diametrically opposed accounts, this book argues that the truth lies somewhere in between.

---

[77] Though see Waldron (2016) 134–43.
[78] Waldron (1999a).
[79] Finnis (2011a) 3–19.
[80] Webber et al. (2018); cf. Jackson (2020) 79–80; Kelly (2020) 104–6; Tsarapatsanis (2020) 617–20.
[81] Waldron (1993b) 31; Waldron (1999a) 224–30.
[82] Whittington (2000) 697; Komesar (1984).

3   The Terror of the Twin Tyrannies

Lying at the heart of the Manichean narrative are the twin fears of the tyranny of the majority on the one hand and the tyranny of juristocracy on the other. Whilst the 'tyranny of the majority' inclines some to support 'judicial supremacy', the 'tyranny of juristocracy' leads others to 'take the constitution away from the courts'.[83] The aim of this section is not to establish which is the most terrifying tyranny, but rather to expose the exaggerations embedded in both. Once shorn of their most hyperbolic expressions, we can move forward to explore more measured and moderate responses to the valid concerns which lie at the root of these rival fears.

Let us start with the 'tyranny of the majority'.[84] Dworkin is right that democratic government is vulnerable to the risk that elected officials will give undue weight to short-term concerns at the expense of long-term interests and guaranteed rights, particularly when those rights attach to unpopular and vilified minorities.[85] Even with the best will in the world, elected legislatures may enact legislation which is contrary to the public interest or violates rights. But those who are terrorised by the 'tyranny of the majority' and rush to the courts for solace, overlook one obvious and commonplace solution: we can structure the Executive and legislature in ways which reduce the likelihood of unjust decisions by instituting checking mechanisms from within.[86] Executives and legislatures are typically large, complex institutions comprising an array of actors with multiple motivations, some of which are specifically designed to curb majoritarian excess and limit the temptation of elected politicians to pander to popular demands.[87] Examples of such checks are documented in Chapter 5. They include vigilant oversight from the Loyal Opposition, the Upper House of a bicameral legislature, Select Committees, and meaningful policy input from independent civil servants, legal advisers, parliamentary drafters, and the Attorney General, to name but a few.[88] Thus, whilst the Government may be elected by a majority of voters at the polls, the legislative process is replete with an array of counter-majoritarian checks and balances, which allow non-majoritarian

---

[83] Tushnet (1999).
[84] Tocqueville (1835 [2003]) 292.
[85] Kavanagh (2009a) 348–52.
[86] Komesar (1994) 204.
[87] Ibid 204.
[88] See Chapters 4 & 5, in this vol.

concerns to be raised and addressed.[89] The question, then, is whether such checks are sufficient to counter the risk which democratically responsive politics undoubtedly creates or, alternatively, whether we need a judicial 'second-look mechanism'[90] activated by individual claimants who believe that their rights have been violated.

But once we mention the prospect of rights-based review enforced by the courts, the 'tyranny of juristocracy' rears its ugly head. As Alexander Bickel observed, if courts are allowed to review, and then strike down, legislation which violates rights, this 'thwarts the will of the representatives of the actual people of the here and now ... exercis[ing] control, not in behalf of the prevailing majority, but against it'.[91] In short, the fear is that the 'second-look mechanism' will become the supreme view, supplanting and suffocating democratic decision-making endorsed by a majority at the polls. So framed, the threat of a rising 'juristocracy' looms large in a constitutional landscape dominated by the 'counter-majoritarian difficulty'.[92]

However, if democratic decision-making includes counter-majoritarian elements at its very core, then constitutional review by the courts looks a lot less difficult – and a lot less 'deviant'[93] – than the 'counter-majoritarian difficulty' would have us believe.[94] The rhetorical charge of the counter-majoritarian difficulty rests on the premise that rights-based review by the courts is a gross deviation from a system of 'pure democracy',[95] where we all have an equal say on matters of principle.[96] But representative democracy is not the purist's heaven of direct, egalitarian, participatory decision-making where we all have a say 'under the auspices of political equality'.[97] Instead, it is an indirect, mediated, and constrained system of government, which combines responsiveness to popular will with independence from that will. Although representative democracy contains majoritarian

---

[89] Mashaw (1997) 71.
[90] Vermeule (2011).
[91] Bickel (1986) 17.
[92] Ibid 16.
[93] Ibid 16.
[94] Sherry (2001) 922.
[95] Mashaw (1997) 201.
[96] Kyritsis (2006) 748. For close examination of the counter-majoritarian difficulty as a 'pathology' and 'obsession' of US constitutional scholarship, see Friedman (2001); Friedman (2002).
[97] Waldron (2016) 38.

components, it is a *mediated majoritarianism* in service of a disciplined democracy.

Consider the fact that in a representative democracy, we typically do not get to decide matters of principle directly. Instead, we get to vote for one representative in a single constituency, based on a restricted set of candidates pre-selected within the higher echelons of a political party.[98] Moreover, all democratic systems strive to ensure that the elected government has an adequate period of elected office – four years in many countries – precisely so that it can implement its policy agenda with a degree of detachment from the pressures of majoritarian, popular will. In doing so, representative democracy creates some 'deliberative distance'[99] between the people and their elected representatives, so that elected politicians have sufficient opportunity to discern and devise policies in the 'true interest of the country',[100] unshackled by the acute pressures of electoral politics. In this way, representative democracy seeks to avoid the corrosive effects of electorally hypersensitive government where elected politicians are 'running scared',[101] perennially tethered to the 'permanent campaign'.[102] In short, representative democracy creates a significant gap between what people want and what legislators decide. To think otherwise is to succumb to the 'populist error that democracy means the direct determination of government policy by the people'.[103]

This has enormous consequences for the twin tyrannies at the heart of the Manichean narrative. First, if the worry about 'the tyranny of the majority' rests on the belief that democracy involves a 'simple-minded mapping of majority preferences onto statutory commands',[104] it is sorely mistaken. Legislation is not 'the plaything of a univocal majority'.[105] Instead, it is the product of a complex, deliberative, mediated, filtered set

---

[98] Crewe (2021) 37 (analysing the role of the party 'selectorate' in framing the choices made by the popular electorate); Mashaw (1997) 13. In Westminster systems, voters do not even get to elect the government directly. Instead, the government is a 'career oligarchy, appointed from within a … partly elected Parliament', Gardner (2010).

[99] Kyritsis (2012) 308; Sabl (2002) 151.

[100] Madison (1788), Federalist Paper 10.

[101] King (1997) (arguing that short electoral cycles in the United States explain why 'America's politicians campaign too much and govern too little', with deleterious consequences for democratic government).

[102] On the 'permanent campaign', see Pildes (2014) 814; Ornstein & Mann (2000); Heclo (2000); Ignatieff (2013b) 71; Gutmann & Thompson (2014) chapter 4.

[103] Weale (2018) xi; Pettit (1999) 186; Mashaw (1997) 105, 201; Kuo (2019) 554, 574.

[104] Mashaw (1997) 69; Webber et al. (2018) 112, 92.

[105] Webber et al. (2018) 108.

of decision-making procedures designed, in part, to distance democratic decision-making from popular will in meaningful ways.[106] Second, whilst the rhetorical purchase of the counter-majoritarian critique rests on a contrast between 'we, the people' and 'they, the judges', what in fact exists is two different types of 'they', each making decisions on our behalf, albeit in different institutional settings and responsive to different institutional incentives.[107] Third, if the legitimacy concern underpinning the counter-majoritarian difficulty rests on a 'lost populist-majoritarian ideal',[108] this bears little resemblance to the indirect and mediated form of representative democracy we actually possess. Representative democracy is a complex alloy of different components, including majoritarian and counter-majoritarian, electoral and non-electoral elements, popular and independent elements. Not only does this reduce the counter-majoritarian difficulty, it also tempers the fear about 'the tyranny of the majority' by presenting the problem in less apocalyptic terms.[109]

In order to assess the threat of a rising 'juristocracy' poised to undermine democratic government, we need to put judicial power in perspective. In constitutional democracies, where courts have the power to invalidate legislation for violation of rights, typically only a tiny fraction of legislative decision-making is ever reviewed by the courts, let alone struck down or declared invalid for failing to comply with judicial understandings of rights.[110] Courts do not get to touch – never mind 'thwart'[111] – the vast majority of legislation enacted by a democratically elected legislature.[112] The 'gargantuan'[113] scale of governmental and legislative activity compared to the 'relatively miniscule judiciary'[114] with heavily circumscribed powers of constitutional review, means that the judicial ability to review governmental action 'is simply dwarfed by the capacity of

---

[106] Manin (1997) 2; Urbinati (2000) 760; Stoker (2006) 137.

[107] Sager (2004) 198; Lain (2017) 1612; Kumm (2010) 166–7.

[108] Mashaw (1997) 201.

[109] Sherry (2001) 922; Barrett (2017).

[110] Ferejohn & Kramer (2002) 1033 (referring to the 'microscopic fraction of cases' which present constitutional issues); Hiebert (2004b) 1986; Sathanapally (2012) 70; Hiebert & Kelly (2015) 7–9; Garrett & Vermeule (2001) 1283; Schauer (2006b); Jowell (2006) 4; Barrett (2017) 79–80.

[111] Bickel (1986) 16.

[112] Komesar (1988) 659.

[113] Garrett & Vermeule (2001) 1283.

[114] Ibid 1283.

governments to produce such action'.[115] Across vast swathes of the policy agenda, including taxation, healthcare, housing, unemployment, education, crime control, policing, immigration, social security, foreign policy, inflation, and economic growth – in short, all the issues most people care about, most of the time – it is the Government and legislature, not the courts, that drive and control the policy-making agenda.[116] In those crucial areas, the legislative first word is the last word – rightly so, because the judiciary has neither the competence nor the legitimacy to make overarching policy decisions in these fraught fields.

Even within the tiny percentage of legislative output which courts get to adjudicate for compliance with rights, judges typically only find against the Executive or legislature in a small subset of that already narrow range. In over two centuries of constitutional review by the American Supreme Court, it has 'invalidated less than one congressional statute per year . . . and in most cases the ruling of unconstitutionality affected only some, often correctable, provision of the statute, and interfered only modestly with Congress's power to work its will'.[117] For all the hand-wringing about the counter-majoritarian difficulty, 'the fact of the matter is that [US] courts usually *approve* the work of legislative and executive officials'.[118] Relatively low rates of strike-down are evident across many other jurisdictions, including those commonly identified as being the strongest constitutional courts in the world.[119] The reality is that courts empowered to

---

[115] Komesar (1994) 252, 268; Komesar (1988) 659; Garrett & Vermeule (2001) 1283; Wiseman (2006) 518.

[116] Komesar (1994) 53–150, 259; Hilbink (2006); Schauer (2006b) 9ff (providing an empirically grounded argument that the UK Supreme Court 'operates overwhelmingly in areas of low public salience' at a considerable 'distance from the centre of gravity of the nation's policy portfolio'); Levinson (2011) 735–6; Graber (2004) (demonstrating that de Tocqueville's famous claim that 'most political questions become legal questions' was demonstrably false both in de Tocqueville's time and in contemporary American politics).

[117] Mashaw (1997) 50.

[118] Friedman (1993) 591; Ferejohn & Kramer (2002) 964, 997–1035 (canvassing 'the full panoply of institutionalised forms of judicial restraint' in US jurisprudence, noting the 'remarkable' degree of judicial restraint, and the 'ubiquity' of the light touch 'rational basis scrutiny' at US Supreme Court level).

[119] Whittington (2014) 2226–8 (United States); Hogan, Kenny & Walsh (2015) (Ireland); King (2015a) 171 (Canada, Germany, the UK); Justice Kate O'Regan (2012) 122–3 (South Africa); Kingreen & Poscher (2018) 358 (observing that the Federal Constitutional Court of Germany invalidates legislation in less than 2 per cent of the constitutional complaints brought before it); see also Determan & Heinzten (2018); Official Annual Report of the FCC 2021, available at www.bundesverfassungsgericht.de/SharedDocs/Downloads/DE/Ja hresbericht/jahresbericht_2021.pdf?__blob=publicationFile&v=6 41 (observing that the success rate of constitutional complaints has averaged at about 1.85 per cent over the last ten years).

invalidate legislation for compliance with rights typically *uphold* legislation rather than strike it down.[120] Indeed, when we examine cases in context, we see that judges in many jurisdictions employ a variety of doctrinal devices, including the presumption of constitutionality, doctrines of judicial deference and restraint, and 'rational basis' or 'reasonableness' standards of review, precisely in order to limit court interference with democratically determined priorities, and to hold back from striking down.[121]

This is not to deny the significant power of apex courts in a constitutional democracy. Far from it. It is simply to highlight the point that in order to assess the legitimacy of rights-based review in a democracy, we need to put judicial power in a broader institutional perspective. Whilst the high-octane theoretical debates on the counter-majoritarian difficulty present rights-based review as a 'strong and final veto'[122] which 'completely displaces'[123] legislative judgment in an affront to democratic values, empirical evidence suggests that this 'affront' is not as frequent, as forceful, nor as final as those debates would have us believe.[124] Instead of being a roadblock which bars legislative entry or an absolute brake on desirable social policy, rights-based review 'is often more of a speed bump or detour'[125] which does not prevent our elected representatives from reaching their ultimate policy goal.[126] As Kent Roach observed, the subtle remedial and adjudicatory practices of courts in systems of so-called strong-form review are 'frequently more nuanced than the story of judicial supremacy suggests'.[127]

When Alexander Bickel first coined the catchphrase 'the counter-majoritarian difficulty',[128] he acknowledged that it was a 'highly simplistic',[129] 'indiscriminate',[130] and 'very gross statement of the matter'.[131]

---

[120] Carolan (2016b); Whittington (2014) 2228; Schauer (2006b); Lain (2017) 1642.
[121] Lain (2017) 1621–31; Roach (2016a) 271–2; Barrett (2017) 73–4; Ferejohn & Kramer (2002) 997ff.
[122] Tushnet (2008b) 247.
[123] Ibid 247; cf. O'Regan (2019) 431–2.
[124] Schauer (2006b) 53.
[125] Pickerill (2004) 31; Whittington (2005b) 1138–40; Hogg & Bushell (1997); Roach (2016b) chapter 10.
[126] Devins (2017) 1548; O'Donnell (2017).
[127] Roach (2016a) 273.
[128] Bickel (1986).
[129] Ibid. 18.
[130] Ibid. 235.
[131] Ibid. 34.

His aim was to articulate the democratic worry as forcefully and 'indiscriminately'[132] as he could 'for analytical purposes',[133] before showing how it could be resolved. The main burden of his iconic book was actually to *counter* the counter-majoritarian difficulty, in part by showing that the courts possessed a sophisticated array of doctrinal tools and techniques which rendered rights adjudication more 'responsive'[134] to democracy than may have at first appeared.[135] As Bickel reminded us in the title of his book, the courts were *The Least Dangerous Branch*,[136] recalling Alexander Hamilton's famous insight that without the power of 'the sword or the purse', the courts 'will always be the least dangerous to the political rights of the Constitution; because it will be least in a capacity to annoy or injure them'.[137] Without the help and support of the other branches of government, judges are effectively impotent. Therefore, we should beware of presenting the weakest branch of government as the Leviathan itself.[138]

When we look around the world today, we are reminded that the most formidable and frightening usurpers of democracy are not unelected judges brandishing Bills of Rights, but rather the military, the moneyed, and megalomaniac authoritarians, all of whom possess the raw physical and financial force to bend people and institutions to their brutal will.[139] Gavels are no match for guns. Once we add to the picture 'the puppet-masters of global finance'[140] – the bankers, transnational corporations, and media conglomerates – the threat of a rising 'juristocracy'[141] determined to protect minority rights, looks decidedly less tyrannical. In fact, scholars who analyse the rise of populist authoritarianism all agree that what these countries sorely lack is *not* the right to participate on equal terms in popular elections (which they typically possess), but rather the independent, counter-majoritarian institutions designed to keep an

---

[132] Ibid. 33.
[133] Ibid. 34.
[134] Ibid 19.
[135] Friedman (1993) 587; O'Donnell (2017) 208.
[136] Bickel (1986).
[137] Hamilton (1788) 78th Federalist Paper ('The Judges as Guardians of the Constitution').
[138] Lain (2017) 1653–6; Devins & Fisher (2015) 67.
[139] Green (2014); Elster (2018).
[140] Holmes (2018) 401.
[141] Hirschl (2004).

aggrandising Executive in check.[142] Before resorting to loaded rhetoric about judges in Western democracies being 'a nine man junta dressed in black clothes',[143] we should spare a thought for the real juntas around the world – both elected and non-elected – which still pose the most devastating threats to democratic government in the twenty-first century. [144]

The key problem with the 'counter-majoritarian difficulty' is that it narrows 'the legitimacy register'[145] to electoral credentials alone, thereby averring that all public officials in a democracy must be elected and accountable in order to make legitimate decisions.[146] But to criticise the courts for being unelected is to criticise them for possessing the key institutional characteristic which underpins their legitimate role in the constitutional scheme. The truth is that we *want* independent or 'counter-majoritarian' judges in a well-functioning democracy, and we abhor the idea of elected judges.[147] Once we recognise that representative government involves the exercise of independent political judgement at some remove from 'popular will', it makes sense to inquire into how to check the decision-making power of our elected representatives.[148] Periodic election is one such check, but rights-based review may be another.[149] Even accepting that the legislature should play the lead law-making role in the constitutional scheme, this does not preclude a meaningful role for courts in checking legislation for compliance with rights.[150]

A final word on the right to participate in democratic decision-making. Whilst popular participation in public decision-making is intrinsically important in a democracy, I conceive of the courtroom as a valuable participatory forum, complementary to democratic decision-

---

[142] Sadurski (2018); Levitsky & Ziblatt (2019) 2, 22–4, 39, 79; Müller (2017) 3, 9; Ginsburg & Huq (2018) 8, 95, 150, 186; Gardbaum (2020b) 1, 28–59; Issacharoff (2018) 449–50; Sunstein (2018b) 78–80.

[143] Waldron (1999b) 309.

[144] Hilbink (2008) 229.

[145] Kyritsis (2020) 1.

[146] Kavanagh (2020) 1488; Lovell (2003) 19.

[147] On the 'unique history' of elected judges in some US states, see Pildes (2014) 810; Croley (1995).

[148] Kyritsis (2006) 746.

[149] The fact that we disagree about what rights require does not undermine the legitimacy of rights-based review, because that argument is 'contingently self-defeating', see Raz (1998a) 47; Kavanagh (2003b) 467–8; Christiano (2000) 520.

[150] Jackson (2020) 79.

making but responsive to different criteria for access, influence and success.[151] Access to rights-based review can empower individuals and groups to challenge decisions made by the Executive and legislature – especially those who might otherwise be 'vulnerable to majoritarian bias or neglect'[152] – in a forum where their claim is adjudicated 'without fear or favour'. This is not the naïve claim that the most excluded and downtrodden people in society can simply walk into court to get their rights protected. Problems with access to court are too well-known to recount here. My point is simply that the criteria for access to court differ in substantial ways to the challenge of leveraging momentum in electoral politics, such that excluded groups can some-times achieve success they could not hope for in ordinary politics, especially when supported by strategic litigators and human rights NGOs.[153] Far from perceiving judicial decisions as a form of insult, dishonour and disempowerment on questions of rights, many of the most marginalised members of our society may welcome independent rights-based review as their only hope of getting the recognition and respect they deserve.[154]

4   Political versus Legal Constitutionalism

Although UK courts do not possess the power to strike down legislation enacted by the democratic legislature, the UK debate about the 'demo-cratic deficit'[155] of judicially enforced rights rages with a ferocity which matches, if not exceeds, the broader Manichean narrative.[156] Why so? The main reason is that there is a long-standing and deep-seated

---

[151] Kavanagh (2003b) 456–65; Gardner (2010) 15; Raz (1995b) 43–4; Raz (1998b) 45; King (2013) 143–6; Peretti (2001) 232; Hilbink (2008) 232.

[152] King (2012) 166–8 (making the sobering point that extreme poverty and social exclusion are often directly linked to low levels of civic engagement and voting in elections).

[153] For analysis of the way in which rights-advocacy groups typically pursue political advocacy alongside strategic litigation, see Duffy (2018) 244, 265–6; Schlanger (1999) 2013; King (2013) 148. For an iconic account of this dual strategy, see Martin Luther King (2000) [1964] 28–9 ('Direct action is not a substitute for work in the courts and halls of government . . . Indeed, direct action and legal action complement one another; when skilfully employed, each becomes more effective').

[154] Pettit (1999) 181, 185.

[155] Hunt, Hooper & Yowell (2015).

[156] Campbell, Ewing & Tomkins (2001); cf. Hunt (2015); Kavanagh (2019); Dyzenhaus (2015); Roach (2015).

scepticism about judicial power in the British constitutional culture.[157] Precisely because the UK has relied on inherited traditions of responsible government for centuries without the need for a codified constitution, there is an acute sensitivity in the UK constitutional culture to the creeping encroachments of an unelected judiciary in the domain of democratic politics.[158] Often described as 'the political constitution',[159] the British constitution has long embodied a preference for constitutional self-regulation within the political system, instead of looking to the courts to impose legally enforced checks from without.[160] Given this tradition, there is fierce resistance to any legal development which seems to threaten the unwritten constitutional order, which is an undeniably impressive achievement of stable constitutional government stretching over centuries. Any rise in judicial power touches a constitutional nerve.[161] Even as the ideological colouration changes from Left to Right – as it seems to be in contemporary times – the underlying fear of 'government by judiciary' remains stable over time.[162]

This explains why the HRA elicited such a visceral and vehement response amongst some UK public lawyers, despite the fact that it did not give the courts the power to strike down or invalidate legislation found to violate rights.[163] Rallying to the cry of the political constitution, these scholars feared an impending judicialisation of politics and a tragic undermining of the 'matchless constitution'.[164] In previous work, I argued that these fears were largely exaggerated.[165] The HRA did not lead to an unbridled 'juristocracy'.[166] Nor did it 'suffocate'[167] political modes of accountability, notwithstanding political rhetoric to that effect.

---

[157] Bentham famously described rights as 'nonsense upon stilts', in Bentham (1843) 501; Kavanagh (2009b) 102–3; Dyzenhaus (2004b) 61; Dyzenhaus (2004c) 10–11.

[158] Kavanagh (2019).

[159] Griffith (1979). For an attempt to disambiguate the multiple meanings of the 'political constitution', see Kavanagh (2019); Gee (2008); Gee & Webber (2010).

[160] Barendt (1998) 49; McHarg (2008) 856; McLean (2016) 121–2.

[161] Thornhill (2016) 210.

[162] The scholarship on the political constitution stemming from John Griffith's scholarship was on the Left of the political spectrum, its contemporary iterations fit more easily within a right-wing political agenda, see Gee (2019).

[163] For a key set of essays encapsulating this visceral scepticism, see Campbell, Ewing & Tomkins (2001); cf. Feldman (2002a); Kavanagh (2019) 72–3; Dyzenhaus (2015).

[164] Loughlin (2013) 6; Kavanagh (2019) 53–63.

[165] Kavanagh (2009a) chapter 13; Kavanagh (2009b).

[166] Ewing (2004) 831; Hirschl (2004).

[167] Tomkins (2001) 9; cf. Kavanagh (2009a) 396–400.

But my concern here is with the form and tenor of the scholarly debate which ensued, not with the accuracy or veracity of the substantive claims.

In launching a crusade against the HRA, 'political constitutionalists' waged war on so-called legal constitutionalists, claiming that the latter wished to 'throw away the British political constitution, give up on Parliament, and turn instead to the courts'.[168] Presenting us with a stark choice between the 'political constitution' where Parliament reigns supreme, and a 'legal constitution' where unelected judges call all the constitutional shots, political constitutionalists presented the two institutions at the heart of this dispute – Parliament and the courts – as vying for supremacy and pole position 'at the heart of the constitutional control room'.[169] In a 'bipolar contest between political and legal constitutionalism',[170] scholars sparred about 'where supremacy lies – with the legislature, as political constitutionalists desire, or the judiciary, as legal constitutionalists wish'.[171] For political constitutionalists, the answer to that question was as clear as it was emphatic: 'democratic legislatures prove superior to courts'.[172] In the early twenty-first century, UK public law theory became dominated by the discourse about the 'competing models of political and legal constitutionalism'.[173] With the unassailable virtue of democracy in one corner and the unequivocal evil of 'juristocracy' in the other, rival scholars 'battled for the soul of the British constitution'.[174]

But by framing the debate as 'a public law of competing supremacies',[175] the UK debate was afflicted by the same problems which marred the broader Manichean narrative.[176] It led to an unduly polarised, dichotomous, reductivist, and ultimately distortive picture of constitutional governance in the British constitutional order.[177] The key problems were as

---

[168] Tomkins (1998) 271.

[169] Tomkins (2003) 19.

[170] McHarg (2008) 877; Phillipson (2014) 271; Dyzenhaus (2015); Gardbaum (2013b) 23.

[171] Bellamy (2011) 89.

[172] Ibid 91–2.

[173] Gardbaum (2013b) 23.

[174] McHarg (2008) 853.

[175] Hunt (2003) 337; Dyzenhaus (2006) 7.

[176] In fact, the two narratives are interconnected because many UK political constitutionalists relied heavily on Waldron's arguments in making their case against rights-based review, see in particular Bellamy (2011). As Jeff King observed, the parallels between Waldron's and John Griffith's arguments are closer than is often appreciated, see King (2015b) 114.

[177] Kavanagh (2019) 57ff.

follows. First, the contrast between political and legal constitutionalism rested on a false dichotomy.[178] The UK constitution – like all other constitutions – envisages a role for both Parliament and the courts in holding the Executive to account, thus relying on a combination of political and legal modes of accountability.[179] In fact, judicial review of executive action has been a keystone of the traditional English constitution since medieval times.[180] The real question, then, is not whether to choose between *either* a political *or* a legal constitution but to establish which modes of accountability are suitable for which kinds of governmental decision within a composite, multi-institutional constitutional framework.[181]

Second, by casting Parliament and the courts as rivals for constitutional supremacy, political constitutionalists overlooked the fact that parliamentary and judicial controls can – and often do – work in combination rather than in combat, complementing and reinforcing each other in mutually supportive ways.[182] Political and legal forms of accountability are neither mutually exclusive nor mutually destructive.[183] Nor are they necessarily a 'zero-sum game',[184] where increased legal accountability in the courts entails a diminution of legislative control. In fact, many commentators have argued that the enhanced judicial powers under the HRA led to an increase, not a decrease, in parliamentary engagement with human rights issues.[185] Instead of a situation where judicial decisions necessarily diminish parliamentary modes of accountability, there are a number of high-profile examples – the *Miller* decision on Brexit prominent amongst them[186] – where the courts actively supported and strengthened Parliament's ability to hold the Executive to account.[187] Thus, by presenting Parliament and the courts as inveterate rivals for constitutional supremacy, the Manichean

---

[178] Kavanagh (2009a) 339, 396, 405, 414; Hunt (2010) 602; Hunt (2015) 17; Phillipson (2016) 1089; Allan (2013) 15, 84, 287, 302; Allison (2007) 35–6; Dyzenhaus (2015) 430; Gardner (2012) 94ff.

[179] Gee (2008) 29–30.

[180] Endicott (2003) 210–11; Joseph (2004) 322; Kavanagh (2019) 65.

[181] Cohn (2007).

[182] Kavanagh (2019) 63–9; Sales (2016a) 457; Phillipson (2016) 1089.

[183] Dyzenhaus (1998) 98; Oliver (2013) 310; Thornhill (2016) 207.

[184] Leigh (1999) 308; Allan (2006b) 174; Craig (2010) 26; Endicott (2003) 210–11; Hilbink (2006) 26.

[185] Hunt (2010).

[186] *R (Miller) v Secretary of State for Exiting the EU* [2017] UKSC 5.

[187] Phillipson (2016); Craig (2017).

narrative occluded the deep interdependence and constructive engagement between the branches of government.[188]

Third, by presenting Parliament and the courts as rivals vying for prime position 'at the heart of the constitutional control room',[189] the Manichean narrative deflected attention away from the most powerful branch of government, namely, the Executive.[190] Eclipsing the Executive is a serious blind spot in any account which seeks to make sense of the British constitutional order, especially given the pivotal role of strong government in the Westminster system.[191] But it is particularly problematic for political constitutionalists whose *credo* was to emphasise, prioritise, and celebrate the political dimensions of the British constitutional order.[192] Trying to understand parliamentary democracy without the Executive is like trying to understand a car without its engine.[193] The remarkable exclusion of the Executive from the domain of the political constitution is another indicator that viewing constitutional issues 'through a binary optic may oversimplify, and so distort'.[194]

All told, the dichotomy between political and legal constitutionalism led to an unfortunate polarisation of the academic debate, presenting us with two exaggerated alternatives which bore little relation to constitutional practice and institutional realities on the ground.[195] Political constitutionalists became so consumed by a jeremiad against judges that they failed to develop a positive conception of constitutionalism which could articulate and accommodate the inherent normativity of the British constitutional order.[196] Determined to prove that political accountability in Parliament was superior to legal accountability in the courts, they overlooked the fact that any constitution needs both political and legal modes of accountability, albeit in different ways and for different purposes.[197] Once the key issues were framed as a stark either/or choice

---

[188] Harlow (2016) 154–6, 172–4; Bamforth (2013) 266; Rawlings (2005) 409.
[189] Tomkins (2002a) 157; Bellamy (2011) 89.
[190] Kavanagh (2019) 58; Carolan (2011) 188.
[191] Griffith (2001) 46; Amery (1964) 4.
[192] Dyzenhaus (2004b) 24–6, 29. For the argument that leading defenders of 'legislated rights' overlook the pivotal role of the Executive branch, see Endicott (2020b); Weis (2020b) 621; Trueblood (2019) 580.
[193] Kyritsis (2015) 160.
[194] Elliott (2015c) 95.
[195] Carolan (2016b) 115.
[196] See further Kavanagh (2019).
[197] Kavanagh (2019); Endicott (2003).

about whether we favour democracy on the one hand or 'juristocracy',[198] on the other, all participants were pressed into one side of a false dichotomy between two extreme positions.[199] The binary optic distorted our vision, blinding us to the multi-institutional nature of the constitutional order and obscuring the more complex institutional reality on which constitutional government depends.[200]

5 Conclusion: A Farewell to Arms

In contemporary constitutional theory, there is a growing realisation that the 'bipolar contest'[201] between political and legal constitutionalism is reaching a dead end.[202] Recognising the ever-decreasing returns of a polarised debate between courts and legislatures locked in a battle for supremacy, political constitutionalists have started to lay down their arms, accepting that constitutional government combines both legal and political dimensions which should be viewed in the round rather than positing a disjuncture or dichotomy between them.[203] Once they are freed from the strictures of the antagonistic narrative, they can begin to imagine a constructive role for the courts in supporting and 'nourishing' the political constitution.[204] In the broader theoretical landscape, too, the most caustic critics of courts are opening their minds to the value of allowing courts to uphold minority rights, whilst simultaneously vindicating the underlying democratic values of equality, participation, representation, and inclusion.[205] As Jeremy Waldron observed, those who are marginalised, excluded, and vilified in the competitive forum of mass electoral politics 'may need special care that only non-elective institutions can provide'.[206]

Now that the fiercest warriors have left the battleground and the remaining members of the academic community see no point in continuing the war, it is time to move on. In place of either judicial or legislative

---

[198] Hirschl (2004).
[199] Hickman (2005a) 311.
[200] Elliott (2015a) 95.
[201] McHarg (2008) 877; Roach (2015) 405.
[202] Hunt (2015) 9–10; Kavanagh (2019) 71–2; Dyzenhaus (2015); Roach (2015).
[203] Campbell, Ewing & Tomkins (2011) 10; Tomkins (2013); Hunt (2015) 9–10; Dyzenhaus (2015).
[204] Tomkins (2013) 2281.
[205] Waldron (2016) 1401–6; Webber et al. (2018).
[206] Waldron (2016) 1403; Roux (2018) 205ff; Dyzenhaus (2009).

romanticism, what is urgently needed to advance this debate is a more realistic view of all three branches of government – one which acknowledges their respective institutional strengths and weaknesses as part of a suitably differentiated role-conception for each branch of government.[207] Turning away from the gladiatorial contest between 'democracy' and 'constitutionalism', many scholars are reaching towards a more constructive and collaborative understanding of the relationship between the branches of government.[208] The aim of this book is to contribute to that broader effort by articulating the collaborative ideal in detail and in depth. Instead of 'prizing law by denigrating politics, or ... prizing politics by denigrating law', this book imagines 'law and politics as respectfully coexisting, as they often do'.[209] The challenge, then, is to articulate the terms of that 'coexistence' whilst mapping out the modes of engagement, interaction, and counterbalancing between them.

Between the dramatic extremes of 'taking the constitution away from the courts'[210] on the one hand, or elevating the courts to a position of solitary supremacy on the other, this book imagines the more measured and variegated possibility of giving the legislature the lead law-making role in the constitutional scheme whilst accepting a significant, but subsidiary, role for the courts in upholding rights. Instead of casting the legislature as a shady character lurking in the wings or the invariable and inveterate villain of the piece, I give the legislature credence as a 'pro-constitutional'[211] actor. Indeed, I broaden out the constitutional *dramatis personae* to include the most powerful and 'least examined branch'[212] of all, the Executive. Not only does this variegated institutional landscape chime more closely with the complex reality of constitutional government on the ground, it also captures the key principles of democracy and constitutionalism which underpin the Manichean narrative, albeit reframing them in more measured, realistic and constructive ways.

---

[207] Kavanagh (2019) 71.

[208] See e.g. King (2012) 11–13; Carolan (2016a); Joseph (2004); Tourkochoriti (2019) 7, 12–15; Leigh & Masterman (2008) 16–18; Dyzenhaus (2006) 3, 11; Hunt (2015) 9; Fredman (2013) 111, 123; Webber et al. (2018) 14, 18, 25; Allan (2013) 327; Phillipson (2014) 272–4; Sager (2004) 5–7, 21; Fallon (2001) 5; Roach (2015) 405ff; Kinley (2015) 32–3; Fowkes (2016b) 221.

[209] Post & Siegel (2003b) 20; Dyzenhaus (2006) 3ff.

[210] Tushnet (1999).

[211] Jackson (2016).

[212] Bauman & Kahana (2006).

If protecting rights is a shared responsibility amongst all three branches of government, then the key theoretical and practical challenge is to articulate the ways in which the branches combine, interact and counteract in a variegated institutional landscape. This book takes up that challenge. The farewell to arms is, therefore, a call for collaboration – not only within and between the branches of government, but also between scholars who perceive themselves as embracing rival positions. Protecting rights is not the solitary task of an omniscient super-judge. Nor is it the sole preserve of an enlightened legislature. Instead, it is a collaborative enterprise where all three branches of government must work together in a way which takes both rights and democracy seriously.

2

The Promise and Perils of Dialogue

1 Introduction

At the beginning of the twenty-first century, the metaphor of 'dialogue' promised to provide an escape route from the Manichean narrative discussed in the previous chapter.[1] Inspired by recent innovations in constitutional design in the UK, Canada, and New Zealand, scholars saw a way of 'decoupling' constitutional rights review 'from judicial supremacy by empowering legislatures to have the last word'.[2] This decoupling could be achieved in various ways. Under the Human Rights Act 1998, the courts could make a declaration that primary legislation violates rights, but that declaration had no impact on the validity or effect of the legislation and placed no obligation on Parliament to change the law.[3] Under the Canadian Charter, the courts were allowed to strike down rights-violating legislation, but the legislature could legislate 'notwithstanding' Charter rights, and even override judicial decisions on what those rights required.[4]

These decoupling mechanisms were viewed as exemplars of a new model of constitutionalism, which was variously described as 'the new Commonwealth model',[5] the 'parliamentary model',[6] the 'hybrid model',[7] the 'dialogue model',[8] or 'weak-form review'.[9] Whichever label was used, the distinctive feature of the new model was that it left 'the last word'

---

[1] This chapter is a significantly revised and updated version of Kavanagh (2016a) ('The Lure and the Limits of Dialogue').

[2] Gardbaum (2001) 709; Stephenson (2016) 2.

[3] Section 4 HRA 1998

[4] Section 33, *Canadian Charter of Rights and Freedoms 1982*.

[5] Gardbaum (2001); Gardbaum (2013b).

[6] Hiebert (2006).

[7] Goldsworthy (2003a) 483.

[8] Young (2009); Young (2017); Hickman (2005a).

[9] Tushnet (2008a); Dixon (2012).

with the legislature.[10] By ensuring that judicial decisions were 'expressly open to legislative revision',[11] the new model combined judicial oversight with legislative override.[12]

As a recent innovation in constitutional design, the new model of constitutionalism elicited great excitement in comparative constitutional law circles. Not only did it seem to provide a viable and attractive alternative to the erstwhile dominant American model of constitutionalism, it also seemed to provide a seductively simple rejoinder to the counter-majoritarian difficulty which had vexed American scholars for decades. After all, if the nerve of that worry was the prospect of courts thwarting the will of the people, the new model removed this democratic deficit by giving the legislature 'the last word'.[13] In a seminal article, two Canadian scholars – Peter Hogg and Alison Bushell – argued that since the Canadian Parliament was free to reverse, modify, or override court rulings on rights under the Canadian Charter, it was meaningful to characterise the relationship between the court and the legislature as a 'productive dialogue'.[14] Instead of giving courts the final say on questions of rights, the legislature could have the last word in the dialogue.

The idea of 'dialogue' caught the imagination of constitutional scholars the world over, swiftly becoming a commonplace, if not 'ubiquitous',[15] way of understanding the dynamics of rights-based review in a democracy.[16] Indeed, it is no exaggeration to say that the metaphor of dialogue 'colonised the constitutional discourse'[17] on rights-based review. Opening up new frontiers in the debate about the legitimacy of rights-based review in a democracy, it seemed to provide the Holy Grail of reconciling judicial protection of rights with democratic

---

[10] Kavanagh (2015a); Kavanagh (2015c) 1009, 1011–12; Tushnet (2008b) ix; Tushnet & Dixon (2014) 102.

[11] Tushnet (2003c) 823.

[12] Ibid 837.

[13] For analysis of role of the institutional 'last word' in constitutional discourse, see Kavanagh (2015a).

[14] Hogg & Bushell (1997) 79.

[15] Bateup (2006) 1109.

[16] For an overview of the global influence of the dialogue metaphor on constitutional discourse, see Sigalet, Webber & Dixon (2019a). For an insightful analysis of the practice of 'dialogic judicial review' in East Asia and 'common law Asia', see Lin (2019); Yap (2015). For its influence on constitutional reform in Australia, see Stephenson (2013); McDonald (2004a).

[17] Carolan (2016a) 211; also see Bateup (2006) 1109; Kavanagh (2016a) 83.

self-government.[18] Instead of taking rights away from the courts, dialogue could let legislatures in. Instead of allowing Hercules to pronounce judicial truths from on high, the legislature could now talk back. Once the relationship between courts and legislatures was shrouded in the alluring aura of dialogue, its 'magnetic appeal'[19] was hard to resist. By 'transforming constitutional rights discourse from a judicial monologue into a richer and more balanced inter-institutional dialogue',[20] dialogue became the constitutional 'elixir of our time'.[21]

There is no doubt that the idea of inter-institutional 'dialogue' injected new insights into constitutional scholarship. By highlighting the iterative and interactive dynamic between the courts and legislature, it provided a way out of the Manichean narrative. Nonetheless, this chapter argues that 'dialogue' is a misleading metaphor which concealed more than it revealed. Charting the promise and perils of dialogue, the aim of the chapter is to examine what dialogue illuminates, what it obscures, and – crucially – what it distorts.

The chapter unfolds in the following way. Part 2 poses the fundamental question: 'what is dialogue'? Parts 3 and 4 examine the Canadian and UK debates about dialogue respectively, charting its stellar rise 'from metaphor to model'[22] in both jurisdictions. Part 5 outlines the promises of dialogue, whilst part 6 addresses its perils. The final part details the 'distortions of dialogue' which afflicted constitutional discourse in Canada, the UK and beyond. In the transition from metaphor to model, dialogue became 'dialogue theory'. But dialogue is not a theory. It is a metaphor in search of a theory, and I argue that it is pointing us in the wrong direction. It is time to turn back. In order to avoid taking similar wrong turnings, we need to revisit the debate about dialogue. Only then can we clear the ground for an alternative route, one that takes constitutional collaboration as its guide.

2 Divining Dialogue

So what is dialogue? For all the talk about dialogue, this question is harder to answer than one might think. Dialogue is a metaphor used to

---

[18] Kavanagh (2016a) 84; Yap (2015) chapter 1.
[19] Cameron (2016) 157; Sathanapally (2012) 37.
[20] Gardbaum (2001) 745.
[21] Smith (1990) 435.
[22] Kavanagh (2016a) 92; Carolan (2016a) 211.

describe the interaction between courts and legislatures under bills of rights.[23] As a metaphor, 'dialogue' evokes an image of an ongoing, iterative process where interlocutors advance their own points of view whilst being open to considering opposing views in a respectful and reflective way. We imagine that parties enter into a dialogue with opposing points of view,[24] but seek to resolve their disagreement in a spirit of 'openness, modesty, and a willingness to learn from others'.[25] Therefore, we associate dialogue with a certain disposition or style of engagement. It connotes an attitude of mutual learning and compromise rather than dogmatism and dictation; mutual adjustment and flexibility rather than predetermined absolutes; argument and persuasion rather than conflict and coercion.[26] 'Dialogue' suggests an equal relationship based on mutual respect rather than a hierarchical relationship based on 'command and control'.[27]

In the literature on constitutional dialogue, these ideas – a relationship between equals; an ongoing exchange; persuasion not coercion; difference and disagreement; openness and transparency; mutual learning and respect – became leitmotivs in the discussion. They led scholars to present the relationship between courts and legislatures as an idealised form of communicative exchange between equals, where persuasion – not coercion – was the order of the day.[28] So what does the metaphor entail for inter-institutional engagement between the branches of government on questions of rights? Whilst the metaphor does not give us concrete conclusions on that question, it nonetheless provides us with some pointers. For example, it may suggest that the branches of government should just 'talk' openly with each other in the fashion of a two-way conversation, offering 'opinions' and sharing 'suggestions' whilst remaining open to contrary views. It may also suggest that no branch of government should ever defer to the other. After all, it is not much like a conversation if someone simply says 'I defer to your view'.[29] Dialogue seems to presuppose an iterative exchange and an open sharing of viewpoints. Perhaps each branch should be wary of making a decision

---

[23] Yap (2012) 528; Carolan (2016a) 212–14; King (2019a) 186.
[24] Waldron (2004) 9.
[25] Roach (2005) 538; Mathen (2007) 128.
[26] Tremblay (2005) 632.
[27] Conger (2008); Kyritsis (2017) 103; Kavanagh (2016a) 85–6; King (2019a) 186–7; Greschner (2000) 55.
[28] Kyritsis (2017) 108–9.
[29] Phillipson (2013) 749; Kavanagh (2016a) 105.

on rights which binds the other branches or coerces them to comply. After all, the duty to comply with a binding decision does not sit easily with the picture of an open dialogue where interlocutors freely advance their own views, unshackled by the threat of compulsion or obligation.[30] If the relationship between courts and legislatures is viewed as a dialogue, maybe the key priority is for all interlocutors to speak their truth about rights in an open and robust fashion whilst listening respectfully to alternative perspectives.

In one form or another, these suggestions entered the constitutional discourse under the spell of the dialogue metaphor.[31] The question, then, is whether these connotations of the metaphor illuminate something important about the judicial/legislative relationship or, alternatively, whether they obscure or distort our understanding of that complex interactive dynamic. Before going on to answer those questions directly, we should pause to consider the potent effect of metaphors on how we think. This is important because the promise and perils of dialogue are due, in no small part, to the promise and perils of metaphors more generally.

Metaphors are figures of speech which suggest a partial similarity – but not an identity – between two things.[32] They conjure up vivid mental pictures which can help to illuminate important features of an object in an evocative and memorable way. By calling to mind a powerful visual image, metaphors can provide a shortcut to understanding complex phenomena.[33] Therefore, whilst metaphors are useful rhetorical and explanatory tools which can 'nudge us into noticing similarities, there is nothing finite in scope nor propositional in nature conveyed by metaphor'.[34] This reminds us of what metaphors are *not*. They are not arguments, based on reasons supporting a conclusion. Instead, they are suggestive pointers about how to look at a problem based on a similarity or likeness between two things. Metaphors suggest, connote, imply, evoke or insinuate, but they do not define the object to which they apply.

---

[30] Kavanagh (2016a) 85, 115ff.
[31] Yap (2012) 528–9; Hickman (2005a) 325; MacFarlane (2012a) 93ff.
[32] For further analysis on the many ways in which 'metaphors matter', see Kavanagh (2016a) 86–91; Greschner (2000); Conger (2008); Lakoff & Johnson (2003) 5; Ritchie (2013), chapter 6; Hills (2012).
[33] Kavanagh (2016a) 87.
[34] Davies (1984) 293.

However, the modesty of metaphors should not lead us to underestimate their potency. Metaphors matter.[35] After all, pictures speak louder than words. A well-chosen metaphor can help make a point vivid, memorable, and, above all, convincing. Metaphors do not simply help us to *explain*; they are also powerful rhetorical tools which help us *persuade*.[36] And if persuasion is a battle of hearts as well as minds, then metaphors are powerful weapons – not least because their potency is often covert or concealed. In subtle and implicit ways, metaphors can lend enormous rhetorical and persuasive force to our arguments. But like all powerful tools, we should handle them with care. Sometimes a metaphor can become entrenched in a discussion, even if it has profoundly misleading or distorting effects.

The 'framing effect'[37] of metaphors is all the more dangerous when we consider that many metaphors are evaluatively loaded, thereby pulling our normative views in directions we might not otherwise pursue.[38] By providing a useful shortcut to understanding complex phenomena, metaphors can also lead to oversimplification. Moreover, when metaphors are introduced into discussion, there is a standing temptation to take them literally or to over-extend them. Recall that the relation between a metaphor and object is one of similarity not identity. If we say that 'life is a journey', we are not suggesting that these two things are identical but that there is an important or illuminating similarity between them. The metaphor suggests a likeness that is only partial. But by illuminating one facet of the 'object', a metaphor can obscure and conceal others. Moreover, if the metaphor is reified or over-extended, the partial similarity may be taken as a comprehensive encapsulation of the object. When this occurs, the partial similarity begins to dominate our understanding of a complex issue. What was introduced as a partial and suggestive insight is given undue salience in our understanding, thus distorting the overall picture.[39]

In my view, many of these problems arose when the metaphor of dialogue entered constitutional discourse. The idea of 'dialogue' became

---

[35] For the role of metaphor in political rhetoric, see Charteris-Black (2006); Reese & Lewis (2009) (on the political potency of the war metaphor in the so-called war on terror post-9/11); Thornburg (1995) (on how images of battle, sports, and sex shape the adversarial legal system).

[36] Conger (2008).

[37] Pinker (2007) 243; Ritchie (2013) chapter 6.

[38] Mashaw (1997) 1.

[39] Greschner (2000) 52; Kavanagh (2016a) 90.

entrenched, despite having some distortive effects. It led to some over-simplification of the complex institutional roles of courts and legislatures. Above all, 'dialogue' became *reified* in constitutional discourse. Rather than playing a purely illustrative, suggestive or rhetorical function which highlighted the similarity between rights-based review and a conversation between equals, the metaphor was itself treated as a source of normative guidance about how the relevant institutional actors should carry out their constitutional roles. In the swift transition from metaphor to full-blown 'model of constitutionalism',[40] the idea of dialogue began to dominate our understanding of the relationship between courts and legislatures, and ultimately distort it. In order to appreciate the transition 'from metaphor to model', we must start our analysis where the idea of 'dialogue' first began in earnest, namely, in an article about dialogue under the Canadian Charter.

3   The Canadian Conversation: From Metaphor to Model

When Hogg and Bushell wrote their influential article on 'Charter Dialogue', their starting point was the counter-majoritarian difficulty. How can it be justified in a democracy for unelected and unaccountable judges to have the 'last word' on what rights require, thus wielding 'a veto over the politics of the nation'?[41] Hogg and Bushell responded by challenging the empirical accuracy of the picture of review on which this question rests. They observed that when judges strike down legislation on Charter grounds, the Canadian legislature still has considerable 'room to advance its objectives, while at the same time respecting the requirements of the Charter as articulated by the courts'.[42] Decisions of the court 'usually leave room for a legislative response, and usually receive one'.[43] Since the effect of the Charter was rarely to block a legislative objective or to raise 'an absolute barrier to the wishes of the democratic institutions',[44] it was therefore a gross exaggeration to portray review under the Canadian Charter as 'the last word' on what rights require, still less a 'veto' on legislative policies. Instead, constitutional rights review was part of a 'dialogue' between courts and legislatures, where legislatures had room

---

[40] Yap (2012) 88.
[41] Hogg & Bushell (1997) 77.
[42] Ibid 82, 80.
[43] Ibid 105, 75.
[44] Ibid 81; Hogg & Amarnath (2017) 1054.

to respond. Therefore, the metaphor of dialogue was first introduced into the scholarship as 'an empirical riposte to allegations of judicial supremacy'.[45]

In light of the fervour with which the metaphor was subsequently embraced by scholars from all sides of the political and ideological spectrum, it is sobering to recall how tentative Hogg and Bushell initially were about the aptness of the metaphor of dialogue to describe the phenomenon they observed:

> At first blush, the word 'dialogue' may not seem particularly apt to describe the relationship between the Supreme Court of Canada and the legislative bodies. After all, when the Court says what the Constitution requires, legislative bodies have to obey. Is it possible to have a dialogue between two institutions when one is so clearly subordinate to the other? Does dialogue not require a relationship between equals?[46]

Hogg and Bushell side-lined these reservations, stipulating that 'where a judicial decision is open to legislative reversal, modification, or avoidance, then it is meaningful to regard the relationship between the Court and the competent legislative body as a dialogue'.[47]

The next question was whether legislative agreement or compliance with a judicial decision would count as 'dialogue'. Despite some reservations about whether agreement or compliance could be squared with the egalitarian and discursive connotations of the metaphor, they stipulated that 'Charter dialogue' comprised all cases where court decisions were followed by 'some action' by the legislature, including legislative agreement or compliance with court rulings.[48] In order to count as dialogue in this specialised sense, it was sufficient that such rulings were open to legislative reversal or avoidance but it was not necessary for this reversal to occur. In short, 'dialogue' included legislative agreement with the courts, but hinged on the possibility of legislative disagreement and dissent.[49]

In later writings, Hogg and Bushell emphasised that their claims about 'dialogue' were largely empirical or descriptive in nature. They had merely documented 'the empirically observable phenomenon'[50] of legislative responses or sequels to court decisions, 'describ[ing] how courts

---

[45] Carolan (2016a) 210; Fredman (2015) 449; King (2019a) 190; Sathanapally (2012) 39.
[46] Hogg & Bushell (1997) 79.
[47] Ibid 79; McMorrow (2018) 91.
[48] Hogg & Bushell (1997) 79.
[49] Ibid 92; Hogg, Thornton & Wright (2007a) 4, 13, 17, 45.
[50] Hogg (2004) 6.

and legislatures *did* behave, rather than how they *should* behave'.[51] It is true that Hogg and Bushell refrained from making explicit normative recommendations about how the institutional actors should behave or interact. However, by invoking the evaluatively loaded metaphor of dialogue, they nonetheless traded on its appealing connotations in order to present the Canadian Charter in a positive light.[52] As the subtitle of their original article revealed, they were not merely describing the facts; they were also endorsing the Charter as a desirable state of constitutional affairs, or at least as 'not such a bad thing after all'.[53] Indeed, some degree of normativity is unavoidable here, because they were applying the metaphor to an inherently normative phenomenon, namely, the roles and relationships between the branches of government in a constitutional scheme.[54] One cannot talk about the roles of the branches of government without implying some ideas of their proper roles and the appropriate boundaries between them. Therefore, Hogg and Bushell could not steer completely clear of normative evaluation in the way that they hoped.[55]

Of course, if Hogg and Bushell were correct in their empirical claim that the courts did not have the last word under the Canadian Charter, this seemed to pose a serious challenge to the counter-majoritarian difficulty, at least in the Canadian context. After all, that claim often rested on the empirical supposition that courts had the last word on issues concerning rights. But if legislative policies were rarely thwarted by judicial review, and if the legislature could usually find a way to limit, override, or reverse judicial decisions about rights, then that seemed to soften the blow of the democratic critique. Hogg and Bushell initially over-claimed on this point, suggesting that the possibility of legislative sequels under the Canadian Charter provided a complete answer to the 'counter-majoritarian difficulty'.[56] They later retracted that claim, falling back on the more modest and plausible suggestion that if Parliament has the last word on what rights require, then the force of the democratic objection is attenuated to some degree.[57]

---

[51] Hogg, Thornton & Wright (2007a) 26; McMorrow (2018) 92.
[52] Carolan (2016a) 210.
[53] Ibid.
[54] Kyritsis (2017) 42; Raz (1979) 47.
[55] Hogg, Thornton & Wright (2007a) 26.
[56] Hogg & Bushell (1997).
[57] Hogg, Thornton & Wright (2007a) at 4, 7, 29, 30, 53, 54; Hogg & Amarnath (2017) 1056, 1065; Roach (2004) 73; McDonald (2004b) 12; Bateup (2007) 3.

The dialogic rendering of rights-based review under the Canadian Charter captured the constitutional imagination in Canada and beyond. It proliferated with breath-taking speed. Already by 1999 – a mere two years after publication of the original article – the idea of dialogue was described as 'the dominant paradigm for understanding the relationship between Charter-based judicial review and democratic governance'.[58] Dialogue was in vogue with a vengeance. The extraordinary popularity of the metaphor in Canada was partly because it appealed to both sides of the polemical debate between Charter enthusiasts and Charter sceptics. For Charter enthusiasts, the attraction of 'dialogue' was that it could provide a partial answer to the legitimacy concerns about judicial review, effectively defending rights-based review by reducing its sense of finality.[59] Rather than portraying the courts as robed elites seizing the last word from the democratically elected legislature, they could be portrayed instead as respectful interlocutors in a democratic dialogue.[60] Dialogue was used a source of legitimation. But Charter sceptics could also rely on the metaphor to oppose the finality of judicial decisions on rights, presenting the legislature as a co-ordinate constitutional actor with the capacity, legitimacy and responsibility to form its own view about rights and, indeed, to assert that view against the courts with confidence and vigour.[61] For critics of the Charter, the idea of dialogue was attractive because it eschewed judicial finality and embraced the legitimacy of the legislative last word.

That is not to say that dialogue ushered in an era of consensus in Canadian constitutional scholarship. Far from it. In the heated debate which ensued, Charter enthusiasts and critics polarised along familiar lines. Yet whilst both camps claimed dialogue as their normative lodestar, they advocated radically opposed understandings of what dialogue meant for the court–legislature relationship. Whilst Charter enthusiasts used dialogue to legitimise robust rights-based review by the courts, Charter sceptics used it to defend legislative override of court rulings on rights. The legislature would 'listen' to what the court had to say, but ultimately cast judicial opinions aside if Parliament disagreed. After all, if legislatures meekly obeyed judicial rulings, that would not count as 'true dialogue'.[62]

---

[58] Manfredi & Kelly (1999) 524.
[59] Roach (2004) 49, 63; Kavanagh (2016a) 84.
[60] Petter (2007) 147, 167.
[61] Webber (2009).
[62] Manfredi & Kelly (1999) 521.

As one scholar observed, 'Merely implementing the view of another is not a dialogue, but rather a monologue, with judges doing most of the talking and legislatures most of the listening'.[63] This led Charter sceptics to ratchet up their normative prescriptions, recommending that both courts and the legislature should behave 'in a dialogically appropriate fashion'.[64] On this view, the legislature should adopt a practice of openly and forthrightly 'challenging court rulings,'[65] whilst the courts should adopt a more modest and respectful disposition towards democratically settled priorities.

Whichever view one held on the appropriate balance of power between courts and legislatures, one thing was clear: scholars on all sides began to deduce detailed normative prescriptions for institutional behaviour from the connotations of a metaphor. Dialogue was being reified in constitutional discourse. From its humble beginnings as a mere metaphor to describe the phenomenon of legislative sequels to judicial decisions, it was now being treated as a 'constitutional talisman'[66] and a demanding normative ideal which should guide legislative and judicial behaviour.[67] In a swift transition from model to metaphor, dialogue was transformed into 'an ideal vision of constitutional democracy'.[68] The only problem was that this ideal was being interpreted in a variety of cross-cutting and sometimes diametrically opposed ways, all riding under the common and capacious banner of 'constitutional dialogue'.

The lure of the metaphor was now so strong that even the judges of the Supreme Court of Canada got in on the action.[69] Initially, the metaphor appeared in the case-law as a source of legitimation.[70] Rather than being portrayed as an omnipotent and hegemonic institutional actor seizing the 'last word' from the democratic legislature, judges argued that they were respectful interlocutors in a constitutional dialogue where the legislature also had an important say.[71] Eventually, however, judges invoked the metaphor to defend particular – often controversial – approaches

---

[63] Webber (2009) 452.
[64] Bateup (2009) 538.
[65] Webber (2009) 458.
[66] McMorrow (2018) 95.
[67] Yap (2012) 528–9.
[68] Yap (2015) 84.
[69] For a detailed examination of the metaphor of dialogue in the Canadian Charter case-law, see Hogg, Thornton & Wright (2007); Roach (2007); Roach (2017); Manfredi (2004).
[70] Carolan (2016a) 210; Greschner (2000) 54; Mathen (2007) 130.
[71] *Vriend v Alberta* [1998] 1 SCR 493, [138]–[139] (Iacobucci J); Carolan (2016a) 210.

to judicial decision-making under the Charter. Some judges relied on it to justify the choice of 'reading in' rather than 'striking down'.[72] Others invoked it to justify striking down rather than reading down, on the basis that striking down essentially remanded the issue to the legislature, thereby fostering greater dialogue.[73] Still others relied on the metaphor to justify increased reliance on delayed declarations of invalidity in preference to immediate strike-downs.[74] This was too much normative weight for a mere metaphor to bear.[75] Was 'reading in' more 'dialogic' than striking down? Or was it the other way around? Did dialogue demand that judges should deliver bold opinions about rights in an open interpretive disagreement?[76] Or would it be more dialogic to adopt a more deferential stance? The answers to these questions were highly contested. It was becoming increasingly clear that the metaphor of 'dialogue' could not provide straight answers.[77]

Since dialogue was now being invoked to support diametrically opposed approaches to how the branches of government should interact in the field of rights, its currency as a useful shorthand to capture the nature and dynamics of the courts/legislature relationship became devalued and discredited. Amidst accusations that judges and scholars were relying on the dialogue metaphor to soft-peddle judicial activism and lend 'false legitimacy'[78] to highly intrusive judicial decisions, the debate began to polarise along familiar 'courts versus legislature' lines.[79] The academic debate was becoming abstruse and jargonistic, focusing ever more closely on the connotations of the metaphor, whilst losing sight of the institutional dynamics to which it was originally applied. Through over-use and over-extension, the metaphor of 'dialogue' became a buzz-word which caused confusion rather than clarification. The Canadian love affair with dialogue was beginning to wane.

---

[72] Hogg, Thornton & Wright (2007a) 9.

[73] Ibid 11.

[74] Ibid 13.

[75] Carolan (2016a); Roach (2007) 51.

[76] Roach (2017).

[77] The judicial experience with dialogue may have provided a cautionary tale for judges in other jurisdictions, most notably in Australia and New Zealand, where the courts refused to rely on the metaphor because it was 'apt to mislead', see *Momcilovic v The Queen* (2011) HCA 34; Stephenson (2016); Ip (2020); Geiringer (2017b).

[78] Morton & Knopff (2000); Morton (1999) 23; Huscroft (2007).

[79] Cossman (2019) 184.

4 The UK Debate about Dialogue

In contrast to Canada, the metaphor of dialogue did not become the dominant paradigm for thinking about the relationship between the branches of government in the UK. Although some scholars embraced the metaphor in the early days of the HRA,[80] many eschewed it altogether,[81] whilst others dismissed it outright as 'fantasy',[82] 'nonsense',[83] and a shameless attempt by supporters of rights review 'to legitimise the illegitimate'.[84] Therefore, the general scholarly response to dialogue in the UK was mixed at best, with many scholars expressing scepticism about its plausibility as a useful way of understanding the inter-institutional dynamics at play under the HRA.[85] Leading judicial figures were also doubtful about dialogue. Speaking before a parliamentary committee, Lord Bingham stated unequivocally that it was an inapt description of the judicial role: 'The business of judges is to listen to cases and give judgment. In doing that, they pay attention to the arguments addressed to them, but I do not see it as the role of the judge to engage in dialogue.'[86]

Crucially, critics of judicial power under the HRA did not rely on the metaphor of dialogue in order to launch a jeremiad against judges. Therefore, 'dialogue' did not become a lightning rod for a polemical debate about the legitimacy of constitutional review, as it did in Canada. However, whilst the discussion lacked the fierceness of the Canadian legitimacy debate, an increasing number of UK scholars rely on the metaphor to describe the UK system.[87] Moreover, it has now featured in a leading UK Supreme Court decision on the right to assisted

---

[80] Hickman (2005a); Young (2009); Klug (2001) 370; Clayton (2004).

[81] Kavanagh (2009a) 128–32, 408–11; Gearty (2004); Feldman (2007); Chandrachud (2017) 7.

[82] Ewing & Tham (2008) 691.

[83] Ewing (2012) 119.

[84] Ibid 119.

[85] For scholarly scepticism about dialogue in the UK context, see Kavanagh (2009a) 128–32, 408–11; Hunt (2015) 20–2; Sales & Ekins (2011) 230–1; Sales (2016a) 469; Duxbury (2017); Ewing (2012) 119; Ewing & Tham (2008) 691; Carolan (2016a); Masterman (2011) 56–9; Elliott (2011) 617.

[86] Lords Bingham, see JCHR, *Minutes of Evidence taken on Monday 26 March 2001: Examination of Witnesses* (2000-01, HL 66-ii, HC 332-ii) [78]. 26 March 2001, HC 66 HC 333, question 78; Masterman (2011) 56–7.

[87] See e.g. Yap (2012); Phillipson (2013) 25; Southerden (2014); Davis & Mead (2014); Crawford (2013); Young (2017); Davis (2014a); Stark (2017a).

suicide.[88] Therefore, it is worth examining the UK debate about dialogue before the tide swells into a tsunami.

Initially, the term 'dialogue' entered the UK debate as a shorthand label to describe the 'model' of rights protection 'implicit in the structural features of the HRA'.[89] The fact that the HRA gave the courts the power to *declare* an incompatibility but not *compel* compliance had unmistakable resonances with dialogue.[90] Though some scholars argued that 'dialogue' could occur following a rights-compatible interpretation under section 3 HRA,[91] many gave pride of place to the declaration of incompatibility. It was not long before the idea of dialogue was infused with normative significance and treated as a touchstone for normative claims about appropriate legislative and judicial behaviour.[92] Dialogue became 'dialogue theory'. But given the malleability of the metaphor, the question inevitably loomed: what was 'dialogue theory'? Even proponents of the metaphor conceded that 'the idea of "dialogic" constitutional theory is opaque and capable of encompassing quite dissimilar approaches to constitutional law'.[93] Beyond the minimal points of consensus that 'dialogue' was opposed to the idea of judicial monopoly or hegemony, there was widespread disagreement within the broad church of dialogue as to what the theory required in concrete terms. Inevitably, a 'multiplicity of meanings'[94] emerged.

Three main lines of debate opened up in the UK debate about dialogue. The first concerned the judicial choice between sections 3 and 4 HRA, with many supporters of dialogue arguing that courts should issue more declarations of incompatibility instead of 'rewriting' legislation using creative tools of interpretation under section 3.[95] Viewed in dialogic terms, the declaration of incompatibility seemed to have better democratic credentials, because it 'enables courts to influence political

---

[88] *R (Nicklinson) v Ministry of Justice* [2014] UKSC 38, [117] Lord Neuberger; Leckey (2015) 162 (who was 'staggered' by 'the extent to which the justices reproduce the paradigmatic language of dialogue and legislative remand').

[89] Clayton (2004) 33; Klug (2003) 126; Nicol (2004b); Young (2009).

[90] Poole (2005) 558; Crawford (2014) 34.

[91] Hickman (2005a) 326; Young (2009).

[92] Davis & Mead (2014) 66.

[93] Hickman (2008) 84.

[94] Carolan (2016a) 212–14.

[95] Gearty (2004) 504; Gearty (2002) 250; Campbell (2001) 99; Bateup (2009) 547 (observing that 'dialogue theorists in the UK tend to disfavour expansive interpretations of section 3')

debate without stifling it'.[96] Rights-compatible interpretation, on the other hand, seemed to shut the legislature out of the dialogue and allow the judges to seize the final word.[97] Therefore, those who viewed the HRA in dialogic terms often urged the courts to rely more heavily on declarations of incompatibility and to 'speak out when they consider that legislation is incompatible with protected rights'.[98] Judges should speak their minds, not bite their tongues.

The second concerned the appropriate legislative response to such declarations, with many scholars urging the legislature to reject, ignore, or disagree with judicial declarations of incompatibility.[99] Some argued that legislative disagreement with judicial decisions on rights should be routine and 'uninhibited',[100] whilst others argued that it should be a matter of last resort after careful democratic deliberation.[101] But the general trend amongst dialogue scholars was to support a practice of legislative disagreement with court rulings on rights. After all, if dialogue suggests 'an exchange of views',[102] then 'talk of dialogue is bogus'[103] unless Parliament uses its power to reject, modify or override a judicial decision on rights.[104]

The third issue concerned the question of judicial deference to Parliament in adjudication under the HRA. On one level, one might have thought that dialogue defenders would support the idea of judicial deference to the democratically elected legislature on the basis that it would give the legislature an important role in protecting rights. However, whilst some accepted such a role, others argued that the logic of dialogue required all three branches of government to 'uncompromisingly tell their truth on rights'[105] without inhibition. The idea of judicial deference sat uneasily with the connotations of the dialogue metaphor. As one scholar put it, 'It is hard to characterise an exchange as a conversation, where one party's contribution is limited to saying "I defer to your view"'.[106]

---

[96] Nicol (2006) 747; Fredman (2000) 119.
[97] Klug (2003) 130; Nicol (2004a) 197; Young (2005) 33.
[98] Klug (2003) 130; Nicol (2006) 747–8; Young (2005) 33; Stark (2017a) 654; Martin (2018) 216.
[99] Davis & Mead (2014).
[100] Nicol (2006) 744.
[101] Davis (2014a).
[102] Leigh & Masterman (2008) 118.
[103] Nicol (2006) 746; Southerden (2014) 255.
[104] Nicol (2006) 746; Leigh & Masterman (2008) 118.
[105] Nicol (2006) 744.
[106] Phillipson (2013) 749.

Whichever view one supported on these contentious issues, three things became clear. First, the metaphor of dialogue was treated as a demanding normative ideal to assess and advocate desirable constitutional behaviour.[107] As in Canada, the metaphor was used to prescribe as well as describe. Second, the metaphor engendered diametrically opposed arguments about the roles and relationships between the branches of government, veering from a respectful, iterative engagement based on mutual learning and persuasion through to a 'no-holds-barred-constitutional politics'[108] marked by 'unrestrained debate' and 'fearless exchanges'[109] between the branches of government locked in combat. Third, as the constitutional practice of litigation and legislation unfolded under the HRA, dialogic disappointments inevitably ensued.[110] The legislature almost always followed and implemented declarations of incompatibility under section 4, and it never overrode an interpretation under section 3. Judges gave great weight to the decisions of the democratically elected legislature and deferred to the legislature on multiple occasions. Indeed, judicial deference was a key leitmotiv of the emerging case-law.[111] Whilst scholars were enthralled by the sound of dialogue, it seemed to be falling on deaf ears in the crucible of constitutional practice.

5 Promises

The test of a good metaphor is whether it captures and illuminates something important and insightful about the object to which it is applied. Therefore, when assessing the idea of dialogue in constitutional discourse, we must ask: what, if anything, does the metaphor of 'dialogue' illuminate about the relationship between courts and legislatures under Bills of Rights? And what, if anything, does it obscure or distort?

Let us start with the positives. When Hogg and Bushell introduced the metaphor of dialogue into constitutional scholarship, they contributed a number of important insights. First, the metaphor of dialogue exposed as exaggerated the idea that when judges engage in rights-based review they

---

[107] Carolan (2016a) 210–11.
[108] Nicol (2006) 747.
[109] Nicol (2002) 276.
[110] Stephenson (2016) 53.
[111] Kavanagh (2009a), chapters 7 & 8.

have 'the last word' on what rights require.[112] The phenomenon of dialogue illustrated 'the implausibility of the notion that the Court left in its wake a humbled Parliament with no options to achieve its policies'.[113] Even when courts strike down legislation, Hogg and Bushell showed that there is usually room for the legislature to respond to court rulings, and that they usually did so respond. Whilst accepting that judges would sometimes have 'the last word' on what rights require, judicially imposed constitutional norms rarely stopped a legislative policy in its tracks. Judicial decisions generally operate at the margins of legislative policy, affecting issues of process, enforcement, and standards, all of which can accommodate most legislative objectives. In this way, the metaphor of dialogue provided a useful – albeit partial – corrective to the image of the courts 'simplistically usurping the role of the legislature'[114] by seizing 'the last word' on rights issues. Therefore, it provided an 'empirical riposte'[115] to the counter-majoritarian difficulty.[116]

Second, the metaphor of dialogue was a useful reminder that protecting rights is not a 'judge-only' affair. Constitutional rights need legislatures as much as – if not more – than courts.[117] Instead of focusing exclusively or myopically on the courts, we should examine the positive role and contribution of the legislature and executive to the joint enterprise of protecting rights. The metaphor of dialogue highlighted the fact that protecting rights is a multi-institutional – rather than single-institutional – task.[118] If the legislature was 'the least examined branch',[119] the metaphor of dialogue promised to put the legislature under the spotlight, treating it as one of the key *dramatis personae* on the constitutional stage.

Third, the metaphor of dialogue seemed to provide a useful counterpoint to the 'nirvana fallacy',[120] namely, the lamentable tendency in constitutional discourse to romanticise one's favoured institution – whether the courts or the legislature – and demonise its perceived rival.[121]

---

[112] See further Kavanagh (2015a).
[113] McDonald (2004b) 18.
[114] Ibid 12.
[115] Carolan (2016a) 210.
[116] Bateup (2006) 24–7; Kelly (2005) 15, 148; Friedman (1993) 586–653.
[117] Webber et al. (2018).
[118] Komesar (1994) 5–6; King (2012) 41.
[119] Bauman & Kahana (2006).
[120] Vermeule (2006) 10; Gyorfi (2016) 141.
[121] Dyzenhaus (2009) 50.

Rather than succumbing to an idealised view of one institution and a jaundiced view of the other, we could imagine that both courts and legislatures may have something valuable to say about rights. The metaphor of dialogue promised to direct our attention to the legitimate contribution each institution can make to the joint endeavour of protecting rights.

Fourth, the metaphor of dialogue provided a useful corrective to a strict and formalistic understanding of the separation of powers, whereby each branch exercises its powers in isolation from the other branches.[122] Instead, the metaphor of dialogue pointed towards an iterative and mutually responsive interaction between them.[123] This had the potential to take us beyond a polarised either/or debate over which institution is the best or which institution should have the 'last word', suggesting instead that we could 'constructively engage both institutions in human rights protection, rather than relying on one institution alone'.[124] Rather than a 'static, one-shot, zero-sum game seeking to determine the location of "final" sovereignty between two binary alternatives', the metaphor of dialogue promised to provide 'a richer, interactive, more dynamic understanding ... of constitutional law and policy'.[125]

One final – though indirect – potential advantage of Hogg and Bushell's analysis was that it brought to light the crucial interdependence of empirical and normative/theoretical analysis of constitutional issues.[126] If we seek to justify judges having 'the last word' on questions of rights, our first question must be: do they actually have the last word? Indirectly, Hogg and Bushell's article reminded us that our theoretical arguments about constitutional law should be disciplined by an appropriately 'fact-sensitive inquiry'[127] grounded in an understanding of institutional roles and the practices which constitute them. Absent such grounding, there is a risk that our theories of constitutionalism become 'theories of a fiction'.[128]

---

[122] For an interactive and relational account of the separation of powers, see Kavanagh (2016b); Kavanagh (2022); Kyritsis (2017); Kyritsis (2015); Carolan (2009) 32, 138–9, 169.
[123] Kyritsis (2017) 105.
[124] Sathanapally (2012) 37.
[125] Palmer (2017) 507.
[126] Kavanagh (2016a) 108; Mashaw (1997) 1–5.
[127] McDonald (2004b) 25, 27; Roach (2004) 76; Bateup (2007) 23; Kavanagh (2016a) 94, 108; MacDonnell (2023a).
[128] Leckey (2015) 181, 197; Kavanagh (2015a) 835.

6 Perils

Despite all these potential insights – mainly as correctives to erroneous or exaggerated views which had come before – the metaphor of dialogue also brought problems and distortions in its wake.[129] The hope that the idea of 'dialogue' could move us beyond an either–or debate about whether the courts or legislature should have the last word was not fully realised in practice. At least in the Canadian context, the ferocious debate about 'dialogue' versus 'true dialogue'[130] became a proxy for the well-worn controversy about which branch of government should have 'the last word' on rights. The issue now was simply: 'who should have the last word in the dialogue?' Similarly, whilst the UK defenders of dialogue championed the values of open deliberation and transparent disagreement, the debate about judging under the HRA polarised along familiar 'court versus legislature' lines.[131] By focusing on the question of who should get 'the last word' on rights, the debate about dialogue reproduced the 'public law of competing supremacies',[132] thus failing to take us beyond the traditional adversarial paradigms.[133]

Furthermore, although Hogg and Bushell's analysis highlighted the importance of fact-sensitive inquiries, the infusion of the metaphor of dialogue into constitutional discourse engendered a more abstract and ethereal account of the institutional roles of the branches of government, detached from the institutional context and constraints under which these actors operate. Though there were some notable exceptions, the discourse about dialogue generally succumbed to 'the lure of abstraction'.[134] Thus, we were told of dialogue's ability to ensure an 'equitable balance between democratic decision-making and compliance with basic human rights',[135] and how dialogue could harness the advantages of all

---

[129] For sceptical perspectives on dialogue, see Carolan (2016a); McDonald (2004b); Schauer (2019); Cossman (2019); MacDonnell (2023a); Mathen (2007); Cameron (2016); MacFarlane (2012b); MacFarlane (2017); Kavanagh (2016a); Law & Chang (2011).

[130] For analysis of the quest for 'true dialogue' in Canadian constitutional discourse, see Kavanagh (2016a) 96–7; Manfredi & Kelly (1999) 521; for the UK, see Nicol (2006) 745–6; Davis (2014a).

[131] Ewing (2004); cf. Kavanagh (2009c).

[132] Hunt (2003) 339.

[133] Hunt (2015) 17–19; Carolan (2016a) 217–19.

[134] Kavanagh (2016a) 109; Leckey (2019b) 68; Cossman (2019) 188.

[135] Southerden (2014) 262.

institutions, whilst doing 'no harm to democracy'.[136] We heard about the value of each institution 'having a say' or 'listening' to another in the context of an 'open interpretative disagreement'[137] about rights.

There is no doubt that these abstracted claims have a pleasing ring to them. They settle like white snow on a troubled landscape. But once their soft covering melts away, we are left with the same old messy picture riven with knotty problems, inevitable tensions and difficult trade-offs. It is not just that easy abstractions like these do not solve the underlying problems. They mask the complexities and lure us into a false sense that we have already solved them. It may well be that – stated in the abstract – open discussion, where everyone shares their point of view and no one is compelled to accept the views of others, is an unadulterated good. It certainly sounds attractive. But these kinds of general, abstract claims do not get us very far in analysing what complex institutions like courts and legislatures actually do given the jurisdictional and institutional constraints under which they labour, still less in grounding bold normative prescriptions about they *should* do.

But whilst the lure of idealisation and abstraction was one concern, the most serious problem was a tendency towards reification of the metaphor of dialogue in constitutional discourse, both in Canada and in the UK. Rather than using the metaphor of 'dialogue' to *illustrate* an argument about the nature of the relationship between courts and Parliament – or illuminate some feature of that relationship – the metaphor of 'dialogue' was itself treated as a source of guidance for understanding the nature of that relationship and providing detailed normative prescriptions to guide institutional behaviour. Recall that the point of using a metaphor is to conjure up a visual image to illuminate – through suggested similarity – something important about the object to which the metaphor is applied. The success of the metaphor hinges, at least in part, on the aptness of the similarity. If a significant dissimilarity arises, then our response should be to question the appropriateness of the metaphor, or reject it outright. In the literature on constitutional dialogue, the opposite response took hold. When divergences between the metaphor and constitutional practice arose, scholars argued that constitutional practice should match the metaphor, not the other way around. They recommended that courts and legislatures should reconfigure their behaviour to comply with a constitutional ideal derived from a mere metaphor.

---

[136] Young (2009); Davis (2014b) 6.
[137] Webber (2009) 458.

Thus, when governments and legislatures refrained from overriding court rulings on rights, scholars urged them to exercise the override under the Canadian Charter, and to defy declarations of incompatibility under the HRA. The argument was that these forms of legislative defiance and disagreement were necessary in order to 'realise the promise of dialogue'[138] and prevent democratic dialogue from 'wither[ing] on the vine'.[139] When the courts invoked standards of deference and restraint when adjudicating rights under the HRA, scholars urged them to engage in a more forthright and robust dialogue with the legislature.[140] They did so despite the fact that some of these normative prescriptions entailed a 'radical reconceptualization of the separation of powers'[141] and a fundamental 'reconfiguration'[142] of the institutional roles and relationships between the branches of government in a constitutional democracy.

What got lost in the discussion was an appreciation that 'dialogue' was merely a metaphor – a vivid word picture which *suggests* a similarity between two things. Instead, it was treated as a 'theory' or 'model' of constitutionalism which *required* institutional actors to behave in various ways. As one commentator observed: 'it is letting the tail wag the dog' for courts or legislatures to orient or change their behaviour to match the metaphor.[143] In order to understand what institutions do – and, crucially, what they *ought* to do as part of their institutional role – we need to examine and appraise their behaviour as part of a contextual institutional analysis. An evocative and alluring metaphor devised in the abstract and then superimposed onto a complex interaction which is 'both like and unlike a dialogue between persons,'[144] is likely to distort. All told, the metaphor of dialogue was taken literally, over-extended and reified, so that it was eventually treated as a fully fledged constitutional ideal which provided a detailed set of prescriptions about institutional behaviour. Rather than encouraging a greater focus on institutional and interactional behaviour,[145] the focus turned on the metaphor itself. Extrapolating connotations from the metaphor became the central focus of discussion, drawing light away from the real

---

[138] Davis (2014a).
[139] Ibid.
[140] Nicol (2006); Stark (2017a).
[141] Hickman (2005a) 309.
[142] King (2019a); Davis (2014b)
[143] Coughlan (2003) 208; Dyzenhaus (2015) 438–9.
[144] Sigalet, Webber & Dixon (2019b) 2.
[145] McDonald (2004b).

phenomenon under scrutiny, namely, the institutional roles of courts and Parliament and the proper relationship between them.

One of the most frequent criticisms of dialogue was the fact that it was indeterminate on the crux constitutional questions concerning the appropriate balance of power between the branches. It was malleable enough to encompass a picture of both an emboldened legislature and a chastened court, or a chastened legislature and an emboldened court.[146] The upshot was that instead of capturing and illuminating something significant and new about the relationship between the branches, 'dialogue' became a capacious catch-all term which could include almost any characterisation of the institutional roles, and almost any relationship between them.[147] Without the analytical resources to distinguish between different modes of engagement, the metaphor became a vague place-holder for any conceivable type of interaction between the branches of government across time and space.[148] Rather than shedding light on a complex phenomenon, dialogue became an opaque, abstruse and malleable term.[149]

This is not to deny that a number of scholars brought more clarity to the conversation, disambiguating dialogue in numerous insightful ways and rendering it more precise and serviceable for analytical purposes. But it was hard to shake off the distortive framing effects of the metaphor, especially given the proliferation of diverging dialogic accounts. The resulting 'avalanche'[150] of dialogue theories – each with its own distinctive analogical or adjectival qualifier[151] – tended to exacerbate rather than

---

[146] Leckey (2015) 167.

[147] For a recent attempt to define dialogue, see Sigalet, Webber & Dixon (2019b) 2–3, 30 (suggesting that dialogue 'may be taken to capture a plurality of different metaphors across institutional contexts and interactions' and that 'dialogue between institutions is both like and unlike dialogue between persons'). Needless to say, if dialogue is broadened out to include further (unspecified) metaphors and further (unspecified) similarities and dissimilarities with actual dialogue, the problem of opacity and indeterminacy is unlikely to be solved any time soon.

[148] MacFarlane (2012a) 97.

[149] Cameron (2001) 1063; Cameron (2016); MacFarlane (2012a) 73, 76, 97 (noting the 'conceptual chaos' caused by dialogue, and arguing that the 'veritable cacophony of different and often competing conceptions of dialogue renders the idea meaningless'); MacFarlane (2017) 127.

[150] Hogg, Thornton & Wright (2007a).

[151] See e.g. Webber (2009) ('dialogue as dialectic'); Tremblay (2005) ('dialogue as deliberation'); Hickman (2005a) (contrasting 'strong-form dialogue' with 'principle-proposing dialogue'); Sathanapally (2012) 41–5 (contrasting 'dialogue as specialisation' with

solve the problem of opacity.[152] After all, it is hard to see the wood for the trees from under an avalanche.

7   Dialogue, Disagreement, Distortion

One of the attractions of dialogue was that it could be all things to all people.[153] Political constitutionalists could invoke the metaphor to justify a strong legislature overriding court rulings on rights, whilst legal constitutionalists could use it to legitimise robust forms of rights-based review by downplaying the finality of judicial decisions in a system of 'weak-form review'. But the attraction of dialogue to both political and legal constitutionalists revealed that it was a false friend to both. The idea of dialogue facilitated a deep ambivalence about the roles and relationships between the branches of government.[154] It could encompass a multitude of different relational dynamics, ranging from a respectful engagement based on mutual learning through to a 'no-holds-barred'[155] argumentative face-off where each branch battled to seize the last word. The problem was that the metaphor of dialogue lacked the analytical resources to distinguish between this dizzying array of options. After all, a dialogue can be a friendly conversation, a fiery argument, or even a no-holds-barred shouting match.[156]

Tellingly, whilst the metaphor of dialogue entered the scholarship as a benign, legitimating discourse which highlighted the values of mutual learning, respect and compromise, as time went on, the language of dialogue was often 'conflated with the language of competition or struggle'.[157] Emphasising the need for 'forthright speech'[158] and 'fearless exchanges'[159] between the branches of government, it was argued that the courts should 'condemn without inhibition what they perceive as human

---

'dialogue as dual review'); Young (2017) ('democratic dialogue'); Levy (2019) ('departmentalist conception of dialogue'); Sigalet (2019) ('constructive dialogue'); Stephenson (2013) (contrasting 'dialogue as legislative response' versus 'dialogue as judicial deference').

[152] Kavanagh (2016a) 111.
[153] Geiringer (2019) 568.
[154] Fredman (2015) 440; Hunt (2015) 17; King (2019a) 187.
[155] Nicol (2006).
[156] Roach (2016b) 308ff; Hunt (2015) 20–1.
[157] Kyritsis (2017) 112.
[158] Nicol (2006) 745.
[159] Ibid 745.

rights violations.'[160] Similarly, the legislature should respond in a 'forth-right' fashion, without any 'inhibitions about putting forward their competing conceptions of rights'.[161] Needless to say, this emphasis on the value of outspoken and 'unrestrained debate'[162] resurrected the old antagonistic narrative, where the inter-institutional dynamics were framed as a matter of 'capitulation and resistance',[163] assertion and 'acquiescence',[164] disagreement and defiance.[165] The legislative *power* to override was converted into the legislative '*right* to disagree'.[166] Little wonder, then, that the idea of dialogue failed to take us beyond the adversarial paradigm of the Manichean narrative. It simply reproduced the rivalry in different form.

There are other reasons why the metaphor of dialogue shaded into antagonism in the constitutional context. One reason was that dialogue was perennially framed as a solution to the notorious counter-majoritarian difficulty. This created a focus on finality and which branch should get 'the last word', thereby resurrecting the dichotomous, binary framing which afflicted the Manichean narrative in the first place. Ironically, therefore, whilst dialogue entered the scholarship as a solution to the counter-majoritarian difficulty and a way out of the 'dead end of polarising positions',[167] it carried the baggage of the Manichean narra-tive with it.[168] Rather than diffusing decision-making responsibility amongst all three branches of government, the idea of dialogue merely shifted the 'last word' from one branch to another, thereby reintrodu-cing the old debate about which branch of government should have the final say.

Far from enhancing understanding, the metaphor of dialogue created a number of distortions, which I will document here.[169] First, it engen-dered an undue emphasis on overrides and legislative disagreement with

---

[160] Ibid 747.
[161] Ibid 745.
[162] Ibid 747.
[163] Tushnet (2008b) 46, 44; Sathanapally (2012) 16.
[164] Tushnet (2008b) 46.
[165] Appleby, MacDonnell & Synot (2020) 447; Sathanapally (2012) 26.
[166] Yap (2012) 532–4 (emphasis added); King (2019a) 194.
[167] Hunt (2015) 20; Roach (2015) 406–7.
[168] Kavanagh (2015a) 846.
[169] For more detailed analysis of the 'distortions of dialogue', see Kavanagh (2016a) 111–20; Carolan (2016a) 214–23.

courts, despite the fact that the legislative override was a peripheral and strikingly under-used feature of the Commonwealth model in practice.[170] The main interactive dynamics between the branches occurred outside of these formal channels, e.g. through the norms of judicial deference and respect, rulings about remedies, and judicial assessments about the justifiability of limitations on rights.[171] By looking at constitutional practice through the lens of dialogue, there was a danger of giving undue salience to peripheral practices, thus occluding the central interactive dynamics at play.

Second, the normative focus on legislative disagreement with courts created a tendency to cast legislative compliance with judicial decisions in a negative light as 'passive acquiescence', forced 'capitulation',[172] and a 'slavish submission'[173] to a hegemonic court.[174] But these diagnoses of failure, capitulation, and passivity are both questionable and problematic. For one thing, they overlook and obscure one important possibility, namely, that the legislature may *agree* with court rulings. In the UK, empirical analysis of legislative responses to declarations of incompatibility reveals that the legislature often agrees with judicial declarations, viewing them as relatively straightforward and uncontroversial 'quiet cases' which cause no legislative resistance or resentment.[175] We should not be lured into assuming – without argument or supporting empirical evidence – that legislative disagreement is the norm, just because it is presupposed by the metaphor of dialogue.

Third, the metaphor of dialogue connoted a dismissive or, at least, uneasy attitude towards the idea of judicial deference to the legislature, despite the fact that this was a pervasive feature of judicial decision-making both under the HRA and the Canadian Charter. Drawing on the leitmotiv of open, transparent disagreement about rights, dialogue scholars argued that courts 'should uncompromisingly tell their truth

---

[170] Carolan (2016a) 214–15; Kavanagh (2016a) 114–15.

[171] Though it is worth noting that some scholars working within the general rubric of 'dialogue' nonetheless emphasised the importance of the dynamics of judicial deference, justification, and limitation of rights, see Roach (2016b) 175ff; Dixon (2009b); Dixon (2019a).

[172] Davis (2014a) 9; Tushnet (2008b) 46.

[173] Webber (2009) 457.

[174] Bateup (2007) 13.

[175] See further chapter 12; King (2015a); Sathanapally (2012) 225–7.

on rights'[176] and engage in 'unapologetic review'[177] on the merits, without any need to compromise, defer, or give weight to the views of the democratically elected legislature. To be sure, when two parties engage in a dialogue, they may have no institutional obligations or social pressures to defer or give weight to the view of their interlocutor. They can simply express their view, and see how the interlocutor responds. But judicial decision-making in a democracy is not like a contribution to an open conversation, where everyone can say what they like. When acting in their judicial capacity – i.e. as part of the judicial role – judges have an obligation to respect the considered opinions of a democratic legislature and to refrain from second-guessing the legislative determination, unless it constitutes a clear violation of rights.[178] So whilst it may be true that judicial deference jars with the connotations of 'dialogue', this may simply be a reason to discard the metaphor, not criticise the practice.

Fourth, by abstracting from institutional context and focusing on the question of which branch of government should get the last word on rights, the idea of 'dialogue' occluded the fact that both courts and legislatures have a shared responsibility to protect rights, which they should each discharge in institutionally specific ways. By invoking the image of a conversational exchange between equals, the metaphor of dialogue abstracted away from the institutional structures, norms, incentives, and context which frame and constrain the actions of judicial and political actors on the ground.[179] Moreover, by riveting on the question of which branch should have 'the last word' in the dialogue, there was a tendency to treat the judicial and legislative voices in the conversation as 'broadly interchangeable contributions'[180] to a dialogue about how to protect rights in a constitutional democracy. The institutional distinctiveness of the judicial and legislative roles got lost in the conversation.

Finally, the idea of dialogue tended to overstate the discursive aspects of legal practice, whilst underplaying the authoritative nature of law.[181] In fact, the distortion of legal authority and finality was one of the most remarkable framing effects of the dialogue metaphor. Many argued that

---

[176] Nicol (2006) 744.
[177] Gardbaum (2013b) 85; cf. Kavanagh (2015a) 840–3; King (2015b) 104–5.
[178] For a more detailed analysis of the dynamics of deference in judicial decision making see Kavanagh (2008); Kavanagh (2010a); Kavanagh (2009b) chapters 7–9; Lawson & Seidman (2020); Chan (2017); Chan (2018).
[179] Carolan (2016a) 221.
[180] Carolan (2016a) 221.
[181] Kyritsis (2017) 107–14; King (2019a) 187, 199–204.

'dialogue should be understood to be a dynamic process involving the interchange of proposals for constitutional meaning',[182] where 'each institutional actor brings forth its understanding for consideration and examination by the other'.[183] In this way of thinking, court rulings on rights should be understood as 'thoughtful opinions'[184] or 'provisional statements'[185] about what rights require, which the legislature should consider but ultimately be free to reject.

But whilst it is certainly true that dialogue may be understood in this way, it is far from clear that judicial and legislative decisions should be understood as an optional exchange of thoughtful suggestions. After all, legislation is much more than a 'proposal for constitutional meaning'. It is an authoritative source of law, which is generally binding on the other branches and all residents in that country.[186] When legislators go through the arduous process of getting a Bill through Parliament, the end result is more than a suggestion. Similarly, when judges make decisions about what the law requires, they produce authoritative rulings, which are binding on the parties to the dispute, and often on all other citizens and state institutions.[187] As Kent Roach observed, if dialogue is viewed as an exchange of ideas as part of an idealised discussion, then it becomes

> an implausible way to describe the authoritative act of judging. At the end of the day, [judges] do not enter into dialogue or a conversation with anyone ... they decide cases according to their view of the law. Institutionally, they expect their decisions will settle disputes and be obeyed, not start conversations.[188]

The mistake was to assume that if court rulings were open to reversal, modification, or even override, this meant that they were merely provisional pointers or optional suggestions, devoid of all authoritative force. But we should be careful not to conflate authority and finality.[189] Judicial decisions on statutory interpretation and common law adjudication are still treated as authoritative rulings, even though they can be overruled by

---

[182] Webber (2009) 457.
[183] Ibid 453.
[184] Nicol (2006) 743; Campbell (1999) 99.
[185] Perry (2003) 635; Tushnet (2008b) xi.
[186] Kyritsis (2017) chapter 5 (entitled 'A Little Less Conversation, a Little More Action Please'); King (2019a) 199ff.
[187] King (2019a) 200–2.
[188] Roach (2005) 537; Greschner (2000) 74; Sales (2016a) 470.
[189] Kyritsis (2017) 109.

the legislature or indeed by the courts themselves. The 'idea of final decisional authority' may be 'foreign to dialogue',[190] but it is absolutely essential to a well-functioning legal system which – whatever else it might claim to do – aims to guide people's behaviour in their day-to-day lives. Dialogue misrepresented and distorted the authoritative nature of legal decisions about rights.[191]

8   Conclusion

The story of the dominance of dialogue in comparative constitutional discourse is a truly remarkable tale. It is testament to the potency of metaphors. In the swift transition from metaphor to model, the connotations of dialogue were used to create an ambitious constitutional ideal and a 'normative template for the legislative/judicial relationship'.[192] However, whilst it opened up a fruitful debate about the interactive dynamics between the branches of government, this chapter has argued that 'dialogue' was a misleading metaphor which ultimately distorted our understanding of the relationship between the branches. Though it promised to take us beyond 'the dead end of polarising positions',[193] it ended up leading us down some more blind alleys. It is time to turn back.

In order to forge an alternative route, we need to tell a deeper story about the relationship between the branches of government, grounded in the foundational principle of the separation of powers and enriched by a contextual institutional analysis which gives more detailed content to institutional roles. Viewed in the context of constitutional practice, the relationship between the branches looks less like a conversation and more like a complex division of labour between differently situated institutions carry out their respective roles, whilst simultaneously working together as partners in a collaborative constitutional enterprise.

---

[190] Webber (2009).
[191] Kyritsis (2017) 101.
[192] Carolan (2016a) 211.
[193] Hunt (2015) 20.

3

The Case for Collaboration

1 Introduction

Underpinning all controversies surrounding the protection of rights is a deeper question about the roles and relationships between the branches of government. In this chapter, I argue that the branches of government are partners in a collaborative enterprise where they each play distinct but complementary roles, whilst working together in mutually respectful, constructive and supportive ways. Instead of squaring off against each other to get the last word on rights in fierce constitutional combat – or having a cosy constitutional conversation about rights – I argue that they must work together in a spirit of constitutional partnership. On this vision of constitutionalism, the branches of government are not enemies. But they are not friends either. Instead, they are partners in a collaborative enterprise where they are required to treat each other with comity and respect. Moving from isolation to interaction – and from conversation to collaboration – this chapter defends the idea of the collaborative constitution.

The challenge, then, is to articulate a relational, interactive and collaborative conception of the separation of powers, where each branch has a distinct role to play, whilst working together towards the shared goal of protecting rights in a democracy. Taking up that challenge, this chapter proceeds in the following way. As with any partnership or collaborative endeavour, we must start with a division of labour. Therefore, Part 2 outlines the dynamic division of labour between the three branches of government. In Part 3, I argue that this division of labour must be supplemented by meaningful checks and balances in order to curb potential abuse of power and counteract the risk of jurisdictional overreach. Part 4 brings the dual dimensions of division of labour and checks and balances together, arguing that they are both underpinned by the deeper constitutional values of comity and collaboration, where the branches of government must work together as part of a joint institutional effort. Part 5 takes up the important question of how the collaborative constitution accommodates conflict and friction between the branches, defending the idea of 'conflict within constitutional constraints'. Instead of engaging in no-holds-barred *constitutional showdowns*, the branches of government should mediate their institutional differences and disagreements through mechanisms of *constitutional slowdown*. Only when the branches of government treat each other with mutual respect - disciplining their interaction with an appropriate degree of self-restraint and forbearance - can they achieve successful and sustainable constitutional government over time.

2   Dividing Constitutional Labour

When we look at constitutional democracies around the world, we are immediately struck by their *institutional plurality*. Instead of unified authority under a single ruler, powers are divided and shared between distinct branches of government. The view that powers should be dispersed amongst a plurality of institutions rather than concentrated in one single branch is often thought to be the 'essence of constitutionalism'[1] and the core of the constitutional separation of powers.[2] The question then arises: how do we demarcate the domains of the different branches and divide the labour between them?

One classic answer is provided by the so-called pure doctrine[3] of the separation of powers, namely, the claim that we should allocate to each branch a single function which gives it its name, whilst prohibiting it from encroaching upon the functions of the others.[4] In its simplest telling, the legislature legislates or makes law; the executive executes or gives effect to it; and the courts adjudicate disputes and apply the law. We can call this the 'one branch–one function' view.[5] It posits a 'one-to-one correlation'[6] between the three branches of government and their

---

[1] Barendt (1997) 137; Möllers (2019) 244–5.
[2] Albert (2010) 207; Magill (2000) 606; Gardbaum (2020b) (describing this as the 'anti-concentration principle').
[3] On the 'pure doctrine' of the separation of powers, see Vile (1998) 13–14; Carolan (2009) 18ff; Kavanagh (2016b) 224–6; Fombad (2016a) 60–4.
[4] Barendt (1995) 601.
[5] Kavanagh (2016b) 225; Merrill (1991) 231.
[6] Kyritsis (2007) 386; Merrill (1991) 231; Carolan (2009) 18.

respective functions, whilst warning each branch not to stray beyond the confines of its single function.[7]

But the claim that there is a tight one-to-one correlation between branch and function cannot be sustained in any constitutional system. It is an open secret that all three branches perform all three functions to some extent.[8] For example, the Executive carries out a legislative function when making 'delegated legislation'. Indeed, in many countries, the Executive also plays a central, if not a predominant, role in enacting primary legislation.[9] Executive power is strikingly multifunctional. When we turn to the legislature, a similarly multifunctional picture emerges. The legislature enacts general laws but it also holds the Executive to account, keeps order in the legislature, administers the process for voting on bills, and resolves disputes over contempt and breach of parliamentary privilege.[10] Similarly, when we look to the courts, judges apply the law and adjudicate legal disputes. But they also make, change, and develop the law in myriad ways. Certainly, in common law systems judicial law-making is widely accepted as an inevitable – and indeed legitimate – part of the judicial role.[11]

Clearly, the strict 'one branch–one function'[12] view cannot be sustained as a descriptive matter. With its monolithic insistence that each branch perform one single function and no other, it does not capture the complex institutional realities in any modern democracy.[13] This undercuts the explanatory power of the 'pure doctrine'.[14] But it also exposes its limits as a normative ideal to which the constitutional system should aspire. After all, we need the legislature to run its internal affairs and we want the Executive to make delegated legislation. We also need the courts to develop the law and sometimes to change it in significant, albeit interstitial, ways. In fact, it is hard to see how any branch could carry out its role in any meaningful way if it was confined

---

[7] Kavanagh (2016b) 225.

[8] Nourse (1999) 754; Griffith (2001) 55; Möllers (2013) 8.

[9] Gwyn (1989) 266.

[10] Packenham (1990); Norton (2013b) 9ff.; Russell & Gover (2017) 283; Sathanapally (2012) 53; Russell & Cowley (2016) 123.

[11] Lord Irvine (2003a) 59; Lord Reid (1972) 22.

[12] Kavanagh (2016b) 225.

[13] Heun (2011) 22; Mendes & Venzke (2018) 6.

[14] Kyritsis (2017) 38; Lawson (1994) 1231; Magill (2000) 1136–7; Kavanagh (2016b) 226.

to the performance of one single function to the exclusion of others.[15] Some intermixture of functions is both necessary and desirable.

The idea that the branches of government should operate in solitary confinement with 'high walls'[16] between them fails to capture a crucial feature of the institutional practice, namely, the interdependence and interaction between the three branches of government when carrying out their respective roles in the constitutional scheme.[17] Consider, for example, the role of the legislature. When the legislature enacts laws using vague statutory terms, it effectively delegates some decision-making authority to other bodies to fill in the gaps in the legislative framework and specify what those terms mean in concrete cases.[18] This is an example of what Joseph Raz describes as 'directed powers',[19] where the legislature sets out the general legal framework using 'deliberately underdetermined rules',[20] thus giving other institutional actors the power and discretion to decide what the law requires in the context of individual cases. As Raz clarifies, the purpose of directed powers is 'to introduce and maintain a certain division of power and labour between various authorities'.[21] Nor should we assume that legislative use of vague statutory terms is a rare or exceptional occurrence. In fact, vagueness is a 'pervasive legislative tool'[22] which legislatures use to divide the constitutional labour and allow the courts to engage in 'particularised equitable decision-making to determine specific cases'.[23] This highlights the fact that the legislature is dependent on courts and other bodies to implement and give effect to the legislation it enacts.

Other forms of interdependence and interaction are manifest when we look at the decisions made by the courts. In fact, from the judicial perspective, the interdependence of the branches of government is even

---

[15] Nourse (1999) 758, 760, 782; Kavanagh (2016b) 222; Fombad (2016a) 68; Pierce (1989) 365.

[16] *Plaut v Spendthrift Farms Inc* 514 US 211 (1995) (Scalia J).

[17] Kavanagh (2016b) 227; Eskridge & Frickey (1994) 28–9; Carolan (2009) 259.

[18] Endicott (1999) 194; Yap (2015) 75.

[19] Raz (1994) 242.

[20] Raz (1979) 194.

[21] Raz (1994) 243.

[22] Endicott (1999); Raz (2001) 419 (arguing that vagueness is a 'power-regulating device' between public organs of government in the collaborative law-making enterprise).

[23] Waldron (2016) 140.

more pronounced, since judges are constitutionally required to respect, implement, and give effect to the law enacted by the legislature.[24] As the 'weakest branch of government',[25] the courts are deeply dependent on the other branches of government to respect and implement judicial decisions.[26] Otherwise, judicial decisions will have no effect. Thus, the idea of each branch operating in solitary confinement, oblivious to the decisions, actions and needs of the other branches, fails to capture the interdependence and constructive interaction between the branches.[27] In order to carry out their roles in the constitutional scheme, each branch must be cognisant of – and responsive to – the roles and responsibilities of the other branches of government which operate within a deeply interdependent and interactive institutional setting.[28] The purity of the 'pure doctrine' is both descriptively inaccurate and normatively implausible.

But if we reject the idea of distinguishing between the branches on the basis of mutually exclusive functions, this begs the question: how can we account for the distinctness of the branches of government in a way which does not conflate their respective powers? After all, 'the desideratum of distinctness'[29] is a necessary component of any meaningful separation of powers. I propose that the answer lies in the idea of *institutional roles*, and the need for distinct but interconnected institutional roles within a joint institutional enterprise.[30]

When we reflect on the nature of governing, we can see that responsible government in any complex society requires the state to carry out a multiplicity of different tasks.[31] But there is no 'one-size-fits-all' decision-making process appropriate for all the tasks the State must carry out.[32] Different tasks call for different decision-making processes. Therefore, it is important to have different institutions carrying out distinct tasks in institutionally differentiated ways.

Typically, we need an institution with energy and efficiency to initiate and propose new policies (the Executive); a deliberative and representative

---

[24] Kyritsis (2017) chapter 7.
[25] Hamilton (1788), Federalist Paper 78.
[26] Whittington (2007) 26; Mendes (2013) 206.
[27] Schacter (2011) 1397 (rejecting the 'separate spheres' approach to understanding the separation of powers).
[28] Eskridge & Frickey (1994) 28–9.
[29] Kyritsis (2007) 386; Kavanagh (2016b) 229, 232.
[30] Kyritsis (2007) 392; MacFarlane (2013) 8–10.
[31] Green (2007) 165.
[32] Kyritsis (2017) 50; Malleson (2010) 109.

body to scrutinise policy proposals and make clear, open, prospective, stable, general rules for the community (a legislative assembly); and an independent body with legal expertise to adjudicate disputes about what the law requires in individual cases (the courts).[33] This provides an outline sketch of the constitutional division of labour between the three main organs of government in a constitutional democracy.

So how do we allocate power to these different branches? We begin by examining the various procedural features of different institutions e.g. their composition, decision-making process, sources of information, and the skills and expertise of the officials who work within them. We then allocate tasks 'to those state organs which by virtue of their composition and decision-making process are suited to perform them well'.[34] But we must also elicit the value these bodies instantiate given their various procedural features, because institutions only make sense in light of the purpose they are supposed to achieve and the value they are designed to embody.[35]

By relating substantive tasks to different institutions based on their institutional characteristics, skills, competence and sources of legitimacy, we try to secure a good division of labour in order to enhance the likelihood of good decision making overall.[36] Thus, if an institution has epistemic or legitimacy-based strengths, it should be allocated tasks which speak to those strengths. And if an institution has epistemic shortcomings, it should not be assigned a task that requires the corresponding epistemic virtues.[37] In short, a good separation of powers channels the multiplicity of decision-making tasks to the forum best placed to carry them out.[38]

Rather than trying to distinguish the branches of government in terms of single, mutually exclusive functions, my approach cashes out the separation of powers in terms of a dynamic division of labour, where

---

[33] Of course, the three main organs of government will typically be joined by a wider cast of constitutional characters, which supplement and support constitutional democracy, including an independent legal profession, police force, civil service, media bodies, electoral commissions, ombudspersons, anti-corruption commissions, etc., see generally Tushnet (2021); Scheppele (2009); Huq & Michaels (2016) 349; Fowkes & Fombad (2016) 1; Pal (2016); Fombad (2016b); Khaitan (2021). On the important role of 'knowledge institutions' in a constitutional democracy (i.e. universities, schools, libraries, a free press, statistics offices, etc.), see Jackson (2021).
[34] Kyritsis (2017) 39, 126; Kavanagh (2016b) 231.
[35] Kyritsis (2017) 42ff (describing this as 'purposive interrelation'); Raz (1979) 106.
[36] Barber (2001) 65.
[37] Kyritsis (2015) 124.
[38] Kavanagh (2016b) 231.

each branch plays a distinct but complementary institutional role.[39] What sets the institutions apart, on this account, is not an injunction to exercise one single function to the exclusion of all others. Instead, it is the imperative to carry out a distinct institutional role in the constitutional scheme as part of a differentiated division of labour. The upshot is a system of 'separated institutions sharing powers'[40] whilst carrying out different roles in a collaborative constitutional scheme.[41]

There are three advantages of thinking in terms of institutional roles rather than mutually exclusive functions. First, institutional roles can encompass a multiplicity of functions, thereby providing a better fit with constitutional practice on the ground. For example, the judicial role of adjudicating and resolving individual disputes can encompass the dual functions of applying and making new law. Similarly, the constitutional role of the Executive can encompass myriad functions, including making delegated legislation, proposing primary legislation, applying or executing legislation enacted by Parliament, and, most broadly, running the country.[42] Therefore, a role-based account can capture the multifunctionality of the branches of government which the traditional 'one branch–one function' view struggles to accommodate.

Second, a role-based account highlights the normative dimension of the separation of powers, emphasising the 'role obligations'[43] which attach to the branches of government in the constitutional scheme. On this view, institutional roles are much more than a laundry list of functions or an enumeration of discrete tasks or jobs to be performed. Instead, they have an irreducibly normative character, constituted by the standards that define what people who perform those tasks can legitimately do in their institutional or official capacity.[44] When we talk about the *role* of judges or legislators in the constitutional scheme, we are not just making factual statements about what they do. We are also making normative statements about what they ought to do *qua* judge or *qua* legislator.[45] In doing so, we situate the functions and tasks of the three branches of government within a 'constitutional role morality'[46] i.e., a set

---

[39] Kyritsis (2015) 107; Kavanagh (2016c).
[40] Neustadt (1964) 43.
[41] Kyritsis (2017) 34.
[42] Endicott (2020b).
[43] Jackson (2016) 1717.
[44] Raz (1979) 105; Weis (2020a); Kyritsis (2017) 42; Sabl (2002) 1–2.
[45] Jackson (2016) 1751; Kyritsis (2015) 9; Heclo (2006) 735–6.
[46] Siegel (2018) 115–18.

of norms, principles, and standards which constitute the role and guide its exercise. This gives us normative benchmarks against which we can appraise and evaluate the institution's performance.[47]

Third, the idea of institutional roles helps focus our attention on the 'position' or 'place' of each institution within a broader constitutional scheme.[48] Given that the three branches of government divide and share the power between them, the challenge of articulating the scope and limits of each institutional role becomes a matter of establishing their relative position within the constitutional division of labour.[49] The question about the allocation of power and responsibility then becomes a question of 'relative authority'[50] within a deeply interdependent, iterative and interactive constitutional scheme. Instead of marking out strict functional boundaries, my account therefore foregrounds the normative constraints of different role conceptions, where the branches of government share powers and functions, whilst remaining mindful of the legitimate role of their constitutional partners in governance.

Of course, once we admit some sharing and overlap of functions between different constitutional actors, this raises a worry about undercutting our ability to distinguish meaningfully between the branches.[51] For example, if both the courts and the legislature make law, how can we mark out the boundaries between them? The answer is that whilst both institutions make law, they do so in different ways, shaped by their different roles and competences within the constitutional division of labour.[52] Judicial law-making powers tend to be piecemeal and incremental, as judges develop the law gradually using existing legal resources. By contrast, legislatures have the power to make radical, wide-ranging changes to the law not based on existing legal norms.[53] Therefore, the distinction between the institutional roles of the courts and legislature does not map onto a distinction between two different functions (such as

---

[47] Heclo (2008) 81, 134, 137–9 (where 'officium' indicates 'the performance of a task, with heavy overtones of a duty to perform them properly, in light of the duties and obligations which accompany those tasks'); Quinlan (1993) 538–10; Kyritsis (2017) 4, 42; Sabl (2002) 14, 52; Cicero (2000) 30. In this book, I treat 'role' and 'office' as interchangeable terms; cf. Weis (2020a).

[48] Weis (2020a) 214; Siegel (2018) 113.

[49] Mendes & Venzke (2018) 3; Roughan (2013) 5, 137ff; Kyritsis (2017) 4.

[50] Mendes & Venzke (2018) 1.

[51] Kavanagh (2016b) 232.

[52] See Ibid 232; Ginsburg & Kagan (2005) 3.

[53] Raz (1979) 194; Gardner (2012) 41.

making law and applying it). Nor does it map directly onto different subject areas or types of issue (such as policies and principles, law and policy, or polycentric and non-polycentric issues).[54] It cuts across those distinctions. The real difference between them resides in the *way* in which each branch of government carries out its respective tasks given the various procedural features of its institutional design and the position it occupies vis-à-vis the other branches.[55] As legal philosopher John Gardner observed:

> What is really morally important under the heading of the separation of powers is not the separation of law-making powers from law-applying powers, but rather the separation of legislative powers of law-making (i.e. powers to make legally unprecedented laws) from judicial powers of law-making (i.e. powers to develop the law gradually using existing legal resources).[56]

In order to secure that meaningful separation, we do not need to erect 'high walls'[57] between the branches in a rigid, compartmentalized allocation of functions. Instead, we need each branch to respect its place in the constitutional scheme, whilst simultaneously respecting the contributions made by its partners in authority.[58] In this way, the branches of government are kept in their place largely by 'the imperatives of role',[59] not by an implausible essentialism about functions.

3   Curbing and Counteracting

Thus far, I have argued that the separation of powers requires a division of labour between the branches of government, where each branch plays a distinct role in the constitutional scheme. But division-of-labour considerations do not exhaust the requirements of the separation of powers.

---

[54] Kavanagh (2016c) 124ff.

[55] Kyritsis (2007); Raz (1979) 106 ('Norm-applying institutions should ... be identified by the way they fulfil their functions rather than by their functions themselves').

[56] Gardner (2012) 41.

[57] *Plaut v Spendthrift Farms Inc* (1995) 514 US 211, 239 *per* Scalia J (arguing that the separation of powers is a 'structural safeguard' and 'prophylactic device, establishing high walls'); though note the warning of Breyer J in the same case that 'the unnecessary building of such walls is, in itself, dangerous, because the Constitution blends, as well as separates, powers in its effort to create a government that will work for, as well as protect the liberties of, its citizens', 245; Greenhouse (1995).

[58] On the difference between legislative and judicial powers of law-making, see further Gardner (2012) 37–42; Raz (1979) 109–10, 194–201; Kavanagh (2004) 270–4.

[59] Quinlan (1993) 538.

In order to curb abuse of power and correct for jurisdictional overreach, we need to supplement the division of labour with checks and balances. Of course, these two dimensions of the separation of powers are not unrelated. After all, one way of curbing abuse of power is to divide it amongst multiple actors so that it is no longer concentrated in few hands.[60] Nonetheless, in order to secure the division of labour whilst preventing the risk of overreach and usurpation, we need to put supplementary safeguards and monitoring mechanisms in place. In short, we need to 'combine separation with supervision'.[61]

In thinking about this issue, it is useful to recall James Madison's canonical account of the value of checks and balances within a system of separated powers. Whilst the first task for the separation of powers is to make some 'division of the government into distinct and separate departments'[62] where each department has a 'will of its own',[63] Madison argued that 'the next and most difficult task is to provide some practical security for each, against the invasion of the others'.[64] Writing in the *Federalist Papers*, Madison famously contended that it was not 'sufficient to mark, with precision, the boundaries of these departments [of government], and to trust to the parchment barriers against the encroaching spirit of power'.[65] In order to avert the risk of abuse of power, we must provide 'auxiliary precautions'[66] in order to defend the institutions from undue incursion and enable them to correct for jurisdictional overreach. As Madison put it, we need to 'contriv[e] the interior structure of the government so that its several constituent parts may, by their mutual relations, be the means of keeping each other in their proper places'.[67] Thus, checks and balances are an important means of buttressing the original division of labour, supporting it with safeguards against the usurpation of power, thereby ensuring that the system as a whole will 'reliably track justice'.[68]

The need to include curbing and counteracting mechanisms within a constitutional system stems from normal precepts of institutional design.

---

[60] Claus (2005) 419; Kyritsis (2015) 107.
[61] Kavanagh (2016b) 233–4; Kyritsis (2017) 142.
[62] Madison (1788), Federalist Paper 51.
[63] Ibid; Möllers (2019) 238.
[64] Madison (1788), Federalist Paper 48; Allan (1993) 53.
[65] Madison (1788), Federalist Paper 51.
[66] Barber (2013).
[67] Madison (1788), Federalist Paper 51; Kinley (2015) 32
[68] Kyritsis (2017) 33.

When setting up institutions, we structure them so that they can play to their institutional strengths, but we also need to mitigate their attendant risks.[69] Therefore, implementing the separation of powers is a 'two-sided exercise'[70] involving the identification of the valuable role each institution can play, as well as an appreciation of their potential downsides and shortcomings. A good governmental structure will not only *allocate* tasks to institutions well suited to carry them out; it will also seek to *curb* potential abuse of power. These safeguards answer to the political imperative to keep power in check, whilst simultaneously providing 'a voice of assurance'[71] to citizens that the branches of government will observe their limitations when carrying out their respective constitutional roles.[72]

In the canonical texts on the separation of powers, writers such as Montesquieu and the US Founding Fathers stressed the importance of checks and balances as a way of controlling political power and curbing its potential abuse.[73] Indeed, many contemporary theorists view these checks as the very 'essence'[74] of the separation of powers, echoing Justice Brandeis' iconic statement that the aim of the separation of powers was 'not to promote efficiency but to preclude the exercise of arbitrary government'.[75] But this is a false dichotomy.[76] We are not forced to choose between efficiency and checks and balances as the sole or supreme rationale of the separation of powers. Instead, we can acknowledge that the separation of powers is a multi-value ideal which promotes a plurality of normative ends, including efficiency and safeguards, autonomy and constraint, specialisation and control.[77] This multifaceted understanding better reflects the institutional and normative complexity of constitutional government, where the constitutional allocation of power is combined with mutual checks and balances in a *system* of constitutional governance.

---

[69] Kyritsis (2012) 303.
[70] Ibid 303.
[71] Strauss (1987) 513, 526; Kyritsis (2015) 109.
[72] Levinson (2011) 657, 659.
[73] Möllers (2013) 10.
[74] Barendt (1995) 599; Möllers (2019) 244–5; Malleson (2010) 102; Albert (2010) 207; Fombad (2016a) 58ff.
[75] *Myers v United States* (1026) 272 US 52, 293 (Brandeis J, dissenting); Fisher (1971) 114.
[76] Pozen (2014) 75; Gwyn (1965) 32–6; Fisher (1971) 114; Malleson (2010) 99ff.
[77] Huq & Michaels (2016) 342; Vile (1998) 303, 368; Möllers (2013) 10.

4   Comity and Collaboration

Thus far, we have seen that the separation of powers comprises both a division-of-labour and a checks-and-balances dimension. The task of this section is to show that these dual dimensions are underpinned by the deeper value of inter-institutional collaboration. Of course, one way of dividing labour between different institutions would be to give each body a discrete set of tasks which they carry out in solitary confinement, without any concern for what the other bodies are doing. But such a disjointed array of isolated and insulated bodies could not function as a workable system of constitutional governance. The branches of government are not 'satellites in independent orbit'[78] or 'latifundia that have no connection between them'.[79] Instead, they are constituent parts of a constitutional system where each depends on the others to carry out their role as part of the 'common project of governance'.[80] Though they have distinct roles, they must work together. Though they are relatively independent from each other, they are also interdependent in subtle ways.[81] As constituent parts of a broader collaborative enterprise, they must therefore coordinate their actions and combine their institutional effort in order to work together as part of a *system* of separated powers.[82]

This idea of separate but interconnected branches was famously expressed by the US Supreme Court:

> While the Constitution diffuses power the better to secure liberty, it also contemplates that practice will integrate the dispersed powers into a workable government. It enjoins upon its branches separateness but interdependence, autonomy but reciprocity.[83]

It is also echoed by a former Lord Chief Justice of England and Wales, Lord Thomas,[84] who observed that just because each branch of government has a distinct role in the constitutional scheme

> does not ... mean that each branch stands in isolation from the other, each carrying out its functions without reference to, understanding of, or

---

[78] Bingham (2000) 230; Roughan (2013) 7.

[79] Barak (2006) 36.

[80] Halberstam (2009) 334; Shane (2003) 506; Levi (1976) 378; Kyritsis (2007) 397; Roughan (2013) 47.

[81] Joseph (2004) 322.

[82] Kavanagh (2022); Kyritsis (2008) 154; King (2008a) 428; Zeisberg (2004) 25.

[83] *Youngstown Sheet and Tube Co v Sawyer* 1953 343 US 579, 635 (Jackson J); Levi (1976) 378; Joseph (2004) 323, 332.

[84] Lord Thomas (2014) [7].

working with the others. The opposite is the case. While careful to ensure
they maintain their distinct roles, and do not intrude upon the functions
and responsibilities of the others, the Executive, Judiciary and Parliament
cannot but work together.[85]

So how should the branches of government relate to each other whilst
working together in the collaborative constitutional scheme? The key
value underpinning the interaction between the branches of government
in the collaborative constitution is the duty of inter-institutional comity.[86]
Comity is 'that respect which one great organ of the State owes to
another'.[87] It is the 'duty of one authority to respect and to support the
proper function of other authorities'.[88] Of course, the detailed requirements of comity in context will vary in accordance with the specific subject
matter, institutional relationship, and configuration of powers in any legal
system. Nonetheless, there are two general features of inter-institutional
comity which underpin those more detailed, context-dependent dynamics. These are the requirements of *mutual self-restraint* and *mutual support*.[89] In order to treat each other with comity and respect, the branches of
government must remain vigilant to avoid interfering with the others'
ability to carry out their respective roles (*mutual self-restraint*); but they
may also be required to actively support each other in various ways in
order to realise the common goal of good government under the
constitution (*mutual support*).[90]

Let us start with the norm of *mutual self-restraint*. Constitutional self-
restraint entails that each branch should refrain from undermining,
usurping, or interfering with the decision-making capacity of the other

---

[85] Lord Thomas (2017b) [16]; Lord Thomas (2014) [40], [11] ('the judiciary, the Executive
and Parliament can work well together whilst still respecting their functional boundaries'); Lord Justice Gross (2016) 25; Lord Burnett of Maldon (2018) 17; Kavanagh (2016b)
235–7.

[86] Endicott (2015a); Endicott (2002); King (2008a) 428; Kavanagh (2009a) 169ff.

[87] *Buckley v Attorney General* [1950] Irish Reports 67 [80] (O'Byrne J); see also Kavanagh
(2008) 187ff; Endicott (2021) xv, 17; Stephenson (2016) 139.

[88] Endicott (2021) xv, 22; Thomas (2017b) [18]; *R (Jackson) v Her Majesty's Attorney
General* [2005] UKHL 56, [125] ('In the field of constitutional law the delicate balance
between the various institutions whose sound and lasting quality ... is maintained to a
large degree by the mutual respect which each institution has for the other').

[89] Kavanagh (2016b) 236.

[90] Bratman (1992); Bratman (2014).

branches of government in the collaborative constitutional scheme.[91] Put more positively, each branch must be 'careful to respect the sphere of action of the other',[92] allowing their coordinate branches sufficient 'leeway'[93] to do their job well. Examples of these norms of self-restraint and non-interference are commonplace in many constitutional systems. For example, UK courts generally refrain from interfering with the privileges or internal workings of Parliament, and from 'questioning proceedings in Parliament' as prohibited by Article 9 of the Bill of Rights 1689.[94] Another example of constitutional self-restraint is the *sub judice* rule which requires Members of Parliament (MPs) to refrain from discussing matters before the courts, in order to avoid prejudicing judicial proceedings and undermining judicial decisions.[95] This reflects 'the long-standing comity between the Parliament and the courts which means that each takes care not to intrude on the other's territory, or to undermine the other's authority'.[96]

Self-restraint is also manifest in the requirement that Ministers and parliamentarians should refrain from denigrating or criticizing the courts in an unduly personalised, intemperate or inaccurate way.[97] Although it is acceptable in the British constitutional order for parliamentarians to criticise judicial rulings, they are expected to do so in a measured and respectful manner which stops short of impugning the integrity of individual judges or undermining the administration of justice.[98] Politicians must walk the fine line between criticism and condemnation, disagreement and denunciation.[99] For the most part, UK Ministers try to stay on the right side of this line. When they disagree with judicial

---

[91] Bickel (1986) 24 (arguing that in discharging their own duties, each branch should strive not to 'lower the quality of the other departments' performance by denuding them of the dignity and burden of their own responsibility').

[92] *AXA General Insurance v HM Advocate* [2011] UKSC 46, [148].

[93] Kavanagh (2016b) 236.

[94] Kavanagh (2014).

[95] See Jack (2011) 518; Gee at al. (2015) 119–22; King (2019a) 203; Lord Woolf (2008) 84; Lord Hodge (2016) 22; HL Select Committee on the Constitution, *Relations between the Executive, the Judiciary and Parliament*, 6th Report of Session 2006–7, para [41]–[42]; Lord Thomas (2017b) [39]–[43] (examining 'the constitutional limits on judicial comment' on controversial topics of acute political moment).

[96] Grieve (2012a) 6.

[97] Gee et al. (2015) 49; O'Brien (2017); Lord Dyson (2018) 18.

[98] Gee et al. (2015) 54, 119, 120.

[99] N Siegel (2017) 15; Justice Ginsburg (1992) 1194–8 (outlining a similar distinction between robust criticism and 'intemperate denunciation' amongst judges on a collegiate court).

rulings, they generally do so without delegitimising the important role of the courts in the constitutional scheme.[100] In exercising such constitutional self-restraint, the political actors help to sustain 'a political culture that respects the authority of judicial decisions'.[101] Mutual self-restraint is necessary to strengthen 'the relationship of comity – the mutual respect and understanding for each other's respective constitutional roles – that ought to exist between Parliament and the judges'.[102]

However, whilst reciprocal self-restraint and mutual non-interference is necessary to discharge the duty of constitutional comity, it is not sufficient. Comity also entails some 'affirmative obligations'[103] which require the branches to positively assist and support one another in carrying out their respective roles in the collaborative constitutional scheme.[104] The requirement of *mutual support* is manifest when the courts give effect to legislation enacted by Parliament, implementing it in a faithful manner, whilst ensuring that legislative enactment hews to constitutional principle. It is also manifest when the Government and Parliament provide adequate funding and structural support for the courts, in order to ensure that they are properly equipped to carry out their adjudicative functions.[105] It is legible, too, when the political branches respect and implement court rulings in good faith[106] and defend the judiciary from illegitimate attacks or damaging critique.[107]

The underlying point here is that judicial independence cannot be secured by judges alone.[108] It only survives in a system of constitutional governance where there is a culture of respect for the law within politics as a whole.[109] As legal scholars on both sides of the Atlantic observe,

---

[100] N Siegel (2017) 15; Gavison (1999) 241; Kavanagh (2010b) 38.

[101] Gee et al. (2015) 116; Shane (2003) 509.

[102] Oliver (2003) 19–20.

[103] Pozen (2014) 38; Sabl (2002) 7; MacDonnell (2013) 624, 636ff.

[104] Kyritsis (2017) 46. The norm of mutual support is also legible in the explicit constitutional duty placed on executives and legislatures in some countries to assist so-called fourth branch institutions in supporting the joint enterprise of governing as a whole, see Pal (2016) 100–2.

[105] Thomas (2017b) [19].

[106] Cranston (2013) 25–6; Burnett (2018) 7.

[107] Thus, when judges were described as 'enemies of the people' in the *Daily Mail* (Slack (2016)), the then Lord Chancellor (Liz Truss MP) was roundly criticised for failing to defend the courts in a prompt and forthright fashion, see Bowcott (2017); Lord Thomas (2017c) [2]–[3]; Lord Thomas (2017b) [41]–[42].

[108] Whittington (2003) 473; Lord Thomas (2015b); Lord Justice Gross (2018) 6.

[109] Gee et al. (2015) 11; Levinson (2011) 733; Oliver (2013) 322.

'a healthy politics of judicial independence has always depended on a functioning partnership between judges and politicians'.[110] Judicial independence ultimately depends on 'the commitment of the executive and legislature in collaboration with the judiciary to maintain a healthy democracy that is committed to the rule of law'.[111]

Now we can begin to put the pieces of the jigsaw together. The collaborative constitution is one where the branches of government have distinct but complementary roles, whilst respecting each other and working together as partners in a joint enterprise of governing.[112] The fact that the branches must work together in a collaborative enterprise frames and shapes the interaction between them. The collaborative constitution is marked by the following features.

First, although the branches of government play distinct roles in the constitutional scheme, they nonetheless share the *common goal* of securing just government under the constitution.[113] By 'just government', I simply mean government which acts justly and fairly on behalf of the community, informed by key constitutional principles including democracy, the rule of law, justice, and the protection of rights.[114] To be sure, the common goal of the collaborative enterprise is stated at a high level of abstraction. Nonetheless, it captures the important point that whilst the three branches of government have distinct roles to play, they must show a 'constitutionally grounded concern for the common constitutional enterprise'[115] and a commitment to the '*res publica* as a whole'.[116] This commitment is legible in the constitutional requirement of many systems that all the key constitutional actors – not just judges – must swear an oath to support and uphold the constitution.[117]

---

[110] Gee et al. (2015) 61, 1, 9, 11, 14, 22, 24; Ferejohn & Kramer (2002) 1039; Katzmann (1988) 2.

[111] Lord Hodge (2015) 473; Lord Justice Gross (2018) 6–7; MacDonnell (2019) 201.

[112] Kumm (2009) 305; Kumm (2017) 56; King (2008a) 428; Joseph (2004) 334; Dyzenhaus (1998) 107; Sager (2004) 5.

[113] Kyritsis (2017) 35; Endicott (2009) 1; *Huddleston* [1986] 2 AER 941, 945, per John Donaldson MR (describing the relationship between the branches as 'a partnership based on a common aim').

[114] Sager (2004) 5–6; MacDonnell (2016) 30.

[115] Jackson (2016) 1743; Halberstam (2004) 801–2; Griffith (1997) 291.

[116] Cicero (2000) 30; Sabl (2002) 1, 141.

[117] Jackson (2016) 1743; Halberstam (2004) 801–2; de Visser (2022) 220; Tushnet (1995) 254–5; Fowkes (2016b) 217.

Second, whilst the branches of government share a common goal, this in no way presupposes identical or equivalent institutional roles. On the contrary, it is *a common goal, differently realised*.[118] Collaboration signposts 'the coming together of distinct elements, espousing complementary goals but responding to different sets of incentives'.[119] Although the branches have joint work, they have different jobs, working together towards a common goal in role-specific ways.[120] Therefore, the collaborative constitution embraces an 'institutional and perspectival diversity'[121] which flows from having 'a plurality of governing institutions'[122] working together.

Third, the collaborative constitution highlights the *heterarchical* – rather than hierarchical – nature of the relationship between the branches.[123] Instead of a hierarchical arrangement of 'command and control' where either the courts or the legislature reigns supreme, collaborative constitutionalism envisages a more complex, heterarchical dynamic where the branches of government must engage with each other in a spirit of mutual accommodation rather than antagonism, compromise rather than combat.[124] Crucially, whilst heterarchy is not hierarchy, it is not equality either. Just because each branch has a valuable and legitimate role in the collaborative enterprise does not mean they play equivalent or interchangeable roles. Instead, they play different roles in the constitutional scheme, whilst working together in the spirit of partnership and mutual respect.[125]

Fourth, the relationship between the branches of government is not a one-off encounter or a single-shot play. Instead, it is a *long-term working relationship* stretching over time.[126] In order to sustain a successful long-term relationship, the interaction between the branches of government is

---

[118] Levi (1976) 391 (describing 'a harmony of purposes differently fulfilled'); Jackson (2016) 1718; Friedman (1992) 772; Mendes (2013) 77; Carolan (2016a) 225–7; Carolan (2016b) 115.

[119] Joseph (2004) 334; Carolan (2009) 124, 139

[120] Joseph (2004) 323; Quinlan (1993) 539.

[121] Carolan (2016b) 118, 225; Stephenson (2016) 9; Sabl (2002) 2, 15, 315–16; Shane (2003) 506–7; Hamilton (1788), Federalist Paper 73, at 443.

[122] Sabl (2002) 2, 15; Sadurski (2019) 23; Carolan (2016b) 220–2.

[123] Halberstam (2009) 326–56; R Siegel (2017) 1757; Krisch (2008) 185; Krisch (2010) 111; Rodriguez (2014) 2097.

[124] Fallon (2001) 11; Halberstam (2009).

[125] Carolan (2016a) 221; Krisch (2008) 185, 196–8.

[126] Balkin (2016) 242–3; Jackson (2016) 1759; Vermeule (2007) 245ff.

framed by the requirements of *reciprocity, repeat-play,* and *reputation.*[127] The ongoing success of a long-term relationship between interdependent actors depends on a spirit of healthy reciprocity between them, and consideration for the medium or long-term impact of their actions on the relationship as a whole. Opportunistic power-play might secure short-term advantage, but it can undermine a branch's reputation as a reliable and trustworthy partner in an ongoing constitutional endeavour.[128] An unduly confrontational move against another branch might trigger open retaliation and a resultant break-down in reciprocal respect, thus unleashing vicious 'cycles of escalating constitutional brinkmanship'[129] which risk corroding the mutual respect and support on which successful long-term relationships rely.[130] Given that the branches of government are involved in a repeat-play rather than one-off relationship, this curbs the incentives to engage in conflictual behaviour. Therefore, the fact that the branches are embedded in long-term working relationships shapes and constrains the interaction between them. In order to sustain good working relations over the long term – and accrue the mutual benefits of a stable constitutional order – the branches of government may be required to pass up on a short-term gain in order to garner long-term advantages for the common good and the democratic polity as a whole.[131]

Finally, the values of comity and collaboration require the branches of government to recognise each other as partners in the joint enterprise of government.[132] In a mutual dynamic of '*role recognition*',[133] each branch must be mindful of the scope and limits of their own institutional role, whilst simultaneously respecting the valuable roles of their partners in authority. Rather than riding roughshod over the contributions made by the other branches - or treating them like pawns in a game where the winner takes all - the branches of government must recognise the legitimacy of all three branches to the common endeavour, building on those contributions in a spirit of comity and collaboration.[134] This does

---

[127] Levinson (2011) 676–7, 684, 711; Pozen (2014) 70; Guzman (2008) 33; Putnam (1994) 88ff; Whittington (2002) 806–8; Elster (2010) 32; Levitsky & Ziblatt (2019) 107.

[128] Heclo (2008) 68–9; Schacter (2011) 1367; Ellickson (1991) 156.

[129] Levitsky & Ziblatt (2019) 112; Nelson (2014); Shane (2003) 543.

[130] Pozen (2014) 2; Matthews (1959) 1072.

[131] Ellickson (1991) 52–6; Bejan (2017) 146; Nagel (1998) 8.

[132] Bratman (2014) 41.

[133] Lord Hodge (2015) 483–4; Lord Hodge (2018) [23].

[134] Sager (2004) 7; Griffith (1997) 291.

not mean that the branches of government must agree with each other.[135] Far from it. In fact, the strength of the collaborative enterprise depends on the varied contributions of diverse institutional actors, and on the dynamic tension and robust contestation between them. Nonetheless, the collaborative constitution requires the branches of government to check each other in a spirit of comity and respect, ever mindful of the fact that they each make a partial contribution to a joint enterprise. Therefore, they must respect the legitimate contributions made by their fellow participants in the joint scheme.

The upshot for our understanding of the separation of powers is profound. It forces us to abandon the 'pure doctrine'[136] where the branches of government work in splendid isolation with 'high walls' between them. In place of high walls, the branches need to build bridges, forging lasting and constructive working relationships between them in a system of 'shared authority'.[137] Instead of a static vision of mutually exclusive functions, the separation of powers is thus recast as 'a dynamic process of engagement',[138] where the branches must carry out their roles in a relationship of interdependence, reciprocity and mutual respect. Moving from isolation to interaction – and 'from rivals to relationships'[139] – the collaborative constitution envisages 'separate branches sharing powers',[140] working together towards the common constitutional goal of securing just government under the constitution. On the collaborative vision, the aim of the separation of powers is not to insulate the branches from each other in a rigid, compartmentalised fashion, but rather to structure their interaction and regulate their relationships as constituent parts of a workable system of constitutional governance.[141]

There is no doubt that this marks a departure from some traditional understandings of the constitutional separation of powers. A static compartmentalisation of functions is replaced with a dynamic division

---

[135] Stephenson (2016) 13.
[136] Vile (1998) 13–14.
[137] Kyritsis (2015); Harlow (2016) 173–4; Cartabia (2016) (using the metaphors of 'bridges and walls' to illuminate the 'Italian style' of constitutional adjudication).
[138] Malleson (2010) 100.
[139] Kavanagh (2019); Barsotti et al. (2017) 63–7, 235–9 (describing the institutional and interpretive 'relationality' involved in the Italian constitutional system).
[140] Neustadt (1964) 43.
[141] Kavanagh (2022); Appleby, MacDonnell & Synot (2020) 441–8.

of labour. High walls are replaced with the hard work of building – and, crucially, *sustaining* – a constitutional partnership over time.[142] But the 'pure doctrine'[143] of the separation of powers posits a purity which exists nowhere in the world, whilst simultaneously exaggerating the stringency of the separation required by the doctrine and inflating the role of conflict and sanctions within it.[144] Between the dual distorted narratives of an essentialist separation of functions on the one hand, and all-out competition and conflict on the other, we have suppressed the underlying collaborative relationships between the branches which make our system work.[145] Instead of emphasising mutual checking and 'sanctioning devices' as the very 'essence'[146] of the separation of powers, the collaborative vision puts those checks in collaborative context, appreciating that the branches of government 'do not merely counteract protectively; they also interact productively'.[147]

By recasting the separation of powers in relational and collaborative terms, our focus of attention shifts away from the competing claims of the courts and legislature to have the last word on rights, towards a more productive inquiry into the nature of the relationship between them. Building constructive constitutional relationships between partners needs more than a set of prohibitions and sanctioning devices to curb potential abuse of power. It also requires norms of constructive engagement and mutual respect which shape, constrain, and discipline the mode of interaction between them.[148] What keeps the branches apart, on this vision, is the distinct institutional roles in the constitutional division of labour. But what holds them together are the relational norms of comity and collaboration which positively frame and shape the interaction between them. It is these norms which provide the 'connective tissue'[149]

---

[142] For reliance on the building metaphor in constitutional scholarship, see e.g. Fowkes (2016a); Von Bogdandy & Paris (2020) (on the way in which the Italian and German constitutional courts 'build judicial authority').

[143] Vile (1998) 13.

[144] Kavanagh (2016b) 229; Posner & Vermeule (2010).

[145] Post & Siegel (2003b) 34; Baker (2019) 407–9.

[146] Barendt (1997) 599.

[147] Hickman (2005a) 335; de Londras (2017); Irvine (2003a) 131.

[148] For an exploration of the negative and positive dimensions of the separation of powers, see Möllers (2019) 246; Möllers (2013) 10, 37, 40–3; Malleson (2010); Hailbronner (2016) 392ff.

[149] Greene (2018) 94; MacDonnell (2019) 204; Kinley (2015) 32.

between the branches of government in a system of 'separatedness but interdependence, autonomy but reciprocity'.[150]

5 Conflict within Constraints: From Showdown to Slowdown

With all this talk of the branches of government working together in a spirit of inter-institutional comity – welcoming rather than eschewing the contributions of the other branches to the collaborative enterprise – the question arises whether the collaborative vision of constitutionalism can accommodate ongoing disagreement, competition and conflict between the branches. After all, when we look at the inter-institutional dynamics in many countries across the world, it seems as if the branches of government are set on a collision course concerning rights, rather than acting as respectful partners in a collaborative enterprise. Indeed, many scholars argue that inter-branch rivalry and conflict is the central normative rationale of the separation of powers, encapsulated in the Madisonian mantra that the branches of government should be pitted against each other so that 'ambition can be made to counteract ambition'.[151] Rather than striving to *work with* the other branches in a spirit of comity and collaboration, we may think that the branches of government should *work against* each other in a spirit of antagonism where the actions of one branch are met with a countervailing force. Is it not more accurate, then, to portray these inter-institutional dynamics in fundamentally conflictual rather than collaborative terms? Indeed, is the principle of the separation of powers not premised on the very idea that the branches of government *should* conflict rather than collaborate, compete rather than combine?

The short answer is 'no'. But the longer response to this question requires us to disaggregate the cluster of concerns it raises, including *contestation, counterbalancing, critique, correction, competition* and *conflict*. Though often conflated, these are not identical phenomena and the collaborative constitution accommodates them in different ways and to different degrees. Let me start with checks and balances. If the Madisonian mantra about 'ambition counteracting ambition' is simply a dramatic way of expressing the value of robust checks and balances in a system of separated powers, then this is clearly part and parcel of the collaborative

---

[150] *Youngstown Sheet and Tube Co v Sawyer* 1953 343 US 579, 635, Jackson J; Post & Siegel (2003a) 1946.
[151] Madison (1788), Federalist Paper 51.

constitution. As emphasised earlier, checks and balances are a constitutive part of the collaborative endeavour. They are axiomatic – not anathema – to the collaborative constitutional scheme. A well-functioning collaborative constitution needs a 'healthy opposition'[152] and creative constitutional tension between the branches of government, precisely so that they can hold each other to account and contribute diverse perspectives to the collaborative effort. By curbing the abuse of power and strengthening the division of labour, checks and balances *help* the individual branches of government – and the common constitutional project as a whole – to work well.

At first blush, it may seem paradoxical to suggest that when one branch checks, corrects, or even vetoes the decision of another branch, this is a form of help. But the paradox disappears once we reflect on the fact that mutual oversight, correction and critique are not necessarily incompatible with participation in a joint activity.[153] We are all familiar with the idea of 'constructive criticism' or *criticism as help*.[154] As academics and scholars, for example, we appreciate critical feedback because it helps us to improve our analysis, deepen our understanding, and contribute to better scholarship overall. In fact, critical feedback is often perceived as more helpful than a purely laudatory response. This is just one example where mutual critique, contestation, and correction can be a central part of a working relationship, rather than being anathema to it.[155] Note that the emphasis here is on *constructive* criticism. There is a difference between constructive criticism intended to help, and vituperative condemnation designed to harm. Whilst the branches of government are required to check and balance each other in constitutionally prescribed ways, they must nonetheless do so within an overarching normative framework of respect for the roles and relationships which lie at the heart of the constitutional order.

Of course, for any system of separated powers to succeed, there must be a 'tension, a tautness'[156] between the branches. Too much agreement

---

[152] Fowkes (2016b) 216.

[153] Kyritsis (2015) 11, 118; Carolan (2009) 203.

[154] Bulman-Pozen & Gerken (2009) 1288 (using the analogous idea of the 'connected critic'); Uhr (2006) 43.

[155] For analogous reflections on the idea of *criticism as help*, see Gee et al. (2015) 150 (using the example of workplace appraisal); Sunstein & Hastie (2015) 107ff (on the value of priming critical thinking within organisations to enhance the overall performance of group decision making).

[156] Griffith (1985) xi; Kavanagh (2019) 69.

or alignment between them and the requisite distance and tension are lost. But too much acrimony and antagonism means that the norms of mutual respect, civility and constructive engagement will become frayed, thereby straining the relationship of comity and partnership between the branches. Navigating a middle course between these two extremes, the collaborative constitution accepts the value of inter-institutional contestation and critique, whilst situating that contestation within the broader collaborative dynamics which underpin a long-term, working relationship between partners. It supports a system of sceptical rather than sanguine cooperation, where each branch is embedded in 'a relationship of mutual tension'[157] as well as mutual respect. As such, the branches must be prepared to check and counterbalance the other as part of an ongoing, collaborative process.[158]

However, there is no denying that the relationship between the branches can 'sharpen into conflict'[159] at times. Elected politicians may feel frustrated to be on the receiving end of an adverse judicial decision which prevents them from pursuing their preferred policy. They may respond by venting their frustration in public, decrying judicial interference with their decisions, and castigating the courts as the enemies of democracy.[160] When such conflicts flare up – as they inevitably do from time to time – what comes to the fore is a fiercely antagonistic dynamic marked by anger and frustration rather than a collaborative relationship marked by respect and restraint. The question, then, is whether this conflictual dynamic captures the fundamental nature of the relationship between the branches?

There are a number of reasons to resist an affirmative response to this question. For one thing, we should beware of assuming that these flashpoints of friction are necessarily representative of the ordinary, everyday modes of engagement between the branches. Media coverage of current affairs tends to foreground controversy and conflict, thereby giving conflictual episodes undue salience in our understanding of political life. One of the truisms of journalism is that conflict is newsworthy.[161] It provides 'good red meat for a media that has an insatiable appetite for news'.[162] But whilst the media feasts on these flashpoints of

---

[157] Loughlin (2013) 109–10; Post & Siegel (2003a) 1952.
[158] Carolan (2009) 186–7 (proposing an attitude of 'sceptical cooperation' between the branches).
[159] Griffith (2001) 49.
[160] Feldman (2015) 96–7.
[161] Simons (2015); Flinders (2012) 147.
[162] Woolf (2008) 155; Lord Dyson (2018) 199; Heclo (2008) 27.

friction – no doubt stoking the fire along the way – we should beware of assuming that these conflictual episodes are replicated in the day-to-day dynamics of constitutional government on the ground. Viewed in diachronic perspective, the engagement between the branches may reveal pockets of conflict, punctuating a broader and longer trajectory of respectful but robust contestation within a framework of collaborative governance.[163]

In the UK, for example, empirical evidence suggests that the occasional but high-profile conflicts between politicians and judges are the exception not the rule.[164] In the mundane, day-to-day working of the British constitution, Government Ministers, parliamentarians, and parliamentary officials work hard – often behind the scenes – to limit, and avoid inflammatory outbursts and corrosive conflict between the key constitutional actors.[165] Similar norms of respect and restraint are legible in other established constitutional democracies.[166] Therefore, the conflictual dimension may be given undue salience in our image of inter-institutional engagement in contemporary constitutional democracies. Whilst we are fascinated by the agonistic drama of dissensus, mesmerised by the rifts and rivalries it portends, the dull realities of constitutional government behind the scenes may nonetheless manifest an ongoing commitment – though shaky at times – to an ethic of comity and collaboration based on mutually respectful modes of engagement.[167]

The deeper point at work here is that successful constitutional governance cannot be a matter of force meeting equal and opposite force in an unbridled battle of wills. If the branches of government were truly at war - locked in a perpetual state of inexorable aggression held only at bay by the threat of sanction from a counteracting force - the constitutional system would degenerate into chaos and lawlessness. Democracy would decay. As in all long-term relationships, it is inevitable that there will be disagreement and inter-branch conflict at times. Indeed, it is a sign of a healthy relationship that it can tolerate a measure of conflict and friction without this undermining the relationship completely. However, if

---

[163] Krisch, Corradini & Reimers (2020).
[164] Gee at al. (2015) 27.
[165] Gee et al. (2015) 24.
[166] Geyh (2006) 234; Pozen (2014) 34; Halberstam (2009) 336–7; Levinson (2011) 733.
[167] Chafetz (2011); Webber (2000) 126.

antagonism, hostility, and open confrontation become the daily *modus vivendi*, the relationship will likely fall apart.

Consider the analogy with marriage. Marriages are long-term relationships marked by mutual respect and love in the service of common endeavours. But as we all know, there is no marriage without disagreement, and all marriages experience conflict at some stage. However, this does not mean that the institution of marriage is accurately understood or normatively oriented towards no-holds-barred conflict across the board. In fact, the opposite is the case. The rationale of the institution of marriage – and the ideal it embodies – is to secure the commitment of two people to a long-term loving relationship, underpinned by the norms of mutual respect, support, trust, and self-restraint, all of which are required to sustain a long-term relationship over time. Good marriages can weather a certain amount of conflict. But if antagonism becomes pervasive and entrenched, then the marriage is likely to break down.

The same is true of the relationship between the branches of government. The existence or prevalence of sharp conflict and angry contestation between the branches does not mean that this is how the constitutional relationships ought to be conducted. If political actors try to eviscerate the jurisdiction of the courts or discredit the legitimacy of the courts in a way which undermines their ability to carry out their judicial role, then those actors have violated the norms of the collaborative constitution on which a well-functioning constitution depends. Whilst the branches of government can tolerate a degree of antagonism and confrontation at times, it cannot be conflict all the way down.[168] Nor can there be conflict all the time. For a healthy system of constitutional government to exist – and, crucially, to *per*sist over time – the interaction between the branches must be based on unwritten conventions and 'tacit understandings'[169] that the branches of government will treat each other with comity and respect. As with all long-term relationships, the relationship between the branches cannot plausibly be based on conflict.[170]

---

[168] Chafetz (2011); Pozen (2014).

[169] Le Sueur (1996) 26; Huq (2018) 1530 (suggesting that a healthy constitutional democracy is better served by 'the restraining friction of formal conventions and expectations of mannered interaction', rather than 'sharp, and even angry, contestation').

[170] Le Sueur (1996) 26; Hay (2007) 161.

The key problem with the conflictual narrative is that it overlooks and underplays the constitutional norms and constraints which frame and shape the inevitable contestation between the branches.[171] It presents a distorted and exaggerated picture of inter-branch dynamics which foregrounds collision whilst occluding the underlying collaborative dynamics at play. As a former British Prime Minister, Lord John Russell, put it,

> every political constitution in which different bodies share the supreme power is only enabled to exist by the forbearance of those among whom this power is distributed ... each must exercise a wise moderation.[172]

Whilst the Madisonian mantra tempts us to see interaction between the branches as 'conflicts between independent strategic actors seeking to pursue well-defined policy preferences', this frequently masks 'more cooperative interaction between interdependent branches'.[173]

When we appreciate the practice of mutual respect, restraint, recognition and support between the branches of government, we can see that they are more to each other than merely sites of resistance and pushback. Rather, they are partners in a collaborative enterprise, where they must work together constructively as part of a common constitutional project.[174] Therefore, the collaborative constitution seeks forbearance rather than ferocity in inter-institutional relations. It enjoins the branches to avoid the aggressive tactics of 'constitutional hardball',[175] namely, 'a form of unrestrained institutional combat aimed at permanently defeating one's political rivals and not caring about whether the democratic game continues'.[176] It requires them to eschew 'dirty tricks or hardball tactics in the name of civility and fair play'.[177]

Instead of engaging in *constitutional showdowns*,[178] the collaborative vision articulates a preference for *constitutional slowdown* where the branches of government commit to the painstaking processes of constitutional government under the rule of law. This requires them to channel

---

[171] Lovell (2003) xix; Hilbink (2009) 782–3.
[172] Letter of Lord John Russell to Poulett Thomson (14 October 1839), cited in Shane (2003) 508; Siegel (2018) 145; Balkin (2018) 17; Levitsky & Ziblatt (2019) 8, 106ff; Holland (2016) 232.
[173] Lovell (2003) 24.
[174] Sabl (2002) 123–4.
[175] Tushnet (2004); Balkin (2008).
[176] Sadurski (2018) 260; Levitsky & Ziblatt (2019) 109.
[177] Levitsky & Ziblatt (2019) 107; Balkin (2018) 19.
[178] Tushnet (2004); Posner & Vermeule (2010) 67ff.

their disagreements through the required institutional structures, accepting the manifold mechanisms of 'horizontal accountability'[179] which the constitution requires. In order to turn its policies into law, the government must go through the arduous stages of the legislative process, incurring all the 'enactment costs'[180] this entails. Similarly, the courts must comply with the rigours of the adjudicative process in open court.

Without doubt, these mechanisms slow government down.[181] But by proceeding in a way which manifests respect for the constitutional rules of the game and the legitimate role of their coordinate branches in holding them to account, the government evinces a commitment to the common goal of just government under the constitution. It accepts the cost of *constitutional slowdown* in order to win the greater prize of a well-functioning, institutionally pluralistic but constrained constitutional government.[182] Collaborative constitutionalism is a system where the government is allowed to push forward, but only if it accepts the constitutional imperative that the other branches are entitled to push back.[183]

The fact that the key constitutional actors must work '*through* institutions',[184] *within* the constitutional rules of the game, *as part* of an institutional role-morality, and *together with* other actors in a system of 'articulated governance'[185] gives rise to relations of responsibility and constitutional obligation which game-theoretical accounts struggle to accommodate. When constitutional democracy goes well, the interaction between the branches is framed by the norms of comity and collaboration, respect and restraint.[186] But when those norms break down, the relationship can deteriorate into a cycle of mutual confrontation, with casualties on all sides. *Constitutional showdown* can lead to *constitutional shut-down*, where the whole system of constitutional government grinds to a halt.[187] Less dramatically, but no less insidiously, ongoing

[179] O'Donnell (1994) 59; Sadurski (2019) 243, 262; Ginsburg & Huq (2018) 150
[180] Stephenson (2008) 15ff; Metzger (2009) 437.
[181] Issacharoff (2018) 449–50; Jennings (1971) 333; Möllers (2019) 253, 255; Sadurski (2018) 246; Runciman (2019) 145.
[182] Sabl (2002) 64, 85; Jennings (1959) 32, 88; Shane (2003) 508; Norton (2020) 29; Huq (2018) 1522.
[183] Levitsky & Ziblatt (2019) 133; Sabl (2002) 84; Möllers (2019) 253; Runciman (2019) 145; Crewe (2015b) 111.
[184] Heclo (2006) 740; Sabl (2002) 85.
[185] Waldron (2016) 46, 62–5.
[186] Bobbitt (1982) 182; Webber (2000).
[187] Jackson (2016) 1775–6; Young (2014).

confrontation between the branches can lead to a gradual erosion of the norms of comity and constructive engagement, ultimately leading to a breakdown in the mutual trust on which the long-term health and well-being of the system depends.[188] A willingness to *slow down*, on the other hand, signals a commitment to comply with the constitutional rules of the game and accept the burdens as well as the benefits of joint institutional action.

Ultimately, the success of any system of separated and shared powers depends on a constitutional commitment by the key political actors to the principles of constitutional democracy. This is the famous Hartian insight that any legal system depends on the political actors recognising the fundamental principles of the constitutional order, and orienting their behaviour towards those principles.[189] And yet, although this recognition is in some sense voluntary, it does not rest on 'pure public-spirited political altruism'[190] alone. On the contrary, it is bolstered by the institutional architecture, the incentives and the checks and balances embedded in the constitutional scheme, and the dense network of civil society actors who work hard to hold political actors to account. It is also shored up by the norms, values, and 'traditions of conduct'[191] which incline the political actors towards respectful and reputable constitutional behaviour in a context of *reciprocity, repeat-play* and *reputation*.[192] Mechanisms of *constitutional slowdown* can also help. After all, slowing down can lead to cooling off.[193] By elongating the time-frame for decision making in a system of 'articulated governance',[194] the collaborative constitution hews towards stability, comity, and mutual respect.

When we look at the constitutional system as a whole, we can see that there are multiple elements of competition and contestation. Political parties fight fiercely to win elections and there is no doubt that the relationship between the Government and Opposition is adversarial and competitive.[195] But even these overtly competitive dynamics are framed and shaped by the constitutional norms of mutual respect and

---

[188] Oliver (2013) 321–3; Elster (2000) 100.
[189] Hart (2012); Levinson (2011); MacDonnell (2019) 199, 204; Huq (2018) 1530.
[190] Oliver (2013) 329; Chafetz (2011) 2, 5, 10.
[191] Loughlin (2013) 5, 23, 36.
[192] Levinson (2011) 676–7, 684, 711; Pozen (2014) 70.
[193] Issacharoff (2018) 449.
[194] Waldron (2016), chapter 5.
[195] On the relationship between Government and Opposition, see Webber (2016); Gerken (2014); Jennings (1971) 30, 65, 86–92; Fontana (2009).

restraint. Although political parties fight fiercely to win an election, it is a foundational rule of the democratic game that the losing side accepts defeat with grace, courtesy and support for the winning side.[196] Stable democracy requires the 'internalisation of politics as repeat play',[197] where the democratic losers accept the outcome of a fair fight, abiding by the norm that good players should not be sore losers.[198]

Similarly, the competitive and oppositional dynamic between Government and Opposition is framed by norms of comity, collaboration and an 'ethics of constitutional commitment'.[199] As leading political scientists have observed, the Opposition's role is 'to oppose, but not to obstruct'[200] – to scrutinise the government and hold it firmly to account but not to prevent the government from running the country, or undermine the constitutional system as a whole. Within the British parliamentary tradition, the Opposition is described as the '*Loyal* Opposition', thus emphasising that the Opposition is 'an essential *part* of the constitution'.[201] Even as it opposes the government of the day, the Opposition must nonetheless remain loyal to the Crown as a symbol of the constitutional system as a whole.[202] Thus, whilst the House of Commons is undoubtedly a 'site of confrontation'[203] between the Government and Opposition, a responsible Opposition eschews a strategy of inveterate and indiscriminate obstruction and relentless filibustering, whilst a responsible government refrains from using the 'guillotine' at every point to silence the Opposition and prevent it exercising its scrutiny role.[204]

Away from the glare of publicity and the media spotlight on the gladiatorial battles on the floor of the House of Commons, both sides work together behind the scenes through what are tellingly described as 'the usual channels'.[205] There, the Government and Opposition jointly

---

[196] Runciman (2019) 15.
[197] Issacharoff (2018) 448; Waldron (2016) 124.
[198] Ignatieff (2013a).
[199] Chafetz (2011).
[200] Sartori (1966) 151; Johnson (2007) 488; Webber (2016) 1, 10; Waldron (2016); Searing (1982) 242; Jennings (1971) 90 ('Even in normal times, it is not the business of an Opposition to obstruct government. Its purpose is to criticise, not to hinder ... Obstruction brings parliamentary government into contempt').
[201] Jennings (1971) 87 (emphasis added).
[202] Ibid 87.
[203] Webber (2016) 10.
[204] Sartori (1966) 152 (describing political opposition as a form of collaboration); Matthews (1959); Crowe (1983) 909.
[205] Russell & Gover (2017) 87–8, 104, 156.

arrange the legislative business and timetable of the House of Commons, based on a shared understanding that the Government has to a right to govern whilst the Opposition is entitled to oppose.[206] By recognising each other as legitimate adversaries in a common constitutional project, rather than enemies bent on mutual destruction, the Government and Opposition respect each other's valuable role in the democratic system, accepting that the common goal of achieving good government under the constitution runs deeper than 'the fault lines of partisan acrimony'.[207]

The achievement of Opposition is that it brings political dissent into the frame of government, channels it, legitimises it, institutionalises it, and makes it part of the constitutional system.[208] There is competition and rivalry to be sure, but it is a 'regulated rivalry'[209] constrained by the rules of the game and a mutual recognition that they both have a valuable part in the joint project of governance.[210] Even in the relationship between Government and Opposition, conflict and contestation play out against a backdrop of comity, collaboration, and a sense of constitutional fair play.[211] The oppositional dynamics take effect within a collaborative constitutional framework.[212]

In the long term, every constitutional system relies for stability on norms and practices of mutual respect between its institutions and a commitment by the key constitutional actors to work together towards the common goal of achieving just government under the constitution.[213] This does not require the branches to agree or harmonise their positions on all matters. Nor does it preclude robust checks and balances. But it does require them to respect each other's legitimate role in the collaborative endeavour; to *channel* their disagreements through the requisite institutional routes set out by the constitution; and to recognise each other as *part* – not the whole – of the system of constitutional governance.[214] Collaboration is the ideal which constitutional government realises when it goes well. Indeed, it is testament to this ideal that we lament outbreaks of antagonism between the branches, and criticise them

---

[206] Griffith, Ryle & Wheeler-Booth (1989) 297–8; Crick (1990) 276.
[207] Ignatieff (2013b) 126; Anastaplo (2004) 1020; de Jouvenel (1966) 169.
[208] Gerken (2014); Waldron (2016) 99–102.
[209] Rosenblum (2008) 12–13, 133–5, 156–7, 363–4.
[210] Jackson (2016) 1756, 1745; Crick (1990) 276.
[211] Webber (2014b) 107; Norton (2001) 28.
[212] Webber (2014b) 107, 109; Kavanagh (2019) 67.
[213] Le Sueur (1996) 26; Bobbitt (1982) 182; Malleson (2010) 112.
[214] Rosenblum (2008) 12, 17.

for not treating each other with comity and respect. We do so because we believe that such antagonism may flout the norms of comity and collaboration which underpin a well-functioning system oriented towards the common good.

6   Conclusion

This chapter has argued that the relationship between the branches of government is best understood as a collaborative enterprise between all three branches of government, where they each have distinct but complementary roles to play, whilst working together in a spirit of comity and collaboration. Even as the branches of government check and balance each other, they must do so with comity and a commitment to the collaborative enterprise in which they participate. Robust checks must be accompanied by 'robust civility'.[215]

Reconceiving the constitution as a 'multi-actor network',[216] the key constitutional actors interact and counteract as part of a broader and more collaborative vision of constitutionalism. Instead of portraying the branches of government as embroiled in a winner-takes-all adversarial struggle between rivals for supremacy, the collaborative constitution emphasises the need for constructive engagement and mutual respect in the shared responsibility for realising rights. Instead of falsely cleaving the courts from the collaborative enterprise – or vilifying the legislature as an inveterate violator of rights – the collaborative constitution appreciates the valuable role that all three branches of government play in a complex interaction where both rights and democracy get their due.[217]

In the chapters that follow, I illustrate the idea of collaborative constitutionalism in motion, relying on a fine-grained study of inter-institutional interaction in a constitutional democracy. Using the UK as a leading exemplar, I chronicle the complex dynamics of the collaborative constitution. In doing so, I seek to shift constitutional analysis away from the dominant narrative about dialogue, pointing it towards a collaborative account where self-restraint and support, deference and deferral have an important role to play.[218] Constitutional outspokenness has its place

---

[215] Garton Ash (2016) 208–14; Sachs (2009) 148–9; Sadurski (2018) 8.
[216] Cohn (2007) 105; McLean (2018) 412; Murray (2013a) 52.
[217] Appleby, MacDonnell & Synot (2020) 442; de Londras (2017).
[218] Dixon & Issacharoff (2016); Lovell (2003); Graber (1993).

to be sure, but 'constitutional reticence'[219] also has value in a long-term relationship between partners. Whilst the dialogic account took its cues from structural mechanisms and formal powers contained in the texts of 'new Commonwealth'[220] Bills of Rights, the collaborative constitution draws on the deeper well of unwritten constitutional norms and constitutional culture. Talk may be cheap, but collaboration is hard work – disciplined by the requirements of mutual respect, restraint and 'role recognition' which sustain a constitutional partnership over time.

By recasting the constitutional separation of powers in *relational* rather than purely *rivalrous* terms, we can shift our focus away from the blunt question about who gets the last word as a matter of formal finality, and look more closely at *how* the branches of government combine, interact and engage with each other when making decisions about rights.[221] So viewed, we can appreciate a more calibrated, moderated and *mediated* form of inter-institutional engagement, framed and shaped by the values and virtues of collaborative constitutionalism.

Moving from 'rivals to relationships'[222] – and from conversation to collaboration – I articulate a vision of constitutionalism which sounds more in self-restraint than external policing, more give-and-take than tit-for-tat.[223] Alongside friction, we must consider function.[224] But underlying the dual dimensions of function and friction are the norms of comity, collaboration, and constitutional fair play which frame, shape, and discipline the interactions between the branches of government.[225] These norms go to the heart of the collaborative constitution in a system of 'separatedness but interdependence, autonomy but reciprocity'.[226] The upshot is that the onerous task of protecting rights is not realised by the solitary crusade of a Herculean super-judge, nor the dignified legislature expressing the voice of the people. Instead, it is a collaborative enterprise between all three branches of government, where they each have a distinct but interconnected role to play.

[219] Webber (2000).
[220] Gardbaum (2013b).
[221] Kavanagh (2016c) 120; Kavanagh (2015a) 847; Hunt (2015) 2; Roach (2015) 406; Dyzenhaus (2015) 425.
[222] Kavanagh (2019).
[223] King (2008a) 428.
[224] Malleson (2010) 117; Barber (2001) 61.
[225] Pozen (2014).
[226] *Youngstown Sheet and Tube Co v Sawyer* 1953 343 US 579, 635 (Jackson J).

PART II

RIGHTS IN POLITICS

4

Governing with Rights

1 Introduction: A Shared Responsibility

This chapter takes as its starting point the proposition that protecting rights is a shared responsibility between all three branches of government.[1] Instead of asking 'Who is the ultimate guardian of rights – the courts *or* Parliament?', we can now reject the false dichotomy presupposed by this question and acknowledge that all three branches of the state – Parliament, the Executive, and the judiciary – have a shared responsibility for this task.[2] As a former Legal Adviser to the UK Parliament's Joint Committee on Human Rights,[3] David Feldman, observed

> Systematic engagement with human rights in a democratic political process can come about only when it is seen as a goal of all institutions, executive, legislative and judicial, working towards a common goal when exercising their different but complementary functions.[4]

Chapter 3 made the case for collaboration as a way of conceptualising the constitutional relationships under the separation of powers. But we now need to supplement that theoretical argument with a more fine-grained understanding of how these institutions work in practice. In the chapters that follow, I explicate the ways in which the three branches of government engage with rights, whilst simultaneously engaging with each other.

This chapter begins with the role of the Executive, exploring its pivotal role in the joint project of protecting rights, before turning in Chapter 5 to the role of the democratic legislature. The decision to begin the

---

[1] Hunt (2015) 1; Harlow & Rawlings (2016) 320; Harlow (2016) 154–5.
[2] Kavanagh (2019).
[3] Hereafter JCHR.
[4] Feldman (2004b) 92; Harlow & Rawlings (2021) 202, 211; Hunt (2010) 602; Hiebert & Kelly (2015) 9.

analysis with the Executive and legislature – and not with the courts – is deliberate. It bespeaks a constitutional perspective which views the government and legislature as 'pro-constitutional actors'[5] and full partners in the collaborative enterprise of protecting rights.[6] Starting with the political branches also has the advantage of following the constitutional chronology on the ground. After all, when courts adjudicate whether a legislative provision violates rights, they enter the picture *after* the legislation has been proposed, scrutinised, debated and enacted by the Executive and legislature acting in concert.[7] Therefore, in terms of defining and defending rights, the Executive and legislature are typically the 'first movers'[8] in the collaborative enterprise of protecting and promoting rights. Indeed, given that the vast majority of legislation is never litigated before the courts, it follows that, most of the time, the political branches not only get the first word on rights, but the last word as well.[9] Therefore, we need to take the Executive and legislature seriously as pivotal protagonists in the collaborative constitutional scheme.[10]

The aim of this chapter is to bring the most powerful branch of government – the Executive – out of the cold and into the heart of the constitutional picture. Since nearly all legislation in Westminster parliaments begins life as a government initiative to change the law, it makes sense to start the narrative here. This chapter proceeds in the following way. Part 2 sketches out the role of the Executive in the collaborative constitutional scheme. Part 3 examines the process of Executive engagement with rights in the post-HRA era, providing a granular account of the various institutional actors involved in the iterative, interactive, and collaborative process of realising rights within the Executive branch. This points up the importance of the 'internal separation of powers',[11] where the constitutional labour is divided *within* the branches of government, not just between them. Part 4 asks whether the rights-vetting measures within the Executive branch in the post-HRA era have succeeded in raising rights consciousness within government. In part 5,

---

[5] Jackson (2016).
[6] King (2012) 57–8.
[7] Gardbaum (2013b) 80; Kyritsis (2012) 319.
[8] Schacter (2011) 1400; Cossman (2019) 188.
[9] Hiebert & Kelly (2015).
[10] Webber et al. (2018) 14–18, chapters 2–3; King (2012) 41ff.
[11] Katyal (2006); Cane (2016) 7.

I envision a form of *Executive constitutionalism*, i.e. a species of constitutional commitment and constraint legible within the Executive branch.
Transcending the false dichotomies of political and legal constitutionalism, I explore the multiple channels of political and legal accountability
which combine within the Executive branch in dynamic, creative and
collaborative ways.

2   The Executive and the Constitution

In the classical conception of the separation of powers, the legislature
makes the law, the courts apply it, and the Executive 'executes' or gives it
effect.[12] In this picture, the legislature occupies the 'initiating place on the
assembly line of law-making',[13] whilst the Executive is consigned to a
reactive or responsive role. In fact, the Executive emerges as doubly
reactive on this view. Vis-à-vis the legislature, the Executive's role is to
'execute' or implement the law enacted by Parliament; and vis-à-vis the
courts, its job is to comply with the law and implement judicial decisions
in a faithful and compliant manner. Either way, the role of the Executive
is presented as 'essentially passive',[14] i.e. as one of application, implementation and compliance with legal and political rules made elsewhere in
the system.

But as we all know, there is much more to the Executive than being the
mere implementer or 'executor' of legislative or judicial will.[15] In many
systems, the Executive is actually the 'central governing, directing and
initiating element'[16] in the joint project of governing. Whilst the
Executive certainly has an applicative role as 'executor' of law enacted
by Parliament, it is also an 'executive' in the sense of a 'CEO, entrusted
with steering the state in sickness and in health'.[17] Far from being a
passive or purely responsive actor, the Executive is the primary branch of
government, to which the legislature and courts must react.[18] This is why

---

[12] On the 'pure doctrine' of the separation of powers, see Vile (1998) 13–14; Carolan (2009)
     18ff; Kavanagh (2016b) 224–6.
[13] Waldron (2016) 51; cf. Kyritsis (2017) 82–3.
[14] Endicott (2020b) 597.
[15] Cohn (2016) 345; Harlow & Rawlings (2021) 188.
[16] Amery (1964) 1; Kavanagh (2019) 63.
[17] Cohn (2016) 345; Endicott (2020b) 607.
[18] Endicott (2021) 18.

we care so much about who is 'in government'. Indeed, it is also why we refer to the Executive branch as 'the Government'. After all, the Executive branch – in collaboration with the legislature and the courts – has the awesome task of running the country.[19] At best, the passive image of the Executive role is woefully incomplete. At worst, it is positively misleading, enticing us to underestimate and overlook the 'focal importance of the Executive'[20] in any constitutional order.

In parliamentary systems, the pivotal role of the Executive is well-known.[21] In Westminster systems, the Executive branch is 'the dominant institution'[22] to which the courts and the legislature react: 'their reactions can be strong, as when the courts declare decisions or actions of ministers to be invalid, or when Members of Parliament produce reports highly critical of ministerial action'.[23] Either way, the Executive is the *engine* of government, the 'driving force of policies and of political behaviour at the national and international level'.[24] Within the collaborative constitutional order, the Executive has the power of initiative: it initiates policy, drives forward the legislative agenda, and determines the key public policies which govern the country.[25]

Of course, the relationship between the Government and legislature is carved up differently in presidential systems where the Executive and legislature have separate electoral mandates.[26] This means that the legislature may need to develop its own executive functions in order to exercise the power of initiative,[27] thus generating more diffuse patterns of bargaining and negotiation between individual representatives across the Executive and legislative branches.[28] It also creates a higher chance of

---

[19] Griffith (2001) 44; Endicott (2021) 18–20.

[20] Endicott (2020b) 601; Griffith (2001) 48; Möllers (2013) 96.

[21] Griffith (2001) 49.

[22] Ibid 49; Elliott & Thomas (2020) 121.

[23] Griffith (2001) 50–1; Jhaveri (2022) 574.

[24] Griffith (2001) 48; Jhaveri (2022) 563; Le Divellec (2007) 98. 126; Kyritsis (2015) 160.

[25] Elliott & Thomas (2020) 121; Endicott (2017a) 18–19; Stephenson (2016) 39.

[26] Endicott (2021) 19; Albert (2010); Möllers (2013) 110–14 (highlighting the overlooked commonalities between presidential and parliamentary systems, in particular 'the common feature of cooperation between governments and parliaments', albeit with more room for conflict in presidential systems); Cane (2016) 6, 78–94, 80.

[27] Möllers (2013) 111 (arguing that 'in American constitutional practice the law is ... mainly conceived as a common political project undertaken by the initiating congressmen (sponsors) and the president').

[28] Pettit (2012) 284–5.

gridlock and stalemate, in contrast to its more coordinated and streamlined parliamentary counterpart. Nonetheless, the pivotal power of the Executive branch should not be underestimated in presidential systems. For example, the US Presidency is 'the most important source of Congress's legislative agenda and the system's chief policy-maker'.[29] This suggests that the structural differences between the Westminster and Washington systems may 'conceal as much as they reveal'.[30]

The Executive possesses a number of institutional virtues and strengths which enable it to perform the role of initiative in the collaborative constitution. First, the Executive possesses the institutional energy, agency and cohesiveness to formulate and motivate a coherent policy agenda.[31] This agency also equips it to respond with alacrity and decisiveness to emergencies as they arise. Second, the Executive has wide-ranging policy expertise and information-gathering capacity which equips it to govern in the modern era.[32] As Cass Sunstein observed, the Executive is 'the most knowledgeable branch'.[33] Third, the Executive possesses a potent form of democratic legitimacy. Not only has it received a majority of votes at the previous election, it has done so on the basis of an Election Manifesto which sets out the new government's policy commitments and legislative plans in a way which frames the electoral choice. When elected, the Government therefore has a democratic 'mandate' to implement its policy programme.[34] The 'electoral connection'[35] between the Government and the populace is a key feature of the Executive's institutional competence and legitimacy.

Together, these three institutional virtues – *energy, expertise and electoral connection* – explain the pivotal role of the Executive in the constitutional order. They enable the government to glean the public

---

[29] Cane (2016) 80; Renan (2017) 808, 849; Dann (2019) 371 (referring to 'the Presidential branch').

[30] Albert (2009) 531.

[31] Endicott (2017a) 13 (citing William Blackstone's phrase that executive power is 'wisely placed in a single hand by the British constitution, for the sake of unanimity, strength and dispatch', see Blackstone (2016) [1765–69], Book 1, 162); Griffith (2001) 52.

[32] Jhaveri (2022) 573.

[33] Sunstein (2016).

[34] Page (2003) 660; Miers & Page (1990) chapter 2; Russell & Gover (2017) chapter 3.

[35] Mayhew (1974).

will and shape public opinion, thereby ensuring that its policy-making agenda is suitably responsive to popular interests and needs.[36] One of the obligations of government is to explain and justify its policies to the public, thereby garnering public support and buy-in for significant policy change.

However, as with all other actors in the collaborative scheme, the Executive cannot – and should not – govern alone. In a system of separated and shared powers under the collaborative constitution, the Government must work *through* the accepted policy-making and legislative channels and *with* the legislature and courts in a spirit of mutual respect and commitment to the need for constitutional checks and balances. Within this collaborative framework, the Government is entitled to move forward, but only if it accepts that the other branches are entitled to push back.[37] The legislature is empowered to slow the Government down, submitting Executive policy proposals to rigorous scrutiny at each stage of the legislative process.

The upshot is that the law-making process is a collaborative enterprise between the Executive and legislature, where the Executive proposes a policy, to which the legislature responds, critiques, and sometimes amends. Thus, in Westminster systems, 'it is not and never has been the function of Parliament to govern'.[38] The role of the legislature is to sustain and support the Government in office, whilst holding it vigilantly to account and scrutinising government policy in the public interest. In short, the Executive has the power of initiative in the collaborative constitution, whilst the legislature possesses the power of scrutiny, deliberation and review.

In constitutional theory, the pivotal role of the Executive has long been obscured. Whilst scholars engage in gladiatorial battles about whether the courts or legislature should occupy pole position 'at the heart of the constitutional control room',[39] they have long occluded the role of the Executive in any constitutional scheme. This raises the question: why is the most powerful branch of government the 'least examined branch'[40] in constitutional scholarship? There are two main

---

[36] Kateb (1981).
[37] Möllers (2013) 102ff.
[38] Griffith (2001) 52.
[39] Tomkins (2003) 19.
[40] Bauman & Kahana (2006).

reasons. First, the very fact that the Executive possesses the energy, agency and capacity to get things done makes it 'the most dangerous branch'[41] from a constitutional point of view. The greatest threat to constitutional democracy is the prospect of a powerful Executive shaking off the shackles of constitutional constraints to create an authoritarian government. Little wonder, then, that constitutional lawyers treat the *Executive as evil* – the constitutional villain of the piece which poses a standing threat to principles of constitutionalism, a presumptively problematic power which must be constantly cabined and contained.[42]

The second reason why constitutional scholars often overlook the Executive is that they tend to view legislation as the finished work-product of the legislative branch, thereby occluding the pivotal role of the Executive in devising and designing the details of legislative proposals. From this perspective, the *Executive is invisible*. Thus, whilst political constitutionalists eulogise the legislature as the locus of democratic legitimacy – and legal constitutionalists champion the courts as a forum of principle and integrity – hardly anyone stoops to defend the Executive as a potentially 'pro-constitutional'[43] actor.

In the collaborative constitution, I strive to present a picture of constitutional government which captures the constitutional reality on the ground. From this more grounded, institutional perspective, I embrace the Executive as the initiator in the joint project of governing and as a potentially pro-constitutional actor, worthy of our cautious and careful respect. Although the Executive controls the guns and the military, it also employs nurses, provides social security, builds hospitals, funds schools, and combats climate change. Rights may be stated with majestic generality, but they can only be delivered with concrete particularity.[44] Therefore, we cannot afford to treat the Executive as an inevitable villain of the piece. We need the Executive to deliver and get things done.[45] A well-functioning constitutional system depends on the

---

[41] Flaherty (1996).

[42] Jhaveri (2022) 573; Griffith (2001) 45 (arguing that it devalues the institution of Government when we present it as 'the necessary enemy of individual freedom').

[43] Jackson (2016); for emerging literature countenancing the possibility of Executive constitutionalism, see e.g. Jhaveri (2022); Appleby & Olijnyk (2017); MacDonnell (2023a); MacDonnell (2023b).

[44] Endicott (2020b) 600; King (2012) 44–8.

[45] Putnam (1994) 8ff.

Executive to act in the public interest in a spirit of comity and collaboration.

The resulting picture of constitutional government is not a solitary portrait of 'The Executive Unbound'.[46] Far from it. It is a complex, multifaceted collaborative enterprise where the Executive takes its place alongside its partners in authority, driving forward the policy agenda whilst accepting the manifold constraints of 'horizontal accountability'[47] embedded in the constitutional separation of powers.

3   Executive Engagement with Rights

In the collaborative enterprise of protecting and promoting rights, the Executive plays a pivotal leadership role in proposing rights-protective and rights-promoting legislative frameworks to Parliament.[48] In this section, I illustrate the Executive's pro-constitutional role in the UK constitutional order, focusing on the intricate mechanisms of rights protection which the Government put in place in the post-HRA era. Though largely invisible to constitutional lawyers, these complex practices and patterns of behaviour have helped to raise rights-consciousness[49] within, between, and across the political branches of government. In order to capture the complexity of rendering legislation compliant with rights, we need to start by understanding the contours of the pre-legislative process which begins in the Executive branch.

Preparing a legislative Bill for entry into Parliament comprises three analytically distinct tasks: (1) deciding on the policy which is to guide any legislative drafting; (2) producing the legislative clauses that make up an Act of Parliament; and (3) handling the parliamentary process, including stewarding the legislation through its parliamentary stages and developing briefings which Ministers can use in debates on the legislation.[50]

So where and how do rights enter this process? Under section 19 of the Human Rights Act 1998, all Bills introduced to Parliament must be accompanied by a Ministerial Statement announcing the Government's

---

[46] Posner & Vermeule (2010); cf. Huq (2012).
[47] Sadurski (2019) 243.
[48] Endicott (2020b) 597ff.
[49] Gardbaum (2013b) 26.
[50] Page (2003) 653.

views about whether the proposed legislation complies with rights.[51] Crucially, the Government Minister is not obliged to attach a positive Statement of Compatibility to the Bill. Section 19(1)(b) explicitly allows the Minister to 'make a statement to the effect that although he is unable to make a Statement of Compatibility the Government nevertheless wishes to proceed with the Bill'.[52] The heavily qualified wording of this subsection signals the seriousness of proceeding without a positive Statement of Compatibility.

This was affirmed in the parliamentary debates on the Human Rights Bill, where Lord Irvine emphasised that

> Ministers will *obviously* want to make a positive statement whenever possible. That requirement should therefore have a significant impact on the scrutiny of draft legislation within government. Where such a statement cannot be made, parliamentary scrutiny of the Bill would be intense.[53]

By being forced to make a public statement on rights-compatibility, the expectation was that

> Responsible Ministers will have to ensure that the legislation does not infringe guaranteed freedoms, or be prepared to justify its decision openly and in the full glare of parliamentary and public opinion.[54]

Therefore, whilst Ministers are not *legally obliged* to make a positive statement of compatibility, they are *politically expected* to do so whenever possible. As the key political architects of the HRA put it, section 19 was intended to 'promote a culture where positive rights and liberties become the focused concern of legislators, administrators and judges alike'.[55]

When the HRA was enacted, many commentators were sceptical that section 19 would succeed in stimulating enhanced political engagement with rights in the legislative process.[56] However, it has had a powerful catalytic effect on the law-making process, triggering serious rights-vetting within the Executive branch,[57] prompting robust

---

[51] Section 19; Hiebert & Kelly (2015) 252–4.
[52] Section 19(1)(b) HRA 1998.
[53] Lord Irvine (2003a) 15 (emphasis added).
[54] Ibid 23.
[55] Ibid 36; Straw (1999).
[56] Klug (2005) 199; Lester (2002a) 76.
[57] Gardbaum (2013b) 162.

parliamentary scrutiny of the rights implications of Bills during the legislative process.[58] Successive governments over the last two decades have operated a 'strong presumption'[59] that any Bill proposed to Parliament must be compatible with the Convention. With only two significant exceptions,[60] all Bills proposed to Parliament since 1998 have been accompanied with a positive Statement of Compatibility under section 19. In order to evaluate Executive engagement with rights before making the section 19 statement, we need to disaggregate the component parts of the 'plural Executive',[61] examining how the various actors within the Executive combine and collaborate to protect rights.

a Cabinet, Civil Servants, and Bill Teams

Whilst the broad policy steer of any piece of legislation generally comes from central government and the relevant government Minister,[62] the day-to-day work on preparing a Bill for entry into Parliament is done below Cabinet and Ministerial level, within the relevant government departments.[63] In fact, government departments are sometimes described as 'the powerhouses of policymaking'.[64] In any department, the Minister is surrounded by a whole cadre of civil servants, who play a critical role in formulating policy objectives and converting broad policy goals into concrete legislative and administrative programmes.[65] As part of this process, civil servants play a more active and creative policy-making role than is often assumed.[66]

---

[58] White Paper, *Rights Brought Home: The Human Rights Bill* [3.1.]; Hunt (2010) 608; Irvine (2003a) 23, 98; Cooper & Marshal-Williams (2000) 198; Weston (2015) 268; Feldman (2007) 99.

[59] Hiebert & Kelly (2015) 274.

[60] Communications Bill 2002 (discussed in Chapter 6.7) and the Illegal Migration Bill 2023.

[61] Daintith & Page (1999) 380ff.

[62] Page & Jenkins (2005) 136–40; Yong (2014) 26.

[63] Russell & Gover (2017) 47; Yong (2014) 14.

[64] Yong (2014) 14.

[65] Page & Jenkins (2005); MacDonnell (2015) 392. For an insider's insight into the civil servant's role in enacting legislation 'from inception to Royal Assent', see Regan (2012).

[66] Page (2003) (examining the 'civil servant as legislator'); Page & Jenkins (2005); Yong & Hazell (2014) 15–16; Sossin (2005a) 431.

In order to create a Bill, the department sets up a 'Bill team' of civil servants, whose job it is to coordinate work on the Bill.[67] The Bill team works closely with legal advisers within government departments, who advise on the legality of proposed policy initiatives, flagging legal concerns when necessary, and working up solutions when an initial proposal seems to run contrary to the law or violate human rights.[68] Instead of treating rights as roadblocks on policy objectives, legal advisers direct political attention towards 'ways of conceiving of the legislative objective in a rights-compatible manner'.[69] They try to facilitate rights-compliant options, rather than foreclose policy preferences. Only rarely does human rights law present an immovable obstacle standing in the way of a policy goal. More often it impacts on the means by which that goal is achieved.[70] Thus, a significant part of the legal advisers' job is to devise rights-compliant solutions, rather than simply identify problems.[71] When developing the legislative proposal within the government department, there is an ongoing, iterative process of communication, consultation, and collaboration between the 'policy leads'[72] on the Bill team on the one hand, and the government lawyers on the other, who, together, find ways of giving effect to the government's policy aim in a legally compliant manner.[73]

Post-HRA, all Bills must be accompanied by an 'ECHR memorandum' containing the department's 'human rights reasoning'.[74] These memoranda are written by the departmental lawyers, who have to consult with the relevant policy officials.[75] The Cabinet Office *Guide to Making Legislation* clarifies that the potential rights implications of any Bill should be 'an integral part of the policy-making process, not a last-minute

---

[67] Cabinet Office, *Guide to Making Legislation* (2022) [3.4], available at www.gov.uk/government/publications/guide-to-making-legislation; Page (2003) 653; Renan (2017) 33ff.

[68] Garnier (2010) 4; Grieve (2012b) 102; Grieve (2012a); Regan (2012) 33; Windsor (2013) 117–41. For a comparative overview of the role of legal advisers within the Executive branch and an argument that they function as constitutional 'gatekeepers' within the Executive branch, see Casey & Kenny (2022).

[69] Hiebert & Kelly (2015) 273, 269, 287; Garnier (2010) 8; Bethlehem (2012) 26.

[70] Feldman (2002b).

[71] Dawson (1992) 598.

[72] These are the officials with lead responsibility at working level for the policy or policies in a bill, see Cabinet Office Guide (n 67) [6.31].

[73] Russell & Gover (2017) 58–60.

[74] Grieve (2012a) 2; Garnier (2010) 6.

[75] Cabinet Office Guide (n 67) [12.7], [12.16]; Hunt (2013) 231.

compliance exercise'.[76] Hence, 'early discussion with departmental legal advisers is essential'.[77] The 'ECHR memorandum' is expected to provide

> a frank assessment by the department of the vulnerability to challenge in legal and policy terms ... [It] should address the weaknesses as well as the strengths in the department's position. It need not, however, be a compendious discussion of the case law. What is needed is a clear and succinct statement of the human rights considerations and the justification in ECHR terms for any interference.[78]

When the HRA was being enacted, the government considered the option of setting up a specialised department to check for rights compliance of the government's legislative proposals. But this option was rejected in favour of a more decentralised and mainstreamed approach in order to let human rights 'run into the bloodstream of each department',[79] ensuring that 'legal advice on rights-compatibility was informed by the institutional culture and policy priorities within the department'.[80] This mainstreaming approach also ensured that 'the responsibility for complying with human rights requirements rests on the government as a whole'[81] instead of being outsourced to a specialised government department.

b   The Office of Parliamentary Counsel

Once the details of the policy are worked out within the department, the Bill team sends the draft Bill to a centralised office of legally qualified and professionally trained legislative drafters called 'The Office of Parliamentary Counsel'.[82] Despite the nomenclature of *parliamentary* counsel, these drafters work exclusively for the government, not for Parliament.[83] Their role is to convert the departmental instructions into a workable Bill which will stand up to scrutiny and criticism in Parliament.[84] In carrying out this task, Parliamentary

---

[76] Cabinet Office Guide (n 67) [12.6]; Hunt (2021) 12.
[77] Cabinet Office Guide (n 67) chapter 12.
[78] Ibid. [12.11]; Hiebert & Kelly (2015) 275; Grieve (2012b) 102.
[79] Hiebert & Kelly (2015) 271.
[80] White Paper, *Rights Brought Home: The Human Rights Bill* [12.12].
[81] Ibid. [3.5]; Hiebert & Kelly (2015) 254, 271; Gardbaum (2013b) 162.
[82] Office of the Parliamentary Counsel, www.gov.uk/government/organisations/office-of-the-parliamentary-counsel
[83] On the sources of legal advice to Parliament, see Kennon (2013) 121ff.
[84] Page (2003) 661; Page (2009) 791–2, 803, 807–9; Sales (2018a) 631; Bowman (2005) 72, 81.

Counsel engage with the Bill team in a dynamic 'iterative process',[85] where they elicit more information from the Department about the policy, but also draw the Department's attention to potential legal difficulties. Parliamentary Counsel also advise on matters of legal and constitutional propriety and can work up legally viable solutions if necessary.[86] Thus, the policy officials, departmental lawyers, and Parliamentary Counsel work together as part of a 'tripartite relationship',[87] working towards the common end of producing a Bill which implements the Department's policy in clear, defensible, and constitutionally compliant terms.

Although Parliamentary Counsel are required to implement the policy objectives of the current Government, they are also civil servants who are relatively independent from the 'political executive'.[88] As such, they are expected to carry out their role in the public interest, infused by an ethos of objectivity, integrity and impartiality.[89] Their independence from the government is bolstered by the fact that, unlike some civil servants working within departments, Parliamentary Counsel do not directly serve a particular Minister.[90] Far from being mere instruments of the Executive's will, Parliamentary Counsel act as

> internal guardians of values customarily regarded as integral to the legal order such as those of non-retrospection, proper use of delegation, and respect for the liberties of the subject.[91]

They are watchdogs for the rule of law within the Executive branch and the legislative process,[92] providing a valuable 'check on the "constitutionality" of legislation'[93] in the British constitutional order.

---

[85] Russell & Gover (2017) 58–9; Page & Jenkins (2005) 2; Page (2003) 662, 664–5; Hay & Richards (2000) 7–10.

[86] Cabinet Office Guide (n 67) [9.9]; Page (2009) 799–804; Greenberg (2011) 23–4; Sales (2018a) 632; Bowman (2005) 73.

[87] Regan (2012) 33; Greenberg (2011) 24; Burrows (2018) 101.

[88] Sossin (2005b) 4; MacDonnell (2015) 385.

[89] Laws (2013) 89; Civil Service Code, www.civilservice.gov.uk; Rhodes (2011) 190, 306.

[90] Page (2009) 811.

[91] Daintith & Page (1999) 254; Oliver (2013) 326; Page (2009) 811; Hazell (2004) 495; Zander (2018) 19; Burrows (2018) 105.

[92] Daintith & Page (1999) 257; Page (2009) 811; Hazell (2004) 495, 500; Oliver (2013) 326; Engle (1983); Zander (2018) 23; Feldman (2005) 109.

[93] Former Parliamentary Counsel, Stephen Laws, argues that Parliamentary Counsel try to ensure that legislation complies with Lon Fuller's eight desiderata of the rule of law, see Laws (2013) 95–7; Sales (2018b) 631.

c The Attorney General and the Law Officers

In the cast of constitutional actors tasked with defending constitutional values within the Executive branch, the Attorney General and the Law Officers are of pivotal importance. As the senior legal advisers to the Government, the Law Officers have a core responsibility to ensure that the Government acts in accordance with law and the rule of law.[94] In the Westminster system, the Attorney General is simultaneously the Chief Legal Adviser to the government (with a key role in ensuring that legislative proposals are compliant with constitutional and legal principles), and an elected MP and government Minister with political responsibilities to the government of the day.[95] This raises the obvious question: how can the Attorney General be a credible custodian of rights and the rule of law whilst simultaneously being a politically partisan member of the government in power?

The traditional rationale for this curious 'constitutional hybrid'[96] role straddling 'the intersecting spheres of government and parliament, the courts and the executive',[97] is that it embeds an 'independent custodian of fundamental legal values'[98] and 'guardian of the public interest'[99] into the engine room of governmental decision making. As a former Law Officer observed, 'it puts at the heart of government an independent lawyer who is trusted by those he advises because he is one of them'.[100] By combining the legal gravitas of a high-calibre lawyer with the political credibility of a fellow Minister who knows how politics works from the inside, the Attorney General's advice commands authority and respect within Cabinet.[101] Therefore, it is precisely the combination of political acumen and legal stature which equips the Attorney General to 'advise, assist, and if necessary

---

[94] For an overview of the role of the Law Officers, see McCormick & Cowie (2020); Edwards (1984) 286–308; Casey (2021) 293–4; Dodek (2010) 18–19

[95] Appleby (2016) 578; McCormick & Cowie (2020) 10–21; Edwards (1984) 185; Yong (2013) 86–7; Grieve (2015); Casey & Kenny (2022) 8.

[96] Walker (1999) 144; Edwards (1984) 90.

[97] Edwards (1984) viii; Windsor (2013) 127; Wendel (2009) 1336

[98] Walker (1999) 145.

[99] Woodhouse (1997) 97; Hutchinson (2008).

[100] Garnier (2010) 2; Appleby (2016) 578–9, 585; Jowell (2006) 13; HC Constitutional Affairs Committee, *Inquiry into the Constitutional Role of the Attorney General*, Fifth Report of Session 2006–7, HC 306, 19 July 2007, 15.

[101] Lord Goldsmith QC (former AG) (2001) 7.

challenge a fellow Minister'.[102] By simultaneously being a legal expert and a Ministerial colleague who is 'able to speak the language of ministerial government',[103] the AG is well-placed to remind the government of its constitutional obligations, offering 'a guiding hand'[104] – and sometimes 'a restraining hand'[105] – to moderate legislative proposals and help them comply with the rule of law.[106] For this reason, the Law Officers are sometimes described as 'Ministers for the rule of law'.[107]

The fact that the AG has to wear different 'hats' in different constitutional contexts is therefore, less a matter of 'constitutional schizophrenia'[108] in a world of irreconcilable antinomies, and more a matter of providing valuable modes of connection and communication between different parts of the working constitution.[109] By interacting with the other *dramatis personae* within and beyond the Executive branch, the Law Officers provide a vital bridge and channel of communication between the three branches of government at the point where law and politics meet.[110] As intermediary actors between the branches of government, they supply some of the connective tissue which helps to make the body politic work well.

Of course, the challenge of navigating the tensions between membership in the Government and obligations to the rule of law requires sensitive political and legal judgement, combined with an ethos of professionalism, ethical discernment and a strong public-service mentality.[111] Especially in highly charged political contexts where the stakes are high, resolving these tensions will inevitably create controversy, opening the Government up to accusations of

---

[102] Garnier (former Solicitor General) (2010).

[103] Uhr (2006) 53.

[104] Garnier (2010) 5; Appleby (2016) 578–9, 585–6; Silkin (1978) 156.

[105] Garnier (2010) 7; see Oral Evidence of Lord Keen of Elie QC, Advocate General for Scotland 2015–20, to the HL Constitution Committee, on *The Role of the Lord Chancellor and the Law Officers,* 27 April 2022, https://committees.parliament.uk/orale vidence/10156/pdf/

[106] Garnier (2017); Evans & Evans (2011) 341.

[107] Stewart (2021).

[108] Walker (1999) 145, 148.

[109] Kyriakides (2003) 73; see also Waldron (2016) 55ff (describing the idea of different actors wearing different institutional 'hats' as 'separation in thought').

[110] Grieve (2015) (arguing that the AG's office provides a vital 'bridge between the judicial and the political world').

[111] Woodhouse (1997) 97ff; Jowell (2006) 11; Casey & Kenny (2022) 12.

pressurising the Attorney General to bend to its will, and the Attorney General to accusations of bowing to that pressure.[112] However, these points of tension on controversial issues should not obscure the fundamental fact that the Law Officers owe their ultimate allegiance to the rule of law and the constitutional system as a whole, with their obligations to Parliament and Government coming in at second and third place.[113] It is their overarching commitment to the constitution and the public interest, which shapes and defines their constitutional role.[114]

So what role does the Attorney General play in upholding rights? The Attorney General has both an indirect and direct role in this regard.[115] Indirectly, the Attorney General can be consulted by the departmental lawyers for advice when they are drafting the ECHR memorandum, as well as by the Parliamentary Counsel when drafting the Bill. Although the primary responsibility for drafting the memorandum rests with the departmental lawyers, the Attorney General plays a supportive and bolstering role behind the scenes, especially on particularly difficult or sensitive issues of legal or constitutional propriety.[116] The 'special relationship'[117] between the Law Officers, the departmental lawyers and Parliamentary Counsel helps to ensure that the need for legality and propriety is 'woven into the fabric of Bill development right from the very start of the legislative process'.[118] This web of constitutional relationships showcases the collaborative effort to uphold the rule of law within the Executive branch.[119]

As a member of the Cabinet Committee on Parliamentary Business and Legislation (PBL), the Attorney General performs a more direct

---

[112] Luban (2007) 164; Walker (1999); Elgot (2021). For insightful analysis of the controversy surrounding the AG's advice on the legality of invading Iraq, see Yong (2013) 81–93. On the resignation of the Advocate General for Scotland in light of his advice on the Internal Markets Bill, see McCormick (2022) 200–1; Stewart, Carrell & Bowcott (2020); Casey & Kenny (2022) 19–20, 22–4.

[113] Garnier (2010) 2; Tait (1997) 547–9; Windsor (2013) 129; Palmer (2011) 334.

[114] Garnier (2010) 3; Grieve (2012a); Goldsmith (2001) 7–8; Quinlan (1993) 541.

[115] Lord Stewart of Dirleton QC (Advocate General for Scotland) (2021) (also describing the Law Officers as 'Ministers for the rule of law').

[116] Cabinet Office Guide (n 67) 12.7; Grieve (2012b) 101–2; Garnier (2010) 4; Palmer (2011) 334; Windsor (2013) 133.

[117] Grieve (2012b) 101.

[118] Garnier (2010) 5; Daintith & Page (1999) 255; Palmer (2011).

[119] Palmer (2011) 338; Roach (2006) 598.

role in ensuring that legislative proposals are compatible with rights. The job of this Committee is to assess the readiness of all Government Bills for introduction to Parliament.[120] A bill is only deemed 'ready' when all the relevant legal and procedural issues have been resolved, including the completion of a satisfactory ECHR memorandum.[121] The role of the Attorney General is to scrutinise the ECHR memorandum in advance of the meeting, to ensure that the department's 'human rights reasoning'[122] is sufficiently robust. Ultimately, the Law Officers have the power to block a Bill during the Committee meeting if they have serious concerns about its legality or propriety. If this occurs, the Government will generally stand by the AG's decision.[123] But this veto power is rarely used. By engaging in ongoing, iterative exchanges with the departmental lawyers from the outset of the policy formation stage, potential problems are typically flagged up and addressed well in advance.

d   The Minister: Claiming Compatibility between Law and Politics

Once the memorandum is approved, the Minister must decide whether to sign off on the section 19 statement attached to the Bill. Cabinet Office Guidelines state that whilst 'departmental legal advisers will take the lead in providing the formal advice required to justify such statements', the final call on whether to claim compatibility rests with the Minister, who must make a political judgement on the basis of the advice given.[124] In reality, it is extremely unlikely that a Minister will claim compatibility if this contradicts the clear legal advice received, especially if that advice is given by the Attorney General.[125] Of course, legal advice about the rights compatibility of a new Bill is not always clear-cut, because the law on a particular issue may be indeterminate or in a state of flux. In such circumstances, the advice necessarily becomes a complex 'question of probabilities',[126]

---

[120] Grieve (2012b) 105.
[121] Cabinet Office Guide (n 67) [12.13]; [2.1–2.7].
[122] Garnier (2010) 6; Grieve (2012b) 102; McCormick & Cowie (2020) 15–16.
[123] Hiebert & Kelly (2015) 275.
[124] Cabinet Office Guide (n 67) [12.13]–[12.15]; Feldman (2007) 99; Gardbaum (2013b) 163; Hiebert & Kelly (2015) 288.
[125] Hiebert & Kelly (2015) 277; Casey (2021) 295.
[126] Leigh & Masterman (2008) 36; for analysis of rights vetting during the Canadian policy-formation process, see Dawson (1992).

involving reasoning from analogy, predictions about how the case-law might develop in the future, and a risk assessment about the likelihood of successful legal challenge.[127] In the UK, legal advisers recommend that a Minister can make a positive statement of compatibility when they estimate the chances of surviving legal challenge as higher than 50 per cent, i.e. more likely than not.[128] Clearly, this figure is a rough guide not a precise algorithm, given that legal advice sometimes involves extrapolation from analogous cases, predictions about a possible line of legal travel, and a consequent risk-evaluation.[129]

Before any Bill is deemed ready for entry into Parliament, it must be accompanied by a 'robust parliamentary handling strategy',[130] which is designed to flag up any potentially contentious issues that may arise during parliamentary debate.[131] This forces the Bill team to anticipate the Bill's likely reception in Parliament and devise a credible strategy for dealing with any adverse reaction.[132] Indeed, the Cabinet Guidelines now explicitly require the handling strategy to include details of 'possible concessions and fall-back positions'[133] in the event of strong push-back in Parliament. Thus, even when the Government starts to draft a Bill, it anticipates what it can get through Parliament *ex ante*.

e   The Joint Committee on Human Rights

Though a detailed analysis of the role of the JCHR must await the next chapter, it is important to flag up the importance of the JCHR at the pre-legislative stage.[134] The JCHR was set up in the post-HRA era as a specialised parliamentary Committee of both Houses designed to scrutinise all government Bills for rights compliance.[135] It has emerged as a constitutional guardian of rights and the rule of law within and

---

[127] Bethlehem (2012) 28, 33; Windsor (2013) 135–6.
[128] Hiebert & Kelly (2015) 280; Leigh & Masterman (2008) 32–3.
[129] Dawson (1992) 598.
[130] Cabinet Office Guide (n 67) [6.16], chapter 20.
[131] On the phenomenon of 'parliamentary handling' within the Executive, see Russell & Gover (2017) 60–2.
[132] Russell & Gover (2017) 60–2, 82, 246; Regan (2012) 34.
[133] Cabinet Office Guide (n 67); Russell & Gover (2017) 60, 62.
[134] Hunt (2013) 228–9.
[135] For further analysis of the composition, role and functions of the JCHR, see Hunt (2013); Kavanagh (2015b).

beyond the Palace of Westminster.[136] However, it also plays a significant role at the pre-legislative stage, engaging with actors within the Executive branch to ensure that the government is aware of potential problems with rights before it puts its legislative proposals to Parliament.

When working up the ECHR memorandum, the departmental lawyers and Bill team sometimes meet with the legal advisers to the JCHR in order to be fully appraised of the JCHR's concerns.[137] Not only does this allow the Bill team to anticipate the JCHR's concerns, it also gives them the opportunity to accommodate them in the details of the Bill, or at least to prepare a response to them as part of their handling strategy.[138] In general, if a Bill team can preserve the key policy priorities of the Bill whilst simultaneously building in safeguards to protect rights, they have every incentive to do so. This is viewed as a much safer governmental strategy than leaving the issue to flare up publicly on the floor of the House of Commons or Lords, when the public and parliamentary reaction may be difficult to predict and control. At this stage of the legislative game, the government wants to get the Bill through Parliament, and it may be prepared to make concessions to ensure that this occurs.[139]

4   Raising Rights-Consciousness

Having documented the process of rights-vetting within the Executive branch, the question then arises: has the HRA succeeded in raising rights-consciousness within the Executive during the vitally important pre-legislative stage? Does the process outlined above manifest a genuine commitment to protecting rights, or does it betray a perfunctory 'tick-box' mentality masking Executive indifference? Whilst it is difficult to establish reliable causal connections, the following conclusions nonetheless emerge from leading empirical studies of Executive engagement with rights.

First, it seems clear that section 19 HRA has incentivised a higher level of rights-consciousness within the Executive than existed prior to the

---

[136] Hunt (2013).
[137] See Hunt (2013); Feldman (2004b) 91, 113.
[138] Hiebert & Kelly (2015) 407.
[139] Russell & Gover (2017) 60–2, 82, 246.

HRA.[140] The requirement to confront whether Bills implicate rights has generated a greater awareness amongst Executive actors about the importance of rights at the Bill-formation stage.[141] If one of the goals of the Ministerial reporting requirement under section 19 HRA was to prevent the Government from 'unknowingly introducing rights-infringing legislation',[142] then it seems to have succeeded to some meaningful degree. Leading empirical studies confirm that the Government is now likely to be 'fully aware of legal concerns on contested issues before it proceeds to Parliament'.[143]

Second, the Ministerial reporting requirement has 'directed more attention to the importance of justification [for compliance with rights], and the necessity to develop compliant ways to achieve legislative objectives'.[144] In particular, the obligation to produce an ECHR memorandum setting out the Government's 'human rights reasoning'[145] has stimulated a more systematic, conscientious, and probing form of rights engagement across all government departments. It has also succeeded in integrating rights concerns into the policy-development process.[146] The pre-HRA days of simply getting a 'casual confirmation of compatibility'[147] seem to be gone, replaced by 'a clearer and more detailed explanation of the reasons for pursuing policy objectives that implicate rights'.[148] Section 19 has 'sharpened the focus, regularity and rigour of rights-based vetting across departments'.[149] Thus, if one of the aims of the HRA was to ensure that there is meaningful scrutiny of rights compliance within Government rather than a cosmetic or box-ticking exercise, it seems to have succeeded to some degree.[150] There is evidence of some serious

---

[140] Feldman (2004b) 78, 96; Gardbaum (2013b) 166–7; Feldman (2005) 113.

[141] Page & Jenkins (2005) 94–5.

[142] Hiebert & Kelly (2015) 262, 238; Irvine (2003b) 311; Leigh & Masterman (2008) 29.

[143] Hiebert & Kelly (2015) 275; Hiebert (2004b) 1978; Leigh & Masterman (2008) 29; Kenny & Casey (2020) 54.

[144] Hiebert & Kelly (2015) 407; Dawson (1992) 598 (noting that the very existence of an analogous Ministerial reporting requirement under the Canadian Charter 'created a very powerful check on the policy process').

[145] Grieve (2012b) 101.

[146] Hiebert & Kelly (2015) 266, 272; Hunt (2010) 607.

[147] Hiebert & Kelly (2015) 272.

[148] Ibid 273; Feldman (2004b) 96–7.

[149] Hiebert (2012) 34; Hiebert & Kelly (2015) 29, 266, 272, 407; Hiebert (2011) 51; Feldman (2004b) 96; Lester (2002b) 401.

[150] Gledhill (2015) 300–1.

good-faith Executive engagement with rights from the beginning of the policy development process.[151]

Third, there seems to be greater legal expertise on rights embedded within government departments, where the Bill team forges constructive working relationships with departmental lawyers in order to give effect to policy priorities whilst simultaneously taking rights seriously. That expertise is then filtered through an iterative engagement with a multiplicity of other actors across government and the legislature, including the legislative drafters, the Attorney General, the Human Rights Unit at the Ministry of Justice, as well as the legal advisers to the JCHR. This collaborative network of actors helps to strengthen the internal scrutiny of the Bill, exposing its provisions to critique and challenge from multiple perspectives.[152] In terms of assessing whether the legal advice to the Government is 'full and frank',[153] empirical analysis based on interviews with government lawyers suggests that they were not 'subject to overt or implicit political pressure to alter their advice so as to allow a positive statement of compatibility'.[154] Even if such pressure arose, they confirmed that they would 'put their professional reputation as lawyers ahead of good working relationships with Ministers, and therefore were not prepared to alter or abandon their professional judgment about compatibility'.[155]

In controversial cases, the AG can support the legal advisers within Government Departments, thereby strengthening the ability of departmental lawyers to stand their ground, even when the legal advice is not what the Government wants to hear.[156] Even viewed on purely consequentialist grounds, the Government is ill-served by receiving complaisant advice which gives a green light to a legally dubious policy. In general, the Government prefers to be alerted to potential legal and political obstacles, so that it can anticipate parliamentary pushback and then work out a solution prophylactically in a way which preserves its main policy priorities.[157] Moreover, government lawyers have a reputational interest in being able to spot and

---

[151] Appleby & Olijnyk (2021) 1.
[152] Casey (2019) 54.
[153] Stewart (2021).
[154] Hiebert & Kelly (2015) 256.
[155] Ibid 281.
[156] Goldsmith (2001) 5.
[157] Appleby & Olijnyk (2021) 20.

anticipate potential problems, flagging them up at an early stage of the policy development process.[158] They are fully aware that the JCHR, the House of Lords Constitutional Committee, Opposition MPs, the House of Lords, and other parliamentary actors will inevitably raise constitutional concerns during the legislative process. Therefore, hiding such concerns from the government is unhelpful.[159]

Finally, the anticipatory effect of potential parliamentary pushback should not be underestimated. Even though the Executive is in the driving seat of the legislative process, Parliament has significant power and influence over the legislative agenda through the power of 'anticipated reactions'.[160] This is the phenomenon where the Government anticipates opposition to its legislative agenda in Parliament, and takes action to avoid it at the early stages of the policy cycle.[161] Interviews with officials at the Department of Constitutional Affairs (as it then was) in 2006 confirmed that when departmental legal advisers were preparing the rights memorandum, they would ask themselves 'How would this run by the JCHR?',[162] thus inducing the Bill team to make adjustments to the Bill *ex ante* in order to avoid a negative JCHR report *ex post*.[163] This suggests that the JCHR may have a significant anticipatory effect and prophylactic influence on policy at the Bill-formation stage.[164]

5   Envisioning Executive Constitutionalism

In the previous section, I showed how a concern to protect and promote rights has permeated the constitutional consciousness within the Executive branch. This is not to suggest that protecting rights is the

---

[158] Hiebert & Kelly (2015) 296; Renan (2017) 854; Goldsmith (2001) 6 ('No client is well served by a lawyer who tells him what he would like to hear instead of what he ought to be told').

[159] Hiebert & Kelly (2015) 296.

[160] Russell & Gover (2017) 82.

[161] Russell, Gover & Wollter (2016) 289, 301.

[162] Klug, 'Report on the Working Practices of the JCHR', Appendix 1 to JCHR, *The Committee's Future Working Practices* (2005-6), HL 239, HC 1575 [8.4]; Weston (2015) 273.

[163] Hiebert (2011) 63.

[164] Hiebert & Kelly (2015) 296-7, 391, 407; Tolley (2009) 48; Norton (2013b) 159, 165; Gardbaum (2013b) 166.

lodestar of political decision-making. The reality is that elected politicians inhabit a complex and fast-moving political universe where policy
priorities, legislative success, party politics, public image and popular
pressures combine and collide on a daily basis. Elected politicians typically view rights as 'side constraints'[165] on their policy goals, rather than as
'navigational lights'[166] for the entire policy endeavour. Questions about
rights are not often at the forefront of their minds.[167] And when they are,
they may be viewed as irritating impediments to valuable policy priorities, rather than the embodiment of a higher political calling. The
protection of rights is only one political consideration amongst many,
and not always the most important one at that.[168]

Nonetheless, acknowledging that we are not governed by a cast of
angels does not mean that we should swing to the opposite extreme, i.e.
of assuming the Executive to be the invariable villain of the piece whose
only concern is to aggrandise its power and trample on minority rights.
Instead of being the epitome of evil, rotten to its core, a more complex
institutional reality may exist and – in relatively well-functioning constitutional systems – does exist. In order to grasp the complexity of the
Executive, we should resist the anthropomorphising tendencies of constitutional scholarship which treats the Executive as a singular actor with no
moral compass, or as a 'cohesive bloc'[169] of elected politicians focused
only on getting re-elected. Instead of an individual actor gone rogue,
what in fact exists is a 'plural Executive'[170] comprising an intricate web of
differently situated actors, only some of whom are politically partisan and
oriented towards re-election.[171] Whilst Government Ministers are
undoubtedly the most visible Executive actors, they sit atop a composite,
pluralistic, and multifaceted institution which incorporates a myriad of
counter-majoritarian checks and stabilising forces within it.[172] The policy

---

[165] Feldman (2002b) 327; Feldman (2004b) 94; Nicol (2006) 742 (noting that human rights
are 'only one part of the crowded universe of the politician).
[166] Palmer (1985) 6; Hiebert & Kelly (2015) 5.
[167] Feldman (2004b) 94–5.
[168] Weston (2015) 278.
[169] Russell & Gover (2017) 65.
[170] Daintith & Page (1999) 6, 380.
[171] Michaels (2015) 515; Komesar (1994) 203; McLean (2020a) 167; Hickford (2013) 591
(describing 'the complicated Crown' in Westminster systems); Renan (2017) 808
(describing 'the President' in the US system as a complex 'collection of institutional
actors'); Dann (2019) 371.
[172] Page & Jenkins (2005) 184; Pozen (2010) 333.

bureaucracy within the Executive branch is truly 'government with a cast of thousands'.[173] Embedded within a scheme of differentiated authority, differently situated actors combine their efforts, working together in order to convert policy into law.[174] A pluralistic appreciation of the Executive branch enables us to envision a form of 'Executive constitutionalism'.[175]

In Westminster systems, the independent civil service is the stable backbone of the Executive branch, but is nonetheless relatively independent from 'the political executive'.[176] The civil service is politically neutral, obliged to serve different political masters over time. And it is 'permanent' in the sense that civil servants enjoy security of tenure, subject only to dismissal for cause.[177] As a permanent bureaucracy appointed on grounds of merit rather than political patronage, the role of civil servants is imbued with 'an ethic of independence, expertise, and public service'[178] together with 'a highly developed sense of constitutional propriety'.[179] This enables civil servants to act as guardians of long-term constitutional values even in the face of short-term political pressures.[180] Working behind the scenes, they can temper the role of 'raw political calculations'[181] in setting policy priorities, reminding government Ministers to keep the longer-term constitutional perspective in view.[182] The upshot is that 'the will of the government' is channelled and filtered through an

---

[173] Page & Jenkins (2005); Page (2009) 790; Posner & Vermeule (2010) 5–6. Yong and Hazell (2014) estimate that there are about 10,000 senior civil servants who work with and support Ministers within their Departments and (as of 2012) about 422,000 civil servants as a whole, see Yong (2014) 14–15.

[174] Yong (2014) 28.

[175] Jhaveri (2022).

[176] Sossin (2005a) 430. For a contrast with the US system, where there is a more transient civil service, largely, though not exclusively, in ideological alignment with the sitting President, see Renan (2017) 829.

[177] McLean (2020a) 168; Rhodes (2011) 55–6, 61 (describing the Civil Service as a 'constitutional bureaucracy' on grounds of its permanence, neutrality, and ultimate loyalty to the Crown, working in 'close partnership' with Ministers).

[178] Sales (2012) 290.

[179] Feldman (2004b) 114; Daintith & Page (1999) 8; Katyal (2006) 2331–5; Metzger (2009) 430; MacDonnell (2015) 392; Sossin (2005b) 4.

[180] Laws (2016) 24; Daintith & Page (1999) 8; Metzger (2009) 430; Renan (2017) 881.

[181] Metzger (2009) 430.

[182] Laws (2016) 24; Renan (2017) 881. This picture is now complicated by the introduction of 'special advisers', sometimes described pejoratively as 'spin doctors' because of their role as media advisers, see Yong & Hazell (2014); Waller (2014a) 111–27 (arguing that 'special advisers' (Spads) 'add a political dimension to the advice and assistance available to Ministers while reinforcing the political impartiality of the permanent Civil Service'

array of intra-Executive checking mechanisms where various actors evaluate and qualify that will to ensure that it complies with constitutional values and the rule of law.[183] Though often overlooked by constitutional lawyers, civil servants are highly significant constitutional actors who supply some 'stabilising ballast'[184] to the political Executive. Indeed, Government Ministers are obliged under the Ministerial Code to respect and uphold the independence and impartiality of civil servants, ensuring that they do nothing to compromise or undermine that independence.[185]

The civil service ethos of independence also applies to government lawyers, Parliamentary Counsel and the Attorney General, who collaborate in myriad ways to ensure that the Government's policies comply with the law, including rights. Whilst all lawyers have a duty to uphold the integrity of the legal system, public service lawyers have a more pronounced role of 'lawyering for the rule of law'.[186] Given their relative detachment from political will, government lawyers can play a 'mediating role'[187] between law and politics, channelling and signposting the value of rights and the rule of law within the political domain. This applies most acutely to the Attorney General as Chief Legal Adviser to the Government. Rather than being a 'hired gun who meekly accedes to executive policy proposals',[188] the Attorney General is expected to be the constitutional conscience around the Cabinet table. All told, the Executive comprises a complex web of differently situated actors with a dialectic tension between them.[189] Though they are relatively invisible to outside observers, there are multiple guardians of rights and rule of law 'hidden behind the Whitehall curtain'.[190]

---

[1] see Cabinet Office, *Code of Conduct for Special Advisers* (December 2016); McLean (2020a) 168.

[183] Oliver (2013) 310.

[184] Foster-Gilbert (2018) 2.

[185] Ministerial Code, August 2019, https://assets.publishing.service.gov.uk/government/uploads/system/uploads/attachment_data/file/826920/August-2019-MINISTERIAL-CODE-FINAL-FORMATTED-2.pdf, [5.1]; Quinlan (1993) 542; *Constitutional Reform and Governance Act* 2010, section 3(6); *Civil Service Code* (2010) [3].

[186] Dotan (2014); Waldron (2010) 323–4; Dawson (1992) 598; MacNair (2005) 502; MacDonnell (2015) 393.

[187] Donald & Leach (2016) 306; Windsor (2013) 130; Drewry (1981) 15.

[188] Windsor (2013) 117; Pillard (2005) 709; McLean (2020a) 170.

[189] Yong & Hazell (2014) 16.

[190] Gee et al. (2015) 53.

Therefore, whilst we often perceive the Executive as a unitary actor with a singular 'will', the defining dynamic within the Executive branch is a complex interplay between the partisan interests and policy goals of Ministers on the one hand, and the impartial duties of civil servants and other independent actors on the other.[191] In the dialectic tension between the forces of electoral accountability and specialised independence, differently situated actors work together in constructive and mutually respectful ways.[192] Therefore, it is too simplistic to dismiss civil servants as mere instruments of the Executive's will. In fact, they often operate as relatively independent constraints on that will, guiding and shaping it whilst striving to safeguard underlying constitutional values.[193] Their obligation to give 'free and frank advice' to their Ministerial masters emphasises that their ultimate loyalty is owed to the constitution and the political system as a whole, not to any individual Minister who is just passing through.[194]

The upshot is that the Executive branch is not a monolithic actor determined to violate rights. Instead, it is a complex, multifaceted branch of government with obligations to honour the constitution and uphold rights. Here, we can glimpse a form of 'Executive constitutionalism', where the Executive embeds constitutional watchdogs within its walls.[195] When assessing the capacity and performance of the Executive to take rights seriously, we must bear this more variegated picture in mind, acknowledging the importance of an 'internal separation of powers',[196] where checks and balances exist *within* each branch, not just *between* them.[197]

When examining how rights are engaged within the Executive in the UK constitutional order, we discerned an intricate, iterative and collaborative process between differently situated actors. The 'human rights reasoning'[198] underpinning the Minister's section 19 Statement was not

---

[191] Sossin (2005b) 3; Waller (2014b) 97; Heclo (1975) 82.

[192] The Ministerial Code (www.gov.uk/government/publications/ministerial-code) places Ministers under an obligation to respect civil servants in their working relationships with them, see Ministerial Code (2022) [1.2]; Kaufman (1997) 33

[193] Daintith & Page (1999) 254; Metzger (2009) 429; MacDonnell (2015) 392.

[194] Sossin (2005a) 430–2; Heclo (1975) 82.

[195] Jhaveri (2022).

[196] Katyal (2006); Metzger (2009) 423; Daintith & Page (1999) 12; Renan (2017) 903; Pillard (2005) 704; Endicott (2017a) 18.

[197] Endicott (2017a) 18; Möllers (2019) 254–5.

[198] Grieve (2012b) 105.

the pure expression of Ministerial 'will' or political preference. Instead, it was the product of a collaborative interplay between a multiplicity of actors, from civil servants and lawyers on the one hand to policy makers and the political leadership on the other. All of these actors contribute in different ways to a 'reticulated process'[199] of stress-testing the Bill from multiple perspectives in order to ensure that it delivered on the Government's policy objective in an effective, workable and rights-compliant fashion.[200] Though these mechanisms cannot be expected to work perfectly all of the time, our evaluation of the Executive must nonetheless accommodate the multiplicity of mechanisms which 'check the executive from within'.[201] An appraisal of these dynamics allows us to imagine a form of 'Executive constitutionalism'[202] where political will is shaped and constrained by constitutional norms in a pluralist institutional landscape.

6 Conclusion

This chapter uncovered an iterative and collaborative dynamic between a web of constitutional and political actors who, together, crafted legislative proposals which took rights seriously within the Executive branch. That is not to suggest that Executive engagement with rights is either optimal or laudable.[203] Far from it. Nonetheless, instead of vilifying the *Executive as evil* or treating the *Executive as invisible*, this chapter uncovered a serious engagement with rights within the 'plural Executive'[204] – including Ministers, policy advisers, civil servants, government agencies, legal advisers, and legislative draftspersons. The result is a variegated constitutional landscape, where many actors work together in a dynamic interplay to uphold the constitution and the rule of law.

---

[199] Kinley (2015) 31.

[200] Page (2003) 661.

[201] Komesar (1994) 201; Renan (2017) 903; Daintith & Page (1999) 3–4, 12; Jai (1996) 6; McLean (2018) 407; McLean (2016) 123ff (emphasising constitutional checks within the Executive as part of the New Zealand variant of political constitutionalism).

[202] For recent turns towards a theory of 'executive constitutionalism', see Appleby & Olijnyk (2021) 5; MacDonnell (2013); MacDonnell (2015); MacDonnell (2023b); Jhaveri (2022); Renan (2017); Pillard (2005) 728ff.

[203] Appleby & Olijnyk (2021) 1.

[204] Daintith & Page (1999) 380.

Imagining Executive constitutionalism, this chapter emphasised our foundational need for a constitutionally committed Executive at the heart of constitutional governance. Just as the Executive has an unrivalled capacity to do evil, it also has a unique capacity to do good, i.e. to initiate laws in the public interest, and to devise, develop, and drive forward policy change which protects and promotes rights in new and interesting ways. To be clear, in defending the Executive as a pivotal and potentially 'pro-constitutional actor',[205] I do not deny the perennial need for stringent constitutional checks on the Executive branch. Nor am I sanguine about the threat of Executive aggrandisement or the recurring temptation to clamp down on rights in service of other political priorities. Even so, in decrying the Executive as the constitutional axis of evil, we fail to grasp its pivotal importance in a well-functioning constitutional democracy. By highlighting the dialectical tension between constitutionalism and democracy *within* the Executive branch, I seek to move the debate beyond the realm of constitutional caricature in order to capture a more complex reality.

As with all of the partners in the collaborative enterprise, the primary locus of Executive constitutionalism must come from within, i.e. from 'the ethics of constitutional commitment'[206] and the constitutional self-discipline and self-restraint to abide by the fundamental norms of the constitutional system. As Daintith and Page observed,

> Executive self-restraint constitutes one of the essential underpinnings of democracy and the rule of law. To achieve restrained discretion, more is needed than criticism of authority and pressure upon it. The system depends heavily on self-restraint and thus on social mechanisms for building in appropriate values and rules of conduct.[207]

This allows us to imagine a form of endogenous 'Executive constitutionalism'[208] over and beyond the exogenous constitutional constraints. By its nature, such 'self-control' is less visible than external constitutional checks. Nonetheless, this practice of constitutional self-

---

[205] Jackson (2016).
[206] Chafetz (2011).
[207] Daintith & Page (1999) 380; Beatson (2021) 119.
[208] Appleby & Olijnyk (2021) 5ff.

restraint lies at the heart of the collaborative constitutional endeavour. By exploring the labyrinth of decisional pathways which shape and constrain Executive engagement with rights, I hope to have shown that such self-restraint is not a constitutional fairy-tale. Instead, it is a hard-won and inherently fragile achievement of constitutional democracy in the twenty-first century.

5

Legislating for Rights

1 Introduction

In the previous chapter, I explored Executive engagement with rights in the UK constitutional order. However, whilst Executive commitment is necessary for protecting rights, it is not sufficient. The aim of this chapter is to examine the politics of rights as the Government's legislative proposals enter Parliament for scrutiny, deliberation and debate. Moving 'from Whitehall to Westminster',[1] i.e. from the Executive to the legislature, this chapter examines the myriad processes of parliamentary engagement with rights.

When the HRA was enacted, it was explicitly based on the idea that all three branches of government should take rights seriously when carrying out their respective constitutional roles.[2] Instead of relying exclusively on retrospective rights review by the courts, the political architects of the HRA adopted a more prospective, prophylactic and holistic approach to protecting rights in a democracy.[3] As the White Paper preceding the HRA affirmed,

> it is highly desirable for the Government to ensure as far as possible that legislation which it places before Parliament in the normal way is compatible with the Convention rights, and for Parliament to ensure that the human rights implications of legislation are subject to proper consideration before the legislation is enacted.[4]

Instead of portraying rights as the sole preserve of judges, the HRA sought to 'weave acceptance and understanding of [rights] into the

---

[1] Whitehall is the part of London where the government sits, including No. 10 Downing Street. Westminster is the adjacent part of London where the Palace of Westminster is located.
[2] Hunt (2010) 602.
[3] Straw & Boateng (1997) 79; Kinley (2015) 29; Ryle (1994) 192; Harlow & Rawlings (2021) 148.
[4] White Paper, *Rights Brought Home: The Human Rights Bill*, 1997 Cm 3782, [3.1].

democratic process' so that 'positive rights and liberties would become the focus and concern of legislators, administrators and judges alike'.[5] In doing so, it envisaged a multi-institutional model of rights protection, where all three branches would have a shared responsibility for rights as part of a collaborative enterprise.[6] The aim of this chapter, then, is to examine the modes and mechanisms of protecting rights in Parliament. Delving into the details, I will provide a textured narrative of *how* rights are engaged and *who* engages them during the legislative process. The chapter concludes by probing parliamentary performance, examining whether these myriad mechanisms have succeeded in raising 'rights-consciousness'[7] amongst key parliamentary actors.

2 Unpacking Parliament

In order to establish how Parliament engages with rights, we need to appreciate the role of the legislature in the constitutional scheme, examining how the component parts of the legislative machine work together to make law. Whilst the Executive provides the 'central governing, directing and initiating element'[8] in the collaborative law-making process, the main role of the legislature is to publicly scrutinise and critically evaluate the Executive's proposals. In this sense, the role of the legislature is responsive to that of the Executive.[9] As John Stuart Mill famously observed, 'instead of the function of governing, for which it is radically unfit, the proper office of a representative assembly is to watch and control the government: to throw the light of publicity on its acts'.[10]

Thus, whilst legal scholars often describe Parliament as the supreme lawmaker within the British system, this is shorthand for a more complex practice where the Executive initiates and formulates a detailed legislative

---

[5] Irvine (2003a) 36; Straw (1999); Hiebert (2004b) 1968; Hiebert & Kelly (2015) 9, 251ff.

[6] King (2012) 41; Weston (2015) 268; Harlow & Rawlings (2021) 159 (describing the HRA as instantiating 'a pluralist model of rights-formation').

[7] Gardbaum (2011) 198.

[8] Amery (1964) 1; Kavanagh (2019) 63.

[9] Griffith, Ryle & Wheeler-Booth (1989) 5; Amery (1964) 11–12; Griffith (2001) 49.

[10] Mill (1998) [1861] 282; Amery (1964) 12, 20, 30. For the multiplicity of functions carried out by the legislature, see Packenham (1990); Norton (2013b) 7–12; Sathanapally (2012) 49–56; Russell & Gover (2017) 282–3.

proposal, which is then debated and scrutinised in Parliament.[11] When Parliament gives its 'final seal of approval'[12] to Government Bills, we may say that the legislature has 'made' the law. But the details and direction of the legislative framework have already been hammered out within the Executive branch, before going through the various stages of the legislative process.[13] The legislative role is largely one of 'assent and review',[14] not initiation and creation. This is not to diminish the important role of the legislature in a constitutional democracy. After all, no policy becomes law until it has undergone 'the trial of discussion'.[15] Nonetheless, the core role of the legislature is not one of proposing law, but of 'passing judgment'[16] on Executive proposals and calling the Executive to account.

So what are the distinctive institutional values which the democratic legislature brings to the collaborative enterprise? There are many. First, the legislature has an expressive and representative role. It is designed to reflect a relatively diverse range of political, geographical and ideological viewpoints. This diversity of perspectives enables the legislature to scrutinise, debate and contest legislative proposals from a variety of perspectives, including from those who lost the previous election.[17] The legislative assembly brings the electoral losers into the deliberative frame, thereby giving them a voice in shaping policy proposals, which, in turn, contributes to the stability of the system as a whole.[18]

Second, the fact that democratic legislatures are predominantly elected bodies gives legislators an insight into popular needs and an incentive to be responsive to those needs. The 'electoral connection'[19] between voters and representatives means that MPs are well placed to ascertain the

---

[11] Kalitowski (2008) 694; Russell & Cowley (2016) 122; Norton (1990) 177 (arguing that the House of Commons is a 'policy influencer' rather than a policy maker or lawmaker).

[12] Mill (1998) [1861] 106.

[13] Griffith (2001) 54; Gee & Webber (2013) 2145–6.

[14] Sathanapally (2012) 54; Feldman (2007) 94.

[15] Manin (1997) 191; Ekins (2012) 151, 175–6.

[16] Manin (1997) 192; Endicott (2017a) 17; Endicott (2021) 19.

[17] Sathanapally (2012) 52; Waldron (1999a); Barber (2001) 84–8; Manin (1997) 186. The ideal of representative diversity should not blind us to the elite composition of many democratic legislatures, see Eskridge (2000) 580 (describing the US Senate as 'almost a parody of diversity' in terms of class, gender, race, and age, with the House of Representatives also 'relatively homogeneous' along all of these dimensions). On the British House of Commons, see White (2022) 69–70.

[18] Packenham (1990); Norton (2013b) 9–10.

[19] Mayhew (1974).

public will. Ongoing constituency work further strengthens the electoral connection, enabling elected politicians to channel constituency concerns into parliamentary debate.[20] When devising policy proposals, MPs can also consult with relevant stakeholders, commission research and gather information about the potential impact of policy proposals. Through parliamentary debate, Select Committees, and the House of Lords, it can subject those proposals to close analytical scrutiny.[21] Only the political actors are in a position to 'consult on, to explain, and to justify law-creation, to persons or groups interested in or affected by it . . . in a way that can give the law-creation process a measure of moral, as well as legal, authority',[22] even amongst those who disagree with it.

Third, members of the legislative assembly possess the political incentives and skills to forge suitable compromises between rival viewpoints in order to garner majority support between diverse groups.[23] As Amy Gutmann and Dennis Thompson observe: 'Compromise is difficult, but governing in a democracy without compromise is impossible'.[24] Therefore, it behoves all political actors to 'reach across the aisle',[25] in order to forge mutually acceptable and stable solutions in the crucible of contestation. The legislative process is a form of 'constitutional slowdown'[26] writ large, one which facilitates 'sober second thoughts'[27] and compromise at every stage. It ensures that Executive proposals garner support across a wide spectrum of opinion in a diverse political landscape.

In examining how the legislative process works, we must start by acknowledging that Parliament is a 'they' not an 'it'.[28] Rather than being a univocal actor with a singular focus, the legislature is a multi-faceted institution made up of multiple component parts, each with distinct institutional interests, aims and incentives.[29] Most obviously, the UK

---

[20] Norton (2013b) 8; Crewe (2021) 34–6, 44–6, 69–75, 112–15.
[21] Horder (2006).
[22] Ibid 78; Sales (2012) 289.
[23] Gutmann & Thompson (2014); Fumurescu (2013) 5, 184–9, 39; Craiutu (2017) 27–32, 119–20, 212–16, 222–3; Sales (2012) 289; Sumption (2019) 25, 29–31.
[24] Gutmann & Thompson (2014) 1.
[25] Ignatieff (2013b) 80–1, 149–50.
[26] On 'constitutional slowdown', see Chapter 3.5.
[27] Vermeule (2011).
[28] Shepsle (1992) 239, 240.
[29] Evans & Evans (2006a) 553; Kalitowski (2008) 705; Roach (2015); Gee & Webber (2013) 2145; Uhr (2006) 45–6; Elliott & Thomas (2020) 182ff.

Parliament is a bicameral legislature comprising two chambers – the House of Commons and the House of Lords – which differ significantly in their composition, institutional culture and constitutional role.[30] The House of Commons comprises elected politicians from across the country, whereas members of the House of Lords are unelected 'Life Peers', most of whom are appointed by the Prime Minister on grounds of expertise or contribution to public life.[31]

Given its democratic legitimacy, the House of Commons is the primary chamber, to which the House of Lords must ultimately give way if the two chambers cannot agree.[32] Whilst the House of Lords used to possess a veto power over legislative proposals from the House of Commons, this has now been replaced with a delaying power of two parliamentary sessions, in recognition of the superior democratic legitimacy of the House of Commons.[33] Thus, when a Bill is 'defeated' in the House of Lords, it then returns to the House of Commons for its reconsideration. Ultimately, however, if the House of Commons wishes to proceed with the Bill, it is entitled to do so.[34] In recognition of the superior democratic legitimacy of the House of Commons, there is a constitutional convention that the House of Lords will not reject or defeat a Bill that implements an election manifesto pledge.[35]

Whilst the House of Lords lacks the democratic legitimacy to veto legislative proposals, it nonetheless plays a valuable and distinctive[36] role in the legislative process which complements and supplements the House of Commons.[37] In particular, the House of Lords is envisaged as 'a revising chamber',[38] drawing on its members' expertise and relative detachment from party-political demands to perform a valuable scrutiny

---

[30] On bicameralism, see Waldron (2016) chapter 4; Russell (2013) chapter 3.

[31] See further Russell (2013).

[32] Crewe (2015b) 10–11; Crewe (2005) 162; Elliott & Thomas (2020) 204–13.

[33] Elliott & Thomas (2020) 207–8.

[34] The Report of the Royal Commission on Reform of the House of Lords, *A House for the Future* (Cm 4534 2000, 3) (arguing that the 'second chamber should engender second thoughts' and prompt the House of Commons to 'think again').

[35] Joint Committee on Conventions HL 265 HC 1212 2005–6; Elliott & Thomas (2020) 207.

[36] Royal Commission on Reform of the House of Lords (n 34) 3.

[37] Elliott & Thomas (2020) 210.

[38] Griffith, Ryle & Wheeler-Booth (1989) 507; Klug & Wildbore (2007) 242; Rogers & Walters (2015) 212; Crewe (2005) 1, 161, 179; Feldman (2004b) 97. In many bicameral legislatures, the Upper Chamber has this role of being a '*chambre de refléxion*', see De Visser (2004) 25.

role in the Westminster Parliament. The House of Lords is also an important 'constitutional guardian'[39] within the legislature, checking legislation for compliance with standards of constitutional propriety.[40]

But the division between the Commons and Lords is only the most basic delineation. Within and across these two Houses, there are multiple parliamentary actors, each of whom contributes to, and has influence over, the various stages of the legislative process. In the House of Commons, the key protagonist is the Government itself, whose Ministers sit on the Front Bench with the Prime Minister at their epicentre. Behind them sit the Government's own supporters from their political party – government backbenchers – on whose support the Government depends for its continuance in office and for getting its legislative proposals through Parliament.[41] Directly across the aisle is 'Her Majesty's Loyal Opposition', whose primary role is to oppose and contest the Government's policies, exposing their shortcomings and subjecting them to rigorous public contestation and critique.[42]

Other key actors in the Westminster Parliament include the Whips, who are in charge of party organisation and discipline, as well as the arrangement and timing of Commons business on both sides of the House.[43] Whips act as a 'two-way channel of communication'[44] between the party leadership and the backbenches. When the Whips on both sides of the House liaise with each other to manage the business of the House and timing of debates, they are described as 'the usual channels',[45] whose collective job is 'to keep the parliamentary show on the road'.[46] Here, we see the Government and Opposition working together collaboratively to secure agreement on the management, organisation and timing of parliamentary business.

Of crucial importance in scrutinising legislative proposals and holding the Executive to account are the permanent Select Committees, which

---

[39] Russell (2013) HL 225, 187–9; Norton (2016) 134.

[40] See Russell & Gover (2017) 38; Russell & Cowley (2016) 126–8.

[41] Russell & Gover (2017) chapter 5; McGann (2006) 454.

[42] On the Loyal Opposition, see Webber (2016); Waldron (2016) chapter 5.

[43] Rogers & Walters (2015) 81–2 (The name derives from 'whippers-in' or 'whips' in the hunting field).

[44] Rogers & Walters (2015) 81.

[45] Rogers & Walters (2015) 82; Griffith, Ryle & Wheeler-Booth (1989) 298–9; Webber (2016) 17.

[46] Crewe (2015b) 125.

provide a complete set of specialised committees to shadow and scrutinise all government departments.[47] Since their creation in 1979, the Select Committees have grown in strength, gaining a reputation for cross-party collaboration and independent-minded scrutiny which makes them a significant site of Executive accountability in the Westminster Parliament.[48] This reputation for independence is partly because Ministers, Whips and Opposition spokespersons are excluded from these committees, but the emphasis on subject specialisation and evidence-based scrutiny also helps to 'break down knee-jerk partisan hostilities'.[49] These Committees contribute to 'a strong parliamentary culture of backbenchers using committees to hold the Government to account'.[50]

Even this thumbnail sketch reveals the plurality and complexity of actors involved in the legislative process. It also hints at the dialectical tensions between them. Once the Government introduces a Bill to Parliament, it has already invested considerable time, energy, resources and political capital into devising the legislative proposal. From the Government's point of view, the legislative process is like an obstacle course with various hurdles which the Government will want to clear as easily and efficiently as possible. From Parliament's point of view, however, those hurdles are vitally important constitutional checkpoints designed to slow the Government down and give parliamentary actors the opportunity to stress-test and scrutinise bills from a variety of perspectives. The legislative process therefore comprises different stages of sequenced analysis in different parliamentary fora, whether in the public arena of parliamentary debates on the floor of the House of Commons, or the more secluded and less confrontational atmosphere of the Committee rooms, where more detailed line-by-line scrutiny of the Bill occurs under the radar of headline news.[51]

3   The JCHR as a Hybrid Constitutional Watchdog

So how do rights enter this multifaceted process? During the legislative process, any MP or Peer can raise rights concerns at any stage of the

---

[47] Russell & Gover (2017) chapter 8.
[48] Russell & Gover (2017) 278; Rogers & Walters (2015) 325; Russell (2010) 1.
[49] Russell & Gover (2017) 278; Feldman (2002b) 327; Rogers & Walters (2015) 325.
[50] Chang & Ramshaw (2017) 11.
[51] Thompson & McNulty (2018); Russell et al. (2017) 13; Oliver (2006) 223.

legislative process, whether during parliamentary debate on the floor of either House or in Committee. Moreover, any of the accountability actors outlined above – including the Opposition, the House of Lords, Select Committees and even the Government's own backbenchers – can bring pressure to bear on the Government's legislative proposals. Indeed, when these oppositional forces align and combine, they can have an accumulative accountability effect on government proposals.[52] Post-HRA, the House of Lords Constitution Committee and the Joint Committee on Human Rights (JCHR) have emerged as complementary accountability actors and key sites of engagement with rights within and beyond the Houses of Parliament.[53] The JCHR is of particular significance. Set up post-HRA in order to institutionalise sustained parliamentary vigilance concerning rights, this JCHR is a key locus of parliamentary scrutiny for compliance with rights. Therefore, it is worth examining the workings of the Committee in more detail.[54]

The JCHR is a Joint Committee of both Houses of Parliament, consisting of twelve members in total – six from the House of Commons and six from the House of Lords.[55] The party-political composition of the Committee broadly mirrors the party-political composition of each House. The fact that there is a combined membership across both Houses generally means that the Government has no overall majority on the Committee.[56] The JCHR is served by a permanent Legal Adviser drawn from the highest ranks of the Bar, academia or the civil service. Rather than being a legal handmaiden to the Committee, the Legal Adviser can play an active and dynamic agenda-setting role, driving forward the Committee's twin tasks of providing probing legislative scrutiny and vigilant Executive oversight on issues relating to rights.[57] The purpose and remit of the JCHR is to examine all matters relating to the protection of human rights in the UK, but also to provide some regular and rigorous analysis of whether Bills comply with rights.[58]

---

[52] Russell, Gover & Wollter (2016); Russell & Cowley (2016).
[53] On the HL Constitution Committee, see Caird (2012); Le Sueur & Caird (2013); Feldman (2002b) 341–2 (observing that the JCHR and the HL Constitution Committee are complementary accountability actors seeking to achieve 'joined up scrutiny').
[54] See further Kavanagh (2015b); Hunt (2013); Feldman (2004b).
[55] On the role of the JCHR, see www.gov.uk/government/publications/ministerial-code
[56] Evans & Evans (2006b) 788.
[57] See further Kavanagh (2015b) 119; Hunt, Hooper & Yowell (2012) 13; Hunt (2010) 604.
[58] Kavanagh (2015b) 119.

The JCHR can be viewed as a 'hybrid breed of constitutional watch-dog'.[59] Its hybridity is manifest in the following four ways. First, although the JCHR has a partly party-political composition, it operates in a relatively non-partisan, consensual, and cooperative manner.[60] The specialist nature of the JCHR's scrutiny work cuts across – and sometimes counteracts – the pull of party allegiance.[61] Working as part of a parliamentary committee typically makes members 'more policy-focused, contributing to a culture where they are more prepared to think independently and work across party lines'.[62]

Second, the JCHR is a *joint* committee of the House of Commons and the House of Lords, thus combining the diverse perspectives of democratically elected and appointed members of the legislature.[63] Joint Committees of both Houses tend to operate with a lower degree of political partisanship than other Select Committees, thus enhancing the non-partisan and consensual nature of JCHR deliberations.[64]

Third, although the JCHR is composed of politicians and Peers from both Houses of Parliament, the political composition is supplemented by the legal expertise and insight it receives from its permanent Legal Adviser.[65] Therefore, the Committee can mesh legal, political and policy analysis in a hybrid form of 'blended judgment'.[66] In doing so, it combines the perspectives of political and legal constitutionalism.[67]

Fourth, and perhaps most importantly, the JCHR plays a hybrid role by channelling law into politics and politics into law. Working at the interface between legislative and judicial decisions about rights, the JCHR provides an institutional nexus of mutual understanding, engagement and accountability in a complex collaborative scheme. When Parliament deliberates about rights during the legislative process, the JCHR informs and incentivises parliamentary deliberation about rights. As I will show

---

[59] Ibid 117–22.
[60] Hiebert (2006) 15–17; Kavanagh (2015b) 118.
[61] Feldman (2002b) 327.
[62] Russell & Gover (2017) 90.
[63] Klug & Wildbore (2007) 242.
[64] Klug (2006) [5.8].
[65] Hazell (2004) 497.
[66] Renan (2017) 813.
[67] Kavanagh (2015b) 130–1; Hunt (2013) 248.

in Chapter 9, this parliamentary deliberation then informs judicial reasoning about whether the statute has struck a proportionate balance between rights and policy priorities.[68] When adjudicating whether legislation complies with rights, the courts take cognisance of legislative engagement with rights, including the iterative exchange between the JCHR and the government of the day.[69]

Similarly, when the courts hand down decisions about rights, the JCHR incorporates them into their own analysis, explaining their significance for parliamentarians. The JCHR acts as a 'constitutional watchdog'[70] for legislative compliance with judicial decisions,[71] especially judicial declarations of incompatibility.[72] In myriad ways, the JCHR provides a bridge and buckle between the Executive, legislative, and judicial branches of government in a complex, collaborative enterprise where multiple constitutional actors contribute and combine. With its unique combination of political acumen, legal expertise and a specialist focus on rights at some remove from the direct demands of party allegiance, the JCHR has emerged as a valuable 'forum of collaboration between the three branches of government'.[73] For many commentators, the JCHR is a 'pro-compliance actor'[74] for judicial decisions on rights, whilst simultaneously bolstering and catalysing legislative deliberation about what rights require.

From its inception, legislative scrutiny has been a central and influential part of the JCHR's work, where it has been a key guardian of rights in the legislative process.[75] In order for legislative scrutiny to be meaningful, it is vitally important to get in early before the policy and statutory details have already been settled.[76] As seasoned parliamentarians know, 'once a Bill hits the floor [of the House of Commons], you can do nips and tucks at best'.[77] For this reason, the JCHR tries to engage in probing pre-legislative scrutiny

---

[68] See further Chapter 10, this vol; Kavanagh (2014); Lazarus & Simonsen (2015).
[69] Hunt, Hooper & Yowell (2012); Yowell (2015).
[70] Kavanagh (2015b) 117–19.
[71] Sathanapally (2012) 160.
[72] Chapters 8, 11, and 12, this vol.
[73] Murray (2013a) 74.
[74] Donald & Leach (2016) 68.
[75] Hazell (2004) 497.
[76] Klug & Wildbore (2007) 239–40; Lester (2002b) 441; Tolley (2009) 48.
[77] Evans & Evans (2011) 339; Feldman (2004b) 107; Klug & Wildbore (2007) 239–40.

when possible, availing of the opportunity to meet the Bill team before a Bill is published.[78] Not only do these meetings give the Bill team the opportunity to anticipate and accommodate the JCHR's concerns, it also gives the JCHR advance warning of possible rights infringements, thus enabling it to engage in probing and rigorous analysis as the Bill goes through Parliament.

Cabinet Office guidelines on the legislative process explicitly alert departments to the fact that the JCHR will 'examine closely the arguments put forward by the Department justifying interference with Convention rights', observing that it is 'clearly advantageous if the JCHR is satisfied about human rights compatibility early in the bill's passage'. Therefore, the government urges departments 'to identify areas likely to concern the [JCHR] and prepare briefing ahead of time'.[79] This testifies to the anticipatory – and potentially chastening – effect the JCHR may have at the policy-formation stage. Even if the JCHR only gets to meet the Bill team after the Bill has been drafted, this still allows the JCHR to identify any additional information the Government should provide in order to facilitate greater scrutiny during the legislative process. It also allows the Bill team to devise a robust 'handling strategy' for parliamentary passage.[80]

Once the Bill is published, there is an iterative communicative exchange between the JCHR and the relevant Government Minister, where the Committee may probe the Government for justification on particular points.[81] JCHR Reports contain a rich resource of political, legal and policy analysis of the rights implications of legislative proposals. They flag up potential rights problems with a view to informing parliamentary debate and expanding the legal and policy evidence base from which the Bill is assessed.[82] But they also suggest solutions to potentially rights-infringing measures, proposing specific legislative amendments to

---

[78] Klug & Wildbore (2007); Feldman (2015) 117; Casey (2019) 58–60.

[79] Cabinet Office, *Guide to Making Legislation*, 2022 [11.31], www.gov.uk/government/publications/guide-to-making-legislation

[80] Hunt (2013) 228–9; Feldman (2002b) 335.

[81] Feldman (2005) 333.

[82] The current practice of the Committee is to write reports only on those Bills which raise significant rights issues, see Joint Committee on Human Rights, *The Committee's Future Working Practices, Twenty Third Report* (2005–6, HL 239/HC 1575), at [27].

avert rights violations.[83] Here, we see the JCHR acting as both an *alerting mechanism* and an *accountability actor*: warning parliamentarians of potential rights concerns, providing them with the informational and argumentative resources to challenge the Government, supporting them in tabling amendments which could make a real difference to the content of the Bill.[84]

The success of the JCHR depends partly on its reputation as a repository of expert, balanced and well-informed analysis,[85] as well as the strength of its constitutional relationships with key actors across the parliamentary and Executive landscape. In all aspects of its work, the JCHR engages interactively and collaboratively with a number of other parliamentary actors, including Select Committees, the House of Lords Constitution Committee, the Human Rights Unit within the Ministry of Justice, civil servants, government legal advisers, policy bureaucrats, parliamentarians, Government Ministers, and Lords Peers.[86] The House of Lords Constitution Committee scrutinises all Public Bills for compliance with the principles and practices of the constitution, including 'fundamental principles relating to good government, liberty and the rule of law'.[87] Alongside the JCHR, the Constitution Committee has emerged as a 'skilful interrogator of government'[88] on constitutional issues. It acts as a 'constitutional long-stop', ensuring that fundamental constitutional change should not occur 'without full and open debate and an awareness of the consequences'.[89] Together with the JCHR and other parliamentary actors, the Constitution Committee has contributed to the collaborative task of embedding constitutional values into the legislative process.[90] The overall picture suggests that the JCHR does

---

[83] Hunt, Hooper & Yowell (2012) 22; Gardbaum (2013b) 167; Feldman (2004b) 111.

[84] Hunt (2010) 603; Hunt, Hooper & Yowell (2012) 22.

[85] Feldman (2002b) 346.

[86] Donald (2015) 144.

[87] Russell (2013) 216; Hazell (2004) 499; Constitution Committee, Second Report (2003–4 HL 19), para. 6. For analysis of the HL Constitution Committee as instituting a form of 'parliamentary constitutional review', see Caird (2012); Le Sueur & Caird (2013); Caird, Hazell & Oliver (2015).

[88] Oliver (2013) 328.

[89] Report of the Royal Commission on the Reform of the House of Lords, *A House for the Future* (2000) [5.17]; De Visser (2004) 1.

[90] Hunt (2013) 249; Oliver (2013) 327–8; Le Sueur & Caird (2013) 288; Russell (2013) 215; De Visser (2004) 31.

not – and cannot – operate in isolation. In order to achieve its goals, it works interactively and collaboratively with other actors, seeking to develop and maintain constructive working relationships between them.[91]

When writing its reports and scrutinising legislative proposals, the JCHR frequently holds Evidence sessions which actively seek representations from a broader range of interested parties and stakeholders from civil society as a whole, including interest groups, NGOs, specialised charities working in the field, academics, as well as MPs, Peers, and other parliamentary actors.[92] These Evidence Sessions channel the varied voices of those whose rights are affected by the Bill into the chambers and corridors of Westminster.[93] In this way, the JCHR provides a conduit for popular participation and civil society involvement into the legislative process,[94] such that it has become a 'focal point for human rights campaigners'.[95] Far from being the ivory-tower reflections of erudite Peers and expert legal advisers, the JCHR is a key locus for civil society engagement, providing a 'systemic channel'[96] for civil society actors to inform and contribute to the legislative process.

By requiring Ministers to provide cogent justifications for their stance on rights, the JCHR has an *awareness-raising* and '*transparency-promoting*'[97] function. It also acts as a *reason-demanding* body, contributing to what David Dyzenhaus and Murray Hunt have described as 'a culture of justification'.[98] The reason-demanding strand of the JCHR's work can be clearly discerned in the persistent pressure it places on the government to provide Parliament with its justifications for claiming compatibility

---

[91] Anderson (2014) 413ff; Donald & Leach (2016) 234–6.

[92] Harlow & Rawlings (2021) 207.

[93] Hunt (2010) 604; Kavanagh (2015b) 123; Feldman (2004b) 114.

[94] Russell & Cowley (2016) 131; Kavanagh (2015b) 123; Sathanapally (2012) 182, 209. For a forensic examination of the influence of pressure groups in the legislative process, see Russell & Gover (2017) chapter 7.

[95] Harlow & Rawlings (2021) 159. Note that human rights-focused NGOs such as Liberty and JUSTICE circulate regular briefings to MPs on rights issues, see Gardbaum (2013b) 193.

[96] Feldman (2002b) 333; Hunt (2010) 42; Kavanagh (2015b) 123; Benton & Russell (2012) 18.

[97] Chandrachud (2017) 206 (emphasis added).

[98] Dyzenhaus (2007) 143; Hunt (2015) 10ff; Norton (2013b) 190.

under section 19 HRA.[99] In the early years of the HRA, the Government simply published a bald statement of compatibility with no supporting reasons. But thanks to the assiduous efforts of the JCHR, the Government now accompanies its section 19 statement with a more detailed statement of its reasoning on rights in the Explanatory Notes to a Bill.[100] Indeed, it is now increasingly common for departments to supplement the information provided in the Explanatory Notes to a Bill with a much more detailed human rights memorandum.[101] In doing so, the JCHR is 'both watchdog and bloodhound. The bloodhound sniffs out the information and the watchdog barks as necessary to warn the Government, Parliament and the public at large of possible incursions into human rights'.[102]

By engaging in an iterative process with Government Ministers, civil servants, Bill teams and parliamentary actors, the JCHR provides a vital nexus point of constructive engagement within, between and beyond the three branches of government on how to protect rights in a democracy.

4   Raising Rights-Consciousness in Parliament

In his analysis of the political engagement with rights under the HRA, Stephen Gardbaum observed that the aim of section 19 HRA was to ensure that 'laws violating rights are not enacted or, if they are, that the process is undertaken deliberately and deliberatively, with eyes wide open'.[103] The key issue, then, is whether the Government and Parliament have opened their eyes to the importance of rights in the legislative process and, if so, whether this enhanced 'rights-consciousness'[104] is making a real difference to the quality of legislation as judged against the standards of rights. When a Bill passes through Parliament, is it subjected to meaningful scrutiny and accountability for its stance on rights?

---

[99] Lester (2002a) 53, 76; Hiebert (2015) 49.
[100] Hunt (2013) 229ff; Lester (2002b) 448; Hiebert (2006) 25; Kavanagh (2015b) 116, 125–6, 131.
[101] Hunt (2013) 229ff.
[102] Lester (2002b) 434; Kavanagh (2015b) 126; Ryle (1994) 196.
[103] Gardbaum (2013b) 161; Hiebert & Kelly (2015) 5.
[104] Gardbaum (2013b) 26.

The following tentative conclusions can be drawn. First, it seems clear that rights have greater salience and visibility in the Westminster Parliament in the post-HRA era.[105] This is partly due to the catalytic accountability effect of the Ministerial reporting requirement under section 19 HRA. But it is also due to the assiduous work of the JCHR in compelling the government to justify its position on rights before, during and after the legislative process.[106] The JCHR has emerged as a pivotal actor in raising awareness about rights across Parliament, but also in demanding justifications from government. Due to the vigilance of the JCHR, there has been a marked increase in the quantity and quality of information which government provides to Parliament regarding its 'human rights reasoning'.[107] This facilitates enhanced parliamentary scrutiny of government decisions and contributes to a 'culture of justification'[108] when legislative proposals seem to impinge on rights.[109]

The fact that the government now publishes an ECHR memorandum on rights compliance accompanying its section 19 Statement is one of the most notable transparency gains secured by the JCHR in its first decade.[110] Though it is difficult to quantify, the JCHR also seems to be creating a significant anticipatory effect at the Bill preparation and policy formation stages, where various actors within the Executive branch strive to make the Bill as Convention-compliant as they can before it hits the floor of the House of Commons.[111] Once the Bill begins its passage through Parliament, the JCHR Reports equip parliamentarians with the necessary legal and political resources to hold the Government to account for its stance on rights. Given that parliamentarians do not have their own legal advisers, the JCHR Reports provide a vitally important resource which

---

[105] Hunt, Hooper & Yowell (2012); Yowell (2015).
[106] Harlow & Rawlings (2021) 139; Norton (2013a) 158ff.
[107] Grieve (2012b) 101ff.
[108] Mureinik (1994); Hunt (2015); Dyzenhaus (1998).
[109] Norton (2016) 124–5, 134–5.
[110] Hunt (2010) 607; Hunt (2013) 231.
[111] Hiebert & Kelly (2015) 21, 297, 301, 391 (noting that after conducting interviews with more than seventy public and parliamentary officials on the operation of 'political rights review' in the post-HRA era, 'all interviewees agreed that the government has a strong interest in a positive JCHR Report').

parliamentarians can use to challenge the Government's legal advice on a firm footing.[112]

Second, in the post-HRA era parliamentarians are now better resourced, informed and equipped to scrutinise the Government's claim to compatibility than before. This increased 'human rights literacy'[113] is bolstered by various NGOs, which provide parliamentarians with regular briefings on matters of rights-based concern.[114] Moreover, there now seems to be a significant increase in legislative deliberation about rights, including increased in the reliance on JCHR Reports during parliamentary debate.[115] Of course, deliberating about rights is one thing and delivering them is another. How effective has Parliament been in ensuring that rights are better protected in the laws it enacts?

In answering this question, we must bear in mind that measuring parliamentary influence is challenging. It is notoriously difficult to make reliable causal connections between various forms of parliamentary accountability and concrete legislative amendments. As a former Legal Adviser to the JCHR, Murray Hunt, observed, parliamentary influence manifests in various forms which may 'defy crude attempts at measurement'.[116] This chimes with leading political science analysis which identifies the anticipatory influence of parliamentary pushback as pivotal in the policy-making process. By its nature, such influence is 'subtle, largely invisible, and frequently even immeasurable'.[117]

Bearing these caveats in mind, there are some instances where parliamentary pushback forced the Government to back down on some of its key legislative commitments, thus amending the law in a rights-protective manner. Examples of this dynamic can be found across diverse policy areas, including religious discrimination, education, identify cards, safeguarding vulnerable groups, immigration, equality, criminal justice, and counter-terrorism.[118]

---

[112] Casey (2019) 56. For an argument in favour of developing a new role of 'Counsel to the Parliament', see Appleby & Olijnyk (2017).
[113] Hunt (2010) 607.
[114] Feldman (2002b) 340; Hunt (2010); Gardbaum (2013b) 193.
[115] Hunt, Hooper & Yowell (2012); Hunt (2015); Kavanagh (2015b); Hunt (2021) 8.
[116] Hunt (2010) 606.
[117] Russell & Benton (2012) 10.
[118] Hunt, Hooper & Yowell (2012); Yowell (2015).

The most notable instances of strong parliamentary pushback – followed by government concession and compromise – have been in the counter-terrorist field.[119] Legislative resistance to such measures came from a variety of parliamentary actors, including the JCHR, the Constitution Committee, the Opposition, the House of Lords, and, crucially, the Independent Reviewer of Terrorism Legislation.[120] The Independent Reviewer subjects the government's legislative proposals to close analytical scrutiny, and then publishes their 'informed, considered and independent'[121] findings for the benefit of Government Ministers, parliamentarians and the populace at large.[122] A focused case-study on 'legislating for terror' will have to await the next chapter. For the moment, it suffices to note that following robust parliamentary scrutiny and accountability, the government agreed to reduce detention without charge for terrorist suspects under the Terrorist Bill 2006 from ninety days as initially proposed to twenty-eight days in the final statute.[123] Though Parliament did not manage to stop detention of terrorist suspects outright, it nonetheless qualified and ameliorated the government's original proposals.[124] The counter-terrorist context therefore provides an insightful case-study of collaborative constitutionalism in action, where legal and political modes of accountability worked together in a form of dynamic interaction and mutual reinforcement, oriented towards a common goal of striving to ensure that Parliament takes rights and the rule of law seriously.[125]

When we look at the mechanisms for protecting rights in Parliament, we are immediately struck by a multi-institutional land-

---

[119] Kavanagh (2009c); Kavanagh (2011); Tomkins (2011); Ewing (2004); Ewing & Tham (2008); Feldman (2006).

[120] Anderson (2014); Blackbourn (2012).

[121] Anderson (2014) 409.

[122] Ibid 403 ('Any Government that invites review on those terms [i.e. on the basis of independence from Government, with unrestricted access to classified documents and national security personnel, followed by public dissemination of their key findings] deserves respect simply for doing so').

[123] Hiebert & Kelly (2015) 321–2.

[124] Kavanagh (2009c).

[125] For examples of case studies along these lines, see Kavanagh (2011); Kavanagh (2010c); Bamforth (2013) 166; Phillipson (2014) 271; Anderson (2014); Davis & de Londras (2014a) 20.

scape populated by a number of 'hybrid constitutional watchdogs'[126] including the JCHR, the HL Constitution Committee, the Attorney General, Parliamentary Counsel, parliamentary officials, and civil servants more generally. Instead of viewing these actors through 'the false dichotomous lens'[127] of political versus legal constitutionalism, we should adopt a wide-scope vision of how the key constitutional actors act, interact and counteract as part of a collaborative constitutional order.

Once we remove the blinkers of the Manichean narrative, we can see that the secret of the JCHR's success does not reside in the fact that it is a purely political actor designed to uphold the political constitution, but rather that it *combines* legal and political perspectives in deeply interactive and interrogative ways, forging connections and building relationships between myriad legal and political actors across Parliament and beyond.[128] The JCHR defies the compartmentalised and polarised thinking underpinning the idea that there is a sharp dichotomy between the political and legal constitution.[129] Operating at the interface between all three branches of government, the JCHR cuts across that distinction, integrating legal and political dimensions within its own functioning and composition, whilst interacting and counteracting constructively with other constitutional actors in the broader accountability architecture. In this way, the JCHR can be viewed as a key contributor to the 'wider collaborative enterprise'[130] of protecting rights in Parliament.

The portrait of policy development, Bill formation and legislative scrutiny presented in this chapter reveals that legal requirements are not viewed exclusively as exogenous constraints imposed from without, but also as endogenous norms embraced from within.[131] The law-making process at Westminster is a collaborative enterprise where 'Parliament and the executive must work together and respect each other's

---

[126] Kavanagh (2015b). The HL Constitution Committee could also be described as a 'hybrid constitutional watchdog', see Le Sueur & Caird (2013) 282; see also Select Committee on the Constitutional Reform Bill, Report (HL 2003–4, 125-I) [420] (observing that the House of Lord Constitution Committee acts 'as a bridge between Parliament and the judiciary').

[127] Kavanagh (2015b) 131.

[128] Ibid 130–1; King (2013) 149.

[129] Kavanagh (2015b) 130–1.

[130] Ibid 116.

[131] Renan (2017).

responsibilities and functions'[132] in a dynamic interplay between Government and Opposition, majority and minority, elected politicians and unelected Peers, Ministers and civil servants, policy specialists and legal advisers. Instead of a polarised and combative picture of the branches of government as rivals for constitutional supremacy, what in fact exists is a more complex, collaborative form of constitutionalism which integrates the key political and legal actors involved.[133] Protecting rights in politics emerges as an iterative, interactive, integrative and interrogative dynamic between legal and political norms unfolds across, within and between the Executive and legislative branches of government.

5 Conclusion

Whilst political compliance with rights is neither legally nor legislatively mandated by the HRA, this chapter charted the emergence of 'elaborate organic systems of intra-governmental and intra-parliamentary constitutional preview'[134] which, together, raise rights-consciousness across Whitehall and Westminster. Comity, complementarity and collaboration emerged as leitmotivs of the institutional analysis, where the lead *dramatis personae* combined, counteracted and collaborated in complementary and constructive ways. At the heart of this complex collaborative process was the abiding duty on all actors to treat 'different but complementary functions'[135] with respect. Indeed, Parliament's scrutiny and accountability function is simply not possible without the active cooperation of the Government, which must play its role in supplying the legislature with the key information it needs in order to form an accurate picture of the Government's plans.[136] As David Feldman observed, providing meaningful parliamentary scrutiny is only achievable if the various institutions involved in creating and scrutinising law 'see themselves as working together, rather than against each other'.[137]

Viewed from the higher echelons of constitutional theory, the nuts and bolts of institutional decision-making with the Executive and

---

[132] Feldman (2004b) 92; Feldman (2002b) 333.
[133] Hunt (2013) 249; Russell (2013) 225.
[134] Oliver (2013) 329; Hunt (2013) 245.
[135] Feldman (2004b) 92; Kavanagh (2015b) 115.
[136] Feldman (2004b) 113.
[137] Ibid 113–15.

legislative branches may seem pedestrian or even banal. Yet from the perspective of 'making rights real'[138] in a constitutional democracy, these are the mechanisms that matter at the point where policy becomes law. Therefore, if we care about rights and the rule of law, we should also care about how those principles are put into practice by the actors who make all the difference.

---

[138] Leigh & Masterman (2008).

6

Legislated Rights

From Domination to Collaboration

1 Introduction

When the Human Rights Act 1998 was enacted, its central aim was to give litigants remedies for violations of rights in domestic law, whilst preserving the doctrine of parliamentary sovereignty.[1] In order to ensure that parliamentary sovereignty was upheld, the HRA did not give the courts the power to strike down legislation for violation of rights. Nor did it impose a legal obligation on Parliament to legislate compatibly with rights.[2] Whilst all 'public authorities' were obliged to ensure that their decisions comply with rights – including the courts and the Government – Parliament was explicitly excluded from the list.[3]

But beyond exclusions and exemptions, the HRA also envisaged a more positive political constitutionalism, putting Parliament at the centre of the constitutional project of protecting and promoting rights. As the White Paper preceding the HRA stressed, 'Parliament itself should play a leading role in protecting the rights which are at the heart of parliamentary democracy'.[4] The Ministerial Reporting requirement under section 19 HRA was designed to ensure that the Executive and the legislature would 'squarely confront'[5] rights before, during and after the legislative process had begun.[6]

---

[1] Klug & Wildbore (2007) 232.
[2] Section 6 HRA.
[3] Ibid.
[4] White Paper, *Bringing Rights Home: The Human Rights Bill*, Cm 3782 1997 [3.6]; Klug & Wildbore (2007) 233.
[5] *R v SSHD, ex parte Simms* [2000] 2 AC 115, 131 Lord Hoffmann.
[6] Straw & Boateng (1997) 79.

Yet this aspiration for meaningful parliamentary engagement with rights is open to two powerful challenges. The first is the claim that Parliament's capacity and willingness to protect rights is fatally undercut by the Executive dominance of Parliament. Instead of holding the Government to account for its stance on rights, the worry is that Parliament will be cowed into constitutional submission by an overbearing Executive. The second is the fear that governmental and legislative engagement with rights is distorted and debilitated by the overbearing influence of a rising juristocracy.[7] If either or both of these claims are true, then they undercut the potential of parliamentary Bills of Rights to incentivise meaningful legislative engagement with rights. The aim of this chapter, therefore, is to critically evaluate both of these claims, testing them in the crucible of constitutional and legislative practice in the Westminster Parliament.

The chapter will unfold in the following way. Part 2 begins by 'deconstructing Executive dominance'. Drawing on recent political science scholarship, I challenge the orthodoxy that the Westminster Parliament is an eviscerated institution at the beck and call of an almighty Executive.[8] Accepting that the Government is in the driving seat of the legislative process, this does not preclude Parliament from pushing back. Moving from domination to collaboration, I show how key parliamentary actors exert subtle but significant influence over the Government's agenda. Part 3 illustrates these political dynamics through a case-study on 'legislating for terror'. In Part 4, I turn to the charge about judicial domination of Parliament on questions of rights. Whilst acknowledging the influence of judicial decisions in parliamentary deliberation about rights, I question the empirical accuracy of the claim that legislative deliberation has succumbed to judicial domination, distortion, or debilitation. The chapter concludes with a case-study of the Communications Bill 2002, one of the few instances where the Government made a negative statement of incompatibility under section 19(1)(b) HRA. This case-study reveals a constructive and collaborative dynamic between all three branches of government, where they each have a role to play in the joint project of protecting rights.

---

[7] Delaney (2014).
[8] Russell & Gover (2017) 1, 3–6.

2   Deconstructing Executive Dominance

In their magisterial study of Parliamentary Bills of Rights, Janet Hiebert and James Kelly argue that legislative engagement with rights in Westminster Parliaments is seriously compromised by the dominance of the Executive in the legislative process.[9] Whilst accepting that the HRA had a substantial and beneficial impact on pre-legislative scrutiny within the Executive branch,[10] they argue that the key characteristics of Westminster systems – namely, Executive dominance of Parliament, cohesiveness of political parties, and the adversarial dynamic between Government and Opposition – conspire to 'undermine parliamentary capacity and willingness to hold governments to account for decisions that implicate rights in an adverse manner'.[11] Despite evocative political rhetoric that the HRA would mainstream a 'culture of rights'[12] across all three branches, Hiebert and Kelly argue that the reality of legislative rights review falls short of the rhetoric. On their analysis, the Government is typically 'unwilling to accept rights-improving amendments'[13] and Parliament is typically unwilling and unable to push back.[14]

In drawing these conclusions, Hiebert and Kelly acknowledge the significant achievements of the JCHR, echoing Stephen Gardbaum's verdict that the JCHR provides the 'gold standard' for parliamentary committees tasked with upholding rights.[15] However, whilst accepting its good-faith efforts to vindicate rights, Hiebert and Kelly question the JCHR's ability to secure legislative amendments which comply with rights, observing that the Government is 'unlikely to change its mind on the basis of a single but contrary parliamentary committee report'.[16] For all the great expectations that Parliamentary Bills of Rights would usher in a distinctively democratic form of constitutionalism, Hiebert and Kelly conclude that they have not led us to the promised land where politicians engage in 'spirited normative debates about the scope of rights implicated in legislative bills'.[17] A 'focus on compatibility with

---

[9] Hiebert & Kelly (2015).
[10] Ibid 266, 272, 407, 28–9.
[11] Ibid 402.
[12] Straw (1999); Hiebert & Kelly (2015) 236, 251.
[13] Hiebert & Kelly (2015) 406.
[14] Ibid 287, 30, 268; Hiebert (2015) 63; cf. Kavanagh (2015b) 134–5.
[15] Hiebert & Kelly (2015) 396; Gardbaum (2013b) 224.
[16] Hiebert & Kelly (2015) 40, 63.
[17] Ibid 16.

Convention rights' had not become a 'fundamental factor in legislative decision-making'.[18]

These arguments are both formidable and foreboding. If true, they cast a dark shadow over our hopes for meaningful rights scrutiny in Westminster Parliaments, or indeed in any parliamentary system of government. After all, if the central and stubborn dynamic is one of executive dominance and parliamentary impotence, then all hopes of creating a 'democratic charter of rights'[19] in Westminster-style political systems are dashed. Unless we can imagine a radical reconfiguration of the Westminster mode of government, a parliamentary Bill of Rights will always be vulnerable to an omnipotent Executive determined to get its way and a supine Parliament unable to resist.

Yet, whilst Hiebert and Kelly helpfully illuminate the detailed dynamics of bureaucratic and legislative engagement with rights, we might question some of their underlying assumptions about Executive dominance in Westminster parliaments. There is no denying that a government with a strong majority in a Westminster system wields enormous power in the legislative process.[20] In the comparative political science literature, 'the Westminster model' is often used as shorthand for a dominant Executive and acquiescent legislature, in recognition of the Executive's pivotal role in the policy-making process.[21] Indeed, the traditional emphasis of Westminster systems on strong Executive government has engendered accusations that the UK is 'an elective dictatorship',[22] with Parliament consigned to the role of 'an elaborate rubber stamp'.[23] This chimes with the popular public and media perception of the Westminster Parliament as an emasculated institution in deep decline – 'a legislature on its knees'[24] which 'bows and scrapes'[25] before an almighty Executive.[26]

---

[18] Ibid 28.

[19] Campbell (2011) 458.

[20] Norton (2001) 13; though cf. Russell & Cowley (2016) 122; Russell, Gover & Wollter (2016).

[21] Lijphart (2012) chapter 2; Kreppel (2014); McGann (2006) 454–5.

[22] Hailsham (1976); Jenkins (2006).

[23] Kalitowski (2008); Rhodes (2011) 287; King & Crewe (2013) 361; cf. Russell, Gover & Wollter (2016).

[24] Huhne (2009).

[25] William Hague, HC Deb, 13 July 2000, vol 518 col 1084; Russell & Gover (2017) 3.

[26] Flinders & Kelso (2011) 249; Russell & Cowley (2016) 121.

But recent political science scholarship now challenges this orthodoxy about a dominant Executive which brooks no compromise and a
diffident Parliament with no power to resist.[27] In the first detailed study
of the Westminster legislative process for over forty years, leading
political scientists Professor Meg Russell and Daniel Gover reveal that
the Westminster Parliament has significant policy influence and is far
less dominated by the Executive than is commonly assumed.[28]
Parliament's greatest influence comes in the form of anticipated reactions, where the Government anticipates parliamentary pushback from
members of both Houses of Parliament, and takes action to avoid it.[29]
Both at the Bill-formation stage and throughout the legislative process,
Government Ministers and key government officials negotiate behind
the scenes with parliamentarians from both Chambers, offering concessions and compromises to avoid unnecessary conflict on the floor of the
House of Commons.[30] Though less visible and observable than a
straightforward government defeat on the floor of the House of
Commons, this anticipatory and preventive influence is nonetheless
significant and substantial.[31]

Of course, this raises the question: if a government has a strong
majority in the House of Commons, why would it be motivated to offer
concessions when it has the power to bulldoze its Bills through
Parliament without doing so? The answer is that majority support for
the Government is contingent, not guaranteed, and the Government
must work hard to maintain it.[32] Even with a working majority, the
Government must contend with differences of opinion on its own backbenches, strong criticism from the Opposition, potential resistance in the
House of Lords, as well as critical media coverage and sceptical reactions
in the populace as a whole.[33]

---

[27] Russell & Gover (2017).
[28] Russell & Cowley (2016); Russell, Gover & Wollter (2016); Flinders & Kelso (2011);
Kalitowski (2008).
[29] Russell & Cowley (2016) 123; Mezey (1979) 26; Lovell (2003) 27.
[30] Russell & Gover (2017) 66-7.
[31] Russell & Cowley (2016) 126; Blondel (1970) (developing the idea of legislative 'viscosity'
where legislative power is measured by the extent to which it can resist Executive
proposals).
[32] Norton (2001) 24; Flinders (2002) 38; Gee & Webber (2013) 2141; Rhodes (2011) 38;
Webber (2014a) 478.
[33] Griffith, Ryle & Wheeler-Booth (1989) 16-17.

Thus, whilst the Government undoubtedly has the formal power and capacity to drive Bills through Parliament without concessions, it is inhibited from doing so by the need to expend political goodwill and precious parliamentary time.[34] At a surface glance, the confidence relationship between government and Parliament in Westminster systems suggests Executive dominance. But confidence cuts both ways. Executive dependence on Parliament for its continuance in office gives Parliament leverage over the government, enabling the legislature to extract concessions and compromises from the government in order to ease the legislative passage of its Bill.[35]

One reason why observers have assumed inveterate Executive dominance of the Westminster Parliament is the fact that the government rarely suffers an open defeat in the House of Commons, and rarely accepts amendments to its Bills moved by non-governmental actors. But the raw record of legislative success – and the official provenance of amendments apparently coming from the Government – are deeply misleading. Whilst the Government may seem to get its way almost all the time, it has already anticipated and accommodated parliamentary push-back at a much earlier stage of the policy-formation process. The Government 'does not put proposals to Parliament that it will not accept ... compromise is preferred over conflict'.[36] Similarly with amendments, the Government often adjusts and accommodates opposition to its legislative and policy priorities *ex ante*, in order to 'deflect more adversarial approaches'[37] on the floor of the House.

A common scenario is one where an Opposition MP agrees to withdraw an amendment when given assurances that the government Minister will 'reconsider' the issue and amend the legislation itself at a later stage.[38] The government has a strong reputational interest in avoiding the appearance of being defeated on the floor of the House of Commons. Therefore, it often prefers to move amendments itself, rather than let the Opposition visibly 'win'.[39] For its part, the Opposition often

---

[34] Laws (2016) 21; Norton (2001) 17, 24; Feldman (2004b) 110 (observing that opponents of a measure can use 'the ticking of the clock as a way of extracting concessions').
[35] Russell & Cowley (2016) 133.
[36] Ibid 133.
[37] Russell & Gover (2017) 109; Russell & Cowley (2016) 128.
[38] Russell & Gover (2017) 295; Regan (2012) 36–7.
[39] Thompson & McNulty (2018) 93.

agrees to such a 'reconsideration' in order to achieve meaningful policy change, even though a more openly combative stance would allow it to score cheap political points.[40]

Naturally, this arrangement creates the impression not only of parliamentary weakness, but also of Executive dominance, further fuelling the conventional wisdom that the Government can almost always get its way regardless of parliamentary opposition.[41] But this surface picture of Executive dominance and parliamentary impotence masks the subtle, but nonetheless significant, influence of non-governmental parliamentary actors in securing amendments and eliciting vital concessions from Government during the legislative process.[42] A failure to appreciate these complex intra-parliamentary dynamics has led previous generations of scholars to overstate government power and underestimate parliamentary influence in Westminster systems.[43]

Recent developments in the Westminster parliament take it even further from the 'old model of an adversarial, majoritarian Westminster'[44] where the Executive is a dominant, if not omnipotent, force. These include the introduction of a robust 'Select Committee' system in 1979;[45] the increasing independence of backbenchers;[46] the gradual weakening of party cohesion over the last forty years;[47] and the declining power of the whips.[48] Interestingly, the Government's own backbenchers emerge as 'pivotal voters' in the Westminster Parliament, where the interdependence between Government and backbenchers give the latter significant power and leverage.[49] Beneath the surface pattern of backbenchers visibly voting to 'back' the Government, there is a more complex, interactive dynamic

---

[40] Russell & Gover (2017) 89–91, 111–12; Manow & Burkhart (2007) (documenting an analogous process of 'legislative self-restraint' under divided government in Germany).

[41] Russell & Cowley (2016) 305.

[42] Zander (2018) 78; Russell & Gover (2017) 260ff.

[43] Russell & Cowley (2016) 126 ('The impact of retreats is far greater than the impact of defeats').

[44] Russell & Gover (2017) 90.

[45] Brazier & Fox (2011) 354; Benton & Russell (2012) 26; Kelly & Maer (2016) 140, 149–53 (showing how the Wright reforms of Select Committees in 2009 further strengthened their independence and effectiveness as a strong scrutinising force in the Westminster Parliament).

[46] Russell & Gover (2017) 120–1; Stuart (2018) 256–7.

[47] Russell & Gover (2017) 234.

[48] Stuart (2018) 255; Crewe (2015b) 128–34; Crewe (2015a) 8–10, 14–15; Rogers & Walters (2015) 81.

[49] Russell & Gover (2017) chapter 5.

where the Government is often willing to do deals with its backbenchers in order to win their support and goodwill.[50]

The disjuncture between formal powers and practical influence is also illustrated by the role of the House of Lords in the Westminster legislative process. Viewed in purely formal terms, the House of Lords seems weak because it 'only' possesses a delaying power, rather than a veto-power over proposed Bills. But whilst a power to delay or slow down the legislative process may look like a sign of weakness, we should not underestimate the political value of time and publicity as potent bargaining tools to leverage concessions in the legislative process.[51] Even though the House of Commons is entitled to bypass the House of Lords and ignore the remonstrations of unelected Peers, the House of Commons generally prefers to work with and through the Upper Chamber, either by seeking to persuade the Lords of the merits of the Bill or by offering concessions to accommodate their concerns.[52] This belies the claim that the House of Lords is a docile or peripheral actor. It also shows that 'a veto power is not essential for significant influence to occur'.[53] As political scientist Sabrina Kalitowski observes, 'although the Commons has "the final say", this does not preclude forms of negotiation'.[54]

Thus, whilst it is undeniable that the Government's policy proposals eventually find their way into law at Westminster, 'the assertion that the Executive is so dominant that it can discount the views of Parliament is not borne out by close analysis'.[55] The image of an omnipotent Executive which brooks no compromise and an obsequious Parliament which mounts no challenge is revealed as an over-simplification of a more complex and multifaceted institution, where iteration and interaction, contestation and collaboration all have a role to play.[56] Beneath the surface image of Executive supremacy and legislative submission lies a more complex and subtle process of 'intraparty negotiation on the government side, inter-cameral negotiation between Commons and Lords, the legislative process, and select committees'.[57]

---

[50] Russell & Cowley (2016) 125–7; Rhodes (2011) 39; Tushnet (2011b) 302, 306.
[51] Döring (1995); Russell & Gover (2017) 111; Crewe (2005) 190.
[52] Russell & Gover (2017) 28, 83; Crewe (2005) 190.
[53] Russell (2013) 61, 64, 162–4.
[54] Kalitowski (2008) 695–6; Russell (2013) chapter 7.
[55] Kalitowski (2008) 695.
[56] Flinders & Kelso (2011) 249; Russell & Cowley (2016) 134; Flinders (2002) 38–9.
[57] Russell & Cowley (2016) 132; on inter-cameral negotiation, see Russell (2013) chapter 7.

This suggests that the prospects for meaningful parliamentary engagement with rights may be stronger than Hiebert and Kelly suppose. If the Government is less dominant than is commonly assumed, and Parliament has meaningful power to push back, then there is good reason to believe that rights-based concerns will also be part of that accountability endeavour. Hiebert may be right that a government is unlikely to amend its legislation 'in light of a JCHR report *alone*'.[58] But that occludes *the accumulative accountability effect* which occurs when the JCHR acts in tandem with – indeed, in collaboration with – other accountability actors, including the House of Lords, the Opposition, disgruntled backbenchers, Select Committees, legal advisers, not to mention the thick ecosystem of civil society actors poised to raise their voice about rights.[59] The JCHR must be viewed in the context of that broader collaborative endeavour.[60] It is precisely when the JCHR works together 'in constitutional partnership'[61] with other parliamentary actors that its accountability effect is most potent.

The key issue here concerns the standards we use to assess Parliament's performance in protecting rights. Hiebert and Kelly pitch the promise of 'proactive legislative rights review'[62] in highly ambitious and demanding terms, imagining a flourishing legislative 'culture of rights',[63] where political actors 'prioritise the need to confront whether and how legislative initiatives implicated rights'[64] and engage in 'spirited normative debates about the scope of rights'[65] unsullied by pragmatic political or legal concerns. As they rightly observe, the realisation of such an ideal would require 'nothing short of a fundamental change to the very political culture that characterises a competitive, parliamentary and adversarial system of government'[66] in Westminster systems.

But whatever the political architects of the HRA meant when they succumbed to the soundbite that the HRA would create a 'culture of rights',[67] it seems unlikely that they envisaged a 'fundamental shift in

---

[58] Hiebert (2012) 40 (emphasis added); Hiebert (2011) 63.
[59] Russell & Gover (2017) 254–7.
[60] Ibid 234.
[61] Russell (2013) 199, 297.
[62] Hiebert & Kelly (2015) 16.
[63] Straw (1999); Irvine (2003a) 90, 98.
[64] Hiebert & Kelly (2015) 5.
[65] Ibid 16.
[66] Ibid 4, 16, 236, 259, 264, 392.
[67] Straw (1999).

how party leaders and parliamentarians operate'[68] in Westminster systems, still less a complete displacement of the central characteristics of 'Westminster-based parliamentary systems'.[69] The idea of a 'culture of rights' may simply have been a piece of political rhetoric to champion the achievement of the HRA in its early days.[70] Alternatively, it may have encapsulated the political aspiration to increase the salience and significance of rights concerns across all three branches of government, rather than leaving them entirely to the courts.

Measured against this more modest but, I believe, more realistic and appropriate metric, the gap between promise and performance narrows, and the record of meaningful rights engagement in the Executive and Parliament comes into view. As Carol Harlow observed, the HRA envisages that the courts and legislators will 'work together to develop a human rights culture ... *consonant with* the Westminster model of government'.[71] Increasing the salience of rights in shaping legislative outcomes does not require a radical reconfiguration of the parliamentary systems of government. Nor does it require a purified form of normative moral reasoning sublimely detached from questions of political strategy, expediency and electoral politics. Instead, it complicates the legislative process by adding a layer of rights-based political scrutiny and accountability into the Westminster system.

3 Legislating for Terror

The previous section outlined some key political dynamics in the Westminster Parliament. In this section, I illustrate those dynamics with a case-study on counter-terrorism in the post-9/11 era. In successive attempts to legislate for terror, parliamentarians successfully managed to use rights-based arguments in order to put pressure on the Government to moderate and ameliorate its initial legislative proposals.[72] True, parliamentary pushback did not succeed in stopping draconian counter-terrorist legislation in its tracks. Post-9/11, and especially after

---

[68] Hiebert & Kelly (2015) 16, 28.
[69] Ibid 10.
[70] Clements (2005) 35; JCHR, Sixth Report, *The Case for a Human Rights Commission*, HL (2002–3) 67, HC (2002–3) 489, [9] (observing that 'no public official (outside the Lord Chancellor's Department) interviewed in the course of this research could describe what was meant by a 'human rights culture').
[71] Harlow (2016) 155 (emphasis added).
[72] Tham (2010).

the London bombings, stringent counter-terrorist legislation came hard and fast. Nonetheless, I suggest that robust parliamentary engagement with rights shaved the worst excesses off proposed Bills, thereby helping to render them more compliant with rights.[73]

Consider the *Anti-Terrorism, Crime and Security Act 2002* (ATCSA), which sought to detain foreign terrorist suspects without trial on the basis that the UK was facing a 'public emergency threatening the life of the nation'.[74] Despite the speed with which the Bill was enacted,[75] the government faced strong rights-based opposition in Parliament. The Bill was subjected to a forensic analysis and strident critique by the JCHR.[76] It also incurred critical reports from the House of Commons Home Affairs Select Committee (HASC), the House of Lords Constitution Committee, the House of Commons Defence Committee, and the House of Lords Delegated Powers and Regulatory Review Committee.[77] It suffered bruising defeats in the House of Lords, where Peers used the power of publicity and the power of persuasion to draw attention to the serious civil liberties concerns raised by the Bill.

Given the opposition from multiple parliamentary actors, the Government eventually agreed four main concessions. First, the scope of the Secretary of State's power to certify an individual as a 'suspected international terrorist' was confined to cases where the Secretary of State *reasonably* believed the person's presence in the UK was a risk to national security.[78] Second, the Government agreed to submit the detention regime to periodic parliamentary review and a biannual review by a Committee of the Privy Counsellors (which subsequently became the Newton Committee) appointed for that purpose.[79] Third, it agreed to create a Special Immigration Appeals Commission in which a senior judge would hear challenges to the Home Secretary's orders to declare suspected foreign nationals as 'international terrorists', with a right of appeal to the

---

[73] Kavanagh (2009c).

[74] Kavanagh (2011).

[75] Tomkins (2002b) 205 (observing that the Bill was allotted just sixteen hours in the House of Commons, though it took nine days to pass through its various stages, following proposed amendments from the House of Lords).

[76] JCHR, First Report, HL (2001–2) 37; HC (2001–2) 372; Second Report: HL (2001–2) 51; HC (2001–2) 420.

[77] Hiebert & Kelly (2015) 308–9; Tomkins (2011) 19.

[78] Fenwick & Phillipson (2011) 864ff; Tomkins (2002b) 211.

[79] Tomkins (2002b) 211.

Court of Appeal on points of law.[80] Fourth, the power of detention was accompanied by a sunset clause, which would expire in fifteen months unless the Secretary of State extended it for twelve-month periods through a statutory instrument.[81] By reversing the burden of legislative inertia, this significantly enhanced the likelihood that this controversial measure would lapse unless the political stars aligned for the government.[82]

To be sure, neither the JCHR – nor any other single actor within Parliament – prevented the Government from enacting this severe counter-terrorist measure which undoubtedly put pressure on rights. Nonetheless, these concessions were both significant and consequential. The sunset clause was deeply instrumental in leading to the demise of the policy in later years. When the Judicial Committee of the House of Lords (as it then was) held that the indefinite detention of non-national terror suspects without trial violated rights in the *Belmarsh* case,[83] the court cited the chorus of critical voices within Parliament to bolster its decision, including those of the JCHR, the Newton Committee, and an array of international human rights bodies which opposed the policy of indefinite detention without trial.[84]

Similarly, when the *Terrorism Bill 2005* purported to increase the period of detention without charge for terrorist suspects from fourteen to ninety days,[85] Parliament managed to reduce this period to twenty-eight days,[86] and subsequently fourteen days.[87] The proposal to introduce a ninety-day detention without trial was roundly criticised by NGOs, judges, academics, and members of the legal profession.[88] It was also subjected to trenchant criticism by a number of parliamentary committees, including the JCHR, and it engendered strong opposition across both Houses of Parliament.[89] The government suffered a landmark defeat in the House of Commons, where a total of forty government backbenchers – including eleven former Ministers – defied

---

[80] Hiebert & Kelly (2015) 310.
[81] ATCSA section 29. For insightful analysis of sunset clauses in the counter-terrorism context, see Ip (2013) 80.
[82] Ip (2013) 74.
[83] *A (and others) v SSHD* [2004] UKHL 56 (hereafter *Belmarsh*).
[84] Ibid Lord Bingham.
[85] Hiebert & Kelly (2015) 321.
[86] Terrorism Act 2006, section 23.
[87] Ibid, section 25.
[88] Rozenberg (2005).
[89] Feldman (2006) 380.

a three-line whip and voted against the government on this issue.[90] In the end, the government agreed to reduce the period of detention, combined with an additional concession that the power would be subject to annual renewal by Parliament, whereby a failure to secure subsequent parliamentary approval would mean that the detention period would revert back to fourteen days.[91]

A number of instructive points emerge from these examples of Executive and legislative interaction at the point where counter-terrorism and constitutional rights meet. First, whilst parliamentary opposition did not 'divert government from pursuing a Bill to which it was deeply committed',[92] it nonetheless compelled the Government to accept concessions, compromises and hard-won amendments which moderated the Government's original proposals, sometimes in significant ways. These episodes reveal that Parliament is not a menial supplicant with no power to resist. Instead, it is a complex institution comprising a multiplicity of accountability actors who, together, can bring considerable pressure to bear on the government's key policy initiatives.

Second, although it is tempting to dismiss some of these amendments as procedural niceties of marginal importance, that would be a grave mistake. To dismiss these concessions as mere technicalities underestimates the potency of procedural safeguards in upholding rights. It also obscures the way in which those procedural requirements can enable accountability actors across Parliament to leverage broader concessions within a statutory regime. For example, the sunset clause included in ATCSA 2002 was pivotal to the eventual demise of indefinite detention without trial for foreign terrorist suspects in UK law.[93] Sunset clauses and parliamentary reviews increase the 'viscosity'[94] of the legislative process. They slow the Executive down by putting political impediments and justificatory pressures firmly in its path. We should never underestimate the power of *constitutional slowdown* in the legislative process.

Third, even in the context of legislating to combat terrorism, the accountability actors within Parliament are at their strongest when working together in collaboration, rather than in isolation. When parliamentary actors combined forces – including the JCHR, Peers from the

---

[90] Hiebert & Kelly (2015) 322.
[91] Terrorism Act 2006, section 25.
[92] Hiebert & Kelly (2015) 300.
[93] Ip (2013).
[94] Blondel (1970).

House of Lords, the HL Constitutional Committee, Opposition MPs, together with more tailored accountability actors such as the Independent Reviewer of Terrorism Legislation, the Newton Committee on Counter-Terrorism, not to mention broader civil society actors – they managed to extract significant concessions from the Government, attenuating the Government's initial proposals and rendering them more rights compliant.[95] As the Independent Reviewer for Terrorism Legislation, David Anderson QC, insightfully observed: 'few of those actors are decisive in isolation; it is their inter-relationship with each other and with the Government that is crucial'.[96] Showing how different streams of legislative influence can 'run through a variety of channels, intersecting and reinforcing one another',[97] Anderson argued that these channels are best viewed 'not as competitors to each other but as subtly inter-related, often divergent but at their most effective when influencing and flowing alongside each other'.[98] The counter-terrorist context thus provides a vivid illustration of the accumulative accountability dynamics within the Westminster Parliament. It shows the collaborative nature of parliamentary influence on the law-making process.[99]

Finally, whilst this chapter focuses on the legislative process, we should remember that the courts are also part of the accountability architecture in the British constitutional order, where the legal accountability provided by the courts complements, supplements and sometimes strengthens the channels of political accountability in Parliament. The constitutional response to counter-terrorism post-9/11 illustrates how judicial and parliamentary methods of accountability work in tandem as part of the collaborative enterprise of protecting and promoting rights.[100]

Rather than thinking of the political and legal channels of accountability as running on separate tracks – or as set on a constitutional collision course – we should appreciate the political and legal channels of accountability as part of a 'mutually reinforcing matrix of interaction',[101] where 'overlapping remedial channels ... together

---

[95] Anderson (2014) 414; Tomkins (2011); Davis & de Londras (2014b).
[96] Anderson (2014) 414; Blackbourn (2012).
[97] Anderson (2014) 215.
[98] Anderson (2014) 415; de Londras & Davis (2010) 20; Phillipson (2013) 271–9.
[99] Horne & Walker (2014) 203; Bamforth (2013) 266; Phillipson (2013) 272.
[100] Bamforth (2013) 266; Kavanagh (2019) 69.
[101] Hickman (2005b) 1016; Anderson (2014) 413–14.

facilitate and control governance of the state'.[102] In short, judges and parliamentarians are engaged in a 'joint, collaborative enterprise of seeking to hold the national security executive in check'.[103]

4   Legislative Decision, Judicial Distortion, Democratic Debilitation

Given the immense power of the Executive to shake off the shackles of constitutional constraint, the threat of a rising juristocracy must surely pale in comparison.[104] However, an overreaching judiciary can certainly distort democratic decision-making. Therefore, we must take the charge of judicial distortion with the seriousness it deserves. We may want judges to uphold rights, but we do not want 'government by judiciary'.[105]

In an influential analysis, Mark Tushnet argued that even when courts lack the power to veto or strike down legislation, they may nonetheless exercise two subtle but insidious forms of judicial domination which he labelled *policy distortion* and *democratic debilitation*.[106] *Policy distortion* occurs 'when legislators who would otherwise articulate their own constitutional norms instead choose to follow the norms the courts articulate',[107] thereby allowing judicial decisions to 'supplant ... legislative consideration of other arguably more important matters'.[108] Instead of exercising their own normative judgement about what rights require, the worry is that legislators will 'slavishly adopt the *dicta* and dictates of the courts', thus treating court rulings 'as dispositive'[109] about rights.[110] In doing so, the political actors succumb to a cringing 'court mimicry',[111]

---

[102] Poole (2007b) 273.
[103] Phillipson (2014) 273.
[104] Chapter 1, this vol.
[105] Berger (1997).
[106] Tushnet (1995).
[107] Ibid 260; King (2012) 251–3.
[108] Tushnet (1995) 247; Sunstein (1993) 145.
[109] Tushnet (1995) 265; Yap (2015) 29.
[110] For expressions of this concern in the UK context, see Campbell, Ewing & Tomkins (2011) 1, 5; Campbell (2011) 468–9; Davis (2010).
[111] On the danger of legal advisers within the Executive branch adopting a 'quasi-judicial' or 'court-mimicking' approach, see Kenny & Casey (2020) 69, 71; Casey & Kenny (2022) 12–14; Hiebert (2002) 52–4; Tushnet (2008b) 173.

which unduly constrains political decision-making and crowds out broader political, ethical, and moral analysis.[112] As Janet Hiebert pithily observed, the worry here is that 'governing with judges means governing like judges'.[113]

Democratic debilitation expresses a different concern, namely, that rights-based review will encourage the legislature to abdicate its own responsibility, leaving the courts to do the heavy lifting in relation to rights.[114] This outsourcing of rights could manifest in different political ways. On the one hand, the existence of rights-based review might induce a kind of legislative laziness where the political actors will say: 'why bother about rights in the legislative process if the courts will pick up the slack during the litigation process?'[115] Alternatively, the legislature could develop a kind of learnt helplessness, becoming acculturated in the belief that it is not their job to worry about rights. More cynically, the political actors could adopt a cavalier attitude, pushing the boundaries of rights as far as they will go. If the courts declare the resulting law to be incompatible with rights, so be it. Whether by kow-towing acquiescence or cavalier abdication, policy distortion and democratic debilitation are likely to lead to a more 'juridical form of constitutionalism'.[116]

Did either of these pathologies afflict Executive and legislative decision making about rights in the post-HRA era? Before answering the question directly, I want to enter two words of caution. First, if policy distortion or debilitation occurs, it will typically take effect by way of legislative self-restraint or 'auto-limitation'.[117] After all, on Tushnet's definition, policy distortion occurs when legislators are constitutionally *empowered* to articulate their own norms, but instead *choose to follow* the norms laid down by courts.[118] Similarly, democratic debilitation occurs when legislators decide to leave it to the courts, or at least acquiesces in that state of affairs. Therefore, even if the courts end up 'dominating' legislative reasoning, the drivers of dominance will be of a subtle and complex variety, often

---

[112] Renan (2017) 894.
[113] Hiebert (2011) 40; Stone Sweet (2000) 204; Goldsworthy (2010) 271; Sathanapally (2012) 68–70; Renan (2017) 894; Waldron (2009) 23.
[114] Tushnet (1995) 247.
[115] Sadurski (2002) 286–7.
[116] Hiebert (2011) 41.
[117] Stone Sweet (2000) 75–9; Stone Sweet (2007) 87; Hiebert (2011) 44.
[118] King (2012) 252.

involving an active decision by legislators to comply with judicial decisions even though they are not legally required to do so. If governments and legislatures 'slavishly submit'[119] to judicial decisions, there may be an element of self-enslavement – or at least self-restraint – involved.

Second, as presented in the theoretical literature, the dangers of distortion and debilitation are hypothetical speculations about what *might* occur, not empirical claims about what *actually* occurs in any particular constitutional system.[120] Whilst it is certainly possible that constitutional review *might* induce the legislature to defer blindly to the courts, or to abdicate its own responsibility for rights, it is equally plausible – at least as a null hypothesis – that it might strengthen, rather than sap, legislators' commitment to uphold rights.[121] After all, one of the common reasons for having a reviewing or 'second-look' mechanism in any institutional design is to create a 'sentinel effect'[122] i.e. that anticipation of being reviewed will make the primary decision-maker more diligent and conscientious when making the original decision. This opens up the possibility that rights-based review might stimulate *enhanced* legislative attentiveness to rights. Therefore, when assessing the claims about distortion and debilitation, we need to remember that they are hypothetical conjectures which require empirical testing, not universal normative truths.[123] With these caveats in place, let us turn to assess the danger of legislative debilitation, before going on to test for judicial distortion of legislative priorities.

5   Detecting Debilitation?

Democratic debilitation denotes an outsourcing of responsibility for rights by the legislature to the courts. In the post-HRA era, have the political actors vacated the field and left the protection of rights to litigation in the courts, rather than legislation in Parliament? Whilst there is certainly room for discussion about the breadth and depth of

---

[119] Webber (2009) 457.

[120] Tushnet carefully frames his argument in a contingent or speculative way about what 'may' or 'might' occur, see Tushnet (1995) 247–8, 275, 283–4; see also Bickel (1986) 23; Sunstein (1993) 145; Waldron (2016) 1403.

[121] Kyritsis (2017) 53; Landau (2018) 49; Schauer (2018) 649–50.

[122] Vermeule (2011) 1464; Kumm (2010) 163; Jackson (2015) 3146; Appleby (2012) 397.

[123] Dixon (2017) 2231.

political engagement with rights post-HRA, a diagnosis of democratic debilitation seems overdone.

When the HRA was enacted, the Government could have made no effort to incorporate rigorous rights-vetting into the policy-formation stages of the pre-legislative and legislative process, leaving it instead to the courts to catch any problems as they arise. They did not adopt this approach.[124] Right from the outset, the message from central government was that all departments should take responsibility for safeguarding rights when developing policy and proposing Bills. The Lord Chancellor's Department (as it then was)[125] explicitly advised Departments *not* to rely on judicial powers of creative interpretation to 'justify shoddy or incomplete drafting'[126] on issues concerning rights. Instead, the government required all departments to produce a rights memorandum containing a 'frank assessment'[127] of the risk of legal and policy challenge. This helped to embed rights reasoning into the heart of the policy-making process. Whilst there was certainly a danger of the Government 'risking rights' in order to 'see whether it gets away with it',[128] this was 'not the usual attitude'.[129] Though undoubtedly variable in terms of quality and quantity, there is evidence of serious good-faith engagement with rights within the Executive and legislative branches. This belies a 'devil may care' attitude when it comes to rights. Even if governments occasionally try to 'chance their arms',[130] the picture is not one of outright abdication.[131]

When section 19 HRA was enacted, there were fears that it might become a 'parrot provision'[132] – a tick-box exercise where the government would claim compatibility with rights as a matter of course. But this

---

[124] Feldman (2004b) 110.

[125] This has now been disbanded and subsumed within the Department of Justice.

[126] Feldman (2004b) 103.

[127] Cabinet Office, *Guide to Making Legislation* (2022) [12.11], www.gov.uk/government/publications/guide-to-making-legislation.

[128] Feldman (2004b) 110.

[129] Ibid 110.

[130] Ibid 93.

[131] Hunt (2021) 16 (observing that in communication between the Government and the JCHR, the Government sometimes resisted putting more explicit safeguards for rights into Bills on the basis that the courts could supply them through interpretation under section 3 HRA).

[132] Klug (2005) 199; Sedley (2008) 21; Lester (2002a) 76.

did not transpire. Though it was not legally obliged to do so, the government integrated rights-based reasoning into the pre-legislative process. Many commentators agree that the section 19 Ministerial Reporting requirement under the HRA has given rise to a more systematic and detailed pre-legislative review of whether Bills are compliant with rights than existed pre-HRA.[133]

As regards parliamentary actors, the picture regarding potential debilitation is more complex. However, it seems that concerns about rights are 'gaining in influence'[134] across Parliament. A lot of evidence points towards 'Parliament's growing awareness of its responsibilities for human rights when carrying out its legislative functions'.[135] If democratic debilitation occurs when 'democratically elected representatives cease to formulate and discuss constitutional norms, instead relying on the courts to address constitutional problems',[136] then we can say with some confidence that does not accurately capture the current state of play in the Westminster Parliament. Without any legal obligation to do so, Parliament voluntarily set up a specialised, non-partisan parliamentary committee (the JCHR) specifically designed to alert parliamentarians to rights-based concerns and enhance parliamentary accountability for their protection. It also set up the House of Lords Constitution Committee to examine all Bills for compliance with constitutional principles.[137] Together, these Committees provide sustained and systematic scrutiny of government decision making and legislative proposals for compliance with rights, the rule of law and broader constitutional principles.[138] Instead of debilitation, we see Parliament integrating rights-based accountability mechanisms into the checks and balances within the legislative branch.

Of course, there is plenty of room to question whether these parliamentary guardians of rights have succeeded in mainstreaming rights across Parliament. On any view, this mainstreaming effort is a challenging, long-term project.[139] Nonetheless, the rigorous scrutiny provided

---

[133] Hiebert & Kelly (2015) 88; Feldman (2004b); Tomkins (2011); Hunt, Hooper & Yowell (2012).
[134] Feldman (2004b) 91.
[135] Ibid 93.
[136] Tushnet (1995) 275.
[137] https://committees.parliament.uk/committee/172/constitution-committee/ Caird (2012).
[138] Feldman (2004b) 97.
[139] Hunt (2010) 601; Hunt (2013) 247–8; Feldman (2004b) 114.

by these Committees – together with their interaction with a multiplicity of actors across Government and Parliament – belie the claim that Parliament has 'ceased to formulate and discuss constitutional norms',[140] outsourcing such considerations to the courts. Instead, they bespeak a determination to bring rights into the heart of executive and legislative decision-making in order to ensure that rights are protected at source, when policy is being proposed, scrutinised and enacted into law. Indirectly, the JCHR, the Constitution Committee, and other account-ability actors subtly change the parliamentary environment in which laws are enacted, increasing the onus on government to justify its legislative proposals in terms of rights.[141] Instead of debilitation, what we see is enhanced deliberation about rights in the Executive and legislative domains.[142]

6   Discerning Distortion?

If debilitation has not occurred to a substantial degree, what about policy distortion? The worry about judicial distortion of legislative reasoning about rights raises the spectre of political actors succumbing to a cringing 'court mimicry',[143] where judicial rulings have a 'chilling effect'[144] on worthwhile social policies. This is an important issue, not least because the fear about policy distortion underpins a number of normative pre-scriptions that political actors should make a 'full and free legislative judgment about potential rights issue . . . informed by, but not limited to, the types of legal reasoning found . . . in judicial decisions'.[145] Indeed, some scholars argue that political actors should make 'an independent judgment about the merits of legislation . . . without necessarily worrying about whether this political judgment is likely to lead to litigation and judicial censure'.[146]

In order to assess the plausibility of these claims, we need to articulate some normative baselines about whether the political actors

---

[140] Tushnet (1995) 275.
[141] Feldman (2004a) 643.
[142] Hunt, Hooper & Yowell (2012); Yowell (2015).
[143] Casey & Kenny (2022) 12.
[144] Ibid 12; Gyorfi (2016) 240.
[145] Gardbaum (2013b) 82; Hiebert & Kelly (2015) 16.
[146] Hiebert & Kelly (2015) 257.

should consider the likelihood of adverse judicial rulings when proposing and enacting legislation. After all, if we think that judicial
decisions should have no role whatsoever in informing, influencing,
or constraining legislative reasoning, then we will code any such
influence as illegitimate policy distortion.[147] Alternatively, if we
believe that legislatures should sometimes comply with court rulings
on rights – i.e. because it usefully deflects political actors away from
'constitutionally suspect action'[148] – then a more differentiated picture
emerges, with some forms of influence being lauded as legitimate
compliance, whilst others are castigated as illegitimate policy
distortion.[149] The line between constitutional compliance and policy
distortion may be 'fluid and debatable',[150] but we need to put some
markers down if we want to gain traction on the crux questions
concerning the danger of distortion.

Let us begin by posing the open normative question: what role, if
any, *should* judicial decisions on rights play in executive and legislative
decision-making which implicates those rights? A number of options
present themselves. In some contexts, there will be a clear judicial decision directly on point. But on many issues which come up for legislative
deliberation, there will be no pertinent judicial decision bearing directly
on the question, either because it has not arisen in litigation or because
the law is indeterminate or in flux. How should political actors respond
to these possibilities? Should they be oblivious to court rulings on rights,
thus forming their own 'independent' viewpoint on rights without con-
tamination from the courts? Or should they consider judicial rulings but
treat them as optional suggestions they can take or leave as they see fit?
Alternatively, should they treat them as authoritative rulings with binding effect?

I suggest the following approach, grounded in the principles and
practice of the collaborative constitution. If there is a clear judicial
ruling on an issue directly implicated in a proposed legislative provision, the Executive and legislature should operate a general

---

[147] Sathanapally (2012) 73; King (2012) 252; Yap (2015) 24.

[148] Kenny & Casey (2020) 72.

[149] On the need to articulate meaningful normative baselines to differentiate policy distortion from 'the enactment of policies consistent with the constitution's requirements', see
Tushnet (1995) 254, 252, 253–5; Casey & Kenny (2022) 29; Yap (2015) 24.

[150] Kenny & Casey (2020) 73.

presumption of respecting and complying with that ruling. The reason for such a presumption lies in the principle of comity articulated in Chapter 3, namely, the duty of mutual respect which the branches of government owe each other as constitutional partners in authority. In the constitutional division of labour, the courts are given the role of making authoritative rulings on what the law requires in the context of an individual dispute. Given this role, it is incumbent on the political branches of government to respect those rulings and presume – unless there are exceptional and weighty reasons to do otherwise – that they should uphold and comply with them. This duty is given institutional expression in the Ministerial Code, where Ministers in the UK Parliament are under an obligation to comply with the law, including court rulings.[151] Indeed, the authority and integrity of an independent judiciary depends on the Executive and legislature giving credence to judicial decisions as authoritative rulings, not optional suggestions.

Therefore, if there is a clear ruling on rights, it is constitutionally appropriate for the Executive and legislature to operate a presumption in favour of complying with that ruling when proposing and enacting legislation. Not only does this evince respect for the courts as a constitutional partner in authority, it also respects the division of labour on which the constitutional system rests. Empirical analyses of the bureaucratic and legislative process in Whitehall and Westminster reveal that there are 'strong political expectations of compliance with negative judicial rulings'.[152] Whilst some might portray this presumptive compliance with court rulings as evidence of a cringing 'court mimicry'[153], it can be framed otherwise, namely, as evidence of mutual respect between the branches of government in a collaborative constitutional scheme.

Thus far, we have dealt with those situations where there is a clear judicial ruling on an issue directly pertinent to a legislative scheme. What about the scenario where there is no clear ruling directly on

---

[151] *Ministerial Code*, 27 May 2022, refers to the 'overarching duty on Ministers to comply with the law and to protect the integrity of public life' [1.3], see: Ministerial Code, www .gov.uk/government/publications/ministerial-code.

[152] Hiebert & Kelly (2015) 266, 403–5.

[153] Casey & Kenny (2022) 12; Casey (2021) 292; Hiebert & Kelly (2015) 16–17.

point? When the legal terrain is untilled by the courts, there is plenty of room for political actors to decide how to proceed. I see no reason why they should be bound by what the courts may or may not decide in a hypothetical future decision. As a former legal adviser to the British Foreign Office put it, the Government 'is entitled to act on the basis of the law as it is, not required to act on the basis of the law as it might evolve to become at some point in the future'.[154] When the law is indeterminate or in flux, legal advisers should flag the level of legal risk.[155] But it is up to the political actors to make the final call about how much risk they wish to bear as part of a 'holistic'[156] assessment combining all the relevant legal, political and policy considerations.

Should political actors automatically withdraw a legislative provision whenever there is the slightest threat of an adverse judicial ruling on the horizon? No. But should they give serious consideration to the potential costs and benefits of enacting the provision which carries an appreciable or even significant risk of judicial censure? Absolutely. Litigation is costly, time-consuming and labour-intensive, not only for litigants but also for the Government, the courts and the taxpayer at large. Therefore, a desire to avoid unnecessary litigation is not necessarily evidence of slavish submission to a lawyerly elite. It could be viewed instead as part of a constitutionally appropriate sense of legislative responsibility to keep within the bounds of the law, whilst avoiding the burdens of costly and unnecessary litigation. On this view, striving to ensure that legislation is not vulnerable to easy challenge in the courts is both a prudent and a principled concern,[157] especially in situations where a potential incursion on rights can be removed prophylactically at no significant cost to the overall policy objective.[158]

When considering the worry about judicial decisions 'supplanting' legislative consideration of rights, we have to recall that many Bills raise no rights concerns at all or, if they do, they implicate rights in a marginal

---

[154] Bethlehem (2012) 33.
[155] Renan (2017) 873–5, 893.
[156] Appleby (2017) 168.
[157] Hiebert & Kelly (2015) 266.
[158] Ibid 266; Feldman (2004b) 112.

or tangential way. As a former Legal Adviser to the JCHR observed, 'most Bills have objectives which are capable of being pursued in a manner which respects human rights',[159] and many potential rights-violations can be easily averted 'without significant alteration to the scope of the legislative objective'.[160]

Even when there is a clear judicial authority directly on point, we should beware of exaggerating the scope and normative finality of the decision. As Jeff King observed, UK courts

> hardly try to provide expansive or exhaustive definitions of the rights. Rather, they give case-by-case indications of how particular policies fail to comply with abstract rights, leaving much undecided both at the normative stage and in particular at the constructive remedial stage . . . So the 'normative finality' accepted by Parliament . . . is in fact a small part of the normative scope of the right and balancing exercise associated with it.[161]

Given the relatively narrow scope of many judicial rulings on rights, together with the absence of case-law on many issues, the threat of judicial decisions 'supplanting' executive or legislative reasoning about rights is modest at best.

Finally, the government's Guidance to Departments on Legislation is that a Statement of Compatibility should not to be made unless the Minister is satisfied that 'the balance of arguments favours the view that the Bill is likely to survive Convention scrutiny in the courts,'[162] in other words, that it is 'more likely than not that the provisions of the Bill will stand up to legal challenge'.[163] This does not seem like an unduly risk-averse approach.[164] Nor does it suggest a slavish submission to judicial decisions. In fact, it leaves considerable latitude for legislative deliberation about how rights should shape legislative outcomes, beyond what the courts have said or might say in the future.[165]

---

[159] Feldman (2002b) 337.
[160] Hiebert & Kelly (2015) 296.
[161] King (2015a) 177; Sathanapally (2012) 73.
[162] Feldman (2004b) 98–9.
[163] Ibid 100.
[164] Though the legal advice on Convention compatibility may have been unduly risk-averse in the early days of devising the ECHR memorandum, that approach has now been changed, see Hiebert & Kelly (2015) 272–3.
[165] MacDonnell (2015) 396.

When we look at parliamentary debate responding to court rulings on rights, there is very little evidence that legislative deliberation about rights has been supplanted or suffocated by a legalistic focus on judicial doctrine. When examining Parliament's responses to judicial declarations of incompatibility, Jeff King observed that 'we must look with diligence to find any reference to judicial decisions in most parliamentary debates, and in a few cases there is none at all'.[166] Leading empirical studies support the conclusion that judicial declarations of incompatibility have had a relatively 'low profile'[167] in Parliament, with 'almost no engagement with the judicial reasoning itself'.[168] When legal decisions were mentioned in parliamentary debate, they were 'almost always advanced *in tandem* with arguments that the measures violated fundamental political principles and were morally acceptable'.[169] As Aruna Sathanapally observed, they

> did not replace political with court-centred conceptions of human rights, but rather gave parliamentarians additional support for rights-based arguments in some circumstances.[170]

In a political climate which is hostile to rights, it may not come as any surprise to hear that parliamentary debate is neither overawed nor overwhelmed by a fixation on judicial decision-making about rights.[171] As one commentator wryly observed, no one could accuse UK parliamentarians of 'unquestioning genuflexion to Strasbourg norms'.[172]

All told, it is hard to accept the hypothesis that judges 'dominate' legislative deliberation in the UK, or that legislators operate in the dark shadow of judicial decisions about rights.[173] To speak of shadows in this context is to presuppose an ominous influence which puts legislatures in the shade whilst leaving courts in the limelight. But there is nothing

---

[166] King (2015a) 185.
[167] Sathanapally (2012) 131, 138, 169–72, 185, 196–9 (providing an empirical riposte to the suggestion that the political branches have been dominated by judges post-HRA); King (2015a); Hunt (2021) 13–14.
[168] King (2015a) 181.
[169] Sathanapally (2012) 198.
[170] Ibid 199; Jai (1996) 10.
[171] King (2015a) 187.
[172] Nicol (2004b) 463.
[173] Tushnet (1995) 265; Kenny & Casey (2020) 69; Windsor (2013) 117; Sadurski (2002) 285.

necessarily shady going on here. Whilst the fear of policy distortion and debilitation is commonly shrouded in the language of shadows and censure, it can be phrased otherwise – as a constitutionally appropriate degree of respect for a coordinate branch. Legislative respect for judicial rulings does not necessarily take us to the constitutional 'dark side'.[174] Instead, it could simply be one aspect of a collaborative constitutional dynamic, where courts make authoritative rulings on a case-by-case basis – often on narrowly focused issues – while the Government and Parliament propose and enact legislation which strives to be compatible with rights and respectful of judicial decisions about what those rights require. Viewed from the perspective of this normative baseline, a compliance-oriented perspective does not necessarily signify subjugation. Instead, it suggests constructive engagement in a collaborative endeavour, where working relationships between and within the branches are based on mutual respect and support.

7 Claiming Compatibility: A Case-Study of Money in Politics

When putting legislative proposals before Parliament, the government operates a 'strong presumption'[175] in favour of making a positive Statement of Compatibility under section 19. Indeed, in the twenty years the HRA has been in force, there have only been four instances where a Bill was introduced to Parliament without an accompanying positive Statement of Compatibility under section 19(1)(a).[176] Therefore, a negative statement of incompatibility under section 19(1)(b) – or, more accurately, a statement that the Government wishes to proceed with a Bill notwithstanding the fact that it seems to contravene rights – has very much been the exception rather than the rule.

In this section, I will provide a case-study of the Communications Bill 2002, which concerned the role of paid political advertising. As one of the foremost examples where the government relied on s. 19(1)(b), it is worth examining it in detail to see what it tells us about the Executive and legislative approach to their obligations under the HRA.

---

[174] Kenny & Casey (2020) 58, 69.
[175] Hiebert & Kelly (2015) 274.
[176] Local Government Bill 2000 (repealed three years later); Communications Bill 2002; House of Lords Reofrm Bill 2012 (subsequently abandoned); Illegal Migration Bill 2023. See further Hiebert & Kelly (2015) 278–9.

The Communications Bill 2002 contained a provision which banned paid political advertising across all broadcast media. The question, then, was whether this ban was compliant with freedom of expression as guaranteed under Article 10 ECHR.[177] The European Court of Human Rights had very recently handed down a ruling against Switzerland in VgT[178] holding that such a ban contravened the right to freedom of expression. Therefore, it was highly likely that the domestic and Strasbourg courts would follow this precedent and declare the Communications Act to be incompatible with Convention rights.

When introducing the Communications Bill to the House of Commons, the proposing Minister (Tessa Jowell MP) announced that because of the ruling in VgT, the government's legal advisers had flagged a 'significant risk'[179] that the provision would lead to a finding of incompatibility before the courts. Whilst the government believed that the ban was justifiable and 'necessary in a democratic society',[180] it felt unable to make a positive Statement of Compatibility under section 19. The Minister affirmed that the government had not taken this route lightly, emphasising that proposing a Bill without a positive Statement of Compatibility under section 19 was an 'obviously exceptional'[181] course, which had only been contemplated 'after careful deliberation and a full examination of both the legal arguments and the policy alternatives'.[182] The government had

> looked hard at the current ban to see whether some minor changes would make it more certain that it was human rights compatible. Unfortunately, any such change would still allow substantial political advertising ... By denying powerful interests the chance to skew political debate, the current ban safeguards the public and democratic debate, and protects the impartiality of broadcasters.[183]

---

[177] *Animal Defenders International v Secretary of State for Culture, Media and Sport* [2008] UKHL 15.

[178] *Verein Gegen Tier Fabriken (VgT) v Switzerland* (2001) 34 EHRR 159.

[179] Feldman (2004b) 99.

[180] HC Deb 3 December 2002, vol 501 cols 787–9 (Tessa Jowell) (clarifying that the Draft Communications Bill was the product of cross-departmental collaboration between the Department of Trade, the Department of Culture, Media and Sport as well as the Department for E-Commerce and Competitiveness).

[181] Ibid.

[182] Ibid.

[183] Ibid.

Given the concern about rights, the Government published a draft version of the Bill, which received an 'almost unprecedented'[184] level of pre-legislative scrutiny and consultation. During the pre-legislative process, the JCHR reviewed the draft Bill and warned that a complete ban on political advertising might not withstand judicial scrutiny under the Convention.[185] Nonetheless, rather than treating the Strasbourg ruling in *VgT* as dispositive or determinative on the issue, the JCHR shared the Government's concerns that allowing paid political advertising in the UK might lead to 'the annexation of the democratic process by the rich and powerful'.[186] In a constructive and iterative exchange between the government and the JCHR, the JCHR urged the government to explore the possibility of devising a more circumscribed ban.[187] The government explored the options, but ultimately concluded that a compromise solution would be unworkable.[188]

The Communications Bill was also scrutinised by the Joint Committee on the Draft Communications Bill, which was specifically created to provide focused, subject-specific legislative scrutiny of the Bill. This Committee ultimately endorsed the central principles of the Bill.[189] Moreover, the Independent Television Commission (a body with overall responsibility for commercial television) wrote to the Government emphasising the value of preserving the existing ban on political advertising whilst highlighting its view that anything short of a complete ban would prove to be unworkable in practice.[190] Finally, the Minister clarified that although the Government would robustly defend the legislation in court as compatible with the Convention and 'necessary in a

---

[184] HC Deb 3 December 2002, vol 395 cols 782–3 (Tessa Jowell).
[185] JCHR, Nineteenth Report of the Session 2001–2 (19 July 2002, HL Paper No 149, HC 1102), considered in *Animal Defenders* (n 177) [14], [32].
[186] JCHR, 19th Report, Session 2001–2, HL 149/HC 1102; *Animal Defenders* (n 177) [14], [63].
[187] JCHR 19 July 2002, HL Paper No 149 HC 1102 [62]–[64].
[188] Explanatory Note for the House of Commons Library, contained in JCHR, 19th Report paras. 7–8. There was a longstanding resistance to paid political advertising in the British broadcast media throughout the twentieth century, see *Committee on Standards in Public Life* (Neill Committee) in 1998, Fifth Report, 'The Funding of Political Parties in the United Kingdom', Cm 4057-I (1998), R94, pp. 173–4; Lewis & Cumper (2009) 92–3.
[189] Joint Committee on the Draft Communications Bill, 25 July 2002, HL Paper 169-I; HC 876-I [301], cited in *Animal Defenders* (n 177) [15].
[190] Letter, 10 October 2002, by Sir Robin Biggam, chairman of the Independent Television Commission (ITC), cited in *Animal Defenders* (n 177) [16], together with the iterative correspondence between the Government and the ITC on the issue of political advertising.

democratic society' under Article 10(2), it would nonetheless respect the decisions of the courts and amend the ban if it was deemed to violate Convention rights.[191]

As the Bill went through Parliament, the JCHR pressed the Government to justify its stance that a complete ban was necessary to give effect to the Government's policy aim.[192] The Government responded that it had explored the possibility of more tailored approaches, but it could not devise a fair and workable scheme of partial political advertising that would adequately secure the legitimate aim of preventing wealthy interests from distorting democratic debate by buying political influence on the broadcast media.[193] Having considered the government's responses in this constructive iterative exchange, the JCHR concluded it was satisfied that the course of action taken by the government evinced no lack of respect for human rights, and was legitimate and proportionate in the circumstances.[194] The Independent Electoral Commission also reported that the UK's case for retaining the ban on paid advertising was persuasive and justifiable in the public interest.[195] The ban on political advertising commanded cross-party support in Parliament and was not subject to amendment in either House.[196] It was duly passed into law as the Communications Act 2003.

What does this episode reveal about the Executive and parliamentary engagement with rights in the post-HRA era? First, by emphasising the exceptional nature of the decision to propose a Bill to Parliament without a positive Statement of Compatibility, the Government signalled the seriousness of proposing a Bill which was not compliant with

---

[191] *Animal Defenders* (n 177); Hiebert & Kelly (2015) 350.

[192] JCHR, First Report of Session 2001–2 (20 December 2002, HL Paper 24; HC 191), para 16.

[193] Letter, 9 January 2003. For an examination of the problems which attend such partial measures, see Rowbottom (2007) 95.

[194] JCHR, Fourth Report, Session 2002–3 (10 February 2003, HL Paper 50; HC 397, paras. 40–41).

[195] European Commission, *Party Political Broadcasting: Report and Recommendations*, January 2003, 17.

[196] Hiebert & Kelly (2015) 354 suggest that the potential rights violation in the Communications Bill 'did not provoke substantial parliamentary discussion' or elicit strong parliamentary accountability. However, many MPs and parliamentarians pressed the Government to justify its stance on the rights during parliamentary debate on the Bill, see HC Deb 3 December 2002, vol 395 cols 782–864, in particular cols 785, 787–9, 799–800, 837–8, 846–8; House of Lords, HL Deb 25 March 2003, vol 646 cols 655–790, in particular cols 658–9, 688, 694, 724, 790.

Convention rights.[197] Therefore, although the Government rebutted the 'strong presumption'[198] in favour of a positive Statement of Compatibility in this particular case, it nonetheless preserved the exceptionality of that decision, emphasising that the decision to depart from the norm was not taken lightly, unreflectively or without extensive pre-legislative and legislative scrutiny. In doing so, the Government accepted 'the need to justify its measures in terms of human rights'.[199] It also signalled an evolving constitutional norm that a negative statement under section 19 should be restricted to 'exceptional cases, triggering strict legislative scrutiny and a heightened burden of justification on government'.[200]

Second, despite its commitment to the ban on political advertising, the Government nonetheless said that it would reconsider its position if the courts held that it violated rights, affirming that it would ultimately comply with an adverse ruling. By adopting this stance, the Government justified its legislative proposal in Parliament as duly respectful of rights, but simultaneously showed respect for the authoritative role of the courts in the constitutional scheme. Instead of adopting a combative, dismissive or disdainful stance vis-à-vis the courts, it took a more respectful and collaborative approach, marked by rigorous and painstaking scrutiny across Whitehall and Westminster. The Government chose the collaborative route of *constitutional slowdown* in preference to the confrontational route of *constitutional showdown*.

Third, whilst the Government took the legal advice about a likely declaration of incompatibility seriously, it did not treat it 'as dispositive'[201] or conclusive about the justifiability of a ban on political advertising. The spectre of judicial censure did not lead to either policy distortion or democratic debilitation. The legal advice *informed* the Government's decision but did not *supplant* it. In fact, it is arguable that the prospect of an adverse judicial ruling actually stimulated more focused and in-depth parliamentary deliberation about the impact on rights than would have otherwise occurred.

---

[197] McLean (2013) 24.
[198] Hiebert & Kelly (2015) 266 (who note the 'strong political expectations of compliance with negative judicial rulings' amongst UK political actors).
[199] Feldman (2002b) 347; Kavanagh (2015b) 131; Feldman (2004b) 100.
[200] McLean (2013) 25 (suggesting that there may be a constitutional convention beginning to emerge around section 19 statements).
[201] Tushnet (1995).

Fourth, the episode illustrates that claiming compatibility under section 19 was not treated as a mere formality or a tick-box exercise. The Government could easily have kept quiet about its legal advice and made a Statement of Compatibility under section 19, despite the high likelihood of a judicial declaration. Had it done so, it could have tamped down on potential parliamentary and political opposition to the Bill. By coming clean on the advice it had received, the Government manifested respect both for Convention rights and the courts, whilst simultaneously stimulating wide-ranging political deliberation about the impact of the advertising ban on freedom of expression.

Finally, this episode showcases the pivotal role of the JCHR and other parliamentary Committees in securing meaningful accountability for rights in the pre-legislative and legislative process. It also demonstrates the role of other bodies such as the Electoral Commission and the Independent Television Commission in contributing to the broader accountability architecture. By engaging in sustained, informed, and critical evaluation of the Communications Bill, these actors combined to create an *accumulative accountability effect* on government in Parliament and beyond.

Viewed in the round, this episode does not reveal a culture of democratic debilitation or political abdication where political actors are blithely unconcerned about whether legislation complies with rights. Nor does it bespeak a climate of cringing 'court mimicry',[202] where mere mention of judicial rulings suffocates meaningful ethical and political deliberation about the merits of particular policies in a democratic society. Instead, it revealed a cautious, considered and collaborative approach, where key political actors listened to legal advice and gave credence to judicial rulings on rights, whilst weighing the risk of an adverse court ruling into a broader blended judgement about principle and policy in a democratic state.[203]

When the Communications Act 2003 was inevitably litigated in *Animal Defenders International*, the House of Lords (now UK Supreme Court) upheld the ban as compatible with freedom of expression, as did the European Court of Human Rights in Strasbourg.[204] Whilst accepting that the ban restricted freedom of expression to some degree, the House

---

[202] Casey & Kenny (2022) 12.

[203] On the 'anti-distortion' rationale for banning political advertising in the broadcast media, see Rowbottom (2013) 4–8.

[204] *Animal Defenders International v UK* (2013) 57 EHRR 21.

of Lords held that it was nonetheless a 'balanced and proportionate response'[205] which struck a fair balance between the need to protect pluralist democratic debate on the one hand, and ensure that political communication is not skewed in favour of those with deepest pockets on the other.[206] In doing so, the House of Lords gave 'great weight'[207] to Parliament's decision to ban paid political advertising, in part because it was 'reasonable to expect that our democratically-elected politicians will be peculiarly sensitive to the measures necessary to safeguard the integrity of our democracy'.[208] In formulating general, workable rules, a line had to be drawn somewhere and 'it is for Parliament to decide where'.[209]

In coming to this conclusion, the court gave weight to the serious Executive and parliamentary engagement with rights, accepting Parliament's conclusion that a partial ban on political advertising was unworkable, and might corrode the healthy democratic culture on which UK democracy depends.[210] Rather than running on separate tracks – or set on a constitutional collision course – the Executive, legislative, and judicial branches of government acted as mutually responsive and mutually respectful actors embedded in a complex, collaborative enterprise.

8 Conclusion

The aim of this chapter was to critically assess the powerful claims that meaningful parliamentary engagement with rights is thwarted by the twin spectres of Executive or judicial dominance. Shifting our lens from domination to collaboration, I argued that neither of these spectres are as haunting as they seem. Whilst the Executive is undoubtedly in the driving seat of the legislative process, I showed that Parliament is willing and able to push back.[211] In place of an exaggerated and simplistic picture of an omnipotent Executive and compliant Parliament, what in fact exists is a complex interaction between interdependent actors within and beyond the Westminster Parliament. This is not to deny that the Executive is the most powerful branch of government in the

---

[205] *Animal Defenders* (n 177) [51].
[206] Ibid.
[207] Ibid [33] Lord Bingham.
[208] Ibid [33].
[209] Ibid [33].
[210] Hunt, Hooper & Yowell (2012) 56–8.
[211] Feldman (2004b) 112.

constitutional scheme. Nonetheless, it qualifies and complicates assertions of Executive omnipotence and 'elective dictatorship' in the UK constitutional order.[212] Within and between the Executive and legislature there is a 'tangled web'[213] of interdependent actors who act, interact, and counteract in a dynamic where law and politics intersect.

---

[212] Hailsham (1976).
[213] Hay & Richards (2000) (describing the 'tangled webs of Westminster and Whitehall').

PART III

JUDGE AS PARTNER

7

Judge as Partner

1 Introduction: Between Supremacy and Subordination

Constitutional theory has long been dominated by two diametrically opposed visions of the judicial role. For some, courts are viewed as the key custodians of rights, heroically defending our most precious constitutional principles from the inevitable onslaught of legislative attack. For others, courts are castigated as an unelected and unaccountable legal elite who undermine democratic self-government and violate our right to participate in public decisions. But underpinning these rival conceptions of the judicial role is the common assumption that the courts and the legislature are locked in a battle for supremacy. Either courts reign supreme, whilst keeping an errant legislature within constitutional bounds – or the legislature reigns supreme, whilst the courts are relegated to the role of being the legislature's faithful agent.

In this part of the book, I argue that courts are neither supreme constitutional guardians who call the shots nor subordinate minions who cower in fear. Instead, they are *partners* in a collaborative enterprise, where they play a significant – but circumscribed – constitutional role. Rather than elevating courts to a position of supremacy where they issue constitutional commands from on high – or denigrating them as the destroyers of democracy and 'enemies of the people',[1] I articulate a more measured role-conception for courts, grounded in the values of comity and collaboration, partnership and patience, respect and restraint. I defend the idea of 'judge as partner'. Charting a middle course between supremacy and subordination, I articulate a robust but restrained role for courts in the collaborative constitutional scheme. The resulting role-conception for courts is less grandiose than Dworkin

---

[1] Slack (2016); Rozenberg (2020).

dreams, but less menacing and destructive of democracy than
Waldron fears.

This chapter unfolds as follows. Delving into the anatomy of adjudication, Part 2 examines the valuable contribution courts make to the
collaborative enterprise. Part 3 uses the idea of 'Janus-faced judging'
to articulate the epistemic and institutional constraints under which
courts labour in the collaborative scheme. Part 4 addresses the claim
that the role of the courts is one of 'faithful agent' to the legislature.
Rejecting that claim, I show how the courts are more than mere agents
of the legislative branch. Instead, they make an independent and
creative contribution to the collaborative scheme.

Part 5 turns to examine the 'principle of legality' and the powerful
canons of construction which judges have long used to protect constitutional values. Here, I will show how statutory interpretation is an
institutional meeting-point between courts and legislatures, where a collaborative constitutional dynamic unfolds. Part 6 presents the principle
of legality as a presumption of constitutional partnership. I close with the
argument that this presumption can operate in both rights-protective and
democracy-enhancing ways.

2   The Contribution Courts Make

The main role of the courts in the collaborative constitution is to resolve
disputes about what the law requires in the context of a particular case.[2]
At the heart of the judicial role is a dispute-resolution function. Of
course, in resolving disputes about what the law requires, judges are
drawn into an array of complex activities – applying and interpreting
statutes, developing judicial doctrine, filling in gaps in the legal framework, reviewing Executive and legislative decisions for compliance with
legal norms, and ensuring that the law is implemented in a fair, just and
equitable manner.

So what is the key value underpinning the judicial contribution to
the collaborative enterprise? The central value judges bring to the joint
enterprise of governing is their independence.[3] Judicial independence

---

[2] Endicott (2020a) (arguing that dispute resolution is the primary role of the courts);
Stephenson (2013) 897; Bogg (2018).
[3] Devlin (1976) 10; Reid (1997) 181; Kavanagh (2016c) 129ff.

has three dimensions. First, judges must have *adjudicatory independence*, i.e. they should be impartial vis-à-vis the individual parties to the dispute. This equips them to adjudicate legal disputes in an unbiased and impartial manner 'without fear or favour' towards either side of the dispute. Second, the courts must have *electoral independence*, i.e. they should be independent from direct popular control and detached from the ongoing pressures of electoral politics. This equips judges to stand firm against the passions of the moment, resisting the pressures of short-term electoral gains. Third, the courts should have *institutional independence* from the other branches of government. This equips judges to perform a valuable supervisory or checks-and-balances role in the constitutional scheme, strengthening their ability to find against the other branches, safe in the knowledge that they will not be sanctioned or suppressed for doing so.[4]

Though judicial independence is not absolute – structurally so – it gives judges the confidence and security they need to hold a powerful Executive and legislature to constitutional account.[5] This illustrates the idea of 'adjudication as accountability',[6] where judges hold the other branches to account for compliance with rights and the fundamental principles of the constitutional system. On this understanding, courts do double-duty: as impartial adjudicators of individual legal disputes and as accountability actors in the constitutional scheme. All three dimensions of judicial independence – *adjudicatory*, *electoral*, and *institutional* – are institutional assets which courts possess when reviewing legislation for compliance with rights.

Alongside the value of judicial independence, judges have other institutional credentials which strengthen their ability to resolve legal disputes in a fair and even-handed manner. These include legal expertise, procedural fairness, an individualised focus on particular claims, as well as the factual, evidentiary and forensic skills possessed by trained lawyers. Together, these attributes give courts a distinctive dispute-resolution competence, enabling them to evaluate the impact of general rules on the particulars of an individual case.[7] By giving people access to

---

[4] Ferejohn & Kramer (2002) 963; Kyritsis (2012) 320ff; King (2013) 135; Gee et al. (2015) 10–11.
[5] Kyritsis (2012) 321; Gee et al. (2015) 5.
[6] Fredman (2013); King (2013).
[7] King (2013) 124ff; Endicott (2020a) 134.

independent legal adjudicators, the courts also perform a valuable function in upholding the rule of law and allowing individuals to challenge governmental decisions.[8]

3   Janus-Faced Judging in a Joint Enterprise

Whilst judicial independence, legal expertise, individualised legal focus, and dispute-resolution competence are undoubtedly institutional strengths of the judicial role, we must also consider their limits and weaknesses. I will mention two such limitations here: the *epistemic limitations* of the courts stemming from their independence, and the *institutional limitations* of judicial law-making stemming from the constraints of the adjudicatory role and the subsidiary position of the courts in the joint enterprise of governing. Let us start with the epistemic limitations.

The fact that judges are typically confined to adjudicating bivalent disputes in an impartial manner means that judges must base their decisions on a restricted range of evidence presented to them as part of the adversarial process.[9] In contrast to elected politicians who can consult with a variety of stakeholders, seek feedback, and commission research on the likely impact and side-effects of a proposed legal change, judges must wear a blindfold.[10] Focusing only on the admissible evidence pertaining to the legal question before them, judges are prevented from seeing the broader social, political, and economic context in which the dispute arises.

These epistemic and evidentiary constraints undoubtedly enhance judicial independence and facilitate the impartial adjudication of legal disputes. But they also limit judges' broader field of vision. This highlights the trade-off between independence and information which lies at the heart of the judicial role.[11] Therefore, although judges are well-placed to decide individual legal disputes in a fair and independent manner, they are less well suited to evaluating broader policy questions involving a multiplicity of competing interests.[12] As a matter of relative

---

[8] Kavanagh (2003b).
[9] Komesar (1994) 123ff; Komesar (1984) 379; Vermeule (2006) 41.
[10] Komesar (1994) 132; Lord Hodge (2015) 479; Yowell (2018) 5.
[11] Komesar (1994) 123; Vermeule (2006) 47; Yap (2015) 20.
[12] Kavanagh (2004) 273; Komesar (1994) 135.

institutional competence, the political branches are typically better placed to see the big picture on a broad policy canvas. Meanwhile, the courts possess a more focused, pointillistic perspective, oriented towards assessing the concrete impact of general laws on particular people.[13]

But the most significant difference between the institutional capacity of the courts and the other branches of government lies in the institutional limitations on judicial law-making. In contrast to the legislature which can engage in radical, root-and-branch reform of an entire area of the law, judicial law-making is typically piecemeal and incremental.[14] Rarely does an individual case encompass an entire area of the law, or allow for radical reform within it. Typically, it concerns the application of general or vague legal standards to particular circumstances or the reconciliation of ostensibly competing legislative provisions. When judges make law, they do so by filling in gaps in existing frameworks, adapting legal doctrines to new circumstances, or extending them gradually on a case-by-case basis using existing legal resources.[15] Operating within existing legal structures, judges are generally confined to engaging in partial and piecemeal reform, changing the law in one aspect of its application in response to the vagaries of litigation.[16] This creates what Joseph Raz described as 'the dilemma of partial reform',[17] where judges must choose between partial reform of one aspect of the law or conserving existing doctrine.

The fact that the courts must operate within existing legal principles highlights the Janus-faced nature of judging in a joint enterprise.[18] When resolving legal disputes, judges must simultaneously face backward in order to give effect to the law as it is, whilst facing forward with a view to potentially developing and changing the law.[19] Whilst the legislature can make new law on its merits in a forward-looking

---

[13] Möllers (2013) 89; Roach (2016a) 299.
[14] On the distinction between judicial and legislative law-making, see Kavanagh (2004) 270–4; Raz (1979) 194–201; Gardner (2012) 37–47.
[15] Kavanagh (2004) 272.
[16] Komesar (1994) 125; Bingham (2000) 234.
[17] Raz (1979) 194ff.
[18] Raz (1998b) 177ff; Kavanagh (2004) 267, 271–2.
[19] Kavanagh (2004) 267ff.

fashion, the courts are confined to developing the law gradually, applying existing legal norms[20] and 'building incrementally on existing principles'.[21] Even when striving to do justice in the instant case, it must be 'justice *according to law*'.[22] Rather than striking out in new dramatic directions, the courts are hedged in by existing legislative frameworks, relevant judicial precedents, and a whole array of doctrinal, procedural and legal principles. This restricts the lawmaking capacity of the courts and limits their ability to act as the primary 'engine of law reform'.[23] Therefore, if root-and-branch legal change is required, it is often better to leave it to the legislature.

When adjudicating legal disputes, judges must answer to two sets of values which are sometimes in tension. One urges fidelity to existing law underpinned by the values of legal authority, certainty, continuity, and stability. The other points towards legal development and innovation underpinned by the values of justice and equitable application of the law in context.[24] This creates a dualistic dynamic at the heart of the judicial role, where judges must strive to strike an appropriate balance between certainty, continuity and stability on the one hand, and flexibility, individualised justice and equity on the other.[25] Instead of a simple choice between activism and restraint, what in fact exists is a perennial obligation to keep the countervailing values of continuity and creativity in view.[26] Even when they decide to innovate, the creative role of the courts has to be informed by 'the need for stability in doctrine and principle and by adherence to the basic values inherent in the constitutional order'.[27] Judges are aware that legal innovation, however

---

[20] Gardner (2012) 41; Raz (1979) 107, 195; Bogg (2022) 410.

[21] *Elgizouli v SSHD* [2020] UKSC 10 [170], Lord Reed.

[22] Endicott (2020a); *Elgizouli* (n 21) [170] (where Lord Reed observed that when courts develop the law based on established principles, they are faithful to their judicial oath to 'do right to all manner of people *after the laws and usages of the Realm*', emphasis added); Sales (2018c) 692–3.

[23] *Elgizouli* (n 21) [170].

[24] Raz (1996) 357ff; Raz (1998a) 180, 360; Tyler (2005) 1390; Bingham (2011) 134; Endicott (2015a) 130; Tulkens (2022) 2 (arguing that the ECtHR 'oscillates between pairs of opposite values and objectives, the promotion of which relies on reciprocal concessions').

[25] By 'equity', I am not referring to the English law of equity, but to the older, related Aristotelian idea of 'particularised grounds of justice that may justify a departure from a general rule', see Endicott (2020a) 133–4.

[26] Lord Reid (1972) 26; Kavanagh (2004) 269; Lord Justice Gross (2018) 8; Cardozo (1921) 113.

[27] Lord Sales (2018c) 695; Kavanagh (2009a) 140.

desirable, comes at a price which must be paid 'in the coin of legal certainty'.[28]

One way of responding to the dual demands of Janus-faced judging is for judges to proceed incrementally, developing the law 'in small steps, not giant bounds'[29] whilst preserving the values of certainty, stability and coherence to the greatest degree possible.[30] As Francis Bacon observed, judicial work 'tendeth to pruning and grafting the law, and not to ploughing it up and planting it again'.[31] Thus, whilst 'law-making – within certain limits – is an inevitable and legitimate element of the judge's role',[32] it is an *incremental* form of law-making which allows for some creativity, albeit creativity within institutional and constitutional constraints.[33] Those constraints inevitably set 'bounds to the scope of judicial law-reform'.[34]

These epistemic and institutional limits have a significant impact on the proper division of labour between the branches in the collaborative constitutional scheme. They explain why the Government and legislature are 'charged with the primary responsibility for deciding the best way of dealing with social problems',[35] whilst the courts have a significant but nonetheless subsidiary role of resolving disputes about the law, which requires them to apply, develop and change the law in relatively piece-meal, interstitial and incremental ways. The emerging role conception for courts does not deny the legitimacy of judicial law-making. But it emphasises that judicial creativity operates under significant constraints. These constraints do not vanish whenever rights come into view. On the contrary, in order to adjudicate rights in a robust but responsible fashion,

---

[28] *R (Kelly) v Secretary of State for Justice* [2008] EWCA Civ 177 [24] (Lord Justice Laws); Cardozo (1921) 113; Raz (1979) 182; Sales (2016b) 92; Horder (2006) 75-7; Lord Sumption, interview transcript cited in Paterson (2013) 272, 261 (observing that judges must strive to ensure that judicial innovation is 'coherent in relation to the generality of cases in other cognate areas of law').

[29] Lord Bingham (2000) 32; Lord Justice Beatson (2021) 43.

[30] Lord Bingham (2011) 32, 134.

[31] Spedding, Ellis & Heath (1872) [1616] 67.

[32] Irvine (2003b) 352; McLachlin (Chief Justice of Canada) (1999) (observing that the need to fill gaps when the law is indeterminate means that 'no matter how restrained a judge attempts to be, a degree of judicial law-making is inevitable').

[33] For a compelling defence of judicial incrementalism in the context of 'judging social rights', see King (2012).

[34] *Lim Poh Choo v Camden and Islington Area Health Authority* [1980] AC 174, 183, Lord Scarman; Lord Hodge (2015) 480.

[35] *Ghaidan v Mendoza* [2004] 2 AC 557 [10]; *R (Quila) v Home Secretary* [2011] UKSC 45 [46].

judges must remain mindful of the limits of the judicial role in the constitutional scheme.

4   From Faithful Agent to Constitutional Partner

In the previous section, we saw that when adjudicating and resolving legal disputes, courts are under an obligation to apply and uphold existing law, including laws enacted by the democratically elected legislature. This highlights the receptive role of the courts vis-à-vis the legislature, where courts 'receive' the work-product of the legislature (the statute) and apply it to the circumstances of the individual case.[36] By declaring what the law is and applying it to the facts of the case before them, the courts appear in their classical image as 'appliers and enforcers of value decisions made elsewhere'.[37] On this view, judges are 'faithful agents'[38] of the legislature, whose defining role is to give loyal and faithful effect to legislatively created norms.

Yet, whilst it is certainly true that courts owe a duty of respect to the legislature, the idea that judges are the legislature's 'faithful agents' is deeply misleading.[39] For one thing, it overlooks the significant, but circumscribed, law-making role which courts possess – not only in developing the common law and judicial doctrine, but in statutory interpretation as well. We have long rejected the idea of the courts as the mere 'mouthpiece of the law',[40] where judges mechanically discover and retrieve statutory meaning as 'obedient deciphers'.[41] As Lon Fuller observed, statutory interpretation is 'not simply a process of drawing out of the statute what its maker put into it'.[42] It is also a process of supplementing and developing statutory meaning in accordance with fundamental constitutional principles. Whilst the courts certainly have a partly 'receptive role'[43] when interpreting statutes, they give as well as receive. They develop as well as apply the law.

---

[36] On the receptive role of the courts, see Kyritsis (2012) 303.

[37] Gavison (1999) 244.

[38] Manning (2001) 1.

[39] For analysis of the 'faithful agent theory of statutory interpretation', see Mashaw (2005); Barrett (2010) 112–25 (now Justice Amy Coney Barrett of the US SC).

[40] Montesquieu [1748] in Cohler, Miller & Stone (1989) 163; Reid (1997); Bingham (2011) 28. For a theoretical account of 'interpretation without retrieval', see Raz (1995a).

[41] Lord Bingham (2000); Sager (2004) 5; Barak (2006) 16.

[42] Fuller (1968) 85.

[43] Kyritsis (2012) 316; Kavanagh (2016c) 130ff; Cardozo (1921) 17; Lain (2017) 1643.

The active role of the courts in the collaborative law-making enterprise is manifest in the following ways. First, when a statute is vague or unclear, judges have an important role in specifying how it should apply in an individual case, thereby 'filling in the gaps'[44] in the legislative framework. Legislatures often use vague statutory terms precisely in order to enlist the help of the courts in applying, interpreting and implementing the law.[45] In doing so, they effect a division of labour between the branches of government, with the legislature setting out the basic legal framework of the law and the basic principles to be followed, and the courts fleshing out the detail in an ongoing process of application and elaboration.[46] Here we see law-making as a collaborative enterprise where Parliament and the courts work together in constitutional partnership. The courts 'fulfil and complete Parliament's intention'[47] by giving concrete effect to vague statutory provisions.[48]

Second, the courts sometimes assume an active interpretive role over time, gradually adapting legislative measures to fit with changing circumstances and different social needs. Of course, the power to adopt an evolutionary or 'updating construction'[49] is not without limits. It is constrained by the existing legislative framework and the limits of incremental judicial law-making. Nonetheless, in many jurisdictions, courts have a limited role in updating the law and adjusting its application to contemporary conditions, either by narrowing or by expanding a statutory provision's range of application.[50] In doing so, the courts help the legislature to implement the law over time, ensuring that it can be gradually adapted to changing circumstances.[51]

Third, the active and creative dimension of judging is illustrated by the judicial duty to integrate disparate and sometimes conflicting

---

[44] Raz (1979) 194; Mashaw (1988) 1692 (observing that the 'faithful agency' account 'ceases to be informative as soon as it is needed – whenever there is some reason for the agent to wonder what the principal meant').

[45] Endicott (1999) 5.

[46] Yap (2015) 75; Barrett (2010) 123. This delegation is an example of what Joseph Raz described as 'directed powers', see Raz (1994) 249.

[47] Sales (2016a) 464–5; Sales (2012) 292; Kavanagh (2016b) 228.

[48] Sales (2012) 292; Jackson (2016) 1728.

[49] Cross (1995) chapter 7.

[50] Kyritsis (2012) 316; Raz (1979) 192.

[51] For further analysis of the idea of dynamic or 'updating interpretation' as a mode of 'living constitutionalism', see Kavanagh (2003a).

legislative measures into the 'general constitutional and systemic fabric'[52] of the law, thus helping to ensure coherence, stability and 'normative harmony within the system'.[53] By harnessing legislation to legal doctrine, the courts 'mix the fruits of long-established traditions with the urgencies of short-term exigencies',[54] thereby ensuring that legislative decision and judicial doctrine can work together as a relatively coherent whole. In doing so, courts engage in ongoing 'maintenance and repair'[55] of the law, eliminating potential absurdities, smoothing out inconsistencies and contradictions, and helping to prevent unjust applications of the law.[56]

Therefore, judges do not always need to 'down tools whenever they meet a defect in the law'.[57] Using the well-known canons of construction and doctrines of statutory interpretation, courts can rectify some problems as they arise.[58] By successively adjusting the law to gradually changing conditions, courts help to avoid the undesirable and unintended consequences of applying rules to unforeseen circumstances.[59] In these and other ways, the courts maintain a 'relationship of partnership'[60] with the executive and legislature, establishing legal meaning in concert with the other branches of government.

When surveying the law-making tasks carried out by the courts, it is clear that judges are more than mere minions. Instead, they are partners in a collaborative constitutional enterprise, working together with the legislature to implement and develop the law over time. Whilst judges undoubtedly owe the legislature a duty of respect, their ultimate fealty and larger loyalty is owed to the constitution and the legal system as a whole.[61] Instead of being the faithful agents of the legislature, the courts

---

[52] Barak (2006) 254.
[53] Ibid 254, 249–55; Cross (1995) 82–92; Lord Justice Sedley (2009) 249; Bennion (2001) 99–100; Sunstein (1989) 469; Raz (1994) 375; Kavanagh (2016b) 130–1; Lord Reid (1972) 183; Lord Sales (2012) 296; Stone (1936) 15; Tyler (2005) 1390, 1394, 1405; Eskridge & Ferejohn (2001) 1216–17.
[54] Raz (1994) 376; Kavanagh (2019) 66; Sunstein (1989) 469; Cardozo (1921) 17; Lord Sales (2012) 296.
[55] Raz (1979) 200; Kavanagh (2016b) 133.
[56] Cross (1995) 49; Kavanagh (2004) 270; Raz (2009) 233; Brenncke (2018) 112–25.
[57] Lord Devlin (1976) 4.
[58] Kavanagh (2016c) 133.
[59] Raz (1979) 200; Kavanagh (2016c) 129.
[60] Sager (2004) 5; Bogg (2018).
[61] Jackson (2016) 1743ff; Barrett (2010) 124; Mashaw (2005) 505.

are more accurately conceived as 'faithful servants of constitutionalism',[62] carrying out their distinctive role in partnership with the political branches of government. This requires 'principled, as well as faithful, adjudication'[63] in a collaborative constitutional scheme, where judges have a 'will of their own'.[64]

5   Of Common Law Rights and Clear Statements

In documenting the active and partly creative role of the courts in the collaborative law-making enterprise, statutory interpretation emerges as an 'inter-institutional meeting point'[65] between courts and legislatures. On this understanding, statutory interpretation is 'much more than a method of establishing what the law is. It is also a tool for developing the law, changing and reforming it'.[66] It is a key instance of *Janus-faced judging*, where judges face backward in order to elucidate the law as it is, whilst facing forward with a view to potentially developing and improving the law.[67] If interpretation 'lives in spaces where fidelity to an original and openness to novelty mix',[68] then judges work at the cross-cutting interface between the two.

The active and creative contribution of the courts to the collaborative constitution is well illustrated by the familiar canons of construction and presumptions of statutory interpretation developed over centuries in many legal systems.[69] These canons include presumptions against unclear changes in the law, in favour of a strict construction of penal statutes, or in favour of interpreting revenue statutes favourably to the taxpayer, as well as presumptions in favour of protecting individual

---

[62] Katyal (1998) 1794; Bateup (2006) 1125; Sachs (2009) 199; Judge (2015) 147; Pitkin (1967) 116–17.

[63] Raz (1994) 374–6.

[64] Madison (1788), Federalist Paper 51, available at the Library of Congress archive (https://guides.loc.gov/federalist-papers/full-text); Barrett (2010) 113.

[65] Kavanagh (2009a) 231; Leckey (2015) 39; Gageler (2011) 11–12 (arguing that there is a 'symbiotic relationship' between legislation and the common law).

[66] Raz (2009) 353.

[67] Ibid 233ff (describing the values of continuity, authority, legal development, and equity as the 'four foci of interpretation'); Kavanagh (2004) 266–8; Endicott (2020a) 134.

[68] Raz (2009) 357.

[69] On presumptions of statutory interpretation, see Cross (1995) chapter 7.

liberty and rights.[70] Though these presumptions can be rebutted by clear statutory language to the contrary, they nonetheless operate as default rules where judges interpret vague, indeterminate or unclear statutory language compatibly with constitutional principles, such as the rule of law and the liberty of the individual.[71]

Consider the nineteenth-century case of *Cooper v Wandsworth*,[72] where the common law courts implied rights of due process into a statute which was otherwise silent on the issue. As Byles J famously pronounced,

> Although there are no positive words in a statute requiring that a party shall be heard, yet the justice of the common law will supply the omission of the legislature'.[73]

In doing so, the court did not 'wait for direction from Parliament.[74] Instead, it interpreted the legislation in light of values 'founded upon the plainest principles of justice',[75] thereby ensuring that the statute complied with underlying constitutional norms of natural justice.[76] Thus, even absent a codified Bill of Rights, common law courts have significant powers to protect individual rights through the presumptions of statutory interpretation.

In contemporary times, the UK courts rely on a 'familiar and well-established principle'[77] that 'fundamental rights cannot be overridden by general or ambiguous words'.[78] Currently labelled the 'principle of legality',[79] this maxim holds that judges will 'decline to hold that Parliament interfered with fundamental rights unless it has made its

---

[70] Cross (1995) chapter 7.

[71] *Stradling v Morgan* (1560) 1 Plow 199, cited in *R (Morgan Grenfell and Co Ltd) v Special Commissioner of Income Tax and another* [2002] UKHL 21 [8]; Endicott (2017b) 281.

[72] *Cooper v Wandsworth Board of Works* 1863 14 CB (NS) 108.

[73] Ibid 194, cited with approval in *Bank Mellat v HM Treasury (No 2)* [2014] AC 763, [35] *per* Lord Sumption; Cardozo (1921) 16.

[74] *Wiseman v Borneman* [1971] AC 297, 309B *per* Lord Morris; Fordham 7.5.

[75] *Cooper v Wandsworth* (n 72) 190; Endicott (2021) 126–36, 142–3, 194–5.

[76] *Wiseman v Borneman* (n 74) 317G; Cardozo (1921) 16–17, 70.

[77] *Axa General Insurance Ltd v The Lord Advocate* [2011] UKSC 46 [151].

[78] *R v SSHD, ex parte Simms* [2000] 2 AC 115, 131.

[79] For analysis of the principle of legality, see generally Elliott & Hughes (2020); Fordham (2020) chapter 35; Kavanagh (2009a) 96–100, 302–7; Lord Sales (2009a) 598; Meagher (2011) 452–6; Bjorge (2016) 230; Goldsworthy (2010) 304–12.

intentions crystal clear'.[80] As Lord Hoffmann famously observed in his canonical judgment in *Simms*,

> in the absence of express language or necessary implication to the contrary, the courts ... presume that even the most general words were intended to be subject to the basic rights of the individual.[81]

The 'principle of legality' is one of the many 'presumptions of general application' described in Sir Rupert Cross's classic work on statutory interpretation as

> not only supplement[ing] the statutory text but also operat[ing] at a higher level as expressions of fundamental principles governing civil liberties and the relations between Parliament, the Executive and courts. They operate here as constitutional principles which are not easily displaced by statutory text.[82]

Therefore, the 'principle of legality' is a new label for a centuries-old canon of construction enjoining courts to interpret legislation in light of constitutional norms.

Older generations of constitutional scholars described such presumptions as forming a 'common law Bill of Rights',[83] whose requirements were deeply inscribed in the foundations of the unwritten constitution. In contemporary times, scholars and judges have rediscovered the potency of the principle of legality as a way of upholding 'common law constitutional rights'[84] as part of a 'presumptive constitutional order'.[85] Indeed, the potency of this tool led Lord Hoffmann to suggest that the principle of legality enabled UK courts to 'apply principles of constitutionality little different from those which exist in countries where the legislature is expressly limited by a constitutional document'.[86] This brings into sharp relief 'the constitutional significance of statutory construction as a technique for promoting legislative

---

[80] *R (Jackson) v Attorney General* [2005] UKHL 56, [159]; *R (Evans) v Attorney General* [2015] UKSC 21, [56]–[58], [90]; Bjorge (2016) 230.

[81] *Simms* (n 78) 131.

[82] Cross (1995) 166; Spigelman (2005) 773.

[83] Willis (1938) 1; Keir & Lawson (1979) 3; Browne-Wilkinson (1992) 399; Kavanagh (2009a) 98–9, 306; Roach (2016b) 133.

[84] Elliott & Hughes (2020); Allan (2006a) 46; Cooke (2004) 276ff; Sales (2009a) 601; Hunt (1997) 152; Rishworth (2016) 143; Geiringer (2008) 62.

[85] Sales (2009a) 601.

[86] *Simms* (n 78) 131; *Matadeen v Pointu* [1999] 1 AC 98, 110; Kavanagh (2009a) 296; Fordham (2020) [35.1.2]; Burrows (2018) 68–70.

consistency with human rights norms'[87] in all systems, regardless of whether they possess a codified constitutional text.

A key defining feature of these presumptions is that they can be rebutted by the legislature, as long as the legislature articulates its intention to do so in clear statutory terms. This explains the US nomenclature which describes such presumptions as 'clear statement rules,'[88] because they can be rebutted by a clear legislative statement to the contrary. Yet the emphasis on the power of legislative rebuttal should not obscure the fact that the key rationale of these rules is actually to incentivise compliance with the values underlying the presumption. Whilst the legislature can certainly override the principle of legality if it is willing to pay the political price, the underlying constitutional expectation is that 'facing up to what is being done will make legislatures, at least some of the time, less likely to do it'.[89] As Lord Bingham observed extra-judicially, the requirement to spell out a potential rights-violation on the face of the statute must surely 'operate as a discouragement, not least because of the increased risk of media criticism and Parliamentary popular resistance'.[90]

By requiring the Executive and legislature to articulate a contrary intention in clear terms, the principle of legality raises the 'enactment costs'[91] for legislative provisions which seek to override rights, whilst simultaneously lowering the political energy required to comply with them.[92] This shifts the burden of inertia in the rights-protective direction.

Therefore, the systemic aim of the principle of legality is to incentivise and encourage political protection of rights. At the very least, by setting the default position as rights-respecting rather than rights-restricting, the principle guards against inadvertent, casual or easy encroachment on constitutionally protected norms by the democratically elected legislature. It also incentivises Parliament to legislate with caution and consti-

---

[87] Geiringer (2008) 61; Willis (1938) 17.

[88] Coenen (2001); Manning (2010) 399.

[89] Schauer (2006a) 474; Fordham (2020) [35.1]; French (2019) 44–5; Manning (2010) 399, 403, 414 (arguing that 'clear statement rules' impose a 'clarity tax' on the legislature in order to disincentivise rights-violating legislation).

[90] Bingham (2011) 51; Elliott (2002) 347; French (2019) 44–5.

[91] Stephenson (2008) 40ff; Young (2000) 1552, 1597, 1606; Levinson (1999) 889.

[92] Barrett (2010) 171; Eskridge & Frickey (1992) 632–3; Young (2000) 1608–9.

tutional care when statutory provisions seem to encroach on rights.[93] As such, the principle of legality operates as a *constitutional slowdown* mechanism. Though it does not prevent the legislature from limiting or even violating rights, it nonetheless orients the system towards compliance with underlying constitutional values.

Given the pivotal role of this presumption in upholding rights, the nomenclature of 'the principle of legality' may seem misleading.[94] The principle may be more accurately described as a *presumption of non-interference with rights*[95] or, more positively, as a *presumption of parliamentary rights protection*. This new nomenclature highlights its close affinity with 'the presumption of constitutionality' and 'clear statement rules'[96] in countries with codified constitutions.[97] In those countries, the presumptions are sometimes described as a form of 'constitutional common law'[98] or 'sub-constitutional constitutional law',[99] supplementing and complementing the written constitutional text.[100]

When applying this presumption, the courts treat legislation as presumptively protective of rights, regardless of whether the enacting Parliament specifically intended to protect them.[101] In other words, the courts *presume* that Parliament wished to protect the value, without *knowing* whether that was true as a matter of fact. In this respect, the principle of legality operates analogously to the presumption of a *mens rea* requirement in criminal offences, where the courts presume the inclusion of *mens rea* regardless of whether the enacting Parliament specifically intended to include it. The justification for doing so is not that the enacting legislature intended to include it, but rather that the

---

[93] *Miller 1* [2016] EWHC 2768 (Admin) [88], where the Divisional Court described the presumption that Parliament intended to legislate in conformity with constitutional statutes as excluding 'casual implied repeal'; Beatson (2021) 120.

[94] For reservations about the label, see Basten (2017); Sales (2009a) 600; Groves & Meagher (2017) 258; Goldsworthy (2017) 53.

[95] Spigelman (2005) 780.

[96] Manning (2010) 399; Meagher (2014).

[97] For analysis of the presumption of constitutionality in countries with codified constitutions, see e.g. Foley (2008) (Ireland); Schauer (1995) (United States); Brenncke (2018) 248ff (Germany).

[98] Monaghan (1975); Schrock & Welsh (1978); Coenen (2001) 1735.

[99] Coenen (2001); Tushnet (2001); Yap (2015) chapter 5; Eskridge & Frickey (1992) (describing it as 'quasi-constitutional law');

[100] Coenen (2001) 1595, 1604, 1869; Tushnet (2001) 1880; Fisher & Devins (1992) 1.

[101] Joseph (2017) 33; Endicott (2003) 208.

presumption is a good way of ensuring that the liberty of the individual and due process of law are protected by the criminal law.[102]

To be sure, when relying on presumptions of statutory interpretation, judicial rhetoric often emphasises that the resulting interpretations are ones the legislature would have endorsed or intended.[103] Yet, in making such counter-factual claims about Parliament's hypothetical or 'presumed intentions',[104] the courts are not engaging in a form of legislative psychoanalysis.[105] Nor are they asserting an empirical truth.[106] Instead, they are 'emphasis[ing] their comity with Parliament',[107] acknowledging that when adjusting statutes to the demands of constitutionalism, they are *working with* their partners in authority, not against them.[108] In applying the 'principle of legality', the courts *help* the legislature to rise to its own obligations to protect and promote rights during the legislative process.

6   The Principle of Legality as a Presumption of Partnership

When interpreting legislation in light of these presumptions, judges act as partners in a collaborative enterprise, striving to give effect to the law, whilst simultaneously integrating ongoing legislation into the broader backdrop of constitutional principle.[109] In doing so, the courts work

---

[102] *Sweet v Parsley* [1969] 1 AER 347, 349; Young (2000) 1551, 1585–6; Schacter (1995) 652; Endicott (2003) 208.

[103] For example, the Australian High Court has reiterated for over a century that it would be 'in the last degree improbable' that the Australian Parliament would ever legislate contrary to rights, see *Potter v Minahan* (1908) 7 CLR 277, 304.

[104] *R (Privacy International) v Investigatory Powers Tribunal* [2019] UKSC 22, [214]; Coenen (2001) 1607.

[105] Gageler (2015) 14.

[106] Endicott (2003) 209.

[107] Endicott (2003) 209; Spigelman (2005) 770 (where former Chief Justice Spigelman of New South Wales, Australia, argues that such judicial rhetoric is 'an act of constitutional courtesy which the judiciary observes in its collective relationship with Parliament'); Gleeson (2009) 33 (where former Chief Justice Gleeson of the Australian High Court describes the principle of legality as a presumption of 'imputed decency'); Goldsworthy (2017) 47.

[108] Finnis (2007) 417 (arguing that the application of the principle of legality 'qualifies the ordinary subordination of our common law to parliamentary authority', meaning that 'constitutional principles and rights prevail over ordinary norms of statutory interpretation'); Bjorge (2016) 230.

[109] Gageler (2015) 14.

together with Parliament to ensure that legislation enacted by the democratically elected legislature complies with fundamental constitutional values, including rights.[110] Statutory interpretation is thus revealed as a collaborative enterprise between all three branches of government where the courts apply the law whilst 'adjusting statute to the demands of constitutionalism'.[111]

However, there is no doubt that applying the principle of legality may lead courts to forgo a statute's most natural meaning in favour of a strained but 'tenable'[112] construction more protective of rights.[113] As former Chief Justice Sian Elias of the New Zealand Supreme Court observed, 'apparent meaning yields to less obvious meaning under the common law presumptions protective of bedrock values'.[114]

This leaves judges open to the charge that they are using the presumption to modify legislative meaning in ways which go against the legislature's intent,[115] subordinating Parliament's apparent will to 'a judicial policy of protecting rights chosen by the judges'.[116] On this view, the principle of legality does not instantiate a constitutional partnership in progress. Instead, it constitutes 'an inappropriate judicial intrusion into the legislative domain of the democratic arms of government'[117] – 'a recipe for judicial overreach ... which erodes parliamentary sovereignty while claiming to respect it'.[118]

There is no denying that the 'principle of legality' enables courts to interpret legislation in ways the legislature may not have intended.[119] However, as argued earlier, the rationale of the presumption is not to discern the specific intentions of the enacting Parliament, but rather to interpret legislation in light of fundamental constitutional

---

[110] *Jackson v Attorney General* [2006] 1 AC 262 [28] ('General words ... should not be read as authorising the doing of acts which adversely affect the basic principles on which the law of the United Kingdom is based in the absence of clear words authorising such acts', *per* Lord Bingham).

[111] Leckey (2015) 21.

[112] *R (Privacy International) v Investigatory Powers Tribunal* [2019] UKSC 22, [22].

[113] Barrett (2010) 109–10; Perry (2019) 20.

[114] *R v Pora* [2001] 2 NZLE 38 [13] Elias CJ; Geiringer (2008) 75–7.

[115] Goldsworthy (2017) 46; Barrett (2010) 164; Van Zyl Smit (2007) 295; Meagher & Groves (2017) 265.

[116] Goldsworthy (2017) 46.

[117] Meagher (2014) 437; Varuhas (2020) 587.

[118] McLean (2020b) 31.

[119] Endicott (2003) 208; Young (2000) 1551, 1585–6; Schacter (1995) 652.

principles unless a contrary legislative intention is clearly shown. Whilst the principle of legality may licence the courts to adopt 'strained interpretations'[120] which seem to depart from the specific intentions of the enacting legislature, the courts are nonetheless giving effect to Parliament's 'standing commitments'[121] to protect fundamental constitutional values underpinning the legal system as a whole.[122]

By treating legislation as presumptively protective of rights, the courts are not imposing their judicial will against a prior legislative determination. Instead, they are holding the legislature to constitutional account, helping it to ensure that legislation enacted by the democratically elected legislature adheres to the fundamental principles underpinning the constitutional order. Therefore, the principle of legality is a 'working hypothesis'[123] of constitutional partnership, not a usurpation of the legislature's rightful role. In fact, the principle of legality can be 'democracy-reinforcing'[124] in the following ways.

First, the constitutional values protected by the canons of construction are typically 'known both to Parliament and the courts'.[125] They are part of the familiar legal background against which Parliament legislates.[126] Instead of being plucked from the judicial imagination and imposed on an unsuspecting legislature, the principle of legality reflects 'constitutional understandings accepted by the courts and legislature in constitutional partnership'.[127] This puts the legislature on notice that legislation will be interpreted in line with constitutional principle, thus enabling parliamentary drafters to draft Bills accordingly.[128] This illustrates a relationship

---

[120] Perry (2019).

[121] Goldsworthy (1999) 181; Goldsworthy (2010) 305–6.

[122] Elias (2015) 5.

[123] *Electrolux Home Products Ltd v Australian Workers' Union* [2004] 221 CLR 309 [21], Gleeson CJ; French (2019) 45; Spigelman (2005) 781; Willis (2022) 393 (describing the principle of legality as a 'stability mechanism' in the constitutional system, tilting the default position towards a conclusion compliant with fundamental constitutional principle).

[124] McLean (2020b) 38.

[125] *Electrolux* (n 123) 329, Gleeson J; *R v SSHD, ex parte Pierson* [1998] AC 539 at 573; Meagher (2014) 437; Chen (2015) 333; Sales (2016a) 457.

[126] Raz (1996) 267ff; *R (Gujra) v Crown Prosecution Service* [2012] UKSC 52, [108] ('Parliament legislates against the background of rights which the common law treats as fundamental or constitutional' *per* Lord Mance); Sales (2009a) 606.

[127] Sales (2016a) 465; French (2019) 44.

[128] Atiyah (1988) 129, 156; Coenen (2001) 1607; Chen (2015) 338.

of 'mutual dependence'[129] and dynamic interaction between courts and legislatures. The legislature enacts laws, taking into account how they will be interpreted in the courts, whilst the courts interpret laws in light of constitutional principles known to Parliament.[130]

Second, the principle of legality is often used as a way of supporting Parliament's control over the Executive branch, in order to ensure that the Executive complies with parliamentary imperatives. Many of the leading cases on the principle of legality concern the Government or administrative bodies, where the key question is whether the Executive has stayed within the powers granted to them by statute.[131] In these cases, the courts support and bolster parliamentary authority, whilst preventing the Executive from enlarging or subverting their powers at Parliament's expense.[132] So viewed, the judicial demand for greater legislative clarity can be understood 'not as a simple power grab by the courts but as the courts granting Parliament an opportunity to supervise the Executive'.[133] When ensuring that the Executive does not stray beyond statutory bounds, the courts are 'respecting, rather than challenging, the will of Parliament'.[134]

Third, the principle of legality is a rebuttable presumption, not an absolute rule and is, therefore, subject to override by the democratically elected legislature. In many cases, the courts have accepted that the principle of legality has been rebutted by clear statutory language to the contrary.[135] Therefore, whilst the principle of legality incentivises compliance with rights, it does not preclude Parliament from limiting

---

[129] Cross (1995) 14; Burrows (2018) 100ff.

[130] Office of Parliamentary Counsel, www.gov.uk/government/organisations/office-of-the-parliamentary-counsel; Garrett (1999) 691 (articulating some priorities for legal scholarship in 'an age of statutes').

[131] See e.g. Ahmed v HM Treasury [2010] UKSC 2, [122] Lord Phillips; Osborn v The Parole Board [2013] UKSC 61; R (Unison) v Lord Chancellor [2017] UKSC 51.

[132] McLean (2020b) 34; McLean (2018) 405; Elliott (2015a) 97–8; Bjorge (2016) 223–9; Bell (2020); Hickman (2005b) 1018–19.

[133] McLean (2020b) 34; Willis (2022) 393.

[134] R (Limbuela) v Secretary of State [2005] UKHL 66, [75].

[135] See e.g. R (Gillan) v Commissioner of Police for the Metropolis [2006] UKHL 12, [14]–[15]; AKJ v Commissioner of the Police for the Metropolis [2013] EWCA Civ 1342; Bank Mellat v HM Treasury (No 2), [2014] AC 763, [55] Lord Reed; R (Anufrijeva) v Secretary of State for the Home Department [2003] UKHL 36, [20] per Lord Bingham dissenting; R v SSHD, ex parte Stafford (1998); Sheldrake v DPP [2004] UKHL 43 [6]; R (Nicklinson) v Ministry of Justice [2013] EWCA Civ 961, [66]; Jackson (n 80) [159]; Evans (n 80) [56].

or overriding them. By allowing the legislature to limit or restrict rights when that is deemed necessary in the public interest, the 'principle of legality' recognises the primacy of Parliament as the lead law-maker in the constitutional scheme, whilst simultaneously affirming the constitutional role of the courts in upholding rights, unless told otherwise.

Finally, the 'principle of legality' may have a beneficial catalytic effect on democratic deliberation. By requiring the legislature to make a clear statement on rights, the principle of legality may stimulate enhanced 'legislative attentiveness' to rights, 'heightening policymaker care in the making of choices that threaten constitutional values'.[136] This democratic justification for the principle of legality was famously articulated by Lord Hoffmann in *Simms*.[137] In a canonical dictum which echoed across the Commonwealth world,[138] Lord Hoffmann observed:

> Parliamentary sovereignty means that Parliament can, if it chooses, legislate contrary to fundamental principles of human rights ... The constraints upon [the] exercise [of this power] are ultimately political, not legal. But the principle of legality means that Parliament must squarely confront what it is doing and accept the political cost. Fundamental rights cannot be overridden by general or ambiguous words. This is because there is too great a risk that the full implications of their unqualified meaning may have passed unnoticed in the democratic process.[139]

In this guise, judicial reliance on the principle of legality is not only 'democracy reinforcing'[140] but 'democracy-enhancing'[141] and 'deliberation-inducing'[142] as well. As the Australian High Court observed, the expectation is that

> curial insistence on a clear expression of an unambiguous intention to abrogate or curtail a fundamental freedom will enhance the parliamentary

---

[136] Coenen (2001) 1655, 1640ff; Hickman (2005b) 1019.
[137] *Simms* (n 78) 131.
[138] For its influence in Australian and New Zealand law, see Coxon (2014) 38ff; Chen (2015) 336–7; Lim (2013) 391–2; Stephenson (2016) 69–70; Geiringer (2008) 74.
[139] *Simms* (n 78) 131; *Bank Mellat* (n 135) [55].
[140] McLean (2020b) 38; Joseph (2017) 30
[141] Manning (2010) 402; Sunstein (2000) 331–2; Eskridge & Frickey (1992) 631; Landau (2014) 1504.
[142] Coenen (2001) 1301; Vermeule (2006) 118.

process by securing a greater measure of attention to the impact of legislative proposals on fundamental rights.[143]

Of course, whether the principle of legality actually catalyses enhanced legislative focus on rights is an empirical question which needs to be tested in different jurisdictions at different times. It is not an abstract normative truth. Nonetheless, the democratic justification for the principle of legality emphasises the collaborative and complementary relationship between the courts and legislature, where judicial and legislative decisions are embedded in a relationship of mutual influence with 'dynamic feedback effects'[144] between them.

In this guise, the principle of legality operates as both a *coordination device* and a *signalling device* between the branches of government.[145] The courts can use it to send a signal to the legislature that a 'clear statement' by the legislature is required to rebut the constitutional presumption at play. By the same token, the legislature can signal its intention to override that presumption by expressing that intention in crystal clear terms.[146] If it does so, the courts must respect that clear statement and interpret the statutory provision accordingly, reassured that the legislature has made its decision after 'squarely confronting' the implications for rights. However, if the legislation is expressed in broad, general or vague terms, this allows for a greater degree of interpretive creativity, allowing more room for judicial manoeuvre. In a dynamic interplay of mutual signalling and constitutional cues, the courts and the legislature give shape to a shared responsibility, engaging in a dynamic and context-sensitive division of constitutional labour.[147]

The principle of legality is a reminder to Parliament that it must tread carefully when enacting legislation which implicates rights. In this way, judges work together with other actors in the constitutional

---

[143] *Coco v The Queen* (1994) 179 CLR 427, 437–8 (Australian High Court), discussed in Lim (2017) 7ff; Goldsworthy (2017) 50–2. For the idea that 'clear statement rules' can promote enhanced legislative focus and deliberation, see Sunstein (1988) 1582–5; Tyler (2005) 1460; Coenen (2001) 1640–55.

[144] Landau (2014) 1533.

[145] For insightful exploration of the 'signalling role' of judicial decision making, see Lawson & Seidman (2020) 105–6, 147, 167–9.

[146] Cross (1995) 167; Sales (2009a) 605; Coenen (2001) 1609.

[147] For a general portrayal of rights-based judicial review as a 'signalling game of legislative–judicial interaction', see Rogers (2001).

scheme who call for constitutional care when matters of fundamental constitutional principle are at stake. For example, the House of Lords Constitution Committee strives to ensure that legislative change which has constitutional significance should be the product of a 'conscious decision of Parliament, reached where possible after informed debate'.[148] Although the function of the Committee is 'not to resist constitutional change', it nonetheless strives to 'limit the scope for ill-considered constitutional change'.[149] In this way, the HL Constitution Committee acts as a constitutional long-stop, 'ensuring that changes are not made to the constitution without a full and open debate and full awareness of the consequences.[150] When applying the principle of legality, the courts bolster this principle, working together with key parliamentary actors in a 'fruitful collaboration'[151] oriented towards the common goal of securing just government under the constitution.

Viewed as a signalling device and as a constitutional catalyst, the principle of legality chimes with the idea of 'judge as nudge' and 'court as catalyst', which will be fleshed out in more detail in Chapter 10. For the moment, it suffices to note that the principle of legality can have a facilitative rather than a preclusive role. Rather than placing a legally enforceable 'Stop' sign in the legislature's path, the principle of legality is a 'Go Slow' sign, combined with a constitutional warning to drive carefully when fundamental constitutional values lie in their path.[152] This is an example of collaborative constitutionalism in action, where the courts give the Executive and legislature 'pause for thought'[153] when

[148] Constitution Committee, The House of Lords Briefing, HL 2007, www.publications .parliament.uk/pa/jt201314/jtselect/jtprivi/30/30.pdf; see also Constitution Committee, *The Process of Constitutional Change* (HL 2010–12, 177) [22].

[149] Submission of former Prime Minister John Major to the Royal Commission on Reform of the House of Lords, cited in Constitution Committee, 'Reviewing the Constitution: Terms of Reference and Method of Working' (HL First Report, 2001), [6].

[150] HL Constitution Committee, 'Reviewing the Constitution: Terms of Reference and Method of Working' (HL First Report, Session 2000–2001, HL Paper 7), [8]; HL Constitution Committee, *Parliament and the Legislative Process*, 14th Report of Session 2003–4, HL Paper 173-1; HL Constitution Committee, *Parliament and the Legislative Process: The Government's Response*, 6th Report of Session 2004–5, HL Paper 114; De Visser (2004) 1.

[151] Coenen (2001) 1836.

[152] McLean (2020b) 38; Elliott (2020) 202; Schacter (2006) 610; Barrett (2010) 175.

[153] Elliott (2020) 202; Coenen (2001) 1649, 1688–9 (arguing that clear statement rules are 'deliberation-enhancing rules' which encourage the legislature to gives rights a 'sober second thought'); McLean (2020b) 30.

constitutionally protected values are at stake. Rather than overriding legislative will, the principle of legality 'invites a deep collaboration between judicial and political authorities',[154] affording the political branches opportunities to contribute constructively to the shared elaboration of constitutional norms over time.[155]

7 Conclusion

Opening up the theme of 'judge as partner', this chapter argued that courts make an active and creative contribution to the collaborative enterprise of making law. By filling in gaps, developing the law incrementally over time, and engaging in ongoing 'maintenance and repair'[156] of the statutory framework, the courts emerged as key constitutional actors, working alongside and together with their fellow participants in the collaborative constitutional scheme. On this vision, judges are not Herculean heroes embarked on a solitary crusade for justice.[157] Nor are they 'the enemies of the people',[158] determined to destroy democracy. Instead, they are partners in a collaborative enterprise, where all three branches of government have a role to play in securing the common goal of just government under the constitution.

This chapter brought into sharp relief 'the constitutional significance of statutory construction as a technique for promoting legislative consistency with human rights norms'.[159] By interpreting legislation in rights-compliant ways, the courts can be seen as 'adjusting statutes to the demands of constitutionalism'.[160] Though often hidden and submerged in a 'sub-constitutional'[161] realm, this chapter excavated the canons of construction as collaborative devices in the constitutional scheme, enabling the courts and legislature to interact in mutually responsive and mutually respectful ways.

---

[154] Coenen (2001) 1588.
[155] Coenen (2001) 1582.
[156] Raz (1979) 200; Kavanagh (2016b) 133.
[157] Cardozo (1921) 141.
[158] Rozenberg (2020).
[159] Geiringer (2008) 61; Willis (1938) 17.
[160] Leckey (2015) 21.
[161] Tushnet (2001).

When interpreting legislation compatibly with the principle of legality, we saw the *court as corrective*, checking legislation for compliance with rights, supplementing legislative meaning and, when necessary, correcting for potential infringements of rights by interpretive means when the statutory text and context so allowed. But we also saw the *court as catalyst*, spurring legislative engagement with rights and supporting the legislature and raising rights-consciousness across all three branches of government. Whilst high-level theoretical debates about the legitimacy of rights-based review present the courts and legislature as 'locked in an embrace of eternal and inevitable opposition',[162] this chapter depicted a more collaborative and mutually supportive dynamic, where the courts were engaged in 'democracy-reinforcing'[163] and even 'democracy-forcing'[164] activities.

This sets the scene for the next chapter, which focuses on adjudication under the HRA 1998. As we shall see, the HRA gives the courts strong powers of interpretation which built on prior judicial experience with the principle of legality as a potent tool to protect rights. As Lord Hoffmann observed, section 3 HRA 'enacted the principle of legality as a rule of construction',[165] albeit in a way which limited the legislative ability to rebut it by clear and unequivocal language.

It is telling that Lord Hoffman's canonical discussion of the principle of legality took place in the twilight zone just before the HRA came into force, thereby emphasising the continuity between the HRA and traditional methods of statutory interpretation upholding common law rights. Whilst the HRA temporarily eclipsed the case-law on 'common law constitutional rights',[166] its rich resources are now being rediscovered anew. In light of the current political hostility towards the HRA and the European Convention, the UK Supreme Court is demonstrating a 'renewed interest in autochthonous constitutionalism'.[167] Returning to their common law roots and tending to

[162] McLachlin (1999) 35.
[163] McLean (2020b) 38.
[164] Vermeule (2006) 118; Coenen (2009) 2840; Kavanagh (2014) 466; Van Zyl Smit (2016) 11ff.
[165] Simms (n 78) 131.
[166] Elliott & Hughes (2020).
[167] Stephenson (2015) 394.

the centuries-old canons of statutory interpretation, the courts ensure that even if the HRA is repealed, they can still reach for the trusted tools of the common law constitution, employing them in subtle but significant ways to protect rights in the quiet recesses of the sub-constitutional terrain.

8

The HRA as Partnership in Progress

1 Introduction

When the Human Rights Act 1998 was enacted, it was described as 'the first Bill of Rights this country has seen for three centuries'.[1] For the first time in British history, the courts were empowered to review legislation for compliance with an enumerated set of fundamental rights and, in the event of a violation, to declare that the democratically elected legislature had contravened rights. Given the centrality of the principle of parliamentary sovereignty in the UK constitutional order, the main challenge was to find a way of upholding rights, whilst giving Parliament the final say in determining what the law should be. There was no political appetite to give the judiciary the power to strike down legislation on the American model.[2] Therefore, the key concern across the political spectrum was to devise a statutory scheme which would uphold rights without undermining the primacy of Parliament in the UK constitutional order.[3]

The architects of the HRA came up with an ingenious way of reconciling rights-based review and parliamentary democracy.[4] It was achieved in the following ways. First, the HRA was an ordinary Act of Parliament, which can be amended or repealed by simple majority vote in Parliament. It had no formally entrenched status as 'supreme law'. Second, the courts were not given the power to invalidate or strike down legislation if they found that it violated rights. Instead, they were given a

---

[1] Straw (2000); Lester (1998); Klug (2001) 370; Ewing (2004) 836; Hiebert (2006) 7.
[2] Lester (2002a) 58; Gearty (2016) 67; Kavanagh (2009a) 310–13; Irvine (2003a) 98; Feldman (1999) 169.
[3] Klug (2003) 125–6; Malleson (2001) 28, 33, 36–7.
[4] For insightful accounts of the research and consultation commissioned by the Labour Party prior to the enactment of the HRA, see Straw (2012) 274–8; Duxbury (2017) 652–5; Klug (2005); Ewing (1999) 79–82.

set of interpretive and declaratory powers which fell short of striking down. Under section 3 HRA the courts were given a robust interpretive duty to 'read and give effect' to legislation in a rights-compatible manner 'so far as it is possible to do so'.[5] However, if a rights-compatible interpretation was not possible, then the courts could issue 'a declaration of incompatibility' under section 4 HRA which would 'not affect the validity, continuing operation or enforcement of the provision in respect of which it is given'.[6] Using these tools, the courts could adjudicate but not invalidate. They could declare, but not disapply, legislation enacted by the democratically elected legislature.

Finally, Parliament was under no legal duty to comply with court rulings on rights. As with all other decisions handed down by the UK courts, Parliament was free to ignore or override judicial decisions about rights under the HRA. True, once a declaration of incompatibility is issued, this triggers a 'fast-track amendment procedure'[7] under section 10 HRA, where the Government could amend legislation swiftly to comply with the judicial declaration.[8] But this is an option, not an obligation. Moreover, section 6 HRA explicitly excludes Parliament and primary legislation from the general duty placed on other public authorities – including the courts – to act compatibly with Convention rights.[9] And as we saw in previous chapters, section 19 HRA allows Parliament to enact legislation which seems to contravene rights. Through an intricate and novel institutional design, the HRA seemed to have found the Holy Grail of protecting rights whilst preserving the primacy of democratic self-government.

As an innovative constitutional design for the twenty-first century, the HRA ignited intense interest amongst UK public lawyers and comparative constitutional scholars, who hailed it as instantiating a 'new model of constitutionalism'.[10] Variously described as 'the new Commonwealth model of constitutionalism',[11] 'weak-form review',[12] the 'parliamentary

---

[5] Section 3(1) HRA.
[6] Section 4(6)(a) HRA.
[7] Section 10 HRA.
[8] Ibid.
[9] Section 6 HRA; Van Zyl Smit (2011) 67–8.
[10] Gardbaum (2013b).
[11] Ibid.
[12] Tushnet (2008b); Goldsworthy (2003a).

model',[13] or a model of 'democratic dialogue',[14] the distinctive and defining feature of the new model was that it 'decoupled [rights-based] review from judicial supremacy by empowering the legislature to have 'the last word'.[15] Instead of giving the courts a 'veto over the politics of the nation',[16] the HRA allowed the courts to share their views about what rights required, whilst allowing the legislature to disagree.

The oratorical aura of this arrangement gave rise to suggestions that the HRA created a 'dialogue' about rights between the branches of government, albeit a dialogue where the legislature had the final say.[17] The fact that the HRA provided 'judicial oversight of legislation without displacing the ultimate power of legislatures to determine public policy'[18] engendered the related claim that the HRA was a leading exemplar of 'weak-form review'.[19] In contrast to the US system of so-called 'strong-form review', which allowed the courts to invalidate primary legislation in a way that was 'final and unrevisable by ordinary legislative majorities',[20] the power of the UK judiciary seemed relatively weak. Not only were the UK courts prevented from striking down legislation, judicial decisions about rights could be modified, overridden or 'displaced'[21] by the sovereign Parliament.

Yet, regardless of whether the UK system was described as a model of democratic dialogue, weak-form review or the New Commonwealth Model of constitutionalism, the common denominator of all these theories was a normative emphasis on the legislature's right to disagree, defy and displace judicial rulings on rights.[22] By combining judicial oversight with legislative override, the courts could share their 'thoughtful opinion on rights',[23] whilst the legislature would have the last word. The lynchpin

---

[13] Hiebert (2004b); Hiebert (2006).

[14] Young (2009); Hickman (2005a).

[15] Gardbaum (2001) 709; Gardbaum (2011) 197; Stephenson (2016) 2. For a 'hard look at the last word', see Kavanagh (2015a).

[16] Hogg & Bushell (1997) 77.

[17] Hickman (2005a) 308–9; Young (2017); Dixon (2007) 407.

[18] Tushnet (2003c) 831.

[19] Tushnet (2008b); Tushnet (2011a); Dixon (2012).

[20] Tushnet (2008b) 33.

[21] Tushnet (2003a) 2786; Kavanagh (2015c) 1032–5 (arguing that 'the language of "displacement" is too crude to capture the complexity of the inter-institutional dynamics' at stake).

[22] Tushnet (2003c) 831; Tushnet (2003a) 2781; Yap (2015) 1, 9, 20, 27; cf. Kavanagh (2015c) 1009–11.

[23] Nicol (2006) 743; cf. Hickman (2008) 88–9.

of the new model, therefore, was the 'formal legislative power to have the final word on what the law of the land is by ordinary majority vote'.[24]

The aim of this chapter is twofold. The first is to explicate the role of the courts under the HRA, situating them within the broader constitutional scheme. The second is to explore the deeper normative questions surrounding the constitutional relationships between the branches of government in the HRA framework. Departing from the scholarly trend to describe that relationship as a 'dialogue' between constitutional equals, or as an instance of 'weak-form review', I show that the role of the courts under the HRA is neither conversational in form nor weak in fact. Instead, I argue that the HRA is best conceived as a constitutional partnership in progress, where the protection of rights is a shared responsibility between all three branches of government, working together in comity and collaboration.

The chapter will proceed in the following way. Part 2 explores the interpretive obligation under section 3 HRA. Part 3 of the chapter outlines the limits of interpretive possibility, thereby illustrating the deeply contextual and remedial elements of the judicial choice between interpretation and declaration under the HRA. Part 4 examines the dynamics surrounding the declaration of incompatibility, explaining why the courts have treated it as a matter of last resort. Part 5 examines the commonplace claim that the declaration of incompatibility is a dialogic device. Rejecting that claim, I argue that a declaration of incompatibility is a much stronger judicial tool than is often assumed. Drawing the strands of analysis together, I conclude with some reflections on the hidden strengths of 'weak-form review'.

2   The Art of the Possible

Under section 3 HRA, the courts are obliged to 'read and give effect' to all legislation in a way which is compatible with Convention rights 'so far as it is possible to do so'.[25] The crux question, therefore, concerns the 'art of the possible':[26] how far can judges go when interpreting legislation compatibly with Convention rights? In the case-law under the HRA, the courts settled on an expansive understanding of section 3 which allows them to modify the effect of otherwise unambiguous legislative

---

[24] Gardbaum (2010) 169; Tushnet (2008b) xi; cf. Kavanagh (2015a) 832; Kavanagh (2015c).
[25] Section 3(1) HRA.
[26] Lester (1998).

provisions. They do so by adopting a two-stage approach to their inter-pretive obligation under section 3.[27]

At the first stage, the courts work out whether the legislation, as ordinarily understood, seems to interfere with Convention rights. If not, then that is the end of the matter and the litigant loses. However, if the courts believe that the ordinary meaning of the statute gives rise to a *prima facie* infringement of Convention rights, then the judges go on to see whether it is nonetheless possible to find a rights-consistent inter-pretation to remove or 'cure'[28] the apparent incompatibility by relying on 'special interpretive obligations under section 3(1)'.[29] At this second stage, the courts explore whether a statutory provision can be '*rendered* Convention-compatible'[30] using the tools of statutory interpretation. At this stage, the courts have held that section 3 allows them

> to adopt an interpretation which linguistically may appear strained. The techniques to be used will include the reading down of express language in a statute but also the implication of provisions.[31]

As Lord Neuberger observed extra-judicially, 'if legislation does not appear to comply [with Convention rights], we must, if we can, *recast* it so that it does comply'.[32] In this way, section 3 operates as a powerful corrective technique to remedy rights-violations through statutory interpretation.[33]

The leading case on interpretation under section 3(1) is *Ghaidan v Mendoza*.[34] This case concerned the rights of a surviving same-sex partner of a tenant to a statutory tenancy under the Rent Act 1977. The Rent Act granted a right of succession to the 'surviving spouse' of a tenant, where 'spouse' was defined as 'a person who was living with the original tenant as his or her wife or husband'.[35] The question was whether this provision applied to same-sex partners. The House of

---

[27] Kavanagh (2009a) 23–4; Gearty (2002) 248, 252; *R v A* [2002] 1 AC 45 [43]; *Sheldrake v DPP* [2004] UKHL 43 [27]–[28].

[28] *Principal Reporter v K* [2010] UKSC 56 [66]; Lord Bingham (2010) 572.

[29] *R (K) v Hackney London Borough Council* [2020] UKSC 40 [114].

[30] *Principal Reporter v K* (n 28) [66] (emphasis added).

[31] *R v A* (n 27) [44].

[32] Neuberger (2015) [47] (emphasis added).

[33] Sathanapally (2012) 86.

[34] *Ghaidan v Mendoza* [2004] 2 AC 557; see further Kavanagh (2009a) chapter 3; Van Zyl Smit (2007).

[35] Rent Act 1977, section 42, [2(1)], sch. 1.

Lords held that, as ordinarily understood, the 'unambiguous'[36] terms of the Rent Act was confined to heterosexual partners and did not apply to same-sex couples. Indeed, it had been interpreted to preclude same-sex surviving partners only three years previously.[37]

The next question was whether this apparent or prima facie infringement could be eliminated by adopting a section 3(1) interpretation. By a majority of 4:1, the House of Lords held that it could. How was this achieved? The House of Lords held that while the language of the Rent Act seemed to preclude same-sex couples, the 'social policy'[38] underlying the Act was to give secure tenancies to couples who were in a stable and loving relationship, and this policy could be applied equally to same-sex couples. By reading the Rent Act to include same-sex couples, the courts could 'eliminate the discriminatory effect' of the legislation, but would 'do so consistently with the social policy underlying [the Act]'.[39] Admittedly, this involved 'extending the reach'[40] of the Rent Act. Nonetheless, the court argued that this was achieved without contradicting the cardinal principles of the legislative framework.

Ghaidan clarifies some key questions about the scope and limits of the interpretive obligation under section 3. All judges agreed that the interpretive obligation in section 3(1) was 'of an unusual and far-reaching character'[41] that went beyond the pre-existing canons of construction. In contrast to the 'principle of legality', which could only apply if legislation was vague, general or ambiguous, section 3 did not require an ambiguity trigger.[42] It could apply even if the statutory language or original legislative intention was clear. In forming this view, they took their cue from the White Paper preceding the HRA, which emphasized that section 3 goes 'far beyond the present rule which enables the courts to take the Convention into account in resolving an ambiguity in a legislative provision'.[43] Thus,

---

[36] *Ghaidan* (n 34) [35].

[37] *Fitzpatrick* [2001] 1 AC 27.

[38] *Ghaidan* (n 34) [35].

[39] Ibid [35]; Van Zyl Smit (2007) 300.

[40] *Ghaidan* (n 34) [128], *per* Lord Rodger.

[41] Ibid [30]; *Sheldrake* (n 27) [28] *per* Lord Bingham.

[42] *Ghaidan* (n 34) [29]–[30] (Lord Nicholls), [44] (Lord Steyn), [119] (Lord Rodger), [67] (Lord Millett).

[43] White Paper, *Rights Brought Home: The Human Rights Bill*, [2.7], [2.14], cited by Lord Steyn in *Ghaidan* (n 34) [42].

> even if, construed according to the ordinary principles of interpretation, the meaning of the legislation admits of no doubt, section 3 may nonetheless require the legislation to be given a different meaning ... Section 3 may require the courts to depart from the legislative intention, that is, depart from the intention of the Parliament which enacted the legislation[44] ... and from the unambiguous meaning the legislation would otherwise bear.[45]

What interpretive tools can courts use to render legislation compliant with rights under section 3? The courts have held that they can interpret statutes 'restrictively or expansively'[46] in order to achieve a Convention-compatible result. They can also use the interpretive techniques of 'reading in' and 'reading down'.[47] 'Reading in' allows the courts to 'supply by implication words that are appropriate to ensure that legislation is read in a way which is compatible with Convention rights'.[48] 'Reading down' involves 'restricting the scope and effect of apparently broad and clear statutory language to ensure that powers can only be exercised consistently with Convention rights'.[49] The upshot is that section 3 empowers the courts

> to change the meaning of the enacted legislation, so as to make it Convention-compliant; ... to an extent bounded only by what is "possible", a court can modify the meaning, and hence the effect, of primary and secondary legislation.[50]

Although this expansive approach to the interpretive obligation is not without its critics,[51] the two-stage approach has been fully endorsed

---

[44] *Ghaidan* (n 34) [29]; *Sheldrake* (n 27) [28], Lord Bingham.

[45] *Ghaidan* (n 34) [30].

[46] Ibid [32].

[47] Rose & Weir (2003) 48–52.

[48] *Ghaidan* (n 34) [121], Lord Rodger. The practice of reading 'curing words' into legislation in order to render them compatible with rights is a constitutional commonplace across multiple jurisdictions, see Eskridge & Frickey (1992); Vermeule (1997) (describing such interpretations as 'saving constructions') (United States); Young (2010) 408 (South Africa); Brenncke (2018) chapters 2 & 3 (England and Germany); Carolan (2016b) 100–7 (Ireland); Leckey (2015) 94–7 (Canada, UK, South Africa); McLean (2001) (New Zealand).

[49] Rose & Weir (2003) 48.

[50] *Ghaidan* (n 34) [32]. For consideration of the analogy between section 3 HRA and the courts' obligation to interpret national legislation in light of the wording and purpose of EU Directives, see Schaeffer (2005); Sales (2009a) 608.

[51] See Nicol (2006); Davis (2010); Campbell (2001); Ewing (2004).

in the case-law. As Lord Bingham stated simply in *R (Al-Skeini) v Secretary of State for Defence,*

> section 3 provides an important tool to be used where it is necessary and possible to modify domestic legislation to avoid incompatibility with the Convention rights protected by the Act.[52]

Thus, the interpretive obligation under section 3 is treated as a 'very strong and far-reaching one, which may require the court to depart from the legislative intention of Parliament.[53] In short, section 3 has created 'a remarkably powerful interpretative obligation, which goes well beyond the normal canons of statutory construction'.[54]

Using section 3, the courts have adopted some bold and creative interpretations. In a number of cases, the courts have used section 3 to 'read down' statutory provisions which clearly imposed a legal burden of proof on the defendant, to mean that the defendant was only obliged to discharge an evidential burden of proof.[55] In *R (Hammond) v Home Secretary,*[56] the House of Lords treated a statutory provision that a life prisoner's tariff 'is to be determined by a single judge of the High Court without an oral hearing' as giving the judge a discretion to require an oral hearing in order to render it compatible with the right to a fair trial.[57]

In *R v Offen,*[58] the Court of Appeal held that a statute which required courts to impose a mandatory life sentence on defendants convicted of two serious criminal offences unless there were 'exceptional circumstances,' should be read in a way which complied with the right to liberty under Article 5 ECHR.[59] Reasoning that the purpose of this notorious 'two strikes and you're out'[60] provision was to protect the public from dangerous criminals, the court interpreted the term 'exceptional

---

[52] *R (Al-Skeini) v Secretary of State for Defence* [2008] 1 AC 153 [15].

[53] *Sheldrake* (n 27) [28], Lord Bingham.

[54] *Reference by the Attorney General and Advocate General of Scotland on the UNCRC (Incorporation) (Scotland) Bill* (2021) UKSC 42, Lord Reed.

[55] *R v Lambert* [2002] 2 AC 545 [22]. In this case, the court read the words 'to prove' under section 28(2) of the Misuse of Drugs Act, 1971, section 38 to mean 'to give sufficient evidence'; *Sheldrake* (n 27); *R v Johnstone* [2003] UKHL 28.

[56] *R (Hammond) v Home Secretary* [2005] UKHL 69.

[57] Criminal Justice Act, 2003, sch 22, para 1.

[58] *R v Offen* [2001] 2 AER 154.

[59] *Offen* concerned section 2 of the Crime (Sentences) Act 1997; Kavanagh (2009a) 22–3, 74, 395; Gearty (2004) 77.

[60] Dyer (2000).

circumstances' to mean that only those prisoners who posed a threat to public safety would fall within the ambit of section 2.[61] Since Mr Offen posed no threat to the public, he was spared an automatic life-sentence and given a three-year sentence instead. In coming to this conclusion, the court emphasized that the rights-compatible reading would still give effect to the intention of Parliament, 'but would do so in a more just, less arbitrary, and more proportionate manner'.[62]

In the most controversial case decided in the early days of the HRA – *R v A*[63] – the House of Lords held that a recently enacted rape-shield provision[64] (which severely curbed judicial discretion to admit sexual history evidence of complainants in rape trials, including sexual history evidence with the accused), violated the accused's right to a fair trial. Although the relevant statutory provision clearly excluded the admissibility of such evidence – indeed, was enacted specifically in order to curb judicial discretion to admit such evidence[65] – the court read an entire subsection into the Act which gave judges discretion to decide whether such evidence was 'so relevant to the issue of consent that to exclude it would endanger the fairness of the trial under Article 6 of the Convention'.[66] Though 'linguistically strained',[67] this implication of provisions was deemed permissible under section 3 in order to ensure that the accused received a fair trial.[68]

3   Taking Interpretation to the Limit

Whilst section 3 is clearly a 'powerful tool'[69] which judges can use to remove an incompatibility with rights, 'the reach of this tool is not unlimited'.[70] Indeed, the very fact that the HRA made provision for the declaration of incompatibility was an explicit acknowledgement that

---

[61] *Offen* (n 58) [97], [100] Lord Woolf.
[62] *Offen* (n 58) [99]; see further Kavanagh (2009a) 22–3, 74, 395.
[63] *R v A* (n 27); for further analysis of early HRA case law, see Kavanagh (2005); Kavanagh (2009a) chapter 2.
[64] Section 23 *Youth Justice and Criminal Evidence Act* 1999.
[65] Kavanagh (2005) 264.
[66] Kavanagh (2009a) 21ff.
[67] *R v A* (n 27) [67]–[68].
[68] For another example of 'reading in' under section 3, see *R v Waya* [2012] UKSC 51.
[69] *Re S (Children) Care Order: Implementation of Care Plan)* [2002] UKHL 10, [38].
[70] Ibid [38].

there were limits to the 'art of the possible' under section 3.[71] However, the HRA did not specify where those limits lay. Therefore, it was up to the courts to articulate them.[72]

In *Ghaidan*, the courts articulated two such limits.[73] The first was that 'the courts should not adopt a meaning inconsistent with a fundamental feature of the legislation'.[74] Any interpretation must 'go with the grain of the legislation'[75] and be compatible with its 'essential principles',[76] its 'underlying thrust'[77] and 'the pith and substance'[78] of the statute. The second is that the courts should not make decisions 'for which they are not equipped. There may be several ways of making a provision Convention-compliant, and the choice may involve issues calling for legislative deliberation'.[79]

We can call these the *fundamental features limit* and *legislative deliberation limit* respectively.[80] As stated, these limits are not precise enough to enable us to predict when judges will issue a declaration of incompatibility in preference to a rights-compatible interpretation under section 3. The courts have 'declined to try to formulate precise rules'[81] on where those limits lie, believing that they would be 'fairly easy to identify'[82] in practice. Nonetheless, we can extrapolate some general guidelines by viewing the cases in context.

The *fundamental features limit* speaks to the limits of judicial law-making outlined in chapter 7. In contrast to the legislature which can make and change the law in radical and comprehensive ways, the courts are generally confined to partial and piecemeal, incremental and interstitial forms of law-making. Recalling the 'dilemma of partial reform'[83] discussed in Chapter 7, the *fundamental features limit* suggests that if a

---

[71] *R (Morris) v Westminster City Council* [2005] EWCA Civ 1184 [56]; *Wilson v First County Trust* [2003] UKHL 40 [14]; Kavanagh (2015c) 1020; Sathanapally (2012) 83.
[72] Van Zyl Smit (2011) 78.
[73] *Gilham v Ministry for Justice* [2019] UKSC 44 [39], [43]; *R (Z) v Hackney London Borough Council* [2020] UKSC 40 [111]; *McDonald v McDonald* [2016] UKSC 28 [69]; *WB v W District Council* [2018] EWCA Civ 928 [22], [25].
[74] *Ghaidan* (n 34) [33].
[75] Ibid [33].
[76] Ibid [110]–[111].
[77] Ibid [33]
[78] Ibid [111].
[79] Ibid [33].
[80] Kavanagh (2015c) 1020ff.
[81] *Ghaidan* (n 34) [50]; *Sheldrake* (n 27) [28]; *Waya* (n 68) [14].
[82] *Ghaidan* (n 34) [50].
[83] Raz (1979) 200–1; Kavanagh (2004) 279–82.

rights-compatible interpretation would cause too much discordance in the legislative scheme or require comprehensive legal reform beyond the law-making capacity of the courts, then the courts will typically leave it to the legislature to remedy the rights-violation by legislative means.[84] Section 3 may be a powerful interpretive tool, but it 'does not allow the courts to change the substance of the [statutory] provision entirely'[85] or depart from the 'cardinal principles'[86] on which the statute rests. Even when 'reading in' or 'reading down', judicial interpretations must nonetheless 'go with the grain'[87] of the statute and preserve its 'general scheme'.[88]

However, if a proposed interpretation would 'radically alter the effect of the legislation'[89] or undermine its 'entire structure',[90] then the limits of interpretation may have been reached, thereby suggesting that a declaration is the more appropriate remedy.[91] For example, in a case concerning a draconian penalty scheme imposed on hauliers found to have clandestine immigrants in their vehicles upon entering the UK (*Roth*),[92] the judges held that they could not cure the rights violation by interpretive means:

> The troubling features of the scheme are all interlinked: to achieve fairness would require a radically different approach. We cannot 'turn the scheme inside out' . . . We cannot create a wholly different scheme . . . so as to provide for an acceptable means of immigration control. That must be for Parliament.[93]

Since comprehensive legislative reform was required, the court issued a declaration of incompatibility, thereby inviting the legislature to remedy the rights-violation using the wide-ranging tools of legislative law reform, which they duly did.[94]

---

[84] Kavanagh (2015c) 1020; Sales (2009a) 609.
[85] *Ghaidan* (n 34) [33].
[86] Ibid [113].
[87] Ibid [33].
[88] Ibid [118].
[89] *Poplar Housing v Donoghue* [2002] QB 48, [73].
[90] *Ghaidan* (n 34) [111].
[91] *R (Z) v Hackney London Borough Council* [2020] UKSC 40 [111]; Leigh & Masterman (2008) 102.
[92] *International Transport Roth GmBH v SSHD* [2002] EWCA Civ 158.
[93] Ibid [66].
[94] Kavanagh (2009a) 39–40; Sathanapally (2012) 94–7.

Whilst the *fundamental features limit* requires the courts to focus on the contoured constraints of the statutory scheme, the *legislative deliberation limit* speaks to broader questions about relative institutional competence, expertise and legitimacy. In *Ghaidan*, the House of Lords clarified that if a rights-compatible interpretation has 'far-reaching practical ramifications ... raising issues ill-suited for determination by the courts and court procedures',[95] then this may suggest that the limits of interpretive possibility have been reached. Moreover, if there are a number of rights-compatible legislative options, the courts generally leave it to the legislature to make the choice about what the best option would be. But these are broad statements are in need of illustration and instantiation. The case of *Bellinger v Bellinger*[96] on transsexual marriage provides a good example of the *fundamental features limit* and the *legislative deliberation limit* in action.

Mrs Bellinger was a male-to-female post-operative transsexual who argued that the Matrimonial Causes Act 1973 was unjustifiably discriminatory because it stipulated that a valid marriage could only occur between a 'male' and a 'female' where gender was determined at birth. The House of Lords held that the 1973 Act clearly violated Mrs Bellinger's rights. However, whilst a rights-compatible interpretation would have been possible using the judicial techniques of 'reading in' or 'reading down' under section 3, the court refused to engage in this interpretive exercise, preferring instead to issue a declaration of incompatibility under section 4. Why did the court believe that it was 'peculiarly inappropriate'[97] to remedy the rights-violation by interpretive means?

The court advanced four key reasons for this refusal, each stemming from an awareness of the limits of judicial capacity and an appreciation of the relative competence, expertise and legitimacy of the legislature. First, a judicial modification of the law on marriage to include transsexuals would be

> a major change in the law, having far-reaching ramifications ... whose solution calls for extensive inquiry and the widest public consultation and discussion. Questions of social policy and administrative feasibility arise at several points, and their interaction has to be evaluated and balanced.

---

[95] *Ghaidan* (n 34) [34].
[96] *Bellinger v Bellinger* [2003] UKHL 21; see further Kavanagh (2009a) 40–1, 137–42. 290; Sathanapally (2012) 94–7.
[97] *Bellinger* (n 96) [45].

The issues are altogether ill-suited for determination by courts and court procedures. They are pre-eminently a matter for Parliament.[98]

The recognition of gender reassignment for the purposes of marriage was 'part of a wider problem which should be considered as a whole and not dealt with in a piecemeal fashion. There should be a clear, coherent policy'.[99] In short, the legalization of transgender marriage called for 'comprehensive legislative reform rather than piecemeal judicial development'.[100] Therefore, it was pre-eminently a matter for the legislature not the courts.

Second, legal reform on transgender rights required a set of 'objective, publicly available criteria'[101] for determining when someone had successfully transitioned from one gender to another. This was a delicate and difficult line-drawing exercise which was 'ill-suited for determination by the courts or court procedures'.[102] Whilst the court was confident that Mrs Bellinger had successfully transitioned, it was 'not in a position to decide where the demarcation line should be drawn' as a general matter.[103] Deducing general criteria for recognition of gender change from the facts of one single case was not 'a proper or indeed a responsible basis on which to change the law'.[104]

Third, the nature of marriage was 'deeply embedded in the religious and social culture of this country'[105] and was subject to widespread moral and ethical controversy within society as a whole. Therefore, a 'fundamental change in the traditional concept of marriage'[106] should be the product of democratic deliberation, not judicial imposition.

Fourth, following the Strasbourg decision in *Goodwin* requiring recognition of transsexuals in UK law, the Government had already set up an Interdepartmental Working Group to examine the implications of granting full legal status to transsexuals in their acquired gender. Since

---

[98] Ibid [45].
[99] Ibid [45].
[100] *A v Chief Constable of West Yorkshire Police* (2004) UKHL 21 [12] Lord Bingham.
[101] *Bellinger* (n 96) [43].
[102] *Ghaidan* (n 34) [34].
[103] *Bellinger* (n 96) [44].
[104] Ibid [40].
[105] Ibid [40].
[106] Ibid [48].

legislative preparations were already underway, 'intervention by the courts would be peculiarly inappropriate',[107]

> more especially when the government, in unequivocal terms, has already announced its intention to introduce comprehensive primary legislation on this difficult and sensitive topic.[108]

The court was reluctant to change the law when the issue was already in hand and moving forward through the legislative process.

Together, these four reasons pointed towards the conclusion that remedying the rights-violation by judicial interpretation was 'peculiarly inappropriate'.[109] Recognising transgender rights and making them real in policy and practice was pre-eminently a matter for 'deliberation and decision by Parliament'.[110]

4   Interpreting Rights, Declaring Wrongs

In choosing between interpretation and declaration under the HRA, the courts effect a division of labour between the branches of government. If they decide to interpret legislation compatibly with rights, they 'cure'[111] the rights violation at source with immediate effect, thus obviating the need for further legislative action. However, if they issue a declaration of incompatibility, they draw Parliament's attention to a potential violation of rights, thereby inviting it – but, crucially, not compelling it – to fix the problem using the wide-ranging tools of legislative law reform. But how do the courts choose between interpretation and declaration? When we look at the cases in context, some patterns emerge concerning the interplay between interpretation and declaration in judicial reasoning under the HRA.[112]

It is clear from the case-law that the limits of section 3 do not hinge solely on what is linguistically possible, but rather a more rounded assessment of what is institutionally and constitutionally appropriate

---

[107] Ibid [39] see *Goodwin v United Kingdom.*, App. No. 28957/95 (ECtHR July 11, 2002).
[108] Ibid [37].
[109] Ibid [48].
[110] Ibid [49].
[111] *Principal Reporter* (n 28) [66].
[112] For further analysis of the judicial choice between interpretation and declaration, see Kavanagh (2007).

for the courts to do as partners in the constitutional scheme.[113] Both the *fundamental features* and the *legislative deliberation* limits pivot on the scope and limits of the judicial role vis-à-vis the other branches of government, and the constitutional division of labour between them.[114] Thus, whilst the interpretive duty under section 3 is undoubtedly a powerful tool, the courts have tended to use it in a way which takes cognisance of the limits of the judicial law-making role outlined in Chapter 7. In doing so, the courts strive to uphold rights, whilst respecting the relative competence and legitimacy of the legislature to drive forward comprehensive, systemic rights-based reform.

The case-law also reveals that the judicial choice between interpretation and declaration is a deeply context-dependent inquiry, heavily influenced by remedial concerns.[115] Recall that the choice between sections 3 and 4 only arises *after* the court has already determined that the legislation 'in its natural and ordinary meaning'[116] is incompatible with rights.[117] Therefore, the choice is 'explicitly remedial',[118] rooted in whether remedial action would be better coming from the courts or the legislature.

In choosing between these 'different remedial pathways',[119] the courts try to establish whether the issue is more appropriately remedied using the piecemeal tools of judicial rectification, as opposed to the more comprehensive law-making tools available to legislators.[120] In general terms, the courts will issue a declaration of incompatibility if root-and-branch reform of the whole area is required;[121] the legislative provision is deeply imbricated in a complex legislative scheme whose provisions are all interlinked;[122] or if the issue has far-reaching ramifications that the court is ill-placed to assess.[123]

However, if the courts believe that they can remedy the rights-violation effectively using the necessarily piecemeal tools of judicial

---

[113] Kavanagh (2009a) 140ff; Kavanagh (2005) 266; Phillipson (2006) 65; Leigh & Masterman (2008) 101, 109.

[114] Kavanagh (2009a) 54–9.

[115] Kavanagh (2015c) 1021ff; Dixon (2009a) 335; Van Zyl Smit (2011).

[116] *Ghaidan* (n 34) [60], Lord Millett.

[117] *S v L* [2012] UKSC 30, [15], Lord Reed.

[118] Van Zyl Smit (2016).

[119] Sathanapally (2012) 102.

[120] Kavanagh (2004); Sathanapally (2012) 88.

[121] *Bellinger* (n 96); *Roth* (n 92).

[122] *Bellinger* (n 96); *Re K and H* [2015] EWCA Civ 543 [31]; Sathanapally (2012) 94–5.

[123] *Re S* (n 69) [43]; *Bellinger* (n 96).

rectification, without causing undue discordance in the legislative scheme, they will typically choose an interpretation under section 3 in order to do justice in the individual case. As Lord Bingham stated extra-judicially, when choosing between sections 3 or 4, the courts will assess

> whether, when faced with the incompatibility, Ministers and Parliament would have practically-effective options of how to cure it: if so, they should be given the opportunity to find the best remedy; if not, s.3 provides the neatest and most final conclusion.[124]

There is one other feature of the interplay between interpretation and declaration which warrants attention here, namely, that when deciding whether to interpret or declare, the courts have treated section 3 as the 'prime remedial measure'[125] under the HRA, with declarations of incompatibility treated as a 'measure of last resort'.[126] This is now a settled principle in the case law.[127] As the Supreme Court has held on numerous occasions: 'section 3(1) is the primary remedy and resort to making a declaration of incompatibility must always be an exceptional course'.[128]

So why have the courts given priority to their interpretive obligation under section 3, thus rendering declarations of incompatibility a relatively rare and exceptional event? There are three main reasons why the courts have treated section 3 as the primary remedial measure and declarations as a matter of last resort: *remedial potency, legislative purpose*, and *the politics of litigation*.

Let us start with *remedial potency*. The only way of giving litigants an immediate and effective remedy is an interpretation under section 3. By 'recast[ing]'[129] the law in rights-compatible terms, the law is changed with immediate effect to remove or ameliorate the rights-offending element, thereby ensuring that 'damages can be awarded, convictions quashed, and injunctions imposed'.[130] By contrast, a declaration of incompatibility leaves the litigant empty-handed. Even if the declaration prompts the legislature to change the law, that will only have prospective

---

[124] Bingham (2010) 572.
[125] *Ghaidan* (n 34) [46], Lord Steyn.
[126] *Ghaidan* (n 34) [46]. On the principle of last resort, see Kavanagh (2009a) 121–8; Kavanagh (2007) 127.
[127] *Sheldrake* (n 27) [28]; *Waya* (n 68) [14].
[128] *R v A* (n 63) [44]; *Gilham v Ministry of Justice* [2019] UKSC 44 [39].
[129] Neuberger (2015) [47].
[130] Irvine (2003b) 319.

effect and, therefore, be of no avail to the litigant before the court.[131] For example, if the court in *Ghaidan* had not interpreted the Rent Act to include same-sex partners, Mr Mendoza would have lost his home.[132] Similarly, in *R v A*,[133] a declaration of incompatibility would have been of no avail to the defendant, who could have been convicted of a serious sexual offence on the basis of a potentially unfair trial.[134] Therefore, if the courts are aware that the litigant will suffer a severe injustice if they do not receive an immediate remedy, this will incline them towards an interpretation under section 3 rather than a declaration under section 4.[135] This chimes with 'the powerful legal tradition of corrective justice'[136] in English common law and the hallowed maxim *ubi jus ibi remedium*.[137] Ironically, therefore, it is precisely the remedial weakness of the declaration of incompatibility under section 4 which can lead to some of the strongest and most creative interpretations under section 3.[138]

Second, the judicial practice of treating interpretation as the primary remedial measure aligns with the central legislative purpose of the HRA, namely, to 'give people in the United Kingdom the opportunities to enforce their rights under the European Convention in British courts rather than having to incur the cost and delay of taking a case to Strasbourg'.[139] Encapsulated in the political slogan 'bringing rights home',[140] the aim of the HRA was to give litigants 'speedy and effective domestic remedies'[141] for violations of Convention rights in domestic law, thus obviating the need for further recourse to Strasbourg.[142] The political expectation was that judicial interpretation would do a lot of

---

[131] Kavanagh (2015c) 1022.

[132] Kavanagh (2009a) 136.

[133] *R v A* (n 63).

[134] Birch (2003) 378; Kavanagh (2005) 260–1.

[135] Dixon (2009a) 346–7 (arguing that the remedial emptiness of declarations of incompatibility is one reason why there have been so few declarations in the criminal law context); Davis & Mead (2014) 71; Stephenson (2016) 157–8.

[136] Sathanapally (2012) 101; Dicey (1964) 199.

[137] Hickman (2015) 48; Feldman (2009) 827.

[138] Kavanagh (2015c) 1023; Kavanagh (2015d) 1050.

[139] White Paper, *Rights Brought Home: The Human Rights Bill* (CM 3782), [1.14], [1.18], Preface by the PM, Tony Blair.

[140] Ibid.

[141] Straw & Boateng (1997) 74.

[142] Klug & Starmer (2005) 728; Malleson (2001) 42; *R (Elan-Cane) v SSHD* [2021] UKSC 56 [92]; *R (SB) v Governors of Denbigh High School* [2006] UKHL 15 [29], Lord Bingham ('the purpose of the HRA was ... to enable rights and remedies to be asserted and enforced by the domestic courts').

heavy lifting in rendering legislation compatible with rights. The key political architects of the HRA predicted that a rights-compatible interpretation under section 3 would be possible in '99% of cases',[143] with declarations of incompatibility reserved for those 'very rare cases'[144] where it was impossible to cure the incompatibility by interpretive means.[145] As the Lord Chancellor explained in the parliamentary debates preceding the HRA:

> We want the courts to strive to find an interpretation of legislation which is consistent with Convention rights so far as the language of the legislation allows, and *only in the last resort* to conclude that the legislation is simply incompatible with them.[146]

By treating interpretation as the primary remedial measure, the courts were striving to implement this purpose. As Lord Steyn observed in *Ghaidan*: 'Rights could only effectively be brought home if section 3(1) was the prime remedial measure, and section 4 a measure of last resort'.[147]

There is one final reason why judges may be inclined to choose interpretation over declaration when adjudicating under the HRA. This goes to *the politics of litigation*. When defending challenges to primary legislation under the HRA, lawyers for the Government frequently urge the courts to adopt a rights-compatible interpretation under section 3 in preference to a declaration of incompatibility.[148] Commenting on this practice extra-judicially, Lord Phillips observed that, in his judicial experience, the creative use of section 3

> suited [Government Ministers] rather well. Ministers do not like declarations of incompatibility. Provided that the main thrust of their legislation is not impaired they have been happy that the courts should revise it to make it Convention-compliant, rather than declare it incompatible. In my experience, Counsel for the Secretary of State usually invites the court to

---

[143] HL Deb 5 February 1998, col 840 (3rd reading) and HC Deb, 16 February 1998, col 778 (2nd reading).

[144] Cooper & Marshal-Williams (2000) 65 (quoting Lord Irvine in parliamentary debate).

[145] Ibid 62.

[146] HL Deb 18 November 1997, vol 583 col 535, Lord Irvine.

[147] *Ghaidan* (n 34) [46], [106]; *Huang v SSHD* [2007] UKHL 11, [8], *per* Lord Bingham; Beatson (2013) 171.

[148] See e.g. *Hammond* (n 56), [29]; *R (Clift) v Home Secretary* [2007] 1 AC 484 [40]; *SSHD v MB* [2008] 1 AC 440; *SSHD v AF (No 3)* [2009] 3 WLR 74.

read down, however difficult it may be to do so, rather than make a declaration of incompatibility.[149]

Other judges have made similar observations, noting extra-judicially that Ministers 'usually prefer us to solve an incompatibility problem for them rather than make a declaration of incompatibility'.[150] Surmising that no government likes to experience an adverse declaratory ruling from the courts,[151] Lady Hale observed that the Government 'would rather live with our adventurous interpretations, provided that the main thrust of their legislation is not impaired'.[152]

These observations are borne out by the case law. In some of the most adventurous decisions under the HRA, the government has argued strenuously in favour of highly creative interpretations under section 3, in preference to a declaration of incompatibility.[153] In *Ghaidan*, Counsel for the government argued that it was 'not even a marginal case'[154] for the application of section 3, reassuring the court that judicial intervention was entirely appropriate, given that a rights-compatible interpretation would not give rise to far-reaching practical difficulties for the legislature.[155] In *R v A*, Counsel for the government likewise urged the court to interpret the legislation compatibly with rights rather than issue a declaration of incompatibility.[156] In *AF*,[157] which concerned the right to a fair trial of a terrorist suspect under a 'control order', members of the court 'pushed Counsel for the Secretary of State quite hard'[158] to consider supporting a declaration of incompatibility, especially given that the proposed interpretation under section 3 ran counter to the 'clear intention of the 2005 Act'.[159] Yet, Counsel for the government resisted that push – no doubt under instruction to do so – despite the fact that a

---

[149] Phillips (2010); *AF* (n 148) [68], Lord Phillips; Kavanagh (2015c) 1022–4; Phillipson (2013) 43–4.

[150] Hale (2013) 6; Mance (2018) 112; Brown (2020) 229.

[151] Mance (2018) 112.

[152] Hale (2013) 6. For academic commentary on this phenomenon, see Kavanagh (2015c) 1022–3; Van Zyl Smit (2016) 16ff; Mallory & Tyrrell (2021) 470–1.

[153] *Ghaidan* (n 34) [128]; *Hammond* (n 56) [17], [29]; *Clift* (n 15) [40]; *MB* (n 148).

[154] *Ghaidan* (n 34) [144].

[155] Ghaidan (n 34) [128]; Van Zyl Smit (2011) 70.

[156] *R v A* (n 63); *Hammond* (n 56) [17], [29].

[157] *AF* (n 148); see further Kavanagh (2010c).

[158] Hale (2013) 6; *Hammond* (n 56) [29] (Lord Hoffmann); *AF* (n 148) [95]; Van Zyl Smit (2016) 16.

[159] See e.g. *AF* (n 148) [95] where Lord Scott criticised government counsel for conceding a section interpretation; Van Zyl Smit (2011) 70.

rights-compatible outcome would require what Lady Hale described extra-judicially as 'heroic feats of interpretation under section 3'.[160] This complicates the picture of the courts and legislatures as adversaries locked in a power struggle to seize the last word on rights.[161] These cases show that the government may not want the last word. Instead, it may be quite happy to let the courts shoulder the burden of rendering legislation compliant with rights beneath the political radar.

This begs the obvious question: why would the government favour a transformative interpretation under section 3, rather than a legally non-binding declaration under section 4 which ostensibly leaves them at liberty to resist and reject that declaration as they see fit? One possibility is that the government does not want to incur the political costs of a 'headline-grabbing damning verdict'[162] involved in a declaration of incompatibility, preferring instead to let the courts modify the law in the relatively invisible subterranean landscape of statutory interpretation.[163] Strained interpretations tend to go unnoticed outside the legal community.[164]

Furthermore, to the general public with no detailed understanding of the nuances of the HRA, a section 3 interpretation seems like 'a clean bill of health in human rights terms'.[165] After all, the practical effect of a remedial interpretation is that the legislation no longer violates rights because the violation has been 'cured' or 'interpreted away'.[166] Therefore, the public message conveyed by a section 3 interpretation is that the legislation is fully compliant with rights, thus obscuring the fact that the courts have 'refashioned'[167] its terms in order to create that effect.[168] By contrast, it is hard to present a declaration of incompatibility

---

[160] *AF* (n 148) [95], Baroness Hale; Kavanagh (2010c) 848–9; Hale (2012) ('Strangely enough, and despite some provocation from the Bench, the government did not challenge our bold interpretation of the legislation and invite us to make a declaration of incompatibility instead').

[161] Leckey (2015) 195.

[162] Kavanagh (2015c) 1023; Mead (2015) 467 (observing that media coverage of the HRA focuses overwhelmingly on declarations of incompatibility, not interpretive decisions under section 3 HRA).

[163] Kavanagh (2009a) 230–1; Nicol (2004b) 468; Kavanagh (2010c) 849–50.

[164] Nicol (2006) 747.

[165] Kavanagh (2015c) 1023; see Mead (2015) 467.

[166] Endicott (2021) 85; Duxbury (2017) 667; Kavanagh (2010c) 850.

[167] Mance (2018) 112.

[168] Kavanagh (2010c) 849–50 (noting that the Government sometimes claim a 'human rights victory' when legislation is interpreted compatibly with rights, omitting to

as anything other than a straightforward failure by the government to protect human rights.[169] The upshot is that although the declaration of incompatibility is often hailed as a device which gives the legislature 'the last word' on rights, the fact is that legislators may not want the last word, either because they are happy to let the courts do their human rights handiwork for them or because they do not want to bear the political costs of a judicial declaration that they do not respect rights.[170]

5   Declarations as Decision not Dialogue

When the Human Rights Act was enacted, the declaration of incompatibility was hailed as the most distinctive and novel feature of its constitutional design. Instead of giving courts the power to veto or invalidate legislation with final effect, the declaration of incompatibility seemed to provide a checking-point in the system, where courts performed 'an alerting and informing function in relation to rights'.[171] The courts could *adjudicate* but not *invalidate*; they could *coax* but not *coerce*. For this reason, many commentators treated the declaration of incompatibility as 'the dialogic device *par excellence*'.[172] On this view, judges could share their 'thoughtful opinion on rights'[173] whereupon Parliament could exercise its 'sovereign prerogative to disagree with judicial assessments'[174] albeit 'informed by the court's view of the law'.[175] All the declaration did was 'place the ball in Parliament's court'.[176] On this understanding, declarations of incompatibility were 'courteous requests for conversation, not pronouncements of truth from on high'.[177]

This idea of 'declarations as dialogue' also gave rise to normative recommendations that judges should issue declarations in a regular if not 'routine'[178] fashion whenever a rights violation arose. After all, if

---

mention that the courts had to engage in some creative interpretation in order to achieve that result); Phillipson (2013) 44.

[169]   Kavanagh (2010c) 849; Kavanagh (2009a) 230; Phillipson (2013) 43–4.

[170]   Leckey (2015) 88–9.

[171]   Gardbaum (2013b) 64, 68, 86; Gardbaum (2013a) 2243–4; cf. Kavanagh (2016a) 839.

[172]   Poole (2007a) 555; Sathanapally (2012) 46; Murray (2013a) 64; Geiringer (2009) 615.

[173]   Nicol (2006) 743; cf. Hickman (2008) 88–9.

[174]   Marshall (2003) 243–4; Masterman & Leigh (2013) 7; Poole (2007a) 558.

[175]   *R (Nicklinson) v Ministry of Justice* [2014] UKSC 38, [343]–[344] Lord Kerr; Kahana (2002) 248, 260.

[176]   *Nicklinson* (n 175).

[177]   Gearty (2006) 96; Davis (2014a) 142; Mallory & Tyrrell (2021) 466–7.

[178]   Campbell (2001).

declarations are merely optional opinions in a constitutional conversation, then surely the courts should issue them freely and robustly 'safe in the knowledge that they are only contributing to a political debate, rather than determining the necessary outcome'.[179] Why should the courts be 'reticent'[180] and restrained if Parliament has the power or even the 'right to disagree'?[181] Dialogue scholars urged the courts to 'uncompromisingly tell their truth on rights'[182] and to issue declarations in an 'uninhibited'[183] and 'outspoken'[184] manner. If talk is cheap, then 'why not just make the declaration?'[185]

But whilst declarations of incompatibility may look like purely hortatory statements with no strings attached, they tie the government's and legislature's hands in the following significant and substantial ways. First, declarations of incompatibility are not simply optional opinions in an ongoing constitutional conversation between the courts and the legislature. Instead, they are 'reasoned conclusions of incompatibility'[186], where the courts conclude that legislation enacted by the democratic legislature clearly violates rights guaranteed under national and international human rights law.

The gravity of a declaration is signalled by the fact that they are reserved to the higher courts,[187] and can only be made after the Executive has been given a chance to make arguments before the court on the propriety of a declaration.[188] Moreover, judges present such declarations as interpretations of law i.e. as authoritative judicial decisions on what human rights law requires in the context of the individual case.[189] Rather than being opening gambits in a constitutional conversation between the branches, declarations are anchored in the adjudication of a particular case, culminating in a considered judicial finding that

---

[179] Sathanapally (2012) 115; Stark (2017a) 644; Davis & Mead (2014) 70; Mallory & Tyrrell (2021) 489–90.
[180] Adams (2021) 311.
[181] Sathanapally (2012) 105; Davis (2014a) 148. For the argument that judicial restraint is unnecessary in a system where legislatures have 'the last word', see Gardbaum (2013b) 85ff; Gardbaum (2015) 1041–2; cf. Kavanagh (2015a) 840–3, 844.
[182] Nicol (2006) 744.
[183] Davis (2014a) 145 (advocating an 'overt rejection of the court's interpretation').
[184] Nicol (2006) 745–6.
[185] Stark (2017a) 639; Martin (2018) 213.
[186] Leckey (2015) 158.
[187] HRA s 4(5).
[188] HRA s 5(1)–(2); Sathanapally (2012) 83.
[189] Elliott (2011) 615; King (2015b) 187.

this piece of legislation violates *this* litigant's rights.[190] Talk may be cheap, but a carefully reasoned judgment of the higher courts on the merits of a concrete legal dispute after a full adversarial hearing before the higher courts, is a scarce and precious constitutional resource which should be treated with caution and care.[191]

Second, given the crucial international law dimension of the HRA, a declaration of incompatibility is more than a judicial statement about what domestic law requires. It is also a 'municipal alert of non-compliance with international law'.[192] As Lady Hale observed, the declaration of incompatibility was designed as an early warning mechanism to 'alert Government and Parliament that, in our view, the United Kingdom is in breach of its international obligations'.[193] Given that the domestic courts try to anticipate – and to some extent replicate – the reasoning of the Strasbourg court, a declaration is effectively an 'authoritative interpretation by the domestic courts of what the ECtHR would (authoritatively) decide'.[194] Thus, although a declaration of incompatibility creates no immediate legal obligation in the domestic sphere, it announces unlawfulness when judged against the benchmark of the ECHR.[195] This 'supports the framing of each declaration as a legal conclusion about what rights require ... [within] the relevant body of human rights law, with the implication being ... that Parliament acts unlawfully if it fails to conform'.[196] In the acoustic interplay between domestic and international law, the declaration carries some 'anticipatory legal force'[197] which sounds on the supra-national level and reverberates back into the domestic domain.[198]

---

[190] Carolan (2016b) 199; Sathanapally (2012) 31; Leckey (2015) 158. There is a fascinating parallel here between declarations of incompatibility and 'advisory opinions' or 'references' in Canadian constitutional law, which are typically respected and implemented by the key political actors, see Mathen (2019).

[191] Komesar (1994) 270.

[192] Sathanapally (2012) 135, 127; Kavanagh (2015a) 1024; Roach (2016b) 284; *R (Animal Defenders International) v Secretary of State for Culture, Media and Sport* [2008] 1 AC 1312 [53].

[193] *Animal Defenders* (n 192) [53], *per* Baroness Hale; also see *R (Countryside Alliance) v AG* [2007] 3 WLR 922 [113], *per* Baroness Hale; Kavanagh (2009a) 285.

[194] Sales & Ekins (2011) 227–9.

[195] Elliott (2015a) 110; Murray (2013a) 64; Sathanapally (2012) 24 (arguing that declarations are 'not entirely separated from binding, judicially enforceable human rights obligations').

[196] Ekins (2019) 449; Elliott (2015a) 109–10; Feldman (1999) 187.

[197] Elliott (2002) 350.

[198] Elliott (2015a) 114.

Third, if the government does nothing to remedy the rights-violation declared by the court, the government knows that the aggrieved litigant can take their case to Strasbourg, whereupon the Strasbourg court is highly likely to find against the UK government.[199] Therefore, the government knows that if it ignores or defies the declaration of incompatibility, it will only succeed in postponing rather than solving the problem. Once the ECtHR declares a violation of Convention rights, this triggers the UK's obligation in international law to comply with Convention rights. If the violation is not remedied at this stage, the Government will incur all the negative publicity and political costs which the HRA was designed to avoid.[200] Therefore, the UK government has a lot to lose – and potentially very little to gain – by defying the declaration. As Lord Lester observed, the declaration gives the government 'a healthy incentive ... to take speedy remedial action, rather than face the likelihood of eventual defeat before the European Court'.[201]

Fourth, a declaration of incompatibility triggers a 'fast-track amendment procedure'[202] under section 10 HRA, which enables a Minister to 'make such amendments to the legislation as he considers necessary to remove the incompatibility'.[203] There is no legal obligation on government to use such a Remedial Order, nor on Parliament to accept it. Section 10 enacts a '*power* to take remedial action',[204] not a duty to do so. However, the fact that declarations triggers a fast-track amendment procedure is nonetheless significant.

For one thing, it shows that the declaration is more than a purely oratorical device, devoid of any legal or practical effect. Instead, it has a significant impact on the political and legal options open to the government. It also shows that the HRA was designed to incentivise, ease and expedite legislative compliance with declarations of incompatibility, rather than start a constitutional conversation about the meaning of rights.[205] By putting in place a 'fast-track' procedure for remedying

---

[199] Kavanagh (2009a) 284, 286–7.
[200] Irvine (2003a) 245; Straw & Boateng (1997); Kavanagh (2015c) 1024.
[201] Lester (2002a) 67; Cooper & Marshal-Williams (2000) 148 (citing Jack Straw MP in parliamentary debate); White Paper, *Rights Brought Home: Human Rights Bill 1998* [2.17]; Kavanagh (2009a) 284; Lester (1999) 224.
[202] Section 10(1) HRA.
[203] Section 10(2) HRA.
[204] Title of section 10 HRA.
[205] Hickman (2015); Irvine (2003a) 245; Lester (1999) 226.

rights-violations declared by the courts, the HRA was clearly designed to facilitate swift compliance with declarations of incompatibility.

This view is borne out by the legislative history of the HRA. When presenting the Human Rights Bill to Parliament, the key political architects of the Act emphasised that 'in the overwhelming majority of cases',[206] the Government and Parliament would 'certainly be prompted to change the law following a declaration'[207] and would wish 'to do so rapidly'.[208] Indeed, by modelling the declaration of incompatibility on the declaratory judgment employed by the Strasbourg court,[209] the drafters of the HRA sought to harness the pre-existing political practice of compliance with Strasbourg rulings and replicate it at the domestic level.[210] As the Home Secretary, Jack Straw MP, observed, 'for 50 years, there has been ... a fundamental recognition that, in practice, decisions of the Strasbourg court must be implemented'.[211] Therefore, any government would want to comply with domestic declarations of incompatibility 'just as successive governments have sought ... to put right any declaration by the Strasbourg court by way of legislation or Executive action in the United Kingdom'.[212] Sections 4 and 10 of the HRA were part of an intricate and interlocking remedial scheme designed to provide a swift and 'effective procedure'[213] for remedying rights-violations in domestic law.

Finally, when courts issue a declaration, this creates a catalytic accountability effect, which strengthens the onus on government to remedy the incompatibility identified by the courts. As we saw in Chapter 5, all declarations of incompatibility activate a formal response from the JCHR, which in turn catalyses a sustained, iterative

---

[206] Jack Straw, cited in Klug (1999) 264.
[207] Lord Irvine, HL Deb (Committee Stage) 27 November 1997, vol 583 col 1139; Cooper & Marshal-Williams (2000) 149–50, 65; White Paper, *Rights Brought Home* (n 201) [2.10]; King (2015b) 112.
[208] HC Deb 16 February 1998, vol 306 col 778 (Jack Straw MP); HL Deb 3 November 1997, vol 582 col 1231 (Lord Irvine); Cooper & Marshal-Williams (2000) 65, 156; HL Deb 3 November 1997, vol 582 col 1267 (Lord McCluskey) ('In almost every case – and I know of no exception – Parliament will at once move to bring the law into line with what judges say the convention says it is'); Mallory & Tyrrell (2021) 492.
[209] Gearty (2010) 584.
[210] Letsas (2013) 139.
[211] Jack Straw MP, in Cooper & Marshal-Williams (2000) 3.
[212] Cooper & Marshal-Williams (2000) 151; Mallory & Tyrrell (2021).
[213] Lord Irvine, HL Deb 19 January 1998, vol 584 col 1293.

correspondence between the JCHR and the government about how best to implement the declaration of incompatibility.[214] By raising the political visibility of the declaration both inside and outside Parliament, the JCHR reinforces the judicial declaration in the political domain, thereby helping Government and Parliament to honour the UK's commitment to the European Convention on Human Rights.[215] Together with other actors across Parliament – including the HL Constitution Committee, backbench MPs, House of Lords Peers, the Law Officers and government Legal Advisers – the JCHR acts as a key site of political accountability for rights compliance within Parliament, complementing and strengthening the legal accountability coming from the courts.[216]

Declarations of incompatibility may also garner significant media attention, thereby mobilising concerted non-governmental and civil society engagement from human rights NGOs, interest groups, journalists, and academic commentators[217] Indeed, since human rights NGOs are often involved as 'Third Party interveners'[218] in the case which gave rise to the declaration in the first place, they are perennially poised to leverage the declaration in order to precipitate broader political and legal reform. As experienced repeat-players in the legal and the political realms, a dynamic of 'pressure through law'[219] bespeaks an 'iterative symbiosis'[220] between strategic litigation and political advocacy, where NGOs emerge as important 'pro-compliance partners'[221] in the broader collaborative enterprise of protecting rights.

When we consider the legal, political and parliamentary repercussions of ignoring or defying a declaration of incompatibility, combined with the authoritative and rhetorical force of a judicial decision of the higher courts that legislation violates rights, we can see that there is more to declarations of incompatibility than 'simply putting the ball in Parliament's court'.[222] By harnessing political pressure-points in the

---

[214] Hunt (2010) 604–5. I am grateful to Angela Patrick, former Legal Adviser to the JCHR, for helpful discussion on this point.

[215] Hunt (2013) 237–8; Kavanagh (2015b) 121–2; Hillebrecht (2014) 102; Sathanapally (2012) 159–62.

[216] Kavanagh (2015b); Sathanapally (2012) 131, 159–60.

[217] De Londras (2013) 64; Shah, Poole & Blackwell (2014); Harvey (2015); Duffy (2018) 18.

[218] Shah, Poole & Blackwell (2014) 316; Lieven & Kilroy (2003) 129; Singh (2013) 185–6; Leckey (2015) 83–4.

[219] Harlow & Rawlings (1992); Epp (2008) 44.

[220] King (2012) 70; Duffy (2018) 244, 265–6.

[221] Donald & Leach (2016); Murray (2013a) 54.

[222] Ekins & Sales (2011) 230.

domestic system, and activating important legal and political repercussions in the international realm, the declaration becomes a *constitutional catalyst* which sets off a chain reaction of legal and political repercussions which puts the political actors on a path of compliance with declarations of incompatibility. Whilst the declaration of incompatibility may seem like an innocuous judicial 'invitation'[223] to the Government and legislature to remedy rights-violations, it is an invitation they are 'unlikely to refuse'.[224] If they do so, it will only lead the aggrieved litigant to take their case to Strasbourg – an eventuality the HRA was specifically designed to avoid.[225]

This has profound implications for the normative argument that the courts should issue declarations in a regular, robust and forthright manner, safe in the knowledge that the government and Parliament can reject a declaration if they disagree.[226] Far from simply 'placing the ball in Parliament's court',[227] a declaration of incompatibility frames the play, narrows the options, and orients the political response towards a compliant rather than a conversational stance. In this context, judges are ill-advised to issue declarations in a loose and liberal fashion. Instead, they should continue to do what they have already done, namely, to evaluate carefully and conscientiously whether legislation is incompatible with rights and then, bearing all the contextual and remedial considerations in mind, decide whether to issue a declaration of incompatibility, knowing that such a declaration carries enormous legal and political heft in the domestic and international realms.

In adjudication under the HRA, the higher courts have adopted a 'reticent'[228] and cautious approach towards declarations of incompatibility. Not only have they treated them as a matter of last resort for cases where 'construction cannot resolve the incompatibility',[229] they have also declined to issue a declaration even when they have identified a clear or potential violation of rights. This has occurred in cases where the claimant lacked standing,[230] a declaration had already been issued on the

---

[223] Feldman (1999) 188.
[224] Lester (1998) 668; Hazell (2015) 177.
[225] Chapter 11.3.
[226] Nicol (2004b); Stark (2017a); Martin (2018) 213ff; Adams (2021).
[227] Nicol (2006) 747.
[228] Stark (2017a) 649.
[229] *R (Morris) v Westminster City Council* [2005] EWCA Civ 1184 [56]; also see *Wilson v First County Trust* [2003] UKHL 40 [14].
[230] *In the matter of an application by the NIHRC* [2018] UKSC 27.

subject;[231] the legislation under scrutiny had effectively fallen into desuetude;[232] or the court wished to avoid pre-empting or inhibiting the legislature's freedom to determine policy outcomes unconstrained by a declaration from the courts.[233]

This judicial reticence is due to an acute appreciation of the political and legal significance of a declaration of incompatibility in the constitutional scheme. Judicial declarations bear 'the trappings of judicial authority'.[234] They trade on the judiciary's reputation for providing authoritative resolutions of individual disputes, and reliably assessing whether legislation is likely to violate Convention rights in a future case before Strasbourg. This reputation is a valuable currency in a constitutional democracy. It should not be squandered or devalued by treating court rulings as mere idle judicial chat or as judges 'carping without consequence'.[235] As Lord Reed observed when reflecting on the longstanding practice of successive governments complying with declaratory orders in administrative law:

> The Government's compliance with court orders, including declaratory orders, is one of the core principles of our constitution, and is vital to the mutual trust which underpins the relationship between the Government and the courts. The courts' willingness to forbear from making coercive orders against the Government, and to make declaratory orders instead, reflects that trust. But trust depends on the Government's compliance with declaratory orders in the absence of coercion. In other words, it is because ours is a society governed by the rule of law, where the Government can be trusted to comply with court orders without having to be coerced, that declaratory orders can provide an effective remedy.[236]

This passage points to the relationship of mutual respect and reciprocal obligations between the branches of government in a collaborative scheme. In a dynamic interplay of respect, restraint and role-recognition, the political actors are generally expected to comply with authoritative rulings of the higher courts, whereupon the courts will treat legislative decisions with comity and respect, aware of the constitutional and

---

[231] R (Chester) v Secretary of State for Justice [2014] UKSC 25.
[232] Rusbridger [2004] 1 AC 357, [36]; Adams (2021).
[233] Nicklinson (n 175); Chester (n 231); NIHRC (n 230); Adams (2021).
[234] Van Zyl Smit (2015).
[235] Duxbury (2017) 651.
[236] Craig v Her Majesty's Advocate (for the Government of the United States of America) [2022] UKSC 6 [46].

democratic credentials the political branches bring to the collaborative scheme.

In the HRA case-law, the courts have emphasised that they will only grant a declaration of incompatibility to 'a person who is a victim of an actual or proposed breach of a Convention rights',[237] noting 'the practical difficulties involved in attempting to carry out an abstract assessment of compatibility, unanchored by the facts of a particular case'.[238] In doing so, the courts have stood firm against the idea of 'declaration as dialogue', refusing to be drawn into an advisory or expository role detached from the circumstances of a particular case. As the House of Lords (now Supreme Court) put it in emphatic terms, 'the Courts are neither a debating club nor an advisory bureau'.[239] Declarations of incompatibility do not change that. As envisaged by the terms of the HRA, a declaration is grounded in an adjudication of a concrete controversy about whether rights have been violated in a particular case. For all the talk about declarations being 'the dialogic device *par excellence*',[240] judges do not view themselves as interlocutors in a constitutional conversation.[241] Instead, they see their role as authoritatively declaring what the law is as part of a constitutional scheme where judicial rulings on rights are entitled to comity and respect.[242]

6 The Hidden Strengths of Weak-Form Review

When the HRA was enacted, it was hailed as a leading exemplar of a new model of constitutionalism. Variously described as the 'New Commonwealth Model',[243] the 'democratic dialogue model',[244] or a system of 'weak-form

---

[237] *Re S* (n 69) [88]; *NIRHC* (n 230) [70].

[238] *NIHRC* (n 230) [334]; Petrie (2019) 635–8.

[239] *Macnaughton v Macnaughton's Trustees* [1953] SC 387, 392; cited in *Rusbridger* (n 232) [35]; *R (Smith) v Secretary of State for Defence* [2010] UKSC 29, [129] per Lord Walker ('It is not the function of this Court to deliver advisory opinions'); *R (Chester) v Secretary of State for Justice* [2010] EWCA Civ 1439, [31] LJ Laws (opining that a judicial 'advisory opinion as to what legislation, as yet undrafted, might properly contain or omit' would be 'quite beyond the pale'); Murray (2013a) 70.

[240] Poole (2005) 558.

[241] For rejection of the idea of 'courts as constitutional advisers' under the HRA, see King (2015b) 123–6; Hickman (2010) 83–7.

[242] Stephenson (2016) 12–13.

[243] Gardbaum (2013b).

[244] Young (2017).

review',[245] the common denominator was a normative emphasis on the value of giving the legislature 'the last word' on what rights require.[246] Though the labels differed, the underlying idea was the same.[247] In each of these accounts, the courts were portrayed as having a 'provisional',[248] 'dialogic', or 'weakened'[249] role. Instead of ruling authoritatively on rights, judges could flag their concerns for legislative consideration, whereupon the legislature could ultimately reject them outright. By weakening the power of the courts to that of offering legal advice with no binding effect, and strengthening the power of the legislature to dismiss, defy, and displace judicial decisions, these accounts seemed to decouple rights-based review from a system of 'judicial supremacy'.

But neither the judicial nor the political practice in any of the Commonwealth countries followed the logic of these 'weak-form' or 'dialogic' theories. Instead of treating the declaration of incompatibility as an optional opinion with no strings attached, the courts treated them as authoritative rulings. Instead of 'uncompromisingly telling their truth on rights',[250] both the courts and the legislature have exercised considerable constitutional restraint. Despite great expectations of a new constitutional dawn where the legislature would seize the last word in a 'democratic dialogue'[251] about rights, the legislature complied with almost every single judgment of the higher courts under the HRA.

The UK Parliament has never overridden a judicial interpretation under section 3, no matter how adventurous the interpretation seemed to be,[252] and it has a near-perfect rate of compliance with declarations of incompatibility. As Gavin Phillipson observed:

> Neither the government nor Parliament appears to regard the courts as merely making helpful suggestions about what the Convention might require. Instead, the democratic branches appear to adhere to the

---

[245] Tushnet (2008b).

[246] Tushnet (2003c) 834; Dixon (2019b) 925; Stephenson (2016) 2; Stephenson (2013) 895.

[247] Many of these theorists used the terms 'dialogue', 'the Commonwealth approach', 'weak-form review' or 'penultimate review' interchangeably as 'simply alternative terms for the same phenomenon', see Gardbaum (2013b) 13–16; Tushnet (2008b) 205; Dixon (2007); Gardbaum (2001) 710; Stephenson (2016) 6–7, 50–5.

[248] Tushnet (2008b) xi; Perry (2003) 635.

[249] Dixon (2019b); Tushnet (2008a) 209.

[250] Nicol (2006) 745.

[251] Young (2017).

[252] Crawford (2014).

> irritatingly old-fashioned view that the role of the courts is to declare what the law is.[253]

Instead of a dynamic of dialogue, disagreement and judicial displacement, what in fact emerged was a constitutional relationship marked by respect and restraint, comity and collaboration. The courts have exercised constitutional caution before handing down declarations of incompatibility, whilst the elected branches of government treat judicial decisions with comity and respect, faithfully implementing those rulings even when they were controversial on the merits.[254]

The allied idea of 'weak-form review' also failed to capture some of the key dynamics under the HRA. For one thing, the courts treated the interpretive obligation under section 3 as a 'strong adjuration'[255] to 'modify' legislation in order to render it compatible with rights, even if this rights-compatible reading went against the unambiguous wording and clear intention of the statute. Whatever else we may say about this approach, it seems inapt to describe it as weak. Nor is it clear that an interpretation which changes the meaning of a statutory provision is necessarily weaker than a judicial strike-down or invalidation of a legislative provision.[256] After all, when a legislative provision is invalidated, it is then up to the legislature to decide how to amend the legislation in order to rectify the rights violation.[257] But if judges rectify the statute by interpretive means, they effectively engage in a form of 'reconstructive surgery' which cures the rights-violation with immediate effect'.[258] Whilst the declaration of incompatibility is nominally hortatory and theoretically advisory, in reality it has proved to be a much stronger form of remedy than first appears, not radically dissimilar in form and effect to judicial strike-downs under 'supreme' Bills of Rights.[259]

So what explains this striking disjuncture between the dominant scholarly narratives on one hand, and constitutional practice on the other? There are three main reasons why the theories of dialogue and 'weak-form review' failed to capture the key institutional dynamics at

---

253 Phillipson (2013) 39.
254 The prisoner voting saga will be examined in Chapter 12.
255 *R v DPP, ex parte Kebilene* [2000] 2 AC 326, 384.
256 Kavanagh (2015c) 1019, 1032; Schauer (1995) 94–5; Carolan (2016b) 97ff.
257 Kavanagh (2015c) 1019.
258 Kavanagh (2015c) 1019; Ekins & Sales (2011) 230–1; Schauer (1995) 95.
259 Kavanagh (2015c) 1028; Hoffmann (1999b) 160; Elliott (2002) 349; Lester (1998) 668; Sales & Ekins (2011) 230.

stake.[260] First, since these theories were designed to solve the notorious 'counter-majoritarian difficulty', the prospect of a 'legislative last word' seemed like the answer to all their prayers. But this fixation on legislative finality obscured the multiple constraints on the legislature's power embedded within the 'unwritten constitution'. Second, these theories tested Commonwealth practice against the American 'archetype'[261] of rights-based review coupled with a judicial strikedown power which is effectively final and non-revisable by the political actors.[262] From the vantage point of US constitutional theory, the UK and Commonwealth systems inevitably looked weak. But this obscured the remarkable strength of statutory interpretation as a tool of rendering legislation compatible with rights. It also eclipsed the hidden strength of declarations of incompatibility.[263] Though it was nominally hortatory with no strings attached, the declaration of incompatibility drew considerable strength from the hidden wiring of the unwritten constitutional order in ways which rendered it strong in fact, if not in form.

The third reason why the idea of dialogue and 'weak-form review' failed to capture the dynamics at stake was that they attempted to deduce a normative theory of institutional roles from surface features of constitutional design, detached from a deeper understanding of the constitutional roles and relationships between the branches of government in a constitutional democracy.[264] Alighting upon the *power* of the legislature to disagree with the courts and override judicial rulings, they overlooked the legislature's *responsibility* to respect rights, the rule of law and judicial independence. They focused on what the constitutional actors were *entitled* to do according to the text of the HRA, detached from a deeper appreciation of what they are *expected* to do as participants in a collaborative enterprise.

Once we move 'beyond the textual, to the institutional'[265] – and beyond the forms to norms – we can see that the interaction between

---

[260] Landau (2014) 1554.
[261] Tushnet (2008b) 25; Dixon (2007) 418.
[262] Geiringer (2018) 307 (noting how leading figures in the 'Commonwealth model scholarship' came from within the American academy, whether by dint of nationality, institutional location, or educational background); Carolan (2016b) 109–10.
[263] Gardbaum (2013b) 244; Kavanagh (2015a) 832–6; Geiringer (2017a) 1251.
[264] Kavanagh (2015d) 1040–1; Geiringer (2017a) 1248; Geiringer (2018) 322–3.
[265] Elliott (2011) 596.

the branches does not rest exclusively, or even primarily, on what the branches are *empowered* to do, but rather on what they *ought* to do as responsible constitutional actors in a collaborative constitutional scheme. By relying on abstracted accounts of institutional action detached from institutional practice, the champions of dialogue and weak-form review failed to situate the appropriate political responses to judicial rulings on rights within a deeper appreciation of the institutional roles and relationships in a constitutional scheme. Importing the conflictual assumptions underpinning the US debate about the counter-majoritarian difficulty into the UK and Commonwealth context, these theories occluded the constitutional norms of respect, restraint and reciprocity which underpin the inter-institutional interaction between branches of government in a relatively well-functioning constitutional system.[266]

The distinctive feature of the HRA is not that it set up a 'democratic dialogue'[267] about rights. Nor is it that it gave the legislature 'the last word' on rights, thereby combining a strong legislature with a weak court. Its most distinctive feature is that it incentivised the political actors to protect and promote rights, whilst eschewing a strategy of strict legal compulsion to do so. Instead of the courts telling the legislature what to do as a matter of 'command and control', the courts work together with Parliament in a dynamic interplay oriented towards the common goal of protecting rights. In a dynamic interplay between *interpretation as cure* and *declaration as catalyst*, the courts uphold rights by coaxing rather than coercing compliance. It would be a mistake to think of this complex coaxing as a sign of institutional weakness. When situated within a collaborative constitutional scheme where the political actors are expected to comply with judicial rulings without being coerced to do so, judicial declarations have a potency and potentiality which a literal textual reading cannot convey.

The HRA is like an elegant piece of sophisticated clockwork, where one cog turns another in a barely perceptible manner. When reviewing legislation for compliance with rights, section 3 is the main cog which sets the adjudicatory task in motion. In many cases, that cog is sufficient to keep the clock ticking over in a rights-compliant but democratically responsive manner. If section 3 cannot do the work, then section 4 is activated. Once section 4 is set in motion, this triggers the fast-track

---

[266] On the idea that function does not necessarily follow form in constitutional government, using the HRA 1998 as an example, see Chandrachud & Kavanagh (2016).
[267] Young (2017).

amendment procedure under section 10. This catalyses the JCHR and other parliamentary and civil society actors to put pressure on the government to explain and justify its stance on rights. The declaration also raises the international alarm, by foretelling a negative ruling in Strasbourg. This focuses the government's mind on the legal, political and international consequences of failing to implement the declaration. When the HRA system functions like clockwork, this concatenation of responsive interaction should be sufficient to prompt corrective political compliance in the domestic sphere. There should be no further need to travel to Strasbourg, because the domestic mechanisms have already achieved a rights-compliant result. Herein lies the hidden strength of 'weak-form review'.

As I have argued in previous work, measuring the strength of any system of rights protection is a multi-dimensional inquiry, depending on a complex interaction between formal powers and informal norms, which only a fine-grained contextual analysis can uncover.[268] Most likely, the outcome of such an analysis will cut across the 'linearity of the weak-form/strong-form distinction',[269] revealing a complex and dynamic picture of relative institutional strengths and weaknesses which complicate our ability to provide a neat, system-wide diagnosis of 'weak' or 'strong'.

What *is* clear, however, is that the HRA was never designed to facilitate a dialogue between the courts and the legislature, where the courts would make some optional suggestions in a constitutional conversation which the legislature could then reject or discard. Nor was it intended to create a system where the legislature could 'displace'[270] court rulings on rights whenever it so desired. If the government or legislature simply refused to implement the declaration because they disagreed with it, that would disrupt the intricate and interconnected workings of the rights-based machine.

In order to understand the political and legal dynamics at play, we have to bring the normative and organic aspects of constitutional culture back into play.[271] Moving from the textual to the institutional, we can appreciate the HRA as a collaborative enterprise between differently situated actors,

---

[268] Kavanagh (2015c) 1036–7; Kavanagh (2015d) 1049–50; Geiringer (2018) 315–16; Gardbaum (2018); Dixon (2019b).

[269] Geiringer (2018) 305; Carolan (2016b) 118.

[270] On the idea of legislative 'displacement' of judicial decisions in so-called 'weak-form' systems, see Tushnet (2003a) 2786; cf. Kavanagh (2015c) 1032ff.

[271] Kavanagh (2015c) 1031; McDonald (2004a) 30; Dyzenhaus (2009) 48.

where they each make a significant contribution to the collaborative endeavour, whilst treating each other with comity and respect. Respect begets restraint. Instead of a no-holds-barred shouting match between institutions at war, what in fact exists is a mutually respectful and restrained interactive dynamic between partners in a complex, collaborative scheme.

In defending a collaborative conception of the powers and responsibilities under the HRA, this chapter echoes one of the key architects of the HRA, who argued that the HRA envisaged a

> new and dynamic cooperative endeavour ... between the Executive, the judiciary and Parliament; one in which each works within its respective constitutional sphere to give ever developing practical effect to the values embodied in the Act.[272]

7 Conclusion

The HRA contains a carefully crafted remedial scheme which enlists all three branches of government in the shared responsibility of protecting rights in a democracy. The argument of this chapter has been that the HRA undergirds a collaborative dynamic, where each branch carries out its respective role, whilst maintaining a constitutionally appropriate measure of respect for their partners in authority. Illustrating collaboration in context, I showed how the courts upheld rights, whilst simultaneously treating the democratically elected legislature with comity and respect. In doing so, the HRA went with the grain of the pre-existing constitutional culture where common law courts have long used the 'principle of legality' and allied canons of statutory construction to orient governmental and legislative behaviour towards a rights-respecting outcome, without forcing it to do so.

One of the themes of this chapter was the judicial concern to respect the relative institutional competence and legitimacy of the government and legislature. Accepting that the HRA entails 'some adjustment of the respective constitutional roles' of the three branches of government, the UK Supreme Court has repeatedly emphasised that it

> does not eliminate the differences between them: differences ... in relation to their composition, their expertise, their accountability and their legitimacy. It therefore does not alter the fact that certain matters are by

---

[272] Irvine (2003a) 112; Leigh & Masterman (2008) 16.

their nature more suitable for determination by Government or Parliament than by the courts.[273]

In short, the powers of the courts under the HRA must be sensitive to the separation of powers and the duty of comity to which it gives rise. The task of the next chapter, then, is to map out the contours of comity, showing how the courts give shape to a shared responsibility, mediating their relationship with the democratic branches of government in a robust but respectful manner.

---

[273] *Pham v SSHD* [2015] UKSC 19, [92] Lord Reed; *R (Carlile) v SSHD* [2014] UKSC 60 [28]–[29] Lord Sumption; Elliott (2020) 211–12.

9

Calibrated Constitutional Review

1 Introduction: Between Abdication and Usurpation

When courts review legislation for compliance with rights, they are inevitably drawn into complex and contentious policy questions on which people disagree. Human rights claims do not arise in a vacuum. Instead, they surface in complex policy fields such as criminal justice, immigration policy, social security, housing, health, environmental regulation, prison conditions, counter-terrorism, and many more. This presents courts with a dilemma. On the one hand, judges are well placed to evaluate the impact of general laws on particular individuals in the context of a specific case. On the other, judges typically lack the epistemic range, institutional competence and democratic legitimacy to make large-scale, consequential decisions for society in a polycentric policy field.[1] This raises the question of how judges can review legislation for compliance with rights without straining the limits of their institutional capacity.[2]

In the collaborative constitution, the Executive and legislature play the lead law-making role in the constitutional scheme, whilst the courts play a significant – but subsidiary – role in resolving legal disputes and holding the other branches to constitutional account. If the relationship between the branches is one of constitutional partnership, then the courts are 'jurisgenerative junior partners to the political branches'.[3] But this does not get us very far in working out *how* judges should approach their adjudicatory task. As partners in a collaborative enterprise, the courts have to decide when to step in, when to step back, and when to stand firm. Even accepting that courts have a largely 'receptive role'[4] vis-à-vis

---

[1] Fuller (1978) 371; Allison (1994); King (2008b); Kavanagh (2016c) 124–7.
[2] Endicott (2002) 280; Kavanagh (2010b) 23.
[3] Kumm (2017) 56; Bogg (2018).
[4] Kyritsis (2012) 315.

the legislature in the constitutional scheme, their receptive role is inevitably 'intertwined with an element of supervision'.[5] The question, then, is how to prevent judicial supervision becoming substitution.

In this chapter, I argue that the courts do so by engaging in *calibrated constitutional review*. What prevents rights-based review becoming judicial substitution is the duty of comity that courts owe the legislature in the collaborative constitutional scheme. The task of this chapter, therefore, is to map out the contours of comity in the context of adjudicating rights. Cutting across the well-worn binaries of 'activism and restraint', interventionism and abstentionism, this chapter articulates a context-dependent and institutionally sensitive account of adjudication, where courts engage in a fine-tuned calibration of competing legal, constitutional and institutional concerns. On this vision, judges must be responsive to rights, whilst simultaneously remaining responsive to their democratic partners in authority. Delving into the rich record judicial reasoning about rights, this chapter shows how judges chart a carefully calibrated middle course 'between the shoals of [judicial] deference and the reefs of judicial supremacism'.[6] I call this *calibrated constitutional review*.

The chapter unfolds in the following way. Part 2 articulates the subsidiary nature of the judicial role, presenting the courts as a form of constitutional quality-control. Part 3 maps the contours of comity and judicial deference uncovering the dual phenomena of judges *giving space* and *giving weight* to democratic decisions. Part 4 isolates the key calibrating factors which lie at the heart of the calibrated process, whilst Part 5 illustrates those dynamics in a case study on 'courting counter-terrorism'. Part 6 presents the principle of proportionality as a form of *calibrated constitutional review*. Situating proportionality within the collaborative constitution, I foreground the idea of *proportionality in partnership*.

2 Courts as Quality-Control

When courts adjudicate whether legislation complies with rights, they sit in judgment on what the legislature has done. Here we see the *courts as corrective* and *counterweight*, checking legislation for compliance with

---

[5] Ibid 316.
[6] Lord Dyson (2018) 97; Lord Justice Sedley (2009) 183.

fundamental legal norms, evaluating the competing claims of litigant and the state and, ultimately, delivering a judicial verdict on whether legislation complies with rights.

But in carrying out this supervisory role, judicial supervision should not become judicial substitution. Even Ronald Dworkin was prepared to acknowledge that

> Democracy would be extinguished by any general constitutional change that gave an oligarchy of unelected experts power to overrule and replace any legislative decision they thought unwise or unjust.[7]

So how can courts discharge their constitutional duty to uphold rights without exceeding the limits of their constitutional role and usurping the role of the democratic legislature? And how can they show a constitutionally appropriate degree of respect for their partners in authority without ceding questions of rights to the democratically elected branches of government?[8]

The answer is that the courts must adjudicate rights in a way which is sensitive to their institutional limitations, whilst remaining respectful of the institutional competence, expertise and legitimacy of the democratically elected branches of government.[9] The fact that judges participate in a collaborative constitutional endeavour means that they are 'bound to respect the contribution of their fellow-participants in the joint institutional effort'.[10] Whilst rights-based review gives the courts a significant power to check, constrain, counteract and control the other branches of government, this power goes hand in hand with a constitutional responsibility to exercise some judicial self-control. Judges must proceed with caution and care, ever mindful of the relative institutional capacities of their partners in authority.

When adjudicating whether legislation complies with rights, judicial reasoning is governed by two types of consideration.[11] The first is a *substantive legal evaluation* of the merits of the rights claim before the court. This involves an evaluation of the nature of the right and the meaning of the statutory provisions and judicial precedents which bear on the case. These are questions of substantive legal content.

---

[7] Dworkin (1996) 32; Kyritsis (2012) 302.
[8] Kavanagh (2010b) 24; Landau (2014) 1550; Palmer (2007) 127.
[9] Kavanagh (2019) 59–69; King (2015b) 114–15; Brady (2012) chapter 3.
[10] Kyritsis (2017) 162.
[11] Kavanagh (2010a) 27–8; Kavanagh (2010b) 229–34; Kyritsis (2008) 155; Kyritsis (2017) 78.

But determining the content of the law is not 'the sole determinant of judicial duty'.[12] Judges must also engage in an *institutional evaluation* about the scope and limits of the judicial role as part of – and partners in – the shared constitutional project of achieving good government under the constitution.[13] Thus, when adjudicating rights, judges must not only ask themselves the first-order question 'What do rights require?' or 'Has this legislative provision violated rights?' They must also ask themselves the second-order (institutional) question: 'What is in my power to decide *qua* judge, given my role in the constitutional scheme?'[14] In order to decide whether legislation violates rights, judges are required to establish the scope and limits of the judicial role vis-à-vis the elected branches of government. Beyond questions about the meaning of rights, they must also consider the requirements of roles.[15]

In the collaborative constitution, the political branches of government play the lead law-making role in the constitutional scheme. But accepting the political branches as the primary law-making bodies does not obviate a constitutionally significant role for the courts. On the contrary, judges have a vitally important role in resolving legal disputes, checking legislation for compliance with rights and upholding the rule of law.

Nonetheless, the judicial role in the constitutional scheme is *subsidiary* to that of the democratic legislature. This subsidiarity is evident in a number of ways. When adjudicating whether legislation complies with rights, the courts enter the picture *after* the Executive and legislature have already enacted a statutory framework encapsulating their considered view on what the law should be. Thus, in terms of setting the policy agenda and implementing a vision of a just constitutional order, the Executive and legislature *get there first.*[16]

The subsidiary nature of the judicial role is also manifest in the fact that judges have a role of review not replacement, supervision not substitution. This is neatly captured by Lawrence Sager's suggestion that

---

[12] Kyritsis (2017) 162; Fallon (2001) 69, 77, 134.

[13] Kavanagh (2010b) 27–8; Lawson & Seidman (2019) 148; Fowkes (2016a) 99; Sager (2004) 5; Kyritsis (2008) 155.

[14] Kyritsis (2017) 176.

[15] Fallon (2001) 69, 77, 134 (arguing that beyond questions about the meaning of legal terms, the courts must make 'a further, practical judgment about the appropriate judicial role in implementing the Constitution', which Fallon describes as a 'necessarily cooperative project'); Strauss (1988) 194.

[16] Kyritsis (2012) 312.

judges reviewing legislation for compliance with rights are akin to quality-control inspectors in an automobile plant:

> the quality-control inspector has only the job of assuring that the cars
> which leave her plant are well-built. Her role is focused and singular and
> comes on top of the efforts of the people who actually put the cars
> together. Constitutional judges are like that. Their mission is singular –
> to identify the fundamentals of political justice that are prominent and
> enduring in their constitutional regime and to measure legislation or
> other governmental acts by those standards. And their mission is redun-
> dant – they enter the process only after legislators have themselves
> considered the constitutional ramifications of proposals before them.[17]

The quality-control analogy captures the fact that the role of the
inspector is not to design or manufacture cars *ex ante*, but rather to
review the quality of the cars *ex post*. Instead of dictating how cars should
be made, quality-control inspectors monitor and test for particular flaws
and potential malfunctions.[18] Sometimes, the inspectors will pick up on
minor problems which may have been overlooked in the initial manufacturing process. Such flaws may be both easy to detect and easy to
correct. At other times, they may discover a more significant defect which
means that the cars must be returned to the manufacturing process to
remedy the problem at source. Either way, by flagging up flaws and
malfunctions, the quality-control inspector contributes constructively to
the joint enterprise of making cars, without taking over the manufacturing process or rebuilding cars from scratch.[19] As Sager emphasises, the
role of the quality-control inspector is both 'singular' and 'redundant',
detecting particular types of error after the cars have been made.[20]

Of course, we should be careful not to push the quality-control analogy
too far. It does not capture the dynamics of rights-review in all respects.
For one thing, the courts possess some powerful techniques of error-
correction as well as error-detection. Moreover, whilst all cars go through
a rigorous process of quality-control before hitting the road, only a tiny

---

[17] Sager (2002) 15; Kyritsis (2012) 318; Prendergast (2019) 257–8; Kumm (2009) 305;
Kumm (2010) 173; Slattery (1987) 731; O'Regan (2019) 431 (former judge of the South
African Constitutional Court).

[18] For the idea of 'court as monitor', see Mashaw (1988) 1692–3.

[19] Bingham (2000) 233 (arguing that when a judge 'quashes the decision under challenge, he
does not thereby become the decision-maker').

[20] Kyritsis (2012) 319.

fraction of legislation ever gets litigated before the courts.[21] Therefore, rights-based review is an exceptional not a routine checking mechanism in the constitutional scheme.

Yet, despite these differences, the quality-control analogy nonetheless captures the fundamental point that rights-based review is a partial and limited 'second opinion mechanism'[22] within the system of constitutional checks and balances. It also shows that the power to review does not licence judicial second-guessing of legislative decisions on an all-things-considered basis. The judicial role is one of *partner, not substitute*, carried out with due respect for the primary law-making role of the legislature.

When adjudicating whether legislation complies with rights, UK courts have repeatedly emphasised that

> theirs is a reviewing role. Parliament is charged with the primary respon-sibility for deciding whether the means chosen to deal with a social problem are both necessary and appropriate. Assessment of the advan-tages and disadvantages of the various legislative alternatives is primarily a matter for Parliament. The possible existence of alternative solutions does not in itself render the contested legislation unjustified. The court will reach a different conclusion from the legislature only when it is apparent that the legislature has attached insufficient importance to a person's Convention rights.[23]

This *dictum* highlights two important points. First, judicial reasoning about rights is framed and shaped by the duty of comity that judges owe to the democratic legislature. Second, whilst the courts have an important role in reviewing legislation for compliance with rights, this does not entitle them to second-guess legislative choices across the board.[24] Instead, the courts have a more focused brief, namely, to test legislation against the requirements of rights and only intervene if they are certain that the legislature has 'attached insufficient importance' to the

---

[21] Hiebert (2004b) 1986; Sathanapally (2012) 70; Hiebert & Kelly (2015) 7–9; Garrett & Vermeule (2001) 1283.

[22] Vermeule (2011) 1139, 1145 (characterising rights-based review as a '*partial* second opinion', because the reviewing court only considers 'a subset of the questions posed by the legislative or agency action under review').

[23] *Wilson v First County Trust (No 2)* [2003] UKHL 40, [80] Lord Nicholls; *R (Carlile) v SSHD [2014] UKSC 60*, [31] ('a court of review' is not entitled to 'substitute its own decision for that of the constitutional decision-maker').

[24] *R (Corner House Research) v Director of the Serious Fraud Office* [2008] UKHL 60, [41] Lord Bingham; *Carlile* (n 24) [31], Lord Sumption.

claimant's rights. However intense or exacting the standard of review, it must stop short of 'transferring the effective decision-making power to the courts'.[25] If rights-based review is a second-look mechanism, we need to ensure that the second look does not become the supreme view.

3   Mapping the Contours of Comity

So how do courts steer a middle course between the Scylla of abdication and the Charybdis of substitution? They do so, in part, by treating legislative decisions with a constitutionally appropriate measure of respect and comity, calibrating the intensity of review in light of rights-based and role-based concerns. As outlined in chapter 3, comity is 'that respect which one great organ of the State owes to the other'.[26] It is the 'duty of one authority to respect and support the proper function of other authorities'.[27] So how do the courts discharge their duty of respect to the Executive and legislature? They do so in two main ways: (1) by *giving the legislature leeway* to make complex policy choices with constitutional confines; and (2) by *giving weight* to legislative decisions about what rights require as embedded in a statutory scheme.[28]

Before examining these two modes of curial respect – *giving leeway* and *giving weight* – there is one terminological point which bears emphasis at the outset. In the early case-law under the HRA, judges frequently spoke in terms of their 'duty of deference' towards the elected branches of government when reviewing legislation for compliance with rights.[29] In recent years, the term 'deference' has fallen out of judicial vogue, with leading judicial figures rejecting the term as inapt to describe the role of the courts because of its 'overtones of servility ... and gracious concession'[30] or even 'cringing abstention in the face

---

[25] *Carlile* (n 24) [30]; *In the matter of Lorraine Gallagher* [2019] UKSC 3, [61].

[26] *Buckley v Attorney General* [1950] IR 67, 80; Endicott (2015a).

[27] Endicott (2021) xv, 22; Lord Thomas (2017b) [18]; *R (Jackson) v Her Majesty's Attorney General* [2005] UKHL 56, [125].

[28] In previous work on the dynamics of deference, I concentrated on the dimension of 'giving weight', underestimating the leeway dimension, see Kavanagh (2009a) chapter 7. For insightful analysis, see Lawson & Seidman (2020) 143–53, esp. 146; Kyritsis (2017) chapter 7.

[29] See Kavanagh (2009a) chapter 7.

[30] *R (Pro-Life Alliance) v British Broadcasting Corporation* [2003] UKHL 23, [75]–[76], *per* Lord Hoffmann.

of superior status'.[31] The worry is that the term 'deference' seems to imply either courteous acquiescence or blind submission to legislative will.[32]

But the idea that judges should pay a degree of deference to the elected branches of government does not necessarily signify a servile or spineless attitude. Nor does it connote unquestioning submission or a blanket surrender of judgement.[33] A judge can 'defer more or less, and on some questions and not others'.[34] In fact, when the term 'deference' was used in the early case-law under the HRA, it was typically used in this variable and context-sensitive manner, where judges emphasised that they would accord the legislature 'an appropriate *degree* of deference'[35] to the legislature, which would 'vary according to the subject matter under consideration, the importance of the human rights in question, and the extent of the encroachment on that right'.[36] Academic commentary also emphasised the idea of 'deference as respect' rather than 'deference as submission',[37] counselling the courts to accord a variable degree of weight or latitude to the elected branches under a suitably calibrated 'due deference'[38] approach. Far from advocating a supine or timid judiciary, these scholars defended a robust but responsible role for judges in upholding rights in a constitutional democracy.

Nonetheless, in order to avoid confusion and focus the analysis on the dynamics at stake rather than the terminology employed, I will generally speak in terms of comity and respect, which can then be parsed into two more specific modes of respect, namely, *giving space* and *giving weight* to the legislature. By emphasising the variability of calibrated constitutional review, I avoid the danger of going to 'the dark side of

---

[31] Sumption (2014) 10; *Carlile* (n 24) [22] Lord Sumption; *Huang v SSHD* [2007] UKHL 11, [16] Lord Bingham; *R (Quila) v SSHD* (2011) UKSC 45, [46], [91], Lord Wilson. For analysis of the judicial reluctance to use the term 'deference', see Hunt (2009) 116–18; Kavanagh (2009a) 178–81; Endicott (2021) 339–440; Steyn (2005) 349–50.

[32] Kavanagh (2009a) 178–9.

[33] Kavanagh (2009a) 169–76; Hunt (2009) 116–18; Lawson & Seidman (2019) 116–19, 122; King (2008a); Elliott (2015b) 72; Kyritsis (2017) 154, 166.

[34] Endicott (2021) 259; Daly (2017) 178ff (arguing for a 'differential deference' approach).

[35] *R v Lambert* [2001] 2 WLR 211, [16]; Steyn (2005).

[36] *A (and others) v SSHD* [2004] UKHL 56 (hereafter *Belmarsh*), [80] Lord Nicholls; *R v Lichniak* [2002] UKHL 47, [14] Lord Bingham; King (2012) 140.

[37] Dyzenhaus (1997); Hunt (2003); Daly (2012) 7–10.

[38] Hunt (2003); Kavanagh (2009a) 169–76, 237–41; Leigh & Masterman (2008) 94; Barak (2012) 396–8.

deference'.[39] Under the collaborative constitution, comity requires calibration not capitulation. It enjoins the courts to review with respect, not submit without question.[40] The key task, then, is to examine how courts discharge their duty of respect, and what impact this has on judicial reasoning about rights.

Let us start by considering the idea of *legislative leeway*. When reviewing legislation for compliance with rights, judges must allow the legislature some space or *legislative leeway* to make detailed and complex policy choices for the community. Variously described as the 'margin of appreciation',[41] 'discretionary area of judgment',[42] or legislative 'latitude',[43] the UK Supreme Court has recognised that it must 'allow room for the exercise of judgment by the executive and legislative branches of government, which bear democratic responsibility for these decisions'.[44] In doing so, the courts are mindful of the fact that 'the making of government and legislative policy cannot be turned into a judicial process'.[45] They acknowledge that reconciling competing interests is a multifaceted policy choice better suited to the legislative function of Parliament than the interpretative role of the courts'.[46]

The width of the margin and degree of discretion is variable. It can be widened or narrowed depending on all the circumstances of the individual case. For example, in cases concerning national security, the government may be entitled to 'a particularly wide measure of discretion'[47] on the basis that the Executive bears key responsibility for deciding how to combat terrorism and the courts may suffer from epistemic deficits in evaluating these sensitive policy choices. But where the expertise of the courts is more directly engaged, e.g. on the requirements of a fair trial in a criminal context or matters of procedural fairness, the margin may be narrowed considerably.

When reviewing legislation for compliance with rights, the courts have observed that the existence of various policy alternatives to realise a

---

[39] Soper (2002) 181; Solove (1999) 941; Barak (2012) 398–9.
[40] Dyzenhaus (1997); Endicott (2021) 46; Krisch (2010) 10.
[41] *R (Z) v Hackney London Borough Council* [2020] UKSC 40, [54] *per* Lord Sales.
[42] *R v DPP, ex parte Kebilene* [2000] 1 AC 326, 384; Fordham (2020) 734.
[43] *Tweed v Parades Commission for Northern Ireland* [2006] UKHL 64 [55].
[44] *Bank Mellat v HM Treasury (No 2)* [2014] AC 763 [93] Lord Reed; *Carlile* (n 24) [33] Lord Sumption.
[45] *Bank Mellat* (n 45) [93]; *Carlile* (n 24) [33] Lord Sumption.
[46] *Fitzpatrick* (1998) Ch 304, 319, *per* Waite LJ; Kavanagh (2004) 194.
[47] *R (Farrakhan) v SSHD* (2002) EWCA Civ 606, [71].

legislative goal 'does not in itself render the contested legislation unjusti-fied'.[48] As long as the legislative provision 'falls within a reasonable range of alternatives', the courts will not find against it 'merely because they can conceive of a better alternative'.[49] This opens up some logical space between what judges believe to be optimal or desirable in their personal capacity and what is appropriate for them to decide in their official capacity *qua* judge.[50] The fact that judges may disagree with a particular legislative provision is not, therefore, a sufficient reason for them to conclude that it violates rights.[51] If legislation is based on a complex choice between multiple policy alternatives, all of which may comply with rights albeit to varying degrees, the courts often acknowledge that such line-drawing exercises should be left to the democratic legislature, not overtaken by the courts.[52]

A judicial concern to avoid usurpation of the legislative function is also legible in the judicial awareness that the courts should not lightly or easily disturb a considered legislative settlement. As the courts have held, a statute 'approved by democratically elected Parliament ... should not be at all readily rejected'.[53] The courts will 'think long and hard'[54] before interfering with in complex policy areas, especially those with significant resource implications.[55] In the *Animal Defenders* case concerning whether a ban on paid political advertising violated freedom of expres-sion, Lord Bingham observed that 'the judgment of Parliament should not be lightly overridden',[56] especially given the detailed evaluation of rights-based concerns during the legislative process:

> In deference to the legislature, courts should not easily be persuaded to condemn what has been done, especially where it has been done in primary legislation after careful evaluation.[57]

---

[48] *Wilson* (n 24) [70] Lord Nicholls.
[49] *R (Pearson) v SSHD* [2001] HRLR 39. For a Canadian comparator case, see *RJR-MacDonald Inc v Attorney-General of Canada* [1995] 3 SCR 199; Lewans (2016) 200, 223.
[50] Kyritsis (2015) 168; Kavanagh (2009a) 240; Kumm (2010) 169.
[51] *R (SG) v Secretary of State for Work and Pensions* [2015] UKSC 16 [155] Lord Hughes ('To say that one disagrees is not the same as saying that the decision is unlawful').
[52] *Wilson* (n 24) [70], Lord Nicholls.
[53] *Kay v Lambeth London Borough Council* [2006] UKHL 10, [28] Lord Bingham.
[54] Ibid [187] Baroness Hale.
[55] Kavanagh (2009a) 222–8.
[56] *R (Animal Defenders International) v Secretary of State for Culture, Media and Sport* [2008] UKHL 15, [33] Lord Bingham (discussed in Chapter 6.7).
[57] Ibid [33].

By giving credence to the legislative settlement, the courts took legislation seriously as the embodiment of a considered decision of a coordinate constitutional actor.[58]

The *Bellinger* case discussed in chapter 7 provides a good example of judges allowing the legislature leeway to make its own contribution to the joint project of protecting rights.[59] Whilst the court held that the Matrimonial Causes Act 1973 clearly violated transgender rights, it nonetheless declined to issue a declaration of incompatibility, because protecting transgender rights in a comprehensive and coherent fashion was 'pre-eminently a matter for Parliament'[60] and 'altogether ill-suited for determination by courts and court procedures.[61] *Bellinger* is a good example of the courts acting as *partner not substitute*, clearly articulating a violation of rights, whilst simultaneously allowing the legislature leeway to decide how that violation should be remedied as part of a broader legislative scheme.

The second way in which courts manifest their duty of respect towards the legislature is by *'giving weight* to the decisions of a representative legislature and a democratic government'.[62] In the case-law under the HRA, the courts have repeatedly said that they will accord an appropriate degree of 'weight to the decisions of the representative legislature and a democratic government';[63] 'principles of institutional competence and respect indicate that they must attach appropriate weight to informed legislative choices'.[64]

The obligation to give weight to the decisions of the democratically elected legislature does not preclude the court from finding against the government, or from ruling that the impugned legislation violates rights. Nor does it mean that the courts are 'absolutely disabled from forming [their] own view'.[65] As Lord Bingham observed,

> The fact that a statutory provision represents the settled will of a demo-
> cratic assembly is not a conclusive reason for upholding it, but a degree of

---

[58] On the value of institutional settlement, see Waldron (2003a) 45.
[59] *Bellinger v Bellinger* [2003] UKHL 21.
[60] Ibid [46].
[61] Ibid [46]–[48].
[62] *Brown v Stott* [2003] 1 AC 681, [39], per Lord Bingham; Kavanagh (2009a) 169ff.
[63] *Brown v Stott* (n 63) [39].
[64] *Re Recovery of Medical Cost for Asbestos Diseases (Wales) Bill* [2015] UKSC 3 [54].
[65] *Wilson* (n 24) [116]; Kavanagh (2009a) 191–2.

deference is due to the judgments of the democratic assembly on how a social problem is best tackled.[66]

Just as the width of the margin of discretion varies in light of the circumstances of the individual case, *giving weight* to the considered decision of the democratically elected legislature in a particular case is also a matter of degree. It is a variable, partial and context-dependent assessment, attuned to all the circumstances of the individual case.[67]

4 Calibrated Constitutional Review

In adjudication under the HRA, one of the most 'important and uncontroversial principles' underpinning the case-law is that 'substantial respect should be paid by the courts to the considered decisions of democratic assemblies'.[68] Accepting that protecting rights involves 'questions of balance between competing interests',[69] the courts have affirmed that

> In some circumstances it will be appropriate for the courts to recognise that there is an area of judgment within which the judiciary will defer, on democratic grounds, to the considered opinion of the elected body. It will be easier for it to be recognised where the issues involve questions of social or economic policy, much less so if the rights are of high constitutional importance or of a kind where the courts are especially well-placed to assess the need for protection.[70]

Although 'the existence of duly enacted legislation does not conclude the issue . . . the degree of respect to be shown to the considered judgments of a democratic assembly will vary according to the subject matter and circumstances'.[71] So, what are the factors which give shape to the duty of respect judges owe to the legislature when evaluating whether legislation complies with rights?

---

[66] *Lichniak* (n 37) [14]; *R (Countryside Alliance) v AG* [2007] 3 WLR 922, [45], Lord Bingham.
[67] Kavanagh (2009a) 201–9.
[68] *Sheldrake v DPP* [2004] UKHL 43, [23], *per* Lord Bingham.
[69] *Kebilene* (n 43) 384.
[70] *Kebilene* (n 43) 380GG.
[71] *Countryside Alliance* (n 67) [45].

The courts have identified a number of 'calibrating factors'[72] which help to determine the 'width of the margin' or the 'degree of deference' when reviewing legislation for compliance with rights.[73] These include:

- the nature of the right engaged in the dispute (e.g. whether it is an absolute or qualified right under the Convention, or whether it is a right 'of high constitutional importance');[74]
- the degree of interference with that right;[75]
- the impact of the decision on the litigant before the court;[76]
- the subject-matter of the dispute, including whether it

  - involves complex and far-reaching questions of social or economic policy;[77]
  - requires a difficult balancing of competing interests;[78]
  - is subject to deep and pervasive controversy;[79]
  - is subject to 'changing social conditions and attitudes';[80]
  - involves a complex policy choice between multiple alternatives;[81]
  - is regulated by a complex legislative framework;[82]
  - has significant financial or resource implications;[83]

---

[72] Dixon (2020) 92; Kavanagh (2014) 469–72 (describing these factors as 'deference-increasing' or 'deference-decreasing' factors); Edwards (2002) 874ff.

[73] For analysis of the calibrating factors, see Hunt (2013) 353–4; King (2012) 143–8; Fordham (2020) [58.5]; Kavanagh (2014) 469–70; Sales (2009b) 229–31; Gerards (2011) 91–113 (examining the calibrating process in the ECtHR and the ECJ).

[74] *Kebilene* (n 43) 384; *Countryside Alliance* (n 67) [124]; *International Transport Roth GmbH v Secretary of State for the Home Department* [2002] EWCA Civ 158, [82]–[87]; *Carlile* (n 24) [13], Lord Sumption ('the more important the right, the more difficult it will be to justify any interference with it').

[75] *Carlile* (n 24) [40].

[76] *Kebilene* (n 43) 384.

[77] *Countryside Alliance* (n 67) [45]; *Wilson v First County Trust* (n 24) [70]; *R (Williamson) v Secretary of State for Education and Employment* [2005] UKHL 15 [51]; *R (Mahmood) v SSHD* [2001] 1 WLR 840, [18].

[78] *Belmarsh* (n 37) [99]; *Countryside Alliance* (n 67) [76]; *In the Matter of an Application by Lorraine Gallagher for Judicial Review (Northern Ireland)* [2019] UKSC 3, [61].

[79] *R (Elan-Cane) v SSHD* [2021] UKSC 56, [62]; *Belmarsh* (n 37) [38].

[80] *Kebilene* (n 43) [149].

[81] *In Re G* (Adoption: Unmarried Couple) [2008] UKHL 38, [20]; *R (Hooper) v Secretary of State for Work and Pensions* [2005] 1 WLR 681.

[82] *R v A* [2002] 1 AC 45 [69]; *Belmarsh* (n 37) [38].

[83] *Elan-Cane* (n 81); *R (Alconbury Developments Ltd) v Secretary of State for the Environment, Transport and the Regions* [2001] UKHL 23, [69]–[70]; *Wandsworth London Borough Council v Michalak* [2003] 1 WLR 617, [41]; see further Kavanagh (2009a) 222–8; King (2007).

- is an issue which Parliament is about to consider;[84]
- was subjected to the intense parliamentary debate;[85]
- the relative institutional competence and expertise of the government and legislature on the particular issue;[86]
- the need for democratically legitimate decision making on broad, controversial questions of policy.[87]

This list is not exhaustive and the various factors combine and interact in different ways, sometimes pulling in different directions in the context of an individual case.[88] Nonetheless, this schema gives us a good overview of the key 'push and pull factors'[89] which frame and shape judicial decision-making about whether legislation complies with rights. In order to appreciate their significance in judicial reasoning about rights, the following points should be borne in mind.

First, whilst all of these factors are *relevant* to the judicial inquiry about how much weight or leeway to give the legislature, none of them are conclusive or determinative.[90] They operate as pointers or 'directional signals'[91] which exert a normative pull on outcomes, but they are not decisive. They can give way to other considerations.[92] Thus, the fact that legislation concerns an issue requires a difficult balancing of competing interests in a controversial policy area does not automatically mean that the courts should uphold it as compatible with rights.[93] Far from it. But the complexity and controversy surrounding the issue nonetheless gives the courts a *constitutional cue* that they should tread carefully, mindful of the fact that they are entering an area where their epistemic and institutional aptitudes may be under strain. Therefore, polycentricity and complexity do not herald a 'judicial no-go area'.[94] Instead, it suggests

---

[84] *Bellinger* (n 60) [37]; *Chester v Secretary of State for Justice* [2013] UKSC 63, [39], Lord Mance (noting that the prisoner voting issue was 'under active consideration' in Parliament); *Countryside Alliance* (n 67) [47]; *R (SB, BC) v SSWP* [2021] UKSC 26, [180].

[85] *Countryside Alliance* (n 67); Kavanagh (2014).

[86] *Poplar Housing v Donoghue* [2002] QB 48, [69]; Legg (2012) chapter 6.

[87] *SSHD v Rehman* [2002] 1 AER 123, [31]; *Belmarsh* (n 37) [97], Lord Hoffmann; Poole (2005); Kavanagh (2009a) 176–80.

[88] Hunt (2003); Lazarus & Simonsen (2015) 403.

[89] Gerards (2011); Wiseman (2006) 538; Van Zyl Smit (2016).

[90] Hunt (2013) 353–4; *Elan-Cane* (n 80), [50].

[91] Gutmann & Thompson (2014) 84; Taggart (2008) 423.

[92] King (2012) 144; Elliott (2015b); *DPP v Ziegler* [2021] UKSC 23 [71]–[78].

[93] Kavanagh (2009a) 175; Jowell (2003) 599.

[94] King (2007) 224.

that courts should go slow, proceeding cautiously and incrementally in a complex policy field where judges may struggle to see all the twists and turns of the road ahead.[95]

Second, there is no 'magic formula'[96] or 'bright-line rule'[97] which can predict or prescribe how to balance the countervailing considerations in any particular case. None of these factors have a 'pre-ordained weight'.[98] They interact in unpredictable ways, sometimes pulling in different directions in the context of an individual case.[99] Therefore, it is impossible to prescribe an 'optimal calibration' in the abstract. A case can concern an apparently severe limitation on rights (thus pulling the courts towards a strict and intrusive standard of review), whilst simultaneously arising in an acutely controversial, complex, and sensitive area of social and economic policy (thus alerting the courts to the limits of their institutional competence and expertise and pushing them away from interfering with the democratic decision).[100] In this circumstance, the courts must weigh and balance the competing considerations, evaluating the relative strength and weight of the 'push and pull factors'[101] in the particular case. The complex task of calibrating the mode, intensity and scope of review can only be captured in a context-sensitive judgment, not an abstract formula for all seasons.[102]

Third, notice how the factors listed above include questions of legal content *and* institutional role. Roughly, the first three factors refer to substantive legal issues concerning the nature and meaning of the right, the impact of the legislation on the individual litigant, and the severity of the interference with rights. The subsequent three factors capture jurisdictional concerns grounded in the constitutional role of the courts vis-à-vis the elected branches of government. When adjudicating rights, the courts must take issues of legal content *and* institutional design into account, evaluating their relative strength in order

---

[95] Elliott (2015b); *R (Baiai) v SSHD* [2008] UKHL [25].

[96] Hodge (2015) 479; Jowell (2003) 592; Rivers (2006).

[97] *Roth* (n 75) [75]; King (2008a) 438.

[98] *DPP v Ziegler* [2021] UKSC 23 [71], [102].

[99] *Roth* (n 75) [54], [75]; *R (SC, CB) v SSWP* [2021] UKSC 26 [99], [130], [142], [151], [159], Lord Reed.

[100] *R (Limbuela) v Secretary of State* [2005] UKHL 66, [13]; Rivers (2006) 204–5; Nason (2016) 194; Hunt (2009) 120.

[101] Gerards (2011); Wiseman (2006) 538.

[102] *R (SC, CB) v SSWP* [2021] UKSC 26 [99], [130], [142], [151], [159], *per* Lord Reed.

to work out what they can competently and legitimately do in the joint enterprise of governing.

This gives rise to the canonical correlatives of public law adjudication:

'the more important the right, the more difficult it will be to justify any interference with it';[103]

'the more substantial the interference with human rights, the more the court will require by way of justification before it is satisfied that the decision is reasonable';[104]

'the more purely political . . . a question is, the more appropriate it will be for political resolution and the less likely it is to be an appropriate matter for judicial decision . . . Conversely, the greater the legal content of any issue, the greater the potential role of the court'.[105]

'The more the decision challenged lies in . . . the macro-political field, the less intrusive will be the court's supervision.'[106]

These correlatives encapsulate the dualistic dynamics at the heart of the judicial role. They highlight that both the substantive and institutional factors are a matter of degree. Just as an interference with rights may range from slight to substantial, the relative competence and legitimacy of the branches of government may also vary substantially depending on the nature and context of the decision involved.[107] None of these factors are fixed commodities. They are flexible variables which must be assessed and weighed in a context-sensitive evaluation which I call *calibrated constitutional review*.[108]

5   Courting Counter-Terrorism

The discussion so far has been pitched at a relatively abstract level. The purpose of this section, therefore, is to illustrate the dynamics of

---

[103] *Carlile* (n 24) [13].
[104] *R v Ministry for Defence, ex parte Smith* [1996] QB 517, 554D-G, 563A, 564H; *R (Mahmood) v SSHD* [2001] 1 WLR 840, [18]; *Pham v SSHD* [2015] UKSC 19, [106] *per* Lord Sumption.
[105] *Belmarsh* (n 37) [29]; *Kebilene* (n 43) 380; Kavanagh (2009a) 202–3; Hunt (2003) 353.
[106] *R v Secretary of State for Education, ex parte Begbie* [2000] 1 WLR 1115 (CA) 1131; King (2012) 202–3.
[107] Endicott (2021) 244–7; King (2012) chapter 8.
[108] Dyzenhaus (2007) 142 (arguing that 'the second-order reasons for deference, far from excluding consideration of the quality of the first-order reasons, invite the court's evaluation of that quality').

calibrated constitutional review in context, using a case-study from the field of national security law in the post-9/11 era.[109] Traditionally, national security was treated as '*par excellence* a non-justiciable question'[110] on the basis that 'the judicial process is totally inept to deal with the sort of problem which it involves'.[111] Although Lord Atkin famously pronounced in *Liversidge v Anderson* that 'the laws are not silent amidst the clash of arms',[112] this evocative adage was honoured more in the breach than in the observance whenever a national security crisis loomed.[113]

But before dismissing judges as lily-livered cowards who invariably capitulate when the going gets tough, we should bear in mind the enormous challenges judges face in the counter-terrorist field.[114] First, when issues of national security are involved, the Executive often claims that some of the information on which its decisions are based must be kept secret.[115] Therefore, the courts labour under conditions of epistemic uncertainty in the national security field.[116] Without access to independent sources of information or their own intelligence service, it is very difficult for judges to challenge Executive decisions on a sure footing if they are not in possession of all of the facts. As I have argued in previous work, 'deference is a rational response to uncertainty, and uncertainty is heightened in a case where secrecy surrounds some of the relevant facts'.[117]

Second, judicial awareness of the life and death consequences of decisions about terrorism cause judges to 'err, if at all, on the side of safety'.[118] Where there is a

> risk of destruction and mayhem on a very substantial scale, those responsible for deciding whether the risk exists and what measures are necessary

---

[109] For a more detailed analysis of 'constitutionalism, counter-terrorism and the courts' in the post-9/11 era, see Kavanagh (2011); Kavanagh (2009b); Fenwick & Phillipson (2011); Goold & Lazarus (2007); Davis & De Londras (2014a).

[110] *Council of Civil Service Unions v Minister for the Civil Service* [1985] AC 374 (hereafter GCHQ).

[111] Ibid 412; Dyzenhaus (2004a); Lord Brown (1994) 589.

[112] *Liversidge v Anderson* [1942] AC 206.

[113] Dyzenhaus (2004a) (describing the post-HRA case law on counter-terrorism as 'intimations amidst the clash of arms').

[114] Kavanagh (2009a) 211–22; Kavanagh (2011) 177–8.

[115] *Belmarsh* (n 37) [27], [94], [117].

[116] Poole (2008) 234.

[117] Kavanagh (2009a) 171.

[118] *Belmarsh* (n 37) [29].

to try and ensure that it is not translated into a reality must be allowed a reasonably wide margin of discretion.[119]

Third, many decisions in the national security context are anticipatory and prognostic in nature, based on risk assessments about possible future events. Without independent sources of information to assess the factual basis of those risks, it is very difficult for judges to second-guess or even scrutinise those risk-based assessments.[120]

These three reasons – *epistemic uncertainty, fear of drastic consequences*, and the role of *risk analysis* – combine to explain the judicial reluctance to challenge Executive and legislative decisions in the national security field. Set against this backdrop, the *Belmarsh Prison* case[121] – where the House of Lords held that indefinite detention of non-national terrorist suspects without trial violated human rights – is all the more remarkable. It provides an example of robust, but respectful, adjudication under the HRA and illuminating case-study of calibrated constitutionalism in context.

The legislation at issue was the Anti-Terrorism, Crime and Security Act 2001 (ATCSA), which had been swiftly enacted to clamp down on Islamic terrorism in the immediate aftermath of 9/11.[122] In order to detain the suspects without trial, the UK derogated from the right to liberty under the ECHR claiming that it was 'strictly necessary' in light of the 'public emergency threatening the life of the nation'.[123] There were two key questions before the court in the *Belmarsh* case:

(1) was there 'a public emergency threatening the life of the nation' as required by Article 15 ECHR? (*the derogation issue*); and
(2) was the decision to detain non-nationals without trial 'necessary' and proportionate in light of the legitimate aim of protecting national security and the need to uphold Convention rights? (*the discrimination issue*).

On the *derogation issue*, the court was reluctant to second-guess the government's decision for all the reasons outlined above. Recognising the limits of their institutional competence and legitimacy in this fraught

---

[119] *Special Immigration Appeals Commission*, cited in Kavanagh (2011) 178.
[120] Dyzenhaus (2007) 146.
[121] *Belmarsh* (n 37); see further Kavanagh (2011) 180ff; Gearty (2005).
[122] Kavanagh (2009b) 301.
[123] Article 15 ECHR.

field, the court gave 'great weight to the judgment of the Home Secretary, his colleagues and Parliament'[124] on whether there was a public emergency threatening the life of the nation. As Lord Nicholls observed:

> All courts are very much aware of the heavy burden, resting on the elected government and not the judiciary, to protect the security of this country and all who live here. All courts are acutely conscious that the government alone is able to evaluate and decide what counter-terrorism steps are needed and what steps will suffice. Courts are not equipped to make such decisions, nor are they charged with that responsibility.[125]

Given the epistemic uncertainty surrounding the key facts, it would have been 'irresponsible not to err, if at all, on the side of safety.[126]

This is not to say that all the judges were convinced by the government's claim that there was a 'public emergency threatening the life of the nation'. On the contrary, many of them revealed 'misgivings',[127] 'hesitation'[128] and even 'very great doubt'[129] about that claim. Nonetheless, given their epistemic uncertainty in a context of high stakes and high risks, the court gave the government 'the benefit of the doubt on this point'.[130] On the *derogation issue*, therefore, the court set the threshold for judicial intervention high, deciding that they would only intervene if the government's decision on the public emergency seemed 'patently implausible'.[131] That threshold was not met in this case.

On the *discrimination issue*, however, the court ratcheted up the intensity of review, adopting a more probing and stringent approach.[132] There were a number of 'push and pull factors' at play. On the one hand, the subject-matter of national security in the post-9/11 era gave the court a constitutional cue that 'substantial latitude should be accorded to the legislature'.[133] On the other hand, the right to individual liberty was 'one of the most fundamental of human rights'[134] in the UK constitutional

---

124 *Belmarsh* (n 37) [29], [38].
125 Ibid [79] Lord Nicholls; [226] Baroness Hale; [166] Lord Rodger.
126 *Belmarsh* (n 37) [29] Lord Bingham.
127 Ibid [26].
128 Ibid [165], Lord Rodger.
129 Ibid [154], Lord Scott.
130 Ibid [154]; cf. Dyzenhaus (2007) 130; Dyzenhaus (2006) 178ff.
131 *Belmarsh* (n 37) [226]; Kavanagh (2009a) 217–18.
132 For an analysis of the role of judicial deference in the national security context, see Kavanagh (2011) 172–4; Kavanagh (2009a) 211–22; Dyzenhaus (2007); Phillipson (2014); Chan (2014); Fenwick (2014).
133 *Belmarsh* (n 37) [81], Lord Nicholls.
134 Ibid [81].

order.[135] Furthermore, indefinite detention without trial was a significant interference with rights, very much at 'the severe end of the spectrum.'[136] As Lord Rodger observed: 'the greater the inroad [on rights], the greater the care with which the justification for it must be examined'.[137] The standard of review was, therefore, intensified.

In contrast to the severe epistemic uncertainty the court faced on the derogation issue, the court felt much better placed to evaluate whether the detention interfered with the claimants' right to liberty and non-discrimination. Once the government's justifications for interfering with this right were subjected to the 'fullest and most anxious scrutiny',[138] there was 'no escape from the conclusion that Parliament must be regarded as having attached insufficient weight to ... human rights'.[139] In light of the discriminatory targeting of non-nationals, and the severity of the interference with liberty, the court concluded that the detention of non-nationals without trial constituted a disproportionate interference with rights.[140]

The *Belmarsh Prison* case illustrates a number of important points about the contours of comity in the exercise of *calibrated constitutional review*. First, when reviewing legislation for compliance with rights, questions of legal content are inextricably bound up with questions about institutional role and constitutional propriety. In order to decide whether indefinite detention without trial violated Convention rights, the courts had to take a stance on their institutional position vis-à-vis the Government and legislature in the constitutional scheme.

Second, whilst acknowledging that national security is an area where the elected branches of government are entitled to 'the utmost respect',[141] this did not preclude the court from scrutinising the legislation for compliance with rights in a probing manner. The degree of deference the courts owed to the elected branches of government was partial not absolute, variable not inveterate.[142] Rejecting the suggestion that

---

[135] Bingham (2011) chapter 12 (entitled 'Personal Freedoms and the Dilemma of Democracies').
[136] *Belmarsh* (n 37) [178].
[137] Ibid [178].
[138] Ibid [107], [192].
[139] Ibid [80].
[140] *Belmarsh* (n 37) [133].
[141] Ibid [196].
[142] Kavanagh (2009a) 172–3.

Executive decisions in the national security field required the 'unquestioning acquiescence of the court',[143] the court warned that

> Constitutional dangers exist no less in too little judicial activism as in too much. There are limits to the legitimacy of executive or legislative decision-making, just as there are to decision-making by the courts.[144]

Therefore,

> Deference to the view of the government and Parliament ... cannot be taken too far. Due deference does not mean abasement before those views, even in matters relating to national security ... the legitimacy of the court's scrutiny role cannot be in doubt.[145]

Third, the *Belmarsh* decision neatly illustrates the variability and context-dependence of the calibrating process, even within the context of one single case. By adopting different intensities of review on the derogation and discrimination issues, the courts calibrated the appropriate degree of deference in a 'focused, issue-specific'[146] way. This gave the legislature more leeway and weight on the derogation issue than on the question of discrimination. Instead of a 'crude, subject-based approach'[147] cordoning off the whole field of national security as a 'judicial no-go area',[148] *Belmarsh* marked a subtle but nonetheless significant constitutional shift 'from non-justiciability to a variable intensity of review'.[149] To be clear, this did not licence 'audacious judicial interventionism'[150] across the board. Nor did it ignore the institutional limits of the judicial role in the national security field. Instead, the court in *Belmarsh* engaged in robust, but respectful, review – upholding rights whilst giving 'great weight'[151] and an 'appropriate degree of latitude'[152] to the democratic legislature in deciding how to respond to a terrorist threat.

Finally, many of the judges gave credence to the conclusions of numerous parliamentary committees which had looked into the issue,

---

[143] *R (Binyam Mohamed) v Secretary of State for Foreign and Commonwealth Affairs* [2010] EWCA Civ 65 [46].
[144] *Roth* (n 75) [54].
[145] *Belmarsh* (38) [176], [44]; Kavanagh (2009a) 228–9.
[146] Hunt (2003) 344; Kavanagh (2011) 175; King (2007) 224.
[147] Hunt (2003) 344.
[148] Kavanagh (2011) 173; Hunt (2003) 344ff; Roach (2009) 164–7; Kavanagh (2009a) 201–9.
[149] Kavanagh (2011); *DPP v Ziegler* [2021] UKSC 23 [92], Lady Arden.
[150] Kavanagh (2011) 173.
[151] Ibid [29]; *Roth* (n 75) [54].
[152] *Belmarsh* (n 37) [80].

including the JCHR, the Committee of Privy Counsellors, and the Reports of the Independent Reviewer of Terrorism Legislation.[153] This provides another example of legal and political forms of accountability 'working in tandem'[154] rather than in tension. It also illustrates the influence of the political process on judicial reasoning about rights, where meaningful parliamentary engagement with rights feeds into the judicial evaluation about whether the legislation complies with rights.[155]

Instead of treating national security as a 'judicial no-go area',[156] the court in *Belmarsh* entered the field and scrutinised the terrain, but did so with caution and care, aware of the epistemic and institutional limitations they faced, whilst taking the government's and Parliament's views on board.[157] Working together with the other branches in a 'dialectical relationship'[158] of comity and collaboration, the courts helped the government to realise the dual demands of 'keeping control of terrorists' without 'losing control of constitutionalism'.[159]

6   Proportionality in Partnership

In constitutional adjudication across the globe, proportionality is a dominant theme.[160] From its humble beginnings in German administrative law, proportionality has now become the *lingua franca* – or perhaps, more accurately, the *lingua germanica* – of rights-based review.[161] When the HRA was enacted, the UK courts took the path of proportionality when assessing whether legislation complies with rights.[162] Since many of the Convention rights are 'qualified rights' – subject to limitations if 'necessary in a democratic society, in the interest of national security,

---

[153] Bamforth (2013) 283–4; Anderson (2014).
[154] Ibid 283.
[155] *Belmarsh* (n 37) [23], [32], [34], [43], [64], [65]; Bamforth (2013) 281.
[156] Kavanagh (2011) 174.
[157] Kavanagh (2009b); Kavanagh (2011); Fenwick (2011); Scheppele (2012) (arguing that a similar shift from non-justiciability towards a variable degree of deference occurred in the post-9/11 jurisprudence in the United States).
[158] Bamforth (2013) 285; Hiebert (2006) 27; Hunt (2010) 602–8.
[159] Walker (2007).
[160] Cohen-Eliya & Porat (2013); Grimm (2007); Stone Sweet & Mathews (2009); Barak (2012); Huscroft, Miller & Webber (2014); Kyritsis (2014).
[161] Möller (2012) (describing proportionality as 'the global model of constitutional rights adjudication').
[162] *Daly v Secretary of State for the Home Department* [2001] 2 WLR 1622; Hunt (2003) 338ff.

territorial integrity or public safety' – the UK courts decided to follow the Strasbourg practice of using the proportionality standard to test whether limitations on rights were justified in a democracy.[163]

Proportionality is a multi-pronged test which requires courts to ask whether (a) the legislation has a legitimate aim; (b) the legislative means are rationally connected to the aim; (c) the means are no more than necessary to accomplish the legislative objective; and (d) that a fair balance has been struck between the rights of the individual and the importance of the legislative objective.[164] Instead of posing a broad, undifferentiated question about whether legislation complies with rights, the proportionality test disaggregates distinct elements of that inquiry, directing judicial attention to each element in turn.[165] As former Chief Justice of the Supreme Court of Israel, Aharon Barak, put it, proportionality requires judges to 'think in stages.'[166] For its most stalwart defenders, proportionality is a fine-grained filtering device which screens out inadequate justifications for rights-infringing measures.[167]

Yet, no matter how differentiated and structured the proportionality rubric may be, there is no denying that at the final stage – often described as the 'balancing stage'[168] or 'proportionality *stricto sensu*'[169] – the courts are required to answer a relatively open-ended question about whether a limitation on rights is too great relative to the likely benefit of the legislative measure.[170] At this stage, the courts are given 'a very broad discretionary power'[171] to determine whether the legislation has achieved a fair balance between competing interests.[172] Given that this final balancing stage is

---

[163] Article 10(2) ECHR; Kumm (2010) 145–9. Note that whilst the US SC is formally resistant to the proportionality standard, many scholars argue that it employs analogous balancing tests as part of the 'tiered scrutiny' framework, see Gardbaum (2008) 419ff; Jackson (2015) 3127; Yowell (2018) 20–4.

[164] For explication of the four-pronged test, see *Bank Mellat* (n 45) [74]; *Quila* (n 32) [45]; Fordham (2020) 539; Yowell (2018) 16–17.

[165] On the disaggregative nature of the proportionality test, see Kavanagh (2009a) 256ff; Wiseman (2001) 454.

[166] Barak (2012) 460, 459; Kumm (2010) 144; Jackson (2015) 3098–9.

[167] Kumm (2010) 160; Kavanagh (2009a) 233–43; Fordham (2020) 538; Jackson (2015) 3151.

[168] Kyritsis (2014) 2.

[169] Barak (2010) 6; Barak (2012) chapter 12; Stone-Sweet & Mathews (2009) 75.

[170] *Bank Mellat* (n 45) [74], Lord Reed; *Carlile* (n 24) [19]; *R (Nicklinson) v Ministry of Justice* [2014] UKSC 38 [80].

[171] *R (SC, CB) v SSWP* [2021] UKSC 26 [162], Lord Reed.

[172] Ibid [208].

the pivotal step in most cases,[173] we should not be sanguine about the degree of judicial discretion involved.

This has given rise to fierce academic criticism that proportionality licenses an intrusive judicial approach which is 'nakedly legislative in character'.[174] For some commentators, proportionality requires the courts to 'weigh the unweighable'[175] and 'compare the incommensurable'[176] in 'the protean scales of justice'.[177] For its most forceful critics, proportionality's 'appearance of juridical craftsmanship barely conceals the unbounded, essentially legislative character of the assessments it involves'.[178] The question therefore arises: does proportionality lead to judicial supremacy over legislative priorities rather than comity and collaboration between constitutional partners? In short, does proportionality undercut the idea of *calibrated constitutional review*?

The answer is 'no', or at least 'not necessarily'. What prevents proportionality becoming judicial substitution of legislative decision-making is that the courts apply the test with varying degrees of restraint and deference, based on an evaluation of relative institutional competence, expertise and legitimacy.[179] As a former judge of the German Federal Constitutional Court put it, whether proportionality is used to intensify judicial control of state action 'is not determined by the structure of the test but by the degree of judicial restraint practised in applying it'.[180] The 'intensity with which the test is applied – that is to say, the degree of weight or respect given to the assessment of the primary decision-maker – depends on the context'.[181] When applying the proportionality standard, the courts *calibrate* the intensity and intrusiveness of their review depending on the severity of the interference with rights, and 'the expertise, position and overall competence of the court as against the decision-making authority'.[182]

---

[173] *DPP v Ziegler* [2021] UKSC 23 [126].
[174] Heydon (2014) 399; Finnis (2011b) 237–8; Endicott (2014) 315.
[175] Endicott (2014) 315; Petersen (2017) 4, 9, 39–45.
[176] Endicott (2014); Da Silva (2011).
[177] Coffin (1988); Jackson (2015) 3142; Endicott (2014).
[178] Finnis (2016) 119.
[179] Kavanagh (2009a) 252–3; Elliott (2020) 210–11.
[180] Lübbe-Wolff (2014) 16, cited with approval in *Bank Mellat* (n 45) [71]; Kavanagh (2009a) 237–41, 243; Rivers (2006) 202–3; Hoffmann (1999a) 112.
[181] *Bank Mellat* (n 45) [69].
[182] De Búrca (1993) 111.

When applying the proportionality standard, the courts operate a 'sliding scale of review',[183] which is 'sensitive to considerations of institutional competence and legitimacy'.[184] Evaluating the relative burdens and benefits of the legislative measure, the courts use the canonical correlatives of public law adjudication to calibrate the intensity of review. In doing so, they observe the key correlative which lies at the heart of the proportionality standard, namely, the greater the intrusion on rights, the stronger the justification required from the intruder.[185]

In this way, proportionality review covers 'a spectrum from a very deferential approach, to a quite rigorous and searching examination of the justification of the measure which has been challenged'.[186] Instead of substituting political decisions across the board, proportionality is a flexible and pliable tool which judges can modulate and calibrate in a context-sensitive fashion.[187] As the UK courts have repeatedly affirmed, when assessing whether legislation is proportionate,

> the court's task is not to substitute its own view for that of the [primary] decision-makers, but to review their decision with an intensity appropriate to all the circumstances of the case.[188]

There is no doubt that proportionality creates a 'risk of undue interference by the courts in the sphere of political choices'.[189] But, as the UK Supreme Court has recently observed, that risk can be avoided if the courts 'apply the principle in a manner which respects the boundaries between legality and the political process'.[190] Once proportionality is situated within the duty of the courts to respect the decisions of the

---

[183] *Pham* (n 105) [106]–[108], Lord Sumption.
[184] *In the matter of an application by the NIHRC (Northern Ireland)* [2018] UKSC 27, [116] Lord Mance; *Nicklinson* (n 175) [166]; *Kennedy v The Charity Commission* [2014] UKSC 20 [54]; *R (Sinclair Collis Ltd) v Secretary of State for Health* [2011] EWCA Civ 437 [127]–[130] LJ Arden; Rivers (2006) 180.
[185] Jackson (2015) 3118; Allan (2014) 233.
[186] De Búrca (1993) 111; *Pham* (n 106) [60], [95], [114]; Craig (2013) 131; Fordham (2020) 541–2.
[187] *Nicklinson* (n 175) [170], Lord Mance; Fordham (2020) 733.
[188] *Pro-Life Alliance* [139], per Lord Walker; Kavanagh (2009a) 261; Fordham (2020) 717; Grimm (2007) 390–1
[189] *R (SC, CB) v SSWP* [2021] UKSC 26 [162] (the child tax credit case).
[190] Ibid.

democratic legislature, it can be viewed a form of *calibrated constitutional review*, not as a surrepticious form of judicial supremacy.[191]

The contextual calibration of the proportionality standard is manifest in multiple ways. For one thing, the courts typically operate a 'variable intensity of review'[192] at the different stages of the proportionality inquiry. For example, it is common for courts in many jurisdictions to give a wide margin of discretion to the legislature in determining a legitimate object- ive, but to be more probing on whether the legislation imposed an excessive burden on the individual.[193] The light-touch approach to whether the legislature has a legitimate aim reflects a judicial concern to avoid undue agenda control, and to refrain from interfering with legisla- tively determined policy priorities.[194] There is variability within – not just between – cases employing the proportionality rubric.[195]

A calibrated approach is also evident when the courts adjust the intensity of review depending on the subject-matter of the case. In areas of economic and regulatory complexity, the courts tend not to interfere with legislative decisions unless they are 'manifestly without reasonable foundation (MWRF)'.[196] However, if severe burdens are placed on mar- ginalised groups, or there is a evidence of discriminatory treatment based on gender, race or sexual orientation, this triggers a more searching form of review where 'the courts will scrutinise with intensity any reasons said to constitute justification',[197] requiring 'particularly convincing and weighty reasons'[198] to justify the differential treatment. Even at the highest intensity of review, the courts emphasise that their task is 'not to substitute its own view for that of the decision-makers, but to review their decision with an intensity appropriate to all the circumstances of the case'.[199] In doing so, they 'accord appropriate respect to the choices

---

[191] Dyzenhaus (2014) 239; Taggart (2008) 460–1; Poole (2007b) 267.
[192] Rivers (2006).
[193] See e.g. Arnardóttir (2017) 30; Kavanagh (2009a) 237ff.
[194] On judicial agenda control, see Tushnet (1995).
[195] Wiseman (2001); Tew (2020) 205–10, 215 (arguing that proportionality is a 'sensitive but robust' judicial tool).
[196] *R (SC, CB) v SSWP* [2021] UKSC 26 [97]–[162]; *R (DA) & R (DS) v Secretary of State for Work and Pensions* [2019] UKSC 21, [56]; *In Re McLaughlin* [2018] UKSC 48, [34], Lady Hale; King (2012) 186; Arnardóttir (2017) 29.
[197] *Ghaidan* [19]; *Steinfeld & Keidan*, [20] Lord Kerr.
[198] See e.g. *Pham* (n 105) [98], [108]); see generally Elliott (2015b) 77; King (2012) 181–7.
[199] *R (Pro-Life Alliance) v BBC* [2004] 1 AC 185, [139], Lord Walker.

made ... by the Government and Parliament, whilst at the same time providing a safeguard against unjustifiable discrimination'.[200]

The upshot is that proportionality does not dictate a 'one-size-fits-all'[201] approach regarding the appropriate standard or intensity of review. It envisages a variegated and flexible rather than monolithic inquiry, which allows the courts to modulate and moderate the intensity of review. When assessing whether a limitation on rights is proportionate, the courts have stressed that it is not their role to dictate an optimal or uniquely proportionate balance between competing interests.[202] Instead, it is to discern whether the legislation has struck 'a reasonable balance'[203] between competing concerns, or whether there is 'a reasonable relationship of proportionality between the means employed and the aim sought to be realised'.[204] As former Chief Justice McLachlin of the Supreme Court of Canada observed, the process of ensuring that laws are

> carefully tailored so that rights are impaired no more than necessary ... seldom admits of perfection and the courts must accord some leeway to the legislator. If the law falls within the range of reasonable alternatives, the courts will not find it overbroad merely because they can conceive of an alternative which might better tailor objective to infringement.[205]

Finally, it is worth recalling that proportionality is premised on the assumption that rights can be justifiably limited by the legislature in light of important social and policy goals.[206] As the UK Supreme Court

---

[200] *R (SC CB) v SSWP* [2021] UKSC 26 [144], *per* Lord Reed.

[201] *Pro-Life Alliance* (n. 204), [144], Lord Walker.

[202] *R (Keyu) v Secretary of State for Foreign and Commonwealth Affairs* [2015] UKSC 69 [272] Lord Kerr (proportionality 'does not demand that the decision-maker bring the reviewer to the point of conviction that theirs was the right decision in any absolute sense'); *Bank Mellat* (n 45) [75] (observing that the 'least restrictive measure' should be described as the 'less intrusive measure' criterion in order to emphasise the judicial recognition of legitimate legislative leeway in formulating legislative responses to social policy concerns); *Carter v Canada (Attorney General)* [2015] 1 SCR 331 [97]; Yowell (2018) 18; Kavanagh (2009a) 240–1; *R (Johnson) v Secretary of State for Work and Pensions* [2020] EWCA Civ 778 [50].

[203] *Bank Mellat* (n 45) [75].

[204] *James v UK* (1986) 8 EHRR 123, 144–5.

[205] *RJR-MacDonald Inc v Canada (AG)* [1995] 3 SCR 199, [160]; Grimm (2007) 390 (observing the German Federal Constitutional Court 'always emphasised that the legislature enjoys a certain degree of political discretion in choosing the means to reach a legislative objective').

[206] Gardbaum (2014) 267, 271 (presenting proportionality as a form of 'democratic constitutionalism').

observed, the very idea of qualified or limited rights 'opens the door to democratic policy choices',[207] reflecting the fact that policy objectives

> engage responsibilities normally attaching in the first instance to other branches of the state, whether the executive or legislature. When considering whether a particular measure is necessary and all the more when considering whether it is justified on a balancing of competing and often incommensurate interests, the courts should recognise the role of the elected branches in striking the appropriate balance between them.[208]

This means that the elected branches of government are 'often in the best position to determine the necessity for the interference'.[209] In doing so, judges have proceeded with 'a certain humility . . . acutely sensitive to the dangers of making decisions which are better left to those who are politically accountable.'[210]

This goes to a larger point about the nature of proportionality review, namely, that it 'creates a legitimate space for government to explain its reasons for limiting rights in a public forum'.[211] Instead of 'displacing the role of the democratically elected arms of government in assessing how best to protect and promote rights',[212] the courts call on the political actors to justify their legislative choices in a context where judges are attuned to the need to give the legislature leeway and respect when complex, polycentric policy choices are at issue.[213]

Far from precluding the Executive or legislature from pursuing policies which may limit rights – or even excluding them from deliberating about whether legislation complies with rights – the proportionality rubric positively *invites* the Government and legislature to make key political choices. Viewed in this light, proportionality emerges as

> democracy-enhancing, both in providing a shared discourse of justification for action claimed to limit rights and in providing more sensitivity to serious process-deficiencies reflecting entrenched biases against particular groups.[214]

---

[207] *NIHRC* (n 189) [340], Lord Reed.
[208] *Nicklinson* (n 175) [166]; Endicott (2014).
[209] *R (T) Chief Constable of Greater Manchester Police* [2015] AC 49, [114], Lord Reed; Jackson (2015) 3145.
[210] Elias (2018) 10; Lee & Lee (2015).
[211] O'Regan (2019) 431 (formerly Justice Kate O'Regan of the South African Constitutional Court); Yap (2015) 103–5.
[212] O'Regan (2019) 431; Grimm (2007) 396.
[213] O'Regan (2019) 431.
[214] Jackson (2015) 3194; Roach (2021) 62.

This illustrates the idea of *proportionality in partnership*, where courts employ a potentially exacting standard of review, but do so in a way which is 'sensitive to the proper contribution of the other branches of government'[215] in the collaborative scheme. By affirming the importance of constitutional rights whilst remaining attuned to democratic reasons, calibration 'breeds comity and collaboration, which in turn allows legal accountability to meet the ebb and flow of demand for it'.[216] Proportionality gives judges new tools to vindicate rights – tools which can cut deep into legislative priorities at times. But the courts can calibrate the depth of the incision and the intrusiveness of review, tempering it with a spirit of comity, collaboration and respect for the democratically elected branches of government. In doing so, the courts 'enlist the political branches as partners in the realisation of . . . rights',[217] acting as a complement not a substitute for democratic government.[218]

7 Conclusion

This chapter defended the idea of *calibrated constitutional review*, where judges engage in robust but responsible review by calibrating the intensity of review in light of a complex matrix of countervailing concerns. The idea of calibrated constitutional review cuts across the polarised pairings of 'activism versus restraint' or 'abstentionism versus interventionism', eschewing accounts of the judicial role which isolate distinct judicial 'stances'[219] or 'postures',[220] whether deferential or interventionist, conversational or peremptory. The problem with these one-sided accounts is that they occlude the dualistic dynamic at the heart of the judicial role – namely, the need to combine and balance the competing demands of Janus-faced judging in a collaborative constitutional scheme. In order to capture the complexity of judicial reasoning about rights, we need to consider the 'push and pull factors' in combination, not in isolation.

---

[215] Rivers (2006) 176.
[216] King (2012) 150–1; Roach (2005) 551; Sathanapally (2012) 14–15.
[217] Roux (2013) 395.
[218] Kumm (2010) 143, 168.
[219] Young (2010) 385.
[220] Leckey (2016) 210–11.

Good judging is neither relentlessly activist nor uniformly restrained. Instead, it is a complex calibration of competing concerns which bear on the individual case. Therefore, restraint in one case and interventionism in another is not necessarily evidence of judicial schizophrenia. Instead, it could be the product of a tailored, calibrated approach which evaluates all the elements carefully in context. In a healthy legal system, judges will see 'both restraint and creativity as duties'.[221]

Instead of judicial decisions being either all acceleration or all brake, the complex challenge of judging in a democracy is to work out how much judicial restraint or creativity is required in the context of an individual case, and what form it should take.[222] By adopting a 'contextual institutional approach'[223] which calibrates the competing values and variables at stake, the skill of judging in a joint enterprise can only be captured in the composite virtues of 'corrective respect',[224] 'creative restraint'[225] and 'constrained creativity'.[226] Good judging requires a 'judicious mix of ... fortitude, forbearance, and fine judgment'.[227]

This fits within the collaborative vision of constitutionalism where all three branches of government have a shared responsibility to protect rights and democracy. Democratically elected actors do their share for rights by enacting rights-protective policies and respecting judicial decisions on what they require. By the same token, the courts 'do their share for democracy'[228] by respecting the primary law-making role of the Executive and legislature in the constitutional scheme.

When reviewing legislation for compliance with rights, judges are neither solitary crusaders for justice nor enemies of the people. Instead, they are partners in a collaborative enterprise, where they play a significant, but subsidiary, role in the constitutional scheme – resolving

---

[221] Endicott (2015b) 110; Lord Justice Gross (2018) [22] (arguing that judges must seek to achieve 'a careful balance between creativity, judgment and reserve or restraint'); Lord Justice Gross (2016) [29].

[222] O'Donnell (2017) 208 (Chief Justice of the Irish Supreme Court); Tulkens (2022) 1–8 (former judge of the ECtHR); Bogg (2018).

[223] King (2008a) 432.

[224] Lord Sales (2016a) 456.

[225] Binnie (2013) 12.

[226] Roach (2016b) 131ff.

[227] Lord Justice Gross (2016) [13] (though the precise quotation refers to 'fortitude, reserve and fine judgment').

[228] Kyritsis (2017) 212.

individual disputes, whilst supervising legislation for compliance with rights. In carrying out their supervisory role, they should supervise with sensitivity to questions of relative institutional competence and legitimacy. In short, they should respect rights whilst remaining responsive to democratic concerns. They do that by engaging in *calibrated constitutional review*.

10

Courting Collaborative Constitutionalism

1 Introduction

In defending the idea of *calibrated constitutional review*, the previous chapter argued that the courts calibrate the intensity, scope, and impact of their review depending on a complex array of contextual variables. The task of this chapter is to take that argument forward by examining the tools and techniques judges use to give the legislature leeway and weight in the collaborative constitutional scheme. If the collaborative enterprise is based on a dynamic division of labour, then we need to examine *how* the branches of government distribute the workload between them. The challenge of this chapter, therefore, is to examine the doctrines and devices of calibrated constitutionalism in context.

In order to illustrate the phenomenon of calibrated constitutionalism, I start by examining the UK Supreme Court's decision in *Nicklinson*,[1] which held that Mr Nicklinson did not have a right to assisted suicide under the European Convention. Whilst showing some sympathy for Mr Nicklinson's plight, the court refrained from issuing a declaration that the existing prohibition violated Convention rights. Though the *Nicklinson* case is unusual in many respects, it nonetheless showcases a broad spectrum of judicial opinions on the scope and limits of the judicial role in circumstances of controversy and contestation. Therefore, *Nicklinson* provides a rich resource of judicial insight on the dilemmas of judging in a democracy.

The chapter will proceed in the following way. Part 2 examines the diversity of judicial perspectives on how the courts should relate to the elected branches of government in the *Nicklinson* case. Using this case as a springboard for further reflection on the tools and techniques of

---

[1] *R (Nicklinson) v Ministry of Justice* [2014] UKSC 38 (hereafter *Nicklinson*).

collaborative constitutionalism, I then go on to address particular tools in context.

Part 3 analyses the emerging trend of 'political process review',[2] probing the question of whether courts should give weight to parliamentary debate when assessing legislation for compliance with rights. Part 4 details the judicial effort to avoid pre-empting ongoing or imminent political engagement with rights. Part 5 turns to an examination of the 'court as catalyst' and the 'judge as nudge'. Instead of viewing the courts as purely reactive or responsive actors, this part explores the catalytic effect of judicial decisions on other constitutional actors. Surveying the varied phenomena of judicial prods and pleas, hints and suggestions, advice and intimations, I uncover a subtle but significant judicial effort to incentivise the Executive and legislature to protect and promote rights. This reveals a complex combination of responsive and catalytic review.

In the final section, I consider Alexander Bickel's canonical claim that the tools and techniques canvassed in this chapter are aptly conceived as 'passive virtues'.[3] Rejecting this characterisation, I argue that they are better conceived as *collaborative devices* which judges use to divide the constitutional labour between the branches of government, whilst playing an active and constructive role in the collaborative constitutional scheme.

2   Legislative Leeway at the End of Life

The question before the court in *Nicklinson*[4] was whether the criminalisation of assisted suicide under the Suicide Act 1961 violated Mr Nicklinson's right to private and family life under Article 8 of the European Convention. Mr Nicklinson was of sound mind and was not terminally ill. But following a severe stroke, he suffered from 'locked-in syndrome' where he was trapped in a life of ongoing suffering and pain. He wanted to end his life and needed help to do so – help which was criminalised under section 2 of the Suicide Act 1961. By a majority of seven to two, the Supreme Court rejected Mr Nicklinson's claim that the Suicide Act violated his 'right to life' under the European Convention. Given the complexity, controversy and sensitivity surrounding this issue,

---

[2] Gardbaum (2020a).
[3] Bickel (1961).
[4] *Nicklinson* (n 1).

the court held that reforming the law on assisted suicide was pre-eminently a matter for Parliament, not the courts.

Despite a clear majority in favour of leaving the matter for Parliament, the *Nicklinson* decision contains a broad spectrum of judicial opinion on the proper role of the courts in the collaborative enterprise. On one end, two minority judges thought that a blanket ban on assisted suicide was a disproportionate interference with rights, thus warranting a declaration of incompatibility in this case.[5] On the other end of the spectrum, two judges believed that the legal regulation of assisted suicide was an 'inherently legislative issue'[6] which only Parliament could resolve.[7] The other five judges lay between these two poles, believing that it would be 'institutionally inappropriate'[8] for the courts to issue a declaration of incompatibility in this case, especially as Parliament was shortly due to debate the issue of assisted suicide.[9] However, if Parliament failed to grasp the legislative nettle, it was 'certainly conceivable'[10] that the courts would issue a declaration of incompatibility in future litigation if a suitable case arose.[11] Therefore, the *Nicklinson* judgment was not a judicial 'no' for all time. It was more like a 'no for now' but 'never say never'.[12]

The reasoning of the court in *Nicklinson* illustrates the dynamics of calibrated constitutionalism in context, echoing many of the themes explored in the previous chapter. The majority began by emphasising the legitimacy of their reviewing role even in contexts of complexity and controversy. As Lord Neuberger observed: 'the mere fact that there are moral issues involved plainly does not mean that the courts have to keep out'.[13] The courts have 'a constitutional role in balancing the relevant interests'[14] and it would be 'an abdication of judicial responsibility'[15] to refuse to engage. This was not a judicial no-go zone.

---

[5] Ibid, Lady Hale and Lord Kerr.
[6] Ibid [234] Lord Sumption.
[7] Ibid, Lords Sumption and Hughes.
[8] Ibid [116] Lord Neuberger.
[9] Ibid, Lords Neuberger, Mance, Clarke, Wilson, and Reed.
[10] Ibid [125] Lord Neuberger; [190] Lord Mance; [198] Lord Wilson; [298] Lord Reed.
[11] Ibid [118] Lord Neuberger; [190] Lord Mance; Murkens (2018) 370.
[12] *Nicklinson* (n 1) [115]–[116] Lord Neuberger.
[13] Ibid [98].
[14] Ibid [191] Lord Mance.
[15] Ibid [113] Lord Neuberger; [191] Lord Mance.

Nonetheless, the court was aware that the issue of assisted suicide engaged 'responsibilities normally attaching in the first instance to the other branches of the state, whether the Executive or the Legislature'.[16] No matter how exacting or probing proportionality review might be, it 'did not entitle the courts simply to substitute their own assessment for that of the primary decision-maker'.[17] In this context, the court decided to 'take matters relatively slowly'[18] and 'tread with the utmost caution'.[19] But if not 'no go', then why 'go slow'?

There were a number of reasons why the court took a cautious and calibrated approach in *Nicklinson*. First, assisted suicide 'raises a difficult, controversial and sensitive issue, with moral and religious dimensions ... which undoubtedly justifies a relatively cautious approach from the courts'.[20] Second, the adversarial process focused on the facts of one particular case prevented the court from fully appreciating the wider implications of a change in the law.[21] In an assessment of relative institutional competence and expertise, the legislature has

> access to a fuller range of expert judgment and experience than forensic litigation can possibly provide. It is better able to take account of the interests of groups not sufficiently represented before the court resolving what is surely a classic polycentric problem.[22]

Third, Parliament had considered the issue of assisted dying and euthanasia on six occasions over the previous decade and had refused to relax the current prohibition on assisted suicide as recently as 2009. The fact that 'a majority of the country's democratically elected representatives' had decided not to change the law warranted a 'degree of respect to be shown to the considered judgment of the democratic assembly'.[23] Indeed, Parliament was due to reconsider the issue of assisted suicide when debating the Assisted Dying Bill, which was due to come before Parliament shortly after the conclusion of the case.[24]

---

[16] Ibid [188] Lord Mance.
[17] Ibid [168] Lord Mance.
[18] Ibid [116] Lord Neuberger.
[19] Ibid [201] Lord Wilson.
[20] Ibid [116], [103] Lord Neuberger.
[21] Ibid [60]; Dyson (2018) 50.
[22] *Nicklinson* (n 1) [232] Lord Sumption.
[23] Ibid [102] Lord Neuberger; [232] Lord Sumption.
[24] Ibid [118].

Therefore, the majority decided to 'accord Parliament the opportunity of considering whether to amend' the law,[25] unconstrained by a declaration of incompatibility by the courts.

Fourth, relaxing the ban on assisted suicide would effect a radical change in the law and be an 'unheralded *volte face*.'[26]. As Lord Neuberger observed, it would be 'a radical step'[27] to declare a statutory provision incompatible with rights when such a declaration 'involved effectively stating that the law should be changed so as to decriminalise an act which would unquestionably be characterised as murder or manslaughter'.[28]

All of these factors 'militate[d] strongly against the courts intervening in this area, at least at this stage'.[29] In the decisional vortex of 'push and pull factors'[30] in an acutely controversial case, the court decided that Parliament was the 'preferable forum in which any such decision should be made, after full investigation and consideration, in a manner which will command popular acceptance'.[31] Though many judges had great sympathy for the Mr Nicklinson's situation, the court nonetheless gave the legislature the benefit of the doubt 'even if the evidence appears to a court weaker and less conclusive than it might otherwise be'.[32] In short, the majority of the judges in *Nicklinson* were keen to give the legislature *leeway* to regulate the issue as it saw fit, whilst simultaneously attaching 'very considerable *weight*[33] to the balance struck by successive Parliaments.

A number of preliminary points can be made about this case. First, all nine judges *proceeded interactively*, viewing the protection of rights as a multi-institutional, not a single-institutional, endeavour. All judges addressed questions of legal content alongside institutional and constitutional concerns about the appropriate division of labour in a collaborative constitutional scheme. As Lord Mance observed, proportionality is a 'flexible doctrine ... not insensitive to considerations of institutional

---

[25] Ibid [113].
[26] Ibid [116].
[27] Ibid [116].
[28] Ibid [110].
[29] Ibid [116] Lord Neuberger.
[30] Gerards (2014) 19.
[31] *Nicklinson* (n 1) [190] Lord Mance.
[32] Ibid [189] Lord Mance.
[33] Ibid [297] Lord Reed (emphasis added); [166] Lord Mance.

competence and legitimacy'.[34] Therefore, *Nicklinson* is a good example of *proportionality in partnership*.

Second, the majority of judges *proceeded respectfully*, aware of the limits of the courts' institutional capacity and the institutional strengths of the legislature in a context of polycentricity, policy complexity, and moral disagreement. Although this did not create a judicial 'no-go area', it nonetheless encouraged the court to enter the field with caution and care.

Third, the majority *proceeded incrementally*, allowing the legislature leeway and time to grapple with the issue. Aware of the dangers of proceeding 'too far, too fast', the court was concerned to avoid pre-empting the democratic process. In this chapter draw out some facets of this reasoning, using them to illustrate the dynamic division of labour between the branches of government in a collaborative enterprise.

3 Proportionality and Political Process Review

When deciding whether the ban on assisted suicide was a proportionate limitation on rights, the Supreme Court in *Nicklinson* gave some weight to the fact that the ban had been 'debated in Parliament at least six times in the last nine years'[35] and each time, Parliament had 'deliberately re-enacted'[36] the prohibition 'after lively public and parliamentary debate'.[37] Two questions then arise: (1) Should the courts consider, and then give weight to, parliamentary deliberation when reviewing legislation for compliance with rights? (2) How does such a practice fit into the relationship of comity, reciprocity and respect between the courts and the legislature in the collaborative constitutional enterprise?

On the first question, it seems intuitively plausible to think that the degree of judicial respect due to a legislative measure should be influenced, at least to some degree, by whether the legislature took rights seriously during the legislative process.[38] After all, if proportionality requires that a 'fair balance must be struck between the rights of the

---

[34] Ibid [166].
[35] Ibid [51] Lord Neuberger.
[36] Ibid [260] Lord Hughes.
[37] Ibid [260] Lord Hughes; [99] Lord Neuberger.
[38] Kavanagh (2014) 444–6.

individual and the interests of the community',[39] then it seems natural to think that judges should inquire into whether such a careful balancing exercise actually took place and, if so, to give it weight in their own evaluation of proportionality. On this view, giving weight to parliamentary debate seems to be both 'rights-respecting' and 'democracy-enhancing'.[40]

However, this issue is more complicated than these intuitive thoughts may suggest. For one thing, the duty of constitutional comity generally requires the courts and legislature to 'abstain from interference with the functions of the other, and to treat each other's proceedings and decisions with respect'.[41] Out of respect for the constitutional separation of powers and the autonomy of internal decision-making processes, many jurisdictions therefore resist the idea of 'political process review'[42] for fear it will lead to a judicial usurpation of the political process. The worry is that judges will assess legislative deliberation against unduly legalistic criteria which fail to grasp the distinctiveness of democratic deliberation, thereby distorting and possibly debilitating democratic decision-making.[43] If this occurs, then political process review might 'undermine the democratic goals it seeks to serve'.[44]

In the UK, the prohibition on judicial supervision of the internal workings of the political process is centuries-old. It is embodied in the principle of parliamentary privilege in Article 9 of the Bill of Rights 1689.[45] According to that principle, UK courts are constitutionally barred from entering the 'forbidden territory'[46] of questioning or criticising parliamentary debate, so that freedom of speech in the Houses of

---

[39] *R (H) v City Council* [2011] EWCA Civ 403, [38]; *Huang v SSHD* [2007] UKHL 11, [19]–[20].

[40] Spano (2014); Spano (2018); Arnardóttir (2017) 12.

[41] *R (SC, CB) v SSWP* [2021] UKSC 26, [165], *per* Lord Reed.

[42] Gardbaum (2020a); Kavanagh (2020); Hailbronner (2020). Judicial reference to, and review of, aspects of the political process appears under different labels in different jurisdictions, including Linde (1976) ('due process of lawmaking'); Rose-Ackerman, Egidy & Fowkes (2015) ('structural review' or 'semi-substantive constitutional review'); Coenen (2009); 'semi-procedural judicial review', Bar-Simon-Tov (2011), Gerards & Brems (2017) ('procedural review').

[43] Bar-Siman-Tov (2011) 1915–27 (examining the persistent resistance to judicial review of the legislative process in the US context).

[44] Hailbronner (2020) 1459.

[45] On the principle of parliamentary privilege, see Kavanagh (2014) 445–7, 453–5.

[46] *Wilson v First County Trust (No 2)* [2003] UKHL 40; Kavanagh (2014) 446.

Parliament is not stifled by fear of judicial censure.[47] On this view, the most 'democracy-enhancing'[48] judicial approach may well be to give the legislature considerable leeway to debate, deliberate and decide as it sees fit.

This presents us with a dilemma. On the one hand, judicial respect for the Executive and legislature as lead lawmakers in the collaborative scheme seems to require judges to give weight to parliamentary debate when assessing proportionality. On the other hand, allowing judges to engage in 'political process review' creates the risk that they will assume the role of 'institutional overseers'[49] of the quality of political deliberation, thereby distorting and debilitating the political dynamics of democratic decision-making.[50]

In an effort to reconcile these competing concerns, UK courts have adopted 'a halfway-house approach',[51] where they strive to give weight to meaningful parliamentary engagement with rights, whilst avoiding the spectre of judges pronouncing on the detailed requirements of democratic deliberation.

When deciding whether legislation strikes a fair balance between competing interests, the courts take account of whether the issue was considered during the legislative process and, if so, to what extent. In doing so, they do not evaluate 'the quality of the reasons advanced in favour of the legislation in the course of parliamentary debate'.[52] Nor do they presume to evaluate 'the sufficiency of the legislative process leading up to the enactment of the statute'.[53] Instead, they carry out a more indirect and light-touch assessment of *whether* the implications for rights were considered during the political process and, if so, *to what extent* and *with what intensity*. If legislation can be shown to be 'the product of considered democratic debate',[54] including 'a carefully considered balancing of individual and community interest',[55]

---

[47] *R (HS2 Action Alliance Ltd) v Secretary of State for Trade and Industry* [2014] UKSC 3, [79]; *Office of Government Commerce v Information Commissioner (AG intervening)* [2008] EWHC 774 [58]; Kavanagh (2014) 453–4.

[48] Spano (2018).

[49] Carolan (2016a) 216.

[50] Saul (2015) 759; Saul (2016) 1080.

[51] Kavanagh (2014) 455–63.

[52] *Wilson v First County Trust* (n 46) [64].

[53] Ibid [67].

[54] *In the Matter of an Application by the (NIHRC) for Judicial Review (Northern Ireland)* [2018] UKSC 27, [350] Lord Reed.

[55] *R (Chester) v Justice Secretary* [2013] UKSC 63, [90] Lady Hale.

following 'full and intense democratic debate',[56] 'careful evaluation'[57] and 'considerable scrutiny',[58] then the courts will give 'appropriate weight to informed legislative choices.'[59] However, if no such balancing exercise occurred or there is a lack of parliamentary engagement with rights, then heightened judicial scrutiny may be in order.[60] In short, the existence and extent of parliamentary engagement with rights becomes a 'calibrating factor'[61] which courts use to determine the degree of weight they should give to the legislature when assessing whether legislation strikes a fair balance between competing considerations.

In rights-based adjudication in the UK, the courts have assessed the quality of legislative deliberation about rights along three main axes: *legislative focus, active and informed debate,* and *deliberative diversity*.[62] For *legislative focus,* the courts ask whether the legislature 'squarely addressed'[63] the implications of rights during the legislative process. Evidence of this might be whether the matter was explicitly 'mentioned in the course of debate in both Houses of Parliament'[64] or whether it was considered or scrutinised by parliamentary committees.[65]

On the issue of *active and informed debate,* the courts observe whether the legislation was 'the produce of active debate in Parliament'[66] or whether there was 'a reasoned and closely-considered judgment of a

---

[56] *R (SG) v Secretary of State for Work and Pensions* [2015] UKSC 16, [95], [155]; *R (Conway) v Secretary of State for Justice* [2017] EWHC 640, [25] (opining that 'despite full investigation and consideration', Parliament decided not to change the law relating to assisted suicide).

[57] *R (Pearson) v SSHD* [1002] EWHC Admin 239, [33].

[58] *R (SC, CB) v SSHD* (n 41), [16].

[59] *In Re Recovery of Medical Costs for Asbestos Diseases (Wales) Bill* [2015] UKSC 3, [54].

[60] *R (SC, CB) v SSHD* (n 41) [180], *per* Lord Reed; Rose-Ackerman, Egidy & Fowkes (2015) 59–72.

[61] Dixon (2020) 92; Kavanagh (2014) 472.

[62] Kavanagh (2014) 463; King (2012) 164–5 (though note that King uses the term 'legislative focus' to encompass all the different facets of legislative engagement outlined above).

[63] *R (Al Skeini) v Secretary of State for Defence* [2007] UKHL 26 [23].

[64] *Williamson v Secretary of State for Education and Employment* [51], [85]–[86].

[65] Ibid [51]; *R (Animal Defenders International) v Secretary of State for Culture, Media and Sport* [2008] UKHL 15, [14]–[19]; Kavanagh (2014) 457.

[66] *Huang* (n 39) [17].

democratic assembly'[67] following a 'prolonged',[68] 'intense',[69] 'thoughtful and well-informed'[70] consideration of the rights issue involved. On *deliberative diversity*, the courts have noted whether 'all opposing views were ... fully represented'[71] in parliamentary debate or whether the legislative framework was 'the result of substantial research and intensive consultation with a wide range of interested and expert groups and individuals'.[72]

In doing so, the courts take cognisance of the breadth and depth of parliamentary engagement with rights, as well as the 'participatory pedigree'[73] of the legislative process. Whilst abjuring a direct qualitative analysis of the content of democratic deliberation, they nonetheless give constitutional credence to focused, thoughtful, inclusive and well-informed engagement with rights during the political process.

The halfway-house approach bespeaks an acknowledgement that it is not the judges' job to determine what counts as 'good' or 'bad' parliamentary debate.[74] Suitably calibrated in a context-sensitive way, this indirect and limited form of 'political process review'[75] is a useful technique of collaborative constitutionalism. The halfway-house approach enables the courts to pay due respect to the deliberative capacities of the democratic legislature, without usurping or debilitating the democratic process.

Of course, the existence of meaningful legislative engagement with rights is neither conclusive nor determinative on the question of whether legislation is compatible with rights. As the ECtHR observed in *Shindler v UK*,[76] the fact that the legislature debates an issue 'possibly even

---

[67] *R (Countryside Alliance) v Attorney General* [2007] UKHL 52, [47]

[68] *R v Shayler* [2003] 1 AC 247, [25]; *Countryside Alliance* (n 67) [128], [157], [76].

[69] *Countryside Alliance* (n 67) [45].

[70] *R (Purdy) v DPP* [2009] UKHL 45, [58].

[71] *Huang* (n 39) [17]; Kavanagh (2014) 459.

[72] *In the Matter of an Application by Lorraine Gallagher for Judicial Review (Northern Ireland) v SSHD* [2019] UKSC 3, [60]; *SG v Secretary of State for Work and Pensions* (n 56) [155] *per* Lord Hughes; Legg (2012) 72.

[73] Legg (2012) 72.

[74] Sales (2009b) 179 ('Judges should not seek to hold the legislature to account by reference to standards and norms of legal practice'); Carolan (2016a) 216; Carolan (2017) 192; Sathanapally (2017) 63.

[75] Gardbaum (2020a); Kavanagh (2020); Hailbronner (2020); Dixon (2023) 271.

[76] *Shindler v UK* App No 19849/09, 7 May 2013, [117]; Kavanagh (2014) 475; Lazarus & Simonsen (2015) 401.

repeatedly' does not automatically mean that the statute is compatible with rights. It simply means that the legislative deliberation is 'taken into consideration by the court for the purpose of deciding whether a fair balance has been struck between competing interests'.[77]

In most of the UK cases concerning political process review, the courts have tended to draw 'positive inferences' from evidence of meaningful engagement with rights, rather than 'negative inferences' from an apparent lack of legislative focus on the rights issue.[78] Judicial respect for legislative debate has generally led to judicial restraint – not judicial intervention – on questions of rights. In fact, there is a 'conspicuous asymmetry'[79] between the 'positive inference' and 'negative inference' cases in UK human rights law. This may be partly due to the importance of parliamentary privilege in the UK constitutional order. But it may also be due to the notorious difficulty of drawing reliable inferences from parliamentary silence or legislative inaction.[80]

This was vividly illustrated by the ECtHR's decision in *Hirst*,[81] where the Strasbourg court famously criticised the UK Parliament for its apparent lack of engagement with prisoners' rights during the legislative process. However, this may have misrepresented the nature of the British parliamentary process, where issues commanding consensual agreement are rarely the subject of parliamentary debate.[82] This underscores the epistemic challenges judges face when evaluating the modes and mechanics of political deliberation in Parliament.[83] It also counsels judicial caution before offering unduly prescriptive or proscriptive comments on the requirements of parliamentary deliberation about rights.

The existence and extent of legislative engagement with rights during the political process plays three main roles in judicial reasoning about rights. First, it plays an *informative role* by providing

---

[77] *Shindler v UK* (n 76) [117].
[78] Kavanagh (2014) 456ff (proposing the distinction between 'positive inference' and 'negative inference' cases); see further Gerards (2017) 141ff; Arnardóttir (2017) 14; Brems (2017) 24.
[79] Kavanagh (2014) 465.
[80] On the danger of judges misunderstanding the significance of apparent legislative inaction, see Bailey (2020a); Bailey (2020b); Kavanagh (2005) 103–4; Howarth (2016).
[81] *Hirst v UK* [2006] 42 EHRR 41.
[82] *Chester v Justice Secretary* (n 55) [136] Lord Sumption; Kavanagh (2014) 476–7.
[83] Nussberger (2017) 169 (German judge of the ECtHR, 2011–19).

'evidentially valuable material'[84] concerning the 'rationale underlying the legislation'[85] and the degree of controversy surrounding it.[86] Second, it can play a *confirmatory role*, reassuring the court that the legislature has 'squarely confronted'[87] the rights issue involved and resolved it in a deliberate – and deliberative – manner. In this guise, judicial cognisance of legislative debate may lead the courts to 'tread carefully'[88] before interfering with a hard-won legislative settlement which reconciles finely-balanced competing interests.[89] However, if there is no evidence of meaningful parliamentary engagement with rights, then this can reassure the court that a judicial intervention will not run contrary to a considered decision of the democratic legislature or upset a hard-won political compromise.[90] Instead, it may be an example of a legislative 'blindspot'[91] or oversight, which the courts may be well placed to correct.

Finally, judicial respect for legislative deliberation on rights can function as a *signalling device*, where courts can incentivise increased parliamentary engagement with rights, acting as a 'catalyst for enhanced democratic deliberation'.[92] In this guise, judicial respect for legislative deliberation can have dynamic feedback effects which are not only 'democracy-enhancing'[93] but 'democracy-inducing'[94] as well.

4   Avoiding Pre-emption

When deciding whether to alter the legal status quo on assisted suicide in *Nicklinson*, the court was reluctant to interfere, because Parliament

---

[84] *Wilson v First County Trust* (n 46) [142].

[85] Ibid [63].

[86] Kavanagh (2014) 470.

[87] *R v Home Secretary, ex p Simms* [2000] 2 AC 115, 131.

[88] Radcliffe (1968) 216; Bingham (2000) 32; *Nicklinson* (n 1) [201].

[89] *C (A Minor) v DPP* [1996] AC 1, 28 *per* Lord Lowry; Walker (2014) 127; Herz (2009).

[90] Kavanagh (2014) 460–3 (describing these as 'negative inference cases').

[91] Dixon (2007) 391.

[92] Kavanagh (2014) 466, 472; Sales (2016a) 456–7; Spielmann (2014) 64; Spano (2018) 492; Lenaerts (2012) 16; Arnardóttir (2017) 15.

[93] Spano (2018).

[94] Gerards & Brems (2017) 5; Eskridge & Ferejohn (2009) 1292; Young (2012) chapter 6; Bar-Siman-Tov (2015); Rose-Ackerman, Egidy & Fowkes (2015) 29 (arguing that the South African Constitutional Court became a 'conscious promoter of participatory democracy' when engaging in 'political process review'); Young (2010) 420.

was 'actively considering the issue'[95] of assisted suicide at that very time. With an imminent parliamentary debate on the horizon, the court was concerned to give the legislature leeway to 'confirm, alter or develop its position'[96] unfettered by a judicial decision oriented towards the facts on one particular case.[97]

The fact that an issue is the subject of current or imminent legislative activity has long been viewed as a *constitutional cue* to the courts that they should tread carefully before precipitous judicial intervention.[98] As Lord Bingham observed extra-judicially:

> if Parliament is actually engaged in deciding what the rule should be in a
> given legal situation, the courts are generally wise to await the outcome of
> that deliberation rather than pre-empt the result by judicial decision.[99]

This chimes with a general practice in common law adjudication for courts to 'walk warily in fields where Parliament has regularly legislated'.[100] The concern to avoid political pre-emption lay at the heart of the *Bellinger* case,[101] where the court refused to interpret the Marriage Act compatibly with transgender rights, in part because the government had already committed to driving forward comprehensive legislative change on the issue. To change the law in response to the immediate case would have pre-empted the democratic process, potentially restricting the array of policy options open to the legislature concerning transgender rights.[102] Significantly, when the Gender Recognition Act 2004 was enacted, it went further than the requirements of the *Bellinger* case, expanding the recognition of transgender rights to those who had not undergone surgical intervention.[103] If the court had issued a

---

[95] *Nicklinson* (n 1), [116]; *In the Matter of an Application by the NIHRC for Judicial Review* [2018] UKSC 27, [116]–[117], *per* Lord Mance.

[96] *Nicklinson* (n 1), [190].

[97] Ibid [118], [190].

[98] Bingham (2000) 31.

[99] Ibid 31–2; Paterson (2013) 277; Sathanapally (2012) 6, 98; Mallory & Tyrrell (2021) 486–8.

[100] Bingham (2000) 32; *Elgizouli v SSHD* [2020] UKSC 10 [105], Lord Kerr; Hodge (2015) 480; Walker (2014) 130–1; Sales (2009a) 606.

[101] *Bellinger v Bellinger* [2003] 1 AC 467.

[102] Kavanagh (2009a) 137–42.

[103] For detailed analysis, see Sharpe (2007a); Sharpe (2007b); Sharpe (2009) (arguing that by removing the condition of surgical intervention for gender recognition, the Gender Recognition Act 2004 put the UK in 'the position of global leader in this area of law reform').

declaration of incompatibility in *Bellinger*, this may have obviated the need for legislative intervention, and possibly prevented the legislature from exploring the more innovative and expansive possibilities it included in the 2004 Act.

The concern to avoid pre-emption reveals a judicial awareness of the dangers of 'agency control' and 'policy distortion'[104] discussed in Chapter 6. This was clearly legible in the US Supreme Court's decision in *Washington v Glucksberg*,[105] which decided that a terminally ill patient did not have 'the right to die' under the US Constitution. In a famous *dictum* – cited with approval by the UK Supreme Court in *Nicklinson*[106] – Justice Rehnquist observed that 'there is currently an earnest and profound debate about the morality, legality, and practicality of assisted suicide' and 'our holding permits this debate to continue, as it should in a democratic society'.[107]

In the context of this highly charged and hotly contested issue of political morality, the US Supreme Court decided 'not to pre-empt, but instead to improve and catalyse democratic deliberation',[108] 'stay [ing] its hand to allow reasonable legislative consideration'[109] to occur. Here, we see a combination of responsive and catalytic review, where the courts are respectful and responsive to the relative institutional capacity and legitimacy of the democratic legislature, whilst simultaneously concerned to stimulate focused legislative deliberation on the issue.

The judicial decision about whether and how to intervene is a deeply context-sensitive and time-sensitive inquiry.[110] This is why many courts employ doctrines of 'ripeness' and 'mootness'[111] to prevent judges from 'entangling themselves in abstract disagreements . . . through premature adjudication'.[112] As American constitutional scholar, Richard Fallon, observed, judges would be

---

[104] Tushnet (1995); Willis (2018) 246.
[105] *Washington v Glucksberg* 521 US 702 (1997).
[106] *Nicklinson* (n 1) [155], [165], [175], [183], [190], [293].
[107] *Washington v Glucksberg* (n 105) 735, cited in *Nicklinson* (n 1) [190]; Katyal (1998) 1767–71.
[108] Sunstein (1996) 94; Coenen (2009) 2840; Dixon (2022).
[109] Sunstein (1996) 94.
[110] Raz (2001) 419.
[111] Ferejohn & Kramer (2002) 1011; Katyal (1998) 1776; Beatson (1998).
[112] *Abbott Labs v Gardner* (1967) 387 US 136, 148; Katyal (1998) 1776.

unfaithful to their roles if, trying to do too much too fast with inadequate resources, they prematurely spoke the truth as they personally saw it and crafted bad doctrine that frustrated reasoned debate and democratic experiment[113]

Indeed, US constitutional jurisprudence provides some cautionary tales about the perils of judges moving 'too far, too fast'[114] in sensitive and complex areas of social policy on which people disagree.

When considering the role of timing as a collaborative device, Rosalind Dixon and Samuel Issacharoff argue that 'judicial deferral'[115] of an issue until the time is right is often the most prudent way of engaging in effective rights-based review. Deferral does not preclude judicial intervention, but it counsels caution before intervening too quickly in matters of immense social, political, and moral controversy. It can also stimulate enhanced legislative focus, democratic deliberation and even participatory pedigree, thus demonstrating its potential to be not only democracy-respecting but democracy-enhancing too.[116] Dixon and Issacharoff's subtle analysis explores the myriad uses of 'democratically sensitive timing'[117] across diverse jurisdictions, emphasising the pragmatic benefits of incremental adjudication which tries not to go 'too far, too fast' with inadequate resources. In the collaborative constitutional understanding, incrementalism is not simply a matter of institutional prudence, or a self-serving strategy to maximise judicial effectiveness. It is also rooted in principled jurisdictional concerns about relative institutional competence and legitimacy which go the heart of a democratic constitutional order.

5   Court as Catalyst, Judge as Nudge

In the high-level theoretical debates about the legitimacy of rights-based review, judges are often portrayed as speaking in peremptory, proscriptive and prescriptive terms. Facing off in a battle for constitutional supremacy, courts are cast as constitutional combatants, 'disabling'[118] the legislature,

---

[113] Fallon (1997) 148.
[114] Ginsburg (1992) 1198; Mikva (1998) 1829; Bateup (2006) 1151.
[115] Dixon & Issacharoff (2016); see also Delaney (2016) 1–4, 7–15, 58–62.
[116] Dixon & Issacharoff (2016); Dinan (2001) 2 (showing that the 'judicial deferral' in *Washington v Glucksberg* (n 105) succeeded in stimulating enhanced legislative engagement with the issue of physician-assisted suicide across many US states).
[117] Dixon (2021) 298; Delaney (2016) 12–16, 58–62.
[118] Tushnet (2003a) 2786; Kavanagh (2015c) 1035.

dictating legal outcomes, and defying the democratic will on complex and controversial policies.

But once we situate rights adjudication in the landscape of what judges do when adjudicating under Bills of Rights, a less dictatorial and more collaborative dynamic comes to the fore. Instead of judges lording it over the democratic legislature in a dictatorial and defiant manner, this section presents the 'court as catalyst'[119] and the 'judge as nudge'.[120] Drawing on an array of judicial tools and techniques, I document a judicial practice of *alerting the legislature*; offering *soft suggestions*; making *judicial pleas* for legislative action; and issuing *warnings* and *threats* with a view to 'prompting'[121] or 'prodding'[122] the legislature to respect rights. What distinguishes these techniques of collaborative constitutionalism is that they are marked by persuasion rather than prescription, coaxing rather than coercion. In place of a hierarchical dynamic of 'command and control', we see a more heterarchical dynamic of comity, collaboration and mutual support.[123]

a   Alerts, Prods, and Pleas

Although the UK Supreme Court did not issue a declaration of incompatibility in *Nicklinson*, it nonetheless alerted the government and Parliament to the urgent need for legal change.[124] Judicial alerts of this kind are familiar to us from ordinary common law adjudication, where judges acknowledge that the law is 'ripe for change',[125] but accept that it is not for the courts to change it. In such situations, the courts may raise a warning flag to the legislature, calling on it to reform the law in a timely and comprehensive fashion.[126] In doing so, judges shine the light of publicity on the issue whilst signalling to

---

[119] Scott & Sturm (2007); Young (2012) 167–91; Roach (2021) 409; Cohn (2007) 105.

[120] Klein (2008); Landau (2014) 258; Davis & De Londras (2014b) 24.

[121] Lord Justice Gross (2016) 18 (observing that the courts can 'stimulate and frame debate and discussion ... and on occasion ... prompt and facilitate a legislative response'); Cohn (2007) 105; Murray (2013a) 52.

[122] Ely (1991) 878–9 (advocating the judicial use of 'Congress-prodding doctrines' in the US); Whittington (2005b) 1157–8.

[123] Judge (2015) 119; Popelier (2017) 80; Yap (2017) 36, 45.

[124] *Nicklinson* (n 1) [117]; Roach (2016a) 272.

[125] Dyson (2018) 50.

[126] See e.g. *Owens v Owens* [2018] UKSC 41 [45], *per* Lord Wilson; *In Re S (Minors) (Care Order: Implementation of Care Plan)* [2002] UKHL 10 [106] (finding no violation of Convention rights but highlighting 'the pressing need for the Government to attend to

other actors in the constitutional scheme that the issue requires urgent attention.[127]

In *Nicklinson*, all nine judges agreed that the judicial branch was not the ideal forum to change the law on assisted suicide.[128] Indeed, when a subsequent Assisted Dying Bill was debated in the House of Lords in 2021,[129] Lord Neuberger endorsed his judicial stance in *Nicklinson*, affirming that 'it was inappropriate, at least at that stage, for the courts to seek to force Parliament to change the law on assisted suicide'.[130] But that was undergirded by a firm belief that Parliament needed to step up to the plate. The judicial concern to avoid pre-emption and allow the legislature leeway to formulate the appropriate policy response, illustrates the dynamics of a constitutional partnership in progress. In that partnership, it is important that the right branch contributes to the right issue in the right way, at the right time.[131]

In the case-law on matters of life and death, the law reports are strewn with *judicial alerts* to the government and legislature about the urgent need for legislative reform using the institutional skills and competence which only the Executive and legislature possess. Indeed, they are also strewn with heartfelt and strongly worded *judicial pleas* imploring the legislature to reform the law in a comprehensive and democratically legitimate fashion.[132] In the earliest cases concerning those on indefinite life-support, the judges repeatedly emphasised that 'the whole matter cries out for exploration in depth by Parliament'.[133] However, as Lord

---

the serious practical and legal problems' surrounding children in care); Burnett (2018) 15.

[127] Kysar & Ewing (2011) 354, 367; Abrahamson & Hughes (1991) 1057; Murray (2013a) 66–7.

[128] *Nicklinson* (n 1) [113], Lord Neuberger.

[129] *Assisted Dying Bill 2021*, Private Members' Bill, introduced to the House of Lords on 26 May 2021, to 'create a legal framework to allow a terminally ill patient to end their life, provided they have the consent of two medical practitioners', and verified by the High Court. Three Private Members' Bills on Assisted Dying have been introduced to the House of Lords since the *Nicklinson* case, but none of them have been enacted.

[130] HL Deb 22 October 2021, vol 815 col 462 (Lord Neuberger); HL Deb 22 October 2021, vol 815 col 408 (Lord Mance).

[131] Draghici (2015) 295; Law (2009) 731–2; Landau (2014) 1534, 1560 (noting a potential 'fire alarm function' for courts); Abrahamson & Hughes (1991) 1058.

[132] Walker (2014) 134; Judge (2015) 115–17; Murray (2013a) 67; Duclos & Roach (1991) 24; Abrahamson & Hughes (1991) 1056–7.

[133] *Airedale NGHS Trust v Bland* [1993] AC 789, 890–1 *per* Lord Mustill; Walker (2014) 134.

Neuberger observed in *Nicklinson*, despite recurrent 'prods and pleas'[134] from the judiciary, 'Parliament has not sought to resolve these questions through statutes, but has been content to leave them to be worked out by the courts'.[135] Judicial alerts and heartfelt pleas sometimes fall on deaf legislative ears.

b   Judicial Advice and Soft Suggestions

When adjudicating whether legislation complies with rights, judges sometimes use *obiter dicta* to make 'soft suggestions'[136] or give 'constitutional hints'[137] about possible legislative changes which might comply with rights.[138] Thus, whilst the majority in *Nicklinson* refrained from changing the law on assisted suicide, many of the judges nonetheless gave hints, intimations, or suggestions about the kind of safeguarded procedure which could be employed to regulate assisted suicide, without risking undue pressure on the weak and vulnerable.

For Lord Neuberger, there was 'much to be said'[139] for having a High Court judge verify the informed intention of a person seeking help to commit suicide. Other judges intimated that 'if a proposal were put forward whereby applicants could be helped to kill themselves, without appreciably endangering the lives of the weak and vulnerable',[140] this might help to reassure the courts that a relaxation of the prohibition on assisted suicide might be justified in some circumstances.

The judicial intimations offered in *Nicklinson* varied in strength and specificity, ranging from obiter asides and 'provisional views'[141] through to Lord Wilson's detailed specification of eighteen criteria which might be relevant to a High Court judge assessing the veracity and commitment of a claimant's professed wish to die.[142] Whilst expressing some

---

[134] Kysar & Ewing (2011).
[135] *Nicklinson* (n 1) [98] *per* Lord Neuberger; Walker (2014) 134.
[136] Chandrachud (2014) 624; Chandrachud (2017) 69–75.
[137] Duclos & Roach (1991) 23ff.
[138] Katyal (1998); cf. Mikva (1998); Heise (2000).
[139] *Nicklinson* (n 1) [127].
[140] Ibid [85].
[141] Ibid [113].
[142] Ibid [205].

'hesitation'[143] about providing this list given the 'absence of submissions'[144] by Counsel on this issue, Lord Wilson defended his approach in explicitly collaborative terms, arguing that his list of factors could inform legislative debate and enable 'Parliament to appreciate the scrupulous nature of any factual inquiry which it might see fit to entrust to the judges'.[145] Drawing on his considerable expertise in the family courts, he shared his insight into analogous mechanisms designed to deal with similarly sensitive issues.[146]

What makes these judicial suggestions 'soft' is that they are legally non-binding. They are *dicta* not dictates, pointers not prescriptions. They *inform* the legislature about the legal problems at stake, but they do not *mandate* results.[147] Nonetheless, as pronouncements from the higher courts in the context of high-profile cases about rights, obiter intimations and 'soft suggestions' may become 'harder edged'.[148] Even though they do not carry coercive force, we should not overlook their significance as manifestations of 'judicial agency'.[149] This raises the question: are such hints a help or a hindrance in the collaborative constitutional enterprise? Do they encroach upon the legislative prerogative to determine the details of a chosen regulatory framework under circumstances of legislative complexity and controversy?

There is no formulaic answer to this question. The propriety of judicial advice and 'soft suggestions' depends on the strength and specificity of the *dicta* involved, the relationship between the branches of government, and the overall contextual matrix of the case. If courts have particular experience in a complex area of the law which is ripe for legislative change, then it may be valuable for judges to communicate their obiter views to the legislature about what legal changes may be desirable.[150]

---

[143] Ibid [205].
[144] Ibid [205].
[145] Ibid [205].
[146] Ibid [205].
[147] Bateup (2006) 1123ff.
[148] Leckey (2015) 109–15; Geiringer (2008) 563.
[149] Leckey (2015) 109, 121, 197.
[150] Rogers (2001) (describing the judicial provision of information as a 'signalling game of judicial–legislative interaction'); Murray (2013a) 66–7; see e.g. *R v K* [2001] UKHL 41 (where Lord Bingham warned that the *mens rea* requirement in sexual offences should be defined 'with extreme care and precision', noting that 'consideration will no doubt be given' to the relevant sections of the Law Commission's Draft Criminal Code on the issue [23]).

In this way, 'judicial intimations'[151] and 'constitutional hints'[152] can 'contribute to a constructive relationship between legislatures and courts',[153] where judges inform the political actors about what is legally required.[154] In turn, this information may clarify the outer limits of rights-based justification, whilst forestalling unnecessary future litigation on grounds of legal uncertainty.[155] Recalling the quality-control analogy discussed in chapter 7, if the courts spot some deficiencies in the law, it may be worthwhile to feed that information back to those on the factory floor – even offering some suggestions about what might fix the problem – so that the legislation can pass judicial muster next time around.[156]

In adjudication under the HRA, the courts have sometimes accompanied a declaration of incompatibility with 'soft suggestions'[157] about how the incompatibility might be resolved.[158] In the *Belmarsh Prison* case, for example, Lord Bingham suggested *obiter* that tagging or restricting communication might 'effectively inhibit terrorist activity',[159] thus obviating the need for indefinite detention. The government and Parliament duly took the hint, and devised a system of control orders where suspected terrorists were effectively placed under house arrest.[160] In the *Thompson* case,[161] where the court declared that inclusion on a Sex Offenders Register for life without any possibility of review violated offenders' due process rights, Lord Phillips suggested, *obiter*, that it would be 'open to the legislature to impose an appropriately high threshold for review',[162] which it duly did. In *Secretary of*

---

[151] Chandrachud (2014) 629.

[152] Duclos & Roach (1991) 37.

[153] Ibid 37.

[154] Ibid 37; Heise (2000) 105; Krotoszynski (1998) (on 'constitutional flares'); Yap (2017) 36ff.

[155] Duclos & Roach (1991) 24–5; Katyal (1998) 1714.

[156] Katyal (1998) 1718; Thomas (2015a) [43]; Thomas (2015b) [12]–[14]; Thomas (2017b) [27]ff (where the Lord Chief Justice of England and Wales outlined other channels of communication and information sharing between the courts and Parliament, such as judicial appearances before parliamentary committees).

[157] Chandrachud (2014) 628.

[158] *T* [2013] EWCA Civ 25, [75]; *R v Waya* [2012] UKSC 61 [4]; *Clift* [2006] UKHL 54 [69] *per* Lord Brown; *Thompson* [2010] UKSC 17 [57].

[159] *Belmarsh* [2004] UKHL 56 [35], *per* Lord Bingham.

[160] Crawford (2013) 68; Murray (2013a) 76–7; Nicol (2006) 735.

[161] *Thompson* (n 158).

[162] Ibid [57]; *R (Miranda) v Secretary of State for the Home Department* [2016] EWCA Civ 6, [110].

State v JJ[163] the House of Lords held (3:2) that a control order imposing an eighteen-hour curfew on a suspected terrorist was an unjustifiable deprivation of liberty under Article 5 ECHR. Whilst two of the
majority judges opined that it was 'inappropriate'[164] to make any
suggestions about what length of time might be held to comply with
Article 5, Lord Brown was concerned to ensure that the Government
should not be kept 'guessing as the precise point at which control
orders will be held vulnerable to article 5 challenges'.[165] He suggested
that sixteen hours should be regarded as an acceptable outer limit – a
suggestion which the Government duly implemented in subsequent
legislation.[166]

Thus, whilst *obiter* intimations have no obligatory legal force, they
may have significant political purchase in practice, especially in a
context where the government is actively seeking a policy solution to
forestall future legal challenge. This gives obiter dicta a potency in fact
which they do not possess in form. Therefore, the courts should be
mindful of their political consequences when offering them in their
legal judgments.

It seems legitimate that the government and legislature should know
where they stand on the requirements of rights, especially in circumstances where they are about to enact new legislation in response to a
recent judicial ruling.[167] However, the case of *JJ* reveals the risk that
judicial hints and soft suggestions may end up short-circuiting full
political deliberation about the scope of rights, thereby disincentivising
the political actors from engaging their own deliberative and fact-finding
skills about how to proceed.[168] Indeed, Lord Scott's obiter dictum in *JJ*
may have encouraged the Government to set a higher threshold for
detention than it might have otherwise adopted, safe in the knowledge
that the sixteen-hour threshold had received an explicit stamp of judicial

---

[163] *Secretary of State v JJ* [2007] UKHL 45; Kavanagh (2009b) 294–7.
[164] *Secretary of State v JJ* (n 163) [16] Lord Bingham; [63] Lady Hale; [84] Lord Carswell.
[165] *Secretary of State v JJ* (n 163) [105]; *Ahmed v HM Treasury* [2010] UKSC 2, [235] Lord
Mance; [143] Lord Phillips; Murray (2013a) 77.
[166] Murray (2013a) 77; Ewing & Tham (2008) 679, 688.
[167] HC Deb 23 January 2019, vol 653 col 157WH (Justin Tomlinson) (making the point in
parliamentary debate responding to the DoI in *Re McLaughlin, Re Judicial Review
(Northern Ireland)* [2018] UKSC 48, that a 'clear steer' from the courts 'equals a much
swifter response from us').
[168] Stark (2017a) 645; Ewing & Tham (2008) 684; Roach (2021) 186–7; King (2012) 284.

approval.[169] This alerts us to the fact that judicial suggestions may have 'negative dynamic effects'.[170] It also counsels judicial caution before sharing their suggestions about potentially rights-protective options, however soft they seem. Keeping the government guessing about the scope and limits of rights may have the salutary effect of keeping them on their constitutional toes.

The UK courts are generally circumspect before offering *obiter* judicial advice. In many cases, courts emphasise that it is not for them to 'prescribe the solution that should be adopted', recognising that it should be 'left to Parliament to decide what amendments to make'.[171] A judicial reluctance to make such suggestions was clearly legible in *Wright v Secretary of State for Health*,[172] which held that a provisional listing of care workers accused of gross misconduct as unsuitable to work with vulnerable adults, violated their right to a fair trial. Though the court declared that the provisional listing arrangement violated rights, Lady Hale refused to venture suggestions about how the legislation could be rendered Convention-compliant, observing that 'it is not for us to attempt to rewrite the legislation . . . it is right that the balance be struck in the first instance by the legislature'.[173] Aware that new legislation was being actively contemplated by the government and Parliament, she eschewed any commentary of what the new legislation should include.[174]

The *Wright* case exemplifies 'the virtue of judicial silence'[175] in situations where the legislature faces complex, polycentric issues. Indeed, Lady Hale justified her reticence on the grounds that the issue involved striking a delicate balance between competing values which the legislature was better placed to carry out.[176] Such a 'self-conscious attempt to avoid policy distortion and agenda control'[177] is often appropriate, unless there is a compelling need to do otherwise. It reflects a judicial

---

[169] For a critique of Lord Brown's dictum by the JCHR, see JCHR *Tenth Report* (2007–8); Ewing & Tham (2008) 691–2; Stark (2017a) 645.

[170] Landau (2014) 1544, 1547.

[171] *T* [2013] EWCA Civ 25, [75]; *Miranda* (n 162) [119].

[172] *R (Wright) v Secretary of State for Health* [2009] UKHL 3; King (2012) 185, 284.

[173] *Wright* (n 172) [39]; Lord Dyson (2018) 49.

[174] *Wright* (n 172) [39].

[175] King (2012) 283–5; Sathanapally (2012) 97; Sunstein (1996) 6–8 (noting some 'constructive uses' of judicial silence to 'improve and fortify democratic processes'); Katyal (1998) 1711; Heise (2000) 105.

[176] Chandrachud (2014) 629.

[177] King (2012) 285.

recognition of the limits of their institutional capacity to give advice on polycentric policy choices.[178]

In *Nicklinson*, the majority of judges were reticent about the potential compatibility of future legislative schemes with rights. Lord Neuberger described Lord Wilson's detailed guidance on a specific regulatory framework as 'somewhat premature',[179] emphasising that it was not 'possible or appropriate'[180] for the courts to identify in advance what might constitute a satisfactory legislative solution.[181]

Lord Wilson's detailed criteria raise the spectre of judicial 'agenda control'.[182] Though offered as helpful suggestions, not stringent stipulations, his judgment can nonetheless be read as a blueprint for statutory reform, with a built-in guarantee that such reform would pass muster in future litigation. Indeed, it could also be read as an effort to overcome legislative inertia by offering the government a ready-made, workable solution to the problem.[183] However well-meaning, Lord Wilson's 'constitutional road map'[184] runs the risk of undue democratic distortion.[185] Obiter intimations or soft suggestions intended to inform the legislative process are one thing, but detailed delineations of a proposed regulatory scheme are quite another. As Lord Neuberger emphasised 'it is for Parliament to decide how to respond to a declaration of incompatibility and in particular how to change the law'.[186]

c   Judicial Warnings

When adjudicating whether legislation complies with rights, we have seen that judges sometimes alert the legislature to problems in the law, calling on Parliament to step into the breach. But what if the legislature ignores these judicial alerts and pleas, because it is unable or unwilling to reform

---

[178] Mikva (1998) 1825.
[179] *Nicklinson* (n 1) [118].
[180] Ibid [118].
[181] Ibid [126].
[182] Tushnet (1995).
[183] *Nicklinson* (n 1), [314] *per* Baroness Hale (outlining 'four essential requirements' which the High Court could use to assess whether someone should be allowed help to end their lives).
[184] On the idea of judges providing 'constitutional road maps', see Luna (2000); Bateup (2006) 1124; Katyal (1998) 1718.
[185] Tsereteli (2017) 240ff (on the risks and benefits of judges 'issuing legislative guidance').
[186] *Nicklinson* (n 1) [126].

the law? One judicial solution is to combine the judicial alert with a 'judicial warning'[187] that if the legislature does not tackle the issue, the courts may have to remedy the problem themselves.[188] In one sense, a judicial warning can be viewed as a mode of valuable information-sharing in a collaborative enterprise, where the courts give the legislature a realistic reminder that legislative inaction will not make the problem go away. Here, we see judges alerting the legislature to a problem in the law, whilst 'prompting' and 'prodding'[189] it to do something about it.[190] By warning the legislature of the likelihood of future judicial intervention, the courts give their soft suggestions a harder edge.

On this view, judicial warnings and threats appear to be 'democracy reinforcing'.[191] By flagging the issue for political attention, the courts give the legislature an opportunity to take the lead in a fraught policy field, albeit with a stern warning that if the legislature fails to act, the courts may have to step into the breach.[192] This ensures that an initial stance of judicial reticence and restraint will nonetheless have some 'bite' or 'constructive force'[193] in prompting legislative action and possibly propelling legislative change.[194] At the very least, it puts the legislature on notice that the consequence of indefinite 'legislative foot-dragging'[195] will be judicial intervention.[196] Here, we see the *court as catalyst*, 'overcoming political inertia'[197] and 'prompting the legislature to revisit its commitment to the status quo'.[198] Rather than stopping the legislature from legislating as it wishes, the courts provide a 'stimulus for law reform',[199] inviting the legislature to take the lead on changing the law. In this rendering, judicial warnings may be

---

[187] Katyal (1998) 1721.
[188] Krotoszynski (1998) 7 (describing such warnings as 'constitutional flares').
[189] Kysar & Ewing (2011) (on judicial 'prods and pleas').
[190] Katyal (1998) 1717; Davis & de Londras (2014b) 24.
[191] Katyal (1998) 1760.
[192] Ibid 1763.
[193] Ibid 1721; Yap (2017) 30.
[194] Ginsburg (2010) 6; Leckey (2015) 159.
[195] *Washington v Glucksberg* 521 US 702 (1997), 2293 (Souter J); discussed in Katyal (1998) 1768–72; Fallon (1997) 137–9, 144–9; Spitzer & Omara (2021) 48, 82.
[196] Katyal (1998) 1763.
[197] Markovits (2005) 1933; Kysar & Ewing (2011) 355; Yap (2017) 30.
[198] Leckey (2015) 149; Scott & Sturm (2007); Young (2010) 385, 409, 412–13; Spitzer & Omara (2021).
[199] Jaffe (1969) 84; Sales (2018b) 233.

presented as not only 'democracy-respecting' but 'democracy-indu-cing' as well.[200]

Of course, we can also imagine a less laudatory narrative. Instead of illustrating a constitutional partnership in progress, we could view judicial warnings as a determined effort to hold the legislature to ransom, threatening it to legislate compatibly with rights 'or else'. On this more sinister and combative reading, judicial warnings are more like a push than a nudge, with the courts wielding the Sword of Damocles over the legislature's head, forcing it to address an issue it would rather avoid.

In my view, this combative reading overstates the degree of power judges wield over democratically elected actors. There is no denying that judicial warnings and threats of future litigation are designed to focus the legislative mind, lending some urgency to calls for legislative reform in a particular field. However, judicial warnings of this kind are typically issued in cases where judges *refrain* from declaring a legislative provision to be incompatible with rights, precisely out of recognition that the elected branches of government are the most competent and legitimate branches to remedy the problem.

In *Nicklinson,* the judicial warning about a possible future declaration of incompatibility was the culmination of a long line of cases where judges had repeatedly implored the legislature to confront the issues arising at the end of life.[201] *Judicial pleas* for legislative intervention were typically accompanied by a frank acknowledgment that

> the formulation of the necessary broad social and moral policy [in such a delicate and acutely controversial field] is an enterprise which the courts have neither the means nor ... the right to perform. This can only be achieved by the democratic process through the medium of Parliament.[202]

Far from rushing in to seize the last word on the issue, judges repeatedly begged the legislature to step in. Therefore, if *Nicklinson* is viewed as a judicial 'nudge combined with a threat', then we must put that threat in perspective, aware that it was issued in a case where the courts gave the legislature ample opportunity to grasp the nettle on this thorny issue.

---

[200] Eskridge & Ferejohn (2009) 1292.
[201] *Nicklinson* (n 1) [98]; Perreira (2015) 372.
[202] *Airedale NHS Trust v Bland* [1993] AC 789, 890 *per* Lord Mustill.

Moreover, the judicial warnings in *Nicklinson* were issued with varying degrees of firmness, ranging from tentative and polite intimations that a future declaration was 'certainly conceivable'[203] or that it was 'a real prospect',[204] through to Lord Wilson's stern warning that 'were Parliament for whatever reason, to fail satisfactorily to address the issue of whether to amend the [law]', a future claim had 'a real prospect of . . . success'.[205]

For Lord Neuberger, the judicial refusal to issue a declaration of incompatibility in *Nicklinson* manifested an appropriate degree of judicial reticence and restraint. As he observed, 'there are times when an indication, rather than firm words are more appropriate and can reasonably be expected to carry more credibility'.[206] In other words, sometimes a nudge is better than a push.[207] Even as the courts send a strong signal to the legislature that the law is in urgent need of reform, it takes effect within an inter-institutional dynamic of mutual respect and restraint.

6   Stepping in Where Parliament Fears to Tread

On matters of life and death, judges have regularly pleaded with Parliament to tackle the complex issues surrounding assisted suicide and the 'right to die', but legislation is not forthcoming. Whilst a number of Private Members' Bills on assisted suicide have been put to Parliament in recent years, they have all failed to garner sufficient support to be passed into law.[208] The result is a continuation of the legal status quo, effectively channelling decisions about life and death towards the courts. The preservation of the status quo may be a result of a considered legislative decision to maintain the ban on assisted suicide in light of all the competing moral, ethical, and political considerations involved.[209] As the Court of Appeal observed in *Nicklinson*,

---

[203] *Nicklinson* (n 1) [190].

[204] Ibid [118].

[205] Ibid [203].

[206] Ibid [117].

[207] On judicial nudges and pushes, see Kavanagh (2015d) 1052; Sachs (2014).

[208] The array of Bills on this topic is documented in *Nicklinson* (n 1) [231].

[209] On the Select Committee Reports on assisted dying, see *Nicklinson* (n 1) [54], [178], [183], [221]; Finnis (2015) 4.

Parliament fully understood what a blanket ban meant and why they were imposing it. They have on numerous occasions considered specific proposals for change but have so far chosen not to accede to them.[210]

On this view, the decriminalisation of assisted suicide is not an issue where Parliament 'fears to tread', and more a matter of Parliament concluding, after serious deliberation, that the status quo is the best available option.

But the decision not to legislate on this issue may also be an example of what Rosalind Dixon has described as legislative 'blind spots' and 'burdens of inertia',[211] where the legislature is inhibited from tackling an issue either because it fails to appreciate the plight of the individuals effected or because of political dynamics which prevent such morally controversial issues rising up the legislative agenda.[212]

A former Supreme Court judge suggested extra-judicially that Parliament had not legislated on assisted suicide because the issue was deemed to be 'too difficult, too controversial, too disruptive of the legislative programme [and] too likely to lose votes rather than to win them'.[213] Other judges have also suggested that legislatures sometimes 'out-source political questions that are too hot to handle to the Judiciary',[214] citing assisted suicide as a case in point.[215] Whatever the case may be, the fact remains that harrowing cases on matters of life and death continue to come before the courts, despite the fact that judges acknowledge the limits of judicial capacity to deal with them. If judicial pleas to the legislature fall on deaf ears, then there is a risk that matters of life and death will become caught in an impasse between 'judges who can't and legislators who won't'.[216]

So how should the courts deal with this predicament? Under the collaborative constitution, the ideal is that each branch of government does the job to which it is best suited, whilst respecting and supporting the other branches in carrying out their respective roles. But what happens when one branch is unable or unwilling to play its part in the collaborative scheme? Should the others simply stand by and say 'We are

---

[210] R (Nicklinson) v Ministry of Justice [2013] EWCA Civ 961, [66] Nicklinson (n 1) (SC) [153], [156].
[211] Dixon (2007) 391.
[212] Walker (2014) 132; Cossman (2019).
[213] Walker (2014) 132; Judge (2015) 113; Paterson (2013) 279.
[214] Lord Justice Gross (2018) 2.
[215] Ibid 2; Shetreet & Turenne (2013) 40; Mance (2018) 116; Sedley (2015) 182–3.
[216] Friendly (1963) 787; Abrahamson & Hughes (1991) 1048.

not institutionally best-placed to make this decision', thus allowing a decisional vacuum to open up? Clearly, political deadlock or legislative inertia does not justify judicial intervention in every case.[217] Judges cannot fill every gap in the legislative law-making process; nor do they have the legitimacy to do so.[218]

However, once the jurisdiction of the court is invoked by a litigant with a justiciable claim, judges have no choice but to adjudicate the issue one way or the other, even in cases which stretch their institutional capacity.[219] As Lord Browne-Wilkinson observed in a case concerning a patient on indefinite life-support, 'If Parliament fails to act, then judge-made law will of necessity, through a gradual and uncertain process, provide a legal answer to each new question as it arises. But in my judgment, that is not the best way to proceed'.[220]

This predicament has been aptly described by Lord Sales as 'the absent legislator problem':[221]

> In practical terms, when the legislator is absent, the courts see problems and know that they will not be addressed or resolved through legislative action any time soon; so the moral pressure on the courts to find a fair and workable solution themselves is increased. In legitimacy terms, the courts know that public respect for the law depends in the long term to a considerable degree on the fairness and defensibility of outcomes which the law produces. If the legislator is absent, a court will tend to feel that it is (more) legitimate for it to act to develop or apply the law in an imaginative way.[222]

The more the legislature is withdrawn or absent from the collaborative law-making enterprise, 'the greater the role the courts tend to feel they

---

[217] Landau (2014) 1535 ('Institutional failure creates a vacuum, but not necessarily one that courts can legitimately fill').

[218] Though cf. *Seales v AG* [2015] NZHC 1239, [211] *per* Collins J (arguing that the fact that Parliament 'has not been willing to address the issues ... does not provide me with a licence to depart from the constitutional role of judges in New Zealand'; Ip (2020); Geiringer (2017b).

[219] *Re Z (a minor)* [1997] Fam 1; Lord Walker (2014) 135; Lord Neuberger (2015) [46]; Lord Etherton (2010) 738; Lord Hope (2009) 762.

[220] *Airedale NGHS Trust v. Bland* [1993] AC 789. For commentary on the potential correlations between judicial intervention and parliamentary activity/inactivity, see Paterson (2013) 276–82.

[221] Lord Sales (2020) 194 (Justice of the UKSC).

[222] Lord Sales (2020) 194; *Nicklinson* (n 1) [230]–[234], Lord Sumption (suggesting that he might have considered intervening on the issue of assisted suicide if 'Parliament had abdicated the task of addressing the question').

should assume'[223] – all the more so in a context where failure to act would allow a serious injustice to stand.[224] A judicial willingness to fill a legislative lacuna bespeaks a commitment to the idea of 'judge as partner', where judges accept that there is a difficult problem which some branch of government must sort out, even if they are not the ideal candidate for the job. In such a context, 'parliamentary inactivity may sometimes be a spur to judicial activity'.[225]

Judicial decisions about whether to step in where the legislature is unwilling or unable to do so is contextually, temporally and institutionally contingent, depending on the array of calibrating factors outlined in Chapter 9. Such factors include e.g. the urgency of resolving the particular dispute before them, the severity of the alleged interference with rights, and concerns about the appropriate division of labour in the constitutional scheme. Timing is also important. If the legislature is best-placed to tackle a particular issue, then it should be given time and opportunity to do so. As Lord Reid observed, 'Where Parliament fears to tread it is not the courts to *rush in*'.[226]

In my view, the Supreme Court in *Nicklinson* was right to refrain from issuing a declaration of incompatibility in that case, especially given the limited evidence before the court and the fact that Parliament was about to deliberate on the broader issues. Whilst signalling a principled willingness to intervene in a future case, the court did not *rush in* where legislatures fear to tread. Instead, it held back, at least for the time being, giving the legislature leeway to consider the issue first. If that warning falls on deaf ears, then this may give the courts some enhanced legitimacy to tackle the issue themselves, should an appropriate future case arise.[227]

---

[223] Lord Sales (2020) 198; Lord Hope (2009) 760; Lord Bingham (2011) 169 ('the courts tend to be most assertive, active, and creative when the political organs of the state ... are for whatever reason showing themselves to be least effective').

[224] Lord Justice Gross (2016) 15 (observing that judges may be inclined to take a 'bold step' in changing the law if there is 'no prospect that Parliament would intervene ... [especially if] absent judicial development, the injustice would remain'); Abrahamson & Hughes (1991) 1056; Roach (2021) 8.

[225] Lord Thomas (2017b) 26; Lord Walker (2014) 131; Lord Bingham (2011) 169; Lord Dyson (2018) 135; Lord Sales (2020) 194, 196, 198; Cardozo (1921) 28, 60; Jaffe (1969) 69; Paterson (2013) 278 (quoting Lord Mance).

[226] *Shaw v DPP* [1962] AC 220, 275; Paterson (2013) 307; Lord Sales (2018b) 706 ('Courts should not rush in to fill the void opening up at the heart of politics').

[227] Krotoszynski (1998) 58.

When considering the circumstances in which judges should step into a fraught policy field, we should not make the mistake of assuming that judicial interventions are invariably viewed by the government or legislature an illegitimate judicial power-grab. On the contrary, there are many instances where political actors actively encourage the courts to contribute creatively to the collaborative law-making process.[228]

When reflecting on his role as a Government Minister, Jack Straw MP observed that 'sometimes the political class is willing, praying, that the courts will act where they fear to tread'.[229] He instanced the law of privacy, where Parliament effectively 'passed the parcel to the courts' and was 'only too relieved that [the courts] created an extensive body of law, and procedure, from the skeletons of Article 8 of the Convention'.[230]

He also cited the example of *R v Davis*[231] concerning whether to allow anonymous witnesses to give evidence at a criminal trial in order to counteract the problem of witness intimidation. When the Court of Appeal decided that the judges would develop the common law to allow such a practice, 'there were sighs of relief all round Whitehall'.[232] However, when the House of Lords (now Supreme Court) subsequently overturned this decision in order to prevent a 'creeping emasculation of the common law principle'[233] that defendants in a criminal trial should be confronted by their accusers, there were 'groans in Whitehall, not least from me, since the decision meant that I had to introduce emergency legislation to fill the hole'.[234]

Of course, a crowded legislative timetable and the burden of extra work are not the only reasons why governments may want the courts to tackle difficult legal problems. They may also wish to avoid unwelcome political or electoral costs. 'Passing the parcel' to the courts may,

---

[228] Katzmann (1988); Graber (1993).

[229] Straw (2013) 39; Leckey (2015) 88.

[230] Straw (2013) 39.

[231] *R v Davis* [2008] UKHL 36.

[232] Straw (2013) 39 (Whitehall is the area of London where government buildings are located, including No. 10 Downing Street).

[233] *R v Davis* (n 231).

[234] Straw (2013) 39.

therefore, be a convenient form of political buck-passing and blame avoidance in 'the politics of partnership'.[235]

In *Davis*, the court managed to resist the Government's legal argument that the courts should fill the hole by creative interpretive means, concluding that developing a suitable scheme of witness protection was 'one for Parliament to endorse and delimit and not for the courts to create'.[236] Yet, in doing so, the court combined a stance of judicial restraint with a firm plea to the legislature to give the matter some 'urgent attention'.[237] As the court explained, piecemeal judicial change would 'only be second best ... Parliament is the proper body both to decide whether such a change is now required, and, if so, to devise an appropriate system which still ensures a fair trial'.[238] As Jack Straw MP subsequently observed, the government could hardly criticise the judiciary following the decision, given that the judges had refused to 'stretch the common law as we (the executive) had wanted' on the basis that 'change had to be a matter for Parliament'.[239]

7 From Passive Virtues to Collaborative Devices

The tools and techniques surveyed in this chapter call to mind Alexander Bickel's discussion of the 'passive virtues'.[240] In a canonical analysis, Bickel famously argued that US Supreme Court should use an array of doctrinal tools to 'stay its hand'[241] and 'withhold constitutional judgment'.[242] Such tools included the doctrines of standing, mootness, vagueness, ripeness, clear statement rules, interpretive presumptions, deference, the 'political questions doctrine', and many more. Describing these doctrines as 'passive virtues'[243] or 'devices of not doing',[244] Bickel argued that the shrewd employment of these judicial techniques could

---

[235] Melnick (1985); Graber (1993). On the phenomenon of political buck-passing on rights in the UK context, see Kavanagh (2015c) 1027; Van Zyl Smit (2011); Davis (2010) 92–3; Murray (2013a) 76.
[236] *R v Davis* (n 231) [98].
[237] Ibid.
[238] Ibid.
[239] Straw (2013) 39.
[240] Bickel (1986) 70; Bickel (1961).
[241] Bickel (1986) 70; Bickel (1961).
[242] Bickel (1986) 70; Bickel (1961).
[243] Bickel (1986) 70; Bickel (1961).
[244] Bickel (1986) 71, 125, 169, 188, 201, 206.

enable the courts to achieve 'wide-ranging and effective rule of principle, whilst at the same time eschewing full dominion'.[245]

There is no doubt that the arguments advanced in this chapter chime with some of Bickel's claims. In his attentiveness to doctrinal detail, as well as his concern to articulate a subsidiary and legitimate role for courts in adjudicating rights, there is much commonality of approach. However, I depart from Bickel's characterisation of the various jurisdictional devices he enumerates as *'passive* virtues' or 'techniques of *avoidance'.*[246] When courts calibrate the intensity of their review – or decide that they should give a degree of weight or leeway to the democratic legislature – they are not 'withholding'[247] judgment or 'avoiding adjudication'.[248] Instead, they are deliberately determining the scope and limits of the judicial role vis-à-vis the legislature, and actively dividing the constitutional labour between them.

In order to adjudicate whether legislation complies with rights, the courts must evaluate the competing legal, constitutional and institutional considerations which bear on the individual case. At times, this will result in a judicial decision to change the law in order to remedy a rights violation. At others, it will warrant a degree of judicial caution and restraint, where judges will give the legislature leeway to devise policy solutions to balance the competing considerations in a politically stable and democratically legitimate fashion. But regardless of which option the courts choose, it will be the product of an active deliberation and positive decision about what responsible adjudication requires in a collaborative scheme. Courts must strive to do their best for rights whilst simultaneously respecting their partners in authority.[249]

On my analysis, the doctrines and devices which Bickel and I discuss are better described as *collaborative devices* than passive virtues. Viewed in the context of the collaborative scheme, judges must balance substantive and institutional reasons in order to work out what they should do in the context of an individual case. As argued in Chapter 7, the idea of 'judge as partner' goes beyond a passive, receptive or acquiescent role. On any reckoning, there is plenty of 'doing' going on when courts

---

[245] Ibid 200.

[246] Bickel (1961) 77; see also Mann (2018) 36; Delaney (2016).

[247] Bickel (1986) 70, 127, 183.

[248] Bickel (1986) 128, 169, 206; Delaney (2016) 1.

[249] Kysar & Ewing (2011) 357–8, 409ff (describing these adjudicatory techniques as 'active virtues'); Katyal (1998) 1711–12.

interpret legislation compatibly with rights using the 'principle of legality',[250] or when they cleverly combine the virtues of responsive and catalytic review in order to prompt, prod and catalyse legislative engagement with rights. Indeed, even the subtle devices of obiter intimations and 'soft suggestions' can be presented as manifestations of judicial agency.

In short, the doctrines and devices courts use to give shape to their relationship with the other branches must be located within an active and creative role-conception where courts 'complement and ultimately collaborate with other institutions, even if that involves prodding those institutions into action'.[251]

8   Conclusion

This chapter has documented the devices courts use to determine the scope and limits of their reviewing role whilst giving shape to their constitutional relationship with the democratically elected branches of government. Faced with issues that strain their institutional capacity and legitimacy, courts may decline to remedy the problem using their necessarily piecemeal law-making tools. Instead, they may reach out to their partners in the collaborative scheme, imploring them to remedy the problem comprehensively and democratically, as only the government and legislature can.

Even when judges hand over the remedial reins to Parliament, they are not consigned to an entirely passive role. On the contrary, they may actively call on the legislature to remedy the problem using judicial alerts, warnings, prods, and pleas. In doing so, judges place an issue on the legislative agenda, thereby raising political consciousness about the urgency and seriousness of the problem. If judicial pleas fall on deaf ears, the courts may have no other option but to step into the breach in order to avert injustice.

The judicial devices surveyed in this chapter complicate the theoretical claim that we should view judges as dictators and disablers of democracy, determined to seize the last word on rights. Rather than speaking in peremptory, prescriptive or proscriptive tones, this chapter uncovered a more complex collaborative dynamic, where judges combine responsive and catalytic review, avoiding pre-emption of democratic decisions whilst

---

[250] Chapter 7, this vol.
[251] King (2012) 325; Lazarus & Simonsen (2015) 389.

prompting and occasionally pleading with the political actors to discharge their own responsibility to protect and promote rights. If no help is immediately forthcoming, the courts have some subtle ways of signalling to their constitutional partners that there is a job of work to do, accompanied by incentivising reminders to catalyse activity elsewhere in the constitutional system.

But once we are in the realm of soft suggestions, subtle signals, helpful hints, and even heartfelt pleas, we have left the dictatorial domain of 'judicial supremacy' and entered a more variegated constitutional landscape, where judges contribute constructively and creatively to the broader collaborative enterprise. In this collaborative endeavour, we see courts highlighting problems which need to be solved and calling on those best placed to fix them to pull their weight in the collaborative endeavour.[252] Judicial alerts, suggestions, warnings, prods, and pleas do not mandate outcomes. Instead, they invite contributions and spur political action as part of a shared responsibility to protect and promote rights in a democracy.[253]

---

[252] Duclos & Roach (1991) 24, 37; Roach (2016a) 299.
[253] Katyal (1998) 1710; Eskridge & Frickey (1994) 40.

PART IV

RESPONSIVE LEGISLATURES

11

Underuse of the Override

1   Great Expectations

In previous chapters, I have explored the role of the Executive, legislature and courts in the collaborative enterprise of protecting and promoting rights. In this part of the book, I turn to the role of governments and legislatures when responding to court rulings on rights. This responsive role is important in any system, but it is particularly important in systems of so-called 'weak-form review' where legislatures are explicitly empowered to adjust, amend and override court rulings on rights. This aim of this chapter is to enhance our understanding of these override mechanisms, by placing them in collaborative context. The task of the next chapter is to examine whether there is a constitutional convention in favour of compliance with declarations of incompatibility under the HRA.

But let us start by looking at the most striking and innovative feature of the so-called Commonwealth model of constitutionalism,[1] namely, the power of the legislature to override court rulings on rights. The most famous override mechanism is section 33 of the Canadian Charter of Rights and Freedoms 1982 which empowers the Parliament of Canada and the provincial legislatures to legislate 'notwithstanding' some of the rights guaranteed in the Charter. The UK HRA also included some institutional innovations designed to give the legislature 'the last word'. Section 19 HRA 1998 allows Parliament to enact legislation notwithstanding its apparent incompatibility with rights.[2] And as we saw in chapter 8, judicial declarations of incompatibility are not legally binding on Parliament and have no direct legal impact on the validity or effect of the legislation.[3]

---

[1] Gardbaum (2013b).
[2] Section 19 HRA.
[3] Section 4 HRA 1998.

The idea of giving courts the power to review the consistency of legislation with protected rights 'while preserving the authority of legislatures to have the last word'[4] generated great expectations amongst comparative constitutional lawyers. For one thing, it seemed to provide a beguilingly simple solution to the perennial counter-majoritarian difficulty.[5] Instead of giving judges a veto over democratic politics, the courts could act as a checking-point in the system, performing 'an interpretative, alerting and informative function.'[6,7] Given the non-finality of judicial decisions – and the possibility of legislatures disagreeing with court rulings on rights – the legislative override was presented as a key feature of 'dialogic constitutionalism,'[8] and the distinctive lynchpin of the New Commonwealth model of constitutionalism.[9] By combining judicial oversight with legislative override, we could protect rights whilst preserving democracy.[10] We could have our constitutional cake and eat it too.

But despite great expectations of a new constitutional dawn, the best-known fact about these override mechanisms is that they are hardly ever used.[11] The Canadian notwithstanding clause has never been used by the Federal Parliament of Canada, and it has only been used occasionally by the provincial legislatures, most prominently and frequently by Quebec.[12] The invocation of the Canadian override was so rare for over three decades that it was widely assumed to have fallen into desuetude.[13] True, there has been a spate of provincial threats to use the notwithstanding clause in recent years, thus putting the override back onto the political agenda as a live issue.[14] Yet very few of these proposed uses have actually materialised, either because the override became unnecessary or

---

[4] Tushnet (2008b) ix; Goldsworthy (2010) 63; Gardbaum (2013b) 61; Tushnet (2003c) 831.
[5] Gardbaum (2001) 748; Tushnet (2008b) 62, 52.
[6] Gardbaum (2013b) 64, 68, 86.
[7] Gardbaum (2013b); Waldron (2006) 1354–5.
[8] Roach (2004) 63; Yap (2012) 534; Kyritsis (2017) 104.
[9] Gardbaum (2013b); Kyritsis (2017) 110–14.
[10] Goldsworthy (2010) 63; Gardbaum (2013b) 61; Tushnet (2003c) 831.
[11] Kavanagh (2015a) 825, 833; Bateup (2009) 549; Stephenson (2016) 2.
[12] Kahana (2002) 221; Kahana (2001) 255.
[13] Huscroft (2007) 96; Vermeule (2012) 425; Yap (2015) 28–9; Stephenson (2013) 880, 897; Roach (2016b) 297–8; Geiringer (2019) 568.
[14] Lake (2022); Smith (2019); Albert (2018) 152–3. Provincial Premiers in Saskatchewan, Ontario, New Brunswick, and Quebec have threatened to invoke the override in recent years, but only four such overrides have survived, two in Quebec and one each in Saskatchewan and Ontario, see further Lake (2022); Nicolaides & Snow (2021) 60 (documenting the media coverage of the override in Saskatchewan and Ontario).

because of widespread public outcry and strident political pushback.[15] There have only been twenty-two successful uses of the override by the provinces in almost four decades, with Quebec accounting for seventeen of those uses.[16] Thus, notwithstanding the increased salience of the override in recent times, there is still a marked reluctance to use it in Canada. Even factoring in the recent resurgence at the provincial level, the overall picture is one of relatively rare use.[17]

In the UK, a similar pattern of non-use or underuse has emerged. In the two decades since the HRA was enacted, the UK government has only made a negative statement of *in*compatibility under section 19(b) HRA on four occasions, only two of which were of major significance.[18] As regards declarations of incompatibility, there has been a near-perfect rate of compliance with declarations of incompatibility since the HRA was enacted.[19] This is all the more remarkable when we consider that Parliament benefits from the burden of inertia following a declaration. By simply doing nothing and ignoring the declaration, Parliament can maintain the *status quo ante*.[20] Nonetheless, in almost every case in which a declaration of incompatibility has been issued, the UK government and Parliament have eventually introduced remedial measures to comply with the judicial declarations. Despite great expectations of a new constitutional dawn, there has been a curious and conspicuous underuse of the override.

This presents something of a puzzle for constitutional theorists and comparative law scholars alike. If the perennial problem of US-style constitutional review is that the legislature is unjustifiably thwarted by the courts, surely we would expect legislators to use an override if given the opportunity to do so. If the purpose of the override was to promote dialogue and disagreement between courts and legislatures, then why have Canadian and UK legislatures adopted a consistently compliant rather than conversational stance towards judicial

---

[15] Albert (2018) 152–3; Valiante (2019); Rizza (2018).

[16] Rousseau & Côté (2017).

[17] Hiebert (2017) 695.

[18] *R (Animal Defenders International) v Culture Secretary* [2008] UKHL 15 [53] (concerning the Communications Bill 2002–3, HC Bill); see further Chapter 6.7. At the time of writing, the Illegal Migration Bill 2023 is going through Parliament, without a positive Statement of Compatibility.

[19] Kavanagh (2015c) 1023–8; King (2015a).

[20] Bateup (2009) 569–70; Vermeule (2012) 442; Sathanapally (2012) 24; Kahana (2002) 250–1.

rulings?[21] Regardless of whether one's constitutional vision of court–legislature relations rests on *confrontation* (where the branches battle for supremacy to get the 'the last word' on rights) or *conversation* (where the branches engage in an ongoing dialogue about the meaning of rights), the underuse of the override remains a mystery. So how do we solve it?

The dominant narrative in both countries is that legislatures wanted to use the override more frequently, but were prevented from doing so due to the exorbitant political costs of being branded as a 'human rights contravener'.[22] Since overriding rights and defying courts is both bad press and bad politics, the override was discredited and delegitimised, thus putting it off-limits as an effective mode of legislative dialogue and disagreement with courts.

The aim of this chapter is to provide an alternative explanation for the underuse of the override. Whilst accepting that the political costs are part of the story, I argue that they are not the whole story, and not the most important part at that. Drawing on a deeper constitutional narrative about the need for the branches of government to forge constructive working relationships between them, I argue that the underuse of the override is an epiphenomenal expression of a set of unwritten but deeply rooted constitutional norms requiring the branches of government to treat each other with comity and mutual respect. I argue further that these norms preclude the legislature from regularly or lightly overriding court decisions merely because they disagree with them. Foregrounding the norms of comity, collaboration and conflict-avoidance, I conclude that legislatures *should* apply – and in Canada and the UK *do* apply – a general presumption in favour of compliance with judicial decisions, unless that presumption is rebutted by exceptional or egregious circumstances.

This chapter proceeds in the following way. Parts 2 and 3 put the Canadian and UK constitutional schemes in context, exploring the common narratives about the underuse of the override in their respective constitutional habitats. Far from undermining the override, Part 4 shows how the political costs of using it were hardwired into the design of the Canadian Charter and the UK HRA from the outset, in order to ensure that the overrides would only be rarely used. Part 5 provides a normative defence of the rare use of the override, grounded

---

[21] MacFarlane (2013) 51; Leckey (2015) 158–9.
[22] Duxbury (2017) 651.

in the principles of collaborative constitutionalism. Finally, Part 6 reflects on the consequences of understanding the override in collaborative terms. On a collaborative understanding, the root cause of the 'underuse of the override' is that it is an epiphenomenal expression of some unwritten constitutional norms requiring the branches of government to treat each other with comity and respect. Even though Canadian and UK political actors were given the *power* to override court rulings, they generally accepted a *responsibility* to respect the decisions of a coordinate branch.

Two terminological clarifications before I begin. First, I will use the word 'override' to refer to the power of the Canadian and UK Parliaments to legislate notwithstanding rights, and the power of the UK Parliament to override or ignore a declaration of incompatibility. Second, by using the phrase 'underuse of the override', I am not suggesting that these powers have been used less than they should or that there is any culpable underuse at play. In fact, my argument is that it is normatively desirable for the override to be used rarely, reserved for suitably exceptional circumstances. Thus, although many scholars lament 'the underuse of the override', I am simply using this phrase in a neutral way to capture the fact that these override powers are rarely used.

2 Canada in Context

Section 33 of the Canadian Charter of Rights and Freedoms provides that the Parliament of Canada or a provincial legislature '*may expressly declare* in an Act of Parliament or of the legislature ... that the Act or a provision thereof *shall operate notwithstanding* [certain specified Charter rights]';[23] and that a legislative provision or statute subject to such a declaration 'shall have such operation as it would have *but for* the provision of this Charter referred to in the declaration'.[24] Section 33 does not refer to judicial decisions. Therefore, the wording seems to permit legislatures to derogate from the specified Charter rights *pre-emptively* (i.e. regardless of whether there has been a judicial decision on the

---

[23] Section 33(1) (emphasis added). Section 33 cannot be invoked in relation to 'democratic rights' under section 2 of the Charter (e.g. freedom of conscience, freedom of expression, freedom of association, freedom of assembly), or against sections 7–15, which protect the right to life, liberty and security of the person, freedom from unreasonable search and seizure, freedom from arbitrary arrest and detention, and the right to equality).

[24] Section 33(2) (emphasis added).

matter, thereby immunising legislation from future judicial challenges);[25] or *reactively* (in order to avoid or overcome the effects of a judicial decision).[26]

Although the power to legislate notwithstanding rights is set out in fairly broad terms, section 33 nonetheless places significant limits on its exercise. First, there must an *express declaration* to override a particular Charter right. Rights cannot be overridden covertly, implicitly or obliquely.[27] Second, the declaration must be contained within *an Act of Parliament* or the legislature. Therefore, any proposed override must run the strenuous gauntlet of the full legislative process and ultimately command a majority across Parliament in order to be enacted into law.

Third, the override is only allowed with respect to *some specified Charter rights*, not all. Thus, it is precluded for democratic rights, mobility rights, and language rights.[28] Finally, the override is subject to a *sunset and re-enactment clause*. If enacted, the override ceases to have effect five years after it comes into force,[29] whereupon Parliament may re-enact the override if it so wishes for a further five years.[30] By requiring review and renewal at five-year intervals, section 33 ensures that any derogation from the Charter requires repeated mobilisation of a political majority across different electoral cycles.[31]

Therefore, whilst section 33 gives Canadian legislatures the power to legislate notwithstanding rights, it is by no means a constitutional *carte blanche*. Instead, it creates a limited power of restricted temporal and substantive scope, subject to all the publicity, transparency and justificatory requirements embedded in the legislative process.[32] Tellingly, section 33 does not speak in strident terms of legislatures 'overriding'

---

[25] Hiebert (2017) 695; Kahana (2001) 277; Leckey & Mendelsohn (2022); Delaney (2016) 54.

[26] Kahana (2002) 234; Hiebert (2009) 107; Albert (2018) 147; Gardbaum (2013b) 110; Leeson (2001) 315. Much controversy surrounds the issue of pre-emptive derogations, see Leckey (2019a) 2–3; Dodek (2016) 55–6; Kahana (2001) 277.

[27] Hogg (2007) 881; Adams & Bower (2022) 8–9.

[28] Section 33(1); Leckey (2019a) 6; Pal (2022) 19 (arguing that the exclusion of democratic rights from the purview of section 33 suggests that it was structured 'to minimise the change that irresponsible legislative action could permanently harm the democratic foundations of the Canadian constitutional order').

[29] Section 33(3).

[30] Section 33(4).

[31] Goldsworthy (2003b) 468; Leeson (2001) 297; Newman (2019) 223.

[32] Kahana (2002) 231; For the argument that the checks embedded in section 33 operate as 'manner-and-form' conditions on legislation which derogates from the Charter, see Kyritsis (2017) 110; MacDonnell (2016) 25.

rights or 'disregarding' court rulings. Instead, it employs much more careful, reserved and conditional language. It stipulates that legislatures 'may' proceed with legislation 'notwithstanding' some of the rights otherwise entrenched in the Charter, subject to specified conditions and constraints. As the general heading to section 33 clarifies, the power to enact legislation 'notwithstanding' specified rights is an 'exception' to the general norm of Charter compliance, and conditional on the political actors making an 'express declaration' to that effect.[33] Viewed as a whole, therefore, the Charter seeks to ensure that all branches of government comply with rights, whilst nonetheless providing for a limited legislative derogation from some of those rights in strictly defined circumstances.[34]

Section 33 was part of an eleventh-hour compromise to get agreement between the federal government and provincial leaders on the Canadian Charter.[35] Some provincial leaders feared that judicial decisions under the Charter would unduly constrict their ability to protect deeply-held social values and institutions in their province. Therefore, they sought reassurance that democratic legislatures would have some meaningful input into the constitutional debate about 'which rights are fundamental in Canadian society and which should prevail when rights are in conflict'.[36] Whilst accepting that rights should be entrenched in the Charter, they nonetheless wanted to ensure that elected politicians would retain the political capacity to disagree with the courts on particularly contentious issues.[37]

Drawing on the historical precedents of the notwithstanding clause in the Canadian Bill of Rights 1960 – and analogous provisions in other provincial Bills of Rights[38] – some provincial leaders argued that the

---

[33] The title above section 33 reads 'Exception where express declaration'; Weinrib (1990) 541; Kahana (2002) 236; Dodek (2016) 48–9; Leckey (2019a) 3–6 (arguing that the override allows for an exceptional derogation from Charter rights, but is not a 'nuclear privative clause').

[34] For this reason, it is apt to describe section 33 as a 'derogation clause' or a 'nevertheless clause', see Leckey (2015) 136, 158, 225; Gardbaum (2013b) 162; Weinrib (2016) 74; Webber (2003) 16.

[35] For analysis of the Charter negotiations, see Lougheed (1998); Leeson (2000) 3; Weinrib (1990) 554; Weinrib (2016) 68, 74–81; Hiebert (2017); MacDonnell (2016) 25.

[36] Wayne McCulloch, cited in Johansen & Rosen (2012) 5; Blakeney (2010) 1–9. For a subtle and insightful historical analysis of the override, see Adams & Bower (2022); Newman (2019).

[37] Russell (2007) 66; Lougheed (1998) 14; Newman (2019) 221, 215; Blakeney (2006) 31–2; Hiebert (2010) 113, 116.

[38] Canadian Bill of Rights 1960; Saskatchewan Human Rights Code, s 44, the Alberta Bill of Rights 2000, s 2 and the Quebec Charter of Human Rights and Freedoms, s 52. For an

Charter should include a legislative power 'to override a court decision which might affect the basic social institutions of a province or region'.[39] In order to reconcile entrenched rights with Canadian traditions of parliamentary democracy, they supported 'the constitutionalisation of rights, subject to a final political judgment in certain instances, rather than a final judicial determination as to the extent of all rights'.[40] Ultimately, section 33 was the 'deal maker'[41] which broke the log-jam in the Charter negotiations. In short, without the notwithstanding clause, the Canadian Charter may never have existed.

Although the notwithstanding clause eventually basked in the glow of international admiration as an ingenious solution to the notorious counter-majoritarian difficulty, it received decidedly mixed reviews in its early days on the Canadian constitutional scene.[42] Critics of the clause believed that it was an alien graft onto an otherwise rights-respecting document, castigating it as fundamentally inconsistent with the Charter's commitment to entrenching rights.[43] The then Prime Minister – Pierre Trudeau – believed that it was deeply wrong to allow governments to suspend any part of the Charter, and only reluctantly agreed to section 33 on condition that it contained a sunset clause as a form of damage limitation.[44]

For those like Trudeau who opposed the clause, their concern was that section 33 gave politicians an illegitimate opt-out clause to trample over rights whenever it was politically expedient to do so.[45] The fact that the override was viewed as the product of a 'grubby late-night deal'[46] struck in the 'the raw politics'[47] of constitutional negotiation behind closed doors tainted its reputation from the outset, casting it as an illegitimate child born into a family of noble rights provisions, all of which could claim much higher breeding.

---

analysis of these historical precursors, see Leeson (2000) 5–6; Johansen & Rosen (2012) 2; Leeson (2001) 302 4; Carter (2019).

[39] Johansen & Rosen (2012) 4–6; Newman (2019).

[40] Newman (2019) 218.

[41] Russell (2007) 66; Brosseau & Roy (2018) 4; Tushnet (2008b) 52; Cameron (2004) 141; Hiebert (2009) 108–9 (arguing that section 33 can also be viewed as a 'deal-breaker' because it undermined the rights-protecting purpose of the Charter).

[42] Weiler (1984) 92.

[43] MacDonnell (2016) 25; Weinrib (1990) 563.

[44] Hiebert (2009) 110, 132; Johansen & Rosen (2012) 2–6; Leeson (2001) 307, 309–12.

[45] Richard Hatfield, Premier of New Brunswick, cited in Johansen & Rosen (2012) 4.

[46] Coyne (2017).

[47] Leeson (2000) 3; Leeson (2001) 298; Dodek (2016) 53, 57–8.

But the fears of those who worried that the override would undermine the Charter were not borne out in practice. Mirroring the pattern of non-use of its historical precursor in the 1960 Canadian Bill of Rights,[48] the clause was never invoked by the Parliament of Canada, and only rarely used in the Provinces. Even factoring in the recent flurry of provincial threats to use the clause, the notwithstanding clause has only been used twenty-two times at provincial level in over four decades, the vast majority of which occurred in Quebec.[49] Therefore, provincial use of the override is still extremely rare. If we bracket Quebec, it is rarer still. So what explains the underuse of the override in the Canadian context? Four key reasons are commonly advanced.

The first is the *path-dependence argument*.[50] Just nine weeks after the Charter was proclaimed, the Quebec legislature used the notwithstanding clause in an omnibus fashion to encompass all statutes enacted in Quebec and even to immunise future statutes from constitutional review.[51] Since Quebec was the sole Province not to have signed up to the Constitutional Act 1982, its omnibus use of the override was widely regarded as a form of political protest against the Charter project as a whole.[52] Many Canadian commentators argued that Quebec's 'sweeping and indiscriminate use of the clause'[53] during its delicate incubation period discredited and delegitimised the override as an acceptable constitutional tool which legislatures could use to disagree with the courts.[54] As Canadian political scientist Christopher Manfredi put it, 'Canadians experienced a use of the notwithstanding clause that they found outrageous before they experienced a Supreme Court decision of equivalent political unpopularity'.[55] Therefore, many argue that this historical contingency set Canada on a path of underuse from which there was no going back.[56]

The second reason is the familiar *political costs argument*.[57] This is the claim that although the Canadian Parliament and provincial legislatures

---

[48] Dodek (2016) 51; Carter (2019) 128.
[49] Kahana (2001); Lake (2022).
[50] On 'path dependence', see Snow (2009); Albert (2008) 1042–3.
[51] Roy & Brosseau (2018) 6–8; Snow (2009) 1.
[52] Hiebert (2017) 698–9.
[53] Goldsworthy (2003b) 468.
[54] Ibid 465; Tushnet (2008b) 52; Bateup (2007) 8; Dodek (2016) 59.
[55] Manfredi (2001) 204, 194; Tushnet (2008b) 59; Newman (2019) 224.
[56] Albert (2008) 1042–3; Tushnet (2008b); Snow (2009) 1; Goldsworthy (2003b) 469; Tushnet (1995) 277, 296; Gardbaum (2013b) 110.
[57] Weiler (1984) 82; Gardbaum (2013b) 90, 110, 201, 239; Tushnet (1995) 296, 284; Goldsworthy (2003b) 467; Kavanagh (2015a) 837–8.

wanted to use the override, they were effectively disabled from doing so by the exorbitant political costs accompanying such a move.[58] Since Charter rights are highly prized in Canadian political culture, a political attempt to override them would inevitably cast politicians in the role of 'human rights transgressors'[59] and Charter cheaters, determined to ride roughshod over rights and the rule of law.[60] Canadian politicians are acutely aware that they would suffer significant popular, parliamentary and political pushback if they attempted to override rights or disregard a decision of the Supreme Court of Canada on what those rights require, especially as judges are highly respected actors in Canadian constitutional culture.[61] For many observers, these costs are so onerous that they have rendered the notwithstanding clause 'politically toxic'[62] and even taboo, at least at the Federal level.[63] The upshot is a widespread belief that the override is effectively off-limits as a legitimate tool of political engagement in Canadian political life.[64]

The third reason is a claim about *textual constraints*. This is the argument that the various restrictions on the exercise of the override contained in section 33 effectively rendered it impossible to use.[65] The sunset and re-enactment clause operates as a particularly strong disincentive in this regard, because even if a government manages to mobilise sufficient political support to use it on one occasion, this is only a 'temporary stop-gap'[66] which requires the expenditure of further political capital five years down the line.[67] Given the political costs of invoking the clause and the 'short duration of the reprieve it offers',[68] the political actors are disincentivised from incurring those costs in the first place. Many leading Canadian and comparative constitutional scholars argue further that the wording of section 33 is an added deterrent because it creates the (false) impression that legislatures wish to deny rights

---

[58] Goldsworthy (2003b); Huscroft (2009) 56; Yap (2015) 28–9.
[59] Mandel (1989) 76; Duxbury (2017) 651.
[60] Goldsworthy (2003b) 467 (describing this perception as 'politically lethal').
[61] Russell (2009) 293; Fletcher & Howe (2001); Tushnet (2008b) 48; Hiebert (2004b); Leeson (2000) 18–19; Goldsworthy (2003b) 455–6, 467–70; Tushnet (2003b) 89; Waldron (2004) 9, 36–7.
[62] Albert (2008) 1044; Albert (2018) 147.
[63] McAdam (2009); Smith (2019).
[64] Albert (2018); McAdam (2009) 15.
[65] Kahana (2002) 222; Cameron (2004) 142.
[66] Leeson (2000) 20; Goldsworthy (2010) 202.
[67] Gardbaum (2013b) 110; Weinrib (2016) 97; Huscroft (2009) 55.
[68] Weinrib (2016) 97.

altogether.[69] However, instead of being *antagonists* of rights, these scholars argue that legislatures are typically *advocates* of particular conceptions of rights, albeit ones which differ from those mandated by the courts. As Jeremy Waldron put it, the notwithstanding clause misrepresents the legislature as having disreputable 'rights misgivings', instead of being engaged in reasonable 'rights disagreements' with courts.[70] This reputational cost deters political actors from invoking the override.

The fourth reason for the underuse of the override can be labelled the *less drastic measures* argument. In Canadian constitutional discourse, the override is variously described as a 'nuclear bomb',[71] a 'sledgehammer',[72] a 'cudgel',[73] a 'sword of Damocles',[74] or even a 'dagger pointed at the heart of our fundamental freedoms'.[75] In this context, using the clause may seem like 'radical overkill'.[76] Therefore, it is hardly surprising that politicians will seek out less confrontational and dramatic ways of achieving the same or similar effect.[77] Why use a sledgehammer when you have more subtle and tailored tools to do the work?

The most obvious option is trying to justify a rights limitation under section 1 of the Charter.[78] Another is enacting a law which retains much of the original policy objective, whilst implementing the judicial decision in a minimal fashion. These more subtle and accommodating approaches enable the government and legislature to achieve their policy objectives to some degree, whilst avoiding the popular outcry and political costs involved to seeking to override a court ruling. The availability and utility of these less drastic measures leads to an underuse of the override.

---

[69] Waldron (2004) 9, 34–7; Gardbaum (2013b) 124; Albert (2008) 1052; Morton & Knopff (2000) 231; Huscroft (2009) 56; Manfredi (2001) 191–3; Hiebert (2015) 57 (arguing that section 33 places politicians under a 'burden of having to act in a deliberately defiant manner' vis-à-vis the courts).

[70] Waldron (2004) 36–7.

[71] Leeson (2000) 19; Leeson (2001) 320–1; Snow (2009) 10; Mailey (2019) 11; McAdam (2009) 3; Hutchins (2018) (describing the Ontario Premier Doug Ford's threat to use the notwithstanding clause as 'going straight to the nuclear option').

[72] MacDonnell (2016) 27; Axworthy (2007) 1 (quoting Prime Minister Paul Martin, who described it as 'a hammer that can only be used to pound away at the Charter').

[73] Lake (2022).

[74] Axworthy (2007) 1.

[75] Ibid 3.

[76] Leeson (2000) 19.

[77] For a stylised analysis of the tendency amongst political actors to use lower-cost over high-cost powers, see Vermeule (2012) 432–3.

[78] Roach (2016b) chapter 9.

3   Reconciling Rights and Democracy UK-Style

When the Human Rights Act 1998 was being enacted, the central concern across the political spectrum was to find a way of allowing judges to enforce human rights whilst preserving parliamentary sovereignty.[79] Previous attempts to incorporate Convention rights into UK law had foundered on a deep-seated aversion to the idea of allowing judges to strike down legislation enacted by Parliament.[80] Such a power was perceived to be 'anathema to the political and legal culture of the United Kingdom under which ultimate sovereignty rests with Parliament'.[81] Therefore, all the key political actors knew that a Bill of Rights which included a strike-down power would never get enacted.

The Canadian solution of including a judicial strike-down whilst offsetting it with a legislative override provision, was considered but ultimately rejected. The combination of rights entrenchment and judicial invalidation was thought to violate the doctrine of parliamentary sovereignty which was 'so uncompromisingly embedded in [the British] political and legal culture'.[82] The central challenge, therefore, was to devise a scheme which would give the courts 'as much space as possible to protect rights, short of a power to set aside or ignore Acts of Parliament'.[83]

The solution to this conundrum was a carefully crafted legislative scheme containing two crucial components. The first was a legally non-binding judicial declaration of incompatibility under section 4; the second was a political Statement of Compatibility – and, crucially, a Statement of *In*compatibility – under section 19 HRA.[84] On a surface reading, both provisions seem to leave the UK government and Parliament completely free to legislate contrary to Convention rights and contrary to court rulings on what those rights require. Indeed, they seem specifically designed to do so. So what explains the consistently compliant practice when responding to declarations of incompatibility? Two key reasons are typically advanced.

---

[79] Lord Irvine, HL Debs, vol 582 col 1229 (3 November 1997); Klug (2003) 125; Kavanagh (2009a) 5, 310–13; Leigh & Masterman (2008) 18.

[80] Lester (2002a) 58; Klug (2005) 198; Klug (2007) 709.

[81] Lord Irvine (2003a) 44; Feldman (1999) 169; Straw (2012) 272; Gearty (2016) 67.

[82] Lord Irvine (2003a) 98; Kavanagh (2009a) 4; Feldman (1999) 168–9.

[83] HL Deb 3 November 1997, vol 582 col 1228 (Lord Irvine of Lairg); Lord Irvine (2003a) 9; Leigh & Lustgarten (1999) 536.

[84] Section 19(2) HRA.

The first reason is rooted in the crucially important *international dimension* of the HRA discussed in Chapter 8. If the UK Government decides to ignore or override a declaration of incompatibility by the UK Supreme Court, then the aggrieved litigant can take their case to Strasbourg, armed with a declaration by the UK Supreme Court that domestic legislation clearly violates their rights.[85] In this situation, the Strasbourg court is highly likely to find in the litigant's favour, whereupon the UK is placed under an international law obligation to remedy the rights violation declared by the ECtHR.[86] Therefore, governments are well aware that little will be achieved, and a good deal may be lost, by not amending the incompatible legislation once the declaration is issued.[87] Given the rhetorical force of a domestic judicial ruling that legislation violates human rights, combined with the political and legal repercussions at the international level, Parliament is placed under enormous pressure to amend statutes to accommodate the judicial ruling.[88] This helps to explain why compliance rather than defiance of declarations of incompatibility is the norm in the UK system.

The second reason is the familiar argument from *political costs*. As in Canada, many UK-based scholars have argued that the legislative freedom to enact laws notwithstanding rights or to disregard declarations is effectively negated by the political costs of using that power.[89] They suggest that reverence for rights and esteem for the courts make it 'not only politically difficult but also constitutionally questionable for Parliament to reject a particular interpretation or even question courts' interpretive method'.[90] Although the Westminster Parliament is legally free to disagree with courts, it was forced to adopt a 'compliance oriented mentality'[91] – capitulating to the judiciary rather than questioning or challenging their rulings. Instead of unleashing a laudable 'culture of controversy'[92] where legislatures and courts could disagree openly and fervently about rights, the political dynamics surrounding the HRA created a lamentable 'culture of compliance',[93] where legislatures kowtow to the courts.

---

[85] Kavanagh (2015c) 1024; Chapter 8.4 and 8.5.
[86] Straw & Boateng (1997) 74.
[87] Elliott (2002) 348; Kavanagh (2009a) 284.
[88] Sales & Ekins (2011) 229–30; Kavanagh (2009a) 285; Leckey (2015) 47–8.
[89] Duxbury (2017) 651.
[90] Campbell (2001) 87; Sathanapally (2012) 72.
[91] Tushnet (2008a) 248; Hiebert & Kelly (2015) 9.
[92] Campbell (1999) 6.
[93] Ibid 6.

4   Underuse by Design not Demonisation

Though there are many reasons for the underuse of the override in both countries, they nonetheless converge on a common theme. This is that the override was thwarted by various political costs, contingencies and cultural constraints which prevented legislatures from seizing 'the last word' on rights. The suggestion is that the override failed to realise its full potential, because it was subtly subverted by a set of political dynamics which rendered it 'politically impotent'.[94] Embedded in a culture of judicial supremacy and reverence for rights, the legislative override became delegitimised and fell into desuetude.[95] The constitutional culture and political climate conspired to undermine the override.[96]

If this diagnosis of demise and desuetude is accepted, then a natural cure presents itself. In order to rescue the override from a dismal descent into desuetude, we should try to lower the political costs of using it and change the constitutional culture in order to make it more hospitable to the override. The scholarly landscape on both sides of the Atlantic is strewn with normative claims of this kind. We are urged to 'reframe'[97] popular conceptions of the override and to 'rethink',[98] 'reconstruct',[99] and 'reconfigure'[100] the role of the legislature and the courts, in order to 'revive',[101] 'reincarnate',[102] 'rehabilitate',[103] and 'reinvigorate'[104] a flourishing legislative practice of overriding court rulings on rights.[105] In the UK, scholars have issued a clarion call to Parliament to 'assert its own supremacy'[106] on rights by disagreeing with court rulings and overriding

---

[94]   Davis (2014a) 145; Webber (2009) (lamenting 'the unfulfilled potential' of the Canadian notwithstanding clause).

[95]   Stephenson (2013) 880; Tushnet (1995) 296; Snow (2009).

[96]   Hogg & Bushell (1997) 83.

[97]   Davis (2014a) 144.

[98]   Kahana (2002) 274.

[99]   Kavanagh (2015a) 836.

[100]   King (2019a) 201 (though note that King does not advocate such a 'reconfiguration'. He is simply describing it as a common dialogic move).

[101]   Albert (2018).

[102]   Albert (2008).

[103]   Hiebert (2004a); Gardbaum (2013b) 89; King (2015b) 10; Klug (2003) 131.

[104]   Davis (2014a) 137–50; Davis (2010) 91, 93, 96; Newman (2019) 234.

[105]   Gardbaum (2013b) 88ff (advocating changes in constitutional practice in order to inculcate greater use of the override). Vermeule and others even recommend the 'pointless exercise' of powers which seem to have fallen into desuetude in order to keep them operative, see Vermeule (2012) 439; Albert (2018) 156–7; Davis (2014a) 145.

[106]   Davis (2014a) 145.

them when it sees fit. On this view, a regular practice of overriding judicial decisions would 'reaffirm the "genius" of the HRA'[107] and realise the promise of dialogue.[108]

But this narrative of thwarted potential and unrealised promise is deeply problematic. For one thing, it is not clear that the political costs of using the override are as severe or unequivocal as the argument assumes. In the UK, popular buy-in to the HRA is weak, in part because leading political elites have aligned with the tabloid press to portray the HRA as a 'villain's charter'.[109] In a political climate which is inhospitable or even hostile to rights, political actors who defy court rulings may be hailed as heroic defenders of British values, rather than as villainous violators of fundamental rights.[110] Given this hostile political atmosphere, the claim that the political actors are politically hamstrung from defying court rulings on the rights of sex offenders, terrorist suspects, prisoners, and immigrants, seems tenuous at best.[111] Indeed, one might say that *despite* the political costs of complying with court rulings, the UK government and Parliament have steadfastly and consistently done so.

The political and constitutional context in Canada is very different given the Charter's 'sacrosanct'[112] status in political discourse and its emergence as an important symbol of Canadian self-identity.[113] By all accounts, popular support for the courts and the Charter is strong in the Canadian polity. There is also a strong culture of compliance with judicial rulings amongst political elites.[114] Therefore, it seems plausible to think that the political costs of using the override will typically be high.[115] Indeed, one of the reasons why the recent provincial proposals to

---

[107] Davis (2010) 93, 96.

[108] Ibid 91; Webber (2009).

[109] Gies (2015a); Gies (2015b).

[110] Phillipson (2006) 45–52; Loader (2007) 33; Feldman (2014) 227–34; Gearty (2016) chapter 8; Hillebrecht (2014) 101–2.

[111] For an astute analysis, see Klug (2007).

[112] McAdam (2009) 2.

[113] Russell (2007) 65 (describing the Charter as a 'popular icon' and symbolic focal point for political discourse); McAdam (2009) 2; Smith (2019) (pointing to a 2013 poll where the Charter ranked above the national flag and anthem as an important symbol of Canadian national identity).

[114] Hiebert (2011) 57–8; Russell (2009) 293; Fletcher & Howe (2001); Weinrib (2016) 96; Bateup (2009) 575–6; Leeson (2001) 319; Casey & Kenny (2022) 19.

[115] Weinrib (2016) 79–80.

invoke the notwithstanding clause have failed is precisely because the political and popular pushback has been formidable.[116]

But even in Canada, we cannot assume that the political costs will invariably impede the override. Leading constitutional commentators suggest that Canadian commitment to the Charter varies from issue to issue, time to time, and province to province, such that public opinion could well go against a court ruling on a particularly contentious and sensitive subject.[117] The recent spate of provincial invocations of the notwithstanding clause may suggest that the political aversion to the override may be more fragile than previously assumed. The upshot is that whilst political costs may give us vital clues to the underuse of the override in some contexts, it does not completely solve the mystery of the 'underuse of the override'.

But there is a deeper problem with the narrative of thwarted potential and unrealised promise. This is that it rests on the assumption that the override was intended to realise the promise of facilitating ongoing dialogue and disagreement between legislatures and courts.[118] However, when we look at the legislative history of the override in both countries, it seems clear that these dialogic aspirations were not shared by the political architects who crafted these mechanisms on either side of the Atlantic.[119]

In Canada, the political actors who brokered the compromise on the Charter typically presented the override as 'a safety valve to correct absurd situations',[120] which should only be used in the 'unlikely event of a decision of the courts that is clearly contrary to the public interest'.[121] Rather than viewing it as a vehicle for ongoing dialogue or disagreement between courts and legislatures on the meaning of rights, they conceived it more narrowly as a mechanism for judicial error correction *in extremis* to

---

[116] Nicolaides & Snow (2021) 60.

[117] Russell (2007) 68; Leeson (2000) 18; Leeson (2001) 319–20; Hogg, Thornton & Wright (2007b) 201; Albert (2018) 153; Russell (2009) 293; Gardbaum (2013b) 121; McAdam (2009) 15–16; Dodek (2016) 61, 65.

[118] Gardbaum (2013b) 125, 127; Newman (2019) 212–13; Albert (2018).

[119] King (2015b) 111–12; Adams & Bower (2022); Johansen & Rosen (2012).

[120] Jean Chrétien, Minister of Justice, House of Commons, Canada, Legislative Debates (Nov. 20 1981), cited in Brosseau & Roy (2018) 5; Fraser (2005) 7, 10, 13–14; Bateup (2007) 2; Johansen & Rosen (2012) 5.

[121] McMurtry (1982) 65; Brosseau & Roy (2018) 3–6; Kahana (2002) 223, 7; Cameron (2016) 149; Bateup (2006) 1147; Russell (1991) 295; Russell (2009) 292 (describing section 33 as providing 'a democratic safety valve).

counteract 'absurd decisions'[122] or as an 'exceptional'[123] way of resolving intractable disagreements about what rights require in a democracy. Like a safety valve in a boiler, the override was designed to diffuse tension in a potentially explosive situation, thus keeping the boiler functioning in the longer term.

Once it was apparent that the notwithstanding clause would be included in the Charter, the crux of the political negotiations turned to placing adequate safeguards and constraints on its use, so that it could not be used lightly, hastily, covertly or without due legislative deliberation.[124] The requirement that an override must be clearly expressed in an Act of Parliament was designed to ensure that any proposed derogation from the Charter would be subject to the full glare of political, parliamentary, media, and public attention.[125] The sunset and re-enactment clause was inserted precisely to disincentivise its use *ex ante*, as well as to limit its effects *ex post*.[126] Those who were philosophically opposed to the override nonetheless accepted it, in part, because they were reassured that, just like its forerunner in the Canadian Bill of Rights 1960, it was 'unlikely ever to be used'.[127]

Therefore, although the Charter included a notwithstanding clause which allowed legislatures to legislate notwithstanding some rights guarantees, it ratcheted up the political costs of using the clause whilst reducing the political gains. The aim of section 33 was *not* to enable legislatures to reject and override judicial decisions whenever they disagreed with them, but rather to facilitate a limited derogation from the Charter in circumstances of deep and intractable disagreement where no other solution could be found.[128] By heightening the 'enactment costs'[129] of legislating 'notwithstanding' Charter rights, section 33 was designed to make a legislative override difficult to use.[130] Rather than being 'a bottle

---

[122] Brosseau & Roy (2018) 5; Tasse (1989) 102–3; Tushnet (2008b) 279.
[123] Lorraine Weinrib, quoted in Stone & Gray (2021).
[124] Leeson (2000) 10; Axworthy (2007) 5; Hiebert (2004a) 171; McMurtry (1982) 65; Russell (1991) 295.
[125] Kahana (2002) 222.
[126] Carter (2019) 128 (arguing that a similar rights-respecting rationale underpinned the notwithstanding clause in the *Canadian Bill of Rights* 1960).
[127] Jean Chrétien (Minister for Justice) and Pierre Trudeau (Prime Minister), both cited in Brosseau & Roy (2018) 4–6; McAdam (2009) 7–8.
[128] Johansen & Rosen (2012) 5–6; Carter (2019) 128
[129] Stephenson (2008) 2.
[130] Kahana (2002) 231.

labelled "Drink me" that cheapens the Charter',[131] the override was more like a bottle bearing a large health warning saying: 'This drink may endanger the long-term health of the constitutional system. Only use this strong medicine if you have no other option, and be mindful of negative side effects.' If the purpose of the override was to give the legislature 'the last word', then it was very much the *last word as last resort*. It was not envisaged as a quotidian contribution to an ongoing dialogue.

A similar picture emerges when we examine the legislative history of the UK HRA. The White Paper preceding the HRA emphasised that although the declaration would 'not of itself have the effect of changing the law ... it will *almost certainly prompt* the Government and Parliament to change the law'.[132] This was affirmed in parliamentary debates where the Government Ministers proposing the Human Rights Bill reiterated their belief that 'the government and Parliament will *in almost all cases* certainly be prompted to change the law following a declaration'.[133]

True, they acknowledged that there might be a rare case 'of great controversy'[134] where Parliament might not wish to accept a declaration of incompatibility, but they emphasised the rarity and exceptionality of this occurrence. As Jack Straw MP observed:

> *In the overwhelming majority of cases*, regardless of which party was in government, I think that Ministers would examine the matter and say 'A declaration of incompatibility has been made and *we shall have to accept it*. We shall therefore *have to remedy the defect in the law* spotted by the Judicial Committee of the House of Lords'.[135]

The use of obligatory language here is telling. It reflects the potent combination of constitutional norms, legal principles, political pressures, and international law requirements discussed in Chapter 8 which, together, give the government numerous incentives to comply with a

---

[131] Coyne (2017).

[132] White Paper 2.10; Irvine (2003a) 12.

[133] HL Deb 27 November 1997, vol 583 col 1139, Lord Irvine (emphasis added); Cooper & Marshal-Williams (2000) 149–50, 65.

[134] HC Deb 16 February 1997, vol 307 col 1301, Jack Straw (instancing the hypothetical and remote possibility of the courts declaring the UK's abortion regime to be incompatible with the Convention); Leigh & Masterman (2008) 113.

[135] HC Deb 21 October 1998, vol 317 col 1301 (emphasis added), cited in Klug (1999) 264.

declaration of incompatibility, rather than allow further unnecessary and costly litigation in Strasbourg.[136]

A similar expectation underpinned section 19 HRA. Although section 19 clearly allows the government to propose legislation to Parliament which is contrary to Convention rights, the firm expectation was that this will be a rare rather than regular occurrence. When discussing section 19, the Lord Chancellor, Lord Irvine, stressed that 'Ministers will *obviously* want to make a positive statement whenever possible'[137] and that it was '*obviously* ... incumbent on Ministers ... to do their best to ensure that bills are compatible with the Convention'.[138] The rationale of requiring governments to make a Statement of Compatibility 'openly, in the full glare of parliamentary and public opinion',[139] was *not* to encourage legislative rights-violation as a matter of course. Instead, it was to incentivise the political actors to think hard about – and ultimately refrain from – legislating incompatibly with rights.[140]

Rather than giving politicians a *carte blanche* to disregard rights, section 19 galvanised the power of publicity[141] and allied mechanisms of political accountability to force Ministers 'to stand up and be counted for human rights'.[142] At the very least, it ensured that any deviations from the requirements of the Convention would be 'conscious, reasoned departures, and not the product of rashness, muddle or ignorance'.[143] Just as the judicial declaration of incompatibility was expected to incentivise political compliance, a governmental statement of *incom*patibility under s. 19(1)(b) was intended to heighten political scrutiny and increase the 'enactment costs'[144] of getting a rights-offending legislative proposal through Parliament. Instead of finding ways of reducing those costs, the HRA deliberately increased them in order to ensure that the override could not be used lightly, covertly, obliquely, or rashly. Compliance was eased; defiance was exacerbated. The overall message was that the legislative override was not intended to be an easy

---

[136] Chapter 8, this vol.

[137] Lord Irvine (2003a) 15 (emphasis added).

[138] Ibid 15 (emphasis added).

[139] Ibid 98.

[140] Weill (2016) 128 (arguing that the idea of the override was 'to deter the legislature by shaming it into refraining from infringing rights').

[141] Mill (1998) [1861] 282; Russell & Gover (2017) 270.

[142] Lord Irvine (2003a) 98; HL Deb 27 November 1997, vol 583 col 1163.

[143] Lord Irvine (2003a) 23.

[144] Stephenson (2008) 2.

or everyday occurrence. It was intended, if at all, as a rare and exceptional event following probing political and public scrutiny.

When we look at the genesis of these provisions in Canada and the UK, it seems clear that the key political architects on both sides of the Atlantic intended them as safety valves for exceptional circumstances rather than as a regular mode of conversational exchange between courts and legislatures. Whilst they undoubtedly gave the legislature 'the last word', it was a *last word as last resort.*

This opens up a novel solution to the mystery of the underuse of the override, namely, that 'underuse' – or, more accurately, 'rare use' – was hardwired into the design of these Bills of Rights from the outset. It was a feature, not a bug, in the system. Rather than treating the political costs as unforeseen or unwelcome impediments to their ideal functioning – or as tragic failures of their true dialogic promise – the historical narrative suggests that the anticipated political costs were deliberately employed to incentivise political compliance with court rulings on rights. Underuse emerged by design rather than demonisation, by foresight rather than oversight.

In making this point about constitutional design, I am not succumbing to a crude originalism, which seeks to draw a conclusive connection between legislative history and legal meaning. No doubt, we should read the historical record with a healthy dose of scepticism, alert to the possibility that the statements about the overrides could be 'cheap talk masking other motivations'.[145] However, the consistently expressed views of the key political architects who devised these mechanisms on both sides of the Atlantic should not be cast aside as irrelevant either. Not only are these views borne out by the constitutional texts, they are also reflected in the subsequent political and legal practice in both countries.

Nonetheless, in order to fully understand the override, we cannot rely on the historical record alone. Instead, we need to tell a deeper normative story grounded in constitutional principle and practice. After all, even if the historical narrative is correct, it still leaves open the possibility that the political elites who devised these clauses were normatively misguided, failing to appreciate the dialogic and democratic advantages of allowing – indeed encouraging – legislatures to regularly review, revise and reject court rulings on rights with which they disagree. To evaluate this,

---

[145] Bradley & Siegel (2017) 280.

we must appeal to arguments of constitutional principle. This is the task of the next section.

5 From Dialogue and Disagreement to Comity and Collaboration

In order to understand the operation of the override, we need to situate it within an understanding of the constitutional partnership between the branches of government, and the need for forge constructive working relationships between them. In the collaborative constitution, the relationship between the branches of government rests on a constitutional division of labour between the three branches, where each branch makes a distinct and valuable contribution to the collaborative enterprise, which the other branches must treat with comity and respect.

As we saw in Chapter 3, comity has two dimensions – *mutual self-restraint* and *mutual support*.[146] The requirement of *mutual self-restraint* means that the branches of government should refrain from interfering with the role and function of their coordinate branches. The duty of *mutual support* captures the 'affirmative obligations'[147] which require the branches to positively assist and support one another in carrying out their respective roles in a scheme of constitutional governance.[148] The duty to work together constructively as part of a joint enterprise therefore constrains the proper modes of interaction between them.

As in any well-functioning partnership, mutual respect is the foundational normative requirement. And since the working relationships between the branches need to be sustained over the long term in a relationship of reciprocity and interdependence, the interaction between the branches is guided by the requirements of 'repeat-play, reciprocity and reputation'.[149] An antagonistic move against another branch might trigger open retaliation and a breakdown in reciprocal respect. Opportunistic power-play might secure a short-term advantage, but can undermine a branch's reputation as a reliable partner in the longer term.[150] The upshot is that in order to sustain good working relations over the long term and accrue the mutual benefits of a stable

---

[146] Kavanagh (2009a) 145, 236.
[147] Pozen (2014) 38; MacDonnell (2013) 626–36.
[148] Kyritsis (2017); Kyritsis (2015).
[149] Levinson (2005) 940; Kramer (2000) 215.
[150] Ellickson (1991) 156.

constitutional order, the branches of government should adopt a norm of conflict-avoidance or at least conflict-minimisation. These three norms – comity, collaboration and conflict-avoidance – frame the relationship between the branches of government and constrain the interaction between them.

So how do these norms bear on the operation of the override? They suggest that the override should be used with caution and care, ever attentive to the need to treat the other branches with comity and respect. They preclude the legislature from regularly or lightly overriding court decisions merely because they disagree with them. Instead, they create a presumption in favour of compliance with court rulings on rights, which should only be rebutted in exceptional circumstances. What justifies this presumption? I offer three reasons.

First, if judicial decisions were cast aside whenever the Government or legislature disagrees with them, this would evince disrespect for judicial rulings and potentially undermine the institutional credibility and integrity of the courts in the joint enterprise of governing.[151] In systems which recognise the value of judicial independence, the aim is to create an institutional environment where judges can make decisions 'without fear or favour', confident that they will be sanctioned or ignored if their rulings do not find favour with the powers that be.[152] Therefore, the rule of law creates a rule of thumb that the government and legislature should generally comply with court rulings, even if they disagree with them.[153] Out of respect for the constitutional role of the courts in the collaborative enterprise, Parliament should operate a presumption in favour of complying with court rulings which can only be displaced in exceptional circumstances.

Second, to treat court rulings as optional opinions to be dismissed whenever another branch disagrees with them is to misconceive – and potentially undermine – the authoritative nature of judicial decisions in the collaborative constitutional scheme.[154] After all, it is the mark of authority that it binds even when we disagree.[155] Of course, if we view the interaction between the courts and the legislature as a form of dialogue,

[151] King (2019a) 202–3; King (2015b) 124; Newman (2019) 223–4; Jacobi (2006) 260; Bateup (2009) 567, 569; Webber (2006) 276–7; Vanberg (2005) 27; Lain (2017) 1657–8.
[152] Kavanagh (2009a) 321.
[153] Beatson (2021) 117; Stephenson (2016) 12.
[154] King (2015b) 123; Hickman (2008) 83–7.
[155] Raz (1979) 51.

we might be lured into believing that the branches are involved in 'a dynamic process involving the interchange of proposals for constitutional meaning',[156] where 'each institutional actor brings forth its understanding for consideration and examination by the other'.[157] But in any constitutional democracy worthy of the name, the role of the courts is *not* to offer thoughtful suggestions for the legislature to ponder, but rather to provide authoritative resolutions of legal disputes and to declare what the law is, in a context where that resolution is treated with comity and respect.[158] If the legislature regularly second-guessed court decisions – substituting their decisions for those of the judiciary – this would strain the relations of comity and collaboration between the branches, and subvert the constitutional division of labour on which the constitution rests.[159]

Finally, a regular practice of overriding the courts would create enormous uncertainty, unpredictability and unfairness for litigants.[160] If judicial decisions were merely provisional pronouncements subject to regular reversal by the legislature, this would mean that litigants could not rely on the courts to give them a final, authoritative ruling about what their rights require.[161] Whilst a democratic dialogue between the branches might be 'normatively appealing'[162] to scholars attuned to the counter-majoritarian difficulty, it is not so appealing to litigants, who look to the courts for an authoritative ruling on what their rights require.[163] Allowing parliamentarians to reject judicial decisions they dislike, would be a cruel waste of time and energy for litigants who need an authoritative resolution of their constitutional claim.[164] Judges have a constitutional responsibility to litigants – and to the legal system as a whole – to resolve these cases in an authoritative, fair and impartial way. A regular legislative override of their decisions would undercut this responsibility.[165]

---

[156] Webber (2009) 457.
[157] Ibid 453.
[158] Beatson (2021) 117 (arguing that 'subject to being overruled by a higher court or a statute, a decision of a [UK] court is binding and cannot be ignored or set aside by anyone, and least of all by members of the government who disagree with it').
[159] Weinrib (1990) 569; Slattery (1987) 742; Kahana (2002) 244; Ahmed, Albert & Perry (2020) 1153–4.
[160] King (2015b) 123–4; Kahana (2002) 244.
[161] Newman (2019); King (2015b) 125.
[162] Kavanagh (2015a) 840.
[163] Kavanagh (2015a) 840; Sales (2016a) 469; Leckey (2015) 174.
[164] Newman (2019) 224; King (2015b) 123–4; Hickman (2010) 83–7.
[165] Van Zyl Smit (2015).

The upshot is that the legislative override is correctly conceived as a safety valve in exceptional circumstances, rather than a regular outlet for inter-institutional dialogue and disagreement about rights. Judicial decisions on rights should be treated as authoritative rulings, not advisory ruminations.[166] Indeed, this is what regularly happens in constitutional practice on both sides of the Atlantic. This does not deny the possibility – indeed, the legitimacy – of political override in some circumstances. But it nonetheless requires it to be reserved for rare and exceptional circumstances.[167]

When political actors comply with judicial decisions on what rights require, they are not acting on the basis of first-order reasons for agreeing with a particular ruling on rights. Nor are they motivated by the threat of political costs alone. Instead, they are acting on second-order institutional reasons to respect the work-product of a coordinate branch as part of a collaborative enterprise. Therefore, the question before the political actors is not simply whether they disagree with a particular court ruling, but rather whether the judicial decision is so egregiously wrong or so deeply contrary to the public interest that it warrants displacing the strong institutional presumption in favour of complying with those rulings as part of a working relationship based on comity and respect. The norms of comity and collaboration give the Executive and the legislature content-independent reasons for compliance with court rulings, just as the enactments of the democratic legislature give the courts content-independent reasons to comply with legislative enactments.[168] Mere disagreement is not sufficient to displace this constitutionally grounded presumption.

Once we situate the override in the context of the constructive working relationships between the branches of government, we can see that the legislature does not – and should not – have the kind of 'equal, revisory or dialogic role'[169] attributed to it by dialogue scholars. The relationship between the branches of government is not like a dialogue, where each branch offers an opinion about rights which the others can then evaluate and reject if they disagree. Instead of characterising the legislative

---

[166] Kumm (2017) 57.

[167] This explains why it is plausible to present the Charter rights which are open to override under section 33 as 'entrenched unless overridden by Parliament or a legislature', not that they are merely optional or non-obligatory, see Brosseau & Roy (2018) 2.

[168] Pozen (2014) 31; Schauer (2008) 1935–40.

[169] King (2019a) 186.

reluctance to use the override as evidence of 'legislative capitulation'[170] or even 'slavish submission'[171] to the courts, it can be understood otherwise, namely, as parliamentarians engaging their own responsibility to uphold rights, whilst simultaneously honouring their duties of comity towards a coordinate branch in a collaborative constitutional enterprise.

6 The Upshot of Understanding the Override

Once we accept that the underuse of the override is an epiphenomenal expression of the norms of respectful engagement between the branches of government in a collaborative scheme, a number of important consequences ensue. First, if the override is understood as a safety valve for cases of severe judicial malfunction, then the underuse of the override may be a constitutional success story, rather than an emblem of constitutional failure involving 'the tragic undermining'[172] of the override. Consistent non-use of the override may suggest that the override is operating exactly as it should, lying in wait for the rare or exceptional circumstance which would warrant its use.[173] If my boiler has worked well over the last twenty years without ever needing to release the safety valve, this does not mean that the safety valve is defective or defunct. It may simply mean that my boiler is working well *and* that the safety valve is functioning as a valuable fail-safe which will kick into action if excess pressure builds up at a future point. On this analysis, rare rather than regular use of the override may be lauded as a legitimate outworking of the collaborative constitutional order. It is evidence of Government Ministers and parliamentarians striving to respect rights, whilst simultaneously having due regard to the legitimate role of the courts in the joint enterprise of governing.

Second, if my analysis is correct, it is by no means a foregone conclusion that the override has 'atrophied'[174] or fallen into desuetude.[175] In an influential analysis, Adrian Vermeule has suggested that the underuse of

---

[170] Davis (2014a) 145.
[171] Webber (2009) 457.
[172] Newman (2019) 210; Gardbaum (2013b) 85 ('It is the non-use or underuse of deliberatively granted powers that threatens the distinctness and stability of the [New Commonwealth Model]').
[173] Kavanagh (2015c) 112–4; Kavanagh (2015a) 838.
[174] Vermeule (2012).
[175] Albert (2018); Gardbaum (2013b) 110; Huscroft (2007) 96.

the override represents the 'atrophy of constitutional powers',[176] borne out of a slippage in the modal status of the override power 'from optional to prohibited'[177] over time. But this allegation of atrophy and desuetude rests on a number of problematic premises. For one thing, it seems to presume that the override was originally conceived as a regular mode of inter-institutional dialogue and disagreement, which then lamentably – and somewhat mysteriously – 'fell' into desuetude or 'withered on the vine'.[178]

But a flourishing and vigorous practice of legislative override was never intended in either country. Nor did it ever take place. The true modal status of the power is – and always was – one of cautious and rare use, unless exceptional circumstances arose. To put it more bluntly, the true modal status is one of presumptive non-use, unless rebutted by strong and exceptional reasons to the contrary. The diagnosis of atrophy rests on a dichotomous choice between powers which are either 'optional' or 'prohibited'. But between these polarised possibilities lie a number of intermediary alternatives, such as 'permissible but not desirable on a regular basis'. The override occupies this more complex middle ground. It is available as an option in exceptional circumstances, but should be avoided in the normal run of constitutional affairs.

Third, my argument takes some distance from the commonplace scholarly plea to 'reinvigorate'[179] or 'reincarnate'[180] the override as a regular mechanism for ongoing dialogue and disagreement between legislatures and courts.[181] I oppose such a 'reincarnation' because it would violate the norms of comity and collaboration, upsetting the differentiated division of labour on which the collaborative constitution depends. Indeed, on my analysis, a practice of regular override would not be a matter of 'reinstating' or 'reviving' anything, but rather of inculcating a novel practice of ongoing legislative disagreement with court rulings on rights, which would violate core elements of the constitutional separation of powers.[182] Therefore, a liberal use of the override is less like a 'reincarnation' and more like the dawning of a new constitutional day – and not a good day at

---

[176] Vermeule (2012); Davis (2014a) 144.
[177] Vermeule (2012) 426.
[178] Davis (2014a) 148.
[179] Davis (2014a) 137–50; Davis (2010) 91, 93, 96.
[180] Albert (2008).
[181] Gardbaum (2013b) 89–90 (advocating 'norms for the legitimate exercise of the legislative power of the final word' in New Commonwealth systems).
[182] King (2015b) 120–4; Hickman (2010) 83–7.

that. The argument of this chapter has been that the inauguration of such a practice would in fact corrode fundamental constitutional norms, rather than usher in a new era of desirable democratic constitutionalism.

Fourth, and relatedly, my analysis also casts doubt on recommendations made by Jeremy Waldron, Jeffrey Goldsworthy, Stephen Gardbaum and Richard Albert that we should amend section 33 of the Canadian Charter in order to reinvigorate the override as a legitimate mode of political disagreement with court rulings on rights.[183] For these scholars, section 33 forces political actors to present themselves as *antagonists* of rights, whereas the truth of the matter is that they are *advocates* of one particular, albeit controversial, understanding of rights.[184] Therefore, they argue that section 33 should be amended to signal the true position, namely, that elected politicians are engaged in legitimate and reasonable 'rights disagreements' with the courts, without harbouring illegitimate 'rights misgivings'.[185]

There are serious problems with this recommendation. For one thing, the issue of whether legislators or governments harbour 'rights misgivings' rather than 'rights disagreements' is an empirical question whose answer will most likely be mixed in any system. Even in relatively well-functioning systems, politicians may have serious misgivings about rights, especially in relation to vilified groups such as prisoners, terrorists, rapists, immigrants, and others. Consider Prime Minister David Cameron's statement in the Westminster Parliament that it would make him 'physically ill'[186] to give prisoners the right to vote, or the Quebec government's ban on religious symbols in public employment.[187] In this context, the language of 'misgivings' is putting it mildly. Therefore, we cannot posit a legislative preference for reasonable 'rights disagreements' as a philosophical prior. There is typically a much wider array of political motivations and orientations towards rights than Waldron's optimistic assessment allows.[188]

Even accepting *arguendo* that legislatures are typically committed to rights, it is difficult to see how amending section 33 to clarify that

---

[183] Waldron (2004) 37–8; Gardbaum (2013b) 90; Goldsworthy (2003b) 467; Albert (2018) 154–5.

[184] Albert (2018) 1054.

[185] Waldron (2004) 37–8.

[186] HC Deb 3 November 2010, vol 517 col 921 (David Cameron).

[187] Leckey (2019a) 2–3 (presenting Quebec's invocation of the override as a 'choice to opt out of the business of protecting rights'); Lake (2022).

[188] King (2015b) 120–1

legislators simply disagree with the judicial interpretation would succeed in legitimising its enhanced use. Whilst the distinction between 'rights disagreements' and 'rights misgivings' may gain some traction in the cerebral atmosphere of an academic seminar, it is unlikely to have any serious purchase in the charged political dynamics surrounding a potential legislative override of a judicial decision.[189] In that context, the distinction would be torn apart by the political opposition, the media, and rights campaigners.[190]

But the deepest problem with this recommendation is that it runs contrary to the deeply held self-understandings of the key political actors in both the Canadian and UK constitutional culture, who do not see their constitutional role as one of advancing alternative conceptions of rights in an ongoing dialogue about what rights require.[191] Instead, they view their role as requiring them to respect court rulings on rights, whilst working from those judicial decisions to devise a suitable remedy for rights violations.[192] As argued earlier, political actors have second-order reasons to comply with court rulings which are independent from, and more fundamental than, whether they agree or disagree with a particular judicial decision. In order to understand the operation of the override, we need to move 'beyond disagreement'[193] as the emblematic mode of interaction between legislatures and courts, engaging more deeply with the norms and constraints under which both courts and legislatures labour as part of the collaborative constitutional endeavour.

7 Conclusion

The aim of this chapter was to solve the mystery of the underuse of the override. Departing from the dominant narrative that the override was tragically thwarted by political costs, I argued that these costs were deliberately hardwired into the system to forestall its frequent use. Locating the override in the broader context of the constitutional roles

---

[189] Newman (2019) 220 (arguing that Waldron's proposal would also face difficulties 'in the realm of practical constitutional drafting').
[190] Kavanagh (2015a) 838.
[191] King (2015a) 176.
[192] Ibid 176.
[193] Sathanapally (2012).

and relationships between the branches of government, I argued that it should be viewed – and generally *is* viewed in Canada and the UK – as a safety valve for exceptional circumstances to be used with caution and care, rather than as a regular mode of dialogue and disagreement between legislatures and courts.

In telling this deeper story, I did not discount the vitally important role of political costs in constraining political behaviour and inhibiting a more liberal use of the override. But I put those costs in perspective, presenting them as a useful means of bolstering and undergirding the underlying norms. Whilst the dominant narrative on the override emphasised the political costs from without, it overlooked the constitutional norms which shape political behaviour from within. By focusing on the lively first-order disagreement between legislatures and courts about rights, it underplayed the second-order institutional norms which shape and constrain the interaction between the branches of government in the crucible of constitutional practice.

This goes to the larger point that in order to understand constitutional phenomena, we must supplement our reading of constitutional texts with an appreciation of constitutional culture. The Canadian Charter and UK Human Rights Act gave their respective legislatures the *power* – the option – of overriding judicial decisions on rights. But the unwritten norms and practices of the collaborative constitution gave them a *responsibility* to exercise that power with caution and due regard for their partners in authority.[194] The power to override was 'coupled with a duty to act with care and comity'.[195]

Ironically, my argument in favour of a rare rather regular use of the override gives political actors more credence as 'pro-constitutional actors'[196] than those scholars who champion regular legislative override of courts. After all, those scholars portray legislators as being afflicted by chronic political passivity due to a false consciousness concerning judicial supremacy on the one hand, and raw calculations of political self-interest and preservation on the other. This chapter turns that argument on its head, suggesting that *despite* being given the formal legal power to override court rulings on rights, Canadian and UK legislatures have

---

[194] Pozen (2014) 39; Halberstam (2004).
[195] Levi (1976) 391.
[196] Jackson (2016).

generally succeeded in honouring their constitutional commitment to rights, whilst respecting the role of the courts in the joint enterprise of governing.[197] The underuse of the override, therefore, reflects well on legislatures on both sides of the Atlantic. It is to their credit, not their chagrin.

---

[197] Gearty (2016) 73.

12

Declarations, Obligations, Collaborations

1 Introduction

When the HRA was enacted, the declaration of incompatibility was viewed as an ingenious way of allowing the courts to give a reasoned view about whether legislation violated Convention rights, without placing the government or legislature under a legal obligation to comply with that assessment. But legal obligations do not exhaust the category of binding constitutional norms in the British constitutional order. Declarations could be binding as a matter of constitutional convention and political morality, if not in law. Therefore, one key question which arises is whether there is a constitutional convention of compliance with declarations of incompatibility. The aim of this chapter is to answer that question.

Based on a forensic examination of all the parliamentary debates on every remedial response to a section 4 declaration since 1998, together with relevant government documents, JCHR Reports, political statements to the media, and political memoir and autobiography, I conclude that parliamentarians at Westminster typically treat declarations of incompatibility as authoritative judicial rulings they are obliged to respect, not optional ruminations they are entitled to reject. Echoing the insightful findings of previous empirical analysis,[1] I argue that the political response to declarations of incompatibility has been predominantly collaborative rather than conflictual in nature.[2] I also discern a constitutional convention *in statu nascendi* that parliamentarians should normally comply with a judicial declaration unless exceptional circumstances arise. Whilst this convention allows for the possibility of ignoring or overriding a declaratory ruling in rare and exceptional circumstances, the default position –

---

[1] King (2015a) 182–6; Sathanapally (2012) chapters 6–9; Crawford (2013); Chandrachud (2017) 105–8, 113–15; Young (2011).
[2] King (2015a) 167, 176, 187; King (2021) [28], [46]; Sathanapally (2012) 224.

and the constitutional expectation – is that the political actors should remedy the declared incompatibility in some form. As I will show, parliamentarians of all political stripes believe themselves to be under an obligation to do so.[3]

The chapter will proceed in the following way. Part 2 begins by defining constitutional conventions. Using that definition, Part 3 goes on to sketch out the main pattern of political response to declarations of incompatibility. Part 4 mines the government's Annual Report to the JCHR on *Responding to Human Rights Judgments*[4] for evidence of the government's attitude to declarations of incompatibility. Part 5 explores the political responses to all declarations of incompatibility since the HRA was enacted, arguing that the vast majority of such declarations were both politically and legally uncontroversial, eliciting a general political attitude of workaday acceptance and willing compliance. Part 6 showcases some examples of an open and welcoming response. Part 7 provides a forensic examination of the four most controversial declarations of incompatibility since the HRA was enacted. Even in a context of acute controversy on the merits, my analysis reveals ample evidence of a strong normative commitment to comply with declarations of incompatibility. Drawing the strands of analysis together, Part 8 concludes that there is an emerging constitutional convention of compliance with declarations of incompatibility, albeit one of a general and qualified kind.

2   Uncovering Conventions

a   What Are Conventions?

Writing in the nineteenth century, Albert Venn Dicey famously described conventions as 'a body . . . of constitutional or political ethics';[5] 'a whole system of political morality . . . maxims or practices which . . . regulate the ordinary conduct of the Crown, of Ministers, and of other persons under the constitution'.[6] Though these norms of political morality are legally non-binding and non-justiciable, they are binding as a

---

[3] King (2015a) 167.

[4] Ministry of Justice, *Responding to Human Rights Judgments: Report to the JCHR on the Government's Response to Human Rights Judgments 2021–2022* (December 2022), hereafter MoJ Report (2022) or 'the Report'.

[5] Dicey (1964) 417; Marshall (1984) 10–12.

[6] Dicey (1964) 24.

matter of 'constitutional morality'.[7] Indeed, as Dicey astutely observed, these norms are often obeyed 'as rigorously as the commands of law'.[8] In contemporary times, conventions are described as 'the basic ground rules of constitutional practice,'[9] the constitutional rules of the game which 'regulate the relations between the different parts of our constitution'[10] and are 'accepted as obligatory by those concerned in the working of the constitution'.[11]

The most influential analysis of conventions in UK constitutional law was provided by Sir Ivor Jennings, who posited a three-part test for identifying a constitutional convention: (1) there must be past precedent or practice of compliance with the rule; (2) the rule must be treated as binding or obligatory; and (3) there must be a good reason for the rule.[12] Still accepted today, the 'Jennings test' clarifies that constitutional conventions require regular action combined with a sense of 'normative obligation'.[13] Using this test, can we say that there is a constitutional convention of compliance with declarations of incompatibility? Chapter 11 provided a number of 'reasons for the rule', explaining why political actors *ought* to adopt a presumption of compliance with declarations of incompatibility. This leaves us to concentrate on the first two limbs in this chapter: regular practice and normative obligation. Starting with the first: is there a past practice of compliance?

b   Regular Practice

Thus far, there have been thirty-four final declarations of incompatibility and there has been a near-perfect – if not perfect – pattern of compliance with those declarations.[14] This track record is all the more remarkable when we consider that Parliament benefits from the burden of inertia. By

---

[7] Ibid 24; Freeman (1872) 109; Mill (1861) 87 (describing the 'unwritten maxims of the Constitution' as 'the positive political morality of the country'); Hood Phillips (1966); Vermeule (2015) 284; though cf. Ahmed, Albert & Perry (2019).

[8] Dicey (1964) 21.

[9] Lord Wilson of Dinton (2004) 420.

[10] Ibid 409; McHarg (2008) 859; Morton (1991) 121; Marshall (1984) 2; Willis (2018) 255; Barendt (1998) 40–2; Jaconelli (1999) 44.

[11] Willis (2018) 255; Wheare (1951) 179; Marshall (1984) 7, 11; Hood Phillips (1978) 104–5.

[12] Jennings (1959) 136; McLean (2013) 21.

[13] Vermeule (2015) 287; Jennings (1959) 135; Albert (2018) 150; Ellickson (1991) 183.

[14] MoJ Report (2022) 35ff (There have been forty-four DoIs in total, though ten have been overturned on appeal. The MoJ lists all forty-four declarations, whereas I focus only those which were final and not overturned).

simply doing nothing and ignoring the declaration, Parliament can maintain the *status quo ante*.[15] Nonetheless, the government and legislature have consistently taken positive action to overcome this burden, remedying the rights-violation identified by the courts, even in the face of countervailing political incentives and electoral pay-offs to do otherwise.[16]

The only possible exception to the regular pattern of compliance concerns the declaration of incompatibility on prisoner voting handed down by the Scottish Registration Appeal Court in *Smith v Scott*,[17] following the Strasbourg ruling in *Hirst v UK*.[18] The involutions of the prisoner voting saga will be examined later in the chapter. Suffice it to say here that this issue was exceptional in many ways. The key political focus was on the UK's relationship with the Strasbourg court, not the government's relationship with domestic courts.[19] Moreover, the UK government has now introduced some minor administrative changes to relax the blanket ban on prisoner voting in order to meet its obligations under the ECHR,[20] and the Council of Europe has accepted them as such.[21] Therefore, it is possible to code the prisoner voting case as one of compliance with a declaration of incompatibility. If so, then we have a rate of 100 per cent compliance with every declaration of incompatibility since the HRA was enacted.

Even if we code the prisoner voting case as an (exceptional) example of non-compliance, this does not necessarily undercut the existence of a convention. Most commentators accept that complete uniformity of action is not required in order to establish a constitutional convention, and one exception does not undo the norm.[22] The requirement is one of regular, not inveterate or exceptionless, conformity with the rule. In fact, many conventions are expressed in terms of what should 'normally' but not invariably occur, thus allowing for exceptional cases to justify

---

[15] Bateup (2009) 569–70; Vermeule (2012) 442; Sathanapally (2012) 24; Kahana (2002) 250–1.

[16] Vermeule (2012) 442.

[17] *Smith v Scott* [2007] CSIH 9.

[18] *Hirst v UK* [2006] ECHR 681.

[19] Crawford (2013) 77; Kavanagh (2015c) 1026; Kavanagh (2015d) 1050–1.

[20] *Smith v Scott* (n 17); MoJ Report (2022) 46.

[21] Johnston & Brown (2023) 1, 3, 16–17.

[22] Jaconelli (2005) 153, 165–6; Munro (1999) 81; Heard (1991) 143–4, 146; Heard (2012) 326, 331; Taylor (2014) 325; Vermeule (2013) 1186–9.

departure from the expected norm.[23] Therefore, even if we categorise the prisoner voting case as an instance of non-compliance, this does not necessarily belie the existence of a convention. Either way, the overall picture still reveals a near-uniform trend of regular and ongoing compliance with declarations of incompatibility over a period of two decades. Given that trend, we may assume that the 'regular practice' component of the Jennings test is met.

c Normative Obligation

What about a sense of normative obligation? Getting a reliable answer to this question is more difficult. It poses significant evidentiary and analytical challenges. For one thing, when ethical standards are deeply internalised by political actors, their relevance and obligatory force may be taken for granted and, therefore, not expressed in explicit – let alone explicitly normative – terms.[24] They become 'the done thing' – the givens of any organisation, so obviously and widely accepted that they are 'taken for granted' and 'go without saying'.[25] Ironically, then, it is precisely when norms are deeply internalised in this way that there is no explicitly articulated record of their operative force.

A further complication is that conforming to a convention may be observationally equivalent to habitual behaviour devoid of any normative dimension, or even to forced behaviour driven by fear of sanctions or political costs.[26] Moreover, political actors may claim to be acting 'out of deeply felt principles of political morality'[27] in order to mask their real motives, including a desire to garner favour with the electorate, to save their political skin, or claim political cover for unpopular decisions. Given the complexity of political life, we should probably expect both

---

[23] For example, 'the Sewel convention' states that the Westminster Parliament will not 'normally' legislate for the devolved regions with the consent of the relevant devolved legislature, section 28(7) of the Scotland Act 1998; Hazell (2015) 174–5; Poirier (2001) 153; see also the emerging convention that there should be a parliamentary debate before going to war, 'except when there was an emergency and such action would not be appropriate', Cabinet Manual 2011, para 5.38; Hazell (2015) 183. On the openness of some conventions to deviation in some cases, see further Jennings (1959) 135; Marshall & Moodie (1967) 25; Munro (1999) 82–6.

[24] Feldman (2013) 95; Vermeule (2013) 288.

[25] Bicchieri (2006) 4ff; Levinson (2011) 691; Pozen (2014) 69–70.

[26] Jaconelli (1999) 30; Heard (1991) 14; Levinson (2011) 734; Vermeule (2013) 1185.

[27] See Feldman (2013) 103; Vermeule (2013) 1163.

mixed messages and mixed motives, where seasoned politicians will combine raw politicking, enlightened self-interest, and a sense of constitutional obligation as reasons for political action.[28] Therefore, we need to tread carefully when striving to uncover conventions, alert to the role of political rhetoric in public life.[29] Bearing this in mind, we can now turn to examine the practice and principles surrounding the political response to declarations of incompatibility.

3 Patterns of Political Response

When a declaration of incompatibility is issued, the government has four main options. The first option is to do nothing. Since the HRA places no legal obligation on either the government or the legislature following a declaration of incompatibility, doing nothing is an obvious possibility. The second is to affirmatively state that it will not remedy the incompatibility identified by the courts. Again, with no legal obligation to comply with the declaration, an explicit rejection of the declaration is not precluded by the terms of the HRA.

The third option is to use the fast-track amendment procedure set out in section 10 HRA, which empowers a Government Minister to use a 'Remedial Order' to 'make such amendments to the legislation as he considers necessary to remove the incompatibility'.[30] Remedial orders must be laid before Parliament for an affirmative resolution, but they are generally less cumbersome than the ordinary legislative response.[31] The fourth option is to amend the legislation using the normal legislative process, either by enacting an entirely new statute to respond to the declaration of incompatibility ('whole act responses') or by tacking a provision onto an existing bill ('tacking responses').[32]

So which options have the government and Parliament taken following a declaration of incompatibility? First, there have been no cases where the political branches have simply done nothing following a declaration of incompatibility. Whilst there have been considerable delays in remedial action, as well as some evidence of minimal and

---

[28] Bradley & Ewing (2011) 26; Heard (2012) 323.
[29] Schauer (2013) 1191 (analysing the 'complex rhetorical terrain' in which political claims of legality are made); Huq (2012).
[30] Section 10 HRA 1998.
[31] Schedule 2 HRA 1998; though see Feldman (2021); King (2021) [35]–[38].
[32] I adopt this nomenclature following King (2015a) 167.

'begrudging compliance',[33] some remedial action has always ensued.[34] Second, there have been no cases where the Government has openly repudiated a declaration of incompatibility or made an unequivocal statement that it will not comply with the declaration issued by the higher courts.[35]

Again, the prisoner voting issue may offer a possible counter-example here, given that then Prime Minister, David Cameron, made a statement in the House of Commons (five years after the declaration of incompatibility in *Smith v Scott*[36]) that 'prisoners are not getting the vote under this government'.[37] But this statement was directed towards the Strasbourg decision in *Hirst*, not the domestic declaration in *Smith v Scott*. Therefore, it is not a clear instance of affirmative denunciation of a declaration of incompatibility. Moreover, it is ambiguous. Whilst the Prime Minister emphasised that prisoners would not get the vote under '*this* government', that does not deny that the United Kingdom is under an international law obligation to implement the ruling. Nor does it necessarily contradict the existence of a constitutional obligation to remedy the rights violation declared by the court. As I will show later in the chapter, the prisoner voting saga does not provide a clear-cut example of political defiance of a declaration of incompatibility under the HRA.

Of the thirty-four final declarations of incompatibility, eight were remedied using the 'fast track' remedial order procedure under section 10 HRA.[38] Although there has been an increased reliance on Remedial Orders in recent years, they have not become the standard or default method of implementation. Eighteen declarations were remedied using the ordinary legislative process, most of which were 'tacking'[39] rather than 'whole Act responses'.[40] In five cases, the government and Parliament changed the law before the final declaration was even issued,

---

[33] Hillebrecht (2014) 14, 21; Chandrachud (2017) 114–22; Kavanagh (2015c) 1025.
[34] On 'minimal compliance', see King (2015a); Chandrachud (2017) 114; Hillebrecht (2014) 99. On the problem of delay, see King (2015a) 168–71; King (2021) [39]–[44]; Van Zyl Smit (2011) 75–6.
[35] King (2015a) 167.
[36] *Smith v Scott* (n 17).
[37] Wintour & Sparrow (2012).
[38] MoJ Report (2022) 45; King (2021) [35]ff.
[39] King (2015a) 167.
[40] Ibid 167.

either because the declaration was preceded by an adverse ruling from Strasbourg and/or because the required legal reform is widely accepted as necessary, desirable, and uncontroversial.[41] We can call these 'pre-emptive responses'. The prisoner voting issue was remedied by making administrative changes. Of the four most recent declarations, we await remedial action. However, the Government has publicly committed to remedying three of them by Remedial Order, whilst the most recent declaration is still 'under consideration' as the Government works out how to address it.[42]

The practice of compliance is thus strikingly consistent over time. The crucial question, then, is how the political actors view these declarations from 'the internal point of view'? In particular, how do they describe and appraise their conduct once a declaration of incompatibility had been issued by the courts? In order to get purchase on this issue, I begin by examining the Annual Report of the Ministry of Justice, which documents the government's response to all declarations since the HRA was enacted.

4   Institutionalising a Compliance-Oriented Approach

When a declaration of incompatibility is issued by the higher courts, this triggers a formal response from the JCHR, which then prompts the government to explain how it plans to respond to the declaration of incompatibility. In recent years, the government has formalised its response to declarations of incompatibility, by publishing the Ministry of Justice's Annual Report to the JCHR on *Responding to Human Rights Judgments*.[43] This Report documents the political response to every declaration of incompatibility since the HRA was enacted and therefore provides a good source of evidence about 'the government's position on the implementation of adverse human rights judgments from ... the domestic courts'.[44]

---

[41] MoJ Report (2022) 43.

[42] Ibid 43. The most recent declaration concerns the DoI *In Re JR111 for Judicial Review* [2021] NIQB 48, 13 May 2021, which held that the requirement on applicants for a Gender Recognition Certificate to provide that they suffer from a 'disorder', violates Convention rights.

[43] MoJ Report (2022).

[44] Ibid 3.

In the Report, declarations of incompatibility are described as 'adverse human rights judgments',[45] which provide 'a notification to Parliament that the legislation is incompatible with the Convention rights'.[46] Whilst the Report states that there is 'no legal obligation on the Government to take remedial action following a declaration of incompatibility',[47] it nonetheless highlights the UK's 'longstanding tradition of ensuring our rights and liberties are protected domestically and of fulfilling our international human rights obligations'.[48] It also affirms that

> the Government will continue to protect and respect human rights and liberties both domestically, and through our international obligations. We will maintain our leading role in the promotion and protection of human rights, democracy, and the rule of law.[49]

The Report also emphasises the Government's commitment to 'constructive engagement with the UK's national human rights institutions and interested non-governmental organisations',[50] as well as the compliance machinery of the Council of Europe.

Under the heading 'Coordination of implementation', the Report notes that 'Lead responsibility for implementation of an adverse judgment rests with the relevant Government Department for each case, whilst the Ministry of Justice provides light-touch coordination of the process'.[51] When a new declaration of incompatibility is issued, the relevant Government Department is 'expected to bring it to the Joint Committee's attention',[52] and is 'encourage[d] ... to update the Joint Committee regularly on their plans for responding to declarations of incompatibility'.[53] The Report acknowledges that the implementation of declaratory judgments 'may require changes to legislation, policy, practice, or a combination of these'.[54] Every year, the Report contains updates on outstanding declarations since the previous Report, thereby providing some ongoing public accountability for the government's record of compliance with declarations of incompatibility.

---

[45] Ibid 5.
[46] Ibid 5.
[47] Ibid 5.
[48] Ibid 5.
[49] Ibid 7.
[50] Ibid 7.
[51] Ibid 5.
[52] Ibid 6.
[53] Ibid 6.
[54] Ibid 4.

The overall tenor of the Ministry of Justice's Annual Report is one of 'workaday acceptance'[55] of declarations of incompatibility, together with a general expectation that the Government will comply with each declaration in due course. The Report proceeds on the working assumption that the Government will remedy rights-violations declared by the domestic courts, just as it will address adverse rulings in Strasbourg. No mention is made of the prospect of rejecting or disregarding declarations, and no formal provision is made for that eventuality. If a declaration of incompatibility is left unremedied, it will eventually appear on the list of adverse rulings which the UK is obliged to implement as a matter of international law.

5   Willing Compliance, Workaday Acceptance

For a constitutional convention to exist, there should be evidence of the key political actors (a) commending conformity with the requisite norm, (b) criticising breaches, and (c) using normative language to articulate a sense of obligation to comply with it.[56] When we examine political responses to declarations of incompatibility, is there a pattern of commendation, critique, and normative endorsement?

We can start by noting that the vast majority of declarations were neither politically controversial nor legally remarkable. Of the thirty declarations which have received a remedial response to date, twenty-six were uncontentious. They had a low political salience both inside and outside Parliament, and were implemented by the government and legislature 'without passion or hatred, *sine ira et studio*'.[57] Echoing the tone of the Annual Report, the predominant political attitude towards these declarations was one of willing compliance and 'workaday acceptance'.[58]

When a declaration is issued, a typical pattern is for the relevant Government Minister to make an announcement to Parliament stating that the government is 'carefully considering the full implications of the ruling'[59] and is working out how to implement it. If the government has

[55] King (2015a) 176.
[56] Hart (2012) 56–7, 115, 257; Green (2012) xxi; Shapiro (2016) 1157.
[57] King (2015a) 176; Sathanapally (2012) 224.
[58] King (2015a) 176.
[59] HC Deb 5 September 2018, vol 646 col 188 (Justin Tomlinson), following the DoI in *Re McLaughlin* [2018] UKSC 48.

already decided on remedial action, it will typically give an undertaking to 'rectify the incompatibility',[60] either 'by means of a Remedial Order'[61] or through ordinary legislative amendment, in order 'to ensure that [the law] is compatible with the court judgment'.[62]

Baroness Andrews' statement to the House of Lords following the declarations in *Morris* and *Gabaj*[63] is typical in this regard. Following declarations that the *Housing Act 1996* failed to respect the right to family life by excluding consideration of dependent children with immigrant status in determining priorities for social housing, Baroness Andrews announced:

> We have acknowledged the court's declarations ... and we are now bringing forward the necessary changes in these amendments to ensure that such British citizens and their families who are currently not getting help will be entitled to accommodation.[64]

The majority of declarations have been politically uncontentious and, therefore, have had a 'low profile' in Parliament and beyond.[65] For the majority of such declarations, the necessity and desirability of legal reform is widely accepted across the political spectrum as 'clearly necessary'[66] and desirable in the circumstances. Thus, when introducing a Remedial Order to remove discriminatory provisions of the British National Act 1981, which had prevented the children of unmarried parents from acquiring British citizenship, the Minister for Immigration observed:

> In this day and age, I think we can all agree that the law should not discriminate against people simply because their parents were not married

---

[60] Grand Committee HL Deb 12 December 2018, vol 794 col 104GC (Lord O'Shaughnessy), following the DoI in *Re Z (A Child) (no. 2)* [2016] EWHC 1191 (Fam).

[61] Grand Committee HL Deb 12 December 2018, vol 794 col 104GC (Lord O'Shaughnessy).

[62] HL Deb 14 December 2016, vol 777 col 1331 (Baroness Chisholm of Owlpen), following the DoI in the *Human Fertilisation and Embryology Act 2008*.

[63] *R (Morris) v Westminster City Council* [2005] EWCA Civ 1184 and *R (Gabaj) v First Secretary of State* (Administrative Court 28 March 2006, unreported); Sathanapally (2012) 149–52.

[64] HL Deb 23 June 2008, vol 702 col GC523 (Baroness Andrews).

[65] Sathanapally (2012) 138ff; King (2015a) 171.

[66] HL Deb 11 April 2002, vol 633 col 603–7 (Baroness Noakes) (concerning the Mental Health Act 1983 (Remedial) Order 2001).

when they were born ... This legislation will correct incompatibilities identified by the domestic courts.[67]

It was important to ensure that 'the incompatibilities found by the courts are addressed.[68]

In some cases, parliamentarians have observed that the required legal change following a declaration was 'not out of line with the thrust of government policy intentions'.[69] In others, the prospect of changing the law was already on the political radar. In many cases, remedial action involved a relatively simple, straightforward and uncontroversial amendment of existing legislation, which was accepted across both Houses of Parliament without division or dissent.[70]

There are multiple examples where parliamentarians have described declarations of incompatibility as obligatory and binding. Many parliamentarians have stated that the declaration '*requires* action by Government to remedy an incompatibility'[71] or that it is 'clearly *necessary* for the Government to remedy the incompatibility'.[72] When introducing the Gender Recognition Bill following the declaration of incompatibility in *Bellinger* on transsexual marriage, David Lammy MP explained to the House of Commons: 'Their Lordships stated that transsexual people do not have [the right to marry] at present and that legislation would be *required* to ensure that they do.'[73] The language of obligation is also often echoed in questions from Opposition MPs or other parliamentarians, who press the Government to explain 'how and how soon they will rectify what they are *required to do* under that

---

[67] HC Deb 23 July 2019, vol 633 col 1242 (Caroline Nokes), responding to the DoI in *R (Fenton Bangs) v SSHD* Administrative Court, 4 July 2017.

[68] HC Deb 23 July 2019, vol 633 col 1242.

[69] HL Deb 1 April 2002, vol 633 col 601 (Labour Government Whip, Lord Filkin); HC Deb 28 October 2002, vol 391 col 627 (Jean Corston), following the declaration in *R (H) v London North and East Region Mental Health Review Tribunal* [2001] EWCA Civ 415.

[70] The JCHR observed that the legislative response following the declaration of incompatibility in *R (Clift) v Secretary of State for the Home Department* [2007] 1 AC 484 as a 'simple' remedy to a 'straightforward legal problem'; see JCHR (2008) Thirty-first Report, Monitoring the Government's Response to Human Rights Judgments: Annual Report 2008 (31 October 2008), HL 173/HC 1078 [107].

[71] HL Deb 11 April 2002, vol 663 col 601 (Lord Filkin) (emphasis added).

[72] HL Deb 11 April 2002, vol 663 col 603 (following the DoI in *H v London North and East Region Mental Health Review Tribunal* (n 69)) (Baroness Noakes); Crawford (2013) 48.

[73] HC Deb 23 February 2004, vol 418 col 52 (emphasis added), following the DoI in *Bellinger v Bellinger* [2003] UKHL 21.

judgment'[74] or 'why it is taking us so long to rectify an anomaly identified by our courts'.[75] If a declaration is still under consideration by the time the Ministry of Justice publishes its Annual Report to the JCHR, the Report may state that 'The Government is considering appropriate legislative options to address the issue raised in this case',[76] or that the 'Government announced its intention to take forward a Remedial Order'.[77] If remedial action is slow in coming, the relevant Minister may write to the JCHR 'to assure the Committee that the Government intends to remedy the incompatibility as quickly as possible'.[78]

When introducing legal measures to comply with a declaration of incompatibility, MPs and Peers typically present declarations as authoritative legal determinations that legislation violates human rights law. For example, following the declaration of incompatibility in *Re McLaughlin*,[79] the relevant Government Minister stated: 'We recognise that we currently have incompatible law on the statute books and we are actively considering all options';[80] 'we now know that the legal union requirement violates the human rights of children born to parents who are neither married nor in a civil partnership.'[81] The only question, then, was how to 'correct', 'remedy', or 'rectify the incompatibility'[82] identified by the court in order to ensure that the law is 'compatible with the court judgment'.[83]

When proposing legislative changes in response to declarations of incompatibility, both MPs and Peers regularly present themselves as motivated to 'correct incompatibilities in primary legislation ... and to ensure that the incompatibilities found by the courts are addressed'.[84] In some cases, parliamentarians accept that a declaration of incompatibility

---

[74] HL Deb 14 December 2016, vol 777 col 1331 (Viscount Craigavon) (emphasis added), following the DoI in *Re Z (A Child) (no. 2)* (n 60).

[75] HL Deb 23 July 2019, vol 799 col 699 (Lord Dholakia), following the DoI in *R (Johnson) v SSHD* [2016] UKSC 56, and Consent Order in *Fenton Bangs v SSHD* (n 67).

[76] MoJ Report (2021) 42, concerning *K (A Child) v Secretary of State for the Home Department* [2018] EWHC 1834.

[77] MoJ Report (2021) 42, concerning *Re McLaughlin* [2018] UKSC 48.

[78] JCHR (2006) Appendix 4 (Letter from Yvette Cooper to the JCHR dated 28 June 2006, responding to *R (Morris) v Westminster City Council* [2006] 1 WLR 505); Crawford (2013) 71.

[79] *Re McLaughlin* (n 77).

[80] HC Deb 23 January 2019, vol 653 col 151 (Liz Roberts).

[81] Ibid (Liz Roberts).

[82] HC Deb 15 June 2020, vol 677 col 605 (Chris Philip).

[83] HL Deb 14 December 2016, vol 777 col 1331 (Baroness Chisholm of Owlpen).

[84] HL Deb 3 September 2020, vol 805 col 75GC (Baroness Scott of Bybrook).

reveals an 'injustice', which the Government 'will do all [it] can to remedy'.[85] When responding to a declaration that the automatic disclosure of some criminal records to employers violated Article 8 ECHR,[86] Ministers stated that they wished to 'bring about a system to enact the observations in the ruling by the Supreme Court, but to do so in a way that keeps the purpose of the regime in place' emphasising that they were 'careful to ensure that [they were] following the guidance in that ruling'.[87]

Viewed in the round, the general pattern of political response is accepting not antagonistic, collaborative not conflictual.[88] Across the vast swathe of political responses to declarations of incompatibility, there is little or no mention of defying the declaration. The general focus is on *how* to implement the declarations of incompatibility, not *whether* to do so.[89]

6   An Open and Welcoming Response

Whilst the general trend is one of routine implementation and 'workaday acceptance',[90] there are some declarations which have elicited a positively welcoming and enthusiastic response. For example, after the High Court held that the Human Fertilisation and Embryology Act 1990 violated Convention rights by preventing a deceased father's name appearing on the birth certificate of his child following artificial insemination in *Blood and Tarbuck*,[91] the Minister for Health announced that the Government was 'absolutely committed to remedying legislation as quickly as possible'.[92] Whilst the declaration of incompatibility provided

> 'an additional impetus to change the law ... fundamentally, the Bill represents the right thing to do, the decent thing to do, for those mothers and their children who find themselves in these tragic circumstances'.[93]

---

[85] HC Deb 12 February 2020, vol 671 col 852 (PM Boris Johnson), following the DoI in *R (Jackson) v Secretary of State for Work and Pensions* [2020] EWHC 183, which held that the failure to extend bereavement support payments to unmarried fathers violated Convention rights.

[86] See eg *R (G) v Constable of Surrey Police* [2019] UKSC 3.

[87] HC Deb 14 September 2020, Debate of the Delegated Legislation Committee on the Draft Rehabilitation of Offenders Act 1974 (Exceptions) Order 1975 (Victoria Atkins MP).

[88] Sathanapally (2012) 224; King (2015a) 176; King (2021) [46]–[47].

[89] Sathanapally (2012) 131; King (2021) [33]; Chandrachud (2017) 83.

[90] King (2015a) 176.

[91] *Blood and Tarbuck v Secretary of State for Health*, Unreported 28 February 2003, Sullivan J.

[92] HL Deb 23 June 2008, vol 702 col 522GC (Baroness Andrews).

[93] HC Deb 28 March 2003, vol 403 col 609 (Chris Grayling); Sathanapally (2012) 177–8; Chandrachud (2017) 78.

Similarly, when the Human Fertilisation and Embryology (Deceased Fathers) Bill was introduced to Parliament to remedy the violation, there was cross-party consensus that 'the 1990 Act is in breach of the Convention and needs to be corrected'[94] – 'as quickly as Parliament will allow'[95] – with many MPs affirming that the substance of the Bill was 'absolutely right'.[96] As Chris Grayling MP observed,

> this Bill represents a crucial opportunity for the House to put right earlier attempts to deal with such legislation. That is long overdue and, in reality, what we are doing is righting a wrong.[97]

A similarly open and welcoming response was legible in the debates following the declaration of incompatibility in *Morris* and *Gabaj*,[98] where many MPs and Peers described the legislative amendment following the declaration of incompatibility as 'undo[ing] a serious injustice that has afflicted Gypsies and Travellers for too long'.[99]

In these cases, the declarations of incompatibility can function as 'door openers for marginalised issues',[100] raising them up the legislative agenda and jump-starting legislative action and engagement.[101] But once the door is opened, the political actors then take ownership of the resulting policy change as valuable in its own terms.

For example, following the declaration of incompatibility in *Steinfeld and Keidan*[102] that the exclusion of heterosexual couples from civil partnerships was discriminatory, the Minister proposing the Bill to remedy the incompatibility praised the claimants in the case for pioneering 'equal civil partnerships' and for triggering the campaign to achieve it.[103] The political response was so willing in this case that the Private Member's Bill was started before the issue even reached the Supreme Court. By the time the Supreme Court issued its declaration of

---

[94] HC Deb 28 March 2003, vol 402 col 604 (Tony Clarke).
[95] HC Deb 28 March 2003, vol 402 col 603 (Tony Clarke).
[96] HC Deb 28 March 2003, vol 403 col 611 (Hazel Blears).
[97] HC Deb 13 June 2003, vol 406 col 990 (Stephen McCabe).
[98] *Morris* (n 63); *Gabaj* (n 63).
[99] HC Deb 27 November 2007, vol 468 col 202 (Julie Morgan).
[100] Sathanapally (2012) 167, 62, 66, 70, 218; Mathen (2016) 103.
[101] Roach (2004) 52; Sathanapally (2012) 42.
[102] *R (Steinfeld and Keidan) v Secretary of State for International Development* [2018] UKSC 32.
[103] HC Deb 22 February 2018, vol 635 col 1096 (Tim Loughton).

incompatibility, the legislative process was well underway. However, the declaration still played a bolstering role in persuading parliamentarians to support the Bill in order 'to comply with the highest court of the land'.[104] As one Conservative MP observed, 'We must ensure that we observe the Supreme Court guidance in the important *Steinfeld* case and that we follow not only the letter but the spirit of the law'.[105]

Rather than treating declarations as a form of unwelcome policy distortion or debilitation, parliamentarians have openly embraced them as a valuable spur to legislative action on a topic which had long required, but not received, serious legislative attention. In the parliamentary debates following the ruling in *R (M) v Secretary of State for Health*),[106] where the inability of a mental patient detained under the Mental Health Act to change the person designated as 'their nearest relative' violated that person's rights, there was a widespread recognition across Parliament that the existing legislation was clearly deficient, and needed to be corrected in order to protect rights.[107] As Baroness Corston noted when introducing the new Mental Health Bill to the House of Lords, although the declaration of incompatibility placed the issue on the legislative agenda, reform of this area had been 'on the horizon for 9 years, which indicates the degree to which it is difficult to legislate in this area'.[108] This highlights the way in which judicial declarations can assist the government and legislature in tackling difficult policy issues, by raising them up the legislative agenda and lowering the political costs involved in making the required policy change.[109]

Across the diverse fields of mental health, transgender rights, immigration, the rights of travellers and gypsies, or discrimination on grounds of gender or sexual orientation, parliamentarians have observed that although reforming the law in these areas does not win votes, protecting these rights is the right thing to do. Thus, in the debates on the Gender Recognition Bill following the declaration of incompatibility in *Bellinger*, a Conservative MP noted that this is

---

[104] HC Deb 18 July 2018, vol 645 col 13 (Tim Loughton).
[105] HC Deb 18 July 2018, vol 645 col 16 (Victoria Atkins); Hayward (2019) 938.
[106] King (2015a) 168.
[107] HL Deb 27 March 2006, vol 680 col W544 (Lord Warner); HL Deb 17 January 2007, vol 688 col 667 (Lord Patel); Young (2011) 783–4.
[108] HL Deb 28 November 2006, vol 687 col 717 (Baroness Corston).
[109] Mallory & Tyrrell (2021) 487; Chandrachud (2017) 71.

the sort of legislation that political parties do not like, but that Governments have to face. It is certainly not the sort of issue that any party would put in its manifesto before a general election nor campaign on with any zeal or the expectation of reaping electoral rewards.[110]

Nonetheless, whilst acknowledging that the estimated '5000 transsexuals in this country' were 'extremely unlikely to turn the result of the next general election', MPs emphasised that this 'imposes a duty on us collectively to try to be as helpful to individuals as we properly may',[111] as prompted to do so by the *Bellinger* decision.

Far from being greeted with resistance and resentment, many declarations are welcomed in a spirit of complementarity and collaboration, with political actors treating the declaration as a beneficial catalyst for legislative change. This bears out Rosalind Dixon's argument that the legislative process may sometimes suffer from 'blind spots' or 'burdens of inertia' which the courts may be able to counteract to some degree.[112] It also illustrates the dynamics of 'judge as nudge'[113] discussed in Chapter 10, where declarations can be valuable judicial spurs to political action as part of a broader collaborative dynamic between courts, governments and legislatures.

7   Courting Controversy

Whilst the vast majority of declarations have elicited a willing, compliant, and sometimes even an openly welcoming political response, four declarations have generated controversy and contestation. These are: the *Anderson* case (which declared that the Home Secretary's involvement in criminal sentencing violated Article 6 ECHR);[114] the *Belmarsh prison* case (which declared that Executive detention without trial of non-national terrorist suspects violated the right to non-discrimination);[115] the *Thompson* case (which declared that placing sex offenders on a Sex Offenders Register indefinitely without any possibility of review violated the right to privacy);[116] and the declaration of incompatibility by the

---

[110] HC Deb 23 February 2004, vol 418 col 81 (Robert Salisbury).
[111] HC Deb 23 February 2004, vol 418 col 59 (Tim Daventry).
[112] Dixon (2007) 391.
[113] Chapter 10, this vol.
[114] *R v Home Secretary, ex parte Anderson* [2003] UKHL 46 (*Anderson*).
[115] *A (and others) v SSHD* [2004] UKHL 56 (*Belmarsh*).
[116] *R (Thompson) v SSHD* [2010] UKSC 17.

Scottish Registration Appeal Court in *Smith v Scott*[117] on prisoner voting, following the Strasbourg ruling in *Hirst*.[118] Despite the acute controversy surrounding these cases, the Government eventually complied with the declarations in some form in all four cases. Nonetheless, these cases provide a stringent testing ground for whether a constitutional convention exists, because they provide examples where political self-interest and constitutional principle may pull apart.

a   When Life Means Life

In *Anderson*,[119] the House of Lords declared that the role of the Home Secretary in setting the minimum period or 'tariff' for life sentences for murder violated the right to a fair trial by an independent court under Article 6 ECHR.[120] Though numerous parliamentary committees had recommended the removal of the Home Secretary's role in criminal sentencing for many years,[121] *Anderson* elicited acute controversy within Government, Parliament and wider society, not least because the topic of mandatory life sentences for murder is a recurrent preoccupation of the tabloid press.[122]

So how did the Government respond to the declaration of incompatibility? In a statement to the House of Commons, the Home Secretary (David Blunkett MP) clarified that the decision 'did not rule that the Home Secretary's power is unlawful. All existing tariffs therefore stand'.[123] Whilst acknowledging that the Government would 'need to study the judgment carefully before finalising our proposals', Blunkett emphasised the need to retain a 'paramount role'[124] for Parliament in 'setting a clear framework within which the minimum period to be served will be established'.[125] Such a scheme would be 'compatible with

---

[117] *Smith v Scott* (n 17).
[118] *Hirst v UK* (n 18).
[119] *Anderson* (n 114).
[120] Ibid [78], Lord Bingham of Cornhill.
[121] Bingham (2000) 339–42; Gale & James (2002) 421; Amos (2004) 117, 122; Crawford (2013) 52.
[122] Feldman (2013) 227; Gies (2015a) 11, 66.
[123] HC Deb 25 November 2002, vol 395 col 100W (David Blunkett).
[124] Ibid.
[125] Ibid.

our Human Rights obligations and will also ensure that Parliament has established the framework for dealing with the most dangerous and evil people in our society'.[126]

In statements to the media, the Home Secretary resorted to more bellicose political rhetoric, insisting that 'life means life'[127] for convicted murderers and reiterating that 'Policy on the protection of the public and punishment of the guilty must always be the domain of the elected Parliament'.[128] He presented the ruling to various media outlets as 'overturning what Parliament has enacted'[129] and as unjustly stripping him of his role in setting jail sentences for convicted murderers.[130]

During his tenure as Home Secretary, David Blunkett was well known for his excoriating invective against the courts.[131] Therefore, his quip following *Anderson* that 'out of touch judges should live in the real world'[132] was par for the course. However, despite his strident political rhetoric, none of his public statements articulated an intention to defy the declaration of incompatibility in *Anderson*. Recall that *Anderson* only impugned the Home Secretary's role in criminal sentencing. It did not preclude Parliament from enacting a stringent sentencing regime or from setting mandatory life sentences for murder.[133] Therefore, Blunkett's reiterated emphasis on the need for Parliament to enact a tough sentencing regime for serious crime was fully compliant with the court's ruling in *Anderson*.

Shortly after the declaration in *Anderson*, Parliament enacted the Criminal Justice Act 2003, which removed the Home Secretary's role in criminal sentencing, whilst setting out a statutory scheme of minimum sentences for murder and other serious offences.[134] For all the bravado and combative rhetoric under the media spotlight, the Home Secretary struck a more constructive and collaborative tone in the parliamentary debates on the Criminal Justice Bill 2003. He confirmed that 'no

---

[126] HC Deb 25 Nov 2002, vol 395 col 102W (David Blunkett).
[127] Travis (2003a).
[128] Rozenberg (2002).
[129] Travis (2003b); Steele (2003).
[130] Upton (2003).
[131] Blunkett (2003); Ford & Gibb (2003); Travis (2004); Shetreet & Turenne (2013) 403; Hiebert & Kelly (2015) 264–5; Gee et al. (2015) 49; Sathanapally (2012) 190; Thomas (2017b) [42].
[132] Travis (2003b).
[133] Article 6 ECHR.
[134] King (2015a).

disagreement exists between the Government and the judiciary about the fact that [the courts] should have the discretion to make decisions in relation to individual cases'.[135] He even expressed some relief that the new legislation 'takes the tariff out of the hands of the Home Secretary'.[136]

Interestingly, whilst his initial statement to the House of Commons emphasised that the *Anderson* ruling did not mean that the Home Secretary's power was unlawful,[137] he subsequently described the ruling as having 'overturned'[138] the pre-existing tariff system. Likewise, other Ministers noted that the *Anderson* case had 'removed the Home Secretary's power to set the minimum term'[139] and that the Home Secretary was '*no longer permitted* to play any part in deciding how long a murderer can stay in prison'.[140] Throughout the parliamentary debate in both Houses, there was a sense that the Home Secretary was 'compelled to relinquish his sentencing power because the law required it'.[141] The government's focus was on how to retain a system of tough sentencing *within* the constraints of the *Anderson* ruling, not whether to reject that ruling outright. Thus, even on the politically sensitive issue of life sentences for murder – and even with a Home Secretary who wore his disdain for the judiciary as a badge of political honour – the Government made no effort to defy the declaration in *Anderson*.

When the Bill went to the House of Lords, Mr Blunkett's excoriating rhetoric about the courts was subject to serious censure and critique, where his comments were described as 'grossly misleading'[142] and nothing more than a crude, populist attempt at 'vote-catching'.[143] The former Lord Chancellor, Lord Woolf, told the House of Lords that he wanted the

---

[135] HC Deb 20 May 2003, vol 405 col 866 (David Blunkett).
[136] HC Deb 20 May 2003, vol 405 col 869–70 (David Blunkett); Crawford (2013) 55.
[137] HC Deb 25 November 2002, vol 395 col 100W (David Blunkett).
[138] HC Deb 20 May 2003, vol 405 col 868, 870 (David Blunkett).
[139] HC Deb 20 May 2003, vol 405 col 901 (Paul Goggins); see also HL Deb 11 November 2003, vol 654 col 1253 (Baroness Scotland of Asthal); Sathanapally (2012) 154.
[140] HL Deb 17 November 2003, vol 654 col 1803 (Lord Ackner); HL Deb 14 October 2003, vol 653 col 861 (noting that the Secretary of State 'lost' his powers to determine the minimum tariff 'as a result of the decision of the House in the case of *Anderson*') (Lord Lloyd of Berwick).
[141] Sathanapally (2012) 154.
[142] HL Deb 16 June 2003, vol 649 col 589 (Lord Ackner).
[143] HL Deb 14 October 2003, vol 653 col 863 (Lord Thomas of Gresford); Upton (2003) ('Blunkett's crass proposals can be seen simply as giving *Sun* and *Express* readers what they want').

government 'to lead on such issues, and not to follow public opinion shaped by the tabloids'.[144] Another House of Lords Peer and future Attorney General – Baroness Anelay of St Johns – announced her dismay at

> the intemperate language used by the Home Secretary in describing some of the judiciary. The easy case is always to bash the judges if one disagrees with the sentence given in a particular instance. This is not a mature response for a politician ... Our job is to get the law right in the first place as it passes through our hands here. We should not whinge if the court ... interprets and applies the law in a way that displeases us. It is the job of the court ... to interpret the law and apply it to the facts of the particular case before it. It is our job to amend the law if cases show that we have not achieved our objective. The Bill give us that opportunity. We should seize it.[145]

This statement provides an excellent articulation of the constitutional division of labour within the collaborative constitution. On this understanding, the courts are expected to make authoritative decisions on the law as it applies to particular cases, whereupon the government and legislature are expected to work from those conclusions to refashion policy accordingly.[146]

b   Courting Counter-Terrorism

The *Belmarsh Prison* case was one of the most controversial declarations of incompatibility in the early years of the HRA.[147] By declaring that indefinite detention without trial for foreign terrorist suspects was discriminatory and disproportionate, the decision struck at the heart of the Government's counter-terrorist strategy in the febrile post-9/11 political atmosphere. When writing the leading decision, the Senior Law Lord, Lord Bingham, was careful to use 'very low-key and extremely uninflammatory language with no big rhetorical high spots because one knew perfectly well it was going to be extremely unpopular with the powers that be'.[148] And so it was. The *Belmarsh* decision sent shockwaves throughout Whitehall.[149] Many senior government Ministers, including

---

[144] HL Deb 16 June 2003, vol 649 col 564; Lord Woolf HL Deb 15 March 2004.
[145] HL Deb 16 June 2003, vol 649 col 558 (Baroness Anelay of St Johns).
[146] King (2015a) 187.
[147] Sathanapally (2012) chapter 8; see further Chapter 6.3 and Chapter 9.5.
[148] Paterson (2013) 295 (quoting from an interview with Lord Bingham).
[149] Bright & Hinsliff (2001); Dyer, White & Travis (2004); Elliott (2011) 611; Kavanagh (2011); Fenwick (2011); Bamforth (2013) 278–87; Dyzenhaus (2007) 125.

the Prime Minister Tony Blair, were deeply frustrated by the decision, believing that the 'draconian'[150] step of detaining terrorist suspects without trial was necessary to combat the looming terrorist threat to the UK.[151] As Mark Elliott observed, 'if ever there was an occasion on which the Government might have been tempted to ignore the Court's view, this was it'.[152]

So how did the government and Parliament react to this judgment? Shortly after the decision was handed down, the Home Secretary, Charles Clarke, made a statement to the House of Commons that he would not release the detainees, reminding the House that under the HRA 'Parliament remains sovereign and it is ultimately for Parliament to decide whether and what changes should be made to the law'.[153] Whilst refraining from criticising the *Belmarsh* decision,[154] he said that he would have to study the judgment carefully to see whether it was possible to modify the legislation 'to address the concerns raised by the House of Lords'.[155]

Shortly afterwards, the Government introduced new legislation 'to meet the Law Lords' judgment',[156] replacing prison detention with a form of home arrest called 'control orders'.[157] When proposing the new control order regime to the House of Commons, the Home Secretary affirmed that Parliament 'should not ignore the judgment or flout it, but act on it and try to put in place a regime that is both

---

[150] Blair (2011) 582 (describing them as 'draconian powers, unacceptable in principle except in the most rare circumstances').

[151] Blair (2011) 568 (noting that at this point in his premiership 'the iron had entered [his] soul on the issue of liberty versus anti-terror law', describing Lord Hoffmann's dissenting dictum in *Belmarsh*, that the anti-terror laws posed a greater threat to the country than terrorism itself, as 'grossly stupid'); Blunkett (2006) 750 (describing the *Belmarsh* decision as 'totally unrealistic'); Jack Straw was reported as saying that *Belmarsh* was 'simply wrong', though he subsequently regretted making that statement, see Straw (2012) 284.

[152] Elliott (2011) 611; Bingham (2011) 154 (describing *Belmarsh* as possibly 'the most serious reverse ... any government ever suffered in our domestic courts'). For analysis of the media coverage of *Belmarsh*, see Gies (2015a) 30–3; Brogan (2005); Cash (2005).

[153] HC Deb 20 December 2004, vol 428 col 1911 (Charles Clarke).

[154] Hickman (2010) 344.

[155] HC Deb 20 December 2004, vol 428 col 1914 (Charles Clarke).

[156] HC Deb 23 February 2005, vol 431 col 345 (Charles Clarke).

[157] Prevention of Terrorism Act 2005; Kavanagh (2010c).

proportionate and not discriminatory'.[158] This position aligned with advice from the Attorney General that the government should obey the judgment in *Belmarsh*.[159]

During parliamentary debate in the House of Commons, some Opposition MPs urged the Home Secretary to defy the ruling in *Belmarsh* in order to preserve the *status quo ante*.[160] But the Home Secretary rejected this option in forthright terms:[161]

> I simply do not accept the argument. I do not think that is correct ... when the Law Lords of this country make a set of criticisms about the way that we are operating that is well founded, by a vote of eight to one, it is incumbent on the Government – and, I would argue, on Parliament – to respond to that and decide how to deal with it.[162]
>
> If the Law Lords say that we have discriminatory and disproportionate legislation, I believe that there is an obligation on the whole House, not simply on the Government, to address that, and that is what we are doing.[163]
>
> I do not accept that it would have been appropriate to ignore the Law Lords judgment ... It is not a good state of affairs when the Law Lords take one position and the Executive take another.[164]

In making these statements, the Home Secretary articulated a sense of constitutional obligation to comply with a declaration of incompatibility, grounded in the rule of law, constitutional comity, and duty of political respect for judicial independence.[165] The clear message was that even if parliamentarians disagree with a ruling, there is nonetheless an obligation to comply with it. As one Labour MP observed, 'as a responsible Government ... we *have to* abide by the rules and laws of the land as decreed by the House of Lords'.[166]

---

[158] HC Deb 23 February 2005, vol 431 col 346 (Charles Clarke); Hickman (2010) 344.
[159] Winstone (2010) 518–19 (documenting a meeting at number 10 Downing Street where the Attorney General advised the Government to obey the Lords' judgment, adding 'It will be a big thing, if we don't accept the judgment'); Crawford (2013); Blunkett (2006) 679–80, 692.
[160] HC Deb 23 February 2005, vol 431 col 345–6 (Bill Cash).
[161] Ibid.
[162] HC Deb 23 February 2005, vol 431 col 346 (Charles Clarke).
[163] HC Deb 22 February 2005, vol 431 col 158 (Charles Clarke).
[164] HC Deb 23 February 2005, vol 431 col 346 (Charles Clarke).
[165] King (2015b) 121.
[166] Tom Harris, col 1436 (emphasis added); cf. Blunkett (2006) 749–50, 680.

True, there were some isolated statements in the House of Lords suggesting that 'the declaration of incompatibility... does not prevent the government legally extending the 2001 Part 4 legislation'.[167] But these statements were the exception, not the norm. Moreover, an emphasis on the lack of legal obligation is immaterial to the existence of a constitutional convention. After all, all conventions qualify and regulate the exercise of legally permissible power.

In any event, the general trend across both Houses of Parliament was for MPs and Peers to describe the *Belmarsh* decision as a judicial ruling 'that detention without trial under the anti-terrorism laws *is unlawful*'[168] and therefore needed to be addressed. In fact, some Government Ministers described the *Belmarsh* decision as having 'overturned'[169] or 'struck down'[170] the impugned law, including the Prime Minister, Tony Blair. Overall, the parliamentary debates following the *Belmarsh* decision are infused with an acceptance – subsequently affirmed by Tony Blair in his autobiography – that 'once the House of Lords made the ruling, we *had to* amend the law'.[171] The focus of parliamentary debate was on *how* that could be achieved, not *whether* to do so.[172]

c   Rhetoric, Resistance and Registering Sex Offenders

The Government's response to the *Thompson* case contains the most visceral expressions of opposition to a judicial declaration of incompatibility since the HRA was enacted.[173] *Thompson* concerned the sensitive issue of whether convicted sex offenders could be kept on a Sex Offenders Register for life without any possibility of review. When the Supreme

---

[167]   HL Deb 1 March 2005, vol 670 col 212 (Lord Kingsland).

[168]   HC Deb 20 December 2004, vol 428 col 1911 (David Heath); HL Deb 3 March 2005, vol 670 col 453 (Lord Falconer); HC Deb 24 February 2005, vol 431 col 480 ('The Law Lords ruled that ... the 2001 Act is unlawful, and therefore we had to introduce new legislation ...') (Peter Hain); Sathanapally (2012) 192.

[169]   HC Deb 23 February 2005, vol 431 col 386 (Simon Hughes); HC Deb 24 February 2005, vol 431 col 486 (Peter Hain).

[170]   HC Deb 23 February 2005, vol 431 col 168 (Charles Clarke); HC Deb 2 November 2005, vol 438 col 932 (Bill Cash); Bamforth (2013) 282.

[171]   Blair (2011) 583 (emphasis added); Crawford (2013); HL Deb 1 March 2005, vol 679 col 187 (Lord Truscott); HC Deb 24 February 2005, vol 431 col 480 (Peter Hain).

[172]   HC Deb 28 February 2005, vol 431 col 778 (stating that 'we cannot' reinstate the law in March 'because of the Law Lords' judgment) (John Denham); HC Deb 23 February 2005, vol 431 col 367 (Mark Oaten).

[173]   For insightful discussion of *Thompson*, see Gearty (2016) 65–6, 72–3; Sathanapally (2012) 214–15; Phillipson (2013) 45–9; King (2015a) 176, 185.

Court declared that this violated their rights, the political response was incendiary.

In the House of Commons, the Home Secretary (Theresa May) proclaimed that the Government was 'disappointed and appalled'[174] by the ruling, suggesting that 'most Members of the House are fed up with the way in which decisions by the House are increasingly being overturned by the courts'.[175] It was 'time to assert that it is Parliament that makes our laws, not the courts',[176] she said, affirming that the Government would implement the ruling 'in the most minimal way possible'.[177] The Prime Minister, David Cameron, took a similarly trenchant stance, exclaiming about 'how completely offensive it is, once again, to have a ruling by a court that flies in the face of common sense',[178] echoing the Home Secretary's claim that they would take the minimum steps necessary to comply with the ruling.[179] Indeed, they were both so apparently incensed by this ruling that they promised to set up a Commission to review the general operation of the HRA.[180]

These overt, frontal attacks on the *Thompson* decision are the most striking exception to the general trend of moderate, accepting, and willing compliance with declarations of incompatibility since the HRA has been enacted.[181] Yet, for all fighting talk, it is telling that the inflammatory rhetoric only stretched to the threat of *minimal compliance* with the ruling, not outright defiance or an open refusal to change the law. Neither the Prime Minister nor the Home Secretary ever suggested that they would ignore or reject the ruling.

Indeed, it is often overlooked that the heated exchange on *Thompson* took place whilst introducing a Remedial Order to 'rectify the legislative incompatibility identified by the Supreme Court'.[182] Not only did this Remedial Order allow for the possibility of periodic review to test whether the sex offender still posed risk to the public (as *Thompson*

---

[174] HC Deb 16 February 2011, vol 523 col 959–61 (Theresa May).
[175] HC Deb 16 February 2011, vol 523 col 969 (Theresa May).
[176] HC Deb 16 February 2011, vol 523 col 960 (Theresa May).
[177] HC Deb 16 February 2011, vol 523 col 961 (Theresa May).
[178] HC Deb 16 February 2011, vol 523 col 955 (David Cameron); Gearty (2016) 65–7.
[179] HC Deb 16 February 2011, vol 523 col 955.
[180] An independent Commission on a UK Bill of Rights was set up in 2011, see www.gov.uk/government/news/commission-on-a-uk-bill-of-rights-launched.
[181] King (2015a) 185; King (2021) [45] (describing *Thompson* as an outlier or 'high water mark' for conflictual political dynamics following a DoI).
[182] HC Deb 20 June 2011, vol 529 col 63ws (Lynne Featherstone); HC Deb 5 March 2012, vol 541 col 52WS–53WS (James Brokenshire).

required), it also imposed a high threshold for such review (as Lord Phillips had suggested *obiter* in *Thompson*).[183] Indeed, it also implemented some of the JCHR's recommendations to ensure that the statutory changes would be fully proportionate and compliant with human rights law.[184] As former Legal Adviser to the JCHR, Murray Hunt, observed, 'Notwithstanding the political hyperbole which had greeted the original judgment, the government accepted the Committee's recommendation without fuss'.[185] Therefore, the response to *Thompson* was marked by a striking combination of tough talk in the media spotlight and compliant action behind the scenes.

Interestingly, both the Prime Minister and the Home Secretary presented themselves *as mandated to* comply with the ruling in *Thompson*. When pressed by an Opposition MP (Jack Straw) to confirm that the government was not legally obliged to comply with the ruling,[186] the Home Secretary deflected the challenge, reaffirming that 'we do *have to* make a change [and] will do so in the most minimal way possible'.[187] What explains this emphasis on obligations not options following declarations of incompatibility?

One possibility is that the Prime Minister and Home Secretary recognised that there was a constitutional convention requiring compliance with declarations of incompatibility, though they lamented that obligation in the context of this particular declaration. Another less laudatory hypothesis is that it was a form of political buck-passing and blame avoidance, where the Government sought to distract the public from the fact that the legal responsibility for implementing the declaration lay with them.[188]

A related possibility is that it was a form of political posturing which David Cameron described elsewhere as a 'Daily Mail Special',[189] i.e.

---

[183] *Thompson* (n 116) [39], Lord Phillips; Chandrachud (2017) 86.

[184] Government Response to the Ninth Report of the JCHR 2010–12, HC 1549 [24]; Phillipson (2013) 48–9; Hunt (2013) 238; Gee et al. (2015) 116.

[185] Hunt (2013) 238.

[186] HC Deb 16 February 2011, vol 523 col 961 (Jack Straw).

[187] HC Deb 16 February 2011, vol 523 col 969 (Theresa May) (emphasis added).

[188] Crawford (2013) 82; Davis (2010) 93; Hazarika & Hamilton (2018) 234; Crewe (2015a) 60; Crewe (2015b) 13.

[189] Hazarika & Hamilton (2018) 234–5 (quoting David Cameron, who referred to a 'Daily Mail Special' as an approach to Prime Minister's Questions (PMQs), where the Prime Minister would 'pick an issue that the middle-ranking tabloids are having kittens about and give it some oomph', with the aim of getting on the front pages of the newspapers the following day; 'If the world is outraged about something, then the Prime Minister

where a politician echoes and amplifies tabloid outrage in order to seem tough on crime, strong on action, and sympathetic to public opinion.[190] If that was Mr Cameron's aim, then he succeeded with flying colours. Predictably, the *Daily Mail* ran an article the next day applauding him for 'declar[ing] war on unelected judges ... after they put the human rights of paedophiles and rapists before public safety'.[191] Perhaps all three possibilities have some explanatory purchase here, i.e. that there was a (reluctant) acknowledgement of some sort of obligation to comply with the ruling, combined with a political strategy of damage limitation, blame avoidance and political grandstanding for political and electoral advantage.

However, whilst the political rhetoric in the adversarial theatre of Prime Minister's Questions was both trenchant and visceral,[192] a more measured and moderate stance was audible in the relatively secluded setting of the Delegated Legislation Committee, where a member of the Coalition Government[193] stated:

> We clearly believe that [*Thompson*] was a correct judgment and, as the Government, we comply with Supreme Court judgments ... the ruling was quite clear and unequivocal, and we have responded.[194]

Similarly, in the House of Lords, Baroness Stowell of Beeston affirmed the correctness of the *Thompson* decision, noting that

> as the Government, we comply with Supreme Court judgments ... we have needed to act on the Court judgment, which is what we have done ... the JCHR has agreed that we have moved from incompatibility to compliance.[195]

Again, whilst the public face of the political response to the declaration of incompatibility on this hot-button issue struck a defiant and combative

---

can use PMQs to make it clear that she is just as outraged and indicate that action will be taken').

[190] Hazarika & Hamilton (2018) 234–5; Crewe (2015a) 60; Crewe (2015b) 13.

[191] Shipman & Doyle (2011) (The full headline in the *Daily Mail* was: 'End this human rights insanity: PM's fury as judges rule paedophiles and rapists get a chance to get off sex offenders register'); Phillipson (2013) 47.

[192] For the view of PMQs as adversarial political theatre which is 'out of character with most of parliamentary life', see Hazarika & Hamilton (2018) 322, 317, 308; Russell & Gover (2017) 105; Blair (2011) 109.

[193] Lynne Featherstone, Parliamentary Under-Secretary of State, a Liberal Democrat member of the Coalition Government.

[194] HC Deb 19 June 2012, vol 546 col 10 (Lynne Featherstone); King (2015a) 186.

[195] HL Deb 5 July 2012, vol 547 col 890 (Baroness Stowell of Beeston).

tone, the political practice behind the scenes revealed a more muted, constructive and collaborative approach, couched in the language of constitutional obligation under the rule of law.[196]

The government's use of intemperate language to castigate the courts elicited strong critique across Parliament, even within the ranks of the Conservative party. The Lord Chancellor, Kenneth Clark MP, felt compelled to write to the Prime Minister and Home Secretary to remind them of their statutory duty to uphold judicial independence.[197] Theresa May's dismissive comments about *Thompson* attracted severe criticism in the House of Lords, where she was accused of pandering shamelessly to the *Daily Mail* instead of making a proper, balanced statement to the House of Commons on how the Government would respond to the ruling.[198]

Some Peers expressed their 'sense of shame'[199] at hearing the Home Secretary's 'headline-grabbing language'[200] and her 'intemperate critique' of the courts. Others affirmed the importance of 'respect for the independence of the judiciary',[201] and the need to abide by the European Convention and the HRA 'and our duties under both'.[202] As one Peer put it: 'it undermines the rule of law when senior Ministers attack Supreme Court judges in that way'.[203]

Baroness Stowell of Beeston – a Conservative Peer – articulated the norms of constitutional comity which frame the appropriate political response to declarations of incompatibility in the following way:

> Our constitutional arrangements are such that when the highest court of the land identifies an incompatibility with the European Convention on Human Rights, the Government of the day, whoever is in power, take remedial action. This is for various reasons, not the least of which is to ensure that the Government are not left vulnerable to further legal proceedings, potentially involving millions of pounds of taxpayers' money ... The Government were disappointed with the UK Supreme

---

[196] Gee et al. (2015) 118.
[197] Shetreet & Turenne (2013) 404; Hodge (2018) 12.
[198] Lord West, col 721; Lord MacDonald, Lord Thomas.
[199] HL Deb 16 February 2011, vol 725 col 721–2 (Lord Thomas); vol 725 col 720 (Lord West) (arguing that the Home Secretary should make statements 'not for the *Daily Mail* but for the House'); vol 725 col 721 (Lord MacDonald).
[200] HL Deb 16 February 2011, vol 725 col 721–2 (Lord Thomas).
[201] HL Deb 17 March 2011, vol 726 col 352 (Lord Howard).
[202] HL Deb 16 February 2011, vol 725 col 716–18 (Baroness Neville-Jones).
[203] HL Deb 5 July 2012, vol 738 col 884 (Lord Lester of Sterne Hill).

Court's ruling, but we take our responsibility to uphold the law seriously, and that includes human rights law.[204]

This was echoed by Baroness Neville-Jones who observed that

It is precisely because this is a law-abiding Government who respects the rule of law that we do not regard it as a practical option not to bring forward legislation to ensure that we are compliant with the ruling of the court.[205]

Both of these statements articulate a strong normative obligation to comply with court rulings on rights, including those which result in a declaration of incompatibility.

d   Political Wrangling about Prisoner Voting

When assessing whether there is a constitutional convention of compliance with declarations of incompatibility, the prisoner voting saga is of critical importance.[206] It is often thought to provide the clearest example to date of political defiance of a declaration, thus potentially disproving the existence of an emerging convention of compliance.[207] In order to examine the veracity of such claims, we need to get a clear appreciation of the sequence of events.

After the Strasbourg court handed down its decision in *Hirst v United Kingdom*[208] that the UK's blanket ban on prisoner voting violated the Convention, the initial political response in the UK was neither fierce nor fraught. Though some members of the government disagreed strongly with the ruling,[209] the general response was 'business as usual'.[210] The government affirmed the UK's obligation to implement the ruling, announcing that it needed to consider the issue in more detail. It duly

---

[204] HL Deb 5 July 2012, vol 738 col 875–6 (Baroness Stowell of Beeston).

[205] HL Deb 16 February 2011, vol 725 col 716–18 (Baroness Neville-Jones).

[206] For insightful analysis of the prisoner voting saga, see Bates (2014); Bates (2017); Murray (2010); Murray (2011); Murray (2013b); Crawford (2013) 73–7; Harlow & Rawlings (2016) 320–2; Harlow (2016) 161–4; Hardman (2020).

[207] Gardbaum (2015) 1043; cf. Kavanagh (2015d) 1050–1; Murray (2013a) 79.

[208] *Hirst v UK* (n 18).

[209] One of the most fervent opponents of prisoner voting was Labour MP Jack Straw, who joined forces with Conservative MP David Davis to galvanise coordinated opposition to it across Parliament, see Blackburn (2011).

[210] McLean (2013).

submitted an Action Plan to the Council of Europe, outlining its plans to consult on the appropriate method of implementing the judgment.[211]

In 2007, the Scottish Administration Appeal Court faced repeat litigation on the prisoner voting issue in *Smith v Scott*[212] and decided to issue a declaration of incompatibility following *Hirst*.[213] The Scottish declaration had extremely low political salience. It received little or no media coverage, and elicited virtually no governmental or parliamentary response.[214]

As the years wore on without any legal change forthcoming, the Council of Ministers started to put pressure on the UK to implement *Hirst*. There was a palpable sense that the government was 'playing for time',[215] engaging in a strategy of prevarication by consultation in order to forestall the political fallout from such a controversial policy change. The prisoner voting issue was like a political game of 'pass the parcel', which every government wanted to pass on to their successors. When the Labour party lost the next election, the new Conservative Prime Minister (David Cameron) ratcheted up the rhetoric on prisoner voting and inflamed the issue, pronouncing to the House of Commons that it made him 'physically ill to even to contemplate having to give the vote to anyone who is in prison. Frankly, when people commit a crime and go to prison, they should lose their rights, including the right to vote'.[216] This seemed to be another example of a 'Daily Mail special',[217] where he indulged in some political grandstanding to signify his tough-on-crime credentials in order to garner support from the tabloids, the voting public and possibly his own backbenchers. Needless to say, this expression of raw revulsion was widely reported in the tabloid press and in all other media outlets.[218] Indeed, it is still frequently cited to this day as evidence of the government's fierce opposition to giving prisoners the right to vote.[219]

---

[211] Bates (2014).
[212] *Smith v Scott* (n 17).
[213] Ibid; Murray (2011) 64–6.
[214] Crawford (2013) 76.
[215] Murray (2011); see Hiebert & Kelly (2015) 278–9; Crawford (2013) 74.
[216] HC Deb 3 November 2010, vol 517 col 921 (David Cameron); Mason (2017) 484.
[217] Hiebert & Kelly (2015) 189, 194–8; Ip (2020) 48.
[218] Mason (2017) 484.
[219] Bennett (2022).

However, whilst many parliamentarians did not hide their 'disgust'[220] at the idea of giving prisoners the right to vote, there are a number of reasons why the prisoner voting saga does not provide a clear-cut example of political defiance of a declaration of incompatibility. First, the political fury surrounding prisoner voting was firmly directed towards the Strasbourg ruling in *Hirst*,[221] not the Scottish decision in *Smith v Scott*.[222] Therefore, it is not a clear-cut example of political resistance to declarations of incompatibility by the higher courts.[223]

Second, the Scottish declaration had low political salience. It was eclipsed by the increasingly toxic and 'totemic'[224] discourse about the UK's sovereignty vis-à-vis Strasbourg.[225] In the high-stakes, high-octane political wrangling about the UK's relationship with the Strasbourg court, the Scottish declaration barely flickered on the political radar. The crux issue was how the UK would respond to the ECtHR and the Council of Europe, not how Whitehall or Westminster would respond to a Scottish declaration.

Third, the fact that the declaration was issued by the Scottish Registration Appeal Court rather than the UK Supreme Court further exacerbated its political marginalisation, increasing the sense that it was merely an incidental by-product of *Hirst*, not a significant legal or political issue in its own right.[226]

Whilst Cameron's raw statement of revulsion naturally hit the headlines, his visceral outburst did *not* encapsulate the government's general response either to the Strasbourg ruling in *Hirst* or the Scottish declaration. In fact, what made the Prime Minister physically ill was his realisation that the UK government was bound to comply with Strasbourg rulings as a matter of international law.[227] As one journalist astutely observed, such visceral statements of revulsion are often 'used by

---

[220] Cameron (2019) 508; Roach (2015) 412–16.

[221] *Hirst v UK* (n 18).

[222] *Smith v Scott* (n 17).

[223] See evidence of the Lord Chancellor, Lord Falconer, before the JCHR (2007) Appendix 13 (27 March 2007) (arguing that the declaration of incompatibility in *Smith v Scott* established no new principle beyond *Hirst*, and the Government was consulting on how to respond to *Hirst*); Crawford (2013) 75.

[224] Bates (2017) 286–7; Ziegler (2015) 171; Donald (2015) 148.

[225] HC Deb 23 May 2012, vol 545 col 1127 (It is for 'Parliament to decide, not a foreign court') (David Cameron); Bates (2014) 504–5; Nicol (2011) 683.

[226] Crawford (2013).

[227] HC Deb 3 November 2010, vol 517 col 921 (David Cameron).

politicians who are about to do the very thing they say they hate, and hope to be excused for it'.[228]

There were numerous statements from other Government Ministers and senior civil servants which qualified and contextualised the Prime Minister's inflammatory rhetoric, confirming the UK Government's commitment to implementing the judgment and honouring its obligations under international human rights law.[229]

The day before David Cameron's statement, the Parliamentary Under-Secretary of State at the Cabinet Office, Mark Harper, affirmed in the House of Commons that 'there is a need to change the law [following *Hirst*]. This is not a choice; it is a legal obligation. Ministers are currently considering how to implement the judgment'.[230] This was followed by a Written Statement affirming that 'Governments have an absolute duty to uphold the rule of law'.[231] The Justice Secretary and Lord Chancellor, Kenneth Clarke MP, was publicly reported as saying that the Government had 'no intention of defying the rule of law',[232] affirming that 'the Prime Minister accepts like everyone else that Government complies with its legal obligations'.[233]

When introducing a subsequent Bill concerning the voting eligibility of prisoners, the next Lord Chancellor and Justice Secretary, Chris Grayling, framed Cameron's statements as 'personal views', thus distancing them from the official government position:

> The Prime Minister [David Cameron] has made clear, on the record, his personal views on this subject, and I have done the same. Those views have not changed. However, the Government are under an international law obligation to implement the Court judgment. As Lord Chancellor, as well as Secretary of State for Justice, I take my obligation to uphold the rule of law seriously.[234]

---

[228] Moore (2011).

[229] HL Deb 20 April 2009, col 1247 ('The European of Human Rights has spoken, and we have to implement that judgment. How we implement it is a difficult issue, and would be for any Government') (Lord Bach); HL Deb 7 May 2009, vol 710 col 146W (Lord Bach); HL Deb 17 June 2009, vol 711 col 1065 (Lord Bach).

[230] HC Deb 2 November 2010, vol 517 col 772 (Mark Harper).

[231] HC Deb 20 December 2010, vol 520 col 150WS–151WS (Mark Harper).

[232] Mulholland & Wintour (2011).

[233] Mulholland & Wintour (2011); Hiebert & Kelly (2015) 283–4.

[234] HC Deb 22 November 2012, vol 553 col 745 (Chris Grayling); HC Deb 2 November 2010, vol 517 col 771 ('We have no choice about complying with the law') (Mark Harper); HC Deb 10 November 2010, vol 518 col 287 ('At some point, regrettably, we need to bring our law into line with the court judgments) (Nick Clegg).

By making this statement, the Lord Chancellor was alluding to the role-based imperatives of high government office, articulating the standards of 'constitutionally appropriate behaviour by anyone who occupies the relevant role, even if, on a purely personal level, some of them might think that it would be better if a different set of norms applied'.[235] He was emphasising that a normative political obligation to comply with judicial rulings was not necessarily contra-indicated by the Prime Minister's vituperative personal views on this particular case.

The only reference to *Smith v Scott* in parliamentary debate was by the Parliamentary Under-Secretary of State, Lord Bach, who noted that the Government was 'mindful of the *Smith* case', affirming that it 'remain [ed] committed to implementing the court's judgment'[236] in *Hirst*, which would simultaneously remedy the incompatibility declared in *Smith v Scott*. He subsequently affirmed that the Government accepted its 'legal obligation to comply with the European Court ruling, and that compliance would ultimately mean giving some prisoners the right to vote'.[237]

All told, whilst the Prime Minister's headline-grabbing statements came to epitomise the political response on prisoner voting in the public mind, the vast majority of official government statements to the House of Commons and Lords manifested a constitutional commitment – however reluctant on this specific issue – to abide by the decision of the Strasbourg court. Indeed, despite the inflammatory rhetoric, the general governmental approach was one of deferral and delay rather than defiance and disagreement. Mr Cameron's 'political posturing'[238] and rhetorical grandstanding on the prisoner voting issue did not accurately reflect the broader political response to either *Hirst* or *Smith v Scott*.

After years of prevaricating and political 'foot-dragging',[239] the government eventually brought forward some minor non-legislative changes in 2017 to enable a small number of prisoners released on temporary licence using an electronic tag and prisoners released on home detention curfew to retain the right to vote.[240] Crucially, these administrative measures did not need to be approved by Parliament. This was a shrewd

[235] McHarg (2008) 860–1.
[236] HL Deb 7 May 2009, vol 710 col 127WE–148WA (Lord Bach).
[237] HL Deb 13 December 2010, vol 723 col 409 (Lord Bach).
[238] Elliott (2011) 600; Bates (2019) 220.
[239] Bates (2014) 526.
[240] Bowcott (2017); Hardman (2020) 244.

political manoeuvre to keep the final resolution of this issue out of the political limelight.[241]

This compromise was accepted by the Council of Europe as 'an adequate response'[242] to the judgment in *Hirst*, and the UK prisoner voting issue is now closed at the European level. In the Report of the Ministry of Justice to the JCHR on *Responding to Human Rights Judgments*, the Government confirmed that 'all necessary measures have now been taken'[243] to implement *Hirst*, and to comply with the declaration of incompatibility in *Smith v Scott*.[244] The matter is now closed. If we code this as compliance with the declaration of incompatibility, we now have a record of complete compliance with declarations of incompatibility over two decades.

Of course, there is plenty of room for discussion about whether these meagre measures on prisoner voting are sufficient to rectify the incompatibility declared in *Smith v Scott*.[245] After over a decade of protracted litigation and political wrangling at the highest levels, it is hardly a triumph for either prisoners' rights or parliamentary sovereignty.

But however minimalistic these legal changes may be, they still manifest the government's commitment to be seen to do something to comply with its international law obligations under the ECHR. Even on an issue where there was widespread public and political support for denying any prisoners the right to vote, the government eschewed the route of outright defiance, preferring to find some form of compliance, however minimal, in order to preserve its reputation and standing in Europe and beyond as a 'human rights-observing state'.[246] Even if the claim of compliance is viewed as 'an embarrassing pretence',[247] it was a pretence which affirmed the UK's international law obligation to comply with the decisions of the ECtHR.[248] It evidenced a strategy of reconciliation, not confrontation.

---

[241] Bowcott (2017).
[242] Secretariat of the Council of Europe, Committee of Ministers 1324th meeting, 7 September 2018; Ministry of Justice (2021) 33.
[243] MoJ Report (2021) 13.
[244] Ibid 13.
[245] Bates (2019) 221.
[246] McLean (2013) 32; Sathanapally (2012) 7.
[247] Endicott (2021) 117–18.
[248] Norton (2020) 21.

8   A Convention to Comply with Declarations of Incompatibility?

Drawing together the various strands of evidence across both the low-salience and high-salience declarations, I conclude that there is considerable evidence of an emerging constitutional convention that the Parliament should comply with declarations of incompatibility, unless exceptional circumstances arise.[249] I take the following points to be accumulatively indicative of a convention *in statu nascendi*.

First, throughout the parliamentary debates, parliamentarians across both Houses repeatedly used normative language to articulate a strong sense of obligation to comply with declaratory rulings of the higher courts.[250] As the Home Secretary put it when responding to the declaration in *Belmarsh*, there is 'an obligation on the whole House [of Commons], not just the Government' to remedy the declared violation, and a concomitant sense that it would not be 'appropriate to ignore the Law Lords' judgment'.[251] The sense of obligation was regularly bolstered by critiques of threatened non-compliance, especially in the House of Lords.

Second, the obligation to respect and implement declarations of incompatibility was explicitly grounded in constitutional principle, including the rule of law, judicial independence, and a sense of constitutional role-morality that a 'law-abiding Government who respects the rule of law'[252] complies with a ruling of the higher courts, even when it disagrees with it. When highly controversial cases arose, the Government effectively said, 'we strongly disagree on the substance, but it is important to uphold the law and the rule of law'.[253] In other words, parliamentarians had a content-independent reason to comply with the declaration – to work with it, not against it in a spirit of comity and collaboration.

What emerged was a sense of *constitutionalism as fair play*, where it was perceived to be constitutionally improper for elected politicians to 'whinge if the court ... interprets and applies the law in a way which displeases [them]'.[254] Mere disagreement with the outcome of a case was

---

[249] For other assessments which detect an emerging convention, see King (2015a) 187; Vermeule (2012) 442; Norton (2020) 21; Ahmed, Albert & Perry (2019) 793.

[250] McLean (2013) 33; Campbell (2001) 8.

[251] Charles Clarke; Campbell (2001) 87.

[252] HL Deb 16 February 2011, vol 725 col 717 (Baroness Neville-Jones).

[253] McLean (2013) 31; Harlow & Rawlings (2016) (arguing that the constitutional expectation that Parliament will comply with judicial rulings is 'strongly underpinned by appeal to the rule of law').

[254] HL Deb 16 June 2003, vol 649 col 566 (Baroness Anelay); Lord Irvine (2003b) 323.

viewed as an insufficient reason to justify disregarding a reasoned conclusion of incompatibility by the higher courts.[255] Instead, the political response to declarations of incompatibility is shaped by a second-order constitutional norm that responsible parliamentarians should comply with court rulings, even when they disagree with them. This is a very strong convention in the Westminster system, one which is 'both law-respecting and rights-respecting'.[256]

Third, a key finding of my empirical analysis is that parliamentarians did not tend to distinguish between judicial decisions which culminated in a declaration of incompatibility and those which did not. There was no sense that declarations of incompatibility should be treated as somehow less authoritative or less binding than other judicial rulings,[257] still less as optional suggestions in a constitutional conversation which the government and legislature can take or leave as they see fit.

In general, the political actors treated declarations as authoritative decisions about what the law requires, akin to other legal rulings of the higher courts. Parliamentarians frequently described declarations of incompatibility as '*court judgments of incompatibility* with the European Convention on Human Rights'[258] or as legal rulings which '*identify an incompatibility* with the European Convention on Human Rights'.[259] Instead of treating declarations as optional suggestions in a constitutional conversation, parliamentarians typically viewed the courts as 'authoritatively deciding on compatibility'[260] and providing an 'authoritative alert of non-compliance'[261] with international and domestic human rights law.

Fourth, my analysis echoes and endorses the findings of previous empirical studies that the general tenor of the political responses to declarations of incompatibility has been predominantly collaborative rather than conflictual, accepting rather than antagonistic. Despite some well-publicised

---

[255] McLean (2013) 31; Chandrachud (2017) 244.

[256] McLean (2013) 31.

[257] Sathanapally (2012) 224. For a parallel account of how the 'advisory opinions' on the Canadian constitutional system are treated as authoritative by the key political and judicial actors, despite their formally advisory pedigree, see Mathen (2019); Heard (1991) 9.

[258] Lord Rosser (Labour) HL Deb 23 July 2019, vol 799 col 699.

[259] HL Deb 5 July 2021, vol 738 col 876 (Baroness Stowell of Beeston) (referring to the declaration of incompatibility in *Thompson*).

[260] Sathanapally (2012) 46.

[261] Ibid.

flashpoints of friction, the predominant dynamic between the political and judicial branches has been one of collaboration and compliance, not conflict and condemnation.[262] The main focus of governmental and parliamentary behaviour is on *how* to implement the declaration, not *whether* to do so.[263] As Jeff King observed, the empirical evidence supports a view of

> collaboration and divided responsibilities, with courts adjudicating cases and setting out findings on the narrow issue, whilst the Government and Parliament work from those conclusions to refashion policy accordingly[264] ... Parliamentarians tend to view themselves as accepting and working with the judgments of the courts and not ordinarily being in a position to offer a contrary interpretation of the right once the court has ruled definitely on the issue.[265]

Finally, whilst declarations of incompatibility are undoubtedly 'adverse rulings' of the higher courts in the sense that they declare that a legislative provision enacted by Parliament contravenes rights, they were not always treated by the government as a tragic thwarting of democratic will. In the vast majority of cases, declarations were politically uncontentious and in many, they were viewed as desirable 'steps on the road to better governance'.[266] Though nominally a 'defeat' in court, the political actors often viewed declarations as valuable opportunities to make the law more just and compliant with rights.[267]

Even with respect to the four most controversial declarations, a simple diagnosis of bitter conflict and undifferentiated disagreement masks a more complex constitutional reality. Often, the rhetorical offensive on the floor of the House of Commons was tempered by more measured political statements in the less visible and politically charged environment of parliamentary committees. In each of the four controversial cases, the political actors conspicuously eschewed the route of open political defiance, preferring instead to pursue a more conciliatory approach, sometimes implementing the declaration in a minimal or begrudging fashion.[268] There was a striking

---

[262] Sathanapally (2012) '2'; King (2015a) 187.
[263] King (2015a) 185; Sathanapally (2012) 131; Chandrachud (2014) 636; Chandrachud (2017) 83.
[264] King (2015a) 187; Sathanapally (2012) 5.
[265] King (2015a) 176.
[266] Irvine (2003b) 323.
[267] Mathen (2016) 102.
[268] Sathanapally (2012) 148; Hillebrecht (2014) 99.

combination of combative political rhetoric in public, and willing compliance behind the scenes.

What explains this curious phenomenon of combative rhetoric and collaborative action? Part of the answer resides in the 'performance element of politics',[269] where successful politicians must speak to multiple audiences simultaneously. When talking tough, they are speaking to the public, the tabloids, journalists, the Opposition, their own backbenches, and the electorate at large.[270] But when complying with unpopular judicial decisions, they are doing their job as Ministers of the Crown, honouring their constitutional obligations to respect judicial decisions, even if they dislike the outcome.

In the day-to-day dynamics of democratic politics, elected politicians have no choice but to consider the political optics alongside policy options, especially on issues which illustrate 'the political valence of penal populism'.[271] Politicians operate in a parliamentary and political habitat where 'issue politicisation'[272] and 'political game-playing'[273] are classic Opposition techniques to make political capital out of an electorally damaging policy change. Therefore, in striving to understand the normative landscape in which politicians operate, we need to distinguish between rhetoric and reality, aware that a political sound-bite to deal with today may put pressure on a constitutional norm which has deeper normative resonance over time.

9   Conclusion

This chapter has argued that there is an emerging constitutional convention in favour of compliance with declarations of incompatibility, unless exceptional reasons arise. It is a qualified, not an absolute, convention, giving expression to what is normally and normatively expected of political actors following a declaration of incompatibility by the higher courts. This does not preclude the Government or Parliament from rejecting a declaration of incompatibility in exceptional circumstances. But it certainly precludes them doing so simply because they disagree with it. As argued in Chapter 11, the political obligation to comply with

---

[269] Crewe (2015a) 51; Crewe (2015b) 223–4; Kaufman (1997) 81.
[270] Russell et al. (2017) 11.
[271] Ip (2020) 48.
[272] Russell & Gover (2017) 100.
[273] Ibid 102–4.

declarations is grounded in a second-order reason to comply with court rulings on rights, irrespective of whether the government agrees with the judicial decision on its merits. The empirical analysis in this chapter reveals that parliamentarians across both Houses repeatedly articulated a normative obligation to comply with such rulings, nested in the values of constitutional comity, judicial independence, and the rule of law.

Of course, to be confident that the convention is fully established – not just in *statu nascendi* – we would want to see it tested in some more highly controversial cases. Thus far, the constitutional norm of compliance has weathered the various political storms. Even when political controversy reached dangerously high levels, the convention of compliance was relatively resistant to the political pressures to pander to the passions of the moment in the heated cauldron of political debate.

The argument advanced in this chapter does not rest on a Panglossian faith in pure civic virtue unsullied by the messy realities of quotidian politics. Instead, it rests on a multifaceted picture where the dark side of politics was firmly in view. As we saw, politicians were not above taking some occasional cheap shots at the independent judiciary. Nor did they always publicly announce their constitutional role-obligations to the assembled press and public gallery. Indeed, they often played to the gallery, whilst simultaneously complying with their constitutional obligations behind the scenes.

The important point here is that a constitutional convention does not depend for its survival on an other-worldly sense of political altruism. It is shored up by constitutional checks and balances, and the vocal vigilance of the Opposition, backbench MPs, the House of Lords, parliamentary committees, government advisers, the media, interest groups, and a wide array of civil society actors who, together, bolster adherence to constitutional norms on a quotidian basis. As political scientist Robert Hazell observed, 'Conventions may not be legally enforceable, but that does not mean they do not have enforcers'.[274] The story of declarations of incompatibility illustrates the sobering and restraining force of 'naming and shaming'[275] as a way of coaxing, if not compelling, compliance with constitutional norms.

---

[274] Hazell (2015) 174; McHarg (2008) 869; Pozen (2014) 72.
[275] For anthropological insights into the role of shame as a powerful sanction in the Westminster Parliament, see Crewe (2015a) 13; Crewe (2005) 138.

Instead of a dynamic of dialogue, disagreement and constitutional displacement where court rulings are treated as optional statements in a constitutional conversation, what in fact emerged is a collaborative constitutional relationship where political actors generally treat the declarations of a coordinate branch with comity and respect. Though fraught on occasion and fragile at times, the general picture is one of collaboration rather than conflict, comity rather than condemnation and disdain.

~

Conclusion

The Currency of Collaboration

1 Collaborative Leitmotivs

This argument of this book has been that protecting rights is a collaborative enterprise between all three branches of government, where each branch has a distinct but complementary role to play in the joint endeavour of securing good government under the constitution. Whilst scholars have long debated the relative merits of either judicial or legislative supremacy, I disrupt those dichotomies, showing how the branches combine, counterbalance, and collaborate in complementary and constructive ways. Resting on the belief that the success and sustainability of any constitutional democracy depends on the health of the working relationships between the branches of government, this book articulates a relational and collaborative vision of constitutionalism.

Instead of perceiving the branches as solitary actors in splendid isolation – or sworn enemies in institutional combat – the collaborative constitution appreciates the branches of government *as partners* in a constitutional scheme, where they must engage with each other in a spirit of comity and collaboration. They must each do their own job in the collaborative enterprise, whilst working on their relationships. In order for a healthy body politic to remain resilient over time, there must be some 'play in the joints'.[1] Therefore, the collaborative constitution calls on the branches of government to recognise and respect the roles of their partners in authority, avoiding undue encroachment on each other's rightful domains. But beyond the norms of non-interference and restraint, the collaborative constitution embraces the positive obligations of mutual respect, support and role-recognition which comprise the

---

[1] Post & Siegel (2003b) 38.

'connective tissue'[2] between the branches.[3] These norms of constructive engagement and mutual respect provide the strong sinews of the collaborative constitution.

One of the aims of this book has been to reorient constitutional discourse away from the dominant preoccupation with inter-institutional conflict and crisis, attempting to seed a more productive conversation about the collaborative dynamics which make the system work. In doing so, this book articulates a collaborative conception of constitutionalism that sounds more in responsibility and restraint than in conflict and confrontation.[4]

One of the book's recurring leitmotivs is the value of institutional restraint as vital to the successful working of the collaborative constitution. In place of no-holds-barred *'constitutional showdowns'*,[5] the collaborative constitution foregrounds the value of *constitutional slowdown*, where all actors commit to the painstaking process and demanding discipline of making constitutional democracy work over the long haul. In doing so, this book internalises the insight that 'every political constitution in which different bodies share the supreme power is only enabled to exist by the forbearance of those among whom this power is distributed . . . each must exercise a wise moderation'.[6]

Where norms of forbearance and restraint are strong, the branches 'do not use their institutional prerogatives to the hilt, even if it is technically legal to do so',[7] because such action could imperil the system as a whole. In order to sustain a healthy body politic over time, the key constitutional actors must play by the constitutional rules of the game, rather than tilt the playing field for short-term advantage. The collaborative constitution therefore calls for the seemingly old-fashioned virtues of moderation and self-restraint, comity and compromise, civility and sensitivity, forbearance and fair play.[8] Though often overlooked and undervalued in contemporary times, these are the values and virtues needed to make

---

[2] Greene (2018) 94, 103.
[3] McLean (2018) 414.
[4] Pozen (2014) 63.
[5] Posner & Vermeule (2008).
[6] Letter of Lord John Russell to Poulett Thomson (14 October 1839), cited in Shane (2003) 508; Levitsky & Ziblatt (2019) 8, 106ff; Willis (2022) 391.
[7] Levitsky & Ziblatt (2019) 106.
[8] MacIntyre (1967) 24ff (describing them as the 'secondary virtues'); Pozen (2014) 89.

constitutional democracy work.[9] They lie at the heart of the collaborative constitution.

Of course, we are naturally mesmerised by the agonistic drama of dissensus and the flashpoints of friction where heroes and villains collide. Both at the practical and theoretical levels, we rivet on the moments of conflict and crisis, framing our understanding of constitutional dynamics through the conflictual lens of 'constitutional hardball'.[10] We are jolted to attention when politicians excoriate the courts, but are less attentive when politicians comply with those rulings *sine ira et studio*.[11] We focus our gaze on the blockbuster cases where courts strike down legislation in apparent defiance of democratic will, but overlook the countless cases where the courts validate and vindicate democratically determined priorities. The result is 'an imbalanced discourse around constitutional conflict'[12] and a consequent neglect of the constitutional norms which frame, shape and constrain that conflict when it arises.

One of the aims of this book is to situate decisions about rights in this larger landscape of constitutional practice, where comity and collaboration, respect and restraint, tension and tautness, all have a role to play. In defending the idea of the collaborative constitution, I keep in mind 'the moves that officials do *not* make'[13] – the countless times the government does not rail against an adverse court ruling with vituperative rhetoric, and the numerous cases where courts do not find a violation of fundamental rights out of respect for the institutional capacity and legitimacy of the democratically elected actors. By exploring the constitutional paths not taken, this book uncovers a rich normative terrain of collaborative constitutionalism marked by the norms of mutual respect and restraint in a system of 'shared authority'.[14]

The collaborative constitution does not naively overlook conflict or contestation. Nor does it underestimate the need for healthy tension and robust checks and balances in a well-functioning constitutional order. Instead, it discerns an interactive dynamic framed and shaped by the norms of the collaborative constitution. Though adherence to these norms is difficult and undoubtedly fragile at times, I uncover a set of

---

[9] Craiutu (2012) (describing moderation as a 'virtue for courageous minds').
[10] Tushnet (2004); Balkin (2008).
[11] Max Weber (1919); Jeff King (2015a) 176.
[12] Pozen (2014) 4.
[13] Ibid 69; Devins (2017).
[14] Kyritsis (2015).

collaborative dynamics which suffuse the role-morality of key constitutional actors in a collaborative constitutional order.

In doing so, I seek to reorient constitutional discourse away from the commonplace conflictual rendering of the separation of powers, towards a more constructive, complementary and collaborative appreciation of constitutional dynamics which puts conflict in its place. Contributing to a broader project of 'reshaping constitutionalism'.[15] I argue that we should put working relationships between the key constitutional actors at the core of constitutional theory.[16]

Though the common trajectory of constitutional scholarship has taken us down a conflictual path where the branches of government are framed as 'competing supremacies',[17] the collaborative constitution calls us back from the brink to appreciate the norms of mutual respect and restraint which forestall ferocity and avoid the catastrophe of 'constitutional showdowns'. Prevention is often better than cure. Therefore, the collaborative constitution adopts a preventative and holistic approach to maintaining the long-term health of the body politic.[18]

Instead of facing off against each other in the mode of 'constitutional hardball',[19] this book emphasises the less glamorous, but more important, values and virtues of constitutional collaboration, where the key actors adhere to the rules of the game in order to accrue the mutual benefits of constitutional collaboration. At the core of this book, therefore, lies a fundamental commitment to the idea of *constitutional fair play* marked by the values of reciprocal respect and restraint in service of the common goal of making constitutional democracy work.

In contemporary constitutional and political theory, there is a recurring preoccupation with disagreement. How can we make legitimate and lasting decisions in a democracy if we all disagree on matters of moral, social, and political principle? Foregrounding the theme of deep disagreement, Jeremy Waldron has responded to this conundrum by advocating a system of pure participatory democracy where all voices are factored into the final decision.[20] This theme is echoed in constitutional theoretical debates, where scholars transfer the fact of disagreement to the

---

[15] Hunt (2007) 467.
[16] Cartabia (2020).
[17] Hunt (2007) 468.
[18] Shogimen (2008).
[19] Tushnet (2004).
[20] Waldron (1999b); Waldron (1993a); Waldron (1993b); Waldron (2006); Waldron (2014).

institutional level, urging the branches of government to engage in open disagreement about matters of principle, with the democratic legislature having 'the last word'.

This book charts a different constitutional course. Instead of advocating a dynamic of deep disagreement and no-holds-barred combat, the idea of the collaborative constitution shifts our vision towards the values of inter-institutional respect and restraint – civility and sensitivity – which frame and shape our disagreements about what to do in a democracy. The abiding image is one of *constrained conflict, regulated rivalry* and *disciplined disagreement*, channelled, filtered, and mediated through the inherited institutional pathways of a constitutional democracy. Democratic disagreements are informed by a modicum of respect and restraint. Political disputes are framed by the constitutional rules of the game. Robust disagreement is tempered by 'robust civility'.[21]

Instead of focusing on the fact of disagreement, this book explores the 'secondary virtues'[22] required to enable us to disagree with respect. Given that any political community needs action-in-concert *despite* disagreements, we need to know '*how* to disagree'[23] in order to get things done in a way which commands acceptance across the political spectrum. Of course, the polarised plurality of contemporary politics poses severe challenges for stable and sustainable political decision-making, especially when emotions run high and disagreement goes deep. In this circumstance, learning how to disagree with respect, restraint and civility has never been more important. Perhaps it has never been more difficult. But by embracing a general preference for constitutional slowdown over showdown – and a commitment to the values of mutual respect and constitutional civility – the collaborative constitutional ideal gives us resources to avert or ameliorate some of the worst excesses of constitutional hardball.[24]

An underlying theme of this book is that learning 'how to disagree' means knowing 'how to collaborate' and work together in service of a common goal. The achievement of action-in-concert in circumstances of disagreement needs the collaborative virtues of comity and civility, complementarity and constructive engagement, all framed by the restraining reminders of reciprocity, reputation and repeat-play.

---

[21] Garton Ash (2016); Bejan (2017).
[22] MacIntyre (1967) 24.
[23] Leslie (2022).
[24] Bejan (2017); Leslie (2022).

Therefore, this book portends a paradigm shift from contestation to collaboration. In order to make decisions in a democracy, we need to reach 'beyond disagreement',[25] putting our diverse views and deeply-held principles to work as part of a collaborative constitutional scheme. Action-in-concert is not easy. It is the foundational challenge of the collaborative constitution.

2   Broadening the Collaborative Horizon

In defending the idea of the collaborative constitution, this book opens up new and fruitful lines of constitutional inquiry which, I hope, will stimulate future research and critical engagement. Though these broader horizons lie beyond the scope of this book, I want to gesture at some of them here in order to illustrate the rich resources of the collaborative constitutional ideal.

One future direction is to draw on collaborative ideas to reshape our understanding of the separation of powers, pushing the boundaries of received understandings beyond the misleading misnomer of *separated* powers and institutional silos. By foregrounding the deep interdependence and dynamic interaction between and within the branches of government, I seek to connect constitutional theory to practice in ways which prompt us to view institutional interaction as a species of *positive constitutionalism*. If the separation of powers denotes a system of distinct institutions *dividing labour, curbing abuse* and *working together* in a system of 'shared authority',[26] then we need to make sense of that shared responsibility in new and innovative ways. In doing so, I hope to contribute to the burgeoning literature and broader research agenda of rethinking the separation of powers in the twenty-first century.[27]

Another avenue for future research concerns *the multi-institutional turn* in constitutional scholarship. Whilst this book explores an array of constitutional actors outside the courts, it prefigures a broader inquiry into the largely unmapped terrain of constitutional actors beyond 'the usual constitutional coterie'.[28] These include political

---

[25] Sathanapally (2012).

[26] Kyritsis (2015).

[27] For contemporary contributions towards this endeavour, see Ackerman (2000); McMillan (2010); Kyritsis (2017); Waldron (2016) chapter 3; Möllers (2019); Carolan (2011); Malleson (2010); Baroš, Dufek & Kosař (2020); Baraggia, Fasone & Vasoni (2020); Fowkes & Fombad (2016); Mendes & Venzke (2018); Sandro (2022) chapter 7.

[28] Appleby, MacDonnell & Synot (2020) 449.

parties,[29] Ombudspersons,[30] Electoral Commissions,[31] human rights and equality commissions, the media,[32] Law Reform Commissions,[33] human rights NGOs, anti-corruption watchdogs, government advisers, 'knowledge institutions',[34] and strategic litigators.[35] Looking beyond 'the holy trinity',[36] we can reimagine the variegated constitutional landscape in new and exciting ways.

For some commentators, these bodies comprise a 'New Fourth Branch'[37] of government, whose existence challenges traditional paradigms of the separation of powers. That striking claim warrants deeper reflection and critical engagement in future scholarship. At first glance, it seems hard to imagine that such a wide array of disparate actors and bodies could comprise a singular branch of government. Here is not the place to analyse the 'New Fourth Branch' claim in depth. This must await a future exploration. But whatever the outcome of that inquiry, one thing is crystal clear. This is that these institutions play a vitally important role in a collaborative constitutional scheme. In the words of the South African Constitution, these bodies are institutions supporting and strengthening constitutional democracy.[38] Therefore, we need to include them in a panoptic analysis of the tools and techniques of democratic constitutionalism in the twenty-first century.

The idea of collaborative constitutionalism may also bear fruit at the international level. Whilst this book has focused on collaborative constitutionalism in the domestic constitutional order, future scholarship could consider the viability of collaborative constitutional governance in the international and transnational field. The collaborative theme already resonates with international law scholars who examine international relations 'after hegemony'.[39] It is also implicit in accounts which present

---

[29] Rosenblum (2008).
[30] Abraham (2008a); Abraham (2008b).
[31] Kildea (2020).
[32] Gies (2015a); Gies (2015b).
[33] Stark (2017b).
[34] Jackson (2021), referring to statistical offices, universities, a free press, libraries and museums, etc. Though tellingly, and to my mind correctly, Jackson does not claim that these 'knowledge institutions' are part of a 'new fourth branch' of government.
[35] Duffy (2018).
[36] Ackerman (2010) 129; Carolan (2009) 21.
[37] Tushnet (2021); Scheppele (2009); Landau (2014) 1515–16; Pal (2016); Khaitan (2021); Albert & Pal (2018) 128–32.
[38] South African Constitution 1996, chapter 9; Tushnet (2021) chapter 1.
[39] Keohane (2005); Roughan (2013).

international relations as a complex form of 'cooperative network governance',[40] grounded in iterated interactions, heterarchical relationships, and constructive engagements between a multiplicity of constitutional actors working across borders.[41]

Though international law is often viewed as the poor cousin of its domestic counterpart because of the former's apparent paucity of strict legal sanctions, the collaborative account highlights the striking parallels between them. After all, on the collaborative conception, the domestic order is also grounded in the foundational norms of comity, collaboration and conflict-management, framed in a context of reciprocity, reputation and repeat-play. Therefore, the theory of collaborative constitutionalism is ripe for application and adaptation in the international sphere.[42] Occupying a precarious middle ground between anarchy and utopia, the idea of collaborative governance could help to make sense of 'the common participation of competing visions in a joint endeavour'.[43]

The collaborative vision may also help to navigate the choppy waters at the interface between national and supra-national orders. When we consider the relationship between national courts and the ECtHR, we see 'a dialectical process at work, as the European Court and national courts influence the work of the other'.[44] As a former judge of the Strasbourg court observed, in order to inculcate respect for rights across forty-eight countries, the ECtHR cannot act as a 'lone ranger'.[45] Instead, it must work together with 'compliance partners'[46] at the domestic level, seeking to forge constructive and collaborative relationships with them. Foundational to the success of those relationships are the norms of 'mutual respect and a common will to act together'.[47]

---

[40] Krisch (2010) 183.
[41] Koh (1997) 2602ff; Brunnée & Toope (2010); Halberstam (2009); Krisch (2010) 23, 69, 111; Finnemore & Sikkink (1998); Bates (2014) 1170; Krisch, Corradini & Reimers (2020).
[42] Brunnée & Toope (2010) 7, 23, 38 (proposing an 'interactional account' of international law); Lupo & Fasone (2016) (examining inter-parliamentary cooperation in the 'composite European Constitution').
[43] Krisch (2010) 275; Goldsmith & Levinson (2009).
[44] Lord Reed (President of the UKSC) (2020) vii.
[45] Garlicki (2008) 515.
[46] Donald (2017); Bates (2015).
[47] Garlicki (2008) 530 (articulating a 'cooperation of courts'); Donald & Leach (2016) 306 (presenting the Convention system 'as interactional and collaborative'); Maduro (2009); Mahoney (2015) 27; Bates (2017) 302; Saul (2017) 379.

Probing the potential of the collaborative account, one could compare and contrast the European doctrine of the 'margin of appreciation'[48] with domestic doctrines of deference. One could also explore the mutually responsive and catalytic forms of 'political process review'[49] in the Strasbourg and domestic courts. The idea of collaborative constitutionalism therefore provides a rich resource for those engaged in probing and parsing the dynamic interplay between domestic and international institutions.[50]

3   Collaboration as Currency

This book rests on the insight that unwritten and uncodified constitutional norms are fundamental to any system of constitutional democracy. Beneath the constitutional architecture lie attitudes. Beneath the forms lie norms. The dependence of legal forms on political norms provides a sobering reminder of the inherent fragility of constitutional democracy as a system of governance. These days, we are all living in 'fragile democracies'.[51]

But it should also instil a measure of modesty and scholarly humility before advocating architectural solutions to constitutional problems. As Wojciech Sadurski poignantly observed when commenting on 'Poland's constitutional breakdown',[52] constitutional law scholars must face up to 'the relative irrelevance of formal constitutional design'.[53] In highlighting the '*relative* irrelevance' of constitutional design, Sadurski did not deny the importance of good constitutional design to a well-functioning constitutional order. As he rightly acknowledged, good institutional design can frame, channel and mediate democratic decision-making in numerous, beneficial ways. But Sadurski was reminding us of the deeper, Hartian point that all law bottoms out in non-law. And at that foundational level, what matters most to the viability and vitality of the

---

[48] Letsas (2006); Delaney (2016) 34–43.
[49] Gardbaum (2020a).
[50] Kanetake & Nollkaemper (2016); Daly (2017) 297ff (arguing for 'a more co-ordinated pluralism' between domestic and regional courts). Ideas of collaborative governance have also been used to capture constitutional relationships in federal states, under the rubric of 'cooperative federalism', see Schütze (2009); Gaudreault-Desbiens (2014); Cyr (2014); Powell (2019) 2691.
[51] Issaacharoff (2015).
[52] Sadurski (2019).
[53] Sadurski (2020a) 330.

constitutional order is an abiding commitment by the key political actors to play by the constitutional rules of the game.[54] A healthy constitutional democracy ultimately depends on 'the good faith of those who work it'.[55] If the rules of the constitutional game are cursorily or contemptuously cast aside, no amount of good design – not even the most intricate and exquisite scheme of checks and balances – can compensate for their lack.[56]

Reflections on the fundamentality and fragility of constitutional norms leads us to a critical question about the *currency of collaborative constitutionalism*. By using the term 'currency', I gesture towards two different phenomena. First, I refer to the general acceptance or prevalence of collaborative constitutionalism as an operative ideal in contemporary constitutional democracies. This is *currency as contemporary commitment*. Second, I refer to the idea of collaboration as a form of *constitutional capital*, i.e. a valuable and precious constitutional resource we need to conserve, treasure and enhance, in order to enjoy the fruits of sustainable constitutional democracy over time. This is *currency as constitutional capital*. Let us start with the idea about *currency as contemporary commitment*.

When we look around the world today, we are confronted with the spectre of constitutional corrosion and democratic decay.[57] Though authoritarianism by an omnipotent Executive has always been the key threat to constitutional democracy, today's examples of democratic decline include populist regimes which have come to power through the electoral ballot box, not by the authoritarian iron fist.[58] Even the most established and long-standing constitutional democracies in the world are showing worrying signs of democratic decay. From East to West, and from North to Global South, there is a palpable sense that 'the unwritten norms that facilitate comity and cooperation'[59] in a well-functioning constitutional democracy are in deep decline.

The UK has not been immune from these broader trends. In the fractious and fragmented post-Brexit environment, Prime Minister Boris Johnson was accused of showing 'contempt for the constitution'[60]

---

[54] Levinson (2011); Chafetz (2011); Sadurski (2020a) 330; Huq (2018).
[55] Issacharoff (2020) 1135 (quoting William Gladstone).
[56] Putnam (1994) 10; McLean (2018) 414; Daly (2017) 293.
[57] Graber, Levinson & Tushnet (2018a).
[58] Issacharoff (2018); Sadurski (2020a).
[59] Pozen (2014) 9; Chafetz & Pozen (2018) 1430.
[60] Brazier (2020).

and 'disdain for the decency of our constitutional conventions'.[61] The charge-sheet of Boris Johnson's 'constitutional abuses'[62] included the unlawful prorogation of Parliament in 2019;[63] misleading Parliament;[64] violating the Ministerial Code;[65] threatening to violate international and domestic law;[66] and attacking the independence of various public institutions, including the courts, the independent legal profession[67], civil servants, the BBC,[68] and the Electoral Commission.[69] Academic commentators pronounced a 'full house of ethical violations'[70] of the *Seven Principles of Public Life* as set out by the Nolan Committee in 1995,[71] namely, selflessness, integrity, objectivity, accountability, openness, honesty, and leadership.[72] Johnson also won the ignominious title of being the first serving British Prime Minister to be convicted of a criminal offence for violating the lockdown rules his own government had devised,[73] and then compounding the constitutional problem by (initially) refusing to resign when found to have broken the law.

Abstracting from the particulars, the common thread linking all of these actions was the contempt they showed for the 'tacit understandings'[74] of the British constitution, and a determination to evade the manifold mechanisms of horizontal accountability designed to keep the Executive in check. Constitutional historian Peter Hennessy proclaimed this to be 'the most severe constitutional crisis involving a Prime Minister'[75] in living memory. Former Prime Minister Sir John Major

---

[61] Wells (2022) (quoting Peter Hennessy).

[62] Blick & Hennessy (2019) 3.

[63] On the prorogation, see *R (Miller) v Secretary of State for Exiting the European Union* [2017] UKSC 5 ('the *Miller* case'); Craig (2020); Endicott (2017b); Barber, Hickman & King (2017); Shipman & Wheeler (2019).

[64] Forrest (2022).

[65] Gordon (2022); Culbertson (2022).

[66] Hogarth (2020).

[67] Bowcott (2020); Grierson & Taylor (2020).

[68] Dittert (2021) (on 'the politics of lies' and erosion of the rule of law under the Johnson government).

[69] Toynbee (2022).

[70] Gordon (2022).

[71] Seven Principles of Public Life, established by the Nolan Committee in 1995.

[72] Blick & Hennessy (2019) 6–8.

[73] Young (2022).

[74] Low (1904) 12.

[75] Hennessy, quoted in Mance (2022); Clark (2022).

accused Johnson of 'pulling our constitution to shreds ... and eroding public trust in British democracy'.[76]

By violating constitutional conventions and accepted norms of political behaviour, Johnson exposed the fragility at the foundations of the British constitutional order, leading to renewed arguments in favour a written constitution.[77] If the unwritten norms of *constitutional fair play* ultimately depend on an ingrained sense of constitutional decency backed up by the informal constraints of 'naming and shaming',[78] there was an understandable concern that they will have little purchase with a Prime Minister commonly described as 'shameless'.[79] Instead of a sense of *constitutional fair play*, we saw elected politicians 'gaming the system'.[80] Instead of political actors guarding the long-term principles of constitutional integrity, we saw political opportunism for short-term personal political gain. Instead of embracing a Weberian 'ethics of responsibility',[81] we entered the era of audacity.

Does this spell the end of the collaborative constitution? Should we embark on a 'eulogy for the constitution that was',[82] turning our gaze away from the demanding norms of the collaborative constitution towards a glum acceptance that all constitutional hope is lost? With democratic decay and constitutional corrosion visible to varying degrees across the globe, it is tempting to form a line on desolation row. But it is precisely when the norms of constitutional government are no longer taken for granted by political elites that we should redouble our efforts to protect the principles and practices which lie at the foundation of a successful and sustainable constitutional order. In a context of constitutional corrosion and democratic decay, we should deepen, rather than disregard, the unwritten norms of the collaborative constitution. This recalls the point made in the Introduction to this book, namely, that the collaborative constitution is both practice and ideal. When the practice falls short, we should nonetheless keep sight of the collaborative ideal to

---

[76] Major (2022).

[77] See e.g. King (2019b).

[78] Crewe (2015a) 13.

[79] Taylor (2022) ('For years, Boris Johnson's superpower was his lack of shame'); Nichols (2022); Graham (2022); Neslen (2021); Giordano (2022); O'Toole (2022); Bogg (2018) (arguing that 'shame has ceased to operate as any kind of constraint on populists and demagogues').

[80] McCrea (2022); Sumption (2022a); Sumption (2022b).

[81] Weber (1919).

[82] Webber (2014a).

which all constitutional actors should orient their behaviour. Only then can we steer the ship of state back onto the course of justice.

When assessing the British constitutional order, we should remember that the 'shameless'[83] Prime Minister was eventually shamed and constitutional conventions ultimately won out.[84] In fact, the countless critiques of Boris Johnson's norm-violating behaviour are themselves testament to the abiding value of collaborative constitutional norms. Boris Johnson's premiership is as much a story about the widespread social, political and legal commitment to the 'tacit understandings' of the British constitution as it is about their flagrant violation. In the mass exodus of Ministers, civil servants, and advisers from the Johnson government, many politicians justified their decision to resign by relying on the institutional role-moralities inherent in a well-functioning constitutional order, where the 'duty to office and country [must come] before partisan self-interest'.[85] Even if some of those statements are read as politically self-serving, they are still evidence of the norms political actors believe to be normatively and constitutionally desirable. The constitutional picture is more complicated than might at first appear.

This brings us to the idea of *currency as constitutional capital.* Analogously with the idea of 'social capital'[86] – i.e. the values of reciprocity, collaboration, trust and fair play that ensue from a dense network of reciprocal social relations within a civic community – I suggest that the norms of collaborative constitutionalism constitute a rich resource of *constitutional capital* which we should treasure and treat with constitutional care.

A country that is rich in constitutional capital is one where the key constitutional actors commit to the rules of the game and abide by the norms of constitutional fair play. It is one where the political figures accept the myriad mechanisms of horizontal accountability embedded in a well-functioning constitutional order. Internalising the idea of constitutional relationships based on reciprocity and repeat play,[87] the government respects the Opposition as an adversary, not an enemy.[88] Democracy is not viewed as the knee-jerk reaction to a univocal 'will of

---

[83] Taylor (2022); O'Toole (2022).

[84] McCrae (2022); Young (2022); Sumption (2022b); Gordon (2022).

[85] Sturgeon (2022).

[86] Putnam (2000) 19ff; Putnam (1994) 88ff; Estlund (2003) 50–6, 106–8, 114–18, 164–5, 178–80; Ellickson (1991); Pinker (2018) 235.

[87] Issacharoff (2018) 448; Levinson (2011) 676–7, 684, 711.

[88] Ignatieff (2013a).

the people', but rather as a painstaking process of *mediated majoritarianism* where majority will is filtered, channelled and mediated through the inherited institutions of a constitutional democracy.[89] On this vision, constitutionalism is appreciated *as usufruct*,[90] i.e. as a valuable inheritance from times past and a precious legacy for future generations. The government of the day is merely a temporary custodian of the constitutional order, not its commander and master. Therefore, there is a heavy responsibility on the current custodians to pass it on in good constitutional shape.

By presenting the norms of the collaborative constitution as a form of *constitutional capital*, I am not conjuring a constitutional nirvana. The achievement of collaborative constitutionalism laid out in this book is already discernible – substantially though imperfectly – in many constitutional systems. Indeed, it is not that long ago that the norms of comity, collaboration and constitutional fair play were taken for granted in established constitutional democracies. By framing these norms as a source of *constitutional capital*, I am not telling a sanguine or celebratory story to lull us into a false sense of constitutional complacency. On the contrary, my aim is to underscore their priceless value and to highlight the catastrophic costs of squandering this precious resource for short-term political gain. Collaborative constitutionalism is a valuable currency which we should not devalue by turning our back on the hard, slow and deliberate work it requires.

We all have a duty of constitutional care to ensure that the norms of comity, collaboration and constitutional fair play are preserved and promoted in a shared constitutional order which is sustainable over time. The time for collaboration is now. By investing in the demanding discipline of the collaborative constitution today, we preserve the precious legacy of a constitutional democracy, whilst contributing to a constitutional gift which keeps on giving.

---

[89] Chapter 1.
[90] Heclo (2008) 7; Heclo (2006) 737.

BIBLIOGRAPHY

Abraham, A (2008a) 'The Ombudsman and Individual Rights' (2008) 61 *Parliamentary Affairs* 370

(2008b) 'The Ombudsman as Part of the UK Constitution: A Contested Role?' (2008) 61 *Parliamentary Affairs* 206

Abrahamson, S & Hughes, R (1991) 'Shall We Dance? Steps for Legislators and Judges in Statutory Interpretation' (1991) 75 *Minnesota Law Review* 1045

Ackerman, B (2000) 'The New Separation of Powers' (2000) 113 *Harvard Law Review* 633

(2010) 'Good-bye, Montesquieu' in Rose-Ackerman & Lindseth (eds.) *Comparative Administrative Law: An Introduction* (Edward Elgar)

Adams, E (2021) 'Judicial Discretion and the Declaration of Incompatibility: Constitutional Considerations in Controversial Cases' 2021 *Public Law* 311

Adams, E & Bower, E (2022) 'Notwithstanding History: The Rights-Protecting Purposes of Section 33 of the Charter' (2022) 26 *Review of Constitutional Studies* 121

Ahmed, F, Albert, R & Perry, A (2019) 'Judging Constitutional Conventions' (2019) 17 *International Journal of Constitutional Law* 787

(2020) 'Enforcing Constitutional Conventions' (2020) 17 *International Journal of Constitutional Law* 1146

Albert, R (2008) 'Advisory Review: The Reincarnation of the Notwithstanding Clause' (2008) 45 *Alberta Law Review* 1037

(2009) 'The Fusion of Presidentialism and Parliamentarism' (2009) 57 *American Journal of Comparative Law* 531

(2010) 'Presidential Values in Parliamentary Democracies' (2010) 8 *International Journal of Constitutional Law* 207

(2018) 'The Desuetude of the Notwithstanding Clause – And How to Revive It' in MacFarlane (ed.) *Policy Change, Courts, and the Canadian Constitution* (University of Toronto Press)

Albert, R & Pal, M (2018) 'The Democratic Resilience of the Canadian Constitution' in Graber, Levinson & Tushnet (eds.) *Constitutional Democracy in Crisis?* (Oxford University Press)

Allan, TRS (1993) *Law, Liberty, and Justice: The Legal Foundations of British Constitutionalism* (Clarendon Press)

(2006a) 'Human Rights and Judicial Review: A Critique of "Due Deference"' (2006) 65 *Cambridge Law Journal* 671

(2006b) 'Publication Review: Our Republican Constitution' [2006] *Public Law* 172

(2013) *The Sovereignty of Law: Freedom, Constitution, and Common Law* (Oxford University Press)

(2014) 'Accountability to Law' in Bamforth & Leyland (eds.) *Accountability in the Contemporary Constitution* (Oxford University Press)

Allison, J (1994) 'Fuller's Analysis of Polycentric Disputes and the Limits of Adjudication' (1994) 53 *Cambridge Law Journal* 367

(2007) *The English Historical Constitution: Continuity, Change and European Effects* (Cambridge University Press)

Almond, G & Verba, S (1989) *The Civic Culture: Political Attitudes and Democracy in Five Nations* (Sage Publishing)

Amery, L (1964) *Thoughts on the Constitution* (Oxford University Press)

Amos, M (2004) 'R v Secretary of State for the Home Department, ex p Anderson: Ending the Home Secretary's Sentencing Role' (2004) 67 *Modern Law Review* 108

Anastaplo, G (2004) 'Loyal Opposition in a Modern Democracy' (2004) 35 *Loyola University Chicago Law Journal* 1009

Anderson, D (2014) 'The Independent Review of Terrorism Laws' [2014] *Public Law* 403

Appleby, G (2012) 'The Evolution of a Public Sentinel: Australia's Solicitor-General' (2012) 63 *Northern Ireland Legal Quarterly* 397

(2016) 'Reform of the Attorney General: Comparing Britain and Australia' [2016] *Public Law* 573

(2017) 'Horizontal Accountability: The Rights-Protective Promise and Fragility of Executive Integrity Institutions' (2017) 23 *Australian Journal of Human Rights* 168

Appleby, G, MacDonnell, V & Synot, E (2020) 'The Pervasive Constitution: The Constitution outside the Courts' (2020) 48 *Federal Law Review* 437

Appleby, G & Olijnyk, A (2017) 'Parliamentary Deliberation on Constitutional Limits in the Legislative Process' (2017) 40 *University of New South Wales Law Journal* 976

(2020) 'Executive Policy Development and Constitutional Norms: Practice and Perceptions' (2020) 18 *International Journal of Constitutional Law* 1136

Arnardóttir, O (2017) 'The "Procedural Turn" under the European Convention on Human Rights and Presumptions of Convention Compliance' (2017) 15 *International Journal of Constitutional Law* 9

Atiyah, P (1988) 'Judicial Legislative Relations in England' in Katzmann (ed.) *Judges and Legislators: Towards Institutional Comity* (Brookings Institution)

Axelrod, R (1990) *The Evolution of Cooperation* (Penguin)

Axworthy, T (2007) 'The Notwithstanding Clause: Sword of Damocles or Paper Tiger?' (2007) 25 *Policy Options* 58

Bailey, D (2020a) 'Bridging the Gap: Legislative Drafting Practice and Statutory Interpretation' [2020] *Public Law* 220

    (2020b) 'Interpreting Parliamentary Inaction' (2020) 79 *Cambridge Law Journal* 245

Baker, D (2010) *Not Quite Supreme: The Courts and Coordinate Constitutional Interpretation* (McGill-Queen's University Press)

    (2019) 'A Feature, Not a Bug: A Coordinate Moment in Canadian Constitutionalism' in Sigalet, Webber & Dixon (eds.) *Constitutional Dialogue: Rights, Democracy, Institutions* (Cambridge University Press)

Balkin, J (2008) 'Constitutional Hardball and Constitutional Crises' (2008) 26 *Quinnipiac Law Review* 579

    (2016) 'The Framework Model and Constitutional Interpretation' in Dyzenhaus & Thorburn (eds.) *Philosophical Foundations of Constitutional Law* (Oxford University Press)

    (2018) 'Constitutional Crisis and Constitutional Rot' in Graber, Levinson & Tushnet (eds.) *Constitutional Democracy in Crisis?* (Oxford University Press)

Bamforth, N (2013) 'Accountability of and to the Legislature' in Bamforth & Leyland (eds.) *Accountability in the Contemporary Constitution* (Oxford University Press)

Baraggia, A, Fasone, C & Vanoni, L (2020) *New Challenges to the Separation of Powers: Dividing Power* (Edward Elgar)

Barak, A (2006) *The Judge in a Democracy* (Princeton University Press)

    (2010) 'Proportionality and Principled Balancing' (2010) 4 *Law and Ethics of Human Rights* 1

    (2012) *Proportionality: Constitutional Rights and Their Limitations* (Cambridge University Press)

Barber, N (2001) 'Prelude to the Separation of Powers' (2001) 60 *Cambridge Law Journal* 59

    (2013) 'Self-Defence for Institutions' (2013) 72 *Cambridge Law Journal* 558

Barber, N, Hickman, T & King, J (2017) 'Reflections on *Miller*' (2017) 8 *United Kingdom Supreme Court Yearbook* 212

Barendt, E (1995) 'Separation of Powers and Constitutional Government' [1995] *Public Law* 599

    (1997) 'Is There a UK Constitution?' (1997) 17 *Oxford Journal of Legal Studies* 137

(1998) *An Introduction to Constitutional Law* (Oxford University Press)

Baroš, J, Dufek, P & Kosař, D (2020) 'Unpacking the Separation of Powers' in Baraggia, Fasone & Vanoni (eds.) *New Challenges to the Separation of Powers* (Edward Elgar)

Barrett, A (2010) 'Substantive Canons and Faithful Agency' (2010) 90 *Boston University Law Review* 109

(2017) 'Countering the Majoritarian Difficulty' (2017) 32 *Constitutional Commentary* 61

Bar-Siman-Tov, I (2011) 'The Puzzling Resistance to Judicial Review of the Legislative Process' (2011) 91 *Boston University Law Review* 1915

(2015) 'The Role of Courts in Improving the Legislative Process' (2015) 3 *Theory and Practice of Legislation* 295

Barsotti, V, et al. (2017) *Italian Constitutional Justice in Global Context* (Oxford University Press)

Basten, J (2017) 'The Principle of Legality – an Unhelpful Label?' in Meagher & Groves (eds.) *The Principle of Legality in Australia and New Zealand* (The Federation Press)

Bates, E (2014) 'Analysing the Prisoner Voting Saga and the British Challenge to Strasbourg' (2014) 14 *Human Rights Law Review* 503

(2015) 'Sophisticated Constructivism in Human Rights Compliance Theory' (2015) 25 *European Journal of International Law* 1169

(2017) 'Democratic Override (or Rejection) and the Authority of the Strasbourg Court: The UK Parliament and Prisoner Voting' in Saul, Follesdal & Ulstein (eds.) *The International Human Rights Judiciary and National Parliaments* (Cambridge University Press)

(2019) 'Principled Criticism and a Warning from the "UK" to the ECtHR?' in Breur (ed.) *Principled Resistance to ECtHR Judgments: A New Paradigm?* (Springer)

Bateup, C (2006) 'The Dialogic Promise' (2006) 71 *Brooklyn Law Review* 1109

(2007) 'Expanding the Conversation: American and Canadian Experiences of Constitutional Dialogue in Comparative Perspective' (2007) 21 *Temple International and Comparative Law Journal* 1

(2009) 'Reassessing the Dialogic Possibilities of Weak-Form Bills of Rights' (2009) 32 *Hastings International and Comparative Law Review* 529

Bator, P (1990) 'The Constitution as Architecture: Legislative and Administrative Courts under Article III' (1990) 65 *Indiana Law Journal* 233

Bauman, R & Kahana, T, eds. (2006) *The Least Examined Branch: The Role of Legislatures in the Constitutional State* (Cambridge University Press)

Beatson, J (1998) 'The Need to Develop Principles of Prematurity and Ripeness for Review' (1998) 3 *Judicial Review* 79

(2013) 'Human Rights and Judicial Technique' in Masterman & Leigh (eds.) *The United Kingdom's Statutory Bill of Rights: Constitutional and Comparative Perspectives* (Oxford University Press)

(2021) *The Rule of Law and the Separation of Powers* (Hart Publishing)

Bejan, T (2017) *Mere Civility: Disagreement and the Limits of Toleration* (Harvard University Press)

Bell, J (2016) 'Comparative Law and Fundamental Rights' in Bell & Paris (eds.) *Rights-Based Constitutional Review* (Edward Elgar)

(2020) 'Common Law Constitutional Rights and Executive Action' in Elliott & Hughes (eds.) *Common Law Constitutional Rights* (Hart Publishing)

Bellah, R, et al. (2008) *Habits of the Heart: Individualism and Commitment in American Life* (University of California Press)

Bellamy, R (2011) 'Political Constitutionalism and the Human Rights Act' (2011) 9 *International Journal of Constitutional Law* 86

Bennett, C (2022) 'Boris Johnson's Future: A Philosophical Exercise for a Wavering MP' *The Conversation* article (1 June 2022). Available at: https://theconversation.com/boris-johnsons-future-a-philosophical-exercise-for-wavering-tory-mps-184106

Bennion, F (2001) *Understanding Common Law Legislation* (Oxford University Press)

Bentham, J (1843) *The Works of Jeremy Bentham. Published under the Superintendence of his Executor John Bowring* vol. 2 (W. Tait)

Benton, M & Russell, M (2012) 'Assessing the Impact of Parliamentary Oversight Committees: The Select Committees in the British House of Commons' [2012] *Parliamentary Affairs* 1

Berger, R (1997) *Government by Judiciary: The Transformation of the Fourteenth Amendment* (Liberty Fund)

Bethlehem, D (2012) 'The Secret Life of International Law' (2012) 1 *Cambridge Journal of International and Comparative Law* 23

Bicchieri, C (2006) *The Grammar of Society: The Nature and Dynamics of Social Norms* (Cambridge University Press)

Bickel, A (1961) 'The Supreme Court 1960 Term. Foreword: The Passive Virtues' (1961) 75 *Harvard Law Review* 40

(1986) *The Least Dangerous Branch* 2nd ed. (Yale University Press)

Bingham, T (2000) *The Business of Judging: Selected Essays and Speeches 1985–1999* (Oxford University Press)

(2010) 'The Human Rights Act' (2010) 6 *European Human Rights Law Review* 568

(2011) *Lives of the Law: Selected Essays and Speeches 2000–2010* (Oxford University Press)

Binnie, I (2013) 'Judging the Judges: "May They Boldly Go Where Ivan Rand Went Before' (2013) 26 *Canadian Journal of Law and Jurisprudence* 5

Birch, D (2003) 'Untangling Sexual History Evidence: A Rejoinder to Professor Temkin' [2003] *Criminal Law Review* 370

Bjorge, E (2016) 'Common Law Rights: Balancing Domestic and International Exigencies' (2016) 75 *Cambridge Law Journal* 220

Blackburn, D (2011) 'Davis and Straw Unite against Prisoner Voting Rights' *The Spectator* (18 January 2011)

Blackbourn, J (2012) 'Evaluating the Independent Reviewer of Terrorism Legislation' [2012] *Parliamentary Affairs* 1

Blackstone, W (2016 [1765–69]) *Commentaries on the Laws of England* (Oxford University Press)

Blair, T (2011) *Tony Blair: A Journey* (Arrow Books)

Blakeney, A (2006) 'Judges: Canada's New Aristocracy – An Interview with Alan Blakeney' (2006) 18 *Inroads* 31

    (2010) 'The Notwithstanding Clause, the Charter and Canada's Patriated Constitution: What I Thought We Were Doing' (2010) 19 *Constitutional Forum* 1

Blick, A & Hennessy, P (2019) 'Good Chaps No More? Safeguarding the Constitution in Stressful Times' *The Constitution Society* blogpost (18 November 2019). Available at: https://consoc.org.uk/publications/good-chaps-no-more-safeguarding-the-constitution-in-stressful-times-by-andrew-blick-and-peter-hennessy/

Blondel, J (1970) 'Legislative Behaviour: Some Steps towards a Cross-National Measurement' (1970) 5 *Government & Opposition* 67

Blunkett, D (2003) 'It's Time for Judges to Learn Their Place' *News of the World* (23 February 2003)

    (2006) *The Blunkett Tapes: My Life in the Bearpit* (Bloomsbury)

Bobbitt, P (1982) *Constitutional Fate: Theory of the Constitution* (Oxford University Press)

Bogg, A (2018) 'Judicial Power and the Left: Deference, Partnership, and Defiance' (9 January 2018) in Ekins & Gee (eds.) *Judicial Power and the Left: Notes on a Sceptical Tradition* (Policy Exchange). Available at: https://judicialpowerproject.org.uk/alan-bogg-judicial-power-and-the-left-deference-partnership-and-defiance/

    (2022) 'Can We Trust the Courts in Labour Law? Stranded Between Frivolity and Despair' (2022) 38 *International Journal of Comparative Labour Law* 103

Bowcott, O (2017) 'Lord Chief Justice Attacks Liz Truss for Failing to Back Article 50 Judges' *The Guardian* (22 March 2017)

    (2020) 'Legal Profession Hits Back at Johnson over "Lefty Lawyers" Speech' *The Guardian* (2 October 2020). Available at: www.theguardian.com/law/2020/oct/06/legal-profession-hits-back-at-boris-johnson-over-lefty-lawyers-speech

Bowman, G (2005) 'Why Is There a Parliamentary Counsel?' (2005) 26 *Statute Law Review* 69

Bradley, A & Ewing, K (2011) *Constitutional and Administrative Law*, 15th rev ed. (Longman)

Bradley, C & Siegel, N (2017) 'Historical Gloss, Constitutional Conventions, and Judicial Separation of Powers' (2017) 105 *Georgetown Law Journal* 255

Brady, A (2012) *Proportionality and Deference: An Institutionally Sensitive Approach* (Cambridge University Press)

Bratman, M (1992) 'Shared Cooperative Activity' (1992) 101 *Philosophical Review* 327

(2014) *Shared Agency: A Planning Theory of Acting Together* (Oxford University Press)

Brazier, A & Fox, R (2011) 'Reviewing Select Committee Tasks and Modes of Operation' 2011 *Parliamentary Affairs* 354

Brazier, R (2020) 'Contempt for the Constitution' *UK Constitutional Law Association* blogpost (6 October 2020). Available at: https://ukconstitutionallaw.org/2020/10/06/rodney-brazier-contempt-for-the-constitution/

Brems, E (2017) 'The "Logics" of Procedural-Type Review by the European Court of Human Rights' in Gerards & Brems (eds.) *Procedural Review in European Fundamental Rights Cases* (Cambridge University Press)

Brenncke, M (2018) *Judicial Law-Making in English and German Courts: Techniques and Limits of Statutory Interpretation* (Intersentia)

Bright, M & Hinsliff, G (2001) 'Chaos: How War on Terror Became a Political Dogfight' *The Observer* (11 September 2001)

Brogan, B (2005) 'Blair: Judges Let Us Down' *The Daily Mail* (27 July 2005)

Brosseau, L & Roy, M-A (2018). The Notwithstanding Clause of the Charter: Background Paper. Service, PIaR. Ottawa, Canada, Library of Parliament.

Brown, S (1994) 'Public Interest Immunity' 1994 *Public Law* 579

(2020) *Playing off the Roof and other Stories: A Patchwork of Memories* (Marble Hill London)

Browne-Wilkinson, N (1992) 'The Infiltration of a Bill of Rights' [1992] *Public Law* 397

Brunnée, J & Toope, S (2010) *Legitimacy and Legality in International Law: An Interactional Account* (Cambridge University Press)

Bulman-Pozen, J & Gerken, H (2009) 'Uncooperative Federalism' (2009) 118 *Yale Law Journal* 1256

Burgess, S (1992) *Contest for Constitutional Authority: The Abortion and War Powers Debates* (University of Kansas Press)

Burnett, I (2018) 'Becoming Stronger Together' Paper presented at Commonwealth Judges and Magistrates' Association Annual Conference 2018. Brisbane, Australia.

Burrows, A (2018) *Thinking about Statutes: Interpretation, Interaction, Improvement* (Cambridge University Press)

Burt, R (1992) *The Constitution in Conflict* (Harvard University Press)

Caird, JS (2012) 'Parliamentary Constitutional Review: Ten Years of the House of Lords Select Committee on the Constitution' [2012] *Public Law* 4

Caird, J, Hazell, R & Oliver, D (2015) *The Constitutional Standards of the House of Lords Select Committees on the Constitution* (The Constitution Society)

Calhoun, C (2000) 'The Virtue of Civility' (2000) 29 *Philosophy and Public Affairs* 251

Cameron, D (2019) *For the Record* (William Collins)

Cameron, J (2001) 'Dialogue and Hierarchy in Charter Interpretation: A Comment on R. v. Mills' (2001) 38 *Alberta Law Review* 1051

(2004) 'The Charter's Legislative Override: Feat or Figment of the Constitutional Imagination' in Huscroft & Brodie (eds.) *Constitutionalism in the Charter Era* (LexisNexis Canada)

(2016) 'Collateral Thoughts on Dialogue's Legacy as Metaphor and Theory: A Favourite from Canada' (2016) 35 *University of Queensland Law Journal* 157

Campbell, T (1999) 'Human Rights: A Culture of Controversy' (1999) 26 *Journal of Law & Society* 6

(2001) 'Incorporation through Interpretation' in Campbell, Ewing & Tomkins (eds.) *Sceptical Essays on Human Rights* (Oxford University Press)

(2011) 'Parliamentary Review with a Democratic Charter of Rights' in Campbell, Ewing & Tomkins (eds.) *The Legal Protection of Human Rights: Sceptical Essays* (Oxford University Press)

Campbell, T, Ewing, K & Tomkins, A, eds. (2001) *Sceptical Essays on Human Rights* (Oxford University Press)

(2011) 'Introduction' in Campbell, Ewing & Tomkins (eds.) *The Legal Protection of Human Rights: Sceptical Essays* (Oxford University Press)

Cane, P (2016) *Controlling Administrative Power: An Historical Comparison* (Cambridge University Press)

Cardozo, B (1921) *The Nature of the Judicial Process* (Yale University Press)

Carolan, E (2009) *The New Separation of Powers: A Theory for the Modern State* (Oxford University Press)

(2011) 'The Relationship between Judicial Remedies and the Separation of Powers: Collaborative Constitutionalism and the Suspended Declaration of Invalidity' (2011) 46 *Irish Jurist* 180

(2016a) 'Dialogue Isn't Working: The Case for Collaboration as a Model of Legislative–Judicial Relations' (2016) 36 *Legal Studies* 209

(2016b) 'Leaving Behind the Commonwealth Model of Rights Review: Ireland as an Example of Collaborative Constitutionalism' in Bell & Paris (eds.) *Right-Based Constitutional Review: Constitutional Courts in a Changing Landscape* (Edward Elgar)

(2017) 'A Dialogue-Oriented Departure in Constitutional Remedies? The Implications of NHV v Minister for Justice for Inter-Branch Roles and Relationships' (2017) 40 *Dublin University Law Journal* 191

Cartabia, M (2016) 'Of Bridges and Walls: The "Italian Style" of Constitutional Adjudication' (2016) 1 *Italian Journal of Public Law* 37

(2020) 'Editorial: Courts' Relations' (2020) 18 *International Journal of Constitutional Law* 3

Carter, M (2019) 'Diefenbaker's *Bill of Rights* and the "Counter-Majoritarian Difficulty": The Notwithstanding Clause and Fundamental Justice as Touchstones for the *Charter* Debate' (2019) 82 *Saskatchewan Law Review* 121

Carter, S (1998) *Civility: Manners, Morals, and the Etiquette of Democracy* (Harper Collins)

Casey, C (2019) 'The Constitution outside the Courts – The Case for Parliamentary Involvement in Constitutional Review' (2019) 61 *Irish Jurist* 36

(2021) 'The Law Officers: The Relationship between Executive Lawyers and Executive Power in Ireland and the United Kingdom' in Doyle, McHarg & Murkens (eds.) *The Brexit Challenge for Ireland and the UK: Constitutions under Pressure* (Cambridge University Press)

Casey, C & Kenny, D (2022) 'The Gatekeepers: Executive Lawyers and the Executive Power in Comparative Constitutional Law' (2022) 20 *International Journal of Constitutional Law* 664

Cash, W (2005) 'Terrorism and the Rule of Law' *The Times* (2 August 2005)

Chafetz, J (2011) 'The Political Animal and the Ethics of Constitutional Commitment' (2011) 124 *Harvard Law Review Forum* 1

Chafetz, J & Pozen, D (2018) 'How Constitutional Norms Break Down' (2018) 65 *UCLA Law Review* 1430

Chan, C (2014) 'Business as Usual: Deference in Counter-Terrorism Judicial Review' in Davis & De Londras (eds.) *Critical Debates in Counter-Terrorism Review* (Cambridge University Press)

(2017) 'A Preliminary Framework for Measuring Deference in Rights Reasoning' (2017) 14 *International Journal of Constitutional Law* 851

(2018) 'Rights, Proportionality and Deference: A Study of Post-Handover Judgments in Hong Kong' (2018) 48 *Hong Kong Law Journal* 51

Chandrachud, C (2014) 'Reconfiguring the Discourse on Political Responses to Declarations of Incompatibility' [2014] *Public Law* 624

(2017) *Balanced Constitutionalism: Courts and Legislatures in India and the United Kingdom* (Oxford University Press)

Chandrachud, C & Kavanagh, A (2016) 'Rights-Based Constitutional Review in the UK: From Form to Function' in Bell & Paris (eds.) *Rights-Based Constitutional Review* (Edward Elgar)

Chang, B & Ramshaw, G (2017) *Strengthening Parliamentary Capacity for the Protection and Realisation of Human Rights* (Westminster Foundation for Democracy)

Charteris-Black, J (2006) *Politicians and Rhetoric: The Persuasive Power of Metaphor* (Palgrave Macmillan)

Chen, B (2015) 'The Principle of Legality: Issues of Rationale and Application' (2015) 41 *Monash University Law Review* 329

Christiano, T (2000) 'Waldron on Law and Disagreement' (2000) 19 *Law and Philosophy* 520

Cicero, M (2000) *Cicero: On Obligations* Translated by Walsh (Oxford University Press)

Clark, T (2022) 'Peter Hennessy: Boris Johnson Has Killed off the "Good Chaps" Theory of Government' *Prospect* (21 January 2022). Available at: www.prospectmagazine.co.uk/magazine/peter-hennessy-interview-good-chaps-theory-of-government-boris-johnson

Claus, L (2005) 'Montesquieu's Mistakes and the True Meaning of Separation of Powers' (2005) 25 *Oxford Journal of Legal Studies* 419

Clayton, R (2004) 'Judicial Deference and "Democratic Dialogue": The Legitimacy of Judicial Intervention under the Human Rights Act 1998' 2004 *Public Law* 33

Clements, L (2005) 'Winners and Losers' (2005) 32 *Journal of Law and Society* 34

Coenen, D (2001) 'A Constitution of Collaboration: Protecting Fundamental Values with Second-Look Rules of Interbranch Dialogue' (2001) 42 *William and Mary Law Review* 1575

  (2009) 'The Pros and Cons of Politically Reversible "Semisubstantive" Constitutional Rules' (2009) 77 *Fordham Law Review* 2835

Coffin, F (1988) 'Judicial Balancing: The Protean Scales of Justice' (1988) 63 *New York University Law Review* 16

Cohen-Eliya, M & Porat, I (2013) *Proportionality and Constitutional Culture* (Cambridge University Press)

Cohler, A, Miller, B & Stone, H (1989) *Montesquieu: The Spirit of the Laws* (Cambridge University Press)

Cohn, M (2007) 'Judicial Activism in the House of Lords: A Composite Constitutionalist Approach' [2007] *Public Law* 95

  (2013) 'Sovereignty, Constitutional Dialogues, and Political Networks: A Comparative and Conceptual Study' in Rawlings, Leyland & Young (eds.) *Sovereignty and the Law* (Oxford University Press)

  (2016) 'Tension and Legality: Towards a Theory of the Executive Branch' (2016) 39 *Canadian Journal of Law and Jurisprudence* 321

Colón-Ríos, J (2012) *Weak Constitutionalism: Democratic Legitimacy and the question of constituent power* (Routledge)

(2014) 'A New Typology of Judicial Review of Legislation' (2014) 3 *Global Constitutionalism* 143

Conger, J (2008) *The Necessary Art of Persuasion* (Harvard Business Press)

Cooke, R (2004) 'The Road Ahead for the Common Law' (2004) 53 *International and Comparative Law Quarterly* 273

Cooper, J & Marshal-Williams, A (2000) *Legislating for Human Rights: The Parliamentary Debates on the Human Rights Bill* (Hart Publishing)

Cossman, B (2019) 'Same-Sex Marriage beyond Charter Dialogue: Charter Cases and Contestation within Government' (2019) 69 *University of Toronto Law Journal* 183

Coughlan, S (2003) 'Justification in the Face of Competing Social and Political Philosophies' (2003) 5 *Criminal Reports* 208

Coxon, B (2014) 'Human Rights at Common Law: Two Interpretive Principles' (2014) 35 *Statute Law Review* 35

Coyne, A (2017) 'Notwithstanding Clause Is a Bottle Labelled 'Drink Me' That Cheapens the Charter' *The National Post* (3 May 2017)

Craig, P (2010) 'Political Constitutionalism and Judicial Review' in Forsyth et al. (eds.) *Effective Judicial Review: A Cornerstone of Good Governance* (Oxford University Press)

(2013) 'The Nature of Reasonableness' (2013) 66 *Current Legal Problems* 131

(2017) 'Miller, Structural Constitutional Review and the Limits of Prerogative Power' [2017] *Public Law* 48

(2020) 'The Supreme Court, Prorogation and Constitutional Principle' 2020 *Public Law* 248

Craiutu, A (2012) *A Virtue for Courageous Minds: Moderation in French Political Thought, 1748–1830* (Princeton University Press)

(2017) *Faces of Moderation: The Art of Balance in an Age of Extremes* (University of Pennsylvania Press)

Cranston, R (2013) 'Lawyers, MPs and Judges' in Feldman (ed.) *Law in Politics, Politics in Law* (Hart Publishing)

Crawford, C (2013) 'Dialogue and Declarations of Incompatibility under Section 4 of the *Human Rights Act 1998*' (2013) 25 *Denning Law Journal* 43

(2014) 'Dialogue and Rights-Compatible Interpretations under Section 3 of the Human Rights Act 1998' (2014) 25 *King's Law Journal* 34

Crewe, E (2005) *Lords of Parliament: Manners, Rituals and Politics* (Manchester University Press)

(2015a) *Commons and Lords: A Short Anthropology of Parliament* (Haus Curiosities)

(2015b) *The House of Commons: An Anthropology of MPs at Work* (Bloomsbury)

(2021) *The Anthropology of Parliaments: Entanglements in Democratic Politics* (Routledge)

Crick, B (1990) 'The Reform of Parliament' in Norton (ed.) *Legislatures* (Oxford University Press)

Croley, S (1995) 'The Majoritarian Difficulty: Elective Judiciaries and the Rule of Law' (1995) 62 *University of Chicago Law Review* 689

Cross, R (1995) *Statutory Interpretation* ed. Bell & Engels (Butterworths)

Crowe, E (1983) 'Consensus and Structure in Legislative Norms: Party Discipline in the House of Commons' (1983) 45 *Journal of Politics* 907

Culbertson, A (2022) 'Boris Johnson Changes Ministerial Code so Those Who Breach It Don't Have to Quit or Face Sack' report on *Sky News* (27 May 2022). Available at: https://news.sky.com/story/boris-johnson-changes-min isterial-code-so-those-who-breach-it-dont-have-to-quit-or-face-sack-12622599

Cyr, H (2014) 'Autonomy, Subsidiarity, Solidarity: Foundations of Cooperative Federalism' (2014) 23 *Constitutional Forum constitutionnel* 20

da Silva, VA (2011) 'Comparing the Incommensurable: Constitutional Principles, Balancing and Rational Decision' (2011) 31 *Oxford Journal of Legal Studies* 273

Daintith, T & Page, A (1999) *The Executive in the Constitution: Structure, Autonomy, and Internal Control* (Oxford University Press)

Daly, P (2012) *A Theory of Deference in Administrative Law: Basis, Application and Scope* (Cambridge University Press)

Daly, T (2017) *The Alchemists: Questioning Our Faith in Courts as Democracy-Builders* (Cambridge University Press)

Dann, P (2005) 'Thoughts on a Methodology of European Constitutional Law' (2005) 6 *German Law Journal* 1453

(2019) 'Governments' in Masterman & Schütze (eds.) *The Cambridge Companion to Comparative Constitutional Law* (Cambridge University Press)

Davies, S (1984) 'Truth-Values and Metaphors' (1984) 42 *Journal of Aesthetics and Art Criticism* 291

Davis, F (2010) 'The Human Rights Act and Juridification: Saving Democracy from Law' (2010) 30 *Politics* 91

(2014a) 'Parliamentary Supremacy and the Re-Invigoration of Institutional Dialogue in the UK' (2014) 67 *Parliamentary Affairs* 137

(2014b) 'The Politics of Counter-Terrorism Judicial Review: Creating Effective Parliamentary Scrutiny' in Davis & De Londras (eds.) *Critical Debates in Counter-Terrorism Judicial Review* (Cambridge University Press)

Davis, F & de Londras, F, eds. (2014a) *Critical Debates on Counter-Terrorism Judicial Review* (Cambridge University Press)

(2014b) 'Introduction: Counter-Terrorism Judicial Review: Beyond Dichotomies' in Davis & De Londras (eds.) *Critical Debates in Counter-terrorism Judicial Review* (Cambridge University Press)

Davis, F & Mead, D (2014) 'Declarations of Incompatibility, Dialogue and the Criminal Law' (2014) 43 *Common Law World Review* 62

Dawson, M (1992) 'The Impact of the Charter on the Public Policy Process and the Department of Justice' (1992) 30 *Osgoode Hall Law Journal* 595

de Búrca, G (1993) 'The Principle of Proportionality and Its Application in EC Law' (1993) 13 *Yearbook of European Law* 105

de Jouvenel, B (1966) 'The Means of Contestation' (1966) 1 *Government & Opposition* 155

de Londras, F (2013) 'Declarations of Incompatibility under the ECHR Act 2003: A Workable Transplant?' (2013) 35 *Statute Law Review* 50

  (2017) 'In Defence of Judicial Innovation and Constitutional Evolution' in Cahillane, Hickey & Gallen (eds.) *Judges, Politics and the Irish Constitution* (Manchester University Press)

de Londras, F & Davis, F (2010) 'Controlling the Executive in Times of Terrorism: Competing Perspectives on Effective Oversight Mechanisms' (2010) 30 *Oxford Journal of Legal Studies* 19

de Visser, M (2004) *Constitutional Review in Europe: A Comparative Analysis* (Bloomsbury/Hart Publishing)

  (2022) 'Non-Judicial Constitutional Interpretation: The Netherlands' in Law (ed.) *Constitutionalism in Context* (Cambridge University Press)

Delaney, E (2014) 'Judiciary Rising: Constitutional Change in the United Kingdom' (2014) 108 *Northwestern University Law Review* 543

  (2016) 'Analyzing Avoidance: Judicial Strategy in Comparative Perspective' (2016) 66 *Duke Law Journal* 1

Determan, L & Heinzten, M (2018) 'Constitutional Review of Statutes in Germany and the United States Compared' (2018) 28 *Journal of Transnational Law & Policy* 95

Devins, N (2017) 'Why Congress Does Not Challenge Judicial Supremacy' (2017) 58 *William & Mary Law Review* 1495

Devins, N & Fisher, L (2015) *The Democratic Constitution* 2nd ed. (Oxford University Press)

Devlin, P (1976) 'Judges and Lawmakers' (1976) 39 *Modern Law Review* 1

Dicey, AV (1964) *Introduction to the Study of the Law of the Constitution* 10th ed. (Macmillan)

Dickson, J (2001) *Evaluation and Legal Theory* (Hart Publishing)

  (2015a) 'Ours Is a Broad Church: Indirectly Evaluative Legal Philosophy as a Facet of Jurisprudential Inquiry' (2015) 6 *Jurisprudence* 207

  (2015b) 'Who's Afraid of Transnational Legal Theory? Dangers and Desiderata' (2015) 6 *Transnational Legal Theory* 565

Dinan, J (2001) 'Rights and the Political Process: Physician-Assisted Suicide in the Aftermath of *Washington v Glucksberg*' (2001) 31 *Publius: The Journal of Federalism* 1

Dittert, A (2021) 'The Politics of Lies: Boris Johnson and the Erosion of the Rule of Law' *The New Statesman* (15 July 2021). Available at: www.news tatesman.com/politics/2021/07/politics-lies-boris-johnson-and-erosion-rule -law.

Dixon, R (2007) 'Creating Dialogue about Socioeconomic Rights: Strong-Form versus Weak-Form Judicial Review Revisited' (2007) 5 *International Journal of Constitutional Law* 391

(2009a) 'A Minimalist Charter of Rights for Australia: The UK or Canada as a Model?' (2009) 37 *Federal Law Review* 335

(2009b) 'The Supreme Court of Canada, Charter Dialogue, and Deference' (2009) 47 *Osgoode Hall Law Journal* 235

(2012) 'Weak-Form Judicial Review and American Exceptionalism' (2012) 32 *Oxford Journal of Legal Studies* 487

(2017) 'The Core Case for Weak-Form Judicial Review' (2017) 38 *Cardozo Law Review* 2193

(2019a) 'Constitutional "Dialogue" and Deference' in Sigalet, Webber & Dixon (eds.) *Constitutional Dialogue: Rights, Democracy, Institutions* (Cambridge University Press)

(2019b) 'The Forms, Functions, and Varieties of Weak(ened) Judicial Review' (2019) 17 *International Journal of Constitutional Law* 904

(2020) 'Calibrated Proportionality' (2020) 48 *Federal Law Review* 92

(2021) 'Strong Courts: Judicial Statecraft in Aid of Constitutional Change' (2021) 59 *Columbia Journal of Transnational Law* 298

(2023) *Responsive Judicial Review: Democracy and Dysfunction in the Modern Age* (Oxford University Press)

Dixon, R & Issacharoff, S (2016) 'Living to Fight another Day: Judicial Deferral in Defense of Democracy' [2016] *Wisconsin Law Review* 683

Dixon, R & Stone, A, eds. (2018) *The Invisible Constitution in Comparative Perspective* (Cambridge University Press)

Dodek, A (2010) 'Lawyering at the Intersection of Public Law and Legal Ethics: Government Lawyers and Custodians of the Rule of Law' (2010) 33 *Dalhousie Law Journal* 1

(2016) 'The Canadian Override: Constitutional Model or Bete Noire of Constitutional Politics?' (2016) 49 *Israel Law Review* 45

Donald, A (2015) 'The Implementation of Judgments of the European Court of Human Rights against the UK: Unravelling the Paradox' in Ziegler, Wicks, & Hodson (eds.) *The UK and European Human Rights: A Strained Relationship?* (Hart Publishing)

(2017) 'Parliaments as Compliance Partners in the European Convention on Human Rights System' in Saul, Follesdal & Ulfstein (eds.) *The International Human Rights Judiciary and National Parliaments: Europe and Beyond* (Cambridge University Press)

Donald, A & Leach, P (2016) *Parliaments and the European Court of Human Rights* (Oxford University Press)

Döring, H (1995) 'Time as a Scarce Resource: Government Control of the Agenda' in Doring (ed.) *Parliaments and Majority Rule in Western Europe* (University of Mannheim)

Dotan, Y (2014) *Lawyering for the Rule of Law: Government Lawyers and the Rise of Judicial Power in Israel* (Cambridge University Press)

Draghici, C (2015) 'The Blanket Ban on Assisted Suicide: Between Moral Paternalism and Utilitarian Justice' (2015) 3 *European Human Rights Law Review* 286

Drewry, G (1981) 'Lawyers in the UK Civil Service' (1981) 59 *Public Administration* 15

Duclos, N & Roach, K (1991) 'Constitutional Remedies as "Constitutional Hints": A Comment' (1991) 36 *McGill Law Journal* 1

Duffy, H (2018) *Strategic Human Rights Litigation: Understanding and Maximising Impact* (Hart Publishing)

Duxbury, N (2017) 'Judicial Disapproval as a Constitutional Technique' (2017) 15 *International Journal of Constitutional Law* 649

Dworkin, R (1977) *Taking Rights Seriously* (Duckworth)

(1985) *A Matter of Principle* (Harvard University Press)

(1986) *Law's Empire* (Harvard University Press)

(1996) *Freedom's Law: The Moral Reading of the American Constitution* (Harvard University Press)

Dyer, C (2000) 'Ruling Neutralises "Two Strikes" Law' *The Guardian* (10 November 2000)

Dyer, C, White, M & Travis, A (2004) 'Judges' Verdict on Terror Laws Provokes Constitutional Crisis' *The Guardian* (17 December)

Dyson, J (2018) *Justice: Continuity and Change* (Hart Publishing)

Dyzenhaus, D (1997) 'The Politics of Deference: Judicial Review and Democracy' in Taggart (ed.) *The Province of Administrative Law* (Hart Publishing)

(1998) 'Reuniting the Brain: The Democratic Basis of Judicial Review' (1998) 9 *Public Law Review* 98

(2004a) 'Intimations of Legality amid the Clash of Arms' (2004) 2 *International Journal of Constitutional Law* 244

(2004b) 'The Genealogy of Legal Positivism' (2004) 24 *Oxford Journal of Legal Studies* 39

(2004c) 'The Left and the Question of Law' (2004) 17 *Canadian Journal of Law and Jurisprudence* 7

(2006) *The Constitution of Law: Legality in a Time of Emergency* (Cambridge University Press)

(2007) 'Deference, Security and Human Rights' in Goold & Lazarus (eds.) *Security and Human Rights* (Hart Publishing)

(2009) 'Are Legislatures Good at Morality? Or Better at It than the Courts?' (2009) 7 *International Journal of Constitutional Law* 46

(2012) 'Constitutionalism in an Old Key: Legality and Constituent Power' (2012) 2 *Global Constitutionalism* 229

(2014) 'Proportionality and Deference in a Culture of Justification' in Huscroft, Miller & Webber (eds.) *Proportionality and the Rule of Law: Rights, Justification, Reasoning* (Cambridge University Press)

(2015) 'What is a Democratic Culture of Justification?' in Hunt, Hooper & Yowell (eds.) *Parliaments and Human Rights: Redressing the Democratic Deficit* (Hart Publishing)

Edwards, J (1984) *The Attorney General, Politics, and the Public Interest* (Sweet & Maxwell)

Edwards, R (2002) 'Judicial Deference under the Human Rights Act' (2002) 65 *Modern Law Review* 859

Ekins, R (2012) *The Nature of Legislative Intent* (Oxford University Press)

(2019) 'Constitutional Conversations in Britain (in Europe)' in Sigalet, Webber & Dixon (eds.) *Constitutional Dialogue: Rights, Democracy, Institutions* (Cambridge University Press)

Ekins, R & Sales, P (2011) 'Rights-Consistent Interpretation and the Human Rights Act 1998' (2011) 127 *Law Quarterly Review* 217

Elgot, J (2021) 'Trust in Law is at Risk if Ministers Bypass MPs' *The Guardian* (19 February 2021)

Elias, S (2015) 'Judgery and the Rule of Law' (2015) 14 *Otago Law Review* 1

Elias, P (2018) 'Judicial Power and the Balance of our Constitution: Comment' (2 February 2018). Available at: http://judicialpowerproject.org.uk/sir-patrick-elias-qc-comment/

Ellickson, R (1991) *Order without Law: How Neighbours Settle Disputes* (Harvard University Press)

Elliott, M (2002) 'Parliamentary Sovereignty and the New Constitutional Order: Legislative Freedom, Political Reality and Convention' (2002) 22 *Legal Studies* 340

(2011) 'Interpretative Bills of Rights and the Mystery of the Unwritten Constitution' 2011 *New Zealand Law Review* 591

(2013) 'Ombudsmen, Tribunals, Inquiries: Re-fashioning Accountability Beyond the Courts' in Bamforth & Leyland (eds.) *Accountability in the Contemporary Constitution* (Oxford University Press)

(2015a) 'Beyond the European Convention: Human Rights and the Common Law' (2015) 68 *Current Legal Problems* 85

(2015b) 'From Bifurcation to Calibration: Twin-Track Deference and the Culture of Justification' in Wilberg & Elliott (eds.) *The Scope and Intensity of Substantive Review* (Hart Publishing)

(2015c) 'Legislative Supremacy in a Multi-Dimensional Constitution' in Elliott & Feldman (eds.) *The Cambridge Companion to Public Law* (Cambridge University Press)

(2020) 'The Fundamentality of Rights at Common Law' in Elliott & Hughes (eds.) *Common Law Constitutional Rights* (Hart Publishing)

Elliott, M & Hughes, K, eds. (2020) *Common Law Constitutional Rights* (Hart Publishing)

Elliott, M & Thomas, R (2020) *Public Law* 4th ed. (Oxford University Press)

Elster, J (2000) *Ulysses Unbound* (Cambridge University Press)

(2010) 'Unwritten Constitutional Norms' Unpublished manuscript. Available at: https://perma.cc/YPN8-764G

(2018) 'The Resistible Rise of Louis Bonaparte' in Sunstein (ed.) *Can It Happen Here? Authoritarianism in America* (Harper Collins)

Elster, J, Offe, C, & Preuss, U (1998) *Institutional Design in Post-Communist Societies: Rebuilding the Ship at Sea* (Cambridge University Press)

Ely, JH (1980) *Democracy and Distrust: A Theory of Judicial Review* (Harvard University Press)

(1991) 'Another Such Victory: Constitutional Theory and Practice in a World Where Courts Are No Different from Legislatures' (1991) 77 *Virginia Law Review* 833

Endicott, T (1999) 'The Impossibility of the Rule of Law' (1999) 19 *Oxford Journal of Legal Studies* 1

(2002) '"International Meaning": Comity in Fundamental Rights Adjudication' (2002) 13 *International Journal of Refugee Law* 280

(2003) 'Constitutional Logic' (2003) 53 *University of Toronto Law Journal* 201

(2009) 'Habeas Corpus and Guantánamo Bay: A View from Abroad' (2009) 54 *American Journal of Jurisprudence (Notre Dame)* 1

(2014) 'Proportionality and Incommensurability' in Huscroft, Miller & Webber (eds.) *Proportionality and the Rule of Law: Rights, Justification, Reasoning* (Cambridge University Press)

(2015a) 'Comity Among Authorities' (2015) 68 *Current Legal Problems* 1

(2015b) 'Was *Entick v Carrington* a Landmark?' in Tomkins & Scott (eds.) *Entick v Carrington: 250 Years of the Rule of Law* (Hart Publishing)

(2017a) 'The Stubborn Stain Theory of Executive Power: From Magna Carta to Miller' *The Judicial Power Project* at Policy Exchange. Available at: https://policyexchange.org.uk/publication/the-stubborn-stain-theory-of-executive-power/

(2017b) 'Lord Reed's Dissent in Gina Miller's Case and the Principles of Our Constitution' (2017) 8 *United Kingdom Supreme Court Yearbook* 259.

(2020a) 'How Judges Make Law' in Fisher, King & Craig (eds.) *The Foundations and Future of Public Law: Essays in Honour of Paul Craig* (Oxford University Press)

(2020b) 'Human Rights and the Executive' (2020) 11 *Jurisprudence: An International Journal of Legal and Political Thought* 597

(2021) *Administrative Law*, 5th ed. (Oxford University Press)

Engle, G (1983) 'Bills Are Made to Pass as Razors Are Made to Sell: Practical Constraints in the Preparation of Legislation' (1983) 4 *Statute Law Review* 7

Epp, C (2008) 'Implementing the Rights Revolution: Repeat Players and the Interpretation of Diffuse Legal Messages' (2008) 71 *Law & Contemporary Problems* 41

Eskridge, W (2000) 'The Circumstances of Politics and the Application of Statutes' (2000) 100 *Columbia Law Review* 558

Eskridge, W & Ferejohn, J (2001) 'Super-Statutes' (2015) 50 *Duke Law Journal* 1215

(2009) 'Constitutional Horticulture: Deliberation-Respecting Judicial Review' (2009) 87 *Texas Law Review* 1273

Eskridge, W & Frickey, P (1992) 'Quasi-Constitutional Law: Clear Statement Rules as Constitutional Lawmaking' (1992) 45 *Vanderbilt Law Review* 593

(1994) 'Foreword: Law as Equilibrium' (1994) 108 *Harvard Law Review* 26

Estlund, C (2003) *Working Together: How Workplace Bonds Strengthen a Diverse Democracy* (Oxford University Press)

Etherton, T (2010) 'Liberty, the Archetype and Diversity: A Philosophy of Judging' [2010] *Public Law* 727

Evans, C & Evans, S (2006a) 'Evaluating the Performance of Legislatures' 2006 *Human Rights Law Review* 545

(2006b) 'Legislative Scrutiny Committees and Parliament Conceptions of Human Rights' [2006] *Public Law* 785

(2011) 'Messages from the Front Line: Parliamentarians' Perspectives on Rights Protection' in Campbell, Ewing & Tomkins (eds.) *The Legal Protection of Human Rights: Sceptical Essays* (Oxford University Press)

Ewing, K (1999) 'The Human Rights Act and Parliamentary Democracy' (1999) 62 *Modern Law Review* 79

(2004) 'The Futility of the Human Rights Act' [2004] *Public Law* 829

(2012) 'Doughty Defenders of the Human Rights Act' in Kang-Riou (ed.) *Confronting the Human Rights Act 1998: Contemporary Themes and Perspectives* (Taylor and Francis)

Ewing, K & Tham, J-C (2008) 'The Continuing Futility of the Human Rights Act' [2008] *Public Law* 668

Fallon, R (1997) 'Foreword: Implementing the Constitution' (1997) 111 *Harvard Law Review* 54

(2001) *Implementing the Constitution* (Harvard University Press)

Feldman, D (1999) 'The Human Rights Act 1998 and Constitutional Principles' (1999) 19 *Legal Studies* 165

(2002a) 'Book Review of Sceptical Essays on Human Rights edited by Tom Campbell, KD Ewing and Adam Tomkins' (2002) 22 *Legal Studies* 651

(2002b) 'Parliamentary Scrutiny of Legislation and Human Rights' [2002] *Public Law* 323

(2004a) 'Can and Should Parliament Protect Human Rights?' (2004) 10 *European Public Law* 635

(2004b) 'The Impact of Human Rights on the UK Legislative Process' (2004) 25 *Statute Law Review* 91

(2005) 'None, One or Several? Perspectives on the UK's Constitution(s)' (2005) 64 *Cambridge Law Journal* 329

(2006) 'Human Rights, Terrorism and Risk: The Role of Politicians and Judges' [2006] *Public Law* 364

(2007) 'Institutional Roles and Meanings of "Compatibility" under the Human Rights Act 1998' in Fenwick, Phillipson & Masterman (eds.) *Judicial Reasoning under the Human Rights Act 1998* (Cambridge University Press)

(2009) 'Remedies for Violations of Convention Rights' in Feldman (ed.) *English Public Law* (Oxford University Press)

ed. (2013) *Law in Politics, Politics in Law* (Hart Publishing)

(2014) 'Sovereignties in Strasbourg' in Rawlings, Leyland & Young (eds.) *Sovereignty and the Law: Domestic, European and International Perspectives* (Oxford University Press)

(2015) 'Democracy, Law, and Human Rights: Politics as Challenge and Opportunity' in Hunt, Hooper & Yowell (eds.) *Parliament and Human Rights: Redressing the Democratic Deficit* (Hart Publishing)

(2021) *Submission to the Independent Human Rights Act Review*. Available at: https://assets.publishing.service.gov.uk/government/uploads/system/uploads/attachment_data/file/1040525/ihrar-final-report.pdf

Fenwick, H (2011) 'Recalibrating ECHR Rights and the Role of the Human Rights Act Post 9/11: Reasserting International Human Rights Norms in the "War on Terror"' (2011) 64 *Current Legal Problems* 153

(2014) 'Post 9/11 UK Counter-Terrorism Cases in the European Court of Human Rights: A "Dialogic" Approach to Rights Protection or Appeasement of National Authorities?' in Davis & de Londras (eds.) *Critical Debates on Counter-Terrorism Judicial Review* (Cambridge University Press)

Fenwick, H & Phillipson, G (2011) 'Covert Derogations and Judicial Deference: Redefining Liberty and Due Process Rights in Counter-terrorism Law and Beyond' (2011) 56 *McGill Law Journal* 864

Ferejohn, J & Kramer, L (2002) 'Independent Judges, Dependent Judiciary: Institutionalising Judicial Restraint' (2002) 77 *New York University Law Review* 962

Finnemore, M & Sikkink, K (1998) 'International Norm Dynamics and Political Change' (1998) 52 *International Organisation* 887

Finnis, J (2007) 'Nationality, Alienage and Constitutional Principle' (2007) 123 *Law Quarterly Review* 417

(2011a) *Natural Law and Natural Rights* 2nd ed. (Oxford University Press)

(2011b) *Reason in Action: Collected Essays Volume I* (Oxford University Press)

(2015) 'A British "Convention Right" to Assistance in Suicide?' (2015) 131 *Law Quarterly Review* 1

(2016) 'Judicial Law-Making and the "Living" Instrumentalisation of the ECHR' in Barber, Ekins & Yowell (eds.) *Lord Sumption and the Limits of the Law* (Hart Publishing)

Fisher, L (1971) 'The Efficiency Side of the Separation of Powers' (1971) 5 *Journal of American Studies* 113

Fisher, L & Devins, N (1992) *Political Dynamics of Constitutional Law* (West Publishing)

Flaherty, M (1996) 'The Most Dangerous Branch' (1996) 105 *Yale Law Journal* 1725

Fletcher, J & Howe, P (2001) 'Public Opinion and Canada's Courts' in Howe & Russell (eds.) *Judicial Power and Canadian Democracy* (McGill-Queen's University Press)

Flinders, M (2002) 'Shifting the Balance? Parliament, the Executive and the British Constitution' (2002) 50 *Political Studies* 23

(2012) *Defending Politics: Why Democracy Matters in the Twenty-First Century* (Oxford University Press)

Flinders, M & Kelso, A (2011) 'Mind the Gap: Political Analysis, Public Expectations and the Parliamentary Decline Thesis' (2011) 13 *British Journal of Politics and International Relations* 249

Foley, B (2008) *Deference and the Presumption of Constitutionality* (Institute of Public Administration)

Foley, M (1989) *The Silence of Constitutions: Gaps, 'Abeyances' and Political Temperament in the Maintenance of Government* (Routledge)

Fombad, C (2016a) 'An Overview of Separation of Powers under Modern African Constitutions' in Fombad (ed.) *Separation of Powers in African Constitutionalism* (Oxford University Press)

(2016b) 'The Role of Emerging Hybrid Institutions of Accountability in the Separation of Powers Scheme in Africa' in Fombad (ed.) *Separation of Powers in African Constitutionalism* (Oxford University Press)

Fontana, D (2009) 'Government in Opposition' (2009) 119 *Yale Law Journal* 548

Ford, R & Gibb, F (2003) 'Judges Are Failing to Do Their Jobs, Says Blunkett' *The Times* (8 May 2003)

Fordham, M (2020) *Judicial Review Handbook*, 7th ed. (Hart Publishing)

Forrest, A (2022) 'Boris Johnson "Misled Parliament on Partygate", ex-No 10 Staff Ready to Tell Inquiry' *The Independent* (9 August 2022)

Foster-Gilbert, C (2018) 'Introduction' in Neuberger & Riddell (eds.) *The Power of Judges* (Haus Publishing)

Fowkes, J (2016a) *Building the Constitution: The Practice of Constitutional Interpretation of Post-Apartheid South Africa* (Cambridge University Press)

(2016b) 'Relationships with Power: Re-imagining Judicial Roles in Africa' in Fombad (ed.) *Separation of Powers in African Constitutionalism* (Oxford University Press)

Fowkes, J & Fombad, C (2016) 'Introduction' in Fombad (ed.) *Separation of Powers in African Constitutionalism* (Oxford University Press)

Fraser, C (2005) 'Constitutional Dialogues between Courts and Legislatures: Can We Talk?' (2005) 14 *Constitutional Forum* 7

Fredman, S (2000) 'Judging Democracy: The Role of the Judiciary under the HRA 1998' (2000) 53 *Current Legal Problems* 99

(2013) 'Adjudication as Accountability: A Deliberative Approach' in Bamforth & Leyland (eds.) *Accountability in the Contemporary Constitution* (Oxford University Press)

(2015) 'From Dialogue to Deliberation: Human Rights Adjudication and Prisoners' Rights to Vote' in Hunt, Hooper & Yowell (eds.) *Parliament and Human Rights: Redressing the Democratic Deficit* (Hart Publishing)

Freeman, E (1872) *The Growth of the English Constitution from the Earliest Times* (Macmillan)

French, R (2019) 'The Principle of Legality and Legislative Intention' (2019) 40 *Statute Law Review* 40

Friedman, B (1992) 'When Rights Encounter Reality: Enforcing Federal Remedies' (1992) 65 *Southern Californian Law Review* 735

(1993) 'Dialogue and Judicial Review' (1993) 91 *Michigan Law Review* 577

(2001) 'The Counter-Majoritarian Problem and the Pathology of Constitutional Scholarship' (2001) 95 *Northwestern University Law Review* 933

(2002) 'The Birth of an Academic Obsession: The History of the Countermajoritarian Difficulty, Part Five' (2002) 112 *Yale Law Journal* 153

(2005) 'The Politics of Judicial Review' (2005) 84 *Texas Law Review* 257

Friendly, HJ (1963) 'The Gap in Lawmaking – Judges Who Can't and Legislators Who Won't' (1963) 62 *Columbia Law Review* 787

Fuller, L (1968) *Anatomy of the Law* (Penguin Books)

(1978) 'The Form and Limits of Adjudication' (1978) 92 *Harvard Law Review* 353

Fumurescu, A (2013) *Compromise: A Political and Philosophical History* (Cambridge University Press)

Gageler, S (2011) 'Common Law Statutes and Judicial Legislation: Statutory Interpretation as a Common Law Process' (2011) 37 *Monash University Law Review* 1

(2015) 'Legislative Intention' (2015) 41 *Monash University Law Review* 1

Gale, C & James, A (2002) 'Mandatory Life Sentences and Executive Interference' (2002) 66 *Journal of Criminal Law* 417

Gambetta, D, ed. (1988) *Trust: Making and Breaking Cooperative Relations* (Basil Blackwell)

Gardbaum, S (2001) 'The New Commonwealth Model of Constitutionalism' (2001) 49 *American Journal of Comparative Law* 707

(2008) 'The Myth and the Reality of American Constitutional Exceptionalism' (2008) 107 *Michigan Law Review* 391

(2010) 'Reassessing the New Commonwealth Model of Constitutionalism' (2010) 8 *International Journal of Constitutional Law* 167

(2011) 'How Successful and Distinctive Is the Human Rights Act? An Expatriate Comparatist's Assessment' (2011) 74 *Modern Law Review* 195

(2013a) 'The Case for the New Commonwealth Model of Constitutionalism' (2013) 14 *German Law Journal* 2229

(2013b) *The New Commonwealth Model of Constitutionalism: Theory and Practice* (Cambridge University Press)

(2014) 'Proportionality and Democratic Constitutionalism' in Huscroft, Miller & Webber (eds.) *Proportionality and the Rule of Law: Rights, Justification, Reasoning* (Cambridge University Press)

(2015) 'What's so Weak about Weak-Form Review? A Reply to Aileen Kavanagh' (2015) 13 *International Journal of Constitutional Law* 1040

(2018) 'What Makes for More or Less Powerful Constitutional Courts?' (2018) 29 *Duke Journal of Comparative and International Law* 1

(2020a) 'Comparative Political Process Theory' (2020) 18 *International Journal of Constitutional Law* 1429

(2020b) 'The Counter-Playbook: Resisting the Populist Assault on Separation of Powers' (2020) 59 *Columbia Journal of Transnational Law* 1

Gardner, J (2002) 'Reasons for Teamwork' (2002) 8 *Legal Theory* 495

(2010) 'How to Be a Good Judge' (2010) 32 *London Review of Books* 15

(2012) *Law as a Leap of Faith: Essays on Law in General* (Oxford University Press)

Garlicki, L (2008) 'Cooperation of Courts: The Role of Supranational Jurisdictions in Europe' (2008) 6 *International Journal of Constitutional Law* 509

Garnier, E (2010) The Law Officers – Speech to the Constitutional and Administrative Law Bar Association. Available at: www.gov.uk/govern

ment/speeches/speech-to-the-constitutional-and-administrative-law-bar-association

(2017) 'Parliament Is Sovereign but It Must Still Listen to the Law: The Law Officers Have a Vital Role to Play in Reminding MPs to Respect the Judiciary and the Rule of Law' *The Times* (18 May 2017)

Garrett, E (1999) 'Legal Scholarship in an Age of Legislation' (1999) 34 *Tulsa Law Journal* 679

Garrett, E & Vermeule, A (2001) 'Institutional Design of a Thayerian Congress' (2001) 50 *Duke Law Journal* 1277

Garton Ash, T (2016) *Free Speech: Ten Principles for a Connected World* (Atlantic Books)

Gaudreault-Desbiens, J (2014) 'Cooperative Federalism in Search of a Normative Justification: Considering the Principle of Federal Loyalty' (2014) 23 *Constitutional Forum constitutionnel* 1

Gavison, R (1999) 'The Role of Courts in Rifted Democracies' (1999) 33 *Israel Law Review* 216

Gearty, C (2002) 'Reconciling Parliamentary Democracy and Human Rights' (2002) 118 *Law Quarterly Review* 248

(2004) *Principles of Human Rights Adjudication* (Oxford University Press)

(2005) '11 September 2001, Counter-Terrorism and the Human Rights Act' (2005) 32 *Journal of Law and Society* 18

(2006) *Can Human Rights Survive?* (Cambridge University Press)

(2010) 'The Human Rights Act: An Academic Sceptic Changes His Mind but Not His Heart' (2010) 6 *European Human Rights Law Review* 582

(2016) *On Fantasy Island: Britain, Europe, and Human Rights* (Oxford University Press)

Gee, G (2008) 'The Political Constitutionalism of JAG Griffith' (2008) 28 *Legal Studies* 20

(2015) *The Politics of Judicial Independence in the UK's Changing Constitution* (Cambridge University Press)

(2019) 'The Political Constitution and the Political Right' (2019) 30 *King's Law Journal* 148

Gee, G & Webber, G (2010) 'What Is a Political Constitution?' (2010) 30 *Oxford Journal of Legal Studies* 273

(2013) 'A Grammar of Public Law' (2013) 14 *German Law Journal* 2137

Geiringer, C (2008) 'The Principle of Legality and the Bill of Rights Act: A Critical Examination of *R v Hansen*' (2008) 6 *New Zealand Journal of Public and International Law* 59

(2009) 'On a Road to Nowhere: Implied Declarations of Inconsistency and the New Zealand Bill of Rights Act' (2009) 40 *Victoria University of Wellington Law Review* 613

(2017a) 'Book Review: Scott Stephenson: From Dialogue to Disagreement in Comparative Rights Constitutionalism' (2017) 15 *International Journal of Constitutional Law* 1247

(2017b) 'The Constitutional Role of the Courts under the New Zealand Bill of Rights: Three Narratives from Attorney-General v Taylor' (2017) 48 *Victoria University of Wellington Law Review* 547

(2018) 'Moving beyond the Constitutionalism/Democracy Dilemma: "Commonwealth Model" Scholarship and the Fixation on Legislative Compliance' in Elliott, Varuhas & Stark (eds.) *The Unity of Public Law? Doctrinal, Theoretical and Comparative Perspectives* (Bloomsbury)

(2019) 'A New Commonwealth Constitutionalism?' in Masterman & Schütze (eds.) *The Cambridge Companion to Comparative Constitutional Law* (Cambridge University Press)

Gerards, J (2011) 'Pluralism, Deference, and the Margin of Appreciation Doctrine' (2011) 17 *European Law Journal* 80

(2014) 'The European Court of Human Rights and the National Courts: Giving Shape to the Notion of "Shared Responsibility"' in Gerards & Fleurin (eds.) *Implementation of the European Convention on Human Rights and of the Judgments of the ECtHR in National Case-Law: A Comparative Analysis* (Intersentia)

(2017) 'Procedural Review by the ECtHR: A Typology' in Gerards & Brems (eds.) *Procedural Review in European Fundamental Rights Cases* (Cambridge University Press)

Gerards, J & Brems, E (2017) 'Procedural Review in European Fundamental Rights Cases: Introduction' in Gerards & Brems (eds.) *Procedural Review in European Fundamental Rights Cases* (Cambridge University Press)

Gerken, H (2014) 'The Loyal Opposition' (2014) 123 *Yale Law Journal* 1958

Geyh, C (2006) *When Courts and Congress Collide* (University of Michigan Press)

Gies, L (2015a) *Mediating Human Rights: Culture, Media and Human Rights* (Routledge)

(2015b) 'Human Rights, the British Press and the Deserving Claimant' in Ziegler, Wicks & Hodson (eds.) *The UK and European Human Rights: A Strained Relationship?* (Hart Publishing)

Ginsburg, RB (1992) 'Speaking in a Judicial Voice' (1992) 67 *New York University Law Review* 1185

(2010) 'The Role of Dissenting Opinions' (2010) 95 *Minnesota Law Review* 1

Ginsburg, T & Huq, A (2016) *Assessing Constitutional Performance* (Cambridge University Press)

(2018) *How to Save a Constitutional Democracy* (Chicago University Press)

Ginsburg, T & Kagan, R (2005) 'Institutional Approaches to Courts as Political Actors' in Ginsburg & Kagan (eds.) *Institutions and Public Law: Comparative Approaches* (Peter Lang)

Giordano, C (2022) '"Truly Shameless": Covid Bereaved Families Say Boris Johnson "Took Us All for Mugs" after Lockdown Party Fine' *The Independent* (12 April 2022).

Gledhill, K (2015) *The Human Rights Acts: The Mechanisms Compared* (Hart Publishing)

Gleeson, M (2009) 'The Meaning of Legislation: Context, Purpose and Respect for Fundamental Rights' (2009) 20 *Public Law Review* 26

Goldsmith, J & Levinson, D (2009) 'Law for States: International Law, Constitutional Law, Public Law' (2009) 122 *Harvard Law Review* 1791

Goldsmith, P (2001) '13th Tom Sargent Memorial Lecture: Politics, Public Interest and Prosecutions – A View by the Attorney General' London. Available at: https://web.archive.org/web/20090902161810/http://www.attorneygeneral .gov.uk/attachments/TOM%20SARGENT.doc

Goldsworthy, J (1999) *The Sovereignty of Parliament: History and Philosophy* (Oxford University Press)

    (2003a) 'Homogenizing Constitutions' (2003) 23 *Oxford Journal of Legal Studies* 483

    (2003b) 'Judicial Review, Legislative Override, and Democracy' (2003) 38 *Wake Forest Law Review* 451

    (2010) *Parliamentary Sovereignty: Contemporary Debates* (Cambridge University Press)

    (2017) 'The Principle of Legality and Legislative Intention' in Meagher & Groves (eds.) *The Principle of Legality in Australia and New Zealand* (The Federation Press)

Goold, B & Lazarus, L, eds. (2007) *Security and Human Rights* (Hart Publishing)

Gordon, M (2022) 'The Prime Minister, the Parties, and the Ministerial Code' *UK Constitutional Law Association* blogpost (27 April 2022). Available at: https://ukconstitutionallaw.org/2022/04/27/mike-gordon-the-prime-minis ter-the-parties-and-the-ministerial-code/

Graber, M (1993) 'The Nonmajoritarian Difficulty: Legislative Deference to the Judiciary' (1993) 7 *Studies in American Political Development* 35

    (2002) 'Constitutional Politics and Constitutional Theory: A Misunderstood and Neglected Relationship' (2002) 27 *Law and Social Inquiry* 309

    (2004) 'Resolving Political Questions into Judicial Questions: Tocqueville's Thesis Revisited' (2004) 21 *Constitutional Commentary* 485

Graber, M, Levinson, S & Tushnet, M, eds. (2018a) *Constitutional Democracy in Crisis?* (Oxford University Press)

    (2018b) 'Constitutional Democracy in Crisis? Introduction' in Graber, Levinson & Tushnet (eds.) *Constitutional Democracy in Crisis* (Oxford University Press)

Graham, J (2022) 'At Last the Curtain Falls on Boris Johnson: The Pantomime Prime Minister Utterly Lacking in Character' *The Guardian* (5 September

2022). Available at: –www.theguardian.com/commentisfree/2022/sep/05/cur
tain-falls-boris-johnson-pantomime-prime-minister

Green, L (1986) 'Book Review: Law's Rule – *The Rule of Law: Ideal or Ideology*, by A.C. Hutchinson and P. Monahan (eds)' (1986) 24 *Osgoode Hall Law Journal* 1023

(2007) 'The Duty to Govern' (2007) 13 *Legal Theory* 165

(2012) 'Introduction' in Hart (ed.) *The Concept of Law* 3rd ed. (Oxford University Press)

(2014) 'The Democratic Constitution', unpublished paper on file with author

Greenberg, D (2011) *Laying Down the Law: A Discussion of the People, Processes and Problems That Shape Acts of Parliament* (Sweet & Maxwell)

Greene, J (2018) 'Trump as a Constitutional Failure' (2018) 93 *Indiana Law Journal* 93

Greenhouse, L (1995) 'Justices Rule That Congress Overstepped Bounds: Scalia and Breyer Trade Quotes from "Mending Wall"' *New York Times* (19 April 1995)

Greschner, D (2000) 'The Supreme Court, Federalism and the Metaphors of Moderation' (2000) 79 *Canadian Bar Review* 47

Grierson, J & Taylor, D (2020) 'Home Office Wrong to Refer to "Activist Lawyers", Top Official Admits' *The Guardian* (27 August 2020). Available at: www.theguardian.com/politics/2020/aug/27/home-office-wrong-to-refer-to-activ ist-lawyers-top-official-admits

Grieve, D (2012a) 'Politicians and Judges: Speech Given to BPP Law School' *Counsel Magazine* (October 2012)

(2012b) 'The Role of Human Rights in a Law Officer's Work: Challenges Facing the HRA and the ECHR' (2012) 17 *Judicial Review* 101

(2015) The Role of the Attorney General. *Ministers Reflect Archive*. Riddell, P, Institute for Government. Available at: www.instituteforgovernment.org.uk/ ministers-reflect/person/dominic-grieve/

Griffith, J (1979) 'The Political Constitution' (1979) 42 *Modern Law Review* 1

(1985) 'Foreword' in Gelfand, Loughlin & Young (eds.) *Half a Century of Municipal Decline: 1935–1985* (Routledge)

(1997) 'Judges and the Constitution' in Rawlings (ed.) *Law, Society, and Economy: Centenary Essays for the London School of Economics and Political Science 1895–1995* (Clarendon Press)

(2001) 'The Common Law and the Political Constitution' (2001) 117 *Law Quarterly Review* 42

Griffith, J, Ryle, M & Wheeler-Booth, M (1989) *Parliament: Functions, Practice and Procedures* (Sweet & Maxwell)

Grimm, D (2007) 'Proportionality in Canadian and German Constitutional Jurisprudence' (2007) 57 *University of Toronto Law Journal* 383

Gross, P (2016) 'The Judicial Role Today' *Queen Mary University, Law and Society Lecture* (23 November 2016). Available at: www.judiciary.uk/wp-content/ uploads/2016/11/speech-by-gross-lj-the-judicial-rle-today.pdf

(2018) 'How Can Judges Strengthen the Rule of Law?' Speech given in Argentina (October 2018). Available at: www.judiciary.uk/wp-content/uploads/2018/10/speech-by-lj-gross-J20-conference-sept18.pdf

Groves, M & Meagher, D (2017) 'The Principle of Legality in Australian and New Zealand Law – Final Observations' in Meagher & Groves (eds.) *The Principle of Legality in Australia and New Zealand* (The Federation Press)

Gutmann, A & Thompson, D (2014) *The Spirit of Compromise: Why Governing Demands it and Campaigning Undermines it* updated ed. (Princeton University Press)

Guzman, A (2008) *How International Law Works: A Rational Choice Theory* (Oxford University Press)

Gwyn, W (1965) *The Meaning of the Separation of Powers* (Martinus Nijhoff)
(1989) 'The Indeterminacy of the Separation of Powers in the Age of the Framers' (1989) 30 *William and Mary Law Review* 263

Gyorfi, T (2016) *Against the New Constitutionalism* (Edward Elgar)

Hailbronner, M (2016) 'Constitutional Legitimacy and the Separation of Powers: Looking Forward' in Fombad (ed.) *Separation of Powers in African Constitutionalism* (Oxford University Press)
(2020) 'Political Process Review: Beyond Distrust' (2020) 18 *International Journal of Constitutional Law* 1458

Hailsham, L (1976) 'Elective Dictatorship' 1976 *The Listener* 496

Halberstam, D (2004) 'Of Power and Responsibility: The Political Morality of Federal Systems' (2004) 90 *Virginia Law Review* 731
(2009) 'Constitutional Heterarchy: The Centrality of Conflict in the European Union and the United States' in Dunoff & Trachtman (eds.) *Ruling the World? Constitutionalism, International Law, and Global Governance* (Cambridge University Press)

Hale, B (2012) 'Argentoratum Locutum: Is Strasbourg or the Supreme Court Supreme?' (2012) 12 *Human Rights Law Review* 65
(2013) 'What's the Point of Human Rights?' (Warwick Law Lecture 2013, University of Warwick), available at: https://www.supremecourt.uk/docs/speech-131128.pdf

Hamilton, A (1788) *The Federalist Papers* (US Library of Congress), available at: https://guides.loc.gov/federalist-papers/full-text

Hampshire, S (2000) *Justice Is Conflict* (Princeton University Press)

Hardman, H (2020) 'In the Name of Parliamentary Sovereignty: Conflict between the UK Government and the Courts over Judicial Deference in the Case of Prisoner Voting Rights' (2020) 15 *British Politics* 226

Harel, A (2014) *Why Law Matters* (Oxford University Press)

Harlow, C (2016) 'The Human Rights Act and "Coordinate Construction": Towards a "Parliament Square" Axis for Human Rights?' in Barber, Ekins, & Yowell (eds.) *Lord Sumption and the Limits of the Law* (Hart Publishing)

Harlow, C & Rawlings, R (1992) *Pressure through Law* (Routledge)

   (2016) "'Striking Back" and "Clamping Down": An Alternative Perspective on Judicial Review' in Bell et al. (eds) *Public Law Adjudication in Common Law Systems* (Hart Publishing)

   (2021) *Law and Administration* 4th ed. (Cambridge University Press)

Hart, HLA (2012) *The Concept of Law* 3rd ed. (Clarendon Press)

Harvey, P (2015) 'Third Party Interventions before the ECtHR: A Rough Guide' (28 January 2015). Available at: https://strasbourgobservers.com/2015/02/24/third-party-interventions-before-the-ecthr-a-rough-guide/

Hay, C (2007) *Why We Hate Politics* (Polity)

Hay, C & Richards, D (2000) 'The Tangled Web of Westminster and Whitehall: The Discourse, Strategy and Practice of Networking within the British Core Executive' (2000) 78 *Public Administration* 1

Hayward, A (2019) 'Equal Civil Partnerships, Discrimination and the Indulgence of Time: *R (Steinfeld and Keidan) v Secretary of State for International Development*' (2019) 82 *Modern Law Review* 922

Hazarika, A & Hamilton, T (2018) *Punch and Judy Politics: An Insiders' Guide to Prime Minister's Questions* (Biteback Publishing)

Hazell, R (2004) 'Who Is the Guardian of Legal Values in the Legislative Process: Parliament or the Executive?' [2004] *Public Law* 495

   (2015) 'The United Kingdom' in Galligan & Brenton (eds.) *Constitutional Conventions in Westminster Systems: Controversies, Changes and Challenges* (Cambridge University Press)

Heard, A (1991) *Canadian Constitutional Conventions: The Marriage of Law and Politics* (Oxford University Press)

   (2012) 'Constitutional Conventions: The Heart of the Living Constitution' (2012) 6 *Journal of Parliamentary and Political Law* 319

Heclo, H (1975) 'OMB and the Presidency – The Problem of "Neutral Competence"' (1975) 38 *The Public Interest* 80.

   (2000) 'Campaigning and Governing: A Conspectus' in Ornstein & Mann (eds.) *The Permanent Campaign and Its Future* (American Enterprise Institute)

   (2006) 'Thinking Institutionally' in Rhodes, Binder & Rockman (eds.) *The Oxford Handbook of Political Institutions* (Oxford University Press)

   (2008) *On Thinking Institutionally* (Oxford University Press)

Heise, M (2000) 'Preliminary Thoughts on the Virtues of Passive Dialogue' (2000) 34 *Akron Law Review* 73

Hennessy, P (1995) *The Hidden Wiring: Unearthing the British Constitution* (Indigo)

Herz, M (2009) 'Some Thoughts on Judicial Review and Collaborative Governance' 2009 *Journal of Dispute Resolution* 361

Heun, W (2011) *The Constitution of Germany: A Contextual Analysis* (Hart Publishing)

Heydon, J (2014) 'Are Bills of Rights Necessary in Common Law Systems?' (2014) 130 *Law Quarterly Review* 392

Hickford, M (2013) 'The Historical, Political Constitution – Some Reflections on Political Constitutionalism in New Zealand's History and its Possible Normative Value' 2013 *New Zealand Law Review* 585

Hickman, T (2005a) 'Constitutional Dialogue, Constitutional Theories and the Human Rights Act 1998' [2005] *Public Law* 306

(2005b) 'In Defence of the Legal Constitution' (2005) 55 *University of Toronto Law Journal* 981

(2008) 'The Courts and Politics after the Human Rights Act: A Comment' [2008] *Public Law* 84

(2010) *Public Law after the Human Rights Act* (Hart Publishing)

(2015) 'Bill of Rights Reform and the Case for Going beyond the Declaration of Incompatibility Model' [2015] *New Zealand Law Review* 35

Hiebert, J (2002) *Charter Conflicts: What Is Parliament's Role?* (McGill-Queen's University Press)

(2004a) 'Is It Too Late to Rehabilitate Canada's Notwithstanding Clause?' in Huscroft & Brodie (eds.) *Constitutionalism in the Charter Era* (Lexis-Nexis)

(2004b) 'New Constitutional Ideas: Can New Parliamentary Models Resist Judicial Dominance When Interpreting Rights?' (2004) 82 *Texas Law Review* 1963

(2006) 'Parliament and the Human Rights Act: Can the JCHR Help Facilitate a Culture of Rights?' (2006) 4 *International Journal of Constitutional Law* 1

(2009) 'Compromise and the Notwithstanding Clause: Why the Dominant Narrative Distorts our Understanding' in Kelly & Manfredi (eds.) *The Charter at 25* (University of British Columbia Press)

(2010) 'Compromise and the Notwithstanding Clause: Why the Dominant Narrative Distorts Our Understanding' in Kelly & Manfredi (eds.) *Contested Constitutionalism: Reflections on the Canadian Charter of Rights and Freedoms* (UBC Press)

(2011) 'Governing Like Judges?' in Campbell, Ewing & Tomkins (eds.) *The Legal Protection of Human Rights: Sceptical Essays* (Oxford University Press)

(2012) 'Governing under the Human Rights Act: The Limitations of Wishful Thinking' [2012] *Public Law* 27

(2015) 'Legislative Rights Review: Addressing the Gap between Ideals and Constraints' in Hunt, Hooper & Yowell (eds.) *Parliament and Human Rights: Redressing the Democratic Deficit* (Hart Publishing)

(2017) 'The Notwithstanding Clause: Why Non-Use Does Not Necessarily Equate with Abiding by Judicial Norms' in Oliver, Macklem & Des Rosiers (eds.) *The Oxford Handbook of the Canadian Constitution* (Oxford University Press)

Hiebert, J & Kelly, J (2015) *Parliamentary Bills of Rights: The Experiences of New Zealand and the United Kingdom* (Cambridge University Press)

Hilbink, L (2006) 'Beyond Manicheanism: Assessing the New Constitutionalism' (2006) 65 *Maryland Law Review* 15

(2008) 'Assessing the New Constitutionalism' (2008) 40 *Comparative Politics* 227

(2009) 'The Constituted Nature of Constituents' Interests: Historical and Ideational Factors in Judicial Empowerment' (2009) 62 *Political Research Quarterly* 781

Hillebrecht, C (2014) *Domestic Politics and International Human Rights Tribunals* (Cambridge University Press)

Hills, D (2012) 'Metaphor' *The Stanford Encyclopedia of Philosophy* Winter ed.

Hirschl, R (2004) *Towards Juristocracy: The Origins and Consequences of the New Constitutionalism* (Harvard University Press)

(2011) 'The Nordic Counternarrative: Democracy, Human Development, and Judicial Review' (2011) 9 *International Journal of Constitutional Law* 449

Hodge, P (2015) 'Judicial Law-Making in a Changing Constitution' (2015) 26 *Stellenbosch Law Review* 471

(2016) 'Upholding the Rule of Law: How We Preserve Judicial Independence in the United Kingdom' Speech given to the Lincoln's Inn Denning Society (7 November 2016). Available at: www.supremecourt.uk/docs/speech-161107.pdf

(2018) *Preserving Judicial Independence in an Age of Populism* Speech at the North Strathclyde Sheriffdom Conference, Paisley, available at: https://www.supremecourt.uk/docs/speech-181123.pdf

Hoffmann, L (1999a) 'The Influence of the European Principle of Proportionality upon UK Law' in Ellis (ed.) *The Principle of Proportionality in the Laws of Europe* (Hart)

(1999b) 'Human Rights and the House of Lords' (1999) 62 *Modern Law Review* 159

Hogan, G, Kenny, D & Walsh, R (2015) 'An Anthology of Declarations of Unconstitutionality' (2015) 54 *Irish Jurist* 1

Hogarth, R (2020) 'The Internal Market Bill Breaks International Law and Lays the Ground to Break more Law' *Institute for Government* post (9 September 2020). Available at: www.instituteforgovernment.org.uk/blog/internal-market-bill-breaks-international-law

Hogg, P (2004) 'Discovering Dialogue' in Huscroft & Brodie (eds.) *Constitutionalism in the Charter Era* (Butterworths)

(2007) *Constitutional Law of Canada* 5th ed. (Carswell)

Hogg, P & Amarnath, R (2017) 'Understanding Dialogue Theory' in Oliver, Macklem & Des Rosiers (eds.) *The Oxford Handbook of the Canadian Constitution* (Oxford University Press)

Hogg, P & Bushell, A (1997) 'The *Charter* Dialogue between Courts and Legislatures (or Perhaps the *Charter Of Rights* Isn't Such a Bad Thing After All)' (1997) 35 *Osgoode Hall Law Journal* 75

Hogg, P, Thornton, A & Wright, WK (2007a) '*Charter* Dialogue Revisited: Or "Much Ado About Metaphors"' (2007) 45 *Osgoode Hall Law Journal* 1

(2007b) 'A Reply on "*Charter* Dialogue Revisited"' (2007) 45 *Osgoode Hall Law Journal* 193

Holland, A (2016) 'Forbearance' (2016) 110 *American Political Science Review* 232

Holmes, S (2018) 'How Democracies Perish' in Sunstein (ed.) *Can it Happen Here? Authoritarianism in America* (Harper Collins)

Hood Phillips, O (1966) 'Constitutional Conventions: Dicey's Predecessors' (1966) 29 *Modern Law Review* 137

(1978) *Constitutional and Administrative Law* (Sweet & Maxwell)

Hope, D (2009) 'The Judges' Dilemma' (2009) 58 *International and Comparative Law Quarterly* 753

Horder, J (2006) 'Moral Arguments in Interpreting Statutes' in Endicott, Getzler & Peel (eds.) *Properties of Law: Essays in Honour of Jim Harris* (Oxford University Press)

Horne, A & Walker, C (2014) 'Lessons Learned from Political Constitutionalism? Comparing the Enactment of Control Orders and Terrorism Prevention and Investigation Measures by the UK Parliament' 2014 *Public Law* 267

Howarth, D (2016) 'On Parliamentary Silence' (13 December 2016). Available at: https://ukconstitutionallaw.org/2016/12/13/david-howarth-on-parliamentary-silence

Huhne, C (2009) 'Cleaning up the House' *The Guardian* (27 January 2009). Available at: www.theguardian.com/commentisfree/2009/jan/27/lords-labour

Hunt, M (1997) *Using Human Rights Law in English Courts* (Hart Publishing)

(2003) 'Sovereignty's Blight: Why Contemporary Public Law Needs a Doctrine of "Due Deference"' in Bamforth & Leyland (eds.) *Public Law in a Multi-Layered Constitution* (Hart Publishing)

(2007) 'Reshaping Constitutionalism' in Morison, McEvoy & Anthony (eds.) *Judges, Transition, and Human Rights* (Oxford University Press)

(2009) 'Against Bifurcation' in Dyzenhaus, Hunt & Huscroft (eds.) *A Simple Common Lawyer: Essays in Honour of Michael Taggart* (Hart Publishing)

(2010) 'The Impact of the Human Rights Act on the Legislature: A Diminution of Democracy or a New Voice for Parliament?' (2010) 6 *European Human Rights Law Review* 601

(2013) 'The Joint Committee on Human Rights' in Horne, Drewry & Oliver (eds.) *Parliament and the Law* (Hart Publishing)

(2015) 'Introduction' in Hunt, Hooper & Yowell (eds.) *Parliament and Human Rights: Redressing the Democratic Deficit* (Hart Publishing)

(2021) The Independent Human Rights Act Review: Response to the Call for Evidence. Available at: www.gov.uk/guidance/independent-human-rights-act-review#call-for-evidence-responses

Hunt, M, Hooper, H & Yowell, P (2012) *Parliament and Human Rights: Redressing the Democratic Deficit* (Arts and Humanities Research Council)

eds. (2015) *Parliaments and Human Rights: Redressing the Democratic Deficit* (Hart Publishing)

Huq, A (2012) 'Binding the Executive by Law or by Politics?' (2012) 79 *University of Chicago Law Review* 777

(2018) 'Legal or Political Checks on Apex Criminality: An Essay on Constitutional Design' (2018) 65 *UCLA Law Review* 1506

Huq, A & Michaels, J (2016) 'The Cycles of Separation-of-Powers Jurisprudence' (2016) 126 *Yale Law Journal* 342

Huscroft, G (2007) 'Constitutionalism from the Top Down' (2007) 45 *Osgoode Hall Law Journal* 91

(2009) 'Rationalising Judicial Power: The Mischief of Dialogue Theory' in Kelly & Manfredi (eds.) *Contested Constitutionalism: Reflections on the Canadian Charter of Rights and Freedoms* (UBC Press)

Huscroft, G, Miller, B & Webber, G, eds. (2014) *Proportionality and the Rule of Law: Rights, Justification, Reasoning* (Cambridge University Press)

Hutchins, A (2018) 'Why Doug Ford Went Straight to the Nuclear Option on Toronto City Council' *Macleans* (10 September 2018)

Hutchinson, A (2008) 'In the Public Interest: The Responsibilities and Rights of Government Lawyers' (2008) 46 *Osgoode Hall Law Journal* 105

Ignatieff, M (2013a) 'Enemies vs. Adversaries' *New York Times* (16 October 2013)

(2013b) *Fire and Ashes: Success and Failure in Politics* (Harvard University Press)

Ip, J (2013) 'Sunset Clauses and Counterterrorism Legislation' [2013] *Public Law* 74

(2020) '*Attorney-General v Taylor*: A Constitutional Milestone?' [2020] *New Zealand Law Review* 35

Irvine, D (2003a) *Human Rights, Constitutional Law and the Development of the English Legal System* (Hart Publishing)

(2003b) 'The Impact of the Human Rights Act: Parliament, the Courts and the Executive' [2003] *Public Law* 308

Issacharoff, S (2015) *Fragile Democracies: Contested Power in the Era of Constitutional Courts* (Cambridge University Press)

(2018) 'Populism versus Democratic Governance' in Graber, Levinson & Tushnet (eds.) *Constitutional Democracy in Crisis?* (Oxford University Press)

(2020) 'The Corruption of Popular Sovereignty' (2020) 18 *International Journal of Constitutional Law* 1109

Jack, M, ed. (2011) *Erskine May's Treatise on the Law, Privileges, Proceedings and Usage of Parliament* 24th ed. (Lexis Nexis)

Jackson, V (2015) 'Constitutional Law in an Age of Proportionality' (2015) 124 *Yale Law Journal* 3094

(2016) 'Pro-Constitutional Representation: Comparing the Role Obligations of Judges and Elected Representatives in Constitutional Democracy' (2016) 57 *William and Mary Law Review* 1717

(2020) 'Pro-Constitutional Representation and Legislated Rights' (2020) 21 *Jerusalem Review of Legal Studies* 77

(2021) 'Knowledge Institutions in Constitutional Democracies: Preliminary Reflections' (2021) 7 *Canadian Journal of Comparative and Contemporary Law* 156

Jacobi, T (2006) 'The Impact of Positive Political Theory on Old Questions of Constitutional Law and the Separation of Powers' (2006) 100 *Northwestern University Law Review* 259

Jaconelli, J (1999) 'The Nature of Constitutional Convention' (1999) 19 *Legal Studies* 24

(2005) 'Do Constitutional Conventions Bind?' (2005) 64 *Cambridge Law Journal* 149

Jaffe, L (1969) *English and American Judges as Lawmakers* (Oxford University Press)

Jai, J (1996) 'Policy, Politics and Law: Changing Relationships in Light of the Charter' (1996) 9 *National Journal of Constitutional law* 1

Jenkins, S (2006) 'This House of Commons is God's Gift to Dictatorship' *The Guardian* (1 November 2006). Available at: www.theguardian.com/commen tisfree/2006/nov/01/comment.politics1

Jennings, I (1959) *The Law and the Constitution* 5th ed. (University of London Press)

(1971) *The British Constitution* (Cambridge University Press)

Jhaveri, S (2022) 'Towards a Theory of Executive Constitutionalism' [2022] *Public Law* 562

Johansen, D & Rosen, P (2012) The Notwithstanding Clause of the Canadian Charter (Law and Government Division) Parliamentary Background Paper

Johnson, N (2007) 'Opposition in the British Political System' (2007) 32 *Government & Opposition* 487

Johnston, N & Brown, J (2023) 'Prisoner's Voting Rights', House of Commons Library Research Briefing, 20 January 2023

Joseph, P (2004) 'Parliament, the Courts, and the Collaborative Enterprise' (2004) 15 *King's Law Journal* 321

(2017) 'The Principle of Legality: Constitutional Innovation' in Meagher & Groves (eds.) *The Principle of Legality in Australia and New Zealand* (The Federation Press)

Jowell, J (2003) 'Judicial Deference: Servility, Civility, or Institutional Capacity?' [2003] *Public Law* 592

(2006) 'Politics and the Law: Constitutional Balance or Institutional Confusion' (The Law Society, London) JUSTICE Tom Sargent Memorial Annual Lecture

Judge, I (2015) *The Safest Shield: Lectures, Speeches and Essays* (Bloomsbury)

Kahana, T (2001) 'The Notwithstanding Mechanism and Public Discussion: Lessons from the Ignored Practice of Section 33 of the Charter' (2001) 44 *Canadian Public Administration* 255

(2002) 'Understanding the Notwithstanding Mechanism' (2002) 52 *University of Toronto Law Journal* 221

Kalitowski, S (2008) 'Rubber Stamp or Cockpit? The Impact of Parliament on Government Legislation' (2008) 61 *Parliamentary Affairs* 694

Kanetake, M & Nollkaemper, A, eds. (2016) *The Rule of Law at the National and International Levels: Contestation and Deference* (Hart Publishing)

Kateb, G (1981) 'The Moral Distinctiveness of Representative Democracy' (1981) 91 *Ethics* 357

Katyal, N (1998) 'Judges as Advicegivers' (1998) 50 *Stanford Law Review* 1708

(2006) 'Internal Separation of Powers: Checking Today's Most Dangerous Branch from Within' (2006) 115 *Yale Law Journal* 2314

Katzmann, R (1988) 'Introduction' in Katzmann (ed.) *Judges and Legislators: Toward Institutional Comity* (Brookings)

Kaufman, G (1997) *How to Be a Minister* (Faber & Faber)

Kavanagh, A (2003a) 'The Idea of a Living Constitution' (2003) 16 *Canadian Journal of Law and Jurisprudence* 55

(2003b) 'Participation and Judicial Review: A Reply to Jeremy Waldron' (2003) 22 *Law and Philosophy* 451

(2004) 'The Elusive Divide between Interpretation and Legislation under the Human Rights Act 1998' (2004) 24 *Oxford Journal of Legal Studies* 259

(2005) 'Unlocking the Human Rights Act: The "Radical" Approach to Section 3 (1) Revisited' [2005] *European Human Rights Law Review* 260

(2007) 'Choosing between Section 3 and 4 of the Human Rights Act 1998: judicial reasoning after *Ghaidan v. Mendoza*' in Fenwick, Phillipson & Masterman (eds.) *Judicial Reasoning under the UK Human Rights Act* (Cambridge University Press)

(2008) 'Deference or Defiance? The Limits of the Judicial Role in Constitutional Adjudication' in Huscroft (ed.) *Expounding the Constitution: Essays in Constitutional Theory* (Cambridge University Press)

(2009a) *Constitutional Review under the UK Human Rights Act* (Cambridge University Press)

(2009b) 'Constitutional Review, the Courts, and Democratic Scepticism' (2009) 62 *Current Legal Problems* 102

(2009c) 'Judging the Judges under the Human Rights Act: Deference, Disillusionment and the "War on Terror"' [2009] *Public Law* 287

(2010a) 'Defending Deference in Public Law and Constitutional Theory' (2010) 126 *Law Quarterly Review* 222

(2010b) 'Judicial Restraint in the Pursuit of Justice' (2010) 60 *University of Toronto Law Journal* 23

(2010c) 'Special Advocates, Control Orders and the Right to a Fair Trial' (2010) 73 *Modern Law Review* 836

(2011) 'Constitutionalism, Counterterrorism, and the Courts: Changes in the British Constitutional Landscape' (2011) 9 *International Journal of Constitutional Law* 172

(2014) 'Proportionality and Parliamentary Debates: Exploring Some Forbidden Territory' (2014) 34 *Oxford Journal of Legal Studies* 443

(2015a) 'A Hard Look at the Last Word' (2015) 35 *Oxford Journal of Legal Studies* 825

(2015b) 'The Joint Committee on Human Rights: A Hybrid Breed of Constitutional Watchdog' in Hunt, Hooper & Yowell (eds.) *Parliament and Human Rights* (Hart publishing)

(2015c) 'What's So Weak about Weak-Form Review? The Case of the UK Human Rights Act 1998' (2016) 13 *International Journal of Constitutional Law* 1008

(2015d) 'What's so Weak about Weak-Form Review? A Rejoinder to Stephen Gardbaum' (2016) 13 *International Journal of Constitutional Law* 1049

(2016a) 'The Lure and the Limits of Dialogue' (2016) 66 *University of Toronto Law Journal* 83

(2016b) 'The Constitutional Separation of Powers' in Dyzenhaus & Thorburn (eds.) *Philosophical Foundations of Constitutional Law* (Oxford University Press)

(2016c) 'The Role of Courts in the Joint Enterprise of Governing' in Barber, Ekins & Yowell (eds.) *Lord Sumption and the Limits of the Law* (Hart Publishing)

(2017) 'Article Review: Aileen Kavanagh on Neil Duxbury's Judicial Disapproval as a Constitutional Technique' *I-CONnect blogpost* (November 2017). Available at: www.iconnectblog.com/2017/11/article-review-aileen-kavanagh-on-neil-duxburys-judicial-disapproval-as-a-constitutional-technique/

(2019) 'Recasting the Political Constitution: From Rivals to Relationships' (2019) 30 *King's Law Journal* 43

(2020) 'Comparative Political Process Theory' (2020) 18 *International Journal of Constitutional Law* 1483

(2022) 'Towards a Relational Understanding of the Separation of Powers' [2022] *Public Law* 535

Keir, D & Lawson, F (1979) *Cases in Constitutional Law* 6th ed. (Clarendon Press)

Kelly, J (2005) *Governing with the Charter* (UBC Press)

(2020) 'Legislative Capacity and Human Rights in the Age of Populism: Two Challenges for Legislated Rights' (2020) 21 *Jerusalem Review of Legal Studies* 94

Kelly, J & Hennigar, M (2012) 'The Canadian Charter of Rights and the Minister of Justice: Weak-form review within a constitutional Charter of Rights' (2012) 10 *International Journal of Constitutional Law* 35

Kelly, R & Maer, L (2016) 'Parliamentary Reform and the Accountability of Government to the House of Commons' in Horne & Le Sueur (eds.) *Parliament: Legislation and Accountabiliity* (Hart Publishing)

Kennon, A (2013) 'Legal Advice to Parliament' in Horne, Drewry & Oliver (eds.) *Parliament and the Law* (Hart Publishing)

Kenny, D & Casey, C (2020) 'Shadow Constitutional Review: The Dark Side of Pre-Enactment Political Review in Ireland and Japan' (2020) 18 *International Journal of Constitutional Law* 51

Keohane, R (2005) *After Hegemony: Cooperation and Discord in the World Political Economy* 2nd ed. (Princeton University Press)

Khaitan, T (2021) 'Guarantor Institutions' (2021) 16 *Asian Journal of Comparative Law* 40

Khosla, M (2010) 'Making Social Rights Conditional: Lessons from India' (2010) 8 *International Journal of Constitutional Law* 739

Kildea, P (2020) 'The Constitutional Role of Electoral Management Bodies: The Case of the Australian Electoral Commission' (2020) 48 *Federal Law Review* 1

King, A (1997) *Running Scared: Why America's Politicians Campaign Too Much and Govern Too Little* (Free Press)

King, A & Crewe, I (2013) *The Blunders of Our Governments* (Oneworld)

King, J (2007) 'The Justiciability of Resource Allocation' (2007) 70 *Modern Law Review* 197

(2008a) 'Institutional Approaches to Judicial Restraint' (2008) 28 *Oxford Journal of Legal Studies* 409

(2008b) 'The Pervasiveness of Polycentricity' [2008] *Public Law* 101

(2012) *Judging Social Rights* (Cambridge University Press)

(2013) 'The Instrumental Value of Legal Accountability' in Bamforth & Leyland (eds.) *Accountability in the Contemporary Constitution* (Oxford University Press)

(2015a) 'Parliament's Role following Declarations of Incompatibility under the Human Rights Act' in Hunt, Hooper & Yowell (eds.) *Parliaments and Human Rights: Redressing the Democratic Deficit* (Hart Publishing)

(2015b) 'Rights and the Rule of Law in Third Way Constitutionalism' (2015) 30 *Constitutional Commentary* 101

(2019a) 'Dialogue, Finality and Legality' in Sigalet, Webber & Dixon (eds.) *Constitutional Dialogue: Rights, Democracy, Institutions* (Cambridge University Press)

(2019b) 'The Democratic Case for a Written Constitution' (2019) 72 *Current Legal Problems* 1

(2021) *Submission to the Independent Human Rights Act Review.* Available at: https://assets.publishing.service.gov.uk/government/uploads/system/uploads/attachment_data/file/1040525/ihrar-final-report.pdf

King, ML (2000 [1964]) *Why We Can't Wait* (Signet)

Kingreen, T & Poscher, R (2018) *Grundrechte Staatsrecht II* 34th ed. (CF Müller)

Kinley, D (2015) 'Finding and Filling the Democratic Deficit in Human Rights' in Hunt, Hooper & Yowell (eds.) *Parliament and Human Rights* (Hart Publishing)

Klein, A (2008) 'Judging as Nudging: New Governance Approaches for the Enforcement of Constitution Social and Economic Rights' (2008) 39 *Columbia Human Rights Law Review* 351

Klug, F (1999) 'The Human Rights Act 1998, Pepper v. Hart and All That' [1999] *Public Law* 246

(2001) 'The Human Rights Act – a "Third Way" or "Third Wave" Bill of Rights' [2001] *European Human Rights Law Review* 361

(2003) 'Judicial Deference under the Human Rights Act 1998' [2003] *European Human Rights Law Review* 125

(2005) 'The Long Road to Human Rights Compliance' (2005) 57 *Northern Ireland Legal Quarterly* 186

(2006) *Report on the Working Practices of the JCHR* (Joint Committee on Human Rights)

(2007) 'A Bill of Rights: Do We Need One or Do We Already Have One?' [2007] *Public Law* 701

Klug, F & Starmer, K (2005) 'Standing Back from the Human Rights Act: How Effective Is It Five Years On?' [2005] *Public Law* 716

Klug, F & Wildbore, H (2007) 'Breaking New Ground: The Joint Committee on Human Rights and the Role of Parliament in Human Rights Compliance' [2007] *European Human Rights Law Review* 231

Koh, H (1997) 'Why Do Nations Obey International Law' (1997) 106 *Yale Law Journal* 2599

Komesar, N (1984) 'Taking Institutions Seriously: Introduction to a Strategy for Constitutional Analysis' (1984) 51 *University of Chicago Law Review* 366

(1988) 'A Job for the Judges: The Judiciary and the Constitution in a Massive and Complex Society' (1988) 86 *Michigan Law Review* 657

(1994) *Imperfect Alternatives: Choosing Institutions in Law, Economics, and Public Policy* (University of Chicago Press)

Koskenniemi, M (2006) 'Constitutionalism as Mindset: Reflections on Kantian Themes about Law and Globalisation' (2006) 8 *Theoretical Inquiries in Law* 9

Kramer, L (2000) 'Putting the Politics Back into the Political Safeguards of Federalism' (2000) 100 *Columbia Law Review* 215

Kreppel, A (2014) 'Typologies and Classifications' in Martin, Saalfeld & Strom (eds.) *The Oxford Handbook of Legislative Studies* (Oxford University Press)

Krisch, N (2008) 'The Open Architecture of European Human Rights Law' (2008) 71 *Modern Law Review* 183

  (2010) *Beyond Constitutionalism: The Pluralist Structure of Postnational Law* (Oxford University Press)

Krisch, N, Corradini, F & Reimers, L (2020) 'Order at the Margins: The Legal Construction of Interface Norms over Time' (2020) 9 *Global Constitutionalism* 343

Krotoszynski, R (1998) 'Constitutional Flares: On Judges, Legislatures, and Dialogue' (1988) 83 *Minnesota Law Review* 1

Kumm, M (2009) 'The Cosmopolitan Turn in Constitutionalism: On the Relationship between Constitutionalism in and beyond the State' in Dunoff & Trachtman (eds.) *Ruling the World? Constitutionalism, International Law, and Global Governance* (Cambridge University Press)

  (2010) 'The Idea of Socratic Contestation and the Right to Justification: The Point of Rights-Based Proportionality Review' (2010) 4 *Law & Ethics of Human Rights* 141

  (2017) 'Constitutional Courts and Legislatures: Institutional Terms of Engagement' (2017) 1 *Catolica Law Review* 55

Kuo, M-S (2019) 'Against Instantaneous Democracy' (2019) 17 *International Journal of Constitutional Law* 554

Kutz, C (2000) 'Acting Together' (2000) LXI *Philosophy and Phenomenological Research* 1

Kyriakides, K (2003) 'The Advisory Functions of the Attorney General' (2003) 1 *Hertfordshire Law Journal* 73

Kyritsis, D (2006) 'Representation and Waldron's Objection to Judicial Review' (2006) 26 *Oxford Journal of Legal Studies* 733

  (2007) 'Principles, Policies and the Power of Courts' (2007) 20 *Canadian Journal of Law & Jurisprudence* 379

  (2008) 'What is Good about Legal Conventionalism?' (2008) 14 *Legal Theory* 135

  (2012) 'Constitutional Review in Representative Democracy' (2012) 32 *Oxford Journal of Legal Studies* 297

  (2014) 'Whatever Works: Proportionality as a Constitutional Doctrine' (2014) 24 *Oxford Journal of Legal Studies* 1

(2015) *Shared Authority: Courts and Legislatures in Legal Theory* (Hart Publishing)

(2017) *Where Our Protection Lies: Separation of Powers and Constitutional Review* (Oxford University Press)

(2020) 'Justifying Constitutional Review in the Legitimacy Register' (2020) 40 *Revus: Journal for Constitutional Theory and Philosophy of Law* 1

Kyritsis, D & Lakin, S (2022) 'The Methodology of Constitutional Theory - Introduction' in Kyritsis & Lakin (eds.) *The Methodology of Constitutional Theory* (Hart Publishing)

Kysar, D & Ewing, B (2011) 'Prods and Pleas: Limited Government in an Era of Unlimited Harm' (2011) 121 *Yale Law Journal* 350

Lain, C (2017) 'Soft Supremacy' (2017) 58 *William & Mary Law Review* 1609

Lake, H (2022) 'Overdoing the Override Clause' *The National* (6 September 2022)

Lakoff, G & Johnson, M (2003) *Metaphors We Live By* (University of Chicago Press)

Landau, D (2014) 'A Dynamic Theory of Judicial Role' (2014) 55 *Boston College Law Review* 1501

(2017) 'Substitute and Complement Theories of Judicial Review' (2017) 92 *Indiana Law Journal* 1282

(2018) 'Institutional Failure and Intertemporal Theores of Judicial Role in the Global South' in Bilchitz & Landau (eds.) *The Evolution of the Separation of Powers: Between the Global North and the Global South* (Edward Elgar)

Lavapuro, J, Ojanen, T & Scheinin, M (2011) 'Rights-Based Constitutionalism in Finland and the Development of Pluralist Constitutional Review' (2011) 9 *International Journal of Constitutional Law* 505

Law, D (2009) 'A Theory of Judicial Power and Judicial Review' (2009) 97 *Georgetown Law Review* 723

Law, D & Chang, W-C (2011) 'The Limits of Global Judicial Dialogue' (2011) 86 *Washington Law Review* 523

Laws, S (2013) 'Legislation and Politics' in Feldman (ed.) *Law in Politics, Politics in Law* (Hart Publishing)

(2016) 'What Is Parliamentary Scrutiny of Legislation For?' in Horne & Le Sueur (eds.) *Parliament: Legislation and Accountability* (Hart Publishing)

Lawson, G (1994) 'The Rise and Rise of the Administrative State' (1994) 107 *Harvard Law Review* 1231

Lawson, G & Seidman, G (2020) *Deference: The Legal Concept and the Legal Practice* (Oxford University Press)

Lazarus, L & Simonsen, N (2015) 'Judicial Review and Parliamentary Debate: Enriching the Doctrine of Due Deference' in Hunt, Hooper & Yowell (eds.) *Parliaments and Human Rights: Redressing the Democratic Deficit* (Hart Publishing)

Le Divellec, A (2007) 'Cabinet as the Leading Part of Parliament' in Ziegler, Baranger & Bradley (eds.) *Constitutionalism and the Role of Parliaments* (Hart Publishing)

Le Sueur, A (1996) 'The Judicial Review Debate: From Partnership to Friction' (1996) 31 *Government & Opposition* 8

Le Sueur, A & Caird, J (2013) 'The House of Lords Select Committee on the Constitution' in Horne, Drewry & Oliver (eds.) *Parliament and the Law* 1st ed. (Hart Publishing)

Leckey, R (2015) *Bills of Rights in the Common Law* (Cambridge University Press)

(2016) 'Enforcing Laws That Infringe Rights' [2016] *Public Law* 206

(2019a) 'Advocacy Notwithstanding the Notwithstanding Clause' (2019) 28 *Constitutional Forum constitutionnel* 1

(2019b) 'Assisted Dying, Suspended Declarations, and Dialogue's Time' (2019) 69 *University of Toronto Law Journal* 64

Leckey, R & Mendelsohn, E (2022) 'The Notwithstanding Clause: Legislatures, Courts, and the Electorate' (2022) 72 *University of Toronto Law Journal* 189

Lee, J & Lee, S (2015) 'Humility in the Supreme Court' (2015) 26 *King's Law Journal* 165

Leeson, H (2000) 'Section 33, the Notwithstanding Clause: A Paper Tiger?' (2000) 6 *IRRP Choices* 1

(2001) 'Section 33, the Notwithstanding Clause: A Paper Tiger?' in Howe & Russell (eds.) *Judicial Power and Canadian Democracy* (McGill-Queen's University Press)

Legg, A (2012) *The Margin of Appreciation in International Human Rights Law: Deference and Proportionality* (Oxford University Press)

Leigh, I (1999) 'Secrets of the Political Constitution' (1999) 62 *Modern Law Review* 298

Leigh, I & Lustgarten, L (1999) 'Making Rights Real: The Courts, Remedies and the Human Rights Act' (1999) 58 *Cambridge Law Journal* 509

Leigh, I & Masterman, R (2008) *Making Rights Real: The Human Rights Act 1998 in Its First Decade* (Hart Publishing)

Lemmens, K (2012) 'Comparative Law as an Act of Modesty: A Pragmatic and Realistic Approach to Comparative Legal Scholarship' in Adams & Bomhoff (eds.) *Practice and Theory in Comparative Law* (Cambridge University Press)

Lenaerts, K (2012) 'The European Court of Justice and Process-Oriented Review' (2012) 31 *Yearbook of European Law* 3

Leslie, I (2022) *How to Disagree: Lessons on Productive Conflict at Work and Home* (Faber & Faber)

Lester, A (1998) 'The Art of the Possible – Interpreting Statutes under the Human Rights Act' [1998] *European Human Rights Law Review* 663

(1999) 'Interpreting Statutes under the Human Rights Act' (1999) 20 *Statute Law Review* 218

(2002a) 'The Magnetism of the Human Rights Act 1998' (2002) 33 *Victoria University of Wellington Law Review* 53

(2002b) 'Parliamentary Scrutiny of Legislation under the Human Rights Act 1998' (2002) *European Human Rights Law Review* 432

Letsas, G (2006) 'Two Concepts of the Margin of Appreciation' (2006) 26 *Oxford Journal of Legal Studies* 705

(2013) 'The ECHR as Living Instrument: Its Meaning and Legitimacy' in Ulfstein, Follesdal & Peters (eds.) *Constituting Europe: The European Court of Human Rights in a National, European and Global Context* (Cambridge University Press)

Levi, E (1976) 'Some Aspects of the Separation of Powers' (1976) 76 *Columbia Law Review* 371

Levinson, D (1999) 'Rights Essentialism and Remedial Equilibration' (1999) 99 *Columbia Law Review* 857

(2005) 'Empire-Building Government in Constitutional Law' (2005) 118 *Harvard Law Review* 915

(2011) 'Parchment and Politics: The Positive Puzzle of Constitutional Commitment' (2011) 124 *Harvard Law Review* 657

Levinson, S & Balkin, J (2009) 'Constitutional Crises' (2009) 157 *University of Pennsylvania Law Review* 707

Levitsky, S & Ziblatt, D (2019) *How Democracies Die: What History Reveals about Our Future* (Penguin)

Levy, J (2019) 'Departmentalism and Dialogue' in Sigalet, Webber & Dixon (eds.), *Constitutional Dialogue: Rights, Democracy, Institutions* (Cambridge University Press)

Lewans, M (2016) *Administrative Law and Judicial Deference* (Hart Publishing)

Lewis, T & Cumper, P (2009) 'Balancing Freedom of Political Expression against Freedom of Political Opportunity' [2009] *Public Law* 89

Lieven, N & Kilroy, C (2003) 'Access to the Court under the Human Rights Act: Standing, Third Party Intervenors and Legal Assistance' in Jowell & Cooper (eds.) *Delivering Rights. How the Human Rights Act Is Working* (Hart)

Lijphart, A (2012) *Patterns of Democracy: Government Forms and Performance in Thirty-Six Countries* 2nd ed. (Yale University Press)

Lim, B (2013) 'The Normativity of the Principle of Legality' (2013) 37 *Melbourne University Law Review* 372

(2017) 'The Rationales for the Principle of Legality' in Meagher and Groves (eds.) *The Principle of Legality in Australia and New Zealand* (Federation Press)

Lin, C (2019) 'Dialogic Judicial Review and Its Problems in East Asia' (2019) 17 *International Journal of Constitutional Law* 701

Linde, H (1976) 'Due Process of Law-Making' (1976) 55 *Nebraska Law Review* 197

Loader, I (2007) 'The Cultural Lives of Security and Rights' in Goold & Lazarus (eds.) *Security and Human Rights* (Hart Publishing)

Lougheed, P (1998) 'Why a Notwithstanding Clause' (1998) 6 *Centre for Constitutional Studies Points of View.* Available at: www .constitutionalstudies.ca/wp-content/uploads/2020/08/Lougheed.pdf

Loughlin, M (2003) 'Constitutional Law: The Third Order of the Political' in Bamforth & Leyland (eds.) *Public Law in a Multi-Layered Constitution* (Hart Publishing)

(2006) 'Towards a Republican Revival' (2006) 26 *Oxford Journal of Legal Studies* 425

(2013) *The British Constitution: A Very Short Introduction* (Oxford University Press)

Lovell, G (2003) *Legislative Deferrals: Statutory Ambiguity, Judicial Power, and American Democracy* (Cambridge University Press)

Low, S (1904) *The Governance of England* (T Fisher Unwin)

Luban, D (2007) *Legal Ethics and Human Dignity* (Cambridge University Press)

Lübbe-Wolff, G (2014) 'The Principle of Proportionality in the Case-Law of the German Federal Constitutional Court' (2014) 34 *Human Rights Law Journal* 12

Luna, E (2000) 'Constitutional Road Maps' (2000) 90 *Journal of Criminal Law and Criminology* 1125

Lupo, N & Fasone, C (2016) *Interparliamentary Cooperation in the Composite European Constitution* (Hart Publishing)

MacDonnell, V (2013) 'The Constitution as Framework for Governance' (2013) 63 *University of Toronto Law Journal* 624

(2015) 'The Civil Servant's Role in the Implementation of Constitutional Rights' (2015) 13 *International Journal of Constitutional Law* 383

(2016) 'The New Parliamentary Sovereignty' (2016) 21 *Review of Constitutional Studies* 13

(2019) 'Rethinking the Invisible Constitution: How Unwritten Constitutional Principles Shape Political Decision-Making' (2019) 65 *McGill Law Journal* 176

(2023a) 'Accounting for a Strong Executive in Theories of Rights Interpretation' Unpublished manuscript, on file with author

(2023b) 'Theorising about the Executive in the Modern State' Unpublished manuscript, on file with author

MacFarlane, E (2012a) 'Conceptual Precision and Parliamentary Systems of Rights: Disambiguating "Dialogue"' (2012) 17 *Review of Constitutional Studies* 73

(2012b) 'Dialogue or Compliance? Measuring Legislatures' Policy Responses to Court Rulings on Rights' (2012) 34 *International Political Science Review* 39

(2013) *Governing from the Bench: The Supreme Court of Canada and the Judicial Role* (UBC Press)

(2017) 'Dialogue, Remedies, and Positive Rights: *Carter v. Canada* as Microcosm for Past and Future Issues under the *Charter of Rights and Freedoms*' (2017) 49 *Ottawa Law Review* 107

MacIntyre, A (1967) *Secularisation and Moral Change* (Oxford University Press)

MacNair, D (2005) 'In the Service of the Crown: Are Ethical Obligations Different for Government Lawyers?' (2005) 84 *Canadian Bar Review* 501

Madison, J (1788) *The Federalist Papers* (US Library of Congress). Available at: https://guides.loc.gov/federalist-papers/full-text

Maduro, MP (2009) 'Courts and Pluralism: Essay on a Theory of Adjudication in the Context of Legal and Constitutional Pluralism' in Dunoff & Trachtman (eds.) *Ruling the World? Constitutionalism, International Law, and Global Governance* (Cambridge University Press)

Magill, E (2000) 'The Real Separation in Separation of Powers Law' (2000) 86 *Virginia Law Review* 1127

Mahoney, P (2015) 'The Relationship between the Strasbourg Court and the National Courts – As Seen from Strasbourg' in Ziegler, Wicks & Hodson (eds.) *The UK and European Human Rights: A Strained Relationship?* (Hart Publishing)

Mailey, R (2019) 'The Notwithstanding Clause and the New Populism' (2019) 28 *Constitutional Forum* 9

Major, J (2022) 'Boris Johnson's Government Has Damaged the UK' *BBC News* report (10 July 2022). Available at: www.bbc.co.uk/news/uk-politics-62134391

Malleson, K (2001) 'A British Bill of Rights: Incorporating the European Convention on Human Rights' in Howe & Russell (eds.) *Judicial Power and Canadian Democracy* (McGill-Queen's University Press)

(2010) 'The Rehabilitation of the Separation of Powers in the UK' in de Groot van Leeuwen & Rombouts (eds.) *Separation of Powers in Theory and Practice: An International Perspective* (Wolf Legal Publishers)

Mallory, C & Tyrrell, H (2021) 'Discretionary Space and Declarations of Incompatibility' (2021) 32 *King's Law Journal* 466

Mance, H (2022) '"A Bonfire of the Decencies": Peter Hennessy on Boris Johnson's Government' *Financial Times* (23 May 2022). Available at: www.ft.com/content/37a5b18a-77d0-4f17-ae0a-99802396ff36

Mance, J (2018) 'The Frontiers of Executive and Judicial Power: Differences in Common Law Constitutional Traditions' (2018) 26 *Asia Pacific Law Review* 109

Mandel, M (1989) *The Charter of Rights and the Legalisation of Politics in Canada* (Thompson Educational)

Manfredi, C (2001) *Judicial Power and the Charter: Canada and the Paradox of Liberal Constitutionalism* 2nd ed. (Oxford University Press)

(2004) 'The Life of a Metaphor: Dialogue in the Supreme Court' in Huscroft & Brodie (eds.) *Constitutionalism in the Charter Era* (Butterworths)

Manfredi, C & Kelly, J (1999) 'Six Degrees of Dialogue: A Response to Hogg and Bushell' (1999) 37 *Osgoode Hall Law Journal* 513

Manin, B (1997) *The Principles of Representative Government* (Cambridge University Press)

Mann, R (2018) 'Non-Ideal Theory of Constitutional Adjudication' (2018) 7 *Global Constitutionalism* 14

Manning, J (2001) 'Textualism and the Equity of the Statute' (2001) 101 *Columbia Law Review* 1

(2010) 'Clear Statement Rules and the Constitution' (2010) 110 *Columbia Law Review* 399

Manow, P & Burkhart, S (2007) 'Legislative Self-Restraint under Divided Government in Germany, 1976–2002' (2007) 32 *Legislative Studies Quarterly* 167

Margalit, A (2010) *On Compromise and Rotten Compromises* (Princeton University Press)

Markovits, D (2005) 'Democratic Disobedience' (2005) 114 *Yale Law Journal* 1897

Marshall, G (1984) *Constitutional Conventions: The Rules and Forms of Political Accountability* (Clarendon Press)

(2003) 'The Lynchpin of Parliamentary Intention: Lost, Stolen, or Strained?' [2003] *Public Law* 236

Marshall, G & Moodie, G (1967) *Some Problems of the Constitution* (Hutchinson)

Martin, S (2018) 'Declaratory Misgivings: Assisted Suicide in a Post-Nicklinson Context' [2018] *Public Law* 209

Mashaw, J (1988) 'As-If-Republican Interpretation' (1988) 97 *Yale Law Journal* 1685

(1997) *Greed, Chaos, and Governance: Using Public Choice to Improve Public Law* (Yale University Press)

(2005) 'Between Facts and Norms: Agency Statutory Interpretation as an Autonomous Enterprise' (2005) 55 *University of Toronto Law Journal* 497

Mason, P (2017) 'Prisoners, Human Rights and the Media' in Tumber & Waisbord (eds.) *The Routledge Companion to Media and Human Rights* (Routledge)

Masterman, R (2011) *The Separation of Powers in the Contemporary Constitution: Judicial Competence and Independence in the United Kingdom* (Cambridge University Press)

Masterman, R & Leigh, I (2013) 'The United Kingdom's Human Rights Project in Constitutional and Comparative Perspective' in Masterman & Leigh (eds.) *The United Kingdom's Statutory Bill of Rights: Constitutional and Comparative Perspectives* (Oxford University Press)

Mathen, C (2007) 'Dialogue Theory, Judicial Review, and Judicial Supremacy: A Comment on "*Charter* Dialogue Revisited"' (2007) 45 *Osgoode Hall Law Journal* 125

(2016) 'A Recent History of Government Responses to Constitutional Litigation' (2016) 25 *Constitutional Forum* 101

(2019) *Courts Without Cases: The Law and Politics of Advisory Opinions* (Hart Publishing)

Matthews, D (1959) 'The Folkways of the United States Senate: Conformity to Group Norms and Legislative Effectiveness' (1959) 53 *American Political Science Review* 1064

Mayhew, D (1974) *Congress: The Electoral Connection* (Yale University Press)

McAdam, R (2009) 'The Notwithstanding Taboo' (2009) 6 *Federal Governance* 1

McCormick, C. (2022) *The Constitutional Legitimacy of Law Officers in the United Kingdom* (Hart Publishing)

McCormick, C & Cowie, G (2020). *The Law Officers: A Constitutional and Functional Overview* (HoC Library)

McCrea, R (2022) 'Boris Johnson Has Done Deep and Lasting Damage to the British Constitution' *The Irish Times* (9 July 2022)

McDonald, L (2004a) 'New Directions in the Australian Bill of Rights Debate' [2004] *Public Law* 22

(2004b) 'Rights, "Dialogue" and Democratic Objections to Judicial Review' (2004) 32 *Federal Law Review* 1

McGann, A (2006) 'Social Choice and Comparing Legislatures: Constitutional versus Institutional Constraints' (2006) 12 *Journal of Legislative Studies* 443

McHarg, A (2008) 'Reforming the United Kingdom Constitution: Law, Convention, Soft Law' (2008) 71 *Modern Law Review* 853

McLachlin, B (1999) 'Charter Myths' (1999) 33 *University of British Columbia Law Review* 23

(2019) 'Legislated Rights: Comments by Beverley McLachlin' *Judicial Power Project* post (14 February 2019). Available at: https://judicialpowerproject .org.uk/legislated-rights-comment-by-beverley-mclachlin/

McLean, J (2001) 'Legislative Invalidation, Human Rights Protection and s 4 of the New Zealand Bill of Rights Act' [2001] *New Zealand Law Review* 421

(2013) 'The New Zealand Bill of Rights Act 1990 and Constitutional Propriety' (2013) 11 *New Zealand Journal of Public and International Law* 19

(2016) 'The Unwritten Political Constitution and Its Enemies' (2016) 14 *International Journal of Constitutional Law* 119

(2018) 'The Unwritten Constitution' in Jacobsohn & Schor (eds.) *Comparative Constitutional Theory* (Edward Elgar)

(2020a) 'Between Sovereign and Subject: The Constitutional Position of the Official' (2020) 70 *University of Toronto Law Journal* 167

(2020b) 'The Principle of Legality, Sovereignty and the Structure of the Constitution' in Harris & Mount (eds.) *The Promise of Law: Essays marking the retirement of Dame Sian Elias as Chief Justice of New Zealand* (Lexisnexis New Zealand)

McMillan, J (2010) 'Re-thinking the Separation of Powers' (2010) 38 *Federal Law Review* 423

McMorrow, T (2018) 'MAID in Canada: Debating the Constitutionality of Canada's New Medical Assitance in Dying Law' (2018) 44 *Queen's Law Journal* 70

McMurtry, R (1982) 'The Search for a Constitutional Accord – A Personal Memoir' (1982) 8 *Queens' Law Journal* 28

Mead, D (2015) '"You Couldn't Make It Up": Some Narratives of the Media Coverage of Human Rights' in Ziegler, Wicks & Hodson (eds.) *The UK and European Human Rights: A Strained Relationship?* (Hart Publishing)

Meagher, D (2011) 'The Common Law Principle of Legality in the Age of Rights' (2011) 35 *Melbourne University Law Review* 449

  (2014) 'The Principle of Legality as Clear Statement Rule: Significance and Problems' (2014) 36 *Sydney Law Review* 413

Meagher, D & Groves, M, eds. (2017) *The Principle of Legality in Australia and New Zealand* (The Federation Press)

Melnick, RS (1985) 'The Politics of Partnership' (1985) 45 *Public Administration Review* 653

Mendes, CH (2013) *Constitutional Courts and Deliberative Democracy* (Oxford University Press)

Mendes, J & Venzke, I (2018) 'Introducing the Idea of Relative Authority' in Mendes & Venzke (eds.) *Allocating Authority: Who Should Do What in European and International Law?* (Hart Publishing)

Merrill, T (1991) 'The Constitutional Principle of Separation of Powers' [1991] *The Supreme Court Review* 225

Metzger, G (2009) 'The Interdependent Relationship between Internal and External Separation of Powers' (2009) 59 *Emory Law Journal* 424

Mezey, M (1979) *Comparative Legislatures* (Duke University Press)

Michaels, J (2015) 'An Enduring, Evolving Separation of Powers' (2015) 115 *Columbia Law Review* 515

Michelman, F (1986) 'Traces of Self-Government' (1986) 100 *Harvard Law Review* 4

Miers, D & Page, A (1990) *Legislation* 2nd ed. (Sweet & Maxwell)

Mikva, AJ (1998) 'Why Judges Should Not Be Advicegivers: A Response to Professor Neal Katyal' (1998) 50 *Stanford Law Review* 1825

Mill, JS (1861) *Considerations on Representative Government* (Parker, Son, and Bourn)

  (1998 [1861]) *On Liberty and Other Essays* (Oxford University Press)

Möller, K (2012) *The Global Model of Constitutional Rights* (Oxford University Press)

Möllers, C (2013) *The Three Branches: A Comparative Model of Separation of Powers* (Oxford University Press)

(2019) 'Separation of Powers' in Masterman & Schütze (eds.) *The Cambridge Companion to Comparative Constitutional Law* (Cambridge University Press)

Monaghan, H (1975) 'Constitutional Common Law' (1975) 89 *Harvard Law Review* 1

Moore, C (2011) 'If Strasbourg Has Its Way, We Will All End Up as Prisoners' *The Telegraph* (11 February 2011)

Morton, FL (1999) 'Dialogue or Monologue?' (1999) 20 *Policy Options* 23

Morton, FL & Knopff, FMR (2000) *The Charter Revolution and the Court Party* (Broadview Press)

Morton, PA (1991) 'Conventions of the British Constitution' (1991) 15 *Holdsworth Law Review* 114

Mulholland, H & Wintour, P (2011) 'UK Will Not Defy European Court on Prisoners' Votes, Says Kenneth Clarke' *The Guardian* (9 February 2011)

Müller, J-W (2017) *What Is Populism?* (Penguin Books)

Munro, C (1999) *Studies in Constitutional Law* 2nd ed. (Butterworths)

Mureinik, E (1994) 'A Bridge to Where? Introducing the Interim Bill of Rights' (1994) 10 *South African Journal of Human Rights* 31

Murkens, J (2018) 'Judicious Review: The Constitutional Practice of the UK Supreme Court' (2018) 77 *Cambridge Law Journal* 349

Murray, C (2010) 'We Need to Talk: "Democratic Dialogue" and the Ongoing Saga of Prisoner Disenfranchisement' (2010) 62 *Northern Ireland Legal Quarterly* 57

(2011) 'Playing for Time: Prisoner Disenfranchisement under the ECHR after Hirst v United Kingdom' (2011) 22 *King's Law Journal* 309

(2013a) 'The Continuation of Politics, by Other Means: Judicial Dialogue under the Human Rights Act 1998' in Masterman & Leigh (eds.) *The United Kingdom's Statutory Bill of Rights: Constitutional and Comparative Perspectives* (Oxford University Press)

(2013b) 'A Perfect Storm: Parliament and Prisoner Disenfranchisement' (2013) 66 *Parliamentary Affairs* 511

Nagel, T (1998) 'Concealment and Exposure' (1998) 27 *Philosophy & Public Affairs* 3

Nason, S (2016) *Reconstructing Judicial Review* (Hart Publishing)

Nelson, E (2014) 'Are We on the Verge of the Death Spiral That Produced the English Revolution of 1642–1649?' from History News Network (14 December 2014). Available at: http://historynewsnetwork.org/article/157822

Neslen, A (2021) 'Boris Johnson Was "a Shambolic, Shameless Clot" Says Former Colleague' *Politico* (3 April 2021). Available at: www.politico.eu/article/alan-duncan-boris-johnson-selfish-ill-disciplined-shambolic-shameless-clot/

Neuberger, D (2015) '"Judge Not, That Ye Be Not Judged": Judging Judicial Decision-Making' *F A Mann Lecture 2015*. Available at: www.supremecourt.uk/docs/speech-150129.pdf

Neustadt, R (1964) *Presidential Power* (Wiley)

Newman, D (2019) 'Canada's Notwithstanding Clause, Dialogue, and National Identities' in Sigalet, Webber & Dixon (eds.) *Constitutional Dialogue: Rights, Democracy, Institutions* (Cambridge University Press)

Nichols, T (2022) 'The Shameless Boris Johnson' *The Atlantic* (7 July 2022). Available at: www.theatlantic.com/newsletters/archive/2022/07/the-shameless-boris-johnson/661520/

Nicol, D (2002) 'Are Convention Rights a No-Go Zone for Parliament?' [2002] *Public Law* 438

(2004a) 'Gender Reassignment and the Transformation of the Human Rights Act' (2004) 120 *Law Quarterly Review* 194

(2004b) 'The Human Rights Act and the Pol iticians' (2004) 24 *Legal Studies* 451

(2006) 'Law and Politics after the Human Rights Act' [2006] *Public Law* 722

(2011) 'Legitimacy of the Commons Debate on Prisoner Voting' [2011] *Public Law* 681

Nicolaides, E & Snow, D (2021) 'A Paper Tiger No More? The Media Portrayal of the Notwithstanding Clause in Saskatchewan and Ontario' (2021) 54 *Canadian Journal of Political Science* 60

Norton, P (1990) 'The House of Commons as a Policy Influencer' in Norton (ed.) *Legislatures* (Oxford University Press)

(2001) 'Playing by the Rules: The Constraining Hand of Parliamentary Procedure' (2001) 7 *Journal of Legislative Studies* 13

(2013a) 'A Democratic Dialogue? Parliament and Human Rights in the United Kingdom' (2013) 21 *Asia Pacific Law Review* 141

(2013b) *Parliament in British Politics* 2nd ed. (Palgrave Macmillan)

(2016) 'Legislative Scrutiny in the House of Lords' in Horne & Le Sueur (eds.) *Parliament, Legislation and Accountability* (Hart Publishing)

(2020) *Governing Britain: Parliament, Ministers and Our Ambiguous Constitution* (Manchester University Press)

Nourse, V (1999) 'The Vertical Separation of Powers' (1999) 49 *Duke Law Journal* 749

Nussberger, A (2017) 'Procedural Review by the ECtHR: View from the Court' in Gerards & Brems (eds.) *Procedural Review in European Fundamental Rights cases* (Cambridge University Press)

O'Brien, P (2017) '"Enemies of the People": Judges, the Media and the Mythic Lord Chancellor' [2017] *Public Law* 135

O'Donnell, D (2017) 'The Sleep of Reason' (2017) 40 *Dublin University Law Journal* 191

O'Donnell, G (1994) 'Delegative Democracy' (1994) 5 *Journal of Democracy* 55

Oliver, D (2003) *Constitutional Reform in the UK* (Oxford University Press)

(2006) 'Improving the Scrutiny of Bills: The Case for Standards and Checklists' [2006] *Public Law* 219

(2013) 'Parliament and the Courts: A Pragmatic (or Principled) Defence of the Sovereignty of Parliament' in Horne, Drewry & Oliver (eds.) *Parliament and the Law* (Hart Publishing)

O'Neill, O (2002) *A Question of Trust: The BBC Reith Lectures* (Cambridge University Press)

O'Toole, F (2022) 'Why Was Boris Johnson so Influential at such a Momentous Moment?' *The Irish Times* (9 July 2022).

O'Regan, K (2012) 'Text Matters: Some Reflections on the Forging of a New Constitutional Jurisprudence in South Africa' (2012) 75 *Modern Law Review* 1

(2019) 'Contemporary Challenges for Human Rights: A View from South Africa' in Harris & Mount (eds.) *The Promise of Law: Essays Marking the Retirement of Dame Sian Elias as Chief Justice of New Zealand* (LexisNexis NZ Ltd)

Ornstein, N & Mann, T, eds. (2000) *The Permanent Campaign and Its Future* (American Enterprise Institute)

Packenham, R (1990) 'Legislatures and Political Development' in Norton (ed.) *Legislatures: Oxford Readings in Politics and Government* (Oxford University Press)

Page, E (2003) 'The Civil Servant as Legislator: Law Making in British Administration' (2003) 81 *Public Administration* 651

(2009) 'Their Word Is Law: Parliamentary Counsel and Creative Policy Analysis' [2009] *Public Law* 790

Page, E & Jenkins, B (2005) *Policy Bureaucracy: Government with a Cast of Thousands* (Oxford University Press)

Pal, M (2016) 'Electoral Management Bodies as a Fourth Branch of Government' (2016) 21 *Review of Constitutional Studies* 85

(2022) 'Democracy and the Notwithstanding Clause' *Biannual Public Law Conference*, University College Dublin. Unpublished paper, on file with the author

Palmer, E (2007) *Judicial Review, Socio-Economic Rights and the Human Rights Act* (Hart Publishing)

Palmer, G (1985) *A White Paper for New Zealand* (New Zealand House of Representatives)

Palmer, M (2011) 'The Law Officers and Departmental Lawyers' [2011] *New Zealand Law Journal* 333

(2017) 'Constitutional Dialogue and the Rule of Law' (2017) 47 *Hong Kong Law Journal* 505

Paris, M-L (2016) 'Setting the Scene: Elements of *Constitutional Theory* and Methodology of the Research' in Bell & Paris (eds.) *Rights-Based Constitutional Review* (Edward Elgar)

Paterson, A (2013) *Final Judgment: The Last Law Lords and the Supreme Court* (Hart Publishing)

Peretti, T (2001) *In Defense of a Political Court* (Princeton University Press)

Perreira, N (2015) 'The Supreme Court in a Final Push to Go beyond Strasbourg' [2015] *Public Law* 367

Perry, A (2019) 'Strained Interpretations' (2019) 39 *Oxford Journal of Legal Studies* 316

Perry, M (2003) 'Protecting Human Rights in a Democracy: What Role for the Courts?' (2003) 38 *Wake Forest Law Review* 635

Petersen, N (2017) *Proportionality and Judicial Activism: Fundamental Rights Adjudication in Canada, Germany and South Africa* (Cambridge University Press)

Petrie, N (2019) 'Indications of Inconsistency' (2019) 78 *Cambridge Law Journal* 612

Petter, A (2007) 'Taking Dialogue Theory Much Too Seriously (or Perhaps *Charter* Dialogue Isn't Such a Good Thing After All)' (2007) 45 *Osgoode Hall Law Journal* 147

Pettit, P (1999) 'Republican Freedom and Contestatory Democratisation' in Shapiro & Hacker-Cordon (eds.) *Democracy's Values* (Cambridge University Press)

(2012) *On the People's Terms: A Republican Theory and Model of Democracy* (Cambridge University Press)

Phillips, N (2010) 'The Art of the Possible: Statutory Interpretation and Human Rights' *The First Lord Alexander of Weedon Lecture, Inner Temple* (22 April 2010)

Phillipson, G (2006) 'Deference, Discretion, and Democracy in the Human Rights Act Era' [2006] *Current Legal Problems* 40

(2013) 'The Human Rights Act, Dialogue and Constitutional Principles' in Masterman & Leigh (eds.) *The United Kingdom's Statutory Bill of Rights: Constitutional and Comparative Perspectives* (Oxford University Press)

(2014) 'Deference and Dialogue in the Real-World Counter-terrorism Context' in Davis & De Londras (eds.) *Critical Debates in Counter-terrorism Judicial Review* (Cambridge University Press)

(2016) 'A Dive into Deep Constitutional Waters: Article 50, the Prerogative and Parliament' (2016) 79 *Modern Law Review* 1064

Pickerill, M (2004) *Constitutional Deliberation in Congress: The Impact of Judicial Review in a Separated System* (Duke University Press)

Pierce, R (1989) 'Separation of Powers and the Limits of Independence' (1989) 30 *William & Mary Law Review* 365

Pildes, R (2014) 'Romanticising Democracy, Political Fragmentation, and the Decline of American Government' (2014) 124 *Yale Law Journal* 804

Pillard, C (2005) 'The Unfulfilled Promise of the Constitution in Executive Hands' (2005) 103 *Michigan Law Review* 676

Pinker, S (2007) *The Stuff of Thought: Language as a Window into Human Nature* (Penguin)

(2018) *Enlightenment Now: The Case for Reason, Science, Humanism and Progress* (Penguin)

Pitkin, H (1967) *The Concept of Representation* (University of California Press)

Poirier, J (2001) 'The Functions of Intergovernmental Agreements: Post-Devolution Concordats in a Comparative Perspective' 2001 *Public Law* 134

Poole, T (2005) 'Harnessing the Power of the Past? Lord Hoffmann and the Belmarsh Detainees Case' (2005) 32 *Journal of Law and Society* 534

(2007a) 'Courts and Conditions of Uncertainty in "Times of Crisis"' 2007 *Public Law* 555

(2007b) 'Tilting at Windmills? Truth and Illusion in "The Political Constitution"' (2007) 70 *Modern Law Review* 250

(2008) 'Courts and Conditions of Uncertainty in "Times of Crisis"' [2008] *Public Law* 234

Popelier, P (2017) 'Evidence-Based Lawmaking: Influences, Obstacles and the Role of the European Court of Human Rights' in Gerards & Brems (eds.) *Procedural Review in European Fundamental Rights Cases* (Cambridge University Press)

Posner, E & Vermeule, A (2008) 'Constitutional Showdowns' (2008) 156 *University of Pennsylvania Law Review* 991

(2010) *The Executive Unbound: After the Madisonian Republic* (Oxford University Press)

Posner, R (2000) 'Law and Disagreement' (2000) 100 *Columbia Law Review* 582

Post, R & Siegel, R (2003a) 'Legislative Constitutionalism and Section Five Power: Policentric Interpretation of the Family and Medical Leave Act' (2003) 112 *Yale Law Journal* 1943

(2003b) 'Protecting the Constitution from the People: Juricentric Restrictions on Section Five Power' (2003) 78 *Indiana Law Journal* 1

Powell, C (2019) 'We the People: These United Divided States' (2019) 40 *Fordham Law Review* 2685

Pozen, D (2010) 'Deep Secrecy' (2010) 62 *Stanford Law Review* 257

(2014) 'Self-Help and the Separation of Powers' (2014) 124 *Yale Law Journal* 2

Prendergast, D (2019) 'The Judicial Role in Protecting Democracy from Populism' (2019) 20 *German Law Journal* 245

Putnam, R (1994) *Making Democracies Work: Civic Traditions in Modern Italy* (Princeton University Press)

(2000) *Bowling Alone: The Collapse and Revival of American Community* (Simon & Schuster)

Quinlan, M (1993) 'Ethics in the Public Service' (1993) 6 *Governance: An International Journal of Policy, Administrations, and Institutions* 538

Radcliffe, L (1968) *Not in Feather Beds* (Hamish Hamilton)

Rawlings, R (2005) 'Review, Revenge and Retreat' (2005) 68 *Modern Law Review* 378

Rawls, J (1971) *A Theory of Justice* (Harvard University Press)

    (2005) *Political Liberalism* (Columbia University Press)

Raz, J (1979) *The Authority of Law: Essays on Law and Morality* (Clarendon Press)

    (1994) *Ethics in the Public Domain: Essays in the Morality of Law and Politics* (Clarendon Press)

    (1995a) 'Interpretation Without Retrieval' in Marmor (ed.) *Law and Interpretation* (Clarendon Press)

    (1995b) 'Rights and Politics' (1995) 71 *Indiana Law Journal* 27

    (1996) 'Intention in Interpretation' in George (ed.) *The Autonomy of Law* (Oxford University Press)

    (1998a) 'Disagreement in Politics' (1998) 43 *American Journal of Jurisprudence* 25

    (1998b) 'On the Authority and Interpretation of Constitutions: Some Preliminaries' in Alexander (ed.) *Constitutionalism: Philosophical Foundations* (Cambridge University Press)

    (2001) 'Sorensen: Vagueness Had No Function in Law' (2001) 7 *Legal Theory* 417

    (2009) *Between Authority and Interpretation* (Oxford University Press)

Reese, SD & Lewis, SC (2009) 'Framing the War on Terror: The Internalisation of Policy in the US Press' (2009) 10 *Journalism* 777

Regan, P (2012) 'Enacting Legislation – a Civil Servant's Perspective' (2012) 34 *Statute Law Review* 32

Reid, L (1972) 'The Judge as Lawmaker' [1972] *Journal of the Society of Public Teachers of Law* 22

    (1997) 'The Judge as Lawmaker' (1997) 63 *Arbitration* 180

Renan, D (2017) 'The Law Presidents Make' (2017) 103 *Virginia Law Review* 805

Rhodes, R (2011) *Everyday Life in British Government* (Oxford University Press)

Rishworth, P (2016) 'Writing Things Unwritten: Common Law in New Zealand's Constitution' (2016) 14 *International Journal of Constitutional Law* 137

Ritchie, L (2013) *Metaphor* (Cambridge University Press)

Rivers, J (2006) 'Proportionality and Variable Intensity of Review' (2006) 65 *Cambridge Law Journal* 174

Rizza, A (2018) '400 Legal Professionals Oppose Ontario's Use of the Notwithstanding Clause' *Global News* (17 September 2018)

Roach, K (2004) 'Dialogic Judicial Review and Its Critics' (2004) 23 *Supreme Court Law Review* 49

(2005) 'Constitutional, Remedial, and International Dialogues about Rights: The Canadian Experience' (2005) 40 *Texas International Law Journal* 537

(2006) 'Not Just the Government's Lawyer: The Attorney General as Defender of the Rule of Law' (2006) 31 *Queen's Law Journal* 598

(2007) 'Sharpening the Dialogue Debate: The Next Decade of Scholarship' (2007) 45 *Osgoode Hall Law Journal* 169

(2009) 'Judicial Review of Anti-Terrorism Legislation: The Post-9/11 Experience and Normative Experiences for Judicial Review' (2009) 3 *Indian Journal of Constitutional Law* 138

(2015) 'The Varied Roles of Courts and Legislatures in Rights Protection' in Hunt, Hooper & Yowell (eds.) *Parliament and Human Rights* (Hart Publishing)

(2016a) 'Remedies for Laws That Violate Rights' in Bell, Elliott, Varuhas & Murray (eds.) *Public Law Adjudication in Common Law Systems: Process and Substance* (Hart Publishing)

(2016b) *The Supreme Court on Trial: Judicial Activism or Democratic Dialogue* revised ed. (Irwin Law)

(2017) 'Is Brad Wall Really Defending School Choice with His Use of the Notwithstanding Clause?' *Globe and Mail* (2 May 2017)

(2021) *Remedies for Human Rights Violations: A Two-Track Approach to Supra-National and National Law* (Cambridge University Press)

Rodriguez, C (2014) 'Negotiating Conflict through Federalism: Institutional and Popular Perspectives' (2014) 123 *Yale Law Journal* 2094

Rogers, J (2001) 'Information and Judicial Review: A Signaling Game of Legislative-Judicial Interaction' (2001) 45 *American Journal of Political Science* 84

Rogers, R & Walters, R (2015) *How Parliament Works* 7th ed. (Routledge)

Rose, D & Weir, C (2003) 'Interpretation and Incompatibility: Striking the Balance' in Jowell & Cooper (eds.) *Delivering Rights: How the Human Rights Act Is Working* (Hart Publishing)

Rose-Ackerman, S, Egidy, S & Fowkes, J (2015) *Due Process of Lawmaking: The United States, Sourth Africa, Germany, and the European Union* (Cambridge University Press)

Rosenblum, N (1998) *Membership and Morals: The Personal Uses of Pluralism in America* (Princeton University Press)

(2008) *On the Side of Angels: An Appreciation of Parties and Partisanship* (Princeton University Press)

Roughan, N (2013) *Authorities: Conflicts, Cooperation, and Transnational Legal Theory* (Oxford University Press)

Rousseau, G & Côté, F (2017) 'A Distinctive Quebec Theory and Practice of the Notwithstanding Clause: When Collective Interests Outweigh Individual Rights' (2017) 47 *Revue generale de droit* 343

Roux, T (2013) *The Politics of Principle* (Cambridge University Press)

(2018) 'In Defence of Empirical Entanglement: The Methodological Flaw in Waldron's Case against Judicial Review' in Levy, Kong, Orr & King (eds.) *The Cambridge Handbook of Deliberative Constitutionalism* (Cambridge University Press)

Rowbottom, J (2007) 'The Ban on Political Advertising and Article 10' (2007) 18 *Entertainment Law Review* 91

(2013) '*Animal Defenders International*: Speech, Spending, and a Change of Direction in Strasbourg' (2013) 5 *Journal of Media Law* 1

Roy, M & Brosseau, L (2018) *The Notwithstanding Clause of the Charter* Background Paper

Rozenberg, J (2002) 'Blunkett's Blunder Confuses the Issue' *The Telegraph* (30 May 2002). Available at: www.telegraph.co.uk/news/uknews/1395765/Blunketts-blunder-confuses-the-issue.html

(2005) '90-Day Detention of Suspects "Unlawful"' *The Telegraph* (21 October 2005). Available at: www.telegraph.co.uk/news/uknews/1500305/90-day-detention-of-suspects-unlawful.html

(2020) *Enemies of the People: How Judges Shape Society* (Bristol University Press)

Runciman, D (2019) *How Democracy Ends* (Profile Books)

Russell, M (2010) 'Parliament: Emasculated or Emancipated?' in Hazell (ed.) *Constitutional Futures Revisited: Britain's Constitution in 2020* (Palgrave Macmillan)

(2013) *The Contemporary House of Lords: Westminster Bicameralism Revived* (Oxford University Press)

Russell, M & Benton, M (2012) 'Assessing the Impact of Parliament Oversight Committees: The Select Committees in the British House of Commons' [2012] *Parliamentary Affairs* 1

Russell, M & Cowley, P (2016) 'The Policy Power of the Westminster Parliament: The "Parliamentary State" and the Empirical Evidence' (2016) 29 *Governance: An International Journal of Policy, Administrations, and Institutions* 121

Russell, M & Gover, D (2017) *Legislation at Westminster: Parliamentary Actors and Influence in the Making of British Law* (Oxford University Press)

Russell, M, Gover, D & Wollter, K (2016) 'Does the Executive Dominate the Westminster Legislative Process? Six Reasons for Doubt' (2016) 69 *Parliamentary Affairs* 286

(2017) 'Actors, Motivations and Outcomes in the Legislative Process: Policy Influence at Westminster' (2017) 52 *Government & Opposition* 1

Russell, P (1991) 'Standing Up for Notwithstanding' (1991) 29 *Alberta Law Journal* 293

(2007) 'The Notwithstanding Clause: The Charter's Homage to Parliamentary Sovereignty' [2007] *Policy Options* 65

(2009) 'The Charter and Canadian Democracy' in Manfredi & Kelly (eds.) *Contested Constitutionalism: Reflections on the Canadian Charter of Rights and Freedoms* (University of British Colombia Press)

Ryle, M (1994) 'Pre-Legislative Scrutiny: A Prophylactic Approach to Protection of Human Rights' [1994] *Public Law* 192

Sabl, A (2002) *Ruling Passions: Political Offices and Democratic Ethics* (Princeton University Press)

Sachs, A (2009) *The Strange Alchemy of Life and Law* (Oxford University Press)

(2014) 'Global Constitutionalism: Alumni Weekend 2013' (2014) 61 *Yale Law Report* 53

Sadurski, W (2002) 'Judicial Review and the Protection of Constitutional Rights' (2002) 22 *Oxford Journal of Legal Studies* 275

(2018) 'Constitutional Crisis in Poland' in Graber, Levinson & Tushnet (eds.) *Constitutional Democracy in Crisis?* (Oxford University Press)

(2019) *Poland's Constitutional Breakdown* (Oxford University Press)

(2020a) 'Constitutional Democracy in the Time of Elected Authoritarians' (2020) 18 *International Journal of Constitutional Law* 324

(2020b) 'Constitutional Design: Lessons from Poland's Democratic Backsliding' (2020) 6 *Constitutional Studies* 59

Sager, L (2002) 'Constitutional Justice' 2002 *Journal of Legislation and Public Policy* 11

(2004) *Justice in Plainclothes: A Theory of American Constitutional Practice* (Yale University Press)

Sales, P (2009a) 'A Comparison of the Principle of Legality and Section 3 of the Human Rights Act 1998' (2009) 125 *Law Quarterly Review* 598

(2009b) 'The General and the Particular: Parliament and the Courts under the scheme of the European Convention on Human Rights' in Andenas & Fairgrieve (eds.) *Lord Bingham and the Transformation of the Law: A Liber Amicorum* (Oxford University Press)

(2012) 'Judges and Legislature: Values into Law' (2012) 71 *Cambridge Law Journal* 287

(2016a) 'Partnership and Challenge: The Courts' Role in Managing the Integration of Rights and Democracy' [2016] *Public Law* 456

(2016b) 'Rights and Fundamental Rights in English Law' (2016) 75 *Cambridge Law Journal* 86

(2018a) 'The Contribution of Legislative Drafting to the Rule of Law' (2018) 77 *Cambridge Law Journal* 630

(2018b) 'Law Reform Challenges: The Judicial Perspective' (2018) 39 *Statute Law Review* 229

(2018c) 'Legalism in Constitutional Law: Judging in a Democracy' [2018] *Public Law* 687

(2020) 'Law, Democracy, and the Absent Legislator' in Fisher, King & Young (eds.) *The Foundations and Future of Public Law: Essays in Honour of Paul Craig* (Oxford University Press)

Sales, P & Ekins, R (2011) 'Rights-Consistent Interpretation and the Human Rights Act 1998' (2011) 127 *Law Quarterly Review* 217

Sartori, G (1966) 'Opposition and Control: Problems and Prospects' (1966) 1 *Government & Opposition* 149

Sathanapally, A (2012) *Beyond Disagreement: Open Remedies in Human Rights Adjudication* (Oxford University Press)

(2017) 'The Modest Promise of 'Procedural Review' in Fundamental Rights Cases' in Gerards & Brems (eds.) *Procedural Review in Europeam Fundamental Rights Cases* (Cambridge University Press)

Saul, M (2015) 'The European Court of Human Rights' Margin of Appreciation and the Processes of National Parliaments' (2015) 15 *Human Rights Law Review* 745

(2016) 'Structuring Evaluations of Parliamentary Processes by the European Court of Human Rights' (2016) 20 *International Journal of Human Rights* 1077

(2017) 'Conclusion: How Does, Could and Should the International Human Rights Judiciary Interact with National Parliaments?' in Saul, Follesdal & Ulfstein (eds.) *The International Human Rights Judiciary and National Parliaments* (Cambridge University Press)

Schacter, J (1995) 'Metademocracy: The Changing Structure of Legitimacy in Statutory Interpretation' (1995) 108 *Harvard Law Review* 593

(2006) 'Political Accountability, Proxy Accountability, and the Democratic Legitimacy of Legislatures' in Bauman & Kahana (eds.) *The Least Examined Branch: The Role of Legislatures in the Constitutional State* (Cambridge University Press)

(2011) 'Ely at the Altar: Political Process Theory through the Lens of the Marriage Debate' (2011) 109 *Michigan Law Review* 1363

Schaeffer, A (2005) 'Linking *Marleasing* and s. 3(1) of the Human Rights Act 1998' (2005) 10 *Judicial Review* 72

Schapiro, R (2009) *Polyphonic Federalism: Toward the Protection of Fundamental Rights* (University of Chicago Press)

Schauer, F (1995) 'Ashwander Revisited' (1995) 1995 *Supreme Court Review* 71

(2006a) 'Legislatures as Rule-Followers' in Bauman & Kahana (eds.) *The Least Examined Branch: The Role of Legislatures in the Constitutional State* (Cambridge University Press)

(2006b) 'Foreword: The Court's Agenda – and the Nation's' (2006) 120 *Harvard Law Review* 4

(2008) 'Authority and Authorities' (2008) 94 *Vanderbilt Law Review* 1931

(2013) 'Official Obedience and the Politics of Defining "Law"' (2013) 86 *Southern California Law Review* 1165

(2018) 'Rights, Constitutions and the Perils of Panglossianism' (2018) 38 *Oxford Journal of Legal Studies* 635

(2019) 'Dialogue and its Discontents' in Sigalet, Webber & Dixon (eds.) *Constitutional Dialogue: Rights, Democracy, Institutions* (Cambridge University Press)

Scheppele, K (2009) 'Parliamentary Supplements (Or Why Democracies Need More than Parliaments)' (2009) 89 *Boston University Law Review* 795

(2012) 'The New Judicial Deference' (2012) 92 *Boston University Law Review* 89

Schlanger, M (1999) 'Beyond the Hero Judge: Institutional Reform Litigation as Litigation' (1999) 97 *Michigan Law Review* 1994

Schrock, T & Welsh, R (1978) 'Reconsidering the Constitutional Common Law' (1978) 91 *Harvard Law Review* 1117

Scott, J & Sturm, S (2007) 'Courts as Catalysts: Rethinking the Judicial Role in New Governance' (2007) 13 *Columbia Journal of European Law* 565

Schütze, R (2009) *From Dual to Cooperative Federalism: The Changing Structure of European Law* (Oxford University Press)

Searing, D (1982) 'Rules of the Game in Britain: Can the Politicians Be Trusted?' (1982) 76 *American Political Science Review* 239

Sedley, S (2008) 'No Ordinary Law' *London Review of Books* 20 (5 June 2008)

(2009) 'The Long Sleep' in Andenas & Fairgrieve (eds.) *Tom Bingham and the Transformation of the Law: A Liber Amicorum* (Oxford University Press)

(2015) *Lions under the Throne: Essays on the History of English Public Law* (Cambridge University Press)

Shah, S, Poole, T & Blackwell, M (2014) 'Rights, Interveners, and the Law Lords' (2014) 34 *Oxford Journal of Legal Studies* 295

Shane, P (2003) 'When Inter-Branch Norms Break Down: Of Arms-for-Hostages, "Orderly Shutdowns", Presidential Impeachments, and Judicial "Coups"' (2003) 12 *Cornell Journal of Law and Public Policy* 503

Shapiro, S (2016) 'What Is the Internal Point of View?' (2016) 75 *Fordham Law Review* 1157

Sharpe, A (2007a) 'A Critique of the Gender Recognition Act 2007' (2007) 4 *Journal of Bioethical Inquiry* 33

(2007b) 'Endless Sex: The Gender Recognition Act 2004 and the Persistence of a Legal Category' (2007) 15 *Feminist Legal Studies* 57

(2009) 'Gender Recognition in the UK: A Great Leap Forward' (2009) 18 *Social & Legal Studies* 241

Shepsle, K (1992) 'Congress Is a "They", Not an "It": Legislative Intent as Oxymoron' (1992) 12 *International Journal of Law and Economics* 239

Sherry, S (2001) 'Too Clever by Half: The Problem with Novelty in Constitutional Law' (2001) 95 *Northwestern University Law Review* 921

Shetreet, S & Turenne, S (2013) *Judges on Trial: The Independence and Accountability of the English Judiciary* (Cambridge University Press)

Shils, E (1997) *The Virtue of Civility: Selected Essays on Liberalism, Tradition, and Civil Society* (Liberty Fund)

Shipman, T & Doyle, J (2011) 'End This Human Rights Insanity: PM's Fury as Judges Rule Paedophiles and Rapists Should Have Chance to Get off Sex Offenders' Register' *Daily Mail* (16 February 2011)

Shipman, T & Wheeler, C (2019) '"Sack Me If You Dare", Boris Johnson Will Tell the Queen' *The Times* (6 October 2019)

Shogimen, T (2008) 'Treating the Body Politic: The Medical Metaphor of Political Rule in Late Medieval Europe and Tokugawa Japan' (2008) 70 *Review of Politics* 77

Siegel, N (2017) 'Political Norms, Constitutional Conventions, and President Donald Trump' (2017) 93 *Indiana Law Journal* 1

(2018) 'After the Trump Era: A Constitutional Role Morality for Presidents and Members of Congress' (2018) 107 *Georgetown Law Journal* 109

Siegel, R (2017) 'Community in Conflict: Same-Sex Marriage and Backlash' (2017) 64 *UCLA Law Review* 1728

Sigalet, G (2019) 'On Dialogue and Domination' in Sigalet, Webber & Dixon (eds.) *Constitutional Dialogue: Rights, Democracy, Institutions* (Cambridge University Press)

Sigalet, G, Webber, G & Dixon, R, eds. (2019a) *Constitutional Dialogue: Rights, Democracy, Institutions* (Cambridge University Press)

(2019b) 'Introduction: The "What" and "Why" of Constitutional Dialogue' in Sigalet, Webber & Dixon (eds.) *Constitutional Dialogue: Rights, Democracy, Institutions* (Cambridge University Press)

Silkin, SC (1978) 'The Functions and Position of the Attorney General in the United Kingdom' (1978) 59 *The Parliamentarian* 149

Simons, M (2015) 'What's With all the War Metaphors? We Have Wars when Politics Fails' *The Guardian* (16 February 2015)

Singh, R (2013) 'The Impact of the Human Rights Act on Advocacy' in Masterman & Leigh (eds.) *The United Kingdom's Statutory Bill of Rights: Constitutional and Comparative Perspectives* (Oxford University Press)

Slack, J (2016) 'Enemies of the People' *The Daily Mail* (4 November 2016)

Slattery, B (1987) 'A Theory of the Charter' (1987) 25 *Osgoode Hall Law Journal* 701

Smith, S (1990) 'The Pursuit of Pragmatism' (1990) 100 *Yale Law Journal* 409

(2000) 'Taking Law Seriously' (2000) 50 *University of Toronto Law Journal* 241

Smith, Z (2019) 'Overriding the Constitution: Populism, the Notwithstanding Clause, and Its Implications for Canada's Rights Framework' *Kennedy School Review* (20 May 2019). Available at: https://ksr.hkspublications.org/2019/05/20/over riding-the-constitution-populism-the-notwithstanding-clause-and-its-implica tions-for-canadas-rights-framework/

Snow, D (2009) 'Notwithstanding the Override: Path Dependence, Section 33, and the Charter' (2009) 8 *Innovations: A Journal of Politics* 1

Solove, D (1999) 'The Darkest Domain: Deference, Judicial Review, and the Bill of Rights' (1999) 84 *Iowa Law Review* 941

Soper, P (2002) *The Ethics of Deference: Learning from Law's Morals* (Cambridge University Press)

Sossin, L (2005a) 'From Neutrality to Compassion: The Place of Civil Service Values and Legal Norms in the Exercise of Administrative Discretion' (2005) 55 *University of Toronto Law Journal* 427

(2005b) 'Speaking Truth to Power? The Search for Bureaucratic Independence' (2005) 55 *University of Toronto Law Journal* 1

Southerden, T (2014) 'Dysfunctional Dialogue: Lawyers, Politicians and Immigrants' Rights to Private and Family Life' [2014] *European Human Rights Law Review* 252

Spano, R (2014) 'Universality or Diversity of Human Rights?' (2014) 16 *Human Rights Law Journal* 1

(2018) 'The Future of the European Court of Human Rights: Subsidiarity, Process-Based Review and the Rule of Law' (2018) 18 *Human Rights Law Journal* 473

Spedding, J, Ellis, R & Heath, D (1872) *The Works of Francis Bacon* 2nd ed. (Longmans, Green, Reader and Dyer)

Spielmann, D (2014) 'Whither the Margin of Appreciation?' (2014) 67 *Current Legal Problems* 49

Spigelman, HJ (2005) 'Principle of Legality and the Clear Statement Principle' (2005) 79 *Australian Law Journal* 769

Spitzer, H & Omara, A (2021) 'Catalytic Courts and the Enforcement of Constitutional Educational Funding Provisions' (2021) 49 *Georgia Journal of International and Comparative Law* 45

Stark, S (2017a) 'Facing Facts: Judicial Approaches to Section 4 of the Human Rights Act 1998' (2017) 133 *Law Quarterly Review* 613

(2017b) *The Work of British Law Commissions: Law Reform ... Now?* (Hart Publishing)

Steele, J (2003) 'Blunkett Takes Swipe at Judges' *The Telegraph* (15 May 2003)

Stephenson, M (2008) 'The Price of Public Action: Constitutional Doctrine and the Judicial Manipulation of Legislative Enactment Costs' (2008) 118 *Yale Law Journal* 2

Stephenson, S (2013) 'Constitutional Reengineering: Dialogue's Migration from Canada to Australia' (2013) 11 *International Journal of Constitutional Law* 870

(2015) 'The Supreme Court's Renewed Interest in Autochthonous Constitutionalism' [2015] *Public Law* 394

(2016) *From Dialogue to Disagreement in Comparative Rights Constitutionalism* (Federation Press)

Stewart, H, Carrell, S & Bowcott, O (2020) 'Lord Keen Resigns over Boris Johnson's Brexit Plan' *The Guardian* (16 September 2020)

Stewart, K (2021) 'The Rule of Law and the Role of Law Officers in its Maintenance' Address at the Annual Conference of the Scottish Criminal Bar Association (3 December 2021)

Steyn, J (2005) 'Deference: A Tangled Story' [2005] *Public Law* 346

Stoker, G (2006) *Why Politics Matters: Making Democracy Work* (Palgrave Macmillan)

Stone, A (2008) 'Judicial Review without Rights: Some Problems for the Democratic Legitimacy of Structural Judicial Review' (2008) 28 *Oxford Journal of Legal Studies* 1

Stone, HF (1936) 'The Common Law in the United States' (1936) 50 *Harvard Law Review* 4

Stone, L & Gray, J (2021) 'Ford to Invoke Notwithstanding Clause to Override Supreme Court Ruling on Election Advertising' *The Globe and Mail* (9 June 2021)

Stone Sweet, A (2000) *Governing with Judges. Constitutional Politics in Europe* (Oxford University Press)

(2007) 'The Politics of Constitutional Review in France and Europe' (2007) 5 *International Journal of Constitutional Law* 69

Stone Sweet, A & Mathews, J (2009) 'Proportionality Balancing and Global Constitutionalism' (2009) 47 *Columbia Journal of Transnational Law* 72

Strauss, D (1988) 'The Ubiquity of Prophylactic Rules' (1988) 55 *University of Chicago Law Review* 190

Strauss, P (1987) 'Formal and Functional Approaches to Separation of Powers Questions: A Foolish Inconsistency' (1987) 72 *Cornell Law Review* 488

Straw, J (1999) *Building a Human Rights Culture* Address to Civil Service College Seminar (9 December 1999). Available at: https://webarchive .nationalarchives.gov.uk/ukgwa/20001008031658/http://www.homeoffice .gov.uk:80/hract/cscspe.htm

(2000) Speech to the Institute of Policy Research (13 January 2000).

(2012) *Last Man Standing: Memoirs of a Political Survivor* (Pan Books)

(2013) *Aspects of Law Reform: An Insider's Perspective* (Cambridge University Press)

Straw, J & Boateng, P (1997) 'Bringing Rights Home: Labour's Plans to Incorporate the European Convention on Human Rights into UK Law' [1997] *European Human Rights Law Review* 71

Stuart, M (2018) 'Whips and Rebels' in Leston-Bandeira & Thompson (eds.) *Exploring Parliament* (Oxford University Press)

Sturgeon, N (2022) 'Nicola Sturgeon Calls Boris Johnson "Disgrace to Office of Prime Minister"' *The Guardian* (13 August 2022)

Sumption, J (2014) *Anxious Scrutiny* Administrative Law Bar Association Annual Lecture, available at: https://www.supremecourt.uk/docs/speech-141104.pdf

(2019) *Trials of the State: Law and the Decline of Politics* (Profile Books)

(2022a) 'Partygate Is Really about Leadership, Lies and the Death of Trust' *The Telegraph* (29 May 2022)

(2022b) 'Our System of Conventions Won out This Time. But if Johnson Had Been Mad as Well as Bad, the Whole Edifice Could Have Fallen' *The Times* (10 July 2022)

Sunstein, C (1988) 'Constitutions and Democracy: An Epilogue' in Elster & Slagstad (eds.) *Constitutionalism and Democracy* (Cambridge University Press)

(1989) 'Interpreting Statutes in the Regulatory State' (1989) 103 *Harvard Law Review* 403

(1993) *The Partial Constitution* (Harvard University Press)

(1996) 'Foreword: Leaving Things Undecided' (1996) 110 *Harvard Law Review* 4

(2000) 'Nondelegation Canons' (2000) 67 *University of Chicago Law Review* 315

(2015) *Constitutional Personae* (Oxford University Press)

(2016) 'The Most Knowledgeable Branch' (2016) 164 *University of Pennsylvania Law Review* 1607

ed. (2018a) *Can It Happen Here? Authoritarianism in America* (Harper Collins)

(2018b) 'Lessons from the American Founding' in Sunstein (ed.) *Can It Happen Here? Authoritarianism in America* (Harper Collins)

Sunstein, C & Hastie, R (2015) *Wiser: Getting beyond Groupthink to Make Groups Smarter* (Harvard Business Review Press)

Taggart, M (2008) 'Proportionality, Deference, Wednesbury' (2008) 3 *New Zealand Law Review* 423

Tait, J (1997) 'The Public Service Lawyer, Service to the Client and the Rule of Law' 1997 *Commonwealth Law Bulletin* 542

Tassé, R (1989) 'Application of the Canadian Charter of Rights and Freedoms' in Beaudoin & Ratushny (eds.) *The Canadian Charter of Rights and Freedoms* 2nd ed. (Carswell)

Taylor, A (2022) 'The Cringe of Boris Johnson' *The Washington Post* (7 July 2022). Available at: www.washingtonpost.com/world/2022/07/07/boris-johnson-cring-shameless-liability/

Taylor, G (2014) 'Convention by Consensus: Constitutional Conventions in Germany' (2014) 12 *International Journal of Constitutional Law* 303

Tew, Y (2020) *Constitutional Statecraft in Asian Courts* (Oxford University Press)

Tham, J-C (2010) 'Parliamentary Deliberation and the National Security Executive: The Case of Control Orders' [2010] *Public Law* 79

Thomas, L (2014) *The Judiciary, the Executive and Parliament: Relationships and the Rule of Law* (Institute for Government) Keynote Speech

(2015a) *Judicial Leadership: Overhauling the Machinery of Justice* (UCL Constitution Unit) Conference on the Paradox of Judicial Independence

(2015b) *Judicial Independence in a Changing Constitutional Landscape* Speech to the Commonwealth Magistrates' and Judges' Association

(2017a) *The Judiciary within the State – Governance and Cohesion of the Judiciary* (Hebrew University, Jerusalem) Lionel Cohen Lecture

(2017b) *The Judiciary within the State – The Relationship between the Branches of State* (Palace of Westminster) Michael Ryle Memorial Lecture

(2017c) Speech after Dinner for Her Majesty's Judges (Mansion House, London)

Thompson, L & McNulty, T (2018) 'Committee Scrutiny of Legislation' in Leston-Bandeira & Thompson (eds.) *Exploring Parliament* (Oxford University Press)

Thornburg, E (1995) 'Metaphors Matter: How Images of Battle, Sports, and Sex Shape the Adversary System' (1995) 10 *Wisconsin Women's Law Journal* 225

Thornhill, C (2016) 'The Mutation of International Law in Contemporary Constitutions: Thinking Sociologically about Political Constitutionalism' (2016) 79 *Modern Law Review* 207

Tocqueville, A (1835 [2003]) *Democracy in America*, ed. Bevan & Kramnick (Penguin)

Tolley, M (2009) 'Parliamentary Scrutiny of Rights in the United Kingdom: Assessing the Work of the Joint Committee on Human Rights' (2009) 44 *Australian Journal of Political Science* 41

Tomkins, A (1998) *The Constitution after Scott: Government Unwrapped* (Clarendon Press)

(2001) 'Introduction: On Being Sceptical about Human Rights' in Campbell, Ewing & Tomkins (eds.) *Sceptical Essays on Human Rights* (Oxford University Press)

(2002a) 'In Defence of the Political Constitution' (2002) 22 *Oxford Journal of Legal Studies* 157

(2002b) 'Legislating against Terror: The Antiterrorism, Crime and Security Act 2001' [2002] *Public Law* 205

(2003) *Public Law* (Oxford University Press)

(2011) 'Parliament, Human Rights, and Counter-Terrorism' in Campbell, Ewing & Tomkins (eds.) *The Legal Protection of Human Rights: Sceptical Essays* (Oxford University Press)

(2013) 'What's Left of the Political Constitution?' (2013) 14 *German Law Journal* 2275

Tourkochoriti, I (2019) 'What is the Best Way to Realise Rights?' (2019) 29 *Oxford Journal of Legal Studies* 1

Toynbee, P (2022) 'Today's Elections are the Last Before the Tories Vandalise Our Democratic Rights' *The Guardian* (5 May 2022). Available at: www .theguardian.com/commentisfree/2022/may/05/boris-johnson-poisoned-pol itical-system-electoral-reform

Travis, A (2003a) 'Life Means Life for Child Killers, Says Blunkett' *The Guardian* (7 May 2003)

(2003b) 'Out of Touch Judges Should Live in the Real World, Says Blunkett' *The Guardian* (15 May 2003)

(2004) 'Blunkett on Film Sways Judges' *The Guardian* (17 November 2004)

Tremblay, L (2005) 'The Legitimacy of Judicial Review: The Limits of Dialogue between Courts and Legislatures' (2005) 3 *International Journal of Constitutional Law* 617

Trueblood, L (2019) 'Book Review: Webber et al., *Legislated Rights: Securing Human Rights through Legislation*' (2019) 82 *Modern Law Review* 577

Tsarapatsanis, D (2020) 'Rights, Values and Really Existing Legislatures' (2020) 11 *Jurisprudence: An International Journal of Legal and Political Thought* 610

Tsereteli, N (2017) 'The Role of the European Court of Human Rights in Facilitating Legislative Change in Cases of Long-Term Delays in Implementation' in Saul, Follesdal & Ulfstein (eds.) *The International Human Rights Judiciary and National Parliaments* (Cambridge University Press)

Tulkens, F (2022) 'Judicial Activism v Judicial Restraint: Practical Experience of This (False) Dilemma at the European Court of Human Rights' [2022] *European Human Rights Law Review* 1

Tushnet, M (1995) 'Policy Distortion and Democratic Debilitation: Comparative Illumination of the Countermajoritarian Difficulty' (1995) 94 *Michigan Law Review* 245

(1999) *Taking the Constitution Away from the Courts* (Princeton University Press)

(2001) 'Subconstitutional Constitutional Law: Supplement, Sham, or Substitute?' (2001) 42 *William & Mary Law Review* 1871

(2003a) 'Alternative Forms of Judicial Review' (2003) 101 *Michigan Law Review* 2781

(2003b) 'Judicial Activism or Restraint in a Section 33 World' (2003) 53 *University of Toronto Law Journal* 89

(2003c) 'New Forms of Judicial Review and the Persistence of Rights and Democracy-Based Worries' (2003) 38 *Wake Forest Law Review* 813

(2004) 'Constitutional Hardball' (2004) 37 *Marshall Law Review* 523

(2008a) 'Dialogic Judicial Review' (2008) 61 *Arkansas Law Review* 205

(2008b) *Weak Courts, Strong Rights: Judicial Review and Social Welfare Rights in Comparative Constitutional Law* (Princeton University Press)

(2011a) 'The Rise of Weak-Form Judicial Review' in Ginsburg & Dixon (eds.) *Comparative Constitutional Law: Research Handbooks in Comparative Law* (Edward Elgar)

(2011b) 'The Political Institutions of Rights-Protection' in Campbell, Ewing & Tomkins (eds.) *Legal Protection of Human Rights: Sceptical Essays* (Oxford University Press)

(2021) *The New Fourth Branch: Institutions for Protecting Constitutional Democracy* (Cambridge University Press)

Tushnet, M & Bugaric, B (2021) *Power to the People: Constitutionalism in the Age of Populism* (Oxford University Press)

Tushnet, M & Dixon, R (2014) 'Weak-Form Review and Its Constitutional Relatives: An Asian Perspective' in Dixon & Ginsburg (eds.) *Comparative Constitutional Law in Asia* (Edward Elgar)

Tyler, A (2005) 'Continuity, Coherence, and the Canons' (2005) 99 *Northwestern University Law Review* 1389

Uhr, J (2006) 'The Performance of Australian Legislatures in Protecting Rights' in Campbell, Goldsworthy & Stone (eds.) *Protecting Rights without a Bill of Rights* (Ashgate)

Upton, J (2003) 'He Huffs and He Puffs' *London Review of Books* (19 June 2003)

Urbinati, N (2000) 'Representation as Advocacy: A Study of Democratic Deliberation' (2000) 28 *Political Theory* 758

Valiante, G (2019) 'Canadian Bar Association Calls on Quebec to Drop Notwithstanding Clause from Bill 21' *National Observer* (5 April 2019)

Van Zyl Smit, J (2007) 'The New Purposive Interpretation of Statutes: HRA Section 3 after *Ghaidan v Mendoza*' (2007) 70 *Modern Law Review* 294

(2011) 'Statute Law: Interpretation and Declarations of Incompatibility' in Hoffman (ed.) *The Impact of the UK Human Rights Act on Private Law* (Cambridge University Press)

(2015) 'Promoting the Rule of Courts or Resisting the Misuse of Courts? A Response to Ekins and Forsyth' Judicial Power Project (15 December 2015). Available at: http://judicialpowerproject.org.uk/promoting-the-rule-of-courts-or-resisting-the-misuse-of-courts-a-response-to-professor-ekins-and-professor-forsyth/

(2016) 'The "Institutional Turn" in Statutory Interpretation and Its Pitfalls: The Case of the Human Rights Act 1998' Unpublished manuscript, on file with author

Vanberg, G (2005) *The Politics of Constitutional Review in Germany* (Cambridge University Press)

Varuhas, J (2020) 'The Principle of Legality' (2020) 79 *Cambridge Law Journal* 578

Vermeule, A (1997) 'Saving Constructions' (1997) 85 *Georgetown Law Journal* 945

(2006) *Judging under Uncertainty: An Institutional Theory of Legal Interpretation* (Harvard University Press)

(2007) *Mechanisms of Democracy: Institutional Design Writ Small* (Oxford University Press)

(2011) 'Second Opinions and Institutional Design' (2011) 97 *Virginia Law Review* 1435

(2012) 'The Atrophy of Constitutional Powers' (2012) 32 *Oxford Journal of Legal Studies* 421

(2013) 'Conventions of Agency Independence' (2013) 113 *Columbia Law Review* 1163

(2015) 'Conventions in Court' (2015) 38 *Dublin University Law Journal* 283

Vile, M (1998) *Constitutionalism and the Separation of Powers* 2nd ed. (Oxford University Press)

Von Bogdandy, A & Paris, D (2020) 'Building Judicial Authority: A Comparison Between the Italian Constitutional Courts and the German Federal Constitutional Court' in Barsotti, Carozza, Cartabia & Simoncini (eds.) *Dialogues on Italian Constitutional Justice - A Comparative Perspective* (Routledge)

Waldron, J (1993a) *Liberal Rights: Collected Papers 1981–1991* (Cambridge University Press)

(1993b) 'A Right-Based Critique of Constitutional Rights' (1993) 13 *Oxford Journal of Legal Studies* 18

(1999a) *The Dignity of Legislation* (Cambridge University Press)

(1999b) *Law and Disagreement* (Oxford University Press)

(2003a) 'Authority for Officials' in Meyer, Paulson & Pogge (eds.) *Rights, Culture, and the Law: Themes from the Legal and Political Philosophy of Joseph Raz* (Oxford University Press)

(2003b) 'Legislating with Integrity' (2003) 72 *Fordham Law Review* 373

(2004) 'Some Models of Dialogue between Judges and Legislators' in Huscroft & Brodie (eds.) *Constitutionalism in the Charter Era* (Butterworths)

(2006) 'The Core of the Case against Judicial Review' (2006) 115 *Yale Law Journal* 1346

(2009) 'Judges as Moral Reasoners' (2009) 7 *International Journal of Constitutional Law* 2

(2010) *Torture, Terror and Trade-Offs: Philosophy for the White House* (Oxford University Press)

(2014) 'Judicial Review and Republican Government' in Wolfe (ed.) *That Eminent Tribunal* (Princeton University Press)

(2016) *Political Political Theory: Essays on Institutions* (Harvard University Press)

Walker, C (2007) 'Keeping Control of Terrorists without Losing Control of Constitutionalism' (2007) 59 *Stanford Law Review* 1395

Walker, N (1999) 'The Antinomies of the Law Officers' in Sunkin & Payne (eds.) *The Nature of the Crown: A Legal and Political Analysis* (Oxford University Press)

Walker, R (2014) 'How Far Should Judges Develop the Common Law?' (2014) 3 *Cambridge Journal of International and Comparative Law* 124

Wall, S (2007) 'Democracy and Restraint' (2007) 26 *Law & Philosophy* 307

Waller, P (2014a) 'Special Advisers and Communications' in Yong & Hazell (eds.) *Special Advisers* (Hart Publishing)

(2014b) 'Special Advisers and the Policy-Making Process' in Yong & Hazell (eds.) *Special Advisers* (Hart Publishing)

Walters, M (2008) 'Written Constitutions and Unwritten Constitutionalism' in Huscroft (ed.) *Expounding the Constitution: Essays in Constitutional Theory* (Cambridge University Press)

(2016) 'The Unwritten Constitution as a Legal Concept' in Dyzenhaus & Thorburn (eds.) *Philosophical Foundations of Constitutional Law* (Oxford University Press)

Watt, G (2012) 'Comparison as Deep Appreciation' in Monateri (ed.) *Methods of Comparative Law* (Edward Elgar)

Weale, A (2018) *The Will of the People: A Modern Myth* (Polity)

Webber, G (2009) 'The Unfulfilled Potential of the Court and Legislature Dialogue' (2009) 42 *Canadian Journal of Political Science* 443

(2014a) 'Eulogy for the Constitution That Was' (2014) 12 *International Journal of Constitutional Law* 468

(2014b) 'Parliament and the Management of Conflict' 2014 *Public Law* 101

(2016) 'Loyal Opposition and the Political Constitution' (2016) 26 *Oxford Journal of Legal Studies* 1

et al. (2018) *Legislated Rights: Securing Human Rights through Legislation* (Cambridge University Press)

Webber, J (2000) 'Constitutional Reticence' (2000) 25 *Australian Journal of Legal Philosophy* 125

(2003) 'Institutional Dialogue between Courts and Legislatures in the Definition of Fundamental Rights: Lessons from Canada (and Elsewhere)' (2003) 9 *Australian Journal of Human Rights* 9

(2006) 'Democratic Decision-Making as the First Principle of Contemporary Constitutionalism' in Bauman & Kahana (eds.) *The Least Examined Branch: The Role of Legislatures in the Constitutional State* (Cambridge University Press)

Weber, M (1919 [2004]) *Politik als Beruf* (Duncker & Humblot) trans Owen, Strong & Livingstone in *The Vocation Lectures* (Hackett Publishing)

Weiler, P (1984) 'Rights and Judges in a Democracy: A New Canadian Version' (1984) 18 *University of Michigan Journal of Law Reform* 51

Weill, R (2012) 'Hybrid Constitutionalism: The Israeli Case for Judicial Review and Why We Should Care' (2012) 30 *Berkeley Journal of International Law* 349

(2014) 'The New Commonwealth Model of Constitutionalism Notwithstanding: On Judicial Review and Constitution-Making' (2014) 62 *American Journal of Comparative Law* 127

(2016) 'Juxtaposing Constitution-Making and Constitutional-Infringement Mechanisms in Israel and Canada: On the Interplay between Common Law Override and Sunset Override' (2016) 49 *Israel Law Review* 103

Weinrib, L (1990) 'Learning to Live with the Override' (1990) 35 *McGill Law Journal* 541

(2016) 'The Canadian Charter's Override Clause: Lessons for Israel' (2016) 49 *Israel Law Review* 67

Weinstock, D (2013) 'On the Possibility of Principled Moral Compromise' (2013) 16 *Critical Review of International Social and Political Philosophy* 537

Weis, L (2020a) 'The Constitutional Office of the Legislature' (2020) 70 *University of Toronto Law Journal* 214

(2020b) 'Situating Legislated Rights: Legislative and Judicial Role in Contemporary Constitutional Theory' (2020) 11 *Jurisprudence: An International Journal of Legal and Political Thought* 621

Wells, I (2022) 'No 10 Parties: PM's Lockdown Fine Constitutional Crisis, Says Historian' *BBC News website* (17 April 2022). Available at: www.bbc.co.uk/news/uk-politics-61134002

Wendel, B (2009) 'Government Lawyers, Democracy, and the Rule of Law' (2009) 77 *Fordham Law Review* 1333

Weston, E (2015) 'The Human Rights Act 1998 and the Effectiveness of Parliamentary Scrutiny' (2015) 26 *King's Law Journal* 266

Wheare, K (1951), *Modern Constitutions* (Oxford University Press)

White, H (2022) *Held in Contempt: What's Wrong with the House of Commons?* (Manchester University Press)

Whittington, K (2000) 'In Defense of Legislatures' (2000) 28 *Political Theory* 690

(2002) 'Extrajudicial Constitutional Interpretation: Three Objections and Responses' (2002) 80 *North Carolina Law Review* 773

(2003) 'Legislative Sanctions and the Strategic Environment of Judicial Review' (2003) 1 *International Journal of Constitutional Law* 446

(2005a) '"Interpose Your Friendly Hand": Political Supports for the Exercise of Judicial Review by the United States Supreme Court' (2005) 99 *American Political Science Review* 583

(2005b) 'James Madison Has Left the Building' (2005) 72 *University of Chicago Law Review* 1137

(2007) *Political Foundations of Judicial Supremacy: The Presidency, the Supreme Court, and Constitutional Leadership in U.S. History* (Princeton University Press)

(2014) 'The Least Activist Supreme Court in History? The Roberts Court and the Exercise of Judicial Review' (2014) 89 *Notre Dame Law Review* 2219

Willis, E (2018) 'Political Constitutionalism: The "Critical Morality" of Constitutional Politics' (2019) 28 *New Zealand Universities Law Review* 237

(2022) 'Unwritten Constitutionalism: Stability without Entrenchment' [2022] *Public Law* 386

Willis, J (1938) 'Statute Interpretation in a Nutshell' (1938) 16 *Canadian Bar Review* 1

Wilson, R (2004) 'The Robustness of Conventions in a Time of Modernisation and Change' [2004] *Public Law* 407

Windsor, M (2013) 'Government Legal Advisers through the Ethics Looking Glass' in Feldman (ed.) *Law in Politics, Politics in Law* (Hart Publishing)

Winstone, R, ed. (2010) *A View from the Foothills: The Diaries of Chris Mullin* (Profile Books)

Wintour, P & Sparrow, A (2012) 'I Won't Give Prisoners the Vote, Says David Cameron' *The Guardian* (24 October 2012)

Wiseman, D (2001) 'The Charter and Poverty: Beyond Injusticiability' (2001) 51 *University of Toronto Law Journal* 425

(2006) 'Competence Concerns in *Charter* Adjudication: Countering the Anti-Poverty Incompetence Argument' (2006) 51 *McGill Law Journal* 503

Woodhouse, D (1997) 'The Attorney General' (1997) 50 *Parliamentary Affairs* 97

Woolf, H (2008) *The Pursuit of Justice* (Oxford University Press)

Yap, P-J (2012) 'Defending Dialogue' [2012] *Public Law* 527

(2015) *Constitutional Dialogue in Common Law Asia* (Oxford University Press)

(2017) 'New Democracies and Novel Remedies' 2017 *Public Law* 30

Yong, B (2013) *Risk Management: Government Lawyers and the Provision of Legal Advice within Whitehall* (The Constitution Society)

(2014) 'Special Advisers and British Government' in Yong & Hazell (eds.) *Special Advisers* (Hart Publishing)

Yong, B & Hazell, R, eds. (2014) *Special Advisers: Who They Are, What They Do and Why They Matter* (Hart Publishing)

Young, A (2005) 'Ghaidan v Godin-Mendoza: Avoiding the Deference Trap' [2005] *Public Law* 23

(2009) *Parliamentary Sovereignty and the Human Rights Act* (Hart Publishing)

(2011) 'Is Dialogue Working under the Human Rights Act 1998?' [2011] *Public Law* 773

(2017) *Democratic Dialogue and the Constitution* (Oxford University Press)

(2022) 'Partygate and the Ministerial Code: Changing the Rules to Avoid Punishment?' Blogpost at Constitutional Law Matters (30 May 2022). Available at: https://constitutionallawmatters.org/2022/05/partygate-and-the-ministerial-code-changing-the-rules-to-avoid-punishment/

Young, E (2000) 'Constitutional Avoidance, Resistance Norms, and the Preservation of Judicial Review' (2000) 78 *Texas Law Review* 1549

Young, K (2010) 'A Typology of Economic and Social Rights Adjudication: Exploring the Catalytic Function of Judicial Review' (2010) 8 *International Journal of Constitutional Law* 385

(2012) *Constituting Economic and Social Rights* (Oxford University Press)

(2014) 'American Exceptionalism and Government Shutdowns: A Comparative Constitutional Reflection on the 2013 Lapse in Appropriations' (2014) 94 *Boston University Law Review* 991

Yowell, P (2015) 'The Impact of the Joint Committe on Human Rights on Legislative Deliberations' in Hunt, Hooper & Yowell (eds.) *Parliament and Human Rights: Redressing the Democratic Deficit* (Hart Publishing)

(2018) *Constitutional Rights and Constitutional Design: Moral and Empirical Reasoning in Judicial Review* (Hart Publishing)

Zander, M (2018) *The Law-Making Process* 7th ed. (Hart Publishing)

Zeisberg, M (2004) 'Constitutional Fidelity and Interbranch Conflict' (2004) 13 *The Good Society* 24

Ziegler, R (2015) 'Voting Eligibility: Strasbourg's Timidity' in Ziegler, Wicks & Hodson (eds.) *The UK and European Human Rights: A Strained Relationship?* (Hart Publishing)

Zweigert, K & Kötz, H (1998) *An Introduction to Comparative Law* 3rd ed. (Oxford University Press)

INDEX

Albert, Richard, 87, 125, 335, 341, 342, 346, 357, 358, 359
Anderson, David, 282, 379, 380, 381, 382
Animal Defenders case, 196, 197, 200, 275
Appleby, Gabrielle, 7, 81, 116, 134, 141, 147, 148, 192, 408
assisted suicide, 298–302, 308, 310, 312–15, 322–3
Attorney General, 134–7, 145

Barak, Aharon, 97, 214, 288, 353
Bates, Ed, 391, 392, 393, 395, 396
Bateup, Christine, 59, 68, 74, 82, 315, 335, 366
Bellinger case, 241, 242, 244, 276, 279, 309, 310, 374, 378, 379
Belmarsh prison case, 181, 273, 278, 281, 282, 283, 284, 285, 286, 287, 316, 379, 383, 384, 386, 397
Bickel, Alexander, 21, 43, 45, 47, 99, 298, 327, 328
Bingham, Lord, 70, 97, 181, 201, 211, 212, 218, 221, 234, 235, 237, 242, 245, 247, 267, 270, 271, 275, 277, 284, 285, 309, 316, 353, 380
Blair, Tony, 384, 386
Blunkett, David, 380, 381, 382
Bratman, Michael, 5, 98, 103
burden of inertia, 218, 323, 335, 365, 379

Cameron, David, 60, 359, 369, 387, 392, 393
Canadian Charter, 21, 58, 59, 64–70, 333, 337–44, 347–50, 359–60

Carolan, Eoin, 47, 54, 59, 65, 66, 68, 69, 71, 73, 74, 76, 82, 83, 85, 102, 108, 252, 260, 304
Casey, Conor, 141, 165, 184, 189, 190, 191, 195, 200
Chandrachud, Chintan, 262, 314, 316, 318, 369, 388
civil servants, 144, 145, 146, 147, 161, 167, 168, 415, 416
civility, 13, 16, 108, 111, 116, 407–8
clear statement rules, 218, 219, 225, 327
comity, 3, 7, 9, 11, 16, 23, 37, 97–106, 112–13, 115, 116–17, 168, 191, 220, 264, 271, 294, 312, 336, 353, 354, 355, 356, 358, 361, 385, 390, 397, 401, 402, 403, 404, 408, 416
common law rights, 215–20, 228
compromise, 13, 61, 102, 153, 174, 175
Constitution Committee, House of Lords, 157, 161, 164, 166, 167, 180, 188, 225–6, 255
constitutional capital, 27, 415–16
conventions, constitutional, 9, 110, 364–5, 366, 368, 386, 401, 413, 414
counter-majoritarian difficulty, 43–4, 45, 46, 47–9, 59, 64, 66, 81, 262, 334, 340, 355
counter-terrorism, 179–84, 281–7, 383–6
Craiutu, Aurelian, 5, 13, 405
Crewe, Emma, 44, 154, 155, 400, 401, 414
culture of rights, 129, 172, 178–9

Davis, Fergal, 71, 72, 78, 82, 251, 346, 357, 358
de Londras, Fiona, 255

declaration of incompatibility, 21, 71, 199, 238–58, 260, 318, 335, 344–6, 350–1, 363–6

deference, judicial, 37, 47, 72, 73, 78, 82, 83, 116, 265, 267, 272–4, 275, 277, 282, 285–7, 289, 411

dialogue, 3, 21, 58, 232, 250–64, 335, 348, 350, 353, 356, 358, 402

Dixon, Rosalind, 21, 59, 78, 79, 116, 186, 246, 259, 277, 305, 308, 311, 323, 379

Dworkin, Ronald, 1, 32, 33, 35, 36, 38, 39, 40, 41, 205, 266, 268

Dyzenhaus, David, 35, 38, 40, 53, 54, 74, 162, 273, 282, 283, 284, 291

Ekins, Richard, 252, 255, 345

Elliott, Mark, 54, 55, 124, 154, 216, 217, 226, 228, 231, 251, 252, 261, 280, 285, 291, 345, 384, 395

Ely, John Hart, 33, 312

Endicott, Timothy, 13, 53, 89, 92, 98, 123, 124, 125, 127, 128, 146, 206, 210, 213, 216, 220, 221, 249, 266, 272, 273, 281, 289, 293, 295, 396

European Court of Human Rights, 194, 198, 199, 246, 252–3, 254, 256, 257, 263, 307, 345, 410

Executive branch, 54, 56, 88, 90, 92, 121–42, 151–2, 164, 210

Executive constitutionalism, 142–3

Executive dominance, 172–9, 201

fair play, constitutional, 11, 17, 115, 117, 397, 404, 406, 414, 415, 416

Fallon, Richard, 14, 102, 269, 311

Feldman, David, 108, 121, 131, 137, 140, 143, 144, 158, 160, 161, 162, 165, 168, 181, 187, 188, 193, 196, 199, 201, 256, 367, 368, 380

Finnis, John, 41, 220, 289, 322

forbearance, 13, 111, 295, 404

Fourth branch, 100, 408–9

Fowkes, James, 14, 17, 105, 107, 305

Gardbaum, Stephen, 20, 21, 22, 24, 52, 58, 60, 83, 117, 122, 128, 129, 151, 163, 189, 231, 232, 233, 250, 258,
261, 292, 298, 303, 306, 333, 334, 342, 346, 348, 358, 359, 391, 411

Gearty, Conor, 71, 250, 254, 361, 387

Geiringer, Claudia, 23, 80, 218, 221, 227, 261, 263

Ghaidan, 211, 234, 235, 236, 239, 240, 241, 242, 244, 245, 246, 247, 248, 265, 291

Goldsworthy, Jeffrey, 21, 58, 221, 225, 334, 338, 341, 342, 359

Graber, Mark, 19, 37, 412

Grieve, Dominic, 99, 131, 135, 136, 140, 146

Hailbronner, Michaela, 105, 303

Halberstam, David, 97, 102

Hale, Lady, 248, 249, 252, 275, 291, 299, 304, 318, 319

Harlow, Carol, 54, 162, 164, 179, 255

Hart, HLA, 9, 15, 113, 372

Heclo, Hugh, 15, 93, 103, 112, 416

Hickman, Tom, 4, 55, 70, 71, 78, 105, 183, 232, 246, 253, 384

Hiebert, Janet, 58, 122, 129, 130, 131, 132, 137, 138, 139, 140, 141, 142, 158, 164, 166, 172, 178, 179, 180, 181, 182, 185, 188, 189, 191, 192, 193, 195, 198, 199, 232, 271, 335, 338, 340, 341, 346, 347, 392

Hilbink, Lisa, 2, 31, 40, 49

Hirst, 307, 366, 369, 380, 391, 392, 393, 394, 395, 396

Hoffmann, Lord, 170, 217, 224, 228, 260, 272, 279

Human Rights Act 1998, 22
    HRA and dialogue, 70–3, 78, 262–4
    section 10 HRA, 253–4
    section 19 ECHR memorandum, 132
    section 19 HRA, 128–32, 162–3, 187–9, 195–201
    section 3 and 4 HRA, choosing between, 243–50
    section 3 HRA, interpretation, 233–43
    section 4 HRA, 238–58

Hunt, Murray, 12, 40, 50, 52, 53, 81, 85, 158, 160, 161, 163, 164, 165, 168, 187, 188, 189, 279, 286, 287, 388, 406

Ignatieff, Michael, 114, 115, 153, 415
Independent Reviewer of Terrorism
    Legislation, 166, 183, 287
Irvine, Lord, 20, 88, 129, 151, 211, 245,
    247, 253, 254, 264, 344, 350, 351,
    399, 411

Jackson, Vicki, 24, 40, 49, 56, 92, 101,
    112, 115, 122, 127, 148, 214, 290,
    292, 293, 361, 409
Johnson, Boris, 114, 376, 412, 413, 415
Joint Committee on Human Rights
    (JCHR), 138–9, 156–63, 188, 197,
    198, 200, 254–5, 263, 287, 364, 370
judges, role of, 24–5
    advisory role, 251, 258
    calibrated constitutionalism, 283,
        297, 299
    calibrated proportionality, 289–94
    calibrated review, 266–7, 277–81
    calibrated review and counter-
        terrorism, 282–7
    catalytic review, 25, 254, 329, 411
    court as catalyst, 311–22
    Hercules, 1, 31, 34, 35, 39, 41, 60,
        117, 227
    Janus-faced judging, 208–12
    judge as faithful agent, 212–15
    judge as nudge, 298, 311–22
    judge as partner, 24–5, 205–8,
        212–15, 325, 328
    judge as quality control, 212–15
    judicial advice, 258
    jurisgenerative partner, 266
judicial activism, 69, 210, 267, 286, 294
judicial advice, 259
judicial restraint, 47, 289, 295, 307, 327
juristocracy, 31, 32, 42, 43, 45, 48, 51,
    52, 171, 184

Kelly, James, 67, 122, 129, 130, 131,
    132, 137, 138, 139, 140, 141, 142,
    164, 166, 172, 178, 179, 180, 181,
    182, 188, 189, 191, 192, 195, 198,
    199, 392
Kenny, David, 189, 190, 191, 195, 200
Khaitan, Tarunabh, 91, 409

King, Jeff, 193, 194, 207, 211, 255, 258,
    273, 279, 281, 291, 294, 295, 318,
    329, 346, 348, 354, 355, 356, 358,
    359, 360, 363, 368, 369, 372, 376,
    378, 381, 383, 385, 387, 389, 397,
    399, 405, 416
Komesar, Neil, 2, 15, 25, 32, 36, 39, 40,
    42, 45, 46, 74, 147, 208, 209, 252
Kumm, Mattias, 10, 24, 101, 266, 288,
    294, 356
Kyritsis, Dimitrios, 6, 13, 18, 43, 44, 49,
    54, 61, 66, 75, 80, 83, 84, 87, 88, 90,
    91, 94, 95, 100, 101, 104, 107, 186,
    207, 212, 213, 266, 268, 269, 270,
    275, 288, 295, 353, 405, 408

Landau, David, 38, 225, 261, 318, 324
Leckey, Robert, 14, 15, 37, 70, 75, 79,
    221, 227, 249, 250, 251, 294, 315,
    320, 338, 339, 359
legal constitutionalism, 32, 50–5, 56,
    123, 167
Levinson, Daryl, 9, 17, 19, 37, 96, 103,
    113, 353, 412
Levitsky, Steven, 9, 10, 11, 13, 103, 111,
    112, 404

MacDonnell, Vanessa, 7, 81, 116, 193,
    340, 343, 408
margin of appreciation, 411
Mashaw, Jerry, 35, 43, 44, 45, 46, 63,
    212, 270
Masterman, Roger, 70, 72, 137, 168,
    240, 350
McLean, Janet, 144, 199, 221, 222, 223,
    224, 226, 228, 391, 396, 397, 398,
    404
moderation, 13, 111, 404
Möllers, Christoph, 6, 38, 96, 105, 124,
    126, 209

Newman, Dwight, 340, 355, 357, 360
Nicklinson, 71, 297–302, 308, 310,
    314–16, 319–23, 325
nirvana fallacy, 35, 38, 40, 74
Norton, Philip, 153, 164, 173, 174,
    396

Opposition, 113–15, 400, 401, 415–16
O'Regan, Kate, 37, 293

Parliamentary Counsel, 133, 136, 145, 167
parliamentary sovereignty, 170, 221, 224, 230, 344, 396
passive virtues, 298, 327–9
permanent campaign, 44
Pettit, Philip, 50, 124
Phillipson, Gavin, 53, 61, 72, 184, 260, 347, 388
policy distortion, 184–95, 199, 310, 318, 378
political constitutionalism, 27, 50–6, 170
political process review, 298, 302–8
populism, 16–17, 27, 44, 45, 48, 400, 412, 413
Pozen, David, 9, 11, 14, 17, 18, 96, 100, 103, 107, 117, 353, 356, 361, 404, 405, 412
principle of legality, 206, 215–27, 228, 264
prisoner voting, 335, 366–7, 369, 370, 380, 391–7
proportionality, 287–94, 300, 302, 308, 329
Putnam, Robert, 13, 127, 412, 415

Rawlings, Richard, 162, 164, 255
Raz, Joseph, 14, 17, 18, 49, 89, 92, 93, 209, 210, 213, 214, 215, 222, 227, 239, 310, 354
reading in, 69, 236, 240
reciprocity, 4, 7, 97, 103, 104, 106, 113, 117, 262, 302, 353, 407, 410, 416
Reed, Lord, 210, 237, 244, 257, 265, 274, 280, 288, 292, 293, 299, 301, 303, 304, 305, 410
repeat play, 114, 353, 408, 410, 415
Roach, Kent, 47, 61, 67, 69, 80, 82, 84, 269, 295, 312, 314, 316, 330, 334, 343, 377
Rosenblum, Nancy, 6, 115, 409
Roth, 240, 280, 286, 292

Sabl, Andrew, 5, 12, 102, 111, 112
Sadurski, 16, 27, 32, 49, 111, 128, 185, 411

Sager, Lawrence, 45, 101, 103, 214, 270
Sales, Lord, 144, 210, 213, 217, 219, 222, 252, 255, 274, 295, 306, 324, 325, 345
Sathanapally, Aruna, 75, 152, 159, 190, 194, 234, 244, 246, 251, 252, 360, 373, 376, 377, 382, 383, 386, 398, 399, 408
Schauer, Fred, 47, 218, 368
self-restraint, 116, 117, 148–9, 176, 185, 186, 353, 404
separation of powers
  checks and balances, 94–7
  collaborative conception of, 3–7, 97–115
  division of labour, 87–94
  relational conception of, 3–4
showdown, constitutional, 11, 87, 116, 199, 404, 406, 408
Simms, 217, 224, 228
slowdown, constitutional, 11, 87, 106–16, 153, 199, 219
social capital, 415, 416
Spano, Robert, 303, 304, 308
Stephenson, Scott, 69, 73, 104, 112, 218, 228, 258, 265, 346, 349, 351
Stone, Adrienne, 212, 349
strong-form review, 21, 22, 263
Sunstein, Cass, 27, 125, 310

Thomas, Lord, 88, 97, 100, 124, 154, 285, 325, 382, 390
Thompson case, 316, 379, 386, 387, 388, 389, 390
transgender rights, 242, 243, 276–7, 309, 310, 378
trust, 13, 110, 113, 257, 414, 415
Tushnet, Mark, 11, 19, 21, 27, 42, 47, 56, 58, 60, 81, 91, 111, 184, 185, 186, 188, 189, 190, 194, 199, 227, 231, 232, 259, 261, 263, 291, 310, 311, 319, 334, 345, 405, 406, 409, 411, 412

unwritten constitutional norms, 336, 361, 365, 411, 412, 414

Vermeule, Adrian, 11, 35, 38, 40, 43, 45, 74, 128, 153, 186, 228, 271, 343, 357, 365, 366, 404

Waldron, Jeremy, 1, 2, 15, 22, 31,
    32, 34, 35, 36, 38, 39, 40, 41, 43,
    49, 55, 61, 89, 112, 113, 123,
    154, 206, 276, 343, 359,
    406
Washington v Glücksberg, 310
weak-form review, 259, 260, 261, 263,
    411
Webber, Gregoire, 26, 40, 41, 44, 59, 67,
    68, 74, 77, 78, 79, 82, 84, 85, 113,

114, 115, 122, 155, 186, 355, 357,
    414

Yap, Po-Jen, 25, 61, 62, 64, 68, 70, 81, 213
Young, Alison, 58, 77, 232, 258, 259,
    262, 378, 413
Young, Katharine, 14, 294

Ziblatt, Daniel, 9, 10, 11, 13, 103, 111,
    112, 404

Books in the series

37. *The Collaborative Constitution* Aileen Kavanagh
36. *Non-Statutory Executive Powers and Judicial Review* Jason Grant Allen
35. *The Law as a Conversation among Equals* Roberto Gargarella
34. *Micronations and the Search for Sovereignty* Harry Hobbs and George Williams
33. *Fundamental Rights and the Legal Obligations of Business* David Bilchitz
32. *Courting Constitutionalism: The Politics of Public Law and Judicial Review in Pakistan* Moeen Cheema
31. *Ruling by Cheating: Governance in Illiberal Democracy* András Sajó
30. *Local Meanings of Proportionality* Afroditi Marketou
29. *Property Rights and Social Justice: Progressive Property in Action* Rachael Walsh
28. *Carl Schmitt's Early Legal-Theoretical Writings: Statute and Judgment and the Value of the State and the Significance of the Individual* Lars Vinx and Samuel Garrett Zeitlin
27. *Remedies for Human Rights Violations: A Two-Track Approach to Supranational and National Law* Kent Roach
26. *Europe's Second Constitution: Crisis, Courts and Community* Markus W. Gehring
25. *A. V. Dicey and the Common Law Constitutional Tradition: A Legal Turn of Mind* Mark D. Walters
24. *Administrative Competence: Reimagining Administrative Law* Elizabeth Fisher and Sidney A. Shapiro
23. *Legal Sabotage: Ernst Fraenkel in Hitler's Germany* Douglas Morris
22. *Proportionality in Action: Comparative and Empirical Perspectives on the Judicial Practice* Edited by Mordechai Kremnitzer, Tayla Steiner and Andrej Lang
21. *Constitutional Dialogue: Democracy, Rights, Institutions* Edited by Geoffrey Sigalet, Grégoire Webber and Rosalind Dixon
20. *The Veiled Sceptre: Reserve Powers of Heads of State in Westminster Systems* Anne Twomey
19. *Vigilance and Restraint in the Common Law of Judicial Review* Dean Knight
18. *The Alchemists: Questioning Our Faith in Courts as Democracy-Builders* Tom Gerald Daly
17. *Australia's Constitution after Whitlam* Brendan Lim
16. *Building the Constitution: The Practice of Constitutional Interpretation in Post-Apartheid South Africa* James Fowkes
15. *Dimensions of Dignity: The Theory and Practice of Modern Constitutional Law* Jacob Weinrib
14. *Reason of State: Law, Prerogative, Empire* Thomas Poole

13. *Bills of Rights in the Common Law* Robert Leckey

12. *The Guardian of the Constitution: Hans Kelsen and Carl Schmitt on the Limits of Constitutional Law*, Translated by Lars Vinx, with an introduction, notes by Lars Vinx

11. *Parliamentary Bills of Rights: The Experiences of New Zealand and the United Kingdom* Janet L. Hiebert and James B. Kelly

10. *Lawyering for the Rule of Law: Government Lawyers and the Rise of Judicial Power in Israel* Yoav Dotan

9. *Balancing Constitutional Rights: The Origins and Meanings of Postwar Legal Discourse* Jacco Bomhoff

8. *Judges on Trial: The Independence and Accountability of the English Judiciary* Shimon Shetreet and Sophie Turenne

7. *Proportionality and Constitutional Culture* Moshe Cohen-Eliya and Iddo Porat

6. *The Politics of Principle: The First South African Constitutional Court, 1995–2005* Theunis Roux

5. *The New Commonwealth Model of Constitutionalism: Theory and Practice* Stephen Gardbaum

4. *Searching for the State in British Legal Thought: Competing Conceptions of the Public Sphere* Janet McLean

3. *Judging Social Rights* Jeff King

2. *Proportionality: Constitutional Rights and their Limitations* Aharon Barak

1. *Parliamentary Sovereignty: Contemporary Debates* Jeffrey Goldsworthy

Milton Keynes UK
Ingram Content Group UK Ltd.
UKHW020301230224
438273UK00007B/47

9 781108 493260